FOURTH EDITION

THE WAR ON DRUGS IV

The Continuing Saga of the Mysteries and Miseries of Intoxication, Addiction, Crime, and Public Policy

JAMES A. INCIARDI

University of Delaware

PEARSON

Boston ■ New York ■ San Francisco
Mexico City ■ Montreal ■ Toronto ■ London ■ Madrid ■ Munich ■ Paris
Hong Kong ■ Singapore ■ Tokyo ■ Cape Town ■ Sydney

Series Editor: *Dave Repetto*
Series Editorial Assistant: *Jack Cashman*
Marketing Manager: *Kelly May*
Editorial-Production Service: *Omegatype Typography, Inc.*
Composition Buyer: *Linda Cox*
Manufacturing Buyer: *Debbie Rossi*
Electronic Composition: *Omegatype Typography, Inc.*
Cover Administrator: *Elena Sidorova*

For related titles and support materials, visit our online catalog at www.ablongman.com.

Between the time website information is gathered and then published, it is not unusual for some sites to have closed. Also, the transcription of URLs can result in typographical errors. The publisher would appreciate notification where these errors occur so that they may be corrected in subsequent editions.

Many of the designations used by manufacturers and sellers to distinguish their products are claimed as trademarks. Where those designations appear in this book, and Allyn and Bacon was aware of a trademark claim, the designations have been printed in initial or all caps.

Library of Congress Cataloging-in-Publication Data

Inciardi, James A.
　The war on drugs IV : the continuing saga of the mysteries and miseries of intoxication, addiction, crime, and public policy / James A. Inciardi. — 4th ed.
　　　p.　cm.
　Includes bibliographical references and index.
　ISBN-13: 978-0-205-51321-5 (pbk.)
　ISBN-10: 0-205-51321-2 (pbk.)
　1. Drug abuse—United States.　2. Drug control—United States.　3. Heroin abuse—United States.　4. Cocaine abuse—United States.　5. Drug abuse and crime—United States.　I. Title.　II. Title: War on drugs four.
HV5825.I5432 2008
363.4'50973—dc22

　　　　　　　　　　　　　　　　　　　　　　　　　　　　　2007026046

Printed in the United States of America

10　9　8　7　6　5　4　3　2　1　　　　11　10　09　08　07

Cover art by Clara Pechansky, www.pechansky.com.br/english/index.html

For Hilary

ABOUT THE AUTHOR

James A. Inciardi, Ph.D., is the director of the Center for Drug and Alcohol Studies at the University of Delaware; a professor in the Department of Sociology and Criminal Justice at the University of Delaware; an adjunct professor in the Department of Epidemiology and Public Health at the University of Miami School of Medicine; a guest professor in the Department of Psychiatry at the Federal University of Rio Grande do Sul in Porto Alegre, Brazil; and a member of the Internal Advisory Committee, Executive Office of the President, Office of National Drug Control Policy.

Dr. Inciardi received his Ph.D. at New York University and has a background in law enforcement, corrections, drug abuse treatment, and research. He is currently involved in the development, implementation, and evaluation of prison-based treatment programs for drug-involved offenders, as well as HIV/AIDS epidemiology and prevention studies in the United States, Latin America, and the Caribbean. Finally, Dr. Inciardi is the author, coauthor, or editor of some 50 books and 400 articles and chapters in the areas of substance abuse, criminology, criminal justice, history, folklore, public policy, HIV/AIDS, medicine, and law.

CONTENTS

v

CHAPTER SEVEN

Bars, Footballs, OCs, and Watson 387: Prescription Drug Abuse and Diversion in the Twenty-First Century   153

Part III   SOME CONSEQUENCES OF DRUG TAKING AND DRUG SEEKING   181

CHAPTER EIGHT

Legends of the Living Dead: Unraveling the Drugs–Crime Connection   181

CHAPTER NINE

Mainlining in the Shadow of Death: Probing the HIV/AIDS–Drugs Connection   217

CHAPTER TWELVE

APPENDIX A

APPENDIX B

PREFACE

■ ■ ■ ■ ■

The worlds of heroin, cocaine, crack, crystal meth, LSD, Ecstasy, and other drugs, as well as crime, are curious and often brutal, populated by czars and kings, bikers and diplomats, peasants and slaves, and agents both legitimate and corrupt. There are many other players as well: an odd assembly of drug users, dealers, and traffickers; sex workers, pimps, transvestites, drag queens, and other denizens of the sex industry; mercenaries and assassins, terrorists and insurgents, and arms traders linked to embattled communities in developing nations; and small and scattered battalions of slaves and runners, lookouts, moles and mules, and other bizarre creatures of the streets.

The worlds of drug trafficking, drug taking, and drug seeking are tragic and dangerous ones as well, in which pain, suffering, violence, and death are commonplace. They are alien and exotic worlds, ranging from the poppy fields of Southeast and Southwest Asia, the jungles of Amazonia, the cloud forests of Africa, and the highlands and high cities of the Andes, to the crack dens and shooting galleries, the road houses and rave halls, and the mean streets and back streets of rural and urban America. *The War on Drugs IV* is a series of reflections on these unusual, hidden, and beleaguered places. Much of what is described is based on street research and outreach in Miami and the Florida Keys; the Bahamas, and the Windward, Leeward and other island chains of the Caribbean Basin; across the Florida Straits to the north coasts and hinterlands of South America; and in New York, Chicago, San Francisco, Belfast, Budapest, Lisbon, Papeete, Cairo, Capetown, Sydney, Cabo San Lucas, and other fever ports of call.

The information presented in *The War on Drugs IV* comes from a profusion of interviews and discussions with the drugs users, drug dealers, and drug traffickers who inhabit the streets and street markets; with the police and other law enforcement agents; and with the White House, State Department, and other government officials charged with controlling the underworlds of drugs and crime. As such, the information is both systematic and anecdotal. The descriptions and characterizations are also based on numerous observations and conversations in South America—in the drug trafficking capitals of Colombia, Bolivia, Ecuador, Peru, and Venezuela, in the coca fields and mountain outposts of the Andes, in the jungle labs and drug-selling bazaars of Amazonia, and in the shantytowns and along the tiled avenues of Rio de Janeiro and other Brazilian cities. In these distant places, the informants included peasant laborers; military officials and other foreign government representatives; drug users and sellers; bandits and dealers in contraband; North and South American drug enforcement agents; members of the U.S. diplomatic corps; and drug abuse researchers, clinicians and their patients.

As a series of perspectives and reflections, this book is not intended to provide a definitive statement on any of the topics it covers, although at times the opinionated nature of the commentary may suggest this. The events, viewpoints, and impressions are written to provide an examination of the American drug scene and policy alternatives against the backgrounds of social and cultural change—where it all has been, where it appears to be now, and where it might be going. Moreover, rather than just a revision of its predecessors, this volume represents an expansion and sequel, hence the name *The War on Drugs IV: The Continuing Saga of the Mysteries and Miseries of Intoxication, Addiction, Crime, and Public Policy.*

Chapter 1, "The Mysteries and Miseries of Intoxication and Addiction," is an attempt to discuss the nature of substance abuse and dependence, and to explain why such terms as "addiction" and "psychological dependence" have become meaningless concepts in discussions of the drug problem. It also presents some insights into the extent of drug abuse in the United States.

Part I, "Drug Fads, Fashions, and Epidemics: Some Perspectives on Getting High in America," is composed of three chapters and focuses on the many social and cultural events that served to shape the nature and course of drug use and ultimately, drug control policy. Chapter 2, "From Dover's Powder to the Evil Weed of the Fields," traces the early history of drug taking in the United States from colonial times through the beginning of World War II. Chapter 3, "Everybody Smokes Dope," examines the emerging use of heroin, marijuana, hallucinogens, and other drugs in post–World War II America. And Chapter 4, "Binge Drinking, Raves, Circuit Parties, and the Mickey Finn," explores the intricacies of drugs, youth, and the club culture in contemporary America, including a focus on the problems associated with raves and the so-called "date-rape" or "acquaintance-rape" drugs.

Part II, "Shit, Smack, Superfly, and Hillbilly Heroin: The Most Dangerous Substances on Earth," is composed of three chapters targeting some of the more enduring drugs of abuse in the United States—heroin and cocaine—plus a new chapter on trends in prescription drug abuse. Chapter 5, "China White and Mexican Black," provides an overview of the heroin problem—where the drug comes from, how it is refined and distributed, how it is prepared and used, and what effects it engenders. Chapter 6, "Cocaine, Crack, and Other Analogs of 'Mama Coca,'" takes the reader along the "Cocaine Highway" to the land of the "Cocaine Cowboys" and "Hurricane Crack," and examines the history, pharmacology, and abuse patterns of powder cocaine and crack cocaine, as well as the human suffering associated with their use. Chapter 7, "Bars, Footballs, OCs, and Watson 387," examines the reemergence of the abuse of prescription medications, the wide range of pharmaceuticals being abused, and their diversion from legal channels to the illicit marketplace.

Part III, "Some Consequences of Drug Taking and Drug Seeking," includes two chapters, addressing two of the major difficulties associated with drug abuse—

crime and HIV/AIDS. In Chapter 8, "Legends of the Living Dead," a social history of the criminalization of drug use is provided, combined with an examination of some of the complexities of the drugs–crime connection. Chapter 9, "Mainlining in the Shadow of Death," probes the HIV/AIDS–drugs connection. Topics include the history of AIDS, the characteristics of HIV disease and the myths surrounding AIDS, and the AIDS risk factors associated with drug use and sexual behaviors.

Part IV, "Strategies in the War on Drugs," is also composed of three chapters addressing a range of programs and alternatives in the policy arena. Chapter 10, "The Great Drug War," examines the enforcement and interdiction aspects of American drug policy, as well as the attempts to reduce the demand for drugs through prevention and treatment. Chapter 11, "The Great Drug Debate," discusses the pros and cons of legalizing drugs and what has become known as "harm reduction." And finally, Chapter 12, "War Is Not the Answer," addresses alternatives to the war on drugs.

ACKNOWLEDGMENTS

The total number of debts one incurs in writing a book is surprisingly large. For their help in gathering information and preparing the manuscript, thanks must go to Hilary L. Surratt, Daniela Alder, and Elisa Pujals at the University of Delaware's Center for Drug and Alcohol Studies. Special thanks must also go to the publishing team at Allyn & Bacon. The reflections and comments of many people who populate the worlds of heroin, cocaine, crack, and crime are included throughout this book. Reported verbatim, they are uncensored and often tend to be rather graphic, and their candor is appreciated. And finally, the vast majority of the rest who contributed their thoughts and experiences to the writing of this book must remain anonymous, but they know who they are, and their help is gratefully appreciated.

THE MYSTERIES AND MISERIES OF INTOXICATION AND ADDICTION

Although there are many things in life that are far worse than being perpetually assaulted with commercial messages, the fact that every person in the United States is exposed to an estimated 30,000 to 40,000 commercials each year is not too comforting. There was a time when the hyping of a product was limited to radio and TV or in the press or on a billboard. But now—like politicians, cockroaches, mosquitoes, and ants—the messages are everywhere—on buses and trains, on T-shirts and caps and uniforms and drinking cups, in the names of sports arenas (South Florida's Pro Player Stadium), and sporting events (the PetroSun Independence Bowl, formerly the Poulan Weed Eater Bowl, and the PapaJohns.com Bowl), and even on ring posts in the local boxing arena, the napkins placed under beverages on domestic and international flights, and the movie screen during previews at the neighborhood picture show. And the myriad of products is overwhelming—things of every conceivable ilk, variety, type, shape, size, condition, price, quality, and function. And drugs are a big part of it all, not only in the commercials but in the news and public service messages as well.

Almost daily, in fact, just about everyone who reads a newspaper, watches a television program, sees a movie, listens to the radio, drives a car, or simply walks down the street is confronted with something about drugs, drug use, and drug abuse. It may be an advertisement pushing a product to manage obesity, hair loss, or erectile dysfunction (as impotence is now called). Or the report may be about a drive-by shooting of a local drug dealer, the breakup of a cocaine smuggling ring, the arrest of a police officer or politician for accepting drug money, a traffic accident involving a drunk driver, binge drinking on a college campus, the drug overdose death of an entertainer, a witless message to "just say no," or the latest findings about tobacco smoking and health. Whatever the topic, drugs seem to occupy a considerable amount of time and space in media reporting, classroom exchanges, political debates, and discussions of public health policy and safety.

What accounts for this imposing focus on drugs and the drug problem? Is it some general fascination with reading and hearing about drug use and its consequences, or are drugs in the United States and other parts of the world really a major problem that demands unremitting and concentrated attention? This leads to a series of other questions. What are the differences between drug use, drug abuse, and drug addiction? Have people always abused drugs, or has abuse started just in the past few decades? Finally, how many people use drugs, and what kinds of drugs are people getting into these days?

ROOTS, BERRIES, HERBS, AND GRAINS: THOUGHTS ON COCKTAILS, BREWS, AND OTHER LIBATIONS AND POTATIONS IN STONE-AGE CULTURE

The beginnings of drug use and abuse are buried in antiquity. It is clear, however, that for millennia people have used a wide variety of substances for the sake of enhancing pleasure and performance, and for altering states of perception and consciousness in one way or another. Alcohol was likely the first chemical to be abused. This natural by-product of decaying organic matter was discovered during primitive times. Evidence of the use of beer (made from grains) and wine (from grapes) has been found in the most ancient human settlements. In fact, some anthropologists argue that early tribal groups shifted from hunter/gatherers to farmers for the sake of having stable sources of the roots, berries, fruits, grains, and other plant products needed to concoct beer and wine. Although alcohol seems to have existed everywhere, most of the other chemicals used to alter performance, perception, and consciousness first came from local shrubs and other vegetation.

Both historical and archeological evidence suggests that the earliest uses of drugs were for purposes not unlike those of today.

- *Celebration.* It would appear that alcohol has long since been used for celebrating personal, tribal, and national events and accomplishments. Drinking was a characteristic part of ceremonies marking victory in battle or commemorating the death of an elder or the crowning of a new chief.
- *Ritual.* Many peoples and cultures believed that certain drugs put them into closer contact with their God or gods—the use of wine in the Christian sacraments, for example, or peyote and mushrooms among Native American cultures. In addition, the use of alcohol and other drugs were common to social and political rituals, such as passing the peace pipe or making what are commonly referred to as "toasts" (see Exhibit 1.1).
- *Coping.* Any variety of chemicals were used for contending with the physical and emotional hardships of daily life. One better known example is the indigenous populations in South America's Andes chewing coca leaves for the suppression of both hunger and fatigue.

■ ■ ■ ■ ■ ▬▬▬▬▬▬▬▬▬▬▬▬▬▬▬▬▬▬▬▬▬▬▬▬▬▬▬▬▬▬▬▬▬

EXHIBIT 1.1

TOASTS AND TOASTING

What, in fact, are *toasts* and where did the term come from? As history would have it, toasts and the custom of toasting have likely been around for thousands of years. It is said that a primitive form of toasting dates back to ancient nomadic tribes who splattered a few drops of drink on sacrificial altars to appease the hunting gods. The word *toast,* as applied to drinking and alcohol, dates back to the seventeenth century when it was common to put a piece of bread, toasted and spiced, into beverages as a form of flavoring. It is said that the use of the word arose in Bath, England, when a celebrated beauty at the time of Charles II was observed taking a bath in a public fountain. One of her admirers took a glass of the water in which she stood and drank it, saluting her health and loveliness. A bystander also declared his admiration for the woman, but his distaste for the bath water. Instead, he offered to have the toast (the woman bathing in the fountain).

For a time in both England and France, as well as colonial Massachusetts, toasting was illegal. It was held that the custom was nothing more than an excuse for heavy drinking and profligacy (also known as debauchery). During the eighteenth century, an *old toast* referred to someone fond of his or her liquor. By the beginning of the twentieth century, the expression *toasted,* meaning intoxicated with alcohol (derived from both drinking too many toasts and the expressions *cooked* or *fried* in the sense of being drunk) had become common. See Francis Grose, *A Classical Dictionary of the Vulgar Tongue* (New York: Barnes & Noble, 1963); Richard A. Spears, *Slang and Euphemism* (Middle Village, NY: Jonathan David, 1981).

▬▬

■ *Pain relief.* Using drugs to relieve pain has been done for thousands of years. Opium was perhaps the earliest pain reliever. Also commonly used was the bark of the willow tree, from which aspirin was eventually synthesized.

Going beyond the reasons why drugs were ingested, drugs were first used in their natural states. That is, their unprocessed, organic forms were chewed, swallowed, sniffed, smoked, or sucked on without being refined or crossbred to increase potency. At some point during the eleventh century, however, distillation was discovered. Distillation is a process of vaporization and subsequent condensation that yields a purified or more concentrated liquid. Brandy was first produced on the Arabian Peninsula through the distillation of wine, and whiskey originated in Ireland through the distillation of beer. Until the nineteenth century, distillation was all that was known about increasing the potency of alcohol and other drugs.

The diffusion of drugs across the globe began in the sixteenth century as European explorers and traders ventured into Asia, Africa, and the Americas. Upon their return to Europe, they ferried with them a variety of new stimulants and intoxicants— tobacco, coca, marijuana, and opium. As European colonists crossed the Atlantic to populate the Americas, they brought many different drugs and spirits, both old and newly discovered, introducing them to New World populations.

PROFESSORS, POLITICIANS, WORD GAMES, AND THE FDA: SOME TRIVIAL DISTINCTIONS BETWEEN DRUG USE, DRUG MISUSE, AND DRUG ABUSE

Although drugs have been used and abused for millennia, and although the drug problem has been a topic of extensive conversation and consideration for generations, the meanings of these and related terms are usually taken for granted. In fact, if politicians of any party or persuasion were asked to define their terms as they point their fingers at one another about drug policy during the campaign seasons, it is doubtful that many could provide accurate answers.

The great majority of college textbooks on drug abuse typically begin by inundating students with interminable streams of definitions for drugs, drug use, drug misuse, chronic drug use, legal and illegal drugs, licit and illicit drugs, social and recreational drugs, hard and soft drugs, gateway drugs, deviant drug use, addiction, dependence (physical, psychological, and psychogenic), compulsive drug use, and substance abuse disorders. The list goes on. Some definitions are important, but studying most of them can be monotonous and wearisome. Only a few notable ones are discussed here.

To begin with, the term *drug* is fairly easy to define and understand. Quite simply, it is any natural or artificial substance (aside from food) that by its chemical nature alters the functioning of the body. As such, aspirin is a drug, as well as penicillin, marijuana, cocaine, and alcohol and tobacco—to name but a few. People *use* drugs for many different reasons, but drugs are also *misused* and *abused.* Some observers have gone to great lengths to distinguish the terms *drug misuse* and *drug abuse,*[1] but suffice it to say that the distinctions are not always clear, and even less useful. Drug misuse typically refers to the inappropriate use of a prescription or nonprescription drug, that is, using it in greater amounts or for purposes other than it was intended. For example, taking a painkiller more often than your physician indicated for an injured knee because it gives you a little buzz is drug misuse. Similarly, taking someone else's antianxiety medication to calm you down before an exam also is drug misuse. (But depending on which textbook you consult, either of these might also be described as abuse.)

Some drug misuse is relatively harmless, but in other instances it can be bizarre or life threatening. A rather curious entry in this regard involves the use of bufotenine, which first came to the attention of the popular press during the mid-1980s.[2] It seems that someone claimed that the toxic slime secreted by *Bufo marinus*—the common marine toad—caused hallucinations, and suddenly "toad licking" became a new trend in a few locales. But actually, the practice of toad licking is quite old, and seems to have developed from legendary and mythological uses of toads throughout history. Reports of using bufotenine as a poison, as well as a magical tool, go back as far as Roman times. It was also apparent in a few Central and South American religions and in Native American tradition in the Southeast and Southwest. Scientific evidence suggests, however, that licking toads does not get you high. The toxic compounds present in the secretions of *Bufo marinus* are likely to poison users before they can consume enough bufotenine to have a hallucinogenic effect. For those heavily involved in toad licking, the *Miami Herald* reported several years ago that

Amphibians Anonymous, whose motto is "Never Has It Been So Easy to Just Say No," offered the following telltale signs of toad slime addiction:

> You know you are in the company of a toad-sucker if you are approached in a singles bar by someone who says: "You show me your warts and I'll show you mine."
>   You know you have a toad-sucker in the family if your son or daughter has breath that smells like the Florida Everglades and has an appetite for live flies.[3]

Drugs are categorized by the Food and Drug Administration (FDA) and the Drug Enforcement Administration (DEA) as either *legal* or *illegal* depending on their potential for abuse. As such, *drug abuse* typically refers to any use of an illegal drug, or the inappropriate use of a legal drug in a manner that can cause problems for the user, which, again, can be referred to as *misuse* (which is why trying to differentiate between the two terms comes down to playing with words). Technically any substance can be abused, but it is the psychoactive drugs that are generally abused. Psychoactive drugs are those that alter mood, levels of perception, or brain functioning. The problems they can cause may be physical, psychological, social, or occupational. All of the illegal drugs and many prescription and over-the-counter drugs have psychoactive properties. Confusing, isn't it?

ANSWERING THE ENIGMATIC QUESTION: IS IT DRUG ADDICTION OR DRUG DEPENDENCE? OR MAYBE IT'S SOMETHING CALLED PSEUDOADDICTION

A characteristic effect typically ascribed to the repeated use of many drugs is *addiction,* a phenomenon that has had many meanings and definitions over the years. The addiction label has been used interchangeably with *dependence, habit forming,* and *habituation,* and is related to the concepts of physical dependence and psychological dependence.[4] If addiction truly meant all these things, almost anything could be addicting—from drinking Dr. Pepper and Snapple to having sex, watching YouTube and MTV, listening to rock and rap, or even eating, sleeping, playing chess, exercising, or taking a shower. As a result, the great majority of clinicians and researchers in the drug field rarely use the term *addiction.* In fact, a noted drug abuse researcher and clinician recently remarked: "*Addiction* is a hairball! It's a word with so many different meanings that it is useless as a scientific term. In fact, for thirty years the World Health Organization has been trying to get rid of it."[5]

Having stated the problems with the word *addiction,* a definition is nevertheless offered only because the concept is so widely used. Perhaps the best definition of addiction is drug craving accompanied by physical dependence, which motivates continuing usage, resulting in tolerance to the drug's effects and a complex of identifiable symptoms appearing when it is suddenly withdrawn. Note that the definition of addiction excludes *psychological dependence*—a term that is generally meaningless, impossible to define, and does not appear anywhere else in this book. You will also note that the words *addict* and *addiction* are used sparingly.

The most preferred terms in the drug field are *substance abuse* and *substance dependence,* both of which are based on specific diagnostic criteria as outlined in the American Psychiatric Association's *Diagnostic and Statistical Manual of Mental Disorders* (see Exhibit 1.2). Within this context, substance abuse requires evidence of repeated occurrences within a twelve-month period of any of four possible legal, social, or interpersonal problems related to the substance. More importantly, however, is the definition of dependence, a concept that indicates the central role a substance

■ ■ ■ ■ ■

EXHIBIT 1.2

DSM-IV CRITERIA FOR SUBSTANCE ABUSE AND DEPENDENCE

Methods to formally classify substance abuse disorders, such as substance abuse and substance dependence, began in the 1950s with the publication of the first *Diagnostic and Statistical Manual of Mental Disorders (DSM)* by the American Psychiatric Association. In early editions of the *DSM,* substance abuse disorders were grouped under the broad category of sociopathic personality disturbances, which included a variety of antisocial behaviors, such as sexual deviations. Early definitions of abuse and dependence had implicit moral overtones that were quite negative. But as substance abuse became better understood, both physiological and behavioral elements were incorporated and the focus of the definitions changed. The *DSM-IV* was finalized in 1994 and included the following diagnostic criteria.

SUBSTANCE ABUSE

A maladaptive pattern of substance use leading to clinically significant impairment or distress, as manifested by one or more of the following occurring at any time during a twelve-month period:

1. Recurrent substance use resulting in a failure to fulfill major role obligations at work, school, or home (e.g., repeated absences or poor work performance related to substance use; substance-related absences, suspensions, or expulsions from school; neglect of children or household)
2. Recurrent substance use in situations in which it is physically hazardous (e.g., driving an automobile or operating a machine when impaired by substance use)
3. Recurrent substance-related legal problems (e.g., arrests for substance-related disorderly conduct)
4. Continued substance use despite having persistent or recurrent social or interpersonal problems

SUBSTANCE DEPENDENCE

A maladaptive pattern of substance use leading to clinically significant impairment or distress, as manifested by three or more of the following occurring at any time during a twelve-month period:

1. *Tolerance,* as defined by either (a) the need for markedly increased amounts of the substance to achieve intoxication or desired effect or (b) a markedly diminished effect with continued use of the same amount of the substance

2. *Withdrawal,* as manifested by either (a) the characteristic withdrawal syndrome for the substance or (b) the same (or closely related) substance being taken to relieve or avoid withdrawal symptoms
3. Taking the substance often in larger amounts or over a longer period than was intended
4. A persistent desire or unsuccessful effort to decrease or control substance use
5. Spending a great deal of time in activities necessary to obtain the substance (e.g., visiting multiple doctors or driving long distances), to use the substance (e.g., chain smoking), or to recover from its effects
6. Giving up or limiting important social, occupational, or recreational activities because of substance use
7. Continuing substance use despite knowledge of having had a persistent or recurrent physical or psychological problem that was likely to have been caused or exacerbated by the substance (e.g., current cocaine use despite recognition of cocaine-induced depression, or continued drinking despite recognition that an ulcer was made worse by alcohol consumption)

Source: American Psychiatric Association, *Diagnostic and Statistical Manual of Mental Disorders, Fourth Edition (DSM-IV)* (Washington, DC: American Psychiatric Association, 1994).

has come to play in an individual's life, with evidence of problems of controlling intake, and the development of physical and psychological difficulties, despite which the individual continues to use the substance. Associated with dependence are tolerance and withdrawal. *Tolerance* is a state of acquired resistance to the effects of a drug whereas *withdrawal* or an *abstinence syndrome* is the appearance of physiological symptoms when the drug is stopped too quickly.

Going beyond addiction, there is also something called *pseudoaddiction.* The term was first used in 1989 to describe a situation resulting from the undertreatment of pain. One of the first cases to be described in the literature was that of a seventeen-year-old youth with leukemia, pneumonia, and chest pain. The teenager displayed behaviors (moaning, grimacing, increasing requests for painkillers) wrongly interpreted by his physicians and nurses as indicators of addiction, rather than the undertreatment of pain. Put simply, pseudoaddiction is something that many physicians do to their patients, through fears and misunderstanding of pain, pain treatment, and addiction.[6]

An important concept that also needs to be addressed here is *neuroadaptation,* the chemical and biological changes that occur within the brain in response to the use of psychoactive drugs. Neuroadaptation works in a very complex way. Imagine yourself taking a puff of a cigarette, a swallow of whiskey, a toke of marijuana, a snort of cocaine, or a shot of heroin. The moment you take that puff, swallow, toke, snort, or shot, trillions of potent molecules surge through your bloodstream into your brain. Once there, they set off a cascade of chemical and electrical events, a kind of neurological chain reaction that ricochets around the skull and rearranges the interior reality of your mind.

Specific drugs trigger distinct reactions by acting on different neurotransmitters, chemicals that alter electrical activity in the brain. Neurotransmitters underlie every thought, emotion, memory, and learning process, and they carry the signals between all nerve cells (neurons) in the brain. When normal functioning of one or more neurotransmitters is altered, whether temporarily or permanently, neuroadaptation occurs.

To better understand how neuroadaptation is related to substance abuse or dependence, consider the role of the transmitter dopamine in brain activity. Dopamine is a neurotransmitter found in various parts of the brain and is believed to mediate the effects of a variety of drugs. At a purely chemical level, almost every experience that humans find enjoyable—whether listening to music, embracing a lover, scuba diving, or even enjoying a chocolate shake—amounts to little more than a small explosion of dopamine in certain parts of the brain. But dopamine levels must be kept within strict bounds. Too little in certain parts of the brain can trigger the tremors and paralysis of Parkinson's disease; too much causes the hallucinations and bizarre thoughts of schizophrenia.

With respect to drug abuse and dependence, nicotine and heroin increase dopamine levels, as does alcohol and a number of other drugs, and cocaine keeps dopamine levels elevated. Thus, drug-dependent individuals do not really crave heroin, alcohol, cocaine, or nicotine per se, but rather the rush of dopamine that these drugs produce. Within this context, neuroadaptation is associated with the altered state of biology that occurs with the repeated use of psychoactive drugs (and the continuously high levels of dopamine or other neurotransmitters) and hence the body's desire for them. Although neuroadaptation, dependence, and withdrawal are physiological phenomena, they are related to substance abuse within historical, social, legal, and behavioral contexts—all of which are addressed at length throughout this book.

HOW MANY DRUG ABUSERS ARE THERE?

Trying to figure out how many people abuse alcohol and other drugs is elusive. Because the mere possession of marijuana, cocaine, heroin, LSD, and certain other drugs is a crime, most people are unwilling to admit they use them. Because so much stigma is associated with drug abuse and dependence, the majority of users conceal their drug involvement from employers, family members, and sometimes even close friends. Moreover, many drug users are members of hidden populations that are difficult to access and count.

Since the early 1970s, scientific survey methods similar to those used for political polling and collecting census data have been used to do cross-sectional studies of the general population to estimate the number of drug abusers.[7] In fact, every year a number of widespread survey studies are conducted in schools and households throughout the United States. Samples are drawn in such a way that the findings can be projected to the population as a whole, much like political polling. But are the estimates correct? The answer is probably not, because there are three major problems. First, although anonymity is guaranteed in these surveys, still, not everyone tells the truth. In most cases, there is no way of checking the validity of what is claimed on a questionnaire. Second, many people are missed by these large-scale surveys—runaways, high school dropouts, and students who were absent on the day of the survey; people with no fixed residence who live in the streets, jails, prisons, or other institutions; individuals unwilling to participate in surveys; and many, many more. Furthermore, in all likelihood many of these inaccessible and hidden populations have high concentrations of drug abusers, so survey data underestimate the extent of drug abuse. And third, there are many of us who are so sick and tired of being bothered at home by pollsters, canvassers, telemarketers, campaigners, missionaries, fundraisers, and the many others aligned with the fellowship of stumping, head counting, and bean counting that we go out of their way to avoid being included in surveys.

Yet in spite of these drawbacks, general population survey data are useful. Respondent underreporting (and overreporting) of drug use and abuse tends to be constant from one year to the next; thus findings reflect relative estimates and trends over time. These data, therefore, are useful for determining overall changes in both drug use and drug abuse.

Among the best known of the large-scale studies is the Monitoring the Future survey. Monitoring the Future is an annual survey of tobacco, alcohol, and illegal drug use of nationally representative samples of eighth- and tenth-graders, high school seniors, college students, and young adults. Conducted by the University of Michigan's Institute for Social Research and funded by the National Institute on Drug Abuse, the Monitoring the Future surveys have been collecting systematic data since 1975. The four primary measures are (1) the percentage of students who have used a particular drug at least *once, ever* in their lifetime, (2) the percentage who have used a drug in the *past year,* (3) the percentage who have used a drug in the *past thirty days,* and (4) the percentage who have reported *daily* use during the past thirty days. As illustrated in Exhibit 1.3, almost three-fourths of the class of 2006 reported having tried alcohol, and almost half reported smoking cigarettes and marijuana or hashish at least once in their lives. Much smaller proportions reported having ever used illegal drugs other than marijuana. Also clear from these data is the indication that, with the exception of cigarettes and marijuana, daily use of other drugs is rare.

Whereas Monitoring the Future focuses primarily on students, the National Survey on Drug Use and Health is the primary source of statistical information on the use of illegal drugs by the U.S. population. Conducted annually by the Department of Health and Human Services, the survey covers residents of households, shelters, rooming houses, dormitories, and military bases. The purpose of the survey is to estimate the prevalence of use of alcohol, tobacco, and a variety of illicit drugs among persons aged 12 years and older. As illustrated in Exhibit 1.4, the 2005 survey estimated that almost 20 million people in the United States were current users of illegal drugs, meaning that they had used an illegal drug during the month prior to being interviewed. Although much of this drug use involved marijuana only, there were, nevertheless, millions of current users of other illegal drugs, including cocaine, heroin, and hallucinogenic drugs.

As a final point here, it should be noted that neither the Monitoring the Future nor the National Survey on Drug Use and Health include members of hidden populations—the homeless, the dropouts, those institutionalized at the time of the

EXHIBIT 1.3   Frequency of Use of Various Drugs for the High School Class of 2006

DRUG	LIFETIME *PERCENTAGE USING ONCE EVER*	ANNUAL *PERCENTAGE USING IN PAST 12 MONTHS*	CURRENT *PERCENTAGE USING IN PAST 30 DAYS*	DAILY *PERCENTAGE USING DAILY IN PAST 30 DAYS*
Any illicit drug	48.2	36.5	21.5	—
Any illicit drug other than marijuana	26.9	19.2	9.8	—
Any illicit drug including inhalants	51.2	38.0	22.1	—
Marijuana/hashish	42.3	31.5	18.3	5.0
Inhalants	11.1	4.5	1.5	—
Nitrites	1.2	0.5	0.3	—
Hallucinogens	8.3	4.9	1.5	—
LSD	3.3	1.7	0.6	—
PCP	2.2	0.7	0.4	—
MDMA (Ecstasy)	6.5	4.1	1.3	—
Cocaine	8.5	5.7	2.5	—
Crack	3.5	2.1	0.9	—
Other cocaine	7.9	5.2	2.4	—
Heroin	1.4	0.8	0.4	—
With a needle	0.8	0.5	0.3	—
Without a needle	1.1	0.6	0.3	—
Other narcotics	13.4	9.0	3.8	—
Amphetamines	12.4	8.1	3.7	—
Methamphetamine	4.4	2.5	0.9	—
Ice	3.4	1.9	0.7	*
Sedatives				
Barbiturates	10.2	6.6	3.0	—
Methaqualone	1.2	0.8	0.4	—
Tranquilizers	10.3	6.6	2.7	—
Alcohol	72.7	66.5	45.3	3.0
Drunkenness	56.4	47.9	30.0	1.6
5+ drinks in a row in past 2 weeks	—	—	—	25.4
Cigarettes	47.1	—	21.6	12.2
Half-pack or more per day	—	—	—	5.9
Smokeless tobacco	15.2	—	6.1	2.2
Steroids	2.7	1.8	1.1	—

— indicates data not available.

* indicates less than .05 percent but greater than 0 percent.

Source: Monitoring the Future study, Institute for Social Research, University of Michigan.

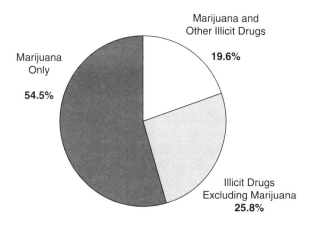

19.7 Million Past Month Illicit Drug Users

EXHIBIT 1.4   Types of Drugs Used in the Past Month by Illicit Drug Users Aged 12 or Older, 2005

Source: Office of Applied Studies, SAMHSA, National Survey on Drug Use and Health, 2005.

surveys, and the many more living in street cultures and countercultures typically bypassed by standard survey methods. As suggested earlier, the proportions of drug users in these populations are significantly higher than in the general population, as is the quantity and frequency of their drug use. As such, the data on drug use in the United States is greatly underestimated.

POSTSCRIPT

Clearly, the number of drug users and abusers is significant, and the different motivations for using drugs are quite numerous. Although a discussion of why people abuse drugs is not the subject matter of this book, it is important to discriminate at least broadly among the different types of abusers. Many separate mechanisms have been used to classify drug abusers into groups. Some classifications have been based on frequency and amount of use whereas others have focused on motivations, routes of administration, or context of use.[8] Perhaps the most practical method of differentiation is the simple fourfold classification of experimenters, social–recreational users, involved users, and dysfunctional abusers—a general categorization that has been widely applied in the drug field for quite some time.

The *experimenters* are by far the largest group of drug abusers. They most frequently try one or more drugs in a social setting, but drugs do not play a significant role in their lives. They use illegal drugs experimentally because their social group relates the effects of drugs as being pleasurable. Experimenters do not seek out drugs but may use marijuana, cocaine, Ecstasy, or some other drug when offered to them in an appropriate setting. In this situation, they may smoke marijuana or snort cocaine once or twice because it does something *to* them. As a University of Delaware senior once commented about his first experience with cocaine:

> I generally don't use drugs, and my only experience with coke was a few weeks ago in the dormitory. My roommate came in with a couple of people and started getting high on it. They kept trying to get me to do some, and finally I snorted some just for the hell of it. When I did, it was quite a blast at first, from my head all the way down, and then I felt like I was floating. After, I felt a little weird. . . .

Similarly, a University of Miami student stated:

> All my life I have stayed away from drugs. I'm one of the people that actually listened to the "just say no" bullshit. But last week at a South Beach club I said "yes." My date had some Xanax, and everyone was trying it, so I did too. I got a buzz. It was nice.

Social–recreational users differ from experimenters primarily in terms of frequency and continuity of consumption. For example, they may use a particular drug when they are at a party and someone presents the opportunity. The drug still does not play a significant role in these users' lives. They still do not actively seek out the drug but use it only because it does something *to* them—makes them feel good. A 28-year-old Miami woman related the following, also about cocaine:

> Partying can be even more fun with a few lines of coke. I never have any of my own, but usually I'll tie in with some guy who does. We'll get a little stoned, and maybe go to bed. It's all in good fun. . . . Another time I was on a double date and this guy had some good toot [cocaine]. We drove up to Orlando and went into Disney World. Do you know what it's like goin' through the haunted mansion stoned like that? It's a whole different trip. . . .

For *involved users,* a major transition takes place after their social–recreational use. As users become involved with illegal drugs, they also become drug seekers, and drugs become significant to their lives. Although they are still quite able to function—in school, on the job, or as a parent or spouse—their proficiency in many areas begins to decline markedly. Personal and social functioning tends to be inversely related to the amount of time involved users spend with drugs. They still have control over their behavior, but their use of drugs occurs with increasing frequency for some adaptive reason; drugs do something *for* them.

Involved drug users are of many types. Some abuse drugs to deal with an unbearable work situation, indulging in controlled amounts of their favorite drug several times a day. Others use one or more drugs to enhance performance or to bolster their self-esteem. Still a third group regularly uses drugs to deal with stress, anxiety, or nagging boredom. As a self-employed New York accountant involved with Dilaudid (a prescription narcotic) put it:

> Life is really crazy. I'm always tense, no matter what I'm doing. And everybody seems to always want something—clients, my wife, the kids, the boss, the bank, the market, the economy, the whole fucking world. . . . A few tabs every few hours seems to get me through things.

The *dysfunctional abusers* are what have become known as the heroin junkies, potheads, cokaholics, cokewhores, and meth freaks. For them, drugs have become the most significant part of their lives. They are personally and socially dysfunctional and spend all of their time taking or seeking drugs. Moreover, they no longer have control over their drug use.

Although dysfunctional drug use is the least common pattern, it is nevertheless widespread. Dysfunctional abusers, furthermore, are not limited to street subcultures; they can be found in all segments of society. In fact, the list of well-known personalities and rock groups who acknowledge to the media dysfunctional drug abuse or overdosing tends to sound like an excerpt from the Who's Who in entertainment and sports and includes, to name but a few, rock groups Nirvana, Smashing Pumpkins, Red Hot Chili Peppers, and Depeche Mode; plus celebrities Gary Busey, James Caan, George Carlin, Chevy Chase, Richard Dreyfuss, Chris Farley (deceased), Corey Feldman, Carrie Fisher, Kelsey Grammer, Stephen King, Sam Kinison (deceased), Garrett Morris, Kate Moss, Nick Nolte, Tatum O'Neal, Richard Pryor (deceased), David Bowie, Glen Campbell, David Crosby, Rick James (deceased), Smokey Robinson, Ringo Starr, and Syd Barrett of Pink Floyd (deceased). In addition, the list includes baseball stars Darryl Strawberry and Dwight Gooden; Argentine soccer idol Diego Maradona; and actors John Belushi (deceased), River Phoenix (deceased), Christian Slater, Charlie Sheen, and Robert Downey Jr. And then there are Whitney Houston and Courtney Love. The list goes on and continues to grow.

NOTES

1. For example, see Erich Goode, *Drugs in American Society* (New York: McGraw-Hill, 1993), pp. 39–42.

2. *Miami Herald,* 31 January 1990, p. 1A; *Washington Post Magazine,* 30 December 1990, p. 22.

3. Thomas Lyttle, "Misuse and Legend in the 'Toad Licking' Phenomenon," *The International Journal of the Addictions,* 28 (1993), pp. 521–538; *Miami Herald,* 2 February 1990, p. 2A.

4. Ronald L. Akers, "Addiction: The Troublesome Concept," *Journal of Drug Issues,* 21 (1991), pp. 777–793; Gilbert Quintero and Mark Nichter, "The Semantics of Addiction: Moving beyond Expert Models to Lay Understandings," *Journal of Psychoactive Drugs,* 28 (1996), pp. 219–228.

5. Edward C. Senay, M. D., personal communication, February 5, 1998.

6. D. E. Weissman and J. D. Haddox, "Opioid Pseudoaddiction—An Iatrogenic Syndrome," *Pain, 36*(3) (1989), pp. 363–366; K. L. Sees and H. W. Clark, "Opioid Use in the Treatment of Chronic Pain: Assessment of Addiction," *Journal of Pain and Symptom Management, 8*(5) (1993), pp. 257–264.

7. For one of these surveys, see Carl D. Chambers, *An Assessment of Drug Use in the General Population* (Albany: New York State Narcotic Addiction Control Commission, 1970).

8. See, for example, Nannette Stone, Marlene Fromme, and Daniel Kogan, *Cocaine: Seduction and Solution* (New York: Pinnacle, 1984).

CHAPTER 2

FROM DOVER'S POWDER TO THE EVIL WEED OF THE FIELDS

The Early History of Drug Taking in America

The beginnings of most social phenomena are relatively easy to trace. American jazz, for example, emerged a little more than a century ago in the city of New Orleans. It was a fusion of the existing musical art forms of black America—the work songs, spirituals, and blues—combined with elements of white folk music, the rhythms of Hispanic America and the Caribbean, the melodies of French dances, and the instrumentation of the marching band.[1] A major impetus for the gay liberation movement in the United States dates back to 1969 to what has become known as "Stonewall." It was a three-day confrontation between police and gay men in New York City's Greenwich Village community sparked by plainclothes police attempts to close down an unlicensed gay bar.*

Similarly, the roots of today's attempt to rid U.S. streets and highways of drunk drivers are also easily targeted. They began on a spring afternoon in 1980 when a 13-year-old California teenager was struck down and killed by a hit-and-run driver. Stunned by the fact that the operator of the automobile was not only drunk at the time, but out on bail for his third drunk-driving offense and unlikely to be punished for the killing, the child's mother organized Mothers Against Drunk Drivers (MADD), which

---

*Just after midnight on June 27, 1969, nine plainclothes police detectives entered the Stonewall Inn at 53 Christopher Street in New York's avant-garde Greenwich Village. When a few of the club's habitués emerged in police custody, a growing mob of onlookers cheered them on: leather boys and drag queens, and butches and femmes, as they sometimes called themselves back in those days, and other assorted demimondaines—the downtrodden and most deviant members of the male homosexual community whom even the majority of gays looked down on. As the crowd expanded to almost four hundred, they began throwing coins, bottles, and bricks. The officers retreated into the Stonewall trying to hole up inside, and when police reinforcements arrived, the crowd began to disperse, and the forty-five-minute riot was suddenly over. On the following night there was a second riot, and a third occurred several days later. Stonewall, as these events have come to be known, was not the beginning of the gay rights movement, but it did mark a generational and ideological shift that brought gay liberation into that vast array of social protest sparked by the sixties generation. See Martin Duberman, *Stonewall* (New York: Dutton, 1993).

ultimately sparked a nationwide movement and campaign for stronger penalties for intoxicated drivers.[2]

The origins of other social trends can be more difficult to uncover. The roots of drug abuse are particularly obscure. The use of opium dates back at least to the ancient Greeks, and references to marijuana appear in early Persian, Hindu, Greek, Arab, and Chinese writings. Similarly, when the Spanish conquistador Francisco Pizarro stumbled upon the Inca empire in 1531, the chewing of coca had already been part of Inca mythology for centuries. Even in the United States, a nation with a relatively short history, the onset of drug abuse as a social phenomenon remains somewhat of a mystery.

THOMAS DOVER, *ROBINSON CRUSOE,* AND THE GREAT AMERICAN MEDICINE SHOW

Perhaps the social phenomenon of drug abuse began sometime during the eighteenth century with Thomas Dover, a student of British physician Thomas Sydenham. Known as the English Hippocrates and the father of clinical medicine, Sydenham had been a strong advocate of the use of opium for the treatment of disease. In fact, he was so committed to the clinical value of opium that sometime before his death in 1689, he stated that "among the remedies which it has pleased the Almighty God to give to man to relieve his sufferings, none is so universal and so efficacious as opium."[3]

Following the path of his mentor, Dover developed a form of medicinal opium. Known as Dover's Powder, it contained one ounce each of opium, ipecac (the dried roots of a tropical creeping plant), and licorice, combined with saltpeter, tartar, and wine.[4] It was introduced in 1709, the same year that Dover, also an adventurer and privateer, rescued castaway Alexander Selkirk from one of the desolate Juan Fernandez Islands off the coast of Chile, thus inspiring Daniel Defoe's *Robinson Crusoe.*[5] Dover's Powder made its way to the United States and remained one of the most widely used opium preparations for almost two centuries.*

The attraction of Dover's Powder was the euphoric and anesthetic properties of opium. For thousands of years, opium had been a popular narcotic. A derivative of the Oriental poppy (*Papaver somniferum L.*)—known by most people as the flower that interrupted Dorothy and Toto on their journey to the land of Oz—it was called the plant of joy some four thousand years ago in the Fertile Crescent of Mesopotamia. In Homer's *Odyssey,* the potion that Helen of Troy mixed to "quiet all pain and strife, and bring forgetfulness of every ill" is believed to have contained opium. There is even speculation that the "vinegar mixed with gall" (mentioned in Matthew 27:34), as an offering to Christ on the cross, contained opium.[6]

The introduction of Dover's Powder apparently started a trend. By the latter part of the eighteenth century, patent medicines containing opium were readily available throughout the urban and rural America. They were sold in pharmacies, grocery and general stores, at traveling medicine shows, and through the mail (see Exhibit 2.1).

---

*Dover's Powder continues to be compounded in both the United States and England, but because of its high opium content, it is rigidly controlled.

EXHIBIT 2.1   1887 Trade Card Advertising Opium Medicine (printed by J. Ottmann, New York)

Source: Image taken from Patricia M. Tice, *Altered States: Alcohol and Other Drugs in America* (New York: The Strong Museum, 1992), p. 42. Also in "Should We Legalize Drugs? History Answers," American Heritage, February/March 1993, p. 44, courtesy of Brown Brothers.

They were marketed under such labels as Ayer's Cherry Pectoral, Mrs. Winslow's Soothing Syrup, McMunn's Elixir, Godfrey's Cordial, Scott's Emulsion, and Dover's Powder. Many of these remedies were seductively advertised as painkillers, cough mixtures, soothing syrups, consumption cures, and women's friends. Others were promoted for the treatment of such varied ailments as diarrhea, dysentery, colds, fever, teething, cholera, rheumatism, pelvic disorders, athlete's foot, and even baldness and cancer. The drugs were produced from imported opium as well as the white opium poppies that were legally grown in the New England states, Florida and Louisiana, the West and Southwest, and the Confederate States during the Civil War.

The medical profession also fostered the use of opium. Dr. William Buchan's *Domestic Medicine,* published in Philadelphia in 1784 as a practical handbook on simple medicines for home use, suggested for the treatment of coughs:

> A cup of an infusion of wild poppy leaves and marsh-mellow roots, or the flowers of coltsfoot, may be taken frequently; or a teaspoonful of the paregoric elixir (flowers of benzoin plus opium) may be put into the patient's drink twice a day. Spanish infusion (liquor combined with the syrup of poppy leaves) is also a very popular medicine in this case, and may be taken in the quantity of a teacuful three or four times a day.[7]

Buchan's treatise on home remedies, which was republished in several editions, also recommended tincture of opium for the treatment of numerous common ailments:

Take of crude opium, two ounces; spirituous aromatic water, and mountain wine, of each ten ounces. Dissolve the opium, sliced, in the wine, with a gentle heat, frequently stirring it; afterward add the spirit, and strain off the tincture.[8]

Yet the mere appearance of Dover's Powder and other patent medicines in the United States was only minimally related to the evolution of drug abuse; other more potent social forces had been of considerably greater significance. Along with Dover's opium concoction, similar remedies were initially shipped to the colonies from London, as were most of the medications of the period. They were available from physicians, or over the counter from apothecaries, grocers, postmasters, and printers, but only in modest quantities.

When trade with England was disrupted during the Revolutionary War, a patent medicine industry emerged in the United States, spirited also by the state of eighteenth-century and early nineteenth-century standard medicine. The prevailing vogue in U.S. medical therapy had stressed extreme bleeding and purging. It was medicine's heroic age, but suspicion of heroic therapy led many people to seek out home remedies or cures available through their local general store.* These suspicions were further intensified with the rise of Jacksonian democracy and its antagonism toward intellectuals.

Expansions in the patent medicine industry were also related to the growth of the U.S. press. The manufacturers of the so-called medicines were the first business entrepreneurs to seek national markets through widespread advertising. They were the first hucksters to use psychological lures to entice customers to buy their merchandise. They were the first manufacturers to help the local merchants who retailed their wares by going directly to consumers with a message about their products. In total national advertising, this segment of the drug industry ranked highest in expenditures. During the post–Civil War decades, some individual proprietors spent in excess of five hundred thousand dollars each year for advertising. In the 1890s, for example, more than one million dollars was spent annually for the promotion of Scott's Emulsion.[9] As to the number of different varieties of patent medicines available, an 1804 New York catalog listed some ninety brands of elixirs; an 1857 Boston periodical included almost six hundred; in 1858 one newspaper account totaled over fifteen hundred patent medicines; and by 1905 the list had stretched to more than twenty-eight thousand.[10]

Curiously, the widespread presence of opium in patent medicines was not altogether understood by the majority of the public, for the so-called patent medicines were actually unpatented. The patenting of a drug required revealing its ingredients so that all might know its composition, but unpatented patent medicines kept their contents secret. In fact, in 1881 the Proprietary Medicine Manufacturers and Dealers Association was organized as an effective lobby for all interests in the trade. For

---

*"Heroic medicine" flourished between 1780 and 1850. It was a time when even educated physicians aggressively used such practices as bloodletting, intestinal purging, vomiting, profuse sweating, and blistering. And it was the patient, rather than the physician, who was considered "heroic."

almost three decades it fought against disclosure laws while Dover's Powder and the other popular opium-containing drugs sold in massive quantities.

Even though opium had been the only known product of the Oriental poppy for the longest time, in 1803 a young German pharmacist, Frederick Serturner, isolated the chief alkaloid of opium.[11] Serturner had hit upon morphine, which he so named after Morpheus, the Greek god of dreams. The discovery was to have profound effects on both medicine and society, for morphine was, and still is, the greatest single pain reliever the world has ever known. When the hypodermic syringe was invented, the use of morphine by injection in military medicine during the Civil War and the Franco-Prussian War granted the procedure legitimacy and familiarity to both physicians and the public.[12]

Furthermore, hypodermic medication had its pragmatic aspects: it brought quick local relief, its dosage could be regulated, and it was effective when oral medication was impractical. The regimen, however, was used promiscuously, for many physicians were anxious to illustrate their ability to quell the pain suffered by their patients, who, in turn, expected instant relief from discomfort. Or as one commentator put it:

> There is no proceeding in medicine that has become so rapidly popular; no method of allaying pain so prompt in its action and permanent in its effect; no plan of medication that has been so carelessly used and thoroughly abused; and no therapeutic discovery that has been so great a blessing and so great a curse to mankind than the hypodermic injection of morphia.[13]

The use of morphine by needle had become so pervasive by the 1890s that technology soon responded with the production of inexpensive equipment for mass use. In the 1897 edition of the Sears Roebuck catalog, for example, hypodermic kits, which included a syringe, two needles, two vials, and a carrying case, were advertised for as little a $1.50, with extra needles available at 25¢ each or $2.75 per dozen.[14]

In addition to the uncontrolled use of opium in patent medicines and morphine by injection, the practice of smoking opium also was prevalent. The Chinese laborers who were imported to build the railroads and work the mines in the trans–Mississippi West introduced it to the United States. It was estimated that by 1875 smoking opium had become widespread, particularly among prostitutes, gamblers, and other denizens of the underworld, but also among more respectable men and women of the middle and upper classes.[15]

As to the full volume of opium and morphine actually consumed during the nineteenth century, the picture is not altogether clear. The domestic production of opium was limited as a result of cultivation techniques that tended to yield a product considerably deficient in morphine, so one indicator of consumption can be drawn from import figures. According to data that the U.S. Public Health Service compiled in 1924, more than seven thousand tons of crude opium and almost eight hundred tons of smoking opium had been imported during the four-decade period ending in 1899.[16] Estimates as to the number of individuals actually dependent on opium during the latter part of the nineteenth century tended to be compiled rather loosely, ranging as high as 3 million.[17] Yet other, more rigorously collected data for the period did indicate that the use of narcotic drugs was indeed pervasive. In 1888, for example, one examination of ten thousand prescriptions from Boston-area pharmacies found that some 15 percent contained opiates,[18] and that was only in Boston. In 1900, it was estimated that in the small state of Vermont, 3.3 million doses of opium were sold each month.[19]

TRIPLEX LIVER PILLS, FRENCH WINE COCA, AND THE INTRODUCTION OF COCAINE TO THE UNITED STATES

Beyond opium and morphine, the patent medicine industry branched even further. Although chewing coca leaves for their mild stimulant effects had been a part of the culture in the Andes Mountains of South America for perhaps a thousand years, for some obscure reason the practice had never become popular in either Europe or the United States. During the latter part of the nineteenth century, however, Angelo Mariani of Corsica brought the unobtrusive Peruvian shrub to the notice of the rest of the world. After importing tons of coca leaves to his native land, he produced an extract

EXHIBIT 2.2   Advertisement for Vin Coca Mariani

Source: Image taken from http://cocaine.org/tonicwine.htm

**EXHIBIT 2.3   Mariani Wine
Endorsed by the Pope**

Source: Image taken from
www.cocaine.org/ popecoke.htm

that he mixed with wine and called Vin Coca Mariani (see Exhibit 2.2).[20] The wine was an immediate success, publicized as a magical beverage that would free the body from fatigue, lift the spirits, and create a lasting sense of well-being. Vin Coca brought Mariani immediate wealth and fame, as well as a medal of appreciation from Pope Leo XIII who used the drink as a source of comfort in his many years of ascetic retirement (see Exhibit 2.3).

Across the ocean during the same years, John Stith Pemberton of Atlanta, Georgia, had been marketing Triplex Liver Pills, Globe of Flower Cough Syrup, and a number of equally curious patent medicines. Noting Mariani's great success, in 1885 Pemberton developed a new product that he registered as French Wine of Coca. The following year he introduced a new drink, Coca-Cola, creating an entirely new category of drink—the cola (see Exhibit 2.4).[21]*

---

*Coca-Cola incorporates decocainized extracts of the coca leaf in one of its flavoring compounds. However, these extracts come not from the species of coca native to the eastern Andes Mountains of South America (*Erythroxylum coca* var. *coca*) from which street cocaine is derived, but from Trujillo coca (*Erythroxylum novogranatense* var. *truxillense*). Trujillo coca is a variety well adapted to the desert conditions found in coastal Peru and has been found in numerous archeological sites, dating back as far as 1750 B.C. See Timothy Plowman, "The Identity of Amazonian and Trujillo Coca," *Botanical Museum Leaflets,* 27 (Harvard University, 1979), pp. 45–51; M. N. Cohen, "Archeological Plant Remains from the Central Coast of Peru," *Nawpa Pacha,* 16 (1978), pp. 36–37; T. C. Patterson, "Central Peru: Its Population and Economy," *Archaeology,* 24 (1971), pp. 316–321.

EXHIBIT 2.4   Coca Cola Bottle, 1899
Source: Courtesy of Coca Cola Company.

The full potency of the coca leaf remained unknown until 1859 when cocaine was first isolated in its pure form.* Yet little use was made of the new alkaloid until 1883 when Dr. Theodor Aschenbrandt secured a supply of the drug and issued it to Bavarian soldiers during maneuvers. Aschenbrandt, a German military physician, noted the beneficial effects of cocaine, particularly its ability to suppress fatigue. Among those who read Aschenbrandt's account with fascination was a struggling young Viennese neurologist, Sigmund Freud. Suffering from chronic fatigue, depression, and various neurotic symptoms, Freud obtained a measure of cocaine and tried it himself. He also offered it to a colleague who was suffering from both a disease of the nervous system and morphine addiction, and to a patient with a chronic and

---

*There appear to be numerous contradictions in the literature as to who first isolated cocaine, and when. Although recent sources hold that it was the German chemist Friedrich Gaedecke in 1855, a more persistent search suggests that Gaedecke only isolated alkaloidal cocaine. It was not until 1859 that Dr. Albert Niemann of the University of Göttingen isolated the chief alkaloid of coca and actually named it *cocaine.* See Carl Koller, "On the Beginnings of Local Anesthesia," paper presented at the annual meeting of the Brooklyn Ophthalmological Society, Brooklyn, New York, April 18, 1940; David F. Allen, *The Cocaine Crisis* (New York: Plenum Press, 1987).

painful gastric disorder. Finding the initial results to be quite favorable in all three cases, Freud decided that cocaine was a magical drug. In a letter to his fiancée, Martha Bernays, in 1884, Freud commented on his experiences with cocaine:

> If all goes well I will write an essay on it and I expect it will win its place in therapeutics by the side of morphium and superior to it. I have other hopes and intentions about it. I take very small doses of it regularly against depression and against indigestion, and with the most brilliant success.... In short it is only now that I feel that I am a doctor, since I have helped one patient and hope to help more.[22]

In July 1884, less than three months after Freud's initial experiences with cocaine, his essay was published in a German medical journal and reprinted in English in the *Saint Louis Medical and Surgical Journal* shortly thereafter.[23] Freud then pressed the drug onto his friends and colleagues, urging that they use it both for themselves and their patients; he gave it to his sisters and his fiancée, and continued to use it himself. By the close of the 1880s, however, Freud and the others who had praised cocaine as an all-purpose wonder drug began to withdraw their support for it in light of an increasing number of reports of compulsive use and undesirable side effects.

By 1890, however, the patent medicine industry in the United States had also discovered the benefits of the unregulated use of cocaine. The industry quickly added the drug to its reservoir of home remedies, touting it as helpful not only for everything from alcoholism to venereal disease, but also as a cure for addiction to other patent medicines. Since the new tonics contained substantial amounts of cocaine, they did indeed make users feel better, at least initially, thus spiriting the patent medicine industry into its golden age of popularity.

THE PECULIAR LEGACY OF BAYER LABORATORIES

Research into the mysteries of opium during the nineteenth century led not only to Serturner's discovery of morphine in 1806, but to that of more than two dozen other alkaloids, including codeine, in 1831. Yet more importantly, in an 1874 issue of the *Journal of the Chemical Society,* British chemist C. R. A.Wright described a series of experiments he had carried out at London's St. Mary's Hospital to determine the effects of combining various acids with morphine. Wright produced a series of new morphinelike compounds, including what became known in the scientific literature as *diacetylmorphine.*[24]

The discovery of both codeine and diacetylmorphine had been the outgrowth of an enduring search for more effective substitutes for morphine. This interest stemmed not only from the painkilling qualities of opiate drugs but also from their sedative effects on the respiratory system. Wright's work, however, went for the most part unnoticed. Some twenty-four years later, though, in 1898, pharmacologist Heinrich Dreser reported on a series of experiments he had conducted with diacetylmorphine for Friedrich Bayer and Company of Elberfeld, Germany, noting that the drug was highly effective in the treatment of coughs, chest pains, and the discomforts

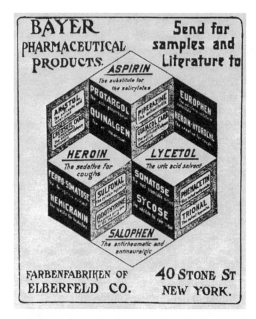

EXHIBIT 2.5   Bayer Pharmaceutical Products, Image circa 1898

Source: Taken from Patricia M. Tice, *Altered States: Alcohol and Other Drugs in America* (New York: The Strong Museum, 1992), p. 45. Also in "Should We Legalize Drugs? History Answers," *American Heritage,* February/ March 1993, p. 45, courtesy of Bettmann Archives.

associated with pneumonia and tuberculosis. Dreser's commentary received immediate notice, for it had come at a time when antibiotics were still unknown, and pneumonia and tuberculosis were among the leading causes of death. He claimed that diacetylmorphine had a stronger sedative effect on respiration than either morphine or codeine, that therapeutic relief came quickly, and that the potential for a fatal overdose was almost nil. In response to such favorable reports, Bayer and Company began marketing diacetylmorphine under the trade name Heroin (see Exhibit 2.5)— so named from the German *heroisch,* meaning heroic and powerful.[25]

Although Bayer's Heroin was promoted as a sedative for coughs and as a chest and lung medicine, it was advocated by some as a treatment for morphine addiction. This situation seems to have arisen from three somewhat related phenomena. The first was the belief that Heroin was nonaddicting. As one physician wrote in the *New York Medical Journal* in 1900:

Habituation [with Heroin] has been noted in a small percentage of the cases. All observers are agreed, however, that none of the patients suffer in any way from this

habituation, and that none of the symptoms which are so characteristic of chronic morphinism have ever been observed. On the other hand, a large number of the reports refer
to the fact that the same dose may be used for a long time without any habituation.[26]

Second, since the drug had a greater potency than that of morphine, only small
dosages were required for the desired medical effects, thus reducing the potential for
the rapid onset of dependence. And third, at the turn of the twentieth century, the
medical community did not fully understand the dynamics of cross dependence.
Cross dependence refers to the phenomenon by which dependence on one drug carries over to certain other pharmacologically related drugs. For the patient suffering
from the unpleasant effects of morphine withdrawal, the administration of Heroin has
the consequence of one or more doses of morphine. The dependence is maintained
and withdrawal disappears, the two combining to give the appearance of a cure. So
given the endorsement of the medical community, with little mention of its potential
dangers, Heroin quickly found its way into routine medical therapeutics and over-
the-counter patent medicines.

HUCKSTERS, THE RED CLAUSE, AND THE
EMERGENCE OF ANTIDRUG LEGISLATION

By the early years of the twentieth century, the steady progress of medical science
had provided physicians with a better understanding of the long-term effects of drugs
they had been advocating. Sigmund Freud had already recognized his poor judgment
in the claims he had made about cocaine; the dependence potential and abuse liability
of morphine had been well established; and the dependence-producing properties of
Bayer's Heroin were being noticed. Yet these drugs—cocaine, morphine, and
heroin—often combined with alcohol, were still readily available from a totally
unregulated patent medicine industry. Not only were they unregulated, but many were
highly potent as well. Birney's Catarrah Cure, for example, was 4 percent cocaine.
Colonel Hoestetter's Bitters had such a generous amount of C_2H_5OH (alcohol) in its
formula to preserve the medicine that the fumes from just one tablespoonful fed
through a gas burner could maintain a bright flame for almost five minutes.

To these and others could be added even more pretentious and sham medications, which, even though not necessarily dangerous to the patient's health, were
pushed on the unsuspecting and gullible public by enterprising and imaginative
hucksters. Perhaps the most curious of these was Samuel M. Kier's Rock Oil. During
the better part of the nineteenth century, salt was typically produced from brine
drawn from deep wells. Occasionally, the utility of such wells was ruined when petroleum found its way into the underground reservoirs.

One Kentucky businessman secured a number of these abandoned, ruined salt
wells; formed the American Medical Oil Company; and sold hundreds of thousands of
bottles of the greasy brine as American Oil, advertising it as an effective remedy for
almost any ailment. But Kier, the profiteering son of a Pennsylvania salt manufacturer,

was even more enterprising. When oil began to flow in quantity from his underground salt deposits, he initiated an active campaign by giving testimony to the wonderful medicinal virtues of "Petroleum, or Rock Oil; A Natural Remedy; Procured from a Well in Allegheny County, Pennsylvania; Four Hundred Feet Below the Earth's Surface." Kier's salespeople, equipped with ornamented wagons and ready supplies of the wonder oil, brought the legendary medicine show to rural and urban America, selling millions of half-pint bottles along the way.[27]

For decades, however, the task of bringing about change in the medicine industry seemed to have few results. As early as the 1870s, while some physicians were actively cashing in on the gullibility of the patient population, others expressed their reservations in print. The medical writings, however, went unnoticed for the most part, for few people other than doctors or pharmacists read the medical journals. Newspapers, on the other hand, were a haven for the patent medicine industry, and most producers of the dubious drugs made sure that they would remain so. They invented a red clause that would appear in advertising contracts. "It is mutually agreed," the red type would indicate, "that this Contract is void, if any law is enacted by your state restricting or prohibiting the manufacture or sale of proprietary medicines."[28] Thus, the newspaper reader saw one column after another of patent medicine advertising, with almost no questioning of the drugs' medical efficacy.

With the new century came a more progressive climate of opinion and a greater willingness to speak out for reform. The American Medical Association purged its journal of questionable advertising; the AMA Council on Pharmacy and Chemistry investigated the patent medicine industry; state chemists undertook analyses of the remedies; and all pooled their findings and turned them over to lay reporters. Then the muckraking journalists took over. William Allen White's *Emporia (Kansas) Gazette* ignored the infamous red clause and hosted a series of articles that pointed out the hazards of self-medication with patent medicines. At the same time, the *Ladies Home Journal* extended the attack to the remedies high in alcoholic content. Yet the most provocative effort was "The Great American Fraud," a long series of articles written by Samuel Hopkins Adams that began in 1905 in the pages of *Collier's* magazine (see Exhibit 2.6). Wrote Adams in his opening essay:

> Gullible America will spend this year $75 million in the purchase of patent medicines. In consideration of this sum it will swallow huge quantities of alcohol, an appalling amount of opiates and narcotics, a wide assortment of varied drugs ranging from powerful and dangerous heart depressants to insidious liver stimulants; and, far in excess of other ingredients, undiluted fraud. For fraud, exploited by the skillfulest of advertising bunco men, is the basis of the trade.[29]

In subsequent articles Adams exposed the institution of the red clause and passionately described the powders and soothing syrups containing heroin, opium, morphine, and cocaine as part of a shameful trade "that stupefies helpless babies and makes criminals of our young men and harlots of our young women." Adams' commentaries in *Collier's* did not go unnoticed, but the final indictment leading to the downfall of the patent medicine industry was totally unrelated to the problems

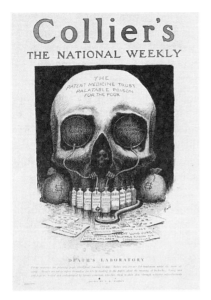

EXHIBIT 2.6   Collier's Weekly, 1905

Source: Taken from Patricia M. Tice, *Altered States: Alcohol and Other Drugs in America* (New York: The Strong Museum, 1992), p. 74.

described in "The Great American Fraud." On five hundred dollars supplied by a socialist periodical, a young novelist lived for seven weeks in the stockyard meat-packing district of Chicago, gathering data among the welter of new emigrant nationalities who were struggling there to adjust to the New World. His name was Upton Sinclair, and his goal was to point out the evils of capitalist exploitation and to bring laborers under the wing of the Socialist party.

With the 1906 publication of Sinclair's account, entitled *The Jungle,* public attention concentrated not on the scandalous miseries of the proletariat in capitalist America, but on the lurid and nauseating details of Chicago's handling of the meat that the entire nation had been eating. It seems that deviled ham was actually minced tripe (stomach lining) dyed red, and much of the packers' lamb and mutton was goat. They kept down infestations of rats in the packing plants by baiting the unsuspecting rodents with poisoned bread. Then, dead rats (poisoned bread and all) typically went into the hoppers of oddments used in sausages and other processed meats for human consumption. What no reader could manage to forget was that, now and then, an employee slipped on a wet floor, fell into a vat of boiling meat scraps, and "was overlooked for days, till all but his bones . . . had gone out to the world as Durham's Pure Leaf Lard."

The Jungle shocked both Congress and the people of America and represented the needed impetus for legislative reform. By mid-1906, the Pure Food and Drug Act was passed, prohibiting the interstate transportation of adulterated or misbranded food and drugs. The act brought about the decline of the patent medicine industry;

henceforth, the proportions of alcohol, opium, morphine, heroin, cocaine, and a number of other substances in each preparation had to be indicated. Thus, because the mass media had pointed out the negative effects of these ingredients, a number of the remedies lost their appeal. Moreover, it suddenly became difficult to market a preparation that contained one or more other narcotic drugs as a cure for morphine dependence.

The new legislation merely imposed standards for quality, packaging, and labeling; it did not actually outlaw the use of cocaine and opiate drugs. Public Law No. 47, 63rd Congress (H.R. 1967), more popularly known as the Harrison Act, sponsored by New York Representative Francis Burton Harrison and passed in 1914, ultimately served in that behalf. At the same time, the new legislation went a long way to alter public and criminal justice responses to drug use in the United States for generations to come.

The Harrison Act required all people who imported, manufactured, produced, compounded, sold, dispensed, or otherwise distributed cocaine and opiate drugs to register with the Treasury Department, pay special taxes, and keep records of all transactions.[30] It was a revenue code designed to exercise some measure of public control over drugs rather than to penalize the estimated 200,000 users of narcotics in the United States. In effect, however, penalization is what occurred.

Certain provisions of the Harrison Act permitted physicians to prescribe, dispense, or administer narcotics to their patients for "legitimate medical purposes" and "in the course of professional practice." But how these two phrases were interpreted ultimately defined narcotics use as a crime. On the one hand, the medical establishment held that addiction was a disease and that addicts were patients to whom drugs could be prescribed to alleviate the distress of withdrawal. On the other hand, the Treasury Department interpreted the Harrison Act to mean that a doctor's prescription for an addict was unlawful.

The United States Supreme Court quickly laid the controversy to rest. In *Webb v. U.S.,*[31] decided in 1919, the High Court held that it was not legal for a physician to prescribe narcotic drugs to an addict for the purpose of maintaining his or her use and comfort. In *U.S. v. Behrman,*[32] decided three years later, this ruling went one step further by declaring that a narcotic prescription for an addict was unlawful, even if the drugs were prescribed as part of a cure program.* The impact of these decisions combined to make it almost impossible for those dependent on narcotics to obtain drugs legally. In 1925, the Supreme Court emphatically reversed itself in *Linder v. U.S.,*[33] disavowing the *Behrman* opinion and holding that addicts (in the words of the High Court) were entitled to medical care like other patients, but the ruling had almost no effect. By that time, physicians were unwilling to treat drug-dependent patients under any circumstances, and a well-developed, illegal drug marketplace had emerged to cater to the needs of the narcotics-using population.

---

*Although cocaine is not a narcotic, the Harrison Act and subsequent court decisions defined it as such. Even in segments of contemporary drug legislation, at both state and federal levels, cocaine is still listed as a narcotic. A discussion of what constitutes a narcotic appears later in this book.

SNOW PARTIES, GERMAN WAR PROPAGANDA, AND THE RISE OF THE CRIMINAL ADDICT

Many commentators on the history of drug use in the United States have argued that the Harrison Act snatched drug users from legitimate society and forced them into the underworld. As attorney Rufus King, a well-known chronicler of U.S. narcotics legislation, once described it, "Exit the addict-patient, enter the addict-criminal."[34] But this naive cause-and-effect interpretation tends to be a rather extreme misrepresentation of historical fact.

Without question, at the beginning of the twentieth century, most users of narcotics were members of legitimate society. In fact, the majority had first encountered the effects of narcotics through their family physician or local pharmacist or grocer. In other words, their dependence had been medically induced during the course of treatment for some other perceived ailment. Yet long before the Harrison Act had been passed, there were indications that this population of users had begun to shrink.[35] Agitation had existed in both the medical and religious communities against the haphazard use of narcotics, defining much of it as a moral disease. For many, the sheer force of social stigma and pressure served to alter their use of drugs.

Similarly, the decline of the patent medicine industry, after the passage of the Pure Food and Drug Act, was believed to have substantially reduced the number of narcotics and cocaine users. Moreover, by 1912, most state governments had enacted legislative controls for dispensing and selling narcotics. Thus, it is possible to assert that the size of the drug-using population had started to decline years before the Harrison Act had become the subject of Supreme Court interpretation. Then too, the combined effects of stigma, social pressure, the Pure Food and Drug Act, and state controls had also served to create an underworld of drug users and black-market drugs. By 1914, a number of commentators had noted this change. Some, however melodramatically, targeted the subterranean economy of narcotics use:

> Several individuals have come to the conclusion that selling "dope" is a very profitable business. These individuals have sent their agents among the gangs frequenting our city corners, instructing them to make friends with the members and induce them to take the drug. Janitors, bartenders, and cabmen have also been employed to help sell the habit. The plan has worked so well that there is scarcely a poolroom in New York that may not be called a meeting place for dope fiends. The drug has been made up in candy and sold to school children. The conspiring individuals, being familiar with the habit-forming action of the drugs, believe that the increased number of "fiends" will create a larger demand for the drug, and in this way build up profitable business.[36]

By the latter part of the decade, other observers were noting that although the medically induced addict was still prominent, a new population had recently emerged.[37] It was an underworld population, composed principally of heroin and cocaine users who had initiated drug use as the result of associations with other criminals. Thus, it would appear that the emergence of the criminal addict was not simply the result of a cause-and-effect criminalization process—the Harrison Act's definition of narcotics use as criminal. Rather, it was likely the result of the effects of legislation combined with the emergence of a new category of users who were already within the underworld.

Although accurate data on the incidence and prevalence of drug use have been available only recently, by the early 1920s readers of the popular media were confronted, almost on a daily basis, with how drug use, and particularly heroin use, had become a national epidemic. Estimates were placed as high as 5 million, with any number of explanations for the increased number of users. Some blamed it on the greed of drug traffickers, others on the inadequate personalities of the users. A few argued that it was a natural consequence of the Prohibition amendment.[38] Most observers generally agreed, however, that more legislation was the answer to the problem. As an editorial in the *Literary Digest* for June 10, 1922, stated:

> "Snow parties," which are said to have become so prevalent as to menace American civilization, will be made impossible by the Jones-Miller bill governing the manufacture, importation and exportation of habit-forming drugs, which has been passed by Congress and signed by President Harding. By striking at the source of supply, the bill goes to the root of the evil, and, in time, will eliminate it altogether.[39]

Snow, as the editorial suggested, referred to heroin and cocaine, and the Jones-Miller Act was a piece of federal legislation that set fines up to five thousand dollars and imprisonment up to ten years for anyone involved in the unlawful importation of narcotics.

Even though the Jones-Miller Act had little impact, other than to further inflate the prices of heroin and morphine on the black market, some people argued that the drug epidemic was a myth. One observer suggested that the exaggerated estimates were no more than German war propaganda. Despite a rumor that those in charge of the draft during World War I would find "no less than 500,000 addicts among the inductees," it was pointed out that of some 3.5 million men examined, only 3,284 were found to be drug dependent. By applying that ratio to 1920 census figures, it was concluded that 100,000 addicts was likely a more accurate estimate, and that drug dependence had actually declined during the previous two decades.[40]

Other data tended to support this conclusion. In 1924, Dr. Lawrence Kolb and Dr. A. G. Du Mez of the U.S. Public Health Service estimated after a careful examination of all the available survey data on drug use that there were probably only 110,000 addicts in the United States at the end of 1922, reflecting a considerable decline since the turn of the century.[41] Yet whatever the correct figures, everyone seemed to agree that narcotics use was indeed a problem that needed to be addressed.

MARIJUANA: THE EVIL WEED OF THE FIELDS, ROADSIDES, AND RIVER BEDS

The national concern over the use of narcotics during the 1930s was not focused solely on heroin, for another substance was considered by some to represent an even greater evil. One might expect that it was cocaine, because the drug's stimulant effects had been promoted in the United States well before the introduction of Bayer's Heroin. But this was not the case. After the passage of the Pure Food and Drug Act in 1906, cocaine use moved underground to the netherworlds of the jazz scene and the bohemia of the avant-garde. There it remained for decades, so much so that the Treasury Department's Bureau of Narcotics, a federal agency that was often accused of grossly exaggerating the extent of drug use in the United States, concluded in 1939 that "the use of cocaine in the illicit traffic continues to be so small as to be without significance."[42] No, it was not cocaine, but rather the more "insidious" marijuana, alternatively called the devil drug, assassin of youth, and weed of madness.

Marijuana, typically referred to a century ago as cannabis or hashish, was introduced to the U.S. public in essentially the same manner as were opium, morphine, cocaine, and heroin. A derivative of the hemp plant from India, *Cannabis sativa L.,* the drug appeared among the patent medicines hawked from the tailgates of medicine show wagons and was sold as a cure for depression, convulsions, hysteria, insanity, mental retardation, and impotence (see Exhibit 2.7). Moreover, during the late 1800s, such well-known pharmaceutical companies as Parke-Davis and Squibb produced tincture of cannabis for the family pharmacist to dispense. As a medicinal agent, however, the drug quickly fell into disfavor. Because of its insolubility, it could not be injected, and taken orally it was slow and generally ineffective. Moreover, its potency was variable, making dosage standardization difficult. Yet as a recreational drug, marijuana had its devotees. By the middle of the 1880s, every major U.S. city had its clandestine hashish clubs catering to a rather well-to-do clientele.

At the beginning of the twentieth century, what was referred to in Mexico as *marijuana* (also *marihuana* and *mariguana*) began to appear in New Orleans and a number of the Texas border towns. Having been used in South America and Central America for quite some time, Mexican ditch weed (as some people called it) was a substance less potent than the hashish (often spelled "hasheesh" in the mass media) that was first smoked in the underground clubs decades earlier. Whereas hashish is the resinous extract of the hemp plant, marijuana is composed of the hemp plant's dried leaves, stems, and flowering tops.*

By 1920, the use of marijuana had become visible among members of minority groups—African Americans in the South and immigrant Mexicans in the Southwest. Given the social and political climate of the period, it is not at all surprising that the use of the drug became a matter of immediate concern. The agitation for reform that had resulted in the passage of the Harrison Act and the Pure Food and Drug Act was still active, and the movement for national prohibition of alcohol was at its peak. Moreover, not only was marijuana an "intoxicant of blacks and wetbacks"[43] that might have a corrupting influence on white society, it was considered particularly dangerous because of its alien (Mexican) origins (see Exhibit 2.8).

Through the early 1930s, state after state enacted antimarijuana laws, usually instigated by lurid newspaper articles depicting the madness and horror attributed to

---

*The etymological roots of the word *marijuana* have been debated at length and still remain unresolved. Some maintain that the word comes from what the Aztec people referred to as *mallihuan,* a term that imparted the idea of a substance that took possession of the user. A second position holds that the word is a corruption of the Portuguese *maranguango,* meaning intoxicating.

■ ■ ■ ■ ■

EXHIBIT 2.7

CANNABIS SATIVA L.

Cannabis sativa L. is an annual plant that flourishes in most warm or temperate climates and varies in height from three to ten feet or more. The leaves are long, narrow, and serrated, and form a fan-shaped pattern; each fan has anywhere from three to fifteen leaves, but typically only five or seven leaves. These leaves are shiny and sticky, and their upper surfaces are covered with short hairs. The psychoactive preparations derivative of cannabis are three:

1. *Marijuana.* The crushed and dried twigs, leaves, and flowers
2. *Hashish.* The resinous extract obtained by boiling in a solvent those parts of the plant that are covered with the resin, or by scraping the resin from the plant
3. *Hashoil.* A dark viscous liquid produced by a process of repeated extraction of cannabis material

The active ingredient in cannabis is delta-9-tetrahydrocannabinol, or simply THC. Whereas the THC content of most marijuana ranges from 1 to 10 percent, in hashish this figure can be as high as 15 to 25 percent, and twice that for hashoil.

Cannabis products vary in both name and form in different parts of the world. In Asia, for example, there is ganga, charas, and bhang. Ganja consists of the young leaves and flowering tops of the cultivated female plant and its resin, pressed or rolled into a sticky mass and then formed into flat or round cakes. Its color is dark green or greenish-brown, and it has a pleasant smell and characteristic taste. Charas is the prepared resin separated from the tops of the female plant. It is pounded and rubbed until it is a grey-white powder and then made into cakes or thin almost transparent sheets, or it is left in dark brown lumps. Bhang consists of the older or more mature leaves of the plant and is often used by boiling in water and adding butter to make a syrup. Bhang is less potent than ganja, which in turn is considerably weaker than charas.

In the Middle East the word *hashish* is usually applied to both the leaves and the resin or a mixture of the two. In North Africa the resin and tops, usually reduced to a coarse powder, are known as *kif* in Morocco, and *takrouri* in Algeria and Tunisia. In Central and Southern Africa *dagga* refers to the leaves and tops.

Despite these many differences in nomenclature, the subjective effects of marijuana are essentially the same, although varying in intensity depending on THC content. At social–recreational use levels, these effects include alteration of time and space perception; a sense of euphoria, relaxation, well-being, and disinhibition; dulling of attention; fragmentation of thought and impaired immediate memory; an altered sense of identity; and exaggerated laughter and increased suggestibility. At doses higher than the typical recreational levels, more pronounced distortions of thought may occur, including a disrupted sense of one's own body, a sense of personal unreality, visual distortions, and sometimes hallucinations, paranoid thinking, and acute psychotic-like symptoms.

the drug's use. Even the prestigious *New York Times,* with its claim of "All the News That's Fit to Print," helped to reinforce the growing body of beliefs surrounding marijuana use. In an article headlined "Mexican Family Go Insane," and datelined Mexico City, July 6, 1927, the *Times* reported:

EXHIBIT 2.8   Marijuana Poster

Source: Available online through the Schaffer Library of Drug Policy www.druglibrary.org/ schaffer/hemp/history/assyouth.htm

> A widow and her four children have been driven insane by eating the Marihuana plant, according to doctors, who say that there is no hope of saving the children's lives and that the mother will be insane for the rest of her life.
>
> The tragedy occurred while the body of the father, who had been killed, was still in a hospital.
>
> The mother was without money to buy other food for the children, whose ages range from 3 to 15, so they gathered some herbs and vegetables growing in the yard for their dinner. Two hours after the mother and children had eaten the plants, they were stricken. Neighbors, hearing outbursts of crazed laughter, rushed to the house to find the entire family insane. Examination revealed that the narcotic marihuana was growing among the garden vegetables.[44]

Popular books of the era were as colorful as the press in describing marijuana and the consequences of its use. A 1928 publication, aptly titled *Dope,* for example, offered the following:

> And the man under the influence of hasheesh catches up his knife and runs through the streets hacking and killing everyone he meets. No, he has no special grievance against mankind. When he is himself, he is probably a good-humored, harmless, well-meaning

creature; but hasheesh is the murder drug, and it is the hasheesh which makes him pick up his knife and start to kill.

Marihuana is American hasheesh. It is made from a little weed that grows in Texas, Arizona, and Southern California. You can grow enough marihuana in a window-box to drive the whole population of the United States stark, staring, raving mad.

. . . but when you have once chosen marihuana, you have selected murder and torture and hideous cruelty to your bosom friends.[45]

In other reports, the link between the antimarijuana sentiment and prejudice was apparent. On January 27, 1929, the *Montana Standard* reported on the progress of a bill that amended the state's general narcotic law to include marijuana:

There was fun in the House Health Committee during the week when the Marihuana bill came up for consideration. Marihuana is Mexican opium, a plant used by Mexicans and cultivated for sale by Indians. "When some beet field peon takes a few rares of this stuff," explained Dr. Fred Fulsher of Mineral County, "he thinks he has just been elected president of Mexico so he starts to execute all of his political enemies. . . ." Everybody laughed and the bill was recommended for passage.[46]

Although marijuana is neither Mexican opium nor a narcotic of any kind, it was perceived as such by a small group of legislators, newspaper editors, and concerned citizens who were pressuring Washington for federal legislation against the drug. Their demands were almost immediately heard by Harry J. Anslinger, the recently installed Commissioner of the Treasury Department's Bureau of Narcotics in 1930. Although it would appear that Anslinger was somewhat of an ultra right-wing conservative who truly believed marijuana to be a threat to the future of U.S. civilization, his biographer maintained that he was an astute government bureaucrat who viewed the marijuana issue as a mechanism for elevating himself and the Bureau of Narcotics to national prominence.[47] In retrospect, however, given what is now known about marijuana, Anslinger's crusade has been interpreted by many to have been no more than the ravings of a madman.

Using the mass media as his forum, Anslinger described marijuana as a Frankenstein drug that was stalking American youth. In an issue of *American Magazine,* he wrote, for example:

The sprawled body of a young girl lay crushed on the sidewalk the other day after a plunge from the fifth story of a Chicago apartment house. Everyone called it suicide, but actually it was murder. The killer was a narcotic known to America as marijuana, and to history as hashish. It is a narcotic used in the form of cigarettes, comparatively new to the United States and as dangerous as a coiled rattlesnake. . . .[48]

Then there was Anslinger's "gore file," a collection of the most heinous cases, most with only the flimsiest of substantiation, that graphically depicted the insane violence that marijuana use engendered. For example, again from *American Magazine:*

An entire family was murdered by a youthful addict in Florida. When officers arrived at the home, they found the youth staggering about in a human slaughterhouse. With an ax he had killed his father, mother, two brothers, and a sister. He seemed to be in a daze. . . . He had no recollection of having committed the multiple crime. The officers knew him ordinarily as a sane, rather quiet young man; now he was pitifully crazed. They sought the reason. The boy said that he had been in the habit of smoking something which youthful friends called "muggles," a childish name for marihuana.[49]

Much of the gore file also touched on the interracial fears in white society. For example:

Colored students at the Univ. of Minn. partying with female students (white), smoking [marijuana] and getting their sympathy with stories of racial persecution. Result pregnancy.

Two Negroes took a girl fourteen years old and kept her for two days under the influence of marihuana. Upon recovery she was found to be suffering from syphilis.[50]

As the result of Anslinger's crusade, on August 2, 1937, the Marijuana Tax Act was signed into law, classifying the scraggly tramp of the vegetable world as a narcotic and placing it under essentially the same controls as the Harrison Act had done with opium and coca products.*

POSTSCRIPT

As was the case with morphine and heroin, observers of the marijuana problem debated about the number of the drug's devotees (as users were often called). What everyone seemed to concur on, however, was that narcotics use was indeed a problem in the United States. Where little agreement existed, however, was in the proper methods for handling it. Throughout the balance of the 1930s, three points of view dominated. The medical establishment argued that addiction was a physical disease and should be treated as such; the law enforcement establishment saw addiction as a criminal tendency and favored harsh punishment for the sake of societal protection and deterrence; and the political establishment believed that drug dependence could be legislated out of existence simply by passing enough comprehensive laws. Each establishment worked in pursuit of its own beliefs and agenda. A few treatment facilities were opened, addicts were arrested and imprisoned, and new legislation was passed.

---

*For decades after the passage of the Marijuana Tax Act, Anslinger continued to write about the evils of marijuana—the Mexican ditch weed—almost as if he had to justify the wisdom of the law. See, for example, Harry J. Anslinger and William F. Tompkins, *The Traffic in Narcotics* (New York: Funk & Wagnalls, 1953); Harry J. Anslinger and Will Ousler, *The Murderers: The Shocking Story of the Narcotics Gangs* (New York: Farrar, Straus, and Cudahy, 1961).

By the early 1940s, narcotic addiction had all but disappeared in the United States. But it was not the result of medical, enforcement, or legislative efforts. World War II had intervened, cutting off the supplies of opium from Asia and interrupting the trafficking routes from Europe. As an editorial in *Time* put it in 1942, "The war is probably the best thing that ever happened to U.S. drug addicts."[51]

NOTES

1. Eric Hobsbawm, *The Jazz Scene* (New York: New Pantheon Books, 1993).
2. Micky Sadoff, *America Gets MADD* (Irving, TX: Mothers Against Drunk Drivers, 1990).
3. Charles E. Terry and Mildred Pellens, *The Opium Problem* (New York: Bureau of Social Hygiene, 1928), p. 56.
4. E. F. Cook and E.W. Martin, *Remington's Practice of Pharmacy* (Easton, PA: Mack Publishing Co., 1951).
5. See Diana Souhami, *Selkirk's Island* (New York: Harcourt, 2001).
6. Peter P. White, "The Poppy," *National Geographic,* February 1985, p. 144. See also Mark David Merlin, *On the Trail of the Ancient Opium Poppy* (Rutherford, NJ: Fairleigh Dickinson University Press, 1984).
7. William Buchan, M.D., *Domestic Medicine: Or, A Treatise on the Prevention and Cure of Diseases by Regimen and Simple Medicines* (Philadelphia: Crukshank, Bell, and Muir, 1784), pp. 225–226.
8. Buchan, p. 520.
9. *Scientific American,* 5 October 1985, p. 214.
10. James Harvey Young, *The Toadstool Millionaires: A Social History of Patent Medicines in America before Federal Regulation* (Princeton, NJ: Princeton University Press, 1961), pp. 19–23.
11. Jerome H. Jaffe and William R. Martin, "Narcotic Analgesics and Antagonists," in *The Pharmacological Basis of Therapeutics,* ed. Louis S. Goodman and Alfred Gilman (New York: Macmillan, 1970), p. 245.
12. See Robert Bartholow, *A Manual of Hypodermatic Medication* (Philadelphia: Lippincott, 1891).
13. H. H. Kane, *The Hypodermic Injection of Morphia* (New York: C. L. Bermingham, 1880), p. 5.
14. *1897 Sears Roebuck Catalogue* (1897; reprinted New York: Chelsea House, 1968), p. 32 of insert on drugs.
15. Terry and Pellens, p. 73.
16. See Lawrence Kolb and A. G. Du Mez, "The Prevalence and Trend of Drug Addiction in the United States and the Factors Influencing It," *Public Health Reports,* 23 May 1924.
17. Terry and Pellens, pp. 1–20. See also H. Wayne Morgan, *Yesterday's Addicts: American Society and Drug Abuse, 1865–1920* (Norman: University of Oklahoma Press, 1974).
18. Virgil G. Eaton, "How the Opium Habit Is Acquired," *Popular Science Monthly,* 33 (1888), pp. 665–666.
19. A. P. Grinnell, "A Review of Drug Consumption and Alcohol as Found in Proprietary Medicine," *Medical Legal Journal,* 1905, cited in Terry and Pellens, pp. 21–22.
20. Hector P. Blejer, "Coca Leaf and Cocaine Addiction—Some Historical Notes," *Canadian Medical Association Journal,* 25 September 1965, p. 702.
21. E. J. Kahn, *The Big Drink: The Story of Coca-Cola* (New York: Random House, 1960).
22. Ernest Jones, *The Life and Work of Sigmund Freud,* Vol. I (New York: Basic Books, 1953), p. 81.
23. Freud's paper "ber Coca" (On Coca) has been reprinted in *Cocaine Papers by Sigmund Freud,* ed. Robert Byck (New York: New American Library, 1975), pp. 49–73.
24. C. R. A. Wright, "On the Action of Organic Acids and Their Anhydrides on the Natural Alkaloids," *Journal of the Chemical Society,* 12 July 1874, p. 1031.
25. Virginia Berridge and Griffith Edwards, *Opium and the People: Opiate Use in Nineteenth-Century England* (New Haven: Yale University Press, 1987), pp. xix–xx.

26. M. Manges, "A Second Report on the Therapeutics of Heroin," *New York Medical Journal,* 20 January 1900, pp. 82–83.

27. James A. Inciardi, "Over-the-Counter Drugs: Epidemiology, Adverse Reactions, Overdose Deaths, and Mass Media Promotion," *Addictive Diseases: An International Journal,* 3 (1977), pp. 253–272.

28. James Harvey Young, *The Medical Messiahs: A Social History of Health Quackery in Twentieth-Century America* (Princeton, NJ: Princeton University Press, 1967), p. 29.

29. Cited in Young, p. 31.

30. The complete text of the Harrison Act, as well as those of other federal drug laws passed from 1909 through 1980, have been reprinted in Gerard P. Walsh ed., *Opium and Narcotic Laws* (Washington, DC: U.S. Government Printing Office, 1981).

31. *Webb v. U.S.,* 249 U.S. 96 (1919).

32. *U.S. v. Behrman,* 258 U.S. 280 (1922).

33. *Linder v. U.S.,* 268 U.S. 5 (1925).

34. Rufus King, "The American System: Legal Sanctions to Repress Drug Abuse," in *Drugs and the Criminal Justice System,* ed. James A. Inciardi and Carl D. Chambers (Beverly Hills, CA: Sage, 1974), p. 22.

35. See Morgan.

36. Perry M. Lichtenstein, "Narcotic Addiction," *New York Medical Journal,* 14 November 1914, p. 962. It should be pointed out here that although Lichtenstein's comments were published almost a year after the passage of the Harrison Act, they were based on his treatment efforts with criminal addicts during prior years while he served as a physician at New York's Manhattan City Prison (more popularly known as "The Tombs"). The complete text of Dr. Lichtenstein's remarks has been reprinted in John A. O'Donnell and John C. Ball, eds., *Narcotic Addiction* (New York: Harper & Row, 1966), pp. 23–34.

37. G.E. McPherson and J. Cohen, "Survey of 100 Cases of Drug Addiction Entering Camp Upton, New York," *Boston Medical and Surgical Journal,* 5 June 1919; Special Committee of Investigation, *Traffic in Narcotic Drugs* (Washington, DC: Department of Treasury, 1919); *Literary Digest,* 26 April 1919, p. 32; *The Outlook,* 25 June 1919, p. 315; *The Survey,* 15 March 1919, pp. 67–68; *American Review of Reviews,* July–December 1919, pp. 331–332.

38. *Literary Digest,* 6 March 1920, pp. 27–28; 16 April 1921, pp. 19–20; 24 February 1923, pp. 34–35; 25 August 1923, pp. 22–23.

39. *Literary Digest,* 10 June 1922, p. 34.

40. *World's Work,* November 1924, p. 17.

41. Lawrence Kolb and A.G. Du Mez, "The Prevalence and Trend of Drug Addiction in the United States and Factors Influencing It," *Public Health Reports,* 23 May 1924, pp. 1179–1204.

42. U.S. Treasury Department, Bureau of Narcotics, *Traffic in Opium and Other Dangerous Drugs* (Washington, DC: U.S. Government Printing Office, 1939), p. 14.

43. Larry Sloman, *Reefer Madness: A History of Marijuana in America* (Indianapolis: Bobbs-Merrill, 1979), p. 26. For a description of a late nineteenth-century hashish club, see H. H. Kane, "A Hashish-House in New York," *Harper's Monthly,* November 1883, pp. 944–949, reprinted in Morgan, pp. 159–170.

44. *New York Times,* 6 July 1927, p. 10.

45. Winifred Black, *Dope: The Story of the Living Dead* (New York: Star & Co., 1928), p. 28.

46. Sloman, pp. 30–31.

47. See John C. McWilliams, *The Protectors: Harry J. Anslinger and the Federal Bureau of Narcotics, 1930–1962* (Newark: University of Delaware Press, 1990).

48. Sloman, p. 34.

49. Sloman, p. 63.

50. Sloman, pp. 58–59.

51. *Time,* 24 August 1942, p. 52.

■ ■ ■ ■ ■

EVERYBODY SMOKES DOPE

Drug Use in Post–World War II America

The crusade against marijuana during the 1930s had attributed to drug use a level of wickedness that could only have been matched by the Victorian imagery of masturbation and its consequences. The 1940s all but ignored the drug problem, principally because if it were indeed a problem, it was an invisible one—hardly a topic that should divert attention away from the events of a world at war. Then came the 1950s, a time when everything seemed right but in many instances was quite wrong.

THE ROAD TO H

Within three years after the close of World War II, the opium and heroin trafficking networks from Southeast Asia and Europe had been reestablished, and illicit narcotics once again began to reach U.S. ports. During the opening years of the 1950s, the prevailing image of drug use was one of heroin addiction on the streets of inner-city America. As summarized by the distinguished author and journalist Max Lerner in his celebrated work *America as a Civilization:*

> As a case in point we may take the known fact of the prevalence of reefer and dope addiction in Negro areas. This is essentially explained in terms of poverty, slum living, and broken families, yet it would be easy to show the lack of drug addiction among other ethnic groups where the same conditions apply.[1]

Lerner went on to explain that drug dependence among African Americans was due to the adjustment problems associated with their rapid movement from a depressed status to the improved standards and freedoms of the era. Yet Lerner's interpretation was hardly a correct one, not only about reefer addiction, but also about the prevalence of drug abuse in other populations—rich and poor, white and black, young and old.

In the popular media of the time, a somewhat more detailed portrait of the problem was offered. *Time, Life, Newsweek,* and other major periodicals spoke of how teenagers, jaded on marijuana, had found greater thrills in heroin. For most, the pattern of initiation had been the same. They began with marijuana, the use of which had become a fad in the "ghetto," as the inner city was referred to then. Then, enticed in schoolyards by brazen Mafia pushers dressed in dark suits, white ties, and wide-brimmed hats, their first dose of heroin was given free. By then, however, it was too late; their fate had been sealed; they were already addicted.[2] Or as a saying of the 1950s went, "It's so good, don't even try it once!"

Hollywood offered a somewhat different image of the situation. The movie industry had banned the portrayal of stories about narcotics from the silver screen in the late 1920s, but *To the Ends of the Earth* starring Dick Powell broke that rule in 1948. *To the Ends of the Earth* was a somewhat benign thriller, but it was followed several years later with the 1955 United Artists' release of *The Man with the Golden Arm.* The film was somewhat controversial in its day, for the Otto Preminger production had touched on a topic that most people felt should remain in the inner city where it belonged. In its actual content, like most films of the comfortable, conservative, prosperous, classless, sexless, and consensual paradise of the 1950s, it reflected majority attitudes and served to confirm established visions of reality. Cast in the role of a would-be professional musician, singer–actor Frank Sinatra was the hero of the story. Plagued by the evils of heroin addiction, he was unable to get his life together. Finally, however, through the help and understanding of his girlfriend Molly (portrayed by Kim Novak), he was saved from a life of pathetic degradation. As in the case of other media images of the drug scene, *The Man with the Golden Arm* offered only a contorted view, failing to probe even the most basic issues.* Even further removed from the real world of heroin use was the portrayal in *The Pusher,* released by United Artists in 1959.

Within the scientific community, much of the literature and research was almost as bizarre. As might be expected, most explanations of drug dependence focused on heroin in the inner city. Young addicts were believed to be either psychotic or neurotic casualties for whom drugs provided relief from anxiety and a means for withdrawing from the stress of daily struggle in the slum. Among the more celebrated studies of the period was psychologist Isidor Chein's *The Road to H.* Concerning youthful heroin use in New York City, Chein concluded:

> The evidence indicated that all addicts suffer from deep-rooted personality disorders. Although psychiatric diagnoses are apt to vary, a particular set of symptoms seems to be common to most juvenile addicts. They are not able to enter into prolonged, close, friendly relations with either peers or adults; they have difficulties in assuming a masculine role; they are frequently overcome by a sense of futility, expectations of failure, and general depression; they are easily frustrated and made anxious, and they find frustrations and anxiety intolerable.[3]

---

*For those interested in viewing *The Man with the Golden Arm,* it is available through both Netflix and Blockbuster.

By focusing on such maladies as weak ego functioning, defective superego, and inadequate masculine identification, Chein was suggesting the notion of a psychological predisposition to drug use—in other words, an addiction-prone personality. The text went on to imply that the series of predispositions could be traced to the addict's family experiences. If the youth received too much love or not enough, or if the parents were overwhelming in terms of their affection or indulgence, then the child would develop inadequately. As a result, the youth would likely be unable to withstand pain and discomfort, to cope with the complexities of life in the neighborhood and community, to assess reality correctly, and to feel competent around others of more varied social experiences. Although this has certainly been the case over the years with a number of heroin users, it does not explain *all* drug dependence. Chein concluded, however, that this type of youth would be more prone to trying drugs than others of more conventional family backgrounds.

The prevailing portrait of drug dependence in the scientific community, then, was one of passive adaptation to stress. Drugs allowed the user to experience fulfillment and the satiation of physical and emotional needs. This general view was also supported by sociological attempts to explain the broader concepts of deviance and delinquency. Given this predisposition, consider what became known in the literature as the "double-failure hypothesis."[4] According to sociologists Richard A. Cloward and Lloyd E. Ohlin, double failures were inner-city youths who were unable to succeed in either the gang subculture or the wider legitimate culture. They embraced drugs, in turn, as a way of finding a place for themselves in society.

For those who lived in the inner city, worked in the inner city, took drugs in the inner city, policed the inner city, or in some other fashion actively observed or participated in inner-city life, the addiction-prone personality, double-failure, and other escapist theories of drug dependence were found humorous. On the contrary, the conduct of most heroin users appeared to be anything but an escape from life. Much of their time was spent in drug-seeking behaviors, in meaningful activities and relationships on the street centers surrounding the economic institutions of heroin distribution. As the late urban anthropologist Edward Preble once put it, they were "taking care of business":

> The brief moments of euphoria after each administration of a small amount of heroin constitute a small fraction of their daily lives. The rest of the time they are aggressively pursuing a career that is exciting, challenging, adventurous, and rewarding. They are always on the move and must be alert, flexible, and resourceful. The surest way to identify heroin users in a slum neighborhood is to observe the way people walk. The heroin user walks with a fast, purposeful stride, as if he is late for an important appointment—indeed, he is. He is *hustling* [robbing or stealing], trying to sell stolen goods, avoiding the police, looking for a heroin dealer with a good *bag* [the street retail unit of heroin], coming back from *copping* [buying heroin], looking for a safe place to take the drug, or looking for someone who *beat* [cheated] him—among other things.[5]

No doubt, there were some who suffered from what was called the "addiction-prone personality," and there might even have been one or two people who were

CHAPTER 3 EVERYBODY SMOKES DOPE   **41**

indeed inner-city "double failures." But on the whole, the early theories could not have been more wrong. Some of the creators of the theories, however, became famous in academic circles for their so-called insights, and students had to read their articles, cite them in term papers, and answer questions about them on midterm and final exams. And interestingly, some of this work continues to appear in textbooks on crime and deviance.

TIMOTHY LEARY IS DEAD

In many ways the 1950s had been a decade of waste. Caught up in a belief that the good life had arrived, people rushed to the suburbs to escape urban congestion. Throughout the country, tract-built developments sprouted as landscapes were bull-dozed flat. This mass migration to the suburbs left the cities to deteriorate. An over-whelming reliance on the automobile, brought about by a sudden romance with the family car and the construction of a forty-thousand-mile interstate highway system, resulted in a breakdown in mass transportation and, in turn, pollution and congestion. These problems were most deeply felt in the inner-city neighborhoods where the poor had been left behind.

Another problem was the racism that had persisted from earlier years. In the growing prosperity of the 1950s, African Americans continued to face the legacy of Jim Crow. In the South, particularly, African Americans were repeatedly the victims of mob murders, lynchings, and all forms of social disenfranchisement.

To compound these problems, youth in the United States faced an enforcement of conformity, a transparency of sexual morals, and a set of cultural prescriptions and proscriptions that stressed achievement, prejudice, waste, compliance, and consensus, yet failed to explain or recognize the confusion and absurdity of it all. As a result of such contradictions, a teenage ethic emerged that made serious negative value judgments about the nature and meaning of life. As social critic Kenneth Rexroth warned in an early issue of *Evergreen Review:*

> Listen You—do you really think your kids are like bobby soxers in those wholesome Coca-Cola ads? Don't you know that across the table from you at dinner sits somebody who looks on you as an enemy who is planning to kill you in the immediate future? Don't you know that if you were to say to your English class, "It is raining," they would take it for granted that you were a liar? Don't you know they never tell you nothing? That they can't? That they simply can't get through, can't, and won't even try anymore to communicate? Don't you know this, really? If you don't, you're in for a terrible awakening.[6]

The enforced conformity, youth rebellion, racism, cultural values that had canonized both consumption and waste, and the numerous other problems in U.S. society that had been festering during the 1940s and 1950s seemed to merge during the following decade, resulting in one of the most revolutionary periods in recent history. The 1960s was a time characterized by civil rights movements, political assassinations, campus and antiwar protests, and inner-city riots.

Among the more startling events was the drug revolution of the 1960s. The use of drugs seemed to have leapt from the more marginal zones of society to the very mainstream of community life. No longer were drugs limited to the inner cities and half-worlds of the jazz scene and the underground bohemian protocultures, where "only jazz musicians were smoking marijuana" as singer Jimmy Buffett later put it. Rather, they had become suddenly and dramatically apparent among members of the adolescent middle class and young adult populations of rural and urban America. By the close of the decade, commentators on the era were maintaining that ours was the addicted society, that through drugs millions had become seekers of instant enlightenment, and that drug taking and drug seeking would persist as continuing facts of American social life.[7]

In retrospect, what were then considered the logical causes of the new drug phenomenon now seem less clear. A variety of changes in the fabric of life had occurred during those years, which undoubtedly had profound implications for social consciousness and behavior. Notably, the revolution in the technology and handling of drugs that had begun during the 1950s was of sufficient magnitude to justify the designation of the 1960s as a new chemical age. Recently compounded psychotropic agents were enthusiastically introduced and effectively promoted, with the consequence of exposing the national consciousness to an impressive catalog of new chemical temptations—sedatives, tranquilizers, stimulants, antidepressants, analgesics, and hallucinogens—that could offer fresh inspiration, as well as simple and immediate relief, from fear, anxiety, tension, frustration, and boredom.[8]

Concomitant with this emergence of a new chemical age, a new youth ethos had become manifest, one characterized by widely celebrated generational disaffection, a prejudicial dependence on the self and the peer group for value orientation, a critical view of how the world was being run, and mistrust for an establishment drug policy whose facts and warnings ran counter to reported peer experiences. On this latter point, it is no wonder that such mistrust had developed. Many teenagers and young adults across the nation had become recreational users of marijuana. For most, the psychoactive effects they experienced included euphoria, fragmentation of thought, laughter, spatial and temporal distortions, heightened sensuality, and increased sociability. A few experienced fear, anxiety, and panic.

Yet what most of the brokers of drug education were saying to users and their peers was something totally different—something reminiscent of Anslinger's pontifications during the reefer madness era of the 1930s. In fact, during the 1950s Anslinger was still saying essentially the same things about marijuana:

> Those who are accustomed to habitual use of the drug are said eventually to develop a delirious rage after its administration during which they are temporarily, at least, irresponsible and prone to commit violent crimes. The prolonged use of this narcotic is said to produce mental deterioration. Much of the most irrational juvenile violence and killing that has written a new chapter of shame and tragedy is traceable directly to this hemp intoxication.[9]

With statements such as these coming from the Commissioner of Narcotics, drug educators, *and parents*—statements that for the most part were contrary to experience and untrue—it is no wonder that the youth of the day turned deaf ears to the antidrug messages.

Whatever the ultimate causes, younger generations in the United States, or at least noticeable segments of them, had embraced drugs. The drug scene had become the arena of happening America; turning on to drugs for relaxation and to share friendship and love seemed to have become commonplace. And the prophet—the high priest as he called himself—of the new chemical age was a psychology instructor at Harvard University's Center for Research in Human Personality. His name was Dr. Timothy Leary.

The saga of Timothy Leary had its roots, not at Harvard in the 1960s, but in Basel, Switzerland, just before the beginning of World War II. It was there, in 1938, that Dr. Albert Hoffman of Sandoz Research Laboratories first isolated a new chemical compound that he called D-lysergic acid diethylamide. More popularly known as *LSD,* it was cast aside in his laboratory where, for five years, it remained unnoticed and unappreciated, its properties awaiting discovery. On April 16, 1943, after absorbing some LSD through the skin of his fingers, Hoffman began to hallucinate. In his diary he explained the effect:

> With closed eyes, multihued, metamorphizing, fantastic images overwhelmed me. . . . Sounds were transposed into visual sensations so that from each tone or noise a comparable colored picture was evoked, changing in form and color kaleidoscopically.[10]

Hoffman had experienced the first consciously induced LSD trip.*

Dr. Humphrey Osmond of the New Jersey Neuropsychiatric Institute neologized a new name for LSD—*psychedelic,* meaning mind expanding. But outside of the scientific community, LSD was generally unknown—even at the start of the 1960s. This was quickly changed by Leary and his colleague at Harvard, Dr. Richard Alpert. They began experimenting with the drug—on themselves, and with colleagues, students, artists, writers, members of the clergy, and volunteer prisoners. Although their adventures with LSD had earned them dismissals from Harvard by 1963, their message had been heard, and LSD had achieved its reputation. Their messages had been

---

*Dr. Hoffman also experienced the first "bad trip." Regarding an April 19, 1943, experience with LSD, he later recalled in his *LSD: My Problem Child* (Los Angeles: J.P. Tarcher, 1983):

> The dizziness and sensation of fainting became so strong at times that I could no longer hold myself erect, and had to lie down on a sofa. My surroundings had now transformed themselves in more terrifying ways. Everything in the room spun around, and the familiar objects and pieces of furniture assumed grotesque, threatening forms. They were in continuous motion, animated, as if driven by an inner restlessness. The lady next door, whom I scarcely recognized, brought me milk—in the course of the evening I drank more than two liters. She was no longer Mrs. R., but rather a malevolent, insidious witch with a colored mask.

numerous and shocking to the political establishment and to hundreds of thousands of mothers and fathers across the nation.

In *The Realist,* a somewhat radical mass-market periodical of the 1960s, Leary commented:

> I predict that psychedelic drugs will be used in all schools in the near future as educational devices—not only marijuana and LSD, to teach kids how to use their sense organs and other cellular equipment effectively—but new and more powerful psychochemicals. . . .[11]

Elsewhere he wrote of the greatest fear that might be generated by psychedelic drug use, what he called *ontological addiction:*

> . . . the terror of finding a realm of experience, a new dimension of reality so pleasant that one will not want to return. This fear is based on the unconscious hunch that normal consciousness is a form of sleepwalking and that somewhere there exists a form of awakeness, of reality from which one would not want to return.[12]

And then, perhaps most frightening of all to the older generation, were Leary's comments to some fifteen thousand cheering San Francisco youths on the afternoon of March 26, 1967. As a modern-day Pied Piper, Leary told his audience: "*Turn on* to the scene, *tune in* to what's happening; and *drop out*—of high school, college, grad school . . . and follow me, the hard way."[13]

Leary's downfall came shortly thereafter, the result of conviction and imprisonment on drug-trafficking charges, followed by a period of time as a fugitive in Algeria and Afghanistan after a prison escape. Some people even thought Leary was dead. His demise was eulogized by the Moody Blues and other rock groups of the era.

Actually, the story of Timothy Leary was not quite over. By 1976 he had straightened out his legal problems and had become a free man and "a cheerleader for scientific optimism," as he once put it. With the onset of the 1980s, Leary joined the ranks of the most highly paid speakers on the college lecture circuit, often debating G. Gordon Liddy of Watergate fame. Quite curiously, Liddy was once his nemesis, having organized a raid in 1966 that led to one of Leary's early drug arrests. During the mid- and late 1980s, Leary became successful in the computer support industry, creating a variety of educational and personal management software.[14] In early 1989, regarding the amount and variety of drugs that were reportedly used during the LSD era, he was quoted as saying: "If you remember the '60s, you weren't there."[15] At the same time, Dr. Leary was heard arguing for a legalization of drugs and suggesting that pharmaceutical firms should be encouraged to develop nonaddicting mood-altering drugs.[16]

On May 31, 1996, at age seventy-five, the man whom the late Richard M. Nixon once called "the most dangerous man in America," died of prostate cancer. But as it might be expected, he didn't go quietly. A few months prior to his death he was quoted in the *Los Angeles Times* as saying: "When I found out that I was terminally ill, I was thrilled. Dying is such a taboo topic and I love the topics the establishment says are taboo."[17] Leary had wanted to meet death on his own terms, declaring that he wished to commit suicide and have it broadcast worldwide on the Internet. But the illness overtook him in his final weeks, and he was unable to carry out what would have been his final act of defiance. However, in January 1997, Timothy Leary took his last and longest trip, when seven grams of his ashes were launched into outer space aboard a commercial rocket and jettisoned 350 miles up as part of an astrofunerary service.*

Getting back to LSD, by 1968 use of the drug was believed to have reached epidemic proportions, and even the parents of young children became frightened when their sons and daughters returned home from their grade schools chanting, to the tune of "Frère Jacques":

In retrospect, the reasons for the hysteria over Leary, LSD, and other psychedelic substances had been threefold. First, the drug scene was especially frightening to mainstream society because it reflected a willful rejection of rationality, order, and predictability. Second, there was the stigmatized association of drug use with antiwar protests and anti-establishment, long-haired, unwashed, radical hippie LSD users. And third, there were the drugs' psychic effects, the reported bad trips that seemed to border on mental illness.

Particularly in the case of LSD, the rumors of how it could blow one's mind became legion. One story told of a youth, high on the drug, taking a swan dive in front of a truck moving at seventy miles per hour. Another spoke of two tripping teenagers who stared directly into the sun until they were permanently blinded. A third described how LSD's effects on the chromosomes resulted in fetal abnormalities.[18] The stories were never documented and were likely untrue.† What *are* true, however, were the reports of LSD flashbacks. Occurring with only a small percentage of the users, individuals would reexperience the LSD-induced state days, weeks, and

---

*Three years after Leary's death, it was learned that the counterculture guru, whose preachings had made him an anti-establishment icon, had become an FBI informant in 1974 to win his freedom from prison. In 2000, fourteen pages of Leary's FBI file were published on the Internet by "The Smoking Gun," an online site that publishes documents obtained through the Freedom of Information Act.

†An additional entry in the annals of LSD folklore is the blue-star acid rumor. Like a recurring nightmare, it has frightened parents for more than thirty years with the warning of LSD in stick-on tattoos. Reports are carried via email, school bulletin boards, copiers, and fax machines, telling parents to be aware of tattoos in the shape of a blue star (and recently Bart Simpson). The messages tell of sinister drug pushers who give out the cartoon tattoos to children to hook them. When the children lick the tattoos and place them on their arms, they become immediately addicted. Interestingly, there has never been a documented case of the phenomenon, and the Drug Enforcement Administration maintains that it is just a hoax that has taken on a life of its own.

■ ■ ■ ■ ■ ▬▬▬▬▬▬▬▬▬▬▬▬▬▬▬▬▬▬▬▬▬▬▬▬▬▬

EXHIBIT 3.1

THE LSD EXPERIENCE

Physiologically, the effects of LSD and other hallucinogens include increased pulse rate and blood pressure, dilated pupils, tremor, cold and sweaty palms, and at times, flushing, shivering, chills, pallor, salivation, and nausea. Drug-induced activity lasts eight to twelve hours, with the most intense changes in mood, sensation, and perception occurring during the first half of the experience. Mood alteration is the first obvious behavioral change observed. Along with this is a significant increase in sensory input, a kind of floating, with perceptual distortions and hallucinations. *Synesthesia* often occurs, involving sensory crossovers: subjects hear colors, taste sounds, and visualize music in colors. There is also tunnel vision, the focusing in on minute details not observed before.

The literature on LSD reports three different experiences when the user is under the influence of the drug: (1) the good trip, a predominantly pleasing experience; (2) the bad trip, a dysphoric experience characterized by anxiety, panic, feelings of persecution and fear, loss of control of time and space perception, and impaired performance; and (3) the ambivalent state, in which the subject may simultaneously experience contrasting feelings of happiness and sadness, relaxation and tension, weakness and power.

The typical LSD dose is about one hundred to two hundred micrograms (one thousand micrograms = one milligram), although experienced abusers who have built up a sufficient level of tolerance may take doses as large as two thousand micrograms. Physical dependence on LSD has not been observed.

sometimes months after the original trip, without having taken the drug again (see Exhibit 3.1).

Despite all the lurid reports and rumors, as it turned out, LSD was not in fact widely used on a regular basis beyond a few social groups that were fully dedicated to drug experiences. In fact, psychedelic substances had quickly earned reputations as being dangerous and unpredictable, and most people avoided them (Exhibit 3.2). By the close of the 1960s, all hallucinogenic drugs had been placed under strict legal control, and the number of users was minimal.[19]

FROM BLACK BEAUTY TO KING KONG

Throughout the 1960s heroin remained the most feared drug, and by the close of the decade estimates as to the size of the addict population exceeded five hundred thousand. Yet despite hysteria about the rising tide of heroin use, LSD and the youth rebellion, Timothy Leary and the psychedelic age, and the growing awareness of drug abuse along the main streets of white America and the mean streets of black America, no one really knew how many people were actually using drugs. In fact, estimates of the incidence and prevalence of marijuana, heroin, psychedelic, and other drug use were, at the very best, only vague and impressionistic.

EXHIBIT 3.2

OTHER HALLUCINOGENIC DRUGS

Other popular hallucinogenic drugs of the era were peyote, mescaline, psilocybin, MDA, and DMT. Peyote is a spineless cactus native to central and northern Mexico whose top crown, or button, is a hallucinogenic drug. The button is dried, then ingested by holding it in the mouth until it is soft, and then swallowed whole. It takes about three to four buttons to experience a trip. Tolerance is not known, and physical dependence has not been reported.

Mescaline is the principle alkaloid in the peyote cactus, and perhaps the first hallucinogen to be chemically isolated (1897). Less potent than LSD, it is ingested orally, smoked, or injected. Tolerance is not known; physical dependence has not been reported; and, interestingly, most confiscated samples of mescaline have been found to be PCP.

Psilocybin is the active ingredient in the *Psilycybe Mexicana* mushroom. Isolated in 1958 by Albert Hoffman, this white crystalline material has a potency somewhere between mescaline and LSD. It is the most rapid acting of the hallucinogens, with onset about fifteen minutes after intake. The maximum intensity of the drug experience occurs after ninety minutes, and effects last some five to six hours. No tolerance or physical dependence has been reported.

MDA is a semisynthetic drug produced by modifying the major psychoactive components of nutmeg and mace. First synthesized in 1910, its effects combine those of mescaline and the amphetamines. MDA can be both toxic and lethal, but no tolerance or physical dependence has been reported.

DMT (dimethyltryptamine), commonly made synthetically, is also found in the seeds of certain South American and West Indian plants. It may appear as a crystalline powder or as a solution, or it may be mixed with substances such as tobacco or parsley. Its effects are similar to those of LSD, but the drug is much weaker and its effects more short-lived.

Although the reliability of political polling had long since demonstrated that the social sciences indeed had the tools to measure the dimensions of the drug problem, no one at any time throughout the 1960s had gone so far as to count drug users in a systematic way. Yet several indicators existed. Studies were suggesting that the annual production of barbiturate drugs (such as phenobarbital and pentobarbital) exceeded one million pounds, the equivalent of twenty-four one-and-one-half-grain doses for every man, woman, and child in the nation—enough to kill each person twice.[20] And for amphetamines and amphetamine-like compounds, the manufacturing figures came to some fifty doses per U.S. resident each year, with half the production reaching the illicit marketplace.[21]

Amphetamines were not new drugs, but their appearance on the street had been relatively recent at the time. Having been synthesized in Germany during the 1880s, their first use among Americans had not come until World War II. Thousands of servicemen in all of the military branches had been issued Benzedrine, Dexedrine, and a variety of other types as a matter of course to relieve their fatigue and anxiety. After the war, amphetamine drugs became more readily available, and they were put to a wider assortment of uses—for students cramming for exams, truck drivers and others who needed to be alert for extended periods of time, for people in weight-control programs, and as nasal decongestants. Yet as strong stimulants with pharmacological effects similar to those of cocaine, in time they became popular drugs of abuse.

As the 1970s began, the first item on the government's agenda for drug reform was amphetamines, with Indiana Senator Birch Bayh conducting hearings. There was a parade of witnesses, and the worst fears about the drugs were confirmed—or so it seemed.[22] Bayh and his committee heard the horror stories of the speed freaks who injected amphetamine and methamphetamine and stalked the city streets suffering from paranoid delusions and exhibiting episodes of violent behavior at the onset of their psychotic states. They heard, too, of the hundreds, thousands, and perhaps hundreds of thousands of children and teenagers stoned on ups, bennies, pinks, purple hearts, black beauties, and King Kong pills. By that time, systematic surveys of the general population had finally begun, with the first, conducted in New York, empirically documenting that amphetamine use and abuse were indeed widespread.[23]

Almost immediately, new legislation was proposed by the Bayh committee and pushed through by the Senate. Tighter controls were placed on prescribing and distributing amphetamines, and legitimate production was ultimately cut by 90 percent. In so doing, it was thought that the drug problem, at least in terms of the dangerous amphetamines, would be measurably solved.

But suddenly something seemed to go terribly wrong. The Senate, oftentimes a sacred repository of culture lag, had, in its infinite wisdom, totally ignored or at least misunderstood the very nature of the youth drug scene of the day. True, many youths *were* getting stoned on amphetamines. And true, speed freaks *were* out on the streets committing random acts of violence. But the actual numbers of amphetamine and methamphetamine freaks were comparatively few, and the frequency of their violent acts was even less. Moreover, the number of youths who had actually become dysfunctional as a result of amphetamine abuse was hardly what any sophisticated researcher or clinician would have called an epidemic.

Most importantly, what the Senate missed was the fact that the amphetamine-using youth in the United States were drug-use habituated. That is, it was not amphetamines that were particularly important to them, but drugs, *any* drugs. So, when amphetamines suddenly dried up on the streets, youthful users simply went to another widely available drug. They chose methaqualone—sopors, ludes, and Captain Quaalude.* Thus, one drug problem was simply replaced by another. But this time, rather than arriving in high school classrooms stoned, users began showing up in hospital emergency rooms and county morgues. Meanwhile, the heroin epidemic continued, and cocaine began to reappear, emerging from the netherworlds of crime and the avant-garde where it had been casually sequestered since the early years of the century.

---

*Other street names for methaqualone include gorilla biscuits, lemons, turkey gizzards, vitamin Q, and mandrax (misspelled as mandrex on the website of the National Institute on Drug Abuse).

THE MANY LIVES OF CAPTAIN QUAALUDE

The U.S. Senate was not the real instigator of the methaqualone problem, for the crisis that followed was one in which everyone seemed to be at fault—the pharmaceutical industry, the medical profession, the Food and Drug Administration, the federal narcotics establishment, and the media. In 1972, the *Washington Post* focused the blame somewhat differently: "The methaqualone boom should make an interesting case study in future medical textbooks: How skillful public relations and advertising created a best-seller—and helped cause a medical crisis in the process."[24]

Methaqualone is a nonbarbiturate sedative/hypnotic drug that was initially synthesized in India during the early 1950s as a possible antimalarial agent. When its hypnotic (sleep-producing) properties were discovered later in the decade, many hoped that, as a nonbarbiturate, methaqualone might be a safer alternative to barbiturates.[25]

Barbiturate drugs had been available for the better part of the century. As potent central nervous system depressants, they were the drugs of choice for inducing sleep. Depending on the dosage level, they were also in common use for anesthesia, sedation, and the treatment of tension, anxiety, and convulsions. However, the barbiturates had their problems. They were widely abused for the "high" they could engender. Moreover, they produced dependence after chronic use, were life-threatening on withdrawal, and could cause fatal overdoses—particularly when mixed with alcohol.

As an alternative to barbiturates, methaqualone was introduced in England in 1959, and in Germany and Japan in 1960. Despite extensive medical reports of abuse in these three countries, the drug was introduced in the United States under the trade names of Quaalude, Sopor, Parest, Somnafac, and, later, Mequin. Although methaqualone was a prescription drug, the federal drug establishment decided that since there was no evidence of an abuse potential, it need not be monitored and the number of times a prescription could be refilled need not be restricted. This, combined with an advertising campaign that promoted the drug as a safe alternative to barbiturates, led to the assumption by the medical profession, the lay population, and the media that methaqualone did not produce dependence—it was "nonaddicting" as the media put it. Even the prestigious *AMA Drug Evaluations* stated, as late as 1973, that no more than "long-term use of larger than therapeutic doses may result in psychic and physical dependence."[26]

The most effective advertising campaign was launched by William H. Rorer pharmaceuticals. Given the success of the catchy double *a* in their antacid Maalox, they named their methaqualone product Quaalude. Their advertising emphasized that it was a nonbarbiturate. Free samples of Quaalude were shipped throughout the country, and physicians began overprescribing the drug.

Looking for a new and safe high, users sought out methaqualone, and the drug quickly made its way to the street. Rather than a safe alternative to whatever they had been taking previously, street users actually had a drug with the same dependence liability and lethal potential as the barbiturates. What they experienced was a pleasant sense of well-being, an increased pain threshold, and a loss of muscle coordination. The high was reputed to enhance sexual performance, for men at least. Although no actual evidence confirmed that effect, it is likely that the depressant effects of the drug were serving to desensitize the nerve endings in the penis, thus permitting intercourse for longer periods without climaxing. Moreover, like alcohol, the drug was acting on the central cortex of the brain to slacken normal inhibitions. Also common was *luding out*—rapidly attaining an intoxicated state by mixing the drug with wine.

In early 1973, after reports of widespread abuse, acute reactions, and fatal overdoses, Birch Bayh convened more Senate hearings, the problems with methaqualone were fully aired, and rigid controls over the drug were put into force.[27] Shortly thereafter, the abuse of methaqualone began to decline.* In the meantime, the heroin problem persisted, and in 1972 West Coast–based cocaine devotees began experimenting with a new variety of smokable cocaine, called *rock.*

EVERYBODY SMOKES DOPE

While legislators, clinicians, and drug educators struggled with the methaqualone problem, marijuana use grew apace. From 1960 through the end of the decade, the number of people in the United States who had used marijuana at least once had increased from a few hundred thousand to an estimated eight million. Given such widespread use, in 1969 the government launched an elaborate and determined effort to cut down the flow of marijuana into the United States. Known as Operation Intercept, and based on the belief that Mexico was and would remain the primary source of marijuana for the United States, the effort was designed principally to tighten inspections of vehicles coming across the border from Mexico and to intercept smuggled drugs.[28]

Set for September 21, 1969, Operation Intercept was timed for the autumn marijuana harvest. Along the twenty-five-hundred-mile-long border, on land as well as in the sea and air, the surveillance network was intense, particularly so at the border crossings where vehicles and passengers could be individually searched. Within an hour after it all started, automobile traffic began to pile up as each vehicle waited to go through inspection. In no time, the backups were three miles long, and in some places they extended to six miles. Members of Congress and other officials immediately began to receive complaints—from Mexico because the effort was hurting tourism, from merchants on both sides of the border because it was affecting business, and from the U.S. travelers who had spent many extra hours waiting to return home.

---

*For those who missed the first wave of methaqualone abuse, another began in 1978 and persisted into the early 1980s. In 1980, some four tons of the drug were produced legally in the United States, and it is estimated that another one hundred million tons were smuggled in, principally from Colombia. In 1982, when tight restrictions were placed on the importation of methaqualone powder from West Germany to Colombia, trafficking in the drug declined substantially. In 1984, all legal manufacturing of methaqualone was halted in the United States, and since that time abuse of the drug has been, at best, modest. However, as recently as 2006, methaqualone could be found on the streets of Miami, Florida, for $7 a pill.

Twenty days later Operation Intercept was abandoned. Although the government deemed it a success, there had been no major seizures of marijuana. In fact, during the three weeks of the operation, the actual seizures averaged 150 pounds per day, a rate no different from that which had existed earlier in 1969. Operation Intercept did have other effects, however. The temporary shortage that it created pushed up the street price of the drug; it led to increased imports of a more potent marijuana from Vietnam and Colombia, and it stimulated the cultivation of domestic marijuana.*

By the early 1970s, marijuana use had increased geometrically throughout all strata of society. Expounding on this situation, a Miami attorney offered an interesting explanation of the prevalence of marijuana use in the United States:

> *Everybody smokes dope!* This profound statement should not be taken to mean that every person in the country smokes marijuana. It merely means: Policemen smoke dope. Probation officers smoke dope. Narcotic agents smoke dope (and sell it). Judges smoke dope. Prosecutors smoke dope. Plumbers, schoolteachers, principals, deans, carpenters, disabled war veterans, Republicans, doctors, perverts, and librarians smoke dope. Legislators smoke dope. Even writers of articles on drug abuse smoke dope. *Everybody smokes dope!*[29]

Given such pervasive use of marijuana, and arrests that were affecting the careers and lives of so many otherwise law-abiding citizens, legislation was introduced that reduced the penalties for the simple possession of the drug—first at the federal level and later by the states. In Alabama, judges were no longer required to impose the mandatory minimum sentence of five years for the possession of even one marijuana cigarette; Missouri statutes no longer included life sentences for second possession offenses; and in Georgia, second-sale offenses to minors were no longer punishable by death.

Then there was the issue of *decriminalization*—the removal of criminal penalties for the possession of small amounts of marijuana for personal use. The movement toward decriminalization began in 1973 with Oregon, followed by Colorado, Alaska, Ohio, and California in 1975; Mississippi, North Carolina, and New York in 1977; and Nebraska in 1978. Given the fact that there were an estimated fifty million users of marijuana in the United States by the close of the 1970s, many hoped that decriminalization, and perhaps even legalization of marijuana use, would become a national affair, but the movement suddenly stalled for a variety of reasons.[30] Principally, Congress had failed to pass legislation that would have decriminalized marijuana under federal statutes. The issue had not been salient enough throughout the nation as a whole to result in concerted action in favor of decriminalization. The lobbying on behalf of marijuana law reform had never demonstrated the power and influence necessary for repeal. Perhaps most important of all, marijuana had always been viewed as a drug favored by youth (see Exhibit 3.3).

---

*A State Department official indicated to the author in 1971 that, given the vast outflow of U.S. dollars into Mexico for wholesale purchases of marijuana, the real purpose of Operation Intercept was to stimulate the production of domestic marijuana and thus to keep the U.S. dollar on this side of the border. Although this reasoning has never been confirmed, Operation Intercept certainly had that effect.

■ ■ ■ ■ ■

EXHIBIT 3.3

A DRUG BY ANY OTHER NAME . . . .

A rather curious but interesting indicator of the popularity of marijuana over the years is the number of different street terms that have been used to designate the substance. Over the past one hundred years, no other drug has generated as many slang labels. Here are just a few: 420, A-bomb, Acapulco Gold, ace, African black, African bush, airplane, Alice B. Toklas, Angola, aromatic sinsemilla, ashes, Atshitsi, aunt mary, B, baby, baby bhang, bale, Bambalacha, bammer, bammy, banji, bar, Barbara Jean, bash, bats, BC bud, Belyando spruce, bhang, binky, birdwood, black, black bart, black ganga, black gold, black gungeon, black gungi, black gunion, black gunny, black maria, black meat, black mo, black moat, blanket, blast, block, blonde, Blue de hue, blunt, bo, bob, Bob Marley, bo-bo, bo-bo bush, bohd, bomb, bomb-diggidy, bomber, bone, boo, boom, brick, broccoli, brown, bud, budda, bullyon, burnie, bush, butter, butter flower, buzz, C-weed, California red, Cambodian red, cam red, cam trip, can, Canadian black, canamo, canappa, cannabis, cannon, canoe, carmabis, carpet weed, charas, charge, catnip, caviteall star, cereal, cess, cheddar, cheeba, cheebo, cheese, cheese stick, chiba, chiba-chiba, Chicago black, Chicago green, chippie, chira, chocolate, chocolate thi, Christmas tree, chronic, churrus, citrol, climb, coli, Colombian, Colombian gold, Colombian red, columbia red, Columbus black, cosa, crazy weed, creeper, creeper bud, cripple, crying weed, cubes, culican, daddy, dagga, daha, dank, dew, dick, dick weed, diggidy, dimba, ding, dinkie dow, dirtgrass, ditch, ditch weed, dizz, djamba, dogie, domestic, donjem, doobie, dope, drafweed, drag weed, dry high, durog, duros, earth, elbow, endo, erb, esra, faggot, Fallbrook redhair, fatty, fine stuff, fingers, flowers, flower tops, frajo, foo, fu, funny stuff, fuck, fuckjoint, fuck-stuff, fuckweed, gage, Gainesville green, ganga, gange, gangster, ganja, gar, garr, gash, gasper, gasper stick, gauge, gauge butt, ghana, gigglesmoke, giggleweed, geek, godfather, gold, gold Colombian, golden leaf, gold star, gong, gonga, gong ringer, good butt, goof, goofball, goofbutt, grass, grass weed, grata, greafa, greapha, greefa, greefp, green, green cigarette, green goddess, greenie, green snacks, greeter, grefa, greta, griefo, grifa, griff, griffo, grillo, grunt, gungun, gunny, gyve, hanhich, happy cigarette, harm reducer, hash, hashish, Hawaiian, hay, hay butt, heathen, he-ho weed, hemp, herb, herba, hit, hocus, homegrown, honey blunt, hooch, hoochie-mama, hooter, hop, hot stick, humble, humble weed, hydro, Illinois green, Indian boy, Indian hay, Indian hemp, indo, Indonesian bud, I.Z.M., J, J's, Jamaican red, jane, Jay, jay smoke, Jersey green, jimmy-john, jive, jive stick, johnnie, Johnson, Johnson grass, joint, jolly green, joy smoke, joystick, joyweed, juane, juanita, Juan Valdez, juiana weed, ju-ju, kali, kaya, K.B., keef, Kentucky blue, K.G.B. (Killer Green Bud), kick, kick stick, kidstuff, kif, killer, killer weed, kilter, kind, kind bud, knuckle samich, kona bud, kona gold, kumba, kushempeng, kutchie, lambsbreath, laughing grass, laughing weed, leaf, lid, lima, limbo, Lipton's, little green friends, L.L., loaf, lobato weed, lobo, loco, loco weed, log, loveboat, love nuggets, loveweed, lumbo, M, mach, machinery, maggie, magic smoke, Manhattan silver, margie, mari, mariquita, maria juana, mariguano, mary, mary and johnnie, maryann, maryjane, maryjane superweed, mary jonas, mary warner, mary weaver, matchbox, Maui, Maui-wowie, megg, meggie, method, merry, messerole, Mexican brown, Mexican ditch weed, Mexican green, Mexican guano, Mexican locoweed, Mexican red, Mexican shit, mezz, mighty mezz, M.J., M.O., mohasky, monte, mooca, moocah, moosters, moota, mootah, mooters, mootie, mootos, moshky, mota, moto, mother, mu, muggie, muggles, musta, muta, mutah, mutha, nail, nick, nickel, Northern Lights, number, O, oboy, O.J., one hitter quitter, oregano, owl, pack, Pakistani black, Panama gold, Panama red, panatella, paper blunts, parsley, pat, philly, philly blunt, pin, pine, pinner, pitillo, pizza, pocket rocket, pod, poke, pot, potiguaya, potten bush, P.R., pretendo, puff the dragon, punk, ragweed, railroad weed, rainy day woman, rama, rasta weed, R.B., reaper, red, red cross, red dirt, reefer, reefer weed, refrigerator weed, reggae, righteous bush, roach, rockets, roof weed, root, rope, rough stuff, rug, salt and pepper, Santa Marta, sassfras, sativa, schwag, scissors, scooby snack, seaweed, seeds, sen, sess, sex weed, sezz, shake, shishi, shit, shitweed, siddi, sinse, sinsemilla, skinny, skunk, skunk weed, smoke, smoochy-woochy-poochy, snop, spinach, splay, spleef, spliff, spliffy, splim, square grouper, stems, stick, stinkweed, stinky, straw, stuff, stum, sugarweed, supergrass, superpot, swag, swisher, sweet lucy, sweet lunch, sweet maryjane, T, Tai, Taima, Tai weed, tea, Texas pot, Texas tea, tex-mex, Thai sticks, thirteen, thumb, tin, torch, tree, tripweed, turf, tweeds, twigs, twist, twistum, Vermont green, viper's weed, vonce, wackytabbacky, wackyweed, weed, weed tea, wheat, white-haired lady, wooz, yellow submarine, yen pop, yerba, yesca, ying, Zacatecas purple, zambi, zigzag, and zol. There are hundreds more (see http://parentingteens.about.com/cs/marijuana/l/bldicmarijuana.htm).

By the close of the 1970s and the onset of the 1980s, evidence indicated that marijuana use in the United States had actually declined. In 1975, surveys showed that some thirty million people were users.[31] By the early 1980s, this figure had dropped to twenty million, with the most significant declines among people aged 25 and under.[32] Perhaps the younger generation had begun to realize that although marijuana was not the devil drug, assassin of youth, or weed of madness that Harry Anslinger and his counterparts had maintained, it was not a totally innocuous substance either. Perhaps the change occurred because of the greater concern with health and physical fitness that became so much a part of U.S. culture during the 1980s, or as an outgrowth of the antismoking messages that appeared daily in the media. Whatever the reason, it was clear that youthful attitudes had changed. Over the period from 1979 through the close of the 1980s, the proportion of seniors in U.S. high schools who saw great risk in using marijuana even once or twice rose from 9.4 to 23.6 percent whereas the proportion who had *ever* experimented with marijuana declined from 60.4 to 43.7 percent—representing a fifteen-year low.[33]

Despite the declining use (and interest) in marijuana within the youth culture during the 1980s, the drug remained in the news. A new organization calling itself The National Anti-Drug Coalition began a crusade against marijuana that was reminiscent of the reefer madness era of the 1930s.[34] Prescription pot became a reality in 1985 when the Food and Drug Administration gave approval to Unimed, Inc., a New Jersey research firm, to produce Marinol, a THC derivative effective for treating the nausea associated with cancer chemotherapy.* And finally, whereas arguments for the legalization of marijuana resurfaced,† the possession of small amounts of marijuana for personal use was *re*criminalized in Oregon through a statewide referendum in 1986, with a similar action occurring in Alaska in 1990.[35]

---

*The debate over marijuana as medicine is addressed in Chapter 11 of this book.
†The debate over the legalization of marijuana and other drugs is also examined at length in Chapter 11.

Meanwhile, the heroin problem endured, cocaine emerged as the new drug of choice, and Caribbean islanders emigrating to Miami and New York brought a variety of smokable cocaine with them—a drug that would become known worldwide as crack. At the same time, most observers were unaware that marijuana use among youth was about to escalate dramatically.

TIC, ROCKET FUEL, AND THE SPECTER OF THE LIVING DEAD

The propaganda campaigns that have periodically emerged to target specific drugs as the root causes of outbreaks of violent crime were not restricted to the Anslinger era of reefer madness. More recently, PCP emerged as the new killer drug, which changes the user into a diabolical monster and a member of the living dead.

PCP, or more formally phencyclidine, a central nervous system excitant agent having anesthetic, analgesic, and hallucinogenic properties, is not a particularly new drug. It was developed during the 1950s, and following studies on laboratory animals, it was recommended for clinical trials on humans in 1957.[36] Parke, Davis & Company marketed the drug under the trade name of Sernyl. Originally, phencyclidine was used as an anesthetic agent in surgical procedures. Although it was found to be generally effective, the drug often produced a number of unpleasant side effects— extreme excitement, visual disturbances, and delirium. As a result, in 1967 the use of phencyclidine was restricted to veterinary use only. Under the trade name of Sernylan, it quickly became the most widely used animal tranquilizer.*

The initial street use of PCP (also known as rocket fuel, horse tranquilizer, animal trank, aurora borealis, DOA, elephant, elephant juice, dust, goon, green snow, mist, sheets, angel dust, fairy dust, dummy dust, embalming fluid, monkey dust, devil's dust, devil stick, hog, THC, Tic, tic tac, supergrass, flakes, and buzz) appeared in the Haight-Ashbury underground community of San Francisco and other West Coast and East Coast cities during 1967. It was first marketed as the *PeaCe Pill*; hence, the name PCP quickly became popular.

Characteristic of the hallucinogenic drug marketplace has been the mislabeling and promotion of one substance as some other more desirable psychedelic, and for a time PCP occupied a conspicuous position in this category. Samples of mescaline (the hallucinogenic alkaloid found in the peyote cactus) sold in Milwaukee, for example, were invariably PCP.[37] During the late 1960s and early 1970s, tetrahydrocannabinol (THC), the active ingredient in marijuana, was frequently sought after in its pure form as a prestigious fad drug. Yet THC has never been sold on the street, for in its isolated form it is so unstable a compound that it quickly loses its potency and effect. During 1970, analyses of street drugs from the greater Philadelphia area revealed that PCP was a common THC substitute.[38]

---

*Dog and cat owners who request medication from a vet to sedate a pet during a plane or long automobile trip are generally given PCP.

In an experiment undertaken in 1971, samples of alleged LSD, THC, mescaline, and PCP were secured from street suppliers in New York City's Greenwich Village. Laboratory analyses identified the THC and mescaline samples to be PCP, and the PCP sample to be LSD, with only the LSD sample having accurate labeling. In a second experiment carried out during early 1972 in Miami's Coconut Grove area, twenty-five individual samples of alleged THC were purchased from an equal number of street drug dealers. Under laboratory analysis, twenty-two of the THC samples were found to be PCP. One was Darvon (a prescription painkiller), another was an oral contraceptive, and the last a chocolate-covered peanut.[39]

It was quickly learned that these apparent deceptions had been aimed at what were then referred to as *plastic,* or *weekend,* hippies and heads—those children of two cultures whose social schizophrenia placed them partially in the straight world and partially in the new underground, never fully being a part of either. In both the New York and Miami drug subcultures, however, and probably in most others, THC was simply accepted as another name for PCP, perhaps explaining why the latter drug was called Tic for more than a decade in many cities.

The stories describing PCP as a killer drug date to its first introduction to the street community. In 1969, for example, a New York City chief of detectives commented:

> Let me tell you, this stuff is bad, real bad. One dose of it and we're talking about some serious instant addiction. I keep telling these kids that if they keep playing around with that shit they are going to blow their fucking minds.*

Similarly, a number of news stories at approximately the same time described PCP as a synthetic drug so powerful that a person could become high simply by touching it—instantly absorbing it through the pores.[40]

These early reports ran counter to both medical and street experiences,[41] and the drug quickly became relegated to the lengthening catalog of street substances that after their initial appearance received little public attention. Most of those using PCP during the early years were not found among the populations addicted to narcotic drugs. Rather, they were multiple-drug users manifesting patterns of long-term involvement with marijuana and/or hashish, combined with the experimental, social–recreational, or spree use of hallucinogens, sedatives, tranquilizers, and stimulants.

During 1978, hysteria over PCP emerged once again, but this time in earnest. In one episode of the popular "60 Minutes" television series, CBS news commentator Mike Wallace described PCP as the nation's number one drug problem, reporting on bizarre incidents of brutal violence—reminiscent of Harry J. Anslinger's gore file—allegedly caused by the new killer drug. Shortly thereafter, a *People* magazine article touted PCP, or the devil's dust, as the most dangerous new drug in the United States.[42] In these and other reports, violence was always associated with PCP use, as well as its

---

*All undocumented quotations in this and subsequent chapters are comments made directly to the author during the course of fieldwork.

propensity to destroy the user's mind and hence to create new recruits to the growing army of the living dead.

During special hearings on August 8, 1978, one senator described PCP as "one of the most insidious drugs known to mankind," and a member of the House of Representatives declared that the drug was "a threat to the national security and that children were playing with death on the installment plan."[43] The syndicated columnist Ann Landers—the seemingly self-proclaimed expert on almost everything from aardvark to zymotechnics—offered the following comment about angel dust (PCP) as part of her ten-year campaign against marijuana use:

> Unless a teenager is a chemist, there is no way he can be sure of what he is ingesting. The possibility of getting angel dust sprinkled in with pot should be enough to scare even the dumbest cluck off the stuff for life. Angel dust can blow your mind to smitherines.[44]

Research during 1978 and 1979 quickly demonstrated that comments such as these may have been overstated. In 1978, when PCP was labeled by "60 Minutes" as the number one drug problem and responsible for more emergency room admissions than any other drug, estimates from the Drug Abuse Warning Network found PCP to account for only 3 percent of all reported drug emergencies.* Furthermore, ethnographic studies of PCP users in Seattle, Miami, Philadelphia, and Chicago demonstrated that the characterizations of users' experiences were slanted and misleading.[45] The studies found something quite different from the monster drug that the media presented as some live enemy overpowering users' rational control and rendering them helpless victims of a psychotic episode, suicide, homicide, or a state of suspended confusion, which only an indefinite confinement in a mental hospital would hopefully reverse.

Users were typically aware that PCP was a potent drug, and except for the few who sought a heavily anesthetized state, most used it cautiously. They aimed to control its effects. Although some had adverse reactions to the drug, violence was rarely a factor. In fact, among the more than three hundred PCP users contacted during the studies, almost all were baffled by the connection of the drug with violent behavior. The only known episodes of violence occurred during bad trips when someone tried to restrain a user, and these were extremely unusual. Furthermore, the few who exhibited aggressive behavior typically had already developed a reputation for violence that was independent of PCP use.

None of this should suggest, however, that PCP is a harmless drug. On the contrary, hallucinations, altered mood states, feelings of depersonalization, paranoia, suicidal impulses, and aggressive behavior have been reported, but not to the extent that some commentators have suggested. In terms of acute drug reactions reported to

---

*The Drug Abuse Warning Network, more commonly known as DAWN, is a large-scale, data-collection effort designed to monitor changing patterns of drug abuse in the United States. Hundreds of hospital emergency rooms and county medical examiners in major metropolitan areas report regularly to the DAWN system. However, since a number of limitations are built into the DAWN data, they are far from representative of the actual character of drug abuse in the United States as a whole.

the DAWN system, the numbers for PCP use resulting in a visit to a hospital emergency room have been significant over the years, reaching a high of almost nine thousand in 2004.[46]

As a final point here, it appeared that PCP use in the general population was relatively low. Among national samples of high school seniors surveyed annually, the proportions having used PCP at least once dropped from 13 percent in 1979 to 2.2 percent in 2006.[47] Moreover, the proportions who used PCP during the thirty-day period prior to the survey contact declined from 2.4 percent to less than 1 percent over the same period. Nevertheless, press reports continued to describe the bizarre behavior that PCP users were exhibiting. Yet despite the media attention, all systematic attempts to study the alleged relationship between PCP use and violent behavior continued to conclude that only a very small minority of users committed bizarre acts while in a PCP-induced state.[48]

POSTSCRIPT

As America moved through the 1980s, 1990s, and the first decade of the twenty-first century, both heroin and cocaine use persisted, and crack-cocaine smoking reached epidemic proportions in many inner-city neighborhoods.* At the same time, a curious variety of fad drugs came to light—some new, and others quite old.

"Crank" (Methamphetamine)

One of the new (yet quite old) drugs to receive attention was "crank," better known as methamphetamine. Also known as crystal, meth, speed, chalk, quartz, go-fast, go, meth, eight ball, glass, 64glass, zip, zoom, Chris, Christy, and a host of other street names, methamphetamine is a central nervous system stimulant chemically related to the amphetamines. It was developed in Japan in 1919 and first used widely during World War II by German soldiers to counter the fatigue of prolonged troop movements. Like the amphetamines, methamphetamine is a potent stimulant with an action on the body similar to the effects of adrenalin. It has been used in the clinical management of psychiatric depression, obesity and weight control, chronic fatigue and narcolepsy, hyperkinetic activity disorders in children, as an analeptic to counter sedative overdose, and as a vasoconstrictor for inflamed mucosal membranes.[49]

Since the early 1970s, the therapeutic applications of methamphetamine have been notably curtailed. Its use in weight control is highly problematic since its appetite-suppressing effects endure for only a short time and its potential for dependence is considerable. Moreover, other drugs have been found to be more effective in the management of psychiatric depression, and for fatigue it is prescribed only in extraordinary circumstances. Significant, as well, in the restricted clinical use of methamphetamine has been its notable abuse potential. It is typically abused for its

---

*Heroin is discussed in Chapter 5, and cocaine and crack are addressed in Chapter 6.

energizing and euphoric properties. Although it can be taken orally for such purposes, the effects tend to be far more profound when taken intravenously. Chronic intravenous use typically leads to psychotic reactions and paranoid delusions.*

Although methamphetamine abuse had been a noticeable part of the American drug scene since the 1960s, it seemed to become more prominent during the latter part of the 1980s and throughout the 1990s, particularly in large urban areas west of the Mississippi. Referred to in the media as the "white man's crack" and the "national drug crisis for the 1990s," crank was being produced in illegal laboratories in California and through Mexican sources, trafficked by Hell's Angels and other biker gangs, and sold primarily to members of the white working class. Although slated to be the drug of the '90s, its popularity remained generally low.[50]

"Ice" (Methamphetamine)

If "crank" was to be the drug of the 1990s, "ice" was the expected "menace," "craze," and "epidemic" of the following decade.[51] Yet, although crank was a relatively familiar drug, ice was something new. Both drugs are chemically the same, in that they are methamphetamine. However, they are structurally quite different. Crank is usually obtained in powder form and in varying levels of purity; it can be ingested orally, smoked, snorted, and injected; the effects last two to four hours. By contrast, ice is a crystalline form of methamphetamine having the appearance of rock salt. Its purity ranges from 90 to 100 percent. It is typically smoked; its effects last seven to twenty-four hours. The drug was initially produced in Hong Kong, Korea, Thailand, and the Philippines, and reports indicated that its rapid onset caused intensive euphoria and often psychoses and violent behavior.[52] Despite the media hype, however, by the beginning of the 1990s the anticipated ice epidemic turned out to be a plague that never was. Although ice appeared to be a problem in Hawaii and parts of California, its use elsewhere appeared to be generally rare.[53]

"Crystal Meth" (Methamphetamine)

Although the so-called "ice age" was described by some observers as no more than media hype and a "moral panic" on the part of government officials,[54] by 2006, "ice," now referred to as "crystal meth," is second only to alcohol and marijuana as the drug used most frequently in many parts of the United States.[55]

In addition to the problems associated with the abuse of crystal meth, other concerns have emerged. The first is the volatile nature of methamphetamine laboratories and their tendency to explode. In addition, they typically contaminate surrounding property. It is estimated that one pound of methamphetamine produced in a clandestine lab yields five to six pounds of hazardous waste. The resultant environmental damage to property, water supplies, farmland, and vegetation where labs have

---

*Two curiosities associated with these effects are *meth monsters* (grotesque, monstrous apparitions) and *meth midgets* (extremely small human shapes), which are commonly hallucinated by chronic methamphetamine users.

operated costs local jurisdictions thousands of dollars in cleanup and makes some areas unusable for extended periods of time. Damage to some areas is extensive. For example, U.S. Forest Service officers have encountered tree "kills" in areas surrounding small toxic labs, and ranchers in Arizona have reported suspicious cattle deaths in areas downstream from labs.[56]

The second issue relates to the thousands of children are neglected because of living with parents, family members, or caregivers who are either crystal meth users or meth cooks. Children who reside in or near meth labs are at great risk of being harmed by toxic ingredients and noxious fumes. As noted earlier, cooking meth is extremely dangerous, and labs often catch on fire and explode. Children whose parents have been using or making meth are often placed in foster homes, straining social services in states hit hard by meth.

Marijuana

In 1979, the use of marijuana among high school students had reached a peak, with 60.4 percent of the class of 1979 reporting use of the drug at some time during their lives. At the same time, 50.8 percent reported using marijuana in the previous twelve months, and 10.3 percent reported daily use. As noted earlier, however, the proportions using the drug declined throughout the 1980s, reaching a 15-year low at the end of the decade.[57] And as the nation moved into the 1990s, the numbers continued to decline, reaching their lowest levels in 1992: lifetime prevalence had dropped to 32.6 percent, use in the past year was down to 21.9 percent, use in the last 30 days declined to 11.9 percent, and the proportion of daily users was at an all-time low (since surveying had begun) of 1.9 percent. Suddenly, parents and politicians and educators and even some drug abuse "experts" began congratulating themselves for their fine work in developing effective drug education programs. "America has finally turned the corner and solved the problem of youthful drug abuse," they exclaimed.

But the jubilation was short-lived. In 1993, data from the Monitoring the Future survey found significant increases in the use of marijuana, and certain other drugs as well, among high school seniors, tenth-graders, and eighth-graders.[58] The use of marijuana in the past year for all three groups had increased, as had the use of cigarettes in the past thirty days. Other significant increases included past year inhalant use among eighth-graders, past year use of LSD among seniors, past year stimulant use among seniors and tenth-graders, and any illicit drug (other than marijuana) use among seniors. And these increases were not simply a mathematical error or statistical fluke. They were indeed *real,* and as it turned out, they represented the beginning of a trend. By the close of the decade, marijuana use had hit a twelve-year high. It became quite clear that after all, the drug problem was anything but over. In fact, other problems seemed to emerge as well—"club drugs," GHB, ketamine, and a number of other brews both familiar and strange. By 2006, marijuana use among high school students had declined somewhat, but it was still well above the levels seen in the early 1990s.

Tobacco

Since 1964, some twenty-eight Surgeon General's reports on smoking and health have concluded that tobacco use is the single most avoidable cause of disease, disability, and death in the United States. In 1988, the Surgeon General concluded that cigarettes and other forms of tobacco, such as cigars, pipe tobacco, and chewing tobacco, are addictive and that nicotine is the drug in tobacco that causes addiction. Nicotine provides an almost immediate "kick" because it causes a discharge of epinephrine from the adrenal cortex. This stimulates the central nervous system and endocrine glands, which causes a sudden release of glucose. Stimulation is then followed by depression and fatigue, leading the user to seek more nicotine.

In addition to nicotine, cigarette smoke is primarily composed of a dozen gases (mainly carbon monoxide) and tar. The tar in a cigarette, which varies from about 15 mg for a regular cigarette to 7 mg in a low-tar cigarette, exposes the user to an increased risk of lung cancer, emphysema, and bronchial disorders. The carbon monoxide in tobacco smoke increases the chance of cardiovascular diseases. The Environmental Protection Agency has concluded that secondhand smoke causes lung cancer in adults and greatly increases the risk of respiratory illnesses in children and sudden infant death.

Women who smoke generally have earlier menopause. Pregnant women who smoke cigarettes run an increased risk of having stillborn or premature infants or infants with low birth weight. Children of women who smoked while pregnant have an increased risk for developing conduct disorders. National studies of mothers and daughters have also found that maternal smoking during pregnancy increased the probability that female children would smoke and would persist in smoking.

Statistics from the Centers for Disease Control and Prevention indicate that tobacco use remains the leading preventable cause of death in the United States, causing approximately 440,000 premature deaths each year and resulting in an annual cost of more than $75 billion in direct medical costs attributable to smoking. Over the past four decades, cigarette smoking has caused an estimated 12 million deaths, including 4.1 million deaths from cancer, 5.5 million deaths from cardiovascular diseases, 2.1 million deaths from respiratory diseases, and 94,000 infant deaths related to mothers smoking during pregnancy.[59]

An important accomplishment since the first Surgeon General's report on smoking and health has been the dramatic reduction in the numbers of people who smoke. In 1965, for example, 42.4 percent of persons aged eighteen and older were smokers; this figure dropped to 24.7 percent by 1997. At the same time, the proportion of adults who have never smoked increased from 44 percent in the mid-1960s to 55 percent by the end of the 1990s.[60] Similarly, among high school seniors, 28.8 percent were daily smokers in 1976, but this dropped to an all-time low of 12.2 percent by 2006. Whereas 19.2 percent of high school seniors smoked at least half a pack of cigarettes a day back in 1976, this figure was down to 5.9 percent by 2006.[61] A remarkable achievement. But 5.9 percent of high school seniors is still too high. Given all the evidence about smoking and health, one wonders how anyone with a functioning brain would still wish to smoke. Many students claim that smoking is cool and glamorous. But is heart disease cool? Is lung cancer glamorous? Is it cool to flunk a job interview because you smelled of tobacco smoke during your meeting with a prospective employer? Is it glamorous to stand out in the rain sucking on a cigarette because your job is a smoke-free workplace?

OxyContin, Crack, and HIV/AIDS

As America worked its way through the first decade of the twenty-first century, the widespread abuse of prescription drugs became evident.* At the same time, a war on drugs had been declared, the legalization of drugs was debated, the use of heroin and cocaine persisted, and the crack epidemic festered in the inner city. Moreover, dealing with problems of drugs became further complicated by the spread of HIV/AIDS within populations of drug users and their sex partners.

---

*See Chapter 7 for more on prescription drugs.

NOTES

1. Max Lerner, *America as a Civilization: Life and Thought in the United States Today* (New York: Simon & Schuster, 1957), p. 666.

2. See *Newsweek,* 20 November 1950, pp. 57–58; 29 January 1951, pp. 23–24; 11 June 1951, pp. 26–27; 25 June 1951, pp. 19–29; 13 August 1951, p. 50; 17 September 1951, p. 60; *Life,* 11 June 1951, pp. 116, 119–122; *The Survey,* July 1951, pp. 328–329; *Time,* 26 February 1951, p. 24; 7 May 1951, pp. 82, 85; *Reader's Digest,* October 1951, pp. 137–140.

3. Isidor Chein, Donald L. Gerard, Robert S. Lee, and Eva Rosenfeld, *The Road to H: Narcotics, Juvenile Delinquency, and Social Policy* (New York: Basic Books, 1964), p. 14.

4. Richard A. Cloward and Lloyd E. Ohlin, *Delinquency and Opportunity* (New York: Free Press, 1960), pp. 178–186.

5. Edward Preble and John J. Casey, "Taking Care of Business: The Heroin User's Life on the Street," *The International Journal of the Addictions,* 4 (1969), p. 2.

6. Kenneth Rexroth, "San Francisco Letter," *Evergreen Review,* Spring 1957, p. 11.

7. See Richard H. Blum and Associates, *Students and Drugs* (San Francisco: Jossey-Bass, 1970); Leslie Farber, "Ours Is the Addicted Society," *New York Times Magazine,* 11 December 1966, p. 43; Joel Fort, *The Pleasure Seekers: The Drug Crisis, Youth, and Society* (New York: Grove Press, 1969); A. Geller and M. Boas, *The Drug Beat* (New York: McGraw-Hill, 1969); Helen H. Nowlis, *Drugs on the College Campus* (New York: Doubleday-Anchor, 1969); J. L. Simmons and B. Winograd, *It's Happening: A Portrait of the Youth Scene Today* (Santa Barbara, CA: Marc-Laired, 1966).

8. James A. Inciardi, "Drugs, Drug-Taking and Drug-Seeking: Notations on the Dynamics of Myth, Change, and Reality," in *Drugs and the Criminal Justice System,* ed. James A. Inciardi and Carl D. Chambers (Beverly Hills, CA: Sage, 1974), pp. 203–222; George Johnson, *The Pill Conspiracy* (Los Angeles: Sherbourne, 1967).

9. Harry J. Anslinger and William F. Tompkins, *The Traffic in Narcotics* (New York: Funk & Wagnalls, 1953), pp. 37–38.

10. Cited in William Manchester, *The Glory and the Dream: A Narrative History of America, 1932–1972* (Boston: Little, Brown, 1974), p. 1362.

11. *The Realist,* September 1966, p. 3.

12. Timothy Leary, "Introduction," in *LSD: The Consciousness-Expanding Drug,* ed. David Solomon (New York: G. P. Putnam's, 1964), p. 17.

13. Cited in Manchester, p. 1366.

14. *Newsweek,* 22 December 1986, p. 48; Steve Ditles, "Artificial Intelligence," *Omni,* 9 April 1987, p. 23; "Timothy Leary," interview by David Sheff in *Rolling Stone,* 10 December 1987, pp. 226–228.

15. *Newsweek,* 13 February 1989, p. 13.

16. Timothy Leary, "On the Drug War," *New Perspectives Quarterly,* 6 (Fall 1989), p. 62.

17. *Los Angeles Times Online,* 1 June 1996.

18. For example, see Bill Davidson, "The Hidden Evils of LSD," *Saturday Evening Post,* 12 August 1967, pp. 19–23.

19. National Commission on Marihuana and Drug Abuse, *Drug Abuse in America: Problem in Perspective* (Washington, DC: U.S. Government Printing Office, 1973), p. 81.

20. Carl D. Chambers, Leon Brill, and James A. Inciardi, "Toward Understanding and Managing Nonnarcotic Drug Abusers," *Federal Probation,* March 1972, pp. 50–55.

21. John C. Pollard, "Some Comments on Nonnarcotic Drug Abuse," paper presented at the Nonnarcotic Drug Institute, Southern Illinois University, Edwardsville, June 1967; John Griffith, "A Study of Illicit Amphetamine Drug Traffic in Oklahoma City," *American Journal of Psychiatry,* 123 (1966), pp. 560–569.

22. U.S. Congress, Senate Subcommittee to Investigate Juvenile Delinquency of the Committee on the Judiciary, *Legislative Hearings on S. 674, "To Amend the Controlled Substances Act to Move Amphetamines and Certain Other Stimulant Substances from Schedule III of Such Act to Schedule II, and for Other Purposes,"* 15–16 July 1971 (Washington, DC: U.S. Government Printing Office, 1972).

23. Carl D. Chambers, *An Assessment of Drug Use in the General Population* (Albany: New York State Narcotic Addiction Control Commission, 1970); James A. Inciardi and Carl D. Chambers, "The Epidemiology of Amphetamine Use in the General Population," *Canadian Journal of Criminology and Corrections,* April 1972, pp. 166–172.

24. *Washington Post,* 12 November 1972, p. B3.

25. For an overview of the history and clinical experiences related to methaqualone, see James A. Inciardi, David M. Petersen, and Carl D. Chambers, "Methaqualone Abuse Patterns, Diversion Paths, and Adverse Reactions," *Journal of the Florida Medical Association,* April 1974.

26. AMA Department of Drugs, *AMA Drug Evaluations* (Acton, MA: Publishing Sciences Group, 1973), p. 313.

27. U.S. Congress, Senate Subcommittee to Investigate Juvenile Delinquency of the Committee on the Judiciary, *Legislative Hearings on the Methaqualone Control Act of 1973, S. 1252* (Washington, DC: U.S. Government Printing Office, 1973).

28. For a thorough analysis of Operation Intercept, see Lawrence A. Gooberman, *Operation Intercept: The Multiple Consequences of Public Policy* (New York: Pergamon Press, 1974).

29. Steven M. Greenberg, "Compounding a Felony: Drug Abuse and the American Legal System," in *Drugs and the Criminal Justice System,* ed. James A. Inciardi and Carl D. Chambers (Beverly Hills, CA: Sage, 1974), p. 186.

30. See Eric Josephson, "Marijuana Decriminalization: Assessment of Current Legislative Status," paper presented at the Technical Review on Methodology in Drug Policy Research, Decriminalization of Marijuana, National Institute on Drug Abuse, Rockville, MD, 20–21 March 1980; James A. Inciardi, "Marijuana Decriminalization Research: A Perspective and Commentary," *Criminology,* May 1981, pp. 145–159.

31. The Domestic Council Drug Abuse Task Force, *White Paper on Drug Abuse* (Washington, DC: U.S. Government Printing Office, 1975), p. 25.

32. The White House, Drug Abuse Policy Office, Office of Policy Development, *National Strategy for Prevention of Drug Abuse and Drug Trafficking* (Washington, DC: U.S. Government Printing Office, 1984), p. 19.

33. *NIDA Notes,* Spring 1990, pp. 11, 20, 27; Office of National Drug Control Policy, *Leading Drug Indicators* (Washington, DC: The White House, 1990); National Institute on Drug Abuse, *National Household Survey on Drug Abuse: Population Estimates 1990* (Rockville, MD: NIDA, 1990).

34. See *War on Drugs,* June 1980. (*War on Drugs* is a publication of the National Anti-Drug Coalition and should not be confused with any book with the same title.) It should be added here that Harry J. Anslinger and the National Anti-Drug Coalition were not the only ones to overstate the problems with marijuana. Consistently conspicuous in this behalf has been Dr. Gabriel G. Nahas, a professor of anesthesiology at Columbia University's College of Physicians and Surgeons. In his *Keep Off the Grass* (Middlebury, VT: Paul S. Eriksson, 1990), Nahas argues that marijuana is a highly addictive drug, and that its use actually eroded a number of ancient civilizations.

35. *Time,* 19 November 1990, p. 47; *Drug Enforcement Report,* 23 November 1990, p. 8.

36. "Phencyclidine (PCP)," *NCDAI Publication 18* (Rockville, MD: National Clearinghouse for Drug Abuse Information, 1973).

37. A. Reed and A. W. Kane, "Phencyclidine (PCP)," *STASH Capsules,* December 1970, pp. 1–2.

38. Sidney H. Schnoll and W. H. Vogel, "Analysis of 'Street Drugs,' " *New England Journal of Medicine,* 8 April 1971, p. 791.

39. Both of these experiments were conducted by the author.

40. *Long Island Press,* 28 November 1970, p. 2.

41. E. F. Domino, "Neurobiology of Phencyclidine (Sernyl), A Drug with an Unusual Spectrum of Pharmacological Activity," *Internal Review of Neurobiology,* 6 (1964), pp. 303–347.

42. *People,* 4 September 1978, pp. 46–48. See also Ronald L. Linder, *PCP: The Devil's Dust* (Belmont, CA: Wadsworth, 1981).

43. Select Committee on Narcotics Abuse Control, Executive Summary, *Hearings on Phencyclidine,* 8 August (Washington, DC: U.S. Government Printing Office, 1978).

44. *Cincinnati Post,* 2 June 1979, p. 23.

45. Harvey W. Feldman, "PCP Use in Four Cities: An Overview," in *Angel Dust,* ed. Harvey W. Feldman, Michael H. Agar, and George M. Beschner (Lexington, MA: Lexington Books, 1979), pp. 29–51.

46. *Emergency Room Data from the Drug Abuse Warning Network* (Rockville, MD: Department of Health and Human Services, 2006).

47. L. D. Johnston, P. M. O'Malley, J. G. Bachman, and J. E. Schulenberg, *Monitoring the Future National Survey Results on Drug Use, 1975–2005. Volume I: Secondary School Student* (NIH Publication No. 06-5883) (Bethesda, MD: National Institute on Drug Abuse, 2006); L. D. Johnston, P. M. O'Malley, J. G., Bachman, and J. E. Schulenberg, *Monitoring the Future National Results on Adolescent Drug Use: Overview of Key Findings, 2006* (NIH Publication No. 07-6202) (Bethesda, MD: National Institute on Drug Abuse, 2007).

48. R. K. Siegel, "PCP and Violent Crime: The People vs. Peace," *Journal of Psychedelic Drugs,* 12 (1980), pp. 317–330; Eric D. Wish, "PCP and Crime: Just Another Illicit Drug?" *Phencyclidine: An Update,* ed. Doris H. Clouet (Rockville, MD: National Institute on Drug Abuse, 1986), pp. 174–189.

49. See Oriana Josseau Kalant, *The Amphetamines: Toxicity and Addiction* (Toronto: University of Toronto Press, 1966); *International Symposium on Amphetamines and Related Compounds,* ed. Erminio Costa and Silvio Garattini (New York: Raven Press, 1970); *Amphetamine Misuse: International Perspectives on Current Trends,* ed. Hilary Klee (Amsterdam: Harwood Academic Publishers, 1997).

50. Community Epidemiology Work Group, *Epidemiologic Trends in Drug Abuse* (Bethesda, MD: National Institutes of Health, 1999).

51. *Drug Enforcement Report,* 24 October 1989, p. 8; *Time,* 18 September 1989, p. 28; *Alcoholism and Drug Abuse Week,* 25 October 1989, pp. 7–8; *Substance Abuse Report,* 15 November 1989, pp. 3–4; *Newsweek,* 27 November 1989, pp. 37–40; *Miami Herald,* 25 October 1989, pp. 1A, 11A.

52. *Street Pharmacologist,* 13 (1989), pp. 3, 10.

53. *Drug Enforcement Report,* 3 January 1990, p. 7; *Substance Abuse Report,* 15 July 1990, pp. 1–2; *Drug Enforcement Report,* 8 January 1991, p. 5; Philip Jenkins, *Synthetic Panics: The Symbolic Politics of Designer Drugs* (New York: New York University Press, 1999).

54. Philip Jenkins, "The Ice Age: The Social Construction of a Drug Panic," *Justice Quarterly,* 11 (1994), pp. 7–31.

55. National Institute on Drug Abuse, *Methamphetamine Abuse,* November 2006. See also, Erich Goode, "Methamphetamine Use in the United States: An Overview," *Law Enforcement Executive Forum, 3*(4) (2003), pp. 43–62.

56. See www.ojp.usdoj.gov/nij/journals/254/methamphetamine_abuse_print.html; D. Hunt, S. Kuck, and L. Truitt, *Methamphetamine Use: Lessons Learned,* Final Report to the National Institute of Justice, February 2006 (NCJ 209730), available at www.ncjrs.gov/pdffiles1/nij/grants/209730.pdf.

57. *NIDA Notes,* Spring 1990, pp. 11, 20, 27; Office of National Drug Control Policy, *Leading Drug Indicators* (Washington, DC: The White House, 1990); National Institute on Drug Abuse, *National Household Survey on Drug Abuse: Population Estimates 1990* (Rockville, MD: NIDA, 1990).

58. L. D. Johnston, P. M. O'Malley, and J. G. Bachman, *Monitoring the Future,* University of Michigan News Release, 19 December 1996.

59. National Institute on Drug Abuse, *NIDA InfoFacts: Cigarettes and other Tobacco Products,* July 2006, Washington, DC: U.S. Department of Health & Human Services.

60. "Achievements in Public Health, 1900–1999: Tobacco Use—United States, 1900–1999," *MMWR Weekly, 48*(43), November 5, 1999, pp. 986–993.

61. L. D. Johnston, P .M. O'Malley, J. G. Bachman, and J. E. Schulenberg, *Monitoring the Future, Trends on Cigarette Smoking and Smokeless Tobacco,* 2006, Table 1. Accessed on June 20, 2007, from www.monitoringthefuture.org/data/06data/pr06cig1.pdf.

CHAPTER 4

BINGE DRINKING, RAVES, CIRCUIT PARTIES, AND THE MICKEY FINN

Drugs and the Youth Culture at the Beginning of the Twenty-First Century

If anything has been learned about drug taking in the United States, it is that patterns of drug abuse are continually shifting and changing. Fads and fashions in the drugs of abuse seem to come and go. Drugs of choice emerge and then disappear from the American drug scene. Still others are rediscovered, reinvented, revitalized, repackaged, recycled, and become permanent parts of the landscape. And as new drugs of abuse become visible, there are the concomitant media and political feeding frenzies, including calls for strengthening the "war on drugs."

Alcohol has been the all-time favorite intoxicant for millennia, and will likely remain so for generations yet to come; opium and other narcotics have been popular in the United States for well over two hundred years; and cocaine, Quaaludes, PCP, heroin, methamphetamine, and LSD just seem to keep coming and going and reinventing themselves. One could say that there is always something old and something new in the American drug scene, and this seems to be especially the case in the adolescent and young adult drug cultures.

ALCOHOL: THE DEVIL'S COCKTAIL

The drug that has been used by more people and in more places and times is the simple by-product of a modest organism's conversion of sugar and water into energy—beverage alcohol, or ethanol. Like a few other significant inventions—the club, the axe, the hammer, and the spear—the discovery of alcohol likely occurred sometime during the early years of the Stone Age.[1] Perhaps some of our Neolithic ancestors left berries or grapes in a vessel for a few days. When they returned, airborne yeasts had already begun fermenting the mixture. The result, undoubtedly, provoked more interest than the original fruit. In time, our primitive ancestors learned that it was possible and desirable to cultivate plants instead of just simply gathering them for food. These prehistoric agriculturalists discovered ways of transforming the starch of their grains into fermentable sugar. Moreover, they quickly discovered not only that fruits, berries, and grains could be used to produce alcohol, but that leaves, tubers, flowers, cacti, milk, and even honey could be fermented as well.

These early beverages (wines and beers), however, were limited in their strength, for the natural fermentation process could generate an alcoholic content of no more than 14 percent. But this all changed during the closing years of the Middle Ages when someone discovered the distillation process—boiling off and isolating the more volatile alcohol from the other fluids—making possible a considerably more potent beverage.

Aqua Vitae, Ambrosia, and the Corruptor of Youth

What, really, is this drug that has been called the water of life, or *aqua vitae* in scholastic Latin; ambrosia, the nectar of the gods; but also the corruptor of youth and the devil's own brew by others? Ethyl alcohol or ethanol is a clear, colorless liquid with little odor but a powerful burning taste. Ethanol is just one of many alcohols; the others include methyl (wood) and isopropyl (rubbing) alcohol, both of which have toxic effects and cannot be readily metabolized by the body, making them quite unsuitable for human consumption.

In addition to ethanol and water, alcoholic beverages generally contain tiny amounts of substances referred to as *congeners.* Many of these chemicals are important to the flavor and aroma of the beverage. Brandy, for example, is relatively rich in congeners whereas vodka contains relatively few. Evidence suggests that the aftereffects of excessive drinking—the inglorious and loathed hangover—are related to the presence of these congeners. The postintoxication effects are greater after consuming drinks higher in congeners.

As drinkers know all too well, alcoholic beverages differ in strength. Beer generally has an alcoholic content of 5 percent, and malt liquors and ice beer are slightly higher. Natural wine varies in alcoholic content between 6 and 14 percent. Fortified wines, such as port and sherry, contain between 17 and 20 percent alcohol. Hard liquor or spirits contain approximately 40 percent ethanol—80 proof. The designation of "proof" originated centuries ago as a test for the potency of a beverage. If gun powder saturated with alcohol exploded upon ignition, this was taken as proof that the liquor was more than half pure alcohol. In the United States and many other parts of the world, proof is calculated as twice the percentage of ethanol by unit volume of beverage. Thus, 86-proof Scotch whiskey is 43 percent alcohol, whereas 151-proof rum is 75 percent alcohol.*

Unlike most other foodstuffs, alcohol is absorbed directly into the bloodstream without digestion. A small amount passes directly through the stomach lining itself; most of it, however, progresses on to the small intestine where it is almost completely

---

*It is important to understand that even though the relative strengths of the beverages differ, one consumes essentially the same amount of ethanol in the standard portions of the drink. In other words, you consume the same quantity of absolute alcohol whether the drink is a twelve-ounce bottle of beer, a three- to four-ounce glass of wine, or a cocktail made with one and one-half ounces (i.e., one shot) of distilled spirits.

absorbed. Although one may experience a burning sensation or diffuse warmth directly following a drink, these responses are the results of the irritating effect that alcohol has on the tissues of the mouth, esophagus, and stomach. Alcohol does not become intoxicating until the blood carrying it reaches the brain. The rapidity with which this occurs is in large measure determined by the condition of the stomach. An empty stomach facilitates absorption of alcohol whereas a full stomach retards it. To some degree the type of beverage involved has an effect on absorption, as well. Beer, for example, contains food substances, which tend to retard absorption. Drinks that are noticeably carbonated—such as champagne and other sparkling wines—seem to go quickly to one's head because the carbon dioxide facilitates the passage of alcohol from the stomach to the small intestine.

Alcohol is held in the tissues of the body before it is broken down like any other food substance. The body oxidizes alcohol at a steady rate, and the drinker can exercise very little control over the process. Therefore, an average-sized man of about 160 pounds drinking three-fourths of an ounce of distilled spirits every hour could consume more than a pint in a twenty-four-hour period and not experience marked intoxication. If the same quantity were consumed over a few hours, however, the person would be quite intoxicated—outright drunk, as a matter of fact.

Alcohol, like other foodstuffs, does have some nutritional value. Undoubtedly, the primitive brews and concoctions were richer in nutritional value, especially vitamins and minerals, than the highly refined beverages available today. Alcohol itself is a rich source of calories that the body can convert into energy and heat. An ounce of whiskey, for example, provides approximately seventy-five calories—or the equivalent of a potato, an ear of corn, a slice of dark bread, or a serving of pasta (without sauce). If one consumes mixed drinks, the caloric content often doubles due to the sweetness of the mixer. These extra calories can be, not surprisingly, somewhat fattening if the drinker does not reduce his or her intake of other foods.

Beer contains additional food value in the form of carbohydrates, and given the national obsession with weight reduction, brewers have put low calorie (lite) beers on the market. But the fact that alcohol offers sufficient calories for a person to subsist on initiates an additional health hazard. Many heavy drinkers, for example, express a preference to drink their meals. Missing, however, are other nutrients, such as the proteins, vitamins, and minerals vital to good health and continued well-being. As a result, heavy drinkers often suffer from chronic malnutrition and related diseases.

Alcohol exerts its most profound effects on the brain. Interestingly, the observable behavior produced by drinking is as much a result of individuals' social situation, mood, and expectations about how drinking will affect them, as it is the actual quantity of alcohol consumed. On two different occasions, for example, an individual drinking the identical quantity and type of beverage might experience euphoria or depression; or he or she may feel energetic or sleepy; or a drink found to be initially stimulating may ultimately encourage sleep. Pharmacologically, alcohol is a central nervous system depressant drug. Little is known about the operation of the specific mechanisms, but some research has suggested that alcohol acts most directly on those portions of the brain that control sleep and wakefulness.

Most drinkers (and nondrinkers as well) are aware of what is known as blood alcohol content (B.A.C.). This is a measure of the proportion of alcohol found in the bloodstream, and for the 160-pound individual previously mentioned, the process works something like this. After two or three drinks taken over a short period of time, he will begin to feel the effects rather quickly. He may feel exhilaration, like being on the top of the world, a freeing of inhibitions and the loosening of one's tongue; he might be more likely to act on impulse than with caution and good judgment, which often take a second place to bravado. Such a person would have an approximate B.A.C. of 0.05 percent.

If he drinks another three drinks in a short period, his B.A.C. would elevate to about 0.1 percent. Now, besides affecting some of the higher centers of thought and judgment located in the cerebral cortex, the alcohol is beginning to impact a few of the more basic motor areas of the brain. By law in most states, our drinker would now be judged incapable of operating a motor vehicle and could be charged with driving under the influence. In addition, he would have some difficulty walking, his hand–eye coordination would be impaired, and there would be slurring in his speech.

At higher concentrations of alcohol from 0.2 percent and up (resulting from the consumption of at least ten ounces of spirits), more of the central nervous system is affected. The drinker has difficulty coordinating even the simplest of movements, and assistance is needed even to walk or undress. By this time, effective sexual function-ing has long since disappeared, and, in addition, emotions become unstable, often shifting from rage to tears and then back again to rage or something else in a matter of moments.* At 0.4 to 0.5 percent, alcohol depresses enough of the central nervous system that the drinker lapses into a coma; at concentrations of 0.7 percent and above the most basic centers of the brain—those that affect respiration and heartbeat—are so suppressed that death is a likely result. Death solely by alcohol overdose is rela-tively rare, however, because one usually lapses into unconsciousness before the crit-ical level of alcohol intake is reached. Nevertheless, it happens, which brings up the issue of binge drinking among college students.

Bladder Busting and Drinking to Get Drunk

There was a time when college students drank to have fun, but on campuses through-out the nation it seems that more and more are drinking for no other reason than to get drunk. Researchers and school administrators call it *episodic heavy drinking,* or *binge drinking,* defined as the consumption of five or more alcoholic beverages in a row for men, or four drinks for women. Although binge drinking is not restricted to any single population group, it appears to occur most often among young people, particularly young men. Researchers estimate that as many as one in four high school

---

*The sexual stimulation that one seems to receive from alcohol occurs through a lessening of inhibitions. However, although it may increase desire, alcohol in sufficient quantity reduces the ability to perform. For men, erection and ejaculation become increasingly more difficult as the B.A.C. increases, and for women achieving an orgasm becomes problematic.

seniors engage in binge drinking, whereas under 10 percent of people aged 35 to 44 do so. And students who begin binge drinking in high school are likely to continue drinking heavily during their college careers.

The atmosphere in many university communities is one that condones or even fosters drinking-related behaviors. College students are frequently targeted by campus promotions from local saloons that advertise nickel beer and bladder buster events, and beer companies spend millions each year marketing their products to students. Research on campus life also reveals that members of fraternities and sororities drink more heavily than nonmembers, and that fraternity and sorority houses operate as functional saloons by hosting keg parties and other social events where alcohol flows freely.

The most comprehensive data documenting the extent of binge drinking on college campuses across the United States come from a series of studies conducted by the Harvard School of Public Health in 1993, 1997, and 1999. The most recent survey included random samples of more than fourteen thousand students from 128 colleges and universities.[2] Although the number of drinkers declined slightly during the course of the decade, in 1999, as in previous years, 44.1 percent of students reported binge drinking

The highest rates of binge drinking in 1999 occurred among men (50.7 percent), whites (49.2 percent), those under 24 years of age (47 percent), those who binged in high school (73.9 percent), and fraternity/sorority members (64.7 percent). In other words, 50.7 percent of male college students reported binge drinking in 1999 (and women were not far behind with 40 percent reporting that they had binged at least once), almost half of all white students had binged, and almost two-thirds of fraternity/sorority members reported binge drinking. Most strikingly, 78.9 percent of students living in sorority or fraternity houses were binge drinkers.

As one might expect, binge drinkers are more likely than non–binge drinkers to have academic problems, drive after drinking, argue with friends, do things that result in injuries, and engage in unsafe sexual practices. Drug Strategies, a nonprofit group whose mission is drug education and prevention, has estimated that underage drinking, including college binge drinking, costs some $58 billion each year in traffic accidents, crime, and treatment.[3] And going further, many students who do not drink have been victims of secondhand binging: physical or sexual assault, property damage, or impaired sleep or study time resulting from other students' binge drinking. The consequences of excessive and underage drinking affect virtually all college campuses, college communities, and college students, whether they choose to drink or not. More specifically, annual statistics show the following.

- *Death.* 1,700 college students between the ages of 18 and 24 die each year from alcohol-related unintentional injuries, including motor vehicle crashes.
- *Injury.* 599,000 students between the ages of 18 and 24 are unintentionally injured under the influence of alcohol.
- *Assault.* More than 696,000 students between the ages of 18 and 24 are assaulted by another student who has been drinking.

- *Sexual Abuse.* More than 97,000 students between the ages of 18 and 24 are victims of alcohol-related sexual assault or date rape.
- *Unsafe Sex.* 400,000 students between the ages of 18 and 24 had unprotected sex and more than 100,000 students between the ages of 18 and 24 report having been too intoxicated to know if they consented to having sex.
- *Academic Problems.* About 25 percent of college students report academic consequences of their drinking including missing class, falling behind, doing poorly on exams or papers, and receiving lower grades overall.
- *Health Problems/Suicide Attempts.* More than 150,000 students develop an alcohol-related health problem, and between 1.2 and 1.5 percent of students indicate that they tried to commit suicide within the past year due to drinking or drug use.
- *Drunk Driving.* 2.1 million students between the ages of 18 and 24 drove under the influence of alcohol last year.
- *Vandalism.* About 11 percent of college student drinkers report that they have damaged property while under the influence of alcohol.
- *Property Damage.* More than 25 percent of administrators from schools with relatively low drinking levels and over 50 percent from schools with high drinking levels say their campuses have a "moderate" or "major" problem with alcohol-related property damage.
- *Police Involvement.* About 5 percent of four-year college students are involved with the police or campus security as a result of their drinking, and an estimated 110,000 students between the ages of 18 and 24 are arrested for an alcohol-related violation such as public drunkenness or driving under the influence.
- *Alcohol Abuse and Dependence.* 31 percent of college students met criteria for a diagnosis of alcohol abuse and 6 percent for a diagnosis of alcohol dependence in the past twelve months, according to questionnaire-based self-reports about their drinking.[4]

Why do so many college students engage in binge drinking? The reasons are numerous. Many binge drinkers were already alcoholics before they entered college. In addition, academic stresses, tensions, and peer pressures, combined with beer companies and bars touting cheap drinks, exacerbate the situation. Not to be forgotten as well is that binge drinking is, for many students, just another aspect of the adolescent acting out that seems to permeate campus life.[5]

To address alcohol's pervasive effects on students, virtually all college campuses have instituted alcohol awareness and education programs, and scores provide students the opportunity to live in alcohol-free dorms. Many universities have banned alcohol at campus social events and instituted tougher penalties for alcohol-related violations, with a particular focus on fraternity and sorority houses. However, most experts agree that these regulations will not end binge drinking, particularly at off-campus private parties and bars.

CLUB CULTURES AND CLUB DRUGS

The club culture in the United States tends to be quite broad and includes raves, dance parties and dance festivals, circuit parties, plus a host of other venues where the nightlife community congregates. The best known of these are raves and circuit parties.

Raves

The term "rave" is said to stand for radical audio visual experience, and when speaking of the rave scene, one is likely to picture youths in garish clothing dancing through the night to electronic music and moving with what appears to be boundless energy. These all-night dance parties, many of which occur without the appropriate licenses or permits required for holding public events, are typically held in abandoned warehouses, airplane hangers, open fields, and other venues where both small and large numbers of participants (25 to 25,000) can be accommodated. Under the motto "Peace, Love, Unity, and Respect" (PLUR), segments of the rave culture stress the importance of strong social bonds, the collective dance experience, spirituality, and a rejection of alcohol and the sex-related aggression that is typically associated with mainstream club reveling.[6]

In the early years, ravers often wore loose, wide-legged jeans that flared out at the bottom. Many were adorned with such childhood items as suckers, pacifiers, and dolls, as well as multiple bands of plastic beads around their necks and blue and green flexible glow sticks. Because of the all-night dancing, ravers dressed in layers, so their clothes could be stripped off as the night heated up.

House, Techno, and Trance

The music of the rave culture dates back to the late 1970s and early 1980s when the popularity of disco was fading and experimentation with electronic music was emerging. Of particular influence during these early years were the Detroit techno, Chicago house, and New York garage styles of dance music. These curious names came from the places where they originated: *techno* from Detroit where computer-generated music had become an emergent art form; *house* from the Warehouse Club in Chicago; and *garage* from the Paradise Garage in the SoHo section of lower Manhattan in New York City.* From these early forms of music sired by computers, keyboards, synthesizers, and sound mixers rather than traditional instruments, a wide variety of techno variations emerged when the styles invaded Europe and raves started to take form. Some of these adaptations include breakbeat, jungle, ambient, ambient house, acid jazz, progressive, and, most recently, trance.[7]

---

*For those unfamiliar with New York City and the unusual names given to some of its Manhattan neighborhoods, SoHo stands for *So*uth of *Ho*uston Street. And for visitors to New York who might have wondered about the trendy section known as "TriBeCa," it refers to the *Tri*angle *Be*low *Ca*nal Street.

When the sound that became techno first appeared in Detroit, the music was primarily instrumental and totally electronic, reaching a speed of some 160 beats per minute.[8] The Detroit sound eventually influenced European groups like Kraftwerk, who were the likely originators of techno when they built their KlingKlang sound factory in the early '70s and launched synth-and-drum-machine tracks like "Autobahn" and "The Man-Machine." At about the same time, house was emerging in Chicago, a musical form that was similar in style to disco, yet with the repetition as well as synthetic and electronic textures of disco intensified. House quickly became popular, particularly among gay and black populations of club-goers in Chicago. And like techno, house was mostly instrumental, but a bit slower at 120–130 beats per minute.*

During the late 1970s, garage was being fashioned in New York City's Paradise Garage. The music at the Garage—opened in 1977 in an indoor truck parking lot—contained gospel-driven extortions that created a pleasure principle–driven religious atmosphere. Regulars of the club referred to the Garage as their church, from which emerged the beginnings of the DJ-as-shaman and the idea of *technoshamanism*.[9] Technoshamanism is based on the notion of bringing the human spirit back into the everyday. True technoshamanism is when shamanistic rituals and practices are done organically and are then combined with the observance of technology in an effort to reach a higher state of consciousness. This movement realizes that the whole human body needs to be brought into the technological age. Many in the rave community seek out the liberation of mind incantations, trance dance, and drugs to reach these heightened states.[10]

With the onset of the 1980s, house and techno began to move in an easterly direction, across the Atlantic, after which the earliest rave parties began to appear in the United Kingdom, and later in Western Europe and Australia. Lighting methods improved and sound systems were enhanced to boost the experiences offered by the music. As each rave party was being organized, flyers were distributed a few days in advance noting the time and place to call on the evening of the event to learn its secret location. Raves began to appear in the larger U.S. cities in the early 1990s and followed the same secretive forms as their European counterparts.

The emergence of trance, a form of techno first associated with the group Tangerine Dream, dates back to the late 1980s. Its most well-known form, Goa trance, began in Europe, but with connections to Goa, India. A tiny emerald land on the west coast of India, Goa has long since been a retreat and vacation spot for British college students. Originally taking place on tropical beaches in India, Thailand, Bali, and the jungles of Asia, Goa trance is said to offer exotic, mystical, and spiritual feelings. Although trance music and dancing appeared in the United States and Britain in the early 1990s, it has been practiced by ancient tribes for centuries as a means to celebrate. The Goa trance craze launched a street style by young women who painted henna designs on their hands using an ancient art called *mendhi* and wore jewels on their foreheads called *bindis*.

---

*Critics of rave music have described it not only as repetitive and cold, but also as faceless and soulless machine music, and a blending of the repetition of disco, the frenzy of punk, and the melodic delicacy of a fire alarm. See John J. Sloan, "It's All the Rave: Flower Power Meets Technoculture," *ACJS Today*, 19 (January 2000), pp. 1–7.

By the early 2000s, the terms "rave" and "raver" were heard less often in the club culture, and traditional rave paraphernalia—facemasks, pacifiers, and glow sticks—ceased to be popular. However, club drugs were still present.

XTC, Special K, and Other Club Drugs

There was a time when the general belief was that raves were alcohol-free parties and that many of the youths and young adults who attended raves, trances, and other dance parties did not use drugs of any kind. At most raves, however, some form of drug use now seems to be the norm. The most notable of the dance drugs—or club drugs as they are often referred to in the media—are MDMA, Ritalin, cocaine, amphetamines and methamphetamine, ketamine, Rohypnol, GHB, whippits, LSD, and a range of other hallucinogens and prescription drugs. Teenagers and young adults who participate in rave and trance events are attracted to these drugs because of the seemingly increased stamina that the substances engender, enabling ravers to dance all night, as well as the intoxicating highs that are said to deepen the rave or trance experience. Many users tend to experiment with a variety of club drugs in combination, oftentimes with alcohol, which can lead to unexpected adverse reactions.

MDMA (Ecstasy).   Over the years, one of the more popular of the club drugs, and a drug of choice among many youths and adults well beyond the dance subcultures, has been MDMA (3,4-methylenedioxymethamphetamine). Better known as Ecstasy and sometimes referred to as X, XTC, E, Adam, Clarity, and Lover's Speed, it is a synthetic compound related to both mescaline and the amphetamines, and commonly (however incorrectly) labeled a hallucinogen.*

Interestingly, Ecstasy was not an altogether new drug when it first received widespread notice. Having been developed by Merck & Company as an appetite suppressant in 1912 (but never marketed), it made its initial appearance on the street in the early 1970s and became the successor to MDA—the love drug of the hippie countercultures in the late 1960s.[11] Information about Ecstasy was first disseminated largely by word of mouth and in anonymously written flight guides that provided instructions on its proper use. For a time it was used by psychiatrists and other therapists for facilitating client communication, acceptance, and fear reduction.[12] It was argued by a number of therapists, for example, that patients opened up while under the influence of the drug, becoming less defensive and less fearful, and recalling events of the past that they had been repressing for years.[13]

As the therapeutic and recreational use of the drug became more widespread during the early 1980s, it drew the attention of both the media and the Drug Enforcement Administration (DEA).[14] In spite of the arguments of several psychiatrists and researchers who strongly believed in Ecstasy's therapeutic potential, a DEA chemist concluded that the drug had a high potential for abuse and should be strictly controlled.[15] By the close of 1986, Ecstasy had become a *Schedule I* drug,

---

*Technically, MDMA is one of a group of drugs designated as *methylated amphetamines.*

which meant that its manufacture, distribution, and sale was a violation of federal law.*

In the aftermath of federal control, the mild euphoric effects of Ecstasy were sought by small segments of undergraduate student populations;[16] Ecstasy parties became popular in a few New York nightclubs;[17] and the drug became a focus of attention in Europe because of its widespread use at disco acid-house parties (later called raves).[18] Deaths related to the use of Ecstacy (and its analog MDEA, also referred to as MDE and known on the street as Eve) were reportedly few in number, but nevertheless apparent, particularly in individuals with cardiac disorders.[19] Moreover, reports of serious and prolonged psychotic reactions to Ecstasy began to accumulate, and preliminary studies at the Addiction Research Center in Baltimore suggested that Ecstasy destroyed nerve cells in the brain that produced the neurotransmitter serotonin—that chemical messenger that modulates feelings, sexual behavior, and responses to pain and stress.[20]

During the late 1980s and early 1990s, Ecstasy moved underground for a time, with a following among members of the dance subculture, New Agers, what was left of America's aging hippie countercultures, and a few segments of the gay community. By the middle of the 1990s, however, Ecstasy seemed to have reemerged as a drug of choice in the United States, Western Europe, and Australia. Its users were not limited to the rave and other dance cultures. By the beginning of 2000, Ecstasy could be found on college campuses, on Wall Street, and in cities and towns across the United States.[21]

Like most other drugs, in small doses MDMA is not particularly problematic. It is taken orally, usually in a tablet or a capsule. MDMA's effects last approximately three to six hours, although confusion, depression, sleep disorders, anxiety, and paranoia have been reported to occur even weeks after the drug is taken. MDMA can produce a significant increase in heart rate and blood pressure, and a sense of alertness like that associated with amphetamine use. The stimulant effects of MDMA, which enable users to dance for extended periods, have led to dehydration, hypertension, and heart or kidney failure. MDMA can be extremely dangerous in high doses. It can cause a marked increase in body temperature (malignant hyperthermia) leading to muscle breakdown and kidney and cardiovascular system failure. MDMA use may also lead to heart attacks, strokes, and seizures in some users.[22] Recent research has also suggested that the chronic abuse of MDMA may produce long-lasting neurotoxic effects in the brain.[23] And as researchers Jerome Beck and Marsha Rosenbaum have noted, other situations are potentially troublesome:

> Overuse ("stacking") and polydrug use are often done for the purpose of fueling marathon bouts of high-energy dancing by young people who feel invulnerable to problematic consequences such as dehydration and overexertion. Other contextual factors also contribute to problematic consequences. These include unfamiliar dealers selling suspect drugs; hot, poorly ventilated settings; alcohol promotion and the lack of readily alternative beverages (including water) needed to combat dehydration.[24]

---

*The regulatory scheme of the federal Controlled Substances Act classifies drugs into five categories, or schedules, based on the drug's accepted medical value and its potential for abuse and dependence (see Appendix B).

Ritalin.   The trade name for methylphenidate, Ritalin is a medication prescribed for children with attention-deficit hyperactivity disorder (ADHD), an abnormally high level of activity. It is also occasionally prescribed for treating narcolepsy, a condition characterized by sudden attacks of deep sleep. Ritalin stimulates the central nervous system, with effects similar to, but less potent than, amphetamines and methamphetamine but more potent than caffeine. Although the actions of the drug are not fully understood, Ritalin has a notably calming effect on hyperactive children and a focusing effect on those with ADHD.

Because of its stimulant properties, however, in recent years the abuse of the drug has become widespread.[25] Adolescents and young adults reportedly use Ritalin for appetite suppression, wakefulness, increased attentiveness, and euphoria— effects that make it ideal for long nights of dancing (or, in the case of some students, studying). Pharmaceutical tablets are typically taken orally or by crushing them and snorting the powder. Others dissolve the tablets in water and inject the mixture. Ritalin is also mixed with heroin, or with both cocaine and heroin for a more potent effect.

Ketamine.   Ketamine, also known as K, Special K, Vitamin K, and Cat, is an injectable anesthetic that has been approved for both human and animal use in medical settings since 1970. Some 90 percent of the ketamine legally sold today, however, is intended for veterinary use. The drug gained popularity for abuse in the 1980s when it was realized that large doses caused reactions similar to those of phencyclidine (PCP), such as dreamlike states and hallucinations.

Ketamine is produced in liquid form or as a white powder that is often snorted or smoked with marijuana or tobacco products. In some cities, ketamine is reportedly being injected intramuscularly. Low-dose intoxication from ketamine results in impaired attention, learning ability, and memory. At higher doses, ketamine can cause delirium, amnesia, impaired motor function, high blood pressure, depression, and potentially fatal respiratory problems.[26]

Gamma-Hydroxybutyrate (GHB).   Known on the street as G, Grievous Bodily Harm, Liquid Ecstasy, and Georgia Home Boy, GHB can be produced as a clear liquid, white powder, tablet, or capsule, and is often used in combination with alcohol, making it extremely dangerous. GHB is often manufactured in homes with recipes and ingredients found and purchased on the Internet. The drug is typically abused either for its intoxicating/sedative/euphoriant properties or for its growth hormone–releasing effects for muscle development.

GHB is a central nervous system depressant that can relax or sedate the body. At high doses it can slow breathing and heart rate to dangerous levels. GHB's intoxicating effects begin ten to twenty minutes after the drug is taken. The effects typically last up to four hours, depending on the dosage. At low doses, GHB can relieve anxiety and produce relaxation; however, as the dose increases, the sedative effects may result in sleep and eventual coma or death. Overdosing on GHB can occur rather quickly, and the signs are similar to those of other sedatives: drowsiness, nausea, vomiting, headache, loss of consciousness, loss of reflexes, impaired breathing, and ultimately death. Because GHB is cleared from the body relatively quickly, it is sometimes difficult to detect in emergency rooms and other treatment facilities.[27]

Whippits.   Whippits are small containers of nitrous oxide (also known as laughing gas for dental anesthesia), intended for home use in whipped cream charging bottles. For whipped cream use, the bottle is filled with heavy cream and pressurized with a whippit cartridge. The nitrous oxide gas causes a frothing action upon depressurization. Whippits are legally sold under the brand name of EZ Whip in boxes of twelve or twenty-four, at a cost of about fifty cents each.

The whippits seen at raves are somewhat different from those used for whipping cream. Generally they are balloons or plastic bags of nitrous oxide, filled and sold by a supplier at or near the rave. The euphoria resulting from *huffing* (inhaling) nitrous oxide, which lasts from two to ten minutes, is considered by some to enhance the dance party experience. However, the effects of nitrous oxide can go well beyond the sought-after high. Nitrous oxide can also cause headaches, nausea, and fainting, and overdoses may result in suffocation, choking, damage to the lungs, liver, and brain, possible stroke, and even sudden death.

Rohypnol.   Sometimes referred to as roofies, rophies, Roche, and the forget-me pill, Rohypnol belongs to the class of drugs known as benzodiazepines (such as Valium, Halcion, Xanax). Rohypnol is tasteless and odorless, and it dissolves easily in carbonated beverages. The sedative and toxic effects of Rohypnol are aggravated by the use of alcohol. Even without alcohol, a dose of Rohypnol as small as one megagram can impair the user for eight to twelve hours.

Rohypnol is usually taken orally, although reportedly it can be ground up and snorted. The drug can cause profound anterograde amnesia; that is, individuals may not remember events they experienced while under the effects of the drug. It is for this reason that one of its street names is the forget-me pill. Other adverse effects associated with Rohypnol include decreased blood pressure, drowsiness, visual disturbances, dizziness, confusion, gastrointestinal disturbances, and urinary retention.* And because of Rohypnol's combined effects, it has become known as a modern-day Mickey Finn.

Circuit Parties

Over the three decades since the advent of the gay civil rights movement, gay male subcultures in large cities have frequently maintained—as an integral and celebrated element of "gay ghetto" life—an intimate connection between recreational drug use, all-night dance parties, and sexual freedom.[28] Although the onslaught of the AIDS epidemic in the 1980s forced a broad-based retrenchment in the more libertine aspects of these subcultures, a number of social forces in the 1990s brought the

---

*Rohypnol, GHB, and ketamine have reportedly been used in sexual assaults as "date-rape" or "acquaintance-rape" drugs. This issue is addressed at length later in this chapter.

drug/sex/dance scenes back with considerable vigor. The most visible facet of this renewed revelry has been the circuit party, which, paradoxically, emerged from AIDS fundraising efforts initiated by the gay community in the early days of the epidemic.

As these one-night fundraising affairs stretched into week-long dance events attracting many thousands of men, recreational drug use became more prevalent. Ecstasy was initially the primary drug of choice for these parties, followed by the additions of other club drugs, like ketamine, GHB, and crystal meth.

In response to the use of crystal meth, the party scene changed again to include the development of harder-edged music and an increasing focus on casual sex encounters rather than dance. Crystal meth has now become embedded in many urban gay communities and is strongly associated with sexual behaviors that put men at risk for HIV infection.

The Emergence of Circuit Parties.   The form and style of the modern circuit party have roots in both the AIDS epidemic and the emergence of rave culture in the late 1980s. The lack of government attention to the growing AIDS crisis in the early 1980s left gay men, by far the most common victims of the disease in the early years, to fend for themselves in helping those already infected and attracting resources to fight the disease. Gay Men's Health Crisis (GMHC) in New York City sponsored, in what some consider to be the very first circuit party, a fundraising event on Fire Island in 1982. The Morning Party (thus named to acknowledge both loss and hope) became an annual, ever-larger dance event that combined fundraising for AIDS with the celebration of life. Miami followed quickly in New York's path, establishing the White Party in 1985. Held at an elegant historic mansion on Biscayne Bay over the Thanksgiving weekend, the White Party became an instant international success. Similar AIDS fundraising affairs soon cropped up in other major cities, gradually spreading to such smaller municipalities as Austin, Texas, and Palm Springs, California. Traveling the "circuit" of parties to support the cause became an important social activity for the mostly white, moneyed gay men who could afford it.

As the circuit phenomenon developed, gay male fashion was also changing. Spurred by a desire to create as much distance as possible from the gaunt appearance of people with AIDS, gay men raised the gym-honed body to icon status. Muscles— often aided by the use of anabolic steroids—became a fashion statement; the shirtless, shaven male chest and "six-pack" abs symbolized circuit party style, while also adding a strong sexual component to the celebrations that defied the power of AIDS to define gay life. As AIDS treatment and prevention technologies—e.g., zidovudine (AZT, the first pharmaceutical treatment for HIV infection), HIV antibody tests, and the "condom code"—emerged in the late 1980s, hope for an end to the epidemic combined with the reinvigoration of gay party life to make the devastation of AIDS less visible and the reinstitutionalization of sexual adventurism in the culture possible.

Drawing on rave cultures, circuit parties increasingly included drug use on a broad scale. As a source of boundless energy and loving, happy feelings, Ecstasy was widely used at gay dance parties that raised money for AIDS. Drug use fueled the extension of the parties into all-night affairs. As men began to travel long distances to attend the events, the parties evolved into extended weekend, and eventually week-long, celebrations. Although most circuit parties across the country still include a sig-nature AIDS fundraising affair, promoters have expanded the concept to include many other events. Miami's Winter Party, begun in 1993 as an afternoon dance party on the beach to raise money for a local gay and lesbian foundation, for example, has become Winter Party Week. In March 2003, the event included twelve "officially sanctioned" dance parties (each from five to nine hours long) that filled both days and nights.

Bars and clubs in the community offer many peripheral "non-official" parties as well. Every event features a dance party with one or more nationally known DJs spinning mostly electronic music. Dance events generally cost $60 to $125 per per-son, with passes for the entire week usually running about $350 to $600, depending on VIP entry status. Municipal governments and mainstream hoteliers have come to provide major support for these events. Corporate sponsors for the 2003 Winter Party included Bacardi, Perrier, Southwest Airlines, and Budweiser. *Circuit Noize,* a national magazine dedicated to articles and advertisements related to circuit events, listed eleven such parties for the month of May 2003, in cities ranging from Chicago and New York to Cancun, Mexico, and Montreal, Canada. The parties are primarily defined by their size (5,000 to 25,000 people are the usual attendance figures), their hours (it is generally possible to stay in party mode twenty-four hours a day), and the recreational drug use that takes place there.

Circuit Parties and Club Drugs.   As drug use increased, the party scene got messier. Ambulances were parked outside of party venues to administer help to the fallen. Bouncers conducted pat down searches for drugs at the entrances. More recently, deaths from drug overdoses caused some charitable organizations, begin-ning with New York's Gay Men's Health Crisis in 1999, to back away from their asso-ciation with the parties.

As the 1990s wore on, there was an explosion in the regular use of club drugs, especially Ecstasy, GHB, ketamine, and crystal meth, among urban gay men. Gay dance clubs, throwing "weekly circuit parties," extended their hours to the limits of municipal tolerance. In entertainment-oriented cities like New York and Miami, after-hours clubs sprang up (*sans* alcohol, but no one cared), opening at 5:00 A.M. and clos-ing in the late afternoon for those who were not yet ready to go home. Thus, the circuit style became an integral part of everyday life in parts of the gay community.

The introduction of crystal meth to the circuit party scene has generated a num-ber of health policy implications. Studies suggest that the use of crystal meth is wide-spread and that the users of crystal meth are at considerable risk for numerous health problems. For example, crystal users are more often users of other drugs as well, with significant numbers using marijuana, cocaine, Ecstasy, ketamine, GHB, and prescrip-tion "uppers" and "downers." As such, they are at increased risk not only for an over-dose on any given drug, but also for potentially lethal drug interactions. In addition, crystal users would appear to be at greater risk for HIV and other sexually transmit-ted infections. For example, they reportedly use drugs more often during their sexual encounters, causing a loss of inhibitions which might serve to increase their willingness to participate in unprotected sex.

Although circuit parties started as events attended by gay men, by the beginning of the year 2000 more and more heterosexual couples and singles have been seen attending, partying, dancing, using drugs, and cruising for partners. As such, it would appear that the circuit party is moving toward the mainstream of the club culture.

THE CHANGING LIFE OF THE MICKEY FINN: ACQUAINTANCE-RAPE DRUGS—YESTERDAY AND TODAY

The Mickey Finn, or simply the Mickey, is commonly believed to be a potion of knockout drops designed to render a given bar patron unconscious. The Mickey Finn has been an enduring part of American folklore, variously portrayed in verbal tradition, the theater, literature, and the mass media. Yet an explanation of its history finds little agreement as to what, exactly, is the Mickey Finn, what it does, and where it comes from. Perhaps even more interestingly, was there a person by the name of Mickey Finn from whom the phenomenon descended? Furthermore, does the Mickey Finn still live; to what extent has the Mickey survived the passing decades; in what form, if any, does it appear today?[29]

Knockout Drops

The traditional conception of the Mickey Finn is knockout drops—a draught or powder slipped into liquor to knock the drinker unconscious—and has been designated as such in popular reference works.[30] By contrast, however, suggesting that bar and saloon owners did not wish an unconscious customer on their hands, some claimed that a Mickey Finn was actually a purgative mixed with whiskey, serving to induce severe cramps and diarrhea.[31] Alternatively, and within segments of the professional underworld generations ago, the Mickey Finn was referred to as double drinks and knockout drops.[32] Although the notion of the Mickey as knockout drops is fairly consistent, no agreement emerges as to its beginnings in place and time.

One version of the Mickey Finn's nature and origin has been offered by Herbert Asbury, a popular historian during the early decades of the twentieth century who compiled informal chronicles of America's urban underworlds.[33] Asbury related that the Mickey Finn was a product of Chicago's Whiskey Row during the 1880s. Whiskey Row, located along the west side of State Street from Van Buren to Harrison, was an expanse where for some thirty years every building and storefront was occupied by a gambling house, a saloon, and/or a wine room. Most of these establishments were known to have been thieves' hangouts—the rendezvous of safe-blowers, pickpockets, sneak thieves, burglars, and confidence men of both amateur and professional status.

At the southern end of Whiskey Row was the Lone Star Saloon, described at that time by a local police inspector as "a low dive, a hangout for colored and white people of the lowest type."[34] The Lone Star opened in 1896, and its owner was an Irish gent by the name of Mickey Finn. Finn first appeared in Chicago during the World's Fair of 1893 as a lush worker, robbing drunks in the Bad Lands and Little Cheyenne districts of South Clark Street. He then worked as a pickpocket in Chicago's red-light district and as a fence for small-time thieves. After Finn opened the doors of his Lone Star Saloon, he continued his thieving by picking the pockets of drunken men in the back room of his establishment.

The story continues with Mr. Finn meeting a black voodoo master known only as Dr. Hall, who sold love potions and charms to brothel tenants, and cocaine and morphine to drug users. Finn reportedly purchased a large bottle of "a sort of white stuff" from which he made two knockout drinks. The first, known as the Mickey Finn Special, was compounded of raw alcohol and the white stuff mixed in the water; Finn's Number Two was beer dosed with the white stuff, fortified with a dash of snuff. The house girls and streetwalkers who worked on a percentage basis with the Lone Star Saloon were instructed to urge one of Finn's concoctions on those with whom they drank. Those who succumbed to the drugged liquor were carried to a back room where Finn systematically robbed them and tossed them into an alley.*

An alternative origin of the Mickey Finn comes from the San Francisco attorney Vincent J. Mullins, who claimed that the disastrous potion was invented on the Barbary Coast, circa 1870, by a discredited Scotch chemist named Michael Finn.[35] Finn, supposedly a fugitive from justice in Scotland and working as a bartender in San Francisco, was reported to be a source of manpower for those ship captains whose crews had deserted to prospect in the gold fields. Under Finn's care, sailors drinking in his bar would suddenly show few signs of life, making them easy to shanghai aboard ships bound for distant ports of call. Unfortunately, there is no corroborating documentation for the story. Furthermore, this supposedly true, historic Mickey was reportedly *tartar emetic* (which is poisonous). This drug, however, was not formulated or introduced until 1918.

The drugging of bar patrons for the purposes of theft, abduction, and sexual assault has existed for generations in the United States, and was reported as early as 1868,[36] and in all likelihood the drug most commonly used was chloral hydrate. Chloral hydrate is the oldest known synthetic sedative-hypnotic drug. It was first prepared in 1832 but remained as a scientific curiosity on the shelves of European

---

*It is difficult to decide whether this was indeed the actual origin of the Mickey Finn, for there is both favorable and confusing evidence in its behalf. Initially, Mr. Mickey Finn—the person and proprietor of the Lone Star Saloon—did exist, for he was known to the Chicago police as a Whiskey Row entrepreneur. Asbury's account of the Mickey Finn Special, without corroboration, was drawn from the testimony of Gold Tooth Mary Thornton, a house girl at the Lone Star Saloon, to a local graft commission in 1903.

On a more confusing note, however, the terms *Mickey* and *Dr. Hall* were both tramp slang for spirituous liquor along the American hobo belt years before the appearance of the Mickey Finn on Chicago's Whiskey Row. Eric Partridge, the well-known specialist in American slang, suggests that *Mickey* was a familiarization of *Michael,* which was likely an early allusion to Irish whiskey (see Eric Partridge, *A Dictionary of the Underworld* [New York: Bonanza Books, 1961]). And finally, *Dr. Hall,* often shortened to *Hall,* was reportedly a tramp slang perversion of the word *alcohol* ("alco-hol" to "alky-hall").

laboratories until 1869 when German physician Leibreich discovered its sedative, hypnotic, and anesthetic properties.[37]

Almost immediately after Leibreich's finding, the sleep-inducing properties of chloral hydrate were praised in the popular literature.[38] Early doses for sleep ranged from 10 to 80 grains of the drug, and sometimes as high as 270 grains. The first documented chloral hydrate overdose was reported at Philadelphia Hospital in 1870 from a dose of 460 grains, and an account of the first known death from the drug appeared in the February 15, 1871, edition of *Medical Times*.[39] Within a year after the introduction of chloral hydrate into medical use, its interactive effects with alcohol were noticed, described as resembling severe alcoholic somnolence.[40] This would suggest that of the possible early candidates for the Mickey Finn preparation, chloral hydrate was the more likely ingredient.

Throughout the twentieth century, chloral hydrate in alcohol was generally considered to be the traditional formula for the Mickey Finn, and the interactive effect of these two drugs has been the subject of considerable medical and pharmacological research.[41] During the closing years of the century, other varieties of the Mickey Finn emerged—Rohypnol, GHB, and ketamine.

Rohypnol: A Twenty-First-Century Mickey Finn

Although GHB and ketamine have been used in sexual assaults, the pharmacological properties of Rohypnol make it a suitable candidate for the acquaintance-rape drug of choice. One in four college women are victims of rape. The term "acquaintance rape" is preferred over "date rape" because although 84 percent of the women know their assailants and 57 percent of the rapes happen on a date, it is not necessarily a woman's date who actually commits the crime. Acquaintance rape, on the other hand, refers to any nonconsensual sexual activity between two or more people who know each other, and it typically happens between friends, spouses, girlfriends and/or boyfriends, and people who just met.

Rohypnol intoxication is characterized by marked sedation and such other effects as extreme disinhibition, severe memory impairment or amnesia, muscle relaxation, visual impediment, and the slowing of psychomotor performance. Most of these effects, specifically the amnesia and disinhibition, demonstrate that a person who unknowingly (or even knowingly) ingested this drug would be an easy target for sexual or other criminal victimization. In fact, the package insert supplied by the drug's manufacturer includes the following comment: "Some patients may have no recollection of any awakenings occurring in the six to eight hours during which the drug exerts its action." Moreover, when Rohypnol is combined with other sedatives, antidepressants, or analgesics, its effects are greatly intensified.

Rohypnol is occasionally used as a primary intoxicant, but reports suggest that when it is used, it is more often ingested along with alcohol.[42] Alcohol and Rohypnol have a mutually potentiating effect—ingestion of one drug strengthens the effects of the other. Rohypnol is unlikely to produce death when taken alone, even in cases of overdose.[43] But in combination with alcohol, it can be life threatening, and extreme disinhibition and blackouts lasting several hours have occurred.

As for Rohypnol's reputation as the rape drug, there is no clear evidence of an epidemic problem, although numerous documented cases have been reported.* Data are limited because Rohypnol-related sex crimes are virtually impossible to detect. Indeed, Dr. Richard Wise of the South Florida Poison Control Center indicated that for every documented case of Rohypnol-induced rape, there are eight to ten suspected cases.[†]

The account of one victim, a 25-year-old student at the University of California at San Diego, appears to be typical of the rape cases in which Rohypnol is suspected. The woman believed that the drug had been put into her wine glass during a concert. She subsequently awakened, stripped of her clothing, unable to remember that she had been raped.[44] Because victims are unable to remember the details of the assault until days later, if at all, it is far too late to examine them for evidence of rape or for the presence of Rohypnol in their bodies. Moreover, because rape goes unreported in the majority of cases anyway—for fear, embarrassment, and the trauma associated with testifying—prosecutions become even more difficult. In addition, victims may have been drinking or using drugs at the time of the offense, thus adding to their apprehension about reporting the crime. As one state attorney recently commented:

> It's very difficult making these cases. Usually the victims don't remember a thing. It's almost like the perfect crime, because *they* [the offenders] don't have to worry about a witness testifying against them.[45]

By the mid-2000s, Rohypnol had all but disappeared from the club scene in many urban areas, from greater awareness of the problematic character of the drug combined with the changing fads in drug abuse. However, it is important to remember that the use of alcohol and other drugs can cause effects similar to those of Rohypnol, and that alcohol remains the most commonly utilized drug by sexual predators. In addition, victims of rape (and of most violent crimes) are themselves frequently under the influence of alcohol or other drugs at the time of assault.

BREWS AND BLENDS BOTH FAMILIAR AND STRANGE: THE ADULTERATION OF CLUB, PARTY, AND DANCE DRUGS

One of the difficulties with virtually all drugs of abuse is that they are rarely pure—some are actually substitutes of other, less expensive compounds, whereas many more are adulterated with various materials. Over the years, for example, caffeine has

---

*The use of Rohypnol in crimes other than rape have been reported as well. Rohypnol has been used on drug victims prior to thefts and robberies. Moreover, like the old-fashioned Mickey Finn, European prostitutes have been using Rohypnol for years to drug their clients and then steal their wallets and other valuables after sedation occurs. See Christine A. Saum, "Rohypnol: The Date Rape Drug?" in *The American Drug Scene,* ed. James A. Inciardi and Karen McElrath (Los Angeles: Roxbury, 1998), pp. 254–261.

[†] Ibid.

been sold as amphetamine, methamphetamine, and cocaine; PCP has been substituted for just about every hallucinogenic drug; such things as over-the-counter painkillers, nasal decongestants, antibiotics, and oral contraceptives have been substituted for Quaaludes; marijuana has been mixed with chewing tobacco, pencil sharpenings, and horse manure to increase its bulk; and heroin and cocaine have been adulterated (cut or padded) with substances such as confectionery sugar, caffeine, aspirin, baking soda, marble powder, and even rat poison.

Caffeine: A Domesticated Drug

Because caffeine is one of the most popular substances used for both adulteration and substitution, a few comments about it seem warranted. As a mild stimulant present in coffee, tea, kola nuts, and cocoa, caffeine was introduced to the Western world just after the European discovery of America.[46] During the two centuries following Columbus's first voyage, explorers and traders brought coffee from Arabia and Turkey, tea from China, kola nuts from West Africa, and cocoa from the West Indies, Mexico, and the tropical Americas. Of these substances, coffee is the most widely used; in the United States alone, it has been so incorporated into our way of life that the annual consumption of this watery extract of the coffee bean is equivalent to almost 200 billion doses of caffeine.

Although the story of coffee's introduction and growth has never been fully documented, myth and fantasy have offered much information that history has failed to provide. Among the Arabs and Persians, it is related that a brew of coffee beans was presented to the Prophet Muhammad by the Archangel Gabriel, whereas others declare that it was discovered along the west coast of the Red Sea. Whatever its true origin may be, history does relate that soon after it had become popular in the East, it was quickly declared as a brew of the devil and, hence, prohibited. In sixteenth-century Egypt, for example, coffee was considered contrary to the spirit of the Koran, and whenever stocks of coffee were found they were immediately burned. Yet the proscription against coffee failed to endure, and the laws against it were repealed. By 1551, it was enjoyed by the populations of Asia Minor, Syria, and Persia. Less than a century later, coffee houses began to appear throughout Europe and in the United States.[47]

The extreme popularity of coffee stems from the stimulating effects of its active ingredient—caffeine. Caffeine stimulates all portions of the cerebral cortex. Its main action produces a more rapid and clearer flow of thought; motor activity is increased and drowsiness and fatigue are appreciably diminished. These effects can become evident after the administration of 150 to 250 milligrams of caffeine, the amount contained in one or two cups of coffee.[48]

Yet caffeine has its hazards. Even in moderate doses, it can affect the heart rate, heart rhythm, blood vessel diameter, coronary circulation, blood pressure, and other bodily functions. Overindulgence in the drug can result in restlessness and disturbed sleep, cardiac irregularities, and gastrointestinal irritation. When taken in extremely large doses, caffeine can be a potent poison. A fatal dose causes convulsions, followed by death resulting from respiratory failure. The fatal caffeine dose is estimated at ten grams—seventy to one hundred cups of coffee.

These severe effects may seem irrelevant to the average coffee drinker, who rarely consumes more than several cups at a single sitting. Yet using caffeine in concentrated tablet form has become a popular U.S. habit. NoDoz, for example, an over-the-counter variety of concentrated caffeine, contains one hundred milligrams of the drug in each tablet. As few as ten tablets simultaneously consumed can initiate the toxic reactions described previously. Even more potent is Vivarin, containing two hundred milligrams per tablet. Problems emerge when students, attempting to forestall sleep while cramming, dissolve ten to twenty tablets into a cup of coffee. The result is a potent stimulant syrup, the use of which can have problematic consequences.

Ersatz XTC

Substitution and adulteration practices that increase profits are common among drug traffickers and dealers. In addition, drugs are often prepared under the poorest hygienic conditions, attaching an extra level of risk to their ingestion. Most recently, these situations have become apparent in the manufacture, trafficking, distribution, and sale of Ecstasy.

The life of the typical Ecstasy tablet found in the United States begins somewhere along the Dutch-Belgian border, in a quiet rural district of northern Europe inhabited primarily by pig farmers.[49] The setting may be rustic, but it is also conveniently close to the Brussels airport. Manufacturers set up Ecstasy factories in abandoned barns and garden sheds, often mixing chemicals in cans, barrels, and drums so unsanitary that, in the words of one director of Belgium's national police force, "I wouldn't even use them for garbage."[50] The production cost for each tablet is just a few cents, but each tablet is sold locally for up to fifty cents. Israeli and Russian organized crime syndicates dominate much of the global trade in Ecstasy and traffic the drug through Canada, the Caribbean, and Latin America into New York, Miami, and other parts of the United States. Tablets usually wholesale for six to eight dollars each, and are resold in raves, other dance clubs, and on the street for anywhere from twenty to forty dollars. At any time during the manufacturing process, adulterants can be introduced; and at any point along the distribution routes, ersatz look-alike drugs might be substituted. Since the beginning of Ecstasy's popularity as a club drug, the most common replacements have included amphetamines, caffeine, LSD, and various inert powders.[51] With the onset of the late 1990s, furthermore, such drugs as atropine and scopolamine have become increasingly used as substitutes for Ecstasy.[52] These drugs typically incorporate one or more of the belladonna alkaloids, a group of organic compounds—*Atropa belladonna, Hyoscyamus niger,* and *Datura stramonium*—that freely occur in nature and have been known for centuries for their strange and stupefying properties.[53]

Atropa belladonna, more commonly known as the deadly nightshade and organically related to the potato and eggplant, is a widely distributed plant with star-shaped flowers, showy red berries, and poisonous qualities. Its name descends initially from Greek mythology, from Atropos, the eldest of the Three Fates who arbitrarily controlled the birth, life, and death of every man. The designation of Atropos was given by

Linnaeus, the eighteenth-century Swedish naturalist who first described the plant. *Belladonna,* meaning beautiful woman in Italian, derives from the ancient use of the drug as an eye beautifier, from its ability to cause dilation of the pupils when smeared on the eyes in small doses.

Datura stramonium, more typically referred to as the jimson weed, Jamestown weed, thornapple, or stink weed, is a spindly plant generally native to temperate and tropical regions in both hemispheres. Its common English name, the jimson weed, derives from the late eighteenth century after a group of soldiers at Jamestown, Virginia, cooked and ate the leaves of the plant and experienced its intoxicating effects (*Jimson* is seemingly a corruption of *Jamestown*). It was this plant, according to Plutarch, that produced fatal effects on the Roman soldiers during their retreat from the Parthians under Mark Antony in 38 and 37 B.C. Similarly, *Hyoscyamus niger,* or black henbane, has been known for centuries and was used in ancient Greece as a poison, to produce madness, and to evoke prophecies.

These organic biologicals have long since been used in preparations, potions, and brews both familiar and strange, many of which fell somewhat beyond the range of orthodox pharmacology. During the Middle Ages, they were reputedly used criminally for inducing madness and for seducing women. Eliphas Levi's *Dogma and Ritual of Magic* suggests that extracts of henbane and deadly nightshade were the active ingredients in many a sorcerer's brew, or were joined in the classic witch's cauldron with more peculiar substances as toad skin, moss from the skull of a parricide (one who murders a relative), or horns from a goat that has cohabited with a young girl.[54] These plants were undoubtedly used in the ancient world in the connection with orgiastic rites characterized by sexual excesses. One might be reasonably certain that at Bacchanalia sexual frenzy was not necessarily produced by plain fermented grape juice. Intoxication of this order was more likely the result of doctoring the wine with leaves or berries of henbane or belladonna.

Sporadic incidents and clusters of poisonings with these plants continue to occur in the United States, mostly among adolescents seeking their hallucinogenic effects. The type of intoxication that occurs is a variety of what is known as *belladonna psychosis,* generated by the atropine and scopolamine contained in the plants.[55] More specifically, atropine can effect severe rises in blood pressure and stimulation of the cerebral cortex. Its prolonged use can cause one to become talkative, to experience disorientation and sometimes hallucinations, followed by depression, stupor, coma, and paralysis of the respiratory system. Scopolamine, more potent than atropine, can produce euphoria, fatigue, restlessness, delirium, and hallucinations. Clearly, the substitution of atropine and scopolamine for Ecstasy, combined with the conditions under which Ecstasy is used in rave settings, has the potential for great harm.

POSTSCRIPT

The history of drug abuse in the United States suggests that club drugs, party drugs, dance drugs, recreational drugs—or whatever other appellations one wishes to attach—have become an integral part of adolescent and young adult cultures. And as noted in the opening comments in this chapter, there are fads and fashions in the drugs of choice, with old and new ones perpetually becoming vogue and then passé. In many parts of the United States during the first half of the 2000s, the more traditional club drugs—Ecstasy, GHB, ketamine, and Rohypnol—began to disappear. At the same time, other drugs began to appear in the clubs, including crystal meth, as well as a wide range of prescription drugs. Moreover, powder cocaine made a comeback as the club drug of choice in many parts of the country. Finally, as the world keeps turning, both teenagers and young adults continue to discover and rediscover the laws of nature and pharmacology. The result is the abuse of almost any substance that promises significant changes in perception and consciousness.

NOTES

1. This section on the history of alcohol is drawn primarily from Harvey A. Siegal and James A. Inciardi, "A Brief History of Alcohol," in *The American Drug Scene,* ed. James A. Inciardi and Karen McErath (Los Angeles: Roxbury, 2007).

2. Henry Wechsler, Jae Eun Lee, Meichun Kuo, and Hang Lee, "College Binge Drinking in the 1990s: A Continuing Problem," *Journal of American College Health,* 48 (March 2000), pp. 199–210.

3. *U.S. News & World Report,* 27 March 2000, p. 53.

4. Ralph W. Hingson, Timothy Heeren, Ronda C. Zakocs, Andrea Kopstein, and Henry Wechsler, "Magnitude of Alcohol-Related Mortality and Morbidity among U.S. College Students Ages 18–24," *Journal of Studies on Alcohol, 63*(2) (2002), pp. 136–144; Ralph Hingson, Timothy Heeren, Michael Winter, and Henry Wechsler, "Magnitude of Alcohol-Related Mortality and Morbidity Among U.S. College Students Ages 18–24: Changes from 1998 to 2001," *Annual Review of Public Health,* 26 (2005), pp. 259–79; C. A. Presley, M. A. Leichliter, and P. W. Meilman, *Alcohol and Drugs on American College Campuses: A Report to College Presidents: Third in a Series, 1995, 1996, 1997* (Carbondale, IL: Core Institute, Southern Illinois University, 1998); J. R. Knight, H. Wechsler, M. Kuo, M. Seibring, E. R. Weitzman, and M. Schuckit, "Alcohol Abuse and Dependence Among U.S. College Students," *Journal of Studies on Alcohol 63*(3) (2002), pp. 263–270; H. Wechsler, J. E. Lee, M. Kuo, M. Seibring, T. F. Nelson, and H. P. Lee, "Trends in College Binge Drinking during a Period of Increased Prevention Efforts: Findings from Four Harvard School of Public Health Study Surveys, 1993–2001," *Journal of American College Health 50*(5) (2002), pp. 203–217; H. Wechsler, B. Moeykens, A. Davenport, S. Castillo, and J. Hansen, "The Adverse Impact of Heavy Episodic Drinkers on Other College Students," *Journal of Studies on Alcohol 56*(6) (1995), pp. 628–634.

5. John Jung, *Under the Influence* (Pacific Grove, CA: Brooks/Cole, 1994); Kate B. Carey and Christopher J. Correia, "Drinking Motives Predict Alcohol-Related Problems in College Students," *Journal of Studies on Alcohol,* 58 (January 1997), pp. 100–105.

6. R. Measham, H. Parker, and J. Aldridge, "The Teenage Transition: From Adolescent Recreational Drug Use to the Young Adult Dance Culture in Britain in the Mid-1990s," *Journal of Drug Issues* 28 (1998), pp. 9–32; R. Newcombe, "A Researcher Reports from the Rave," *DrugLink* 7 (1992), p. 14; Simon Reynolds, *Generation Ecstacy: Into the World of Techno and Rave Culture* (Boston: Little, Brown and Company, 1998).

7. J. J. Sloan, "It's All the Rave: Flower Power Meets Technoculture," *Academy of Criminal Justice Sciences Today,* 19 (January 2000), pp. 1–6; C. R. Knowles, *Up All Night: A Closer Look at Club Drugs and Rave Culture* (New York: Red House Press, 2001); T. McCall, *This Is Not a Rave: In the Shadow of a Subculture* (New York: Thunder's Mouth Press, 2001); M. Silcott, *Rave America: New School Dancescapes* (Toronto, Ontario, Canada: ECW Press, 1999).

8. D. Bradborn, "RAVE On!" *Dance Magazine,* 5 July 1993.

9. S. Reynolds, *Generation Ecstasy* (Boston: Little, Brown and Company, 1998).

10. J. Lopiano-Misdom and J. De Luca, *Street Trends: How Today's Alternative Youth Cultures Are Creating Tomorrow's Mainstream Markets* (New York: Harper, 1997); J. Fritz, *Rave Culture: An Insider's Overview* (Victoria, BC, Canada: SmallFry Press, 1999).

11. See Marsha Rosenbaum, "Why MDMA Should Not Have Been Made Illegal," in *The Drug Legalization Debate,* ed. James A. Inciardi (Newbury Park, CA: Sage, 1991), pp. 135–146.

12. Jerome Beck, "The Popularization and Resultant Implications of a Recently Controlled Psychoactive Substance," *Contemporary Drug Problems,* 13 (1986), pp. 23–63.

13. Joe Klein, "The New Drug They Call 'Ecstasy,'" *New York,* 20 May 1985, pp. 38–43.

14. *Time,* 10 June 1985, p. 64; *New York Times,* 1 June 1985, p. 6; C. Dye, "XTC: The Chemical Pursuit of Pleasure," *Drug Journal News,* 10 (1982), pp. 8–9; *Discover,* August 1986, p. 34.

15. For a thorough history and analysis of the MDMA controversy, see Jerome Beck and Marsha Rosenbaum, "The Scheduling of MDMA ("Ecstasy")," in *Handbook of Drug Control in the United States,* ed. James A. Inciardi (Westport, CT: Greenwood Press, 1990), pp. 303–316.

16. S. J. Peroutka, "Incidence of Recreational Use of 3, 4-Methylenedimethoxymethamphetamine (MDMA, 'Ecstasy') on an Undergraduate Campus," *New England Journal of Medicine,* 317 (1987), p. 1542; D. M. Barnes, "New Data Intensify the Agony over Ecstasy," *Science* 239 (1988), pp. 864–866.

17. *New York Times,* 11 December 1988, p. 58.

18. Charles Kaplan, "Ecstasy in Europe: Acid House Parties," *Street Pharmacologist,* Spring 1989, pp. 6–7; *Bonn Die Welt,* 5 February 1990, p. 3.

19. *Street Pharmacologist,* April 1987, p. 4.

20. G. Ricaurte, G. Bryan, L. Strauss, L. Seiden, and C. Schuster, "Hallucinogenic Amphetamine Selectively Destroys Brain Serotonin Nerve Terminals," *Science,* 229 (1985), pp. 986–988; C. J. Schmidt, "Neurotoxicity of the Psychedelic Amphetamine, Methylenedioxymethamphetamine," *Journal of Pharmacology and Experimental Therapeutics,* 240 (1987), pp. 1–7; Errol B. De Souza and George Battaglia, "Effects of MDMA and MDA on Brain Serotonin Neurons: Evidence from Neurochemical and Autoradiographic Studies," in *Pharmacology and Toxicology of Amphetamine and Related Designer Drugs,* ed. Khursheed Asghar and Errol De Souza (Rockville, MD: National Institute on Drug Abuse, 1989), pp. 196–222.

21. *Time,* 13 March 2000, pp. 64–66; *Time,* 5 June 2000, pp. 60–73.

22. National Institute on Drug Abuse, "Club Drugs," *Community Drug Alert Bulletin,* 10 January 2000.

23. Alan L. Leshner, "A Club Drug Alert," *NIDA Notes,* 14 (March 2000), pp. 3–4.

24. Beck and Rosenbaum, pp. 139–140.

25. John J. Burke, "Ritalin: Potential for Diversion and Abuse," *Pharmaceutical Drug Diversion Conference,* National Association of Drug Diversion Investigators, New York, May 5, 2000.

26. James W. Dotson, Deborah L. Ackerman, and Louis Jolyn West, "Ketamine Abuse," *Journal of Drug Issues,* 25 (1995), pp. 751–757; *Substance Abuse Letter,* 17 January 1996, p. 7; *Drug Enforcement Report,* 9 March 1999, pp. 4–5.

27. *NIDA Infofax,* "Club Drugs," 14 February 2000.

28. Portions of this section were adapted from Steven P. Kurtz and James A. Inciardi, "Crystal Meth, Gay Men, and Circuit Parties," *Law Enforcement Executive Forum, 3*(4), (2003) pp. 97–114.

29. Portions of this section were adapted from James A. Inciardi, "The Changing Life of Mickey Finn: Some Notes of Chloral Hydrate Down Through the Ages," *Journal of Popular Culture,* 11 (1978), pp. 591–596.

30. See, for example, E. C. Brewer, *Brewer's Dictionary of Phrase and Fable* (New York: Harper and Brothers, n.d.), p. 610; Jim Hogshire, *Pills-a-Go-Go: A Fiendish Investigation into Pill Marketing, Art, History, and Consumption* (Venice, CA: Feral House, 1999).

31. For example, William Morris and Mary Morris, *Dictionary of Word and Phrase Origins,* Vol. III (New York: Harper and Row, 1971), pp. 176–177; Harold Wentworth and Stuart Berg Flexner, eds., *Dictionary of American Slang* (New York: Thomas Y. Crowell, 1960), p. 38.

32. Mary Churchill Sharpe, *Chicago May: Her Story* (New York: Macaulay, 1928), p. 99.

33. Herbert Asbury, *The Gangs of New York: An Informal History of the Underworld* (Garden City, NY: Garden City Publishing Company, 1927); ibid., *The Barbary Coast: An Informal History of the San Francisco Underworld* (Garden City, NY: Garden City Publishing Company, 1933); ibid., *The French Quarter: An Informal History of the New Orleans Underworld* (New York: Alfred A. Knopf, 1936); ibid., *Sucker's Progress: An Informal History of Gambling in America from the Colonies to Canfield* (New York: Dodd, Mead, 1938); ibid., *Gem of the Prairie: An Informal History of the Chicago Underworld* (New York: Alfred A. Knopf, 1940); ibid., *The Great Illusion: An Informal History of Prohibition* (New York: Doubleday, 1950).

34. Herbert Asbury, *Gem of the Prairie*, op. cit., p. 172.

35. Herb Caen, *Don't Call It Frisco* (Garden City, NY: Doubleday, 1953), pp. 251–254.

36. See, for example, Edward Winslow Martin, *Secrets of the Great City* (Philadelphia: National, 1868), p. 313; Matthew Hale Smith, *Sunlight and Shadow in New York* (Hartford, CT: J. B. Burr), p. 229.

37. Robert F. Fairthorns, "On Chloral Hydrate," *Journal of the Franklin Institute, 61* (May 1871), pp. 327–332.

38. For example, see "A Few Words on Chloral," *Once a Week,* November 6, 1869, pp. 305–307.

39. Robert F. Fairthorns, op. cit.

40. Benjamin W. Richardson, "Chloral and Other Narcotics," *Popular Science Monthly, 15* (1879), pp. 491–503.

41. W. Lloyd Adams, "The Comparative Toxicity of Chloral Alcoholate and Chloral Hydrate," *Journal of Pharmacology and Experimental Therapeutics, 78* (1943), pp. 340–345; Peter K. Gessner and Bernard E. Cabana, "Chloral Alcoholate: Reevaluation of Its Role in the Interaction between the Hypnotic Effects of Chloral Hydrate and Ethanol," *Journal of Pharmacology and Experimental Therapeutics, 156* (1967), pp. 602–605; H. L. Kaplan, R. B. Forney, F. W. Hughes, and N. C. Jain, "Chloral Hydrate and Alcohol Metabolism in Human Subjects," *Journal of Forensic Sciences,* 12 (July 1967), pp. 295–304; Peter K. Gessner and Bernard E. Cabana, "A Study of the Interaction of the Hypnotic Effects and the Toxic Effects of Chloral Hydrate and Ethanol," *Journal of Pharmacology and Experimental Therapeutics, 174* (1970), pp. 247–259.

42. Drug Enforcement Administration, "Flunitrazepam (Rohypnol)," *DEA Highlights* (Washington, DC: U.S. Department of Justice, 1995).

43. D. E. Smith, D. R. Wesson, and S. Calhoun, *Rohypnol (Flunitrazepam)* (San Francisco: Haight-Ashbury Free Clinic, 1996).

44. J. Laboy, "Date Rape Drug Raises Fear in O.C.," *The Orange County Register,* 26 November 1995, p. B1.

45. D. Kidwell and C. Piloto, "Colorless, Odorless Pills (Roofies) Send Rape Rate Soaring," *The Miami Herald,* 15 February 1996, p. A7.

46. W. Schivelbusch, *Tastes of Paradise: A Social History of Spices, Stimulants, and Intoxicants* (New York: Pantheon Books, 1992).

47. A. Weil and W. Rosen, *Chocolate to Morphine: Understanding Mind-Active Drugs* (Boston: Houghton Mifflin Company, 1983); Schivelbusch; J. Grehan, "Smoking and 'Early Modern' Sociability: The Great Tobacoo Debate in the Ottoman Middle East (Seventeenth to Eighteenth Centuries)", *The American Historical Review, 111*(5) (2006): www.historycooperative.org/journals/ahr/111.5/grehan.html.

48. J. E. James, *Understanding Caffeine: A Biobehavioral Analysis* (London: Sage Publications, 1997).

49. *Time,* 13 March 2000, p. 63.

50. Ibid.

51. See www.Ecstasy.org.

52. See www.Ecstasy.org.

53. See Carl D. Chambers, James A. Inciardi, and Harvey A. Siegal, *Chemical Coping: A Report on Legal Drug Use in the United States* (New York: Spectrum Publications, 1975).

54. Chambers, Inciardi, and Siegal.

55. For example, see "Jimson Weed Poisoning," *Morbidity and Mortality Weekly Report,* 44 (27 January 1995), pp. 41–44; Richard A. Wagner and Samuel M. Keim, "Plant Poisoning, Alkaloids-Tropane," *E-Medicine,* 9 March 2000 (www.emedicine.com).

CHAPTER 5

CHINA WHITE AND MEXICAN BLACK

Comments on the Production, Trafficking, and Use of Heroin

English language usage is replete with any number of rather curious oddities. One of these is *euphemism,* denoting a delightfully ridiculous and roundabout word or phrase used to replace some other term or expression considered to be coarse, repugnant, indelicate, offensive, displeasing, or otherwise painful. Among the most famous of these linguistic fig leaves are *affair* to communicate the idea of marital infidelity; *ethnic cleansing* for genocide; *making love* and *sleeping together* to cover all manners of copulation and fornication; *irregularity,* first posed by a 1930s adman as a genial substitute for that abnormal condition of the bowels known as constipation; and at airports, a "revised departure time" means that your flight will be late. Other recent examples, products of the advertising industry, include *preowned vehicle* as opposed to a used car, *periodic pain* for menstrual cramps, *feminine hygiene* for the vaginal douche and sanitary napkin, and, from the Red Lobster chain of seafood restaurants, there is *call-ahead seating* to replace making a reservation.

Remember that rather bizarre and improbable form of vacation home ownership called the *time share?* In theory, it sounded like a great idea: rather than spending tens or even hundreds of thousands of dollars to purchase a retreat in Florida, Hawaii, the Caribbean, or on the slopes in Aspen or Stowe, for a more modest sum you could purchase your place in the sun or snow for just a week or two. During that time, say, the first week in July every year, it was all yours to enjoy. But time shares quickly became negatively value-laden ventures when owners began to tire of being locked into vacationing the same week or two every year, year after year. In addition, having to move into the grime and disorder left behind by the previous week's owner seemed always to be the case. As sales declined, the time-share industry had to deal with the problem. So it came up with some good euphemisms; although nothing else changed, the time share is now referred to as *interval ownership, second-home membership,* and *vacation clubs,* and for some strange reason, people are buying them once again.

Finally, not to be forgotten are the sweeping changes that have occurred in jailhouse nomenclature. After the riot at New York's Attica Prison in 1971, in a spree of legislative wishful thinking in a number of jurisdictions, prisons and penitentiaries became known as *correctional facilities,* wardens and keepers became *superintendents,* guards became *correction officers,* and prisoners and convicts became *inmates.* *

A second peculiarity of language is the redefinition of words, either through simple ignorance or deliberate intent. This variety of linguistic manipulation has been a particular problem in the drug field for quite some time. Few words in the English language, for example, have been as misdefined, misused, and misunderstood as *narcotic.* The consequences of this linguistic torment have become apparent in the areas of drug abuse legislation, prevention, education, treatment, and research.

WHAT, INDEED, *ARE* NARCOTIC DRUGS?

The wide and inconsistent usage of the term *narcotic* appears not only in the popular media but in legal and scientific circles as well. Sometimes narcotic is used to characterize any drug producing stupor, insensibility, or sleep, thus embracing a breadth of substances ranging from alcohol to heroin. It is used to classify compounds that are addiction producing, creating even further confusion because *addiction,* as already noted in Chapter 1, is defined so haphazardly. In legal matters, *narcotic* often designates any drug that is allegedly dangerous, is widely abused, or has a high potential for abuse. As a result, such substances as marijuana, cocaine, PCP, and amphetamines are considered along with heroin and morphine in narcotics regulations, in spite of the fact that they have little in common with true narcotics. Cocaine, for example, has effects that are almost totally opposite those of heroin. In medicine, a field in which greater specificity would be expected, the terms *narcotics, opiates, opioids, dependence-producing drugs, addicting drugs,* and *morphinelike drugs* are used interchangeably. Elsewhere, narcotics are simply habit-forming drugs.

In pharmacology, a science that focuses on the chemical nature, structure, and action of drugs, the designation of *narcotic* is quite specific.[1] It includes the natural derivatives of *Papaver somniferum L.*—the opium poppy—and any synthetic derivatives of similar pharmacological structure and action. These derivatives have both analgesic and sedative properties. Thus, the range of substances that can be called narcotics is quite limited and encompasses three basic groups.

1. *Natural Narcotics*
   - Opium, derived directly from *Papaver somniferum L.*
   - Morphine, the principal constituent of opium. As noted in Chapter 1, it is one of the more effective drugs known for the relief of severe pain and remains the standard against which new analgesics are measured.

---

*No doubt one of these days someone will invent a substitute term for *hemorrhoid,* a truly ugly word well in need of a euphemism. It would not be surprising if the new expression came from Parke-Davis, the makers of a hemorrhoid relief preparation that they have cleverly named *Anus*ol, and which they even more cleverly pronounce *An*-u-sol.

- Codeine, also derived from opium, is present in both the opium poppy and opium. Most codeine is processed from morphine and is available as a white crystalline powder, in elixirs, and in pill and injectable forms. The drug's analgesic effects are similar to those of morphine, but its potency is considerably less. As a result, abuse and dependence are relatively uncommon since large quantities must to be taken to produce such effects.
- Thebaine, a minor constituent of opium, is chemically similar to both morphine and codeine, but produces stimulatory rather than depressant effects. It is not used therapeutically, but is converted into a variety of compounds including hydrocodone, oxycodone, and oxymorphone (see Chapter 7).

2. *Semi-Synthetic Narcotics*
   - Heroin, processed from morphine
   - Hydrocodone, hydromorphone, oxycodone, and fentanyl*

3. *Synthetic Narcotics*
   - High potency varieties, such as methadone and meperidine*
   - Low potency varieties, such as propoxyphine, pentazocine, and tramadol*

Although all drugs, including narcotics, and their actions should be designated in terms of their chemical structure and their effects on cellular biochemistry or physiological systems, there has been the tendency to classify most according to the prevailing attitudes of the dominant cultural group and its most vocal representatives. Yet defining *narcotic* precisely is not an attempt to engage in any semantic game. The term *narcotic* is based on objective pharmacological criteria, as opposed to the nominalist view that a narcotic is anything that someone may wish to call a narcotic. In the final analysis, however, with so many different applications and usages of the word, *narcotic* has become a somewhat problematic designation.

HEROIN: "THE MOST DANGEROUS SUBSTANCE ON EARTH"

Known to its users as shit, smack, skag, horse, harry, henry, H, jones, boy, brown, black tar, or simply dope or junk, many people in the criminal justice community, the political arena, and the general public have called heroin "the most dangerous substance on earth."[2] Indeed, heroin is a powerful narcotic. Several times more potent than morphine, it suppresses both respiratory and cardiovascular activity and has strong analgesic effects and a high abuse liability and dependence potential. At overdose levels heroin can produce coma, shock, and, ultimately, respiratory arrest and death. For the better part of the past one hundred years, heroin has been one of the

---

*Hydrocodone, hydromorphone, oxycodone, fentanyl, methadone, meperidine, propoxyphine, pentazocine, and tramadol are discussed at length in Chapter 7.

most widely discussed drugs of abuse, and perhaps the most feared. Yet for those involved in the production, distribution, sale, and use of this crystalline powder, heroin is something entirely different. It represents the cornerstone of several unique worlds with their own peculiar goals, values, rules, needs, and achievements.

Adventures on the Opium Express

The "opium express" is a world of production and trafficking networks that stretch around the globe, from Asia and parts of Latin America to Europe, Australia, Canada, and the United States. It is an enterprise that involves millions of peasant farmers, thousands of corrupt government officials, disciplined criminal entrepreneurs, and street-level dealers.

Historically, a focal point in the trafficking complex of opium and heroin has been the Golden Triangle, a vast area of Southeast Asia comprising the rugged Shan hills of Burma (now known as Myanmar),* the serpentine ridges of northern Thailand, and the upper highlands of Laos.† This geographic area emerged during the late 1960s and early 1970s as the world's largest producer of illicit opium,[3] providing yields of some seven hundred metric tons annually.‡ For a time, the Golden Triangle also dominated the heroin-refining markets of Western Europe, and there is considerable agreement that the growing of opium in the region was introduced by Chinese political refugees. Using the Netherlands as their principle importation and distribution area, Chinese traffickers virtually controlled the heroin market—arranging for the purchase of raw opium, overseeing its conversion into heroin, and managing the international smuggling network. By the late 1970s, however, rivalries among the various Chinese drug syndicates, law enforcement efforts against Asian traffickers, and declining production due to poor crop yields served to reduce the importance of the region as a center of opium trade.[4]

A second focal point in the opium–heroin trafficking complex is what has become known as the Golden Crescent, an arc of land stretching across Southwest Asia through sections of Pakistan, Iran, and Afghanistan. Emerging as the leading opium producer in the world during the late 1970s, the Golden Crescent successfully challenged its Southeast Asian counterpart by generating a raw material for heroin that was less expensive and generally more potent. By the mid-1980s, more than half the heroin entering the United States originated as opium in the Golden Crescent. Iran was the key opium producer, and Pakistan and Afghanistan were the primary heroin refiners and shippers, having numerous illicit laboratories on both sides of the

---

*In 1989 the country's official English name was changed from the Union of Burma to the Union of Myanmar. In the Burmese language, the country has been known as Myanma (or, more precisely, Mranma Pran) since the thirteenth century. Also in 1989, the English name of the capital, Rangoon, was dropped in favor of the common Burmese name, Yangon.

†Laos is officially known as the Lao People's Democratic Republic, or more simply, Lao PDR.

‡Both coca and opium production figures are typically expressed in metric tons—1 metric ton is equal to 1,000 kilograms or 2,204.6 pounds. In this example, 700 metric tons would be the equivalent of some 1.54 million pounds.

Khyber Pass. By the close of the decade, however, with estimates suggesting that the combined yield of Southeast and Southwest Asian opium production had exceeded three thousand metric tons, the Golden Triangle had reemerged as the world leader in opium production.[5] By the close of the 1990s, with illicit opium poppy farming apparent in Vietnam, Mexico, Colombia, and perhaps other nations, the annual world production available for refining into heroin exceeded 3,700 metric tons.[6]

Since 2000, many changes have occurred around the world that have affected the extent of poppy cultivation from place to place and the amount of opium available for heroin production, including the U.S. invasion of Afghanistan after 9/11 and the rise and fall and subsequent resurgence of the Taliban in Afghanistan; the eradication of poppy fields in Thailand, Lao PDR, Myanmar, Vietnam, and Colombia; and the growth of poppy cultivation in Mexico.[7] As illustrated in Exhibit 5.1, for example, the 2005 world poppy cultivation totaled 151,500 hectares (1 hectare [ha] equals 2.5 acres), with 68 percent occurring in Afghanistan, 22 percent in Myanmar, and the remaining 10 percent distributed throughout the rest of the world. Exhibit 5.1 also illustrates that of the 4,620 metric tons (1 metric ton [mt] equals 2,200 lbs) of opium produced worldwide, almost all (89%) occurs in Afghanistan. Exhibit 5.2 illustrates these cultivation and production figures over time.

The actual process culminating in the use of heroin around the world begins in the remote sections of the Golden Triangle and Golden Crescent. There, hill-tribe farmers use the most basic agricultural techniques to cultivate the opium poppy.[8] The annual crop cycle begins in late summer as farmers scatter poppy seeds across the surface of their freshly hoed fields. Three months later, the plant is mature—a greenish stem topped by a brightly colored flower. Gradually the petals fall to the ground, exposing a seed pod about the size and shape of a small egg. Inside the pod is a milky white sap that is harvested by cutting a series of shallow parallel incisions across the surface of the pod. As the sap seeps from the incisions and congeals on the

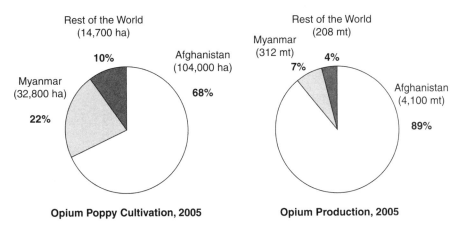

EXHIBIT 5.1   Poppy Cultivation and Opium Production

Source: The United Nations Office on Drugs and Crime, UNODC.

AFGHANISTAN—
Opium poppy cultivation (ha), 1990–2005

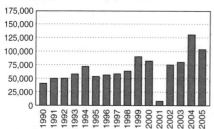

AFGHANISTAN—
Opium production (metric tons), 1990–2005

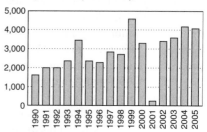

MYANMAR—
Opium poppy cultivation (ha), 1990–2005

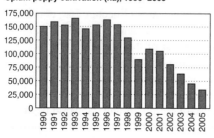

MYANMAR—
Opium production (metric tons), 1990–2005

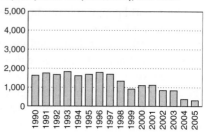

LAO PDR—
Opium poppy cultivation (ha), 1990–2005

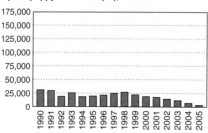

LAO PDR—
Opium production (metric tons), 1990–2005

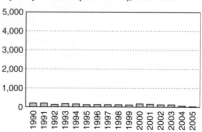

REST OF THE WORLD—
Opium poppy cultivation (ha), 1990–2005

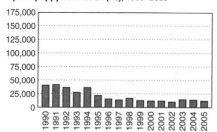

REST OF THE WORLD—
Opium production (metric tons), 1990–2005

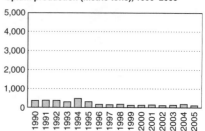

EXHIBIT 5.2   Annual Opium Poppy Cultivation and Opium Production in Main Producing Countries, 1990–2005

Source: The United Nations Office on Drugs and Crime, UNODC.

surface of the pod, it changes to a brownish-black color. This is raw opium, which the farmers collect by scraping the pod with a flat, dull knife.

The farmers then carry the raw opium on horseback to a local refinery, where it is immediately converted into morphine—a practice that traffickers prefer, since compact morphine bricks are easier and safer to smuggle than are bundles of sticky, pungent opium. The conversion of raw opium into pure morphine is an exercise in rudimentary chemistry. The opium is first dissolved in drums of hot water. Lime fertilizer is added to the steaming solution, precipitating out organic wastes and leaving the morphine suspended near the surface. Any residual waste matter is removed, and the morphine is transferred to another drum, where it is heated, stirred, and mixed with concentrated ammonia. The morphine solidifies and drops to the bottom of the container and is filtered out in the form of chunky white kernels. Once dried and packaged, the morphine weighs about 10 percent as much as the original raw opium from which it was extracted.

The process of transforming morphine into heroin is a bit more complex, and at one time, from the end of World War II through the 1960s, Hong Kong and Marseilles were the heroin-refining capitals of the world. More recently, this industry has become increasingly dispersed, with precision laboratories also in the opium-growing regions of Southeast and Southwest Asia, and in Turkey, Malaysia, Colombia, and Mexico. The refining process occurs in five stages that chemically bind acetic acid to the morphine molecule, thereby generating a substance that can be transformed into the powder known as heroin. Ten kilograms of morphine can produce an equivalent amount of heroin that ranges from 80 to 99 percent pure.

The trafficking of the refined heroin from the clandestine laboratories to United States ports involves an elaborate organizational web of transportation routes, couriers, and payoffs. Depending on the particular trafficking organization, the drug may be transshipped by way of established routes through Indonesia, the Philippines, Syria, Egypt, Kenya, Russia, Israel, Nigeria, Italy, France, England, Germany, the Netherlands, Central and South America, Canada, the Caribbean islands, and combinations thereof. If the circumstances demand it, an organization can quickly and ingeniously design alternate routes. For example, a Miami heroin trafficker indicated that, as the result of an arrest in Turkey, an assassination in Kuwait, and a plane crash in Corsica, one shipment of drugs had to be diverted through at least eight countries before it ultimately reached its final destination:

> As the story got to me, which I'm sure is true knowing where it came from, the stuff [heroin] started out in a small lab near Ou Neua. That's a place in north Laos I think somewhere up near the Chinese border. It made its way to Bangkok okay, where it was supposed to be flown to Athens, Amsterdam, New York, and then to Miami by car. But then things really got fucked up. The guy who's supposed to make the transfer in Athens gets picked up for somethin' or other, so they fly it to Singapore instead. They had someone there who could take it most of the way, but he decides to get himself killed in Kuwait before he even gets there.

So get this: It goes to back to Bangkok, to somewhere in India, then somewhere else in the Middle East, and then up (or is it down) the fucking Nile to Egypt. Then there's this mule in Corsica that's gonna take it, but he freaks out when his girlfriend finds out she don't know how to fly her plane too well and ends up cashing it in. Somehow it finds its way to South Africa. It goes by ship to Uruguay, and then up through South America—Ecuador, Colombia, Peru and all that—to Panama, Mexico City, Chicago, Detroit, New York, and then Miami. It's one for the Guinness book of fucking records.*

The couriers who actually carry heroin across the world and into the United States are as diverse as the personalities who use the drug—members of the trafficking organizations traveling alone or with their families as tourists, corrupt diplomats, pilots and other airline personnel, professional athletes, students, ship captains and seamen, teachers, physicians, judges, fashion models, and numerous others. Recently, even members of the most ultraconservative Orthodox Hasidic Jewish sects have been recruited as drug couriers.[9]

Mexican Black Tar and Colombian Death Wish

Although Afghanistan was the largest producer of opium in the world at the beginning of the twenty-first century, most of the heroin entering the United States originates in Colombia and Mexico.[10] Mexican black tar heroin, also known as Mexican brown, has been available in the United States since the 1980s and gets its name from its color, which ranges from dark brown to black, and from its consistency, which may be sticky like roofing tar or hard like coal. The color and consistency of black tar result from the crude processing methods used in Mexico to manufacture the drug. It is typically sold on the street in its tarlike state, with purities ranging from 20 to 80 percent. The Drug Enforcement Administration estimates that as much as 29 percent of the heroin sold in the United States comes from Mexico and that much of it is of the black tar variety.[11]

The Colombian opium and heroin industries date back to the early 1980s when a few growers experimented with the cultivation of the opium poppy in the Orinoco Llanos section of the country. It was not until the latter years of the 1990s, however, that Colombian heroin became visible in trafficking networks, and by 2000, Colombia was ahead of Asia as the principal U.S. supply source. For a glimpse of the author's first exposure to the Colombian heroin trade, see Exhibit 5.3.

Opium poppies are grown along the eastern slopes of the Andes Mountains in the central part of Colombia. Some growers work with specific traffickers, an arrangement under which the trafficker provides the farmer with the necessary seeds and agricultural supplies. Farmers collect the raw opium gum from mature plants

---

*As already noted in Chapter 1, all undocumented quotations throughout this volume are personal communications to the author.

■ ■ ■ ■ ■

EXHIBIT 5.3

A REPORT FROM THE FIELD: OPIUM AND HEROIN IN THE ORINOCO LLANOS

On several occasions during the 1980s, at a time when the violence associated with cocaine trafficking was escalating, I journeyed throughout South America at the behest of the United States Information Agency (USIA). My purpose was to tour the university and media lecture circuits in Bolivia, Colombia, Ecuador, Peru, and Brazil to address the political, social, and economic implications of trafficking for illegal drug producing, refining, and transporting countries. The experiences were both exciting and informative, and I was exposed to a variety of new cultures and peoples. But there were times when I never knew who I was really working for. Maybe it was the USIA, but more likely it was the State Department, the Drug Enforcement Administration (DEA), or even the CIA. Perhaps it was all of them, because representatives of each agency seemed to be present everywhere I went.

On one particular visit to Bogota, Colombia, in early 1982, I spent several hours talking to the editor of *El Colombiano,* the city's largest newspaper. I was accompanied by two interpreters—one from DEA and one from the CIA. One of the questions asked by the editor was: "We have a growing cocaine problem here, but do you think we'll ever see heroin addicts in Colombia, like in the United States?" My answer was "yes, because the traffickers are already growing opium poppies in the Orinoco Llanos region of the country." The DEA and CIA representatives seemed upset by my answer, and later they asked me how I knew about the poppy growing—because it was a high security topic and they had heard about it from confidential sources only a few days earlier. I told them that I had read it in *High Times,* which was my way of telling them that I would not divulge my source. Actually, I didn't really know; it was just a good guess. Before visiting Colombia for the first time, I had learned as much as I could about the country. I came across a discussion of the Colombian *llanos*. The term refers to prairies, specifically those of the Orinoco River basin in eastern Colombia. The *llanos* of the Orinoco is a vast, hot region of rolling savanna broken by low-lying mesas, scrub forest, and scattered palms. It is sparsely populated, and it seemed a likely place for growing poppies. In the more than twenty-five years since that interview at *El Colombiano* (see *El Colombiano,* 2 June 1982, p. 2), Colombia has become a major producer and exporter of heroin, with much of the current cultivation in the mountains, but some still in the *llanos*.

and transport it to opium brokers who, in turn, sell the product to chemists who process it first into morphine base and later into heroin. These chemists often work in a contractual arrangement with the trafficking groups that smuggle the heroin into the United States. Smuggling is accomplished in a variety of ways, including the concealment of heroin inside hollowed-out shoes, luggage, stuffed animals, live animals, dead fish, in the lining of clothes, in the stems of artificial flowers, and even in people's stomachs. It is also smuggled in larger bulky packages, hidden in ships and aircraft, or through passageways tunneled under the Mexico–U.S. border (see Exhibit 5.4).

The Colombian heroin trade is currently dominated by independent trafficking groups who have been able to solidify and expand their position in the U.S. heroin

EXHIBIT 5.4   Cross-Border Drug Tunnel. January 26, 2006: DEA and ICE (Immigration and Customs Enforcement) agents uncovered a massive cross-border drug tunnel between the United States and Mexico. The cement-lined passage linked warehouses in Tijuana, Mexico, and Otay Mesa, California. The nearly 1,000-yard tunnel came complete with electricity, ventilation, and over two tons of marijuana.

Source: Image provided by the U.S. Drug Enforcement Administration.

market by distributing high-quality heroin and by initially undercutting the price of their competitors. They also use marketing strategies, such as including free samples of heroin in cocaine shipments, to build a clientele. Trafficking groups operating in New York and Philadelphia even market their drug using brand names—such as No Way Out and Death Wish—as a way to instill customer recognition and loyalty. These marketing techniques have allowed traffickers from Colombia to expand and ultimately dominate the heroin market.

Once in the United States, heroin may be stepped on (diluted) as many as seven to ten times. What started out in some remote Asian or Colombian laboratory as 99 percent pure heroin is cut with lactose (milk sugar, a by-product of milk processing), quinine, cornstarch, or almost any other powdery substance that will dissolve when heated. Heroin is also mixed with cleansing powder or dirt, or even arsenic or strychnine when the user is singled out for a "hot shot" (fatal dose). Ultimately, the heroin sold on the street ranges anywhere from 10 to 90 percent pure.

H IS FOR HEAVEN, *H* IS FOR HELL, *H* IS FOR HEROIN

Why people use heroin, or any illicit drug for that matter, is not altogether understood. Theories are legion, so much so that one publication of the National Institute on Drug Abuse devoted its entire 488 pages to outlining the major views.[12] A number of investigators have described heroin users as maladjusted, hostile, immature, dependent, manipulative, and narcissistic individuals, suggesting that drug use is just one more symptom of their disordered personalities.[13] Others suggest that because drug use is an integral part of the general culture that surrounds the user, it is learned behavior.[14]

The view of the late Alfred R. Lindesmith, among the more often quoted, most simplistic, and perhaps least helpful theories of heroin use, explains addiction as the result of the user's association of the drug with the distress accompanying the sudden cessation of its use.[15] Using heroin, he contended, is one thing, for people have various motivations for trying the drug. Becoming addicted, Lindesmith argued, is another. Users who fail to realize the connection between the withdrawal distress and the drug manage to escape addiction. Those who link the distress to the drug use, and thereafter use it to alleviate the distress symptoms, invariably become addicted.

Although Alfred Lindesmith was a pioneer in the drug field (there's even a center named after him), his theory is both simplistic and ludicrous because few, if any, heroin users are likely so naive about drugs that they are unaware of tolerance, dependence, and withdrawal. Heroin users, both present and past, including those in the 1930s and 1940s when Lindesmith developed his theory, first experimented with drugs within the context of peer groups in which a new user initiated heroin use under the tutelage of a more experienced user. More realistically, neophyte users typically think that addiction will not happen to them. As one seasoned heroin user commented:

> I had my first taste of heroin back in 1973. I was 14 years old, and I had seen my brother shooting up for years. My brother always told me how bad a heroin habit was, and that I should never do it. But I thought I could use it without getting hooked. Stupid adolescent that I was at the time, never believing that anyone could possibly be smarter than me. So I took a taste, and a few more tastes, and I always thought that it would never happen to me. But after a while I was tasting every day, and then several times every day. I finally realized that it caught me, and I was just like my older brother, just another Brooklyn junkie.

Going beyond Lindesmith, other explanations of heroin use are the bad habit theory, disruptive environment theory, cognitive control theory, social deviance theory, biological rhythm theory, subcultural theory, social neurobiological theory, and many many more.[16] Among the more novel is Sandra Coleman's incomplete mourning theory, an explanation holding that addictive behavior is a function of an unusual number of traumatic or premature deaths, separations, and losses that the drug user has not effectively resolved or mourned.[17]

Then there is the theory of the addiction-prone personality, elucidated by Dr. Kenneth Chapman of the U.S. Public Health Service almost six decades ago:

> The typical addict is emotionally unstable and immature, often seeking pleasure and excitement outside of the conventional realms. Unable to adapt comfortably to the pressures and tensions in today's speedy world, he may become either an extremely dependent individual or turn into a hostile "lone wolf" incapable of attaching deep feelings toward anyone. In his discomfort, he may suffer pain—real or imaginary. The ordinary human being has normal defense machinery with which to meet life's disappointments, frustrations, and conflicts. But the potential addict lacks enough of this inner strength to conquer his emotional problems and the anxiety they create. In a moment of stress, he may be introduced to narcotics as a "sure-fire" answer to his needs. Experiencing relief from his pain, or an unreal flight from his problems, or a puffed-up sense of power and control regarding them, he is well on the road toward making narcotics his way of life.[18]

Stated differently, when stable people are introduced to drugs, they will discard them spontaneously before becoming dependent. Those who have addiction-prone personalities, because of psychoses, psychopathic or psychoneurotic disorders, or predispositions toward mental dysfunctioning, "become transformed into the typical addict."[19]

To the great misfortune of the heroin-using population, the concept of the addiction-prone personality dominated much of the thinking in the drug-abuse treatment industry for generations. Although the theory evolved from studies of heroin users in psychiatric facilities during the early years of addiction treatment, it was applied universally and continues to be accepted by many.[20] Yet researchers who have gone beyond the confines of their laboratories, hospitals, and university campuses to study drug users in their natural environments understand, and likely always did, that users who come to the attention of psychiatric facilities are often quite different from those who remain active on the street for extended periods of time.

The difficulty with the concept of the addiction-prone personality, and all other theoretical explanations of heroin dependence, has been the assumption that one single theory accounts for the entire spectrum of drug-using behaviors—a problem that has plagued discussions of deviant behavior in general. Unfortunately, this kind of thinking is not altogether that remote, at least in its logical structure, from the arguments of Dr. Benjamin Rush two centuries ago that *a* theory of disease, rather than distinct theories of separate diseases, exists. Yet in all likelihood, there are as many reasons for using drugs as there are individuals who use drugs. For some it may be a function of family disorganization, cultural learning, poor self-image, maladjusted personality, addiction-prone personality, childhood trauma, or even incomplete mourning. For others heroin use may be no more than a normal response to the world in which they live. And finally, there may even be one or two heroin users for whom Lindesmith's withdrawal avoidance approach fits.

As the motivations for heroin use vary, so too do the patterns of initiation. Some careers in drug use are therapeutic in origin—through the chronic use of morphine,

OxyContin, Vicodin, or another narcotic analgesic that was prescribed for the treatment of pain or some other ailment. For most, however, heroin is a later stage of a lifestyle of drug taking that began during early adolescence with the use of alcohol, codeine cough syrup, organic solvents, marijuana, and/or amphetamines. Whatever the pattern of initiation, dependence on heroin, if it occurs at all, is a lengthy process. Despite the one-shot-and-you're-hooked myth, to become dependent on heroin, one must work at it—particularly when the heroin available is of low potency. Moreover, most people do not begin their heroin use by mainlining (intravenous injection). The recollections of David K., a New York City heroin user for almost three decades, illustrate a pattern of onset that is not altogether uncommon:

> One day my cousin comes over and he's using heroin, and he throws this 10-dollar bag of junk on the kitchen table and says, "Try some." I say, "Listen Alfie, I ain't about to put any of your shit into my veins." He says, "No man, just snort some of it, it's great."
>
> So I decide to snort some of Alfie's shit. I close off one nostril and sniff the shit out of the shit. . . . It blew my fucking head off, really fucked me up. I got such a bad pain in my head that I thought I was fucking brain damaged. I puked my guts out. I was really sick. . . .
>
> A few weeks later I see Alfie again and ask him for some stuff, you know, just to try it again. You'd think that after that first time I might have learned something. But no. It's like when you try your first cigarette. You get dizzy and upset in your gut, but you do it again anyway because you want to be cool and since everybody else is doin' it there must be something to it.
>
> So I snort again and *ho-ly fucking shit!* I felt like I died and went to heaven. My whole body was like one giant fucking incredible orgasm.

What David K. had experienced was his first rush. Or as described somewhat more vividly by former New York City heroin addict Manual J. Torres:

> . . . it's really something else. I mean, it's like the shit really hit the fan . . . you can't describe it. All the colors of Times Square tumble right over your forehead and explode in your eyeballs like a million, jillion shooting stars. And then, each one of them goddamn stars novas in a cascade of brilliant Technicolor. And the world levels out. You know what I mean? There's no right, no wrong. Everything's beautiful, and it's like nothing's happening baby but clear, crisp light. The mambo beat is like hot fuck notes bouncing off lukewarm street scenes. The drummer downstairs in the park is onto life's whole fucking secret, and the primitive urge of his swinging soul becomes a mellow sharpness in your ears. And you want to gather all of creation inside you; maybe for a minute you do. What a perfect Manny Torres you become for a moment![21]

After snorting on and off for several months, and still not addicted, David K. moved into the next stage of heroin use:

> I ran into this lady that I used to fuck and hang out with a couple of years ago and she asks me if I want to come along with her while she makes her connection [buys heroin] and fixes [injects the drug]. After a while she asks me if I want to try the needle and I say no, but then I decide to go halfway and skin-pop [injecting into the muscle just beneath the skin]. Well, man, it was wonderful. Popping was just like snorting, only stronger, finer, better, and faster.

For David, skin-popping lasted for three months, although not on a daily basis. "I don't think I was addicted then," he said, "because sometimes I'd go for almost a whole week without popping and I didn't get sick." Then he began to mainline (inject the drug directly into his vein):

> Travelin' along the mainline was like a grand slam home run fuck, like getting a blow job from Miss America. The rush hits you instantly, and all of a sudden you're up there on Mount Olympus talking to Zeus.

Two months later David decided that he was hooked (addicted). He was using heroin regularly, spending more than two hundred dollars daily on his habit, and getting sick when more than six to eight hours would pass without fixing. Although he had no intentions of quitting his heroin use, he did admit that addiction had its drawbacks: "Any damn junkie that says that he doesn't like his shit is a fucking liar. They all love their dope. But your whole damn life revolves around your shit." Or as Manny Torres described it:

> See, once you're hooked you're not your own boss any more. You belong to your habit. Plain and simple. You plan and scheme, and con, and lie, and hustle for your habit. Anybody and everybody becomes fair game. Look, you leave mother, brother, sister, father, friend for heroin. When you're hooked you gotta score. It ain't *maybe* I'll score, maybe I won't. It's, man, I'm *gonna* score and all hell ain't gonna stop me! And scoring can take time; it can be downright frustrating and uncomfortable. I've waited for over three hours on a street corner for a cat with a bag to surface. And you don't leave, 'cause he's the only one holding and if you miss him someone else will get the stuff and you'll be left holding air.[22]

As mentioned earlier, Alfred R. Lindesmith and others have claimed that, once addicted, the rush, the kick, and the euphoria that heroin produces become of only minor importance in explaining continued usage; and that it is the fear of the withdrawal symptoms—the yawning, sneezing, crying, running nose, gooseflesh, rapid pulse, hot and cold flashes, nausea and vomiting, diarrhea, stomach cramps, and muscular spasms—that motivates further use.[23] Yet, by contrast, Dr. David P. Ausubel once argued:

The popular misconception that addicted individuals deprived of the drug suffer the tortures of the damned, and that once caught in the grip of physiological dependence the average person is powerless to help himself, are beliefs that have been touted on a credulous public by misinformed journalists and by addicts themselves.[24]

On this point, David K. commented:

Listen, white brother, that's a crock of pure mule shit! Sure, you hurt, you hurt bad all over. But what you're really doin' is chasin' the rush and that wonderful feeling that you and the whole fucking world around you is cool. That's what you're really after, the high, the wonderful high. True, when you get busted and have to kick cold [without medication] in some dirty fucking stinking jail you raise hell and put on a show so maybe you'll get some medicine, but it's never as bad as you make it. . . . When it comes time to die, I want it to be an OD [overdose] on smack. That would be the greatest way to take the ride over the edge of the fucking world.

And, too, a recovering addict counselor in a Florida drug treatment program added:

When we are sure that the new resident has no concurrent addiction to some other drug, we just put him on the couch in the living room, give him a blanket, and ignore him. He'll start putting on his act, trying to get some sympathy. He'll look around the room and see some guy waxing the floor, somebody else at an ironing board, or somebody just reading a book. They're people who were shooting with him once out in the street and now they're all ignoring him. Pretty soon he settles down. He hurts, but it wears off in 24 to 48 hours.

The myth that heroin withdrawal is similar to the tortures of hell has a long history. As early as 1917 in a paper read before the California State Medical Association, Dr. A. S. Tuchler of San Francisco stated: "When one is placed in confinement and deprived of the drug, the suffering, both physical and mental, endured by the addict, is beyond comprehension and belief."[25]

More recently, the myth has been a product of the media, vividly presented in films such as *The Man with the Golden Arm* (1955), *Monkey on My Back* (1957), *French Connection II* (1975), *The Basketball Diaries* (1995), and numerous episodes of "Hill Street Blues," "Police Story," "Miami Vice," "N.Y.P.D. Blue," "Law and Order," and other television series. But researchers and clinicians in the drug field, and many heroin users as well, tend to agree that withdrawal is no different, and no more severe, than the chills, cramps, and muscle pains that are associated with a good dose of the flu—something that almost everyone has experienced.*

---

*It must be emphasized here that this is not necessarily the case with all dependence-producing drugs. The unsupervised nonmedical withdrawal from barbiturates and other sedative drugs can bring on shock, coma, and death.

GAMBLING WITH DEATH

Unlike the situation with many other drugs, chronic heroin use seems to produce little direct or permanent physiological damage. Street heroin users tend to neglect themselves, however, and commonly reported disorders include heart and lung abnormalities, *tracks* (scarred veins), malnutrition, weight loss, endocarditis (a disease of the heart valves), stroke, gynecological and obstetrical problems in women, and particularly hepatitis, local skin infections, and abscesses.[26] Many heroin users live on the street, in alleys or abandoned buildings, and in general ignore the standard practices that encourage good health. In this regard a Philadelphia heroin user stated:

> When you spend most of your time hustling on the streets, scoring, fixing, scoring, fixing, hustling again, and living in some damp cellar that has dripping fungus on the walls you don't have time for such frills as fresh laundry, perfume baths, and gourmet food. . . .

And as David K. remarked:

> . . . Once in a while I go home and I find that my sister has left me some clean clothes, but most of the time I wear the same fucking things from week to week. . . . I don't know how long it's been since I had a good shower, and for food it's either a taco, a Big Mac, or french fries and sour balls washed down with Coca-Cola and cheap wine.

Some women heroin users experience a number of additional problems. A heroin-using part-time sex worker (prostitute) in Miami commented:

> When you find yourself fucking for money, fucking for drugs, and sometimes fucking or sucking a hairy prick for something to eat or a place to sleep, you're not too careful about avoiding the cruds. What's more, since you're stoned most of the time you don't feel much in the way of pain, or either that your whole body hurts and you can't tell where the trouble is. . . . When some kind of mess starts leakin' from my crotch like toothpaste from a tube I know it's time to get my ass off to the clinic.

Even though infections and malnutrition are the result of poor eating habits and lack of personal hygiene, hepatitis B virus (HBV) and hepatitis C virus (HCV) are the result of needle sharing (see Chapter 9). In addition, since 1980 sharing injection paraphernalia has been associated with acquired immune deficiency syndrome (AIDS), a topic that also is addressed in detail in Chapter 9.

Even worse is the problem of heroin overdose, a phenomenon that is still not fully understood. Some users OD as the result of too much heroin or heroin that is too potent. In these instances, if death occurs, it is the result of respiratory depression, that is, suffocation. In other instances death is so rapid that the needle is often still in the user's arm when he or she is found. Such deaths are the result of asphyxiation caused by acute pulmonary edema (an accumulation of fluid in the lungs). Overdose deaths are more often the result of heroin intake combined with the concurrent use of alcohol and another sedative. Adulterants that are used to cut heroin also pose difficulties. Quinine is popular. An irritant, it can cause vascular damage, acute and potentially lethal disturbances in heartbeat, depressed respiration, coma, and respiratory arrest. Moreover, heroin plus quinine can have an unpredictable compounding effect.[27]

Overdose can also be a natural consequence of the drug-taking and drug-seeking behaviors of heroin users. In their endless pursuit of the high, users continually seek out good stuff—strong, potent heroin—and they have several alternatives. They can make their purchases from their regular dealer, with whom they have been successful in the past. They can use the street grapevine—an informal, and often erroneous, communication network that lets them know where they can connect for dynamite stuff and great shit. Finally, associated with the street grapevine are brand names—a phenomenon apparent in New York, Philadelphia, Miami, Chicago, St. Louis, Los Angeles, and other urban areas across the United States where heroin is generally available.

The labeling of drugs with brand names, studied most extensively by ethnographer Paul J. Goldstein, has become a popular merchandising technique in the drug black market. The process occurs chiefly with heroin and involves distinctive packaging prior to sale. The bag containing the heroin is labeled with a name, symbol, or number, usually in a specific color (see Exhibit 5.5). The brand names touted as good stuff in New York City over the years have carried such epithets as Black Magic, Chako Fan, Death Row, 888, Fuck Me Please, Good Pussy, 90%, Kojak, The Beast, 32, and The Witch.[28] In Miami during the late 1980s, the 1990s, and early 2000 some highly sought-after names included Overtown Max, Chain Saw, Mexican Satan, Hand Job, Golden Girl, Jail Bait, Sweet Lucy's Tit, Miami's Vice, Gloria (after singer Gloria Estefan), Celia (after singer Celia Cruz), La Vida Loca (of Ricky Martin fame), Death Wish, and No Way Out. With respect to the functions of heroin labeling, Goldstein explained:

> Most [users] have limited capital to expend on heroin. There are a multitude of street dealers to choose from. Getting beat on a heroin purchase or buying inferior quality heroin is an omnipresent risk. The quality of heroin that is commonly available is poor. Heroin users have either experienced or heard reminiscences of the superior dope of yesteryear and may have occasionally encountered highly potent heroin themselves in more recent years. Heroin users always look to obtain the highest quality heroin in a confusing and uncontrolled marketplace. Most seem to feel that labeling bags of heroin assists them in their quest.[29]

Whether it is through brand names or grapevine rumor, the pursuit of the best heroin can have lethal consequences. To cite a well-known example from the annals of heroin folklore, during February 1975, word quickly spread throughout the Miami drug community that a dealer in North Miami Beach had a supply of heroin so potent that he was hesitant to sell it. As one user put it: "It's supposed to be a gift from God, a god by the name of Bentley." Although the dealer ultimately sold his supply, a sample was obtained for analysis. As it turned out, the drug was etorphine, one of several compounds discovered by K. W. Bentley of Edinburgh during the early 1960s through a manipulation of the morphine molecule.[30] Bentley's compound had a potency several

EXHIBIT 5.5   Sample Heroin Trademark
Labeling is a merchandising technique used not only in legitimate enterprise, but also in the illegal drug trades. In Miami, for example, popular street level brands of heroin include Overtown Max (after the dealer selling it) and Afghan Delight (after the drug's origin); for the cocaine set there is Big-C and Amazonas, and for crack users there is Biscayne Babe, Bogey, and Noriega's Holiday. The Sail Boat Brand label reproduced above was found on a package of heroin from Southeast Asia that was intercepted by the Drug Enforcement Administration.

thousand times that of morphine. Before it finally disappeared from the streets, more than a score of heroin users in South Florida had tried it and fatally overdosed.*

Miami's etorphine incident was not an isolated case, for the drug has periodically reappeared on the streets of South Florida and elsewhere in the years hence. Then there was *China White,* a pure but rare and perhaps mythical strain of heroin from Southeast Asia that was a fantasy among many West Coast users for decades. "Getting down [shooting up] on it is a never-ending dream," said one user from Sacramento. In late 1980, the dream finally came true for some, or so it seemed. Word spread through

---

*Under the Controlled Substances Act of 1971, etorphine is classified as a Schedule I drug, which means that, like heroin and LSD, it has no accepted medical use in the United States and its mere possession is a violation of federal law. Etorphine hydrochloride, a less potent variety, is used occasionally by veterinarians to immobilize wild animals. In fact, even this milder form is so strong that a two-cubic-centimeter dose is capable of immobilizing a four-ton elephant.

southern California that China White had finally arrived on U.S. shores. But the drug was not China White at all, and users began dying from it. It was 3-methylfentanyl, or TMF, a chemical similar in structure to fentanyl, a synthetic narcotic analgesic eighty to one hundred times more potent than morphine.[31]

Moreover, TMF was the first in a continuing series of what have become known as designer drugs. So-named because they are new substances designed by slightly altering the chemical makeup of other illegal or tightly controlled drugs, they are typically more potent and often contaminated versions of either fentanyl, Demerol, or some other synthetic narcotic. One variety has been found to destroy brain cells; another produces the symptoms of Parkinson's disease and accelerated aging; a third paralyzes its users; and a fourth has a potency six thousand times that of heroin—producing instantaneous death.[32] And the California episode was not an isolated one. During the early weeks of 1991 in the New York City area, no less than 18 heroin users died with an additional 233 hospitalized from a designer drug batch sold in the South Bronx under the label Tango & Cash. Again, the drug was either fentanyl or a fentanyl analog.[33] Since then, fentanyl (as China White) has periodically reemerged in numerous locales, including New Jersey, New York, Chicago, Detroit, California, and the United Kingdom.[34] As such, drug cocktails have posed such a threat to heroin users seeking a fix that one testified: "I don't know if the next dose will kill me."*

Heroin overdoses have also been related to higher than expected potency. During much of the 1980s and 1990s, the purity of street heroin ranged from only 1 to 10 percent. With the onset of heroin trafficking from Colombia in the late 1990s, however, purity rates have been as high as 98 percent, with the national average somewhere in the vicinity of 40 percent.[35] Overdoses have also resulted from special drug cocktails. In the early 1990s, for example, dealers started peddling a new combination of heroin and morphine known on the street as New Jack Swing.[36] Named after the 1991 Wesley Snipes/Ice T/Chris Rock/Mario Van Peebles/Vanessa Williams film *New Jack City,* the drug combination turned out to be lethal for several users. In the late 1990s Homicide, Polo, Death Shot, and Super Buick heroin cocktails appeared in northeastern U.S. cities. These were variations of a potent blend of heroin, dextromethorphan (a cough suppressant), thiamine (vitamin B1), and scopolamine, and sent scores of heroin users to hospital emergency rooms in New York, Philadelphia, Baltimore, and Washington, DC.[37]

The precise number of overdoses from heroin (and other illicit narcotics) use is probably impossible to estimate. Users, unless their conditions appear especially life threatening, are rarely brought to hospital emergency rooms for treatment. The exact cause of death in cases of lethal overdoses is not always possible to identify. On the basis of data from the Drug Abuse Warning Network (DAWN), which tracks drug-related emergency room visits and deaths, the number of heroin-related drug emergencies increased substantially during the 1990s, from 36,000 in 1990 to almost 80,000 in 1999 to more than 164,000 by 2005.[38]

---

*Curiously, whereas China White was the purest of the fantasy heroin, more recently the designation of *China White* has also been applied to high-quality heroin arriving from Southeast Asia. Moreover, China White has become synonymous with pure Asian heroin.

Related to overdosing on heroin are the many visits to hospital emergency rooms as a result of contaminated drugs. An example in this regard occurred in Glasgow, Dublin, Liverpool, and other parts of the United Kingdom during 2000.[39] Scores of heroin users were appearing in hospitals, gravely ill with large and painful skin abscesses, dangerously high white blood cell counts, and extremely low blood pressure. The illness would begin as an infection at the place where the heroin was injected. As the primary infection became swollen and painful, killing surrounding tissue, large areas of affected flesh had to be surgically removed. Many cases resulted in heart failure and death. It was suspected that the outbreak was the result of bacteria in a contaminated batch of heroin that worked its way through England, Ireland, and Scotland.

THE HEROIN EPIDEMICS

The use of heroin by injection apparently developed during the 1930s and became widespread after 1945.[40] Between 1950 and the early 1960s, most major cities across the United States experienced a low-level spread of heroin use, particularly among African Americans and other minority populations. Thereafter, use began to grow rapidly, rising to peaks in the late 1960s and then falling sharply. The pattern was so ubiquitous that it came to be regarded as epidemic heroin use.[41] More recent epidemics occurred in 1973–1974, 1977–1978, and 1982–1983, defined as such on the basis of the numbers of new admissions to heroin treatment facilities. Yet interestingly, no one really knew how widespread heroin use was during those years, and even today the estimates are often no more than scientific guesses.

Throughout the 1960s, the Treasury Department's Bureau of Narcotics would periodically announce the number of active narcotics addicts in the United States. As of December 31, 1967, for example, it set the number at 62,045.[42] This figure—not 60,000 or 65,000, but 62,045—suggested considerable precision. New York City's many drug abuse researchers, clinicians, and members of law enforcement groups found the estimate suspect, however, because in their experience the heroin problem was much greater. In fact, a heroin user from New York's Harlem area jokingly stated that "there are more junkies than that just on my street."

The suspicions were justified, of course, for the Bureau's figure was based almost exclusively on reports from local police departments. Moreover, New York had its own such file at the time, one that reported almost twice the national bureau's number of new cases for the same year.[43] In an attempt to foist some scientific rationality into the estimates of heroin prevalence, in 1969 researchers John C. Ball of Temple University and Carl D. Chambers of the New York State Narcotic Addiction Control Commission combined data from the New York and National Bureau of Narcotics files with figures provided by the federal drug treatment facilities in Lexington, Kentucky, and Fort Worth, Texas. Through a complex series of ratios and correction factors, they came up with a figure of 108,424 heroin addicts for the year 1967.[44] Even Ball and Chambers, however, were not altogether confident with their estimate, for they were acutely aware of the potentially vast number of unreported cases.

In 1970, using scientific survey methodology, cross-sectional studies of the general population finally reached the drug field.[45] As indicators of heroin use, however, the data were disappointing. It was known at the outset that general population surveys could access only the more stable at-home populations, thus excluding residents of jails and penitentiaries, mental institutions, migrant workers, the homeless, the residents of welfare hotels and skid-row shelters and lodging houses, others living on the street, and the members of drug subcultures who either had no stable living quarters or were typically away from them.[46]

As the drug field moved through the 1970s, the National Institute on Drug Abuse developed what it called *heroin trend indicators,* relative estimates generated from a composite of reported heroin-related deaths, hospital emergency room visits, heroin treatment admissions, and high school and household surveys. On the basis of these data, the estimated number of heroin users in the United States for 1977 ranged from 396,000 to 510,000.[47]

Throughout the 1980s, government reports were maintaining that the number of heroin users in the United States was somewhere in the vicinity of 500,000, having been at that level for about a decade and a half.[48] At the beginning of the 1990s, however, there were indications that the number of heroin users might be on the increase, a situation brought about, at least in part, by the use of heroin to mediate the stimulant effects of crack cocaine (see Chapter 6). By the close of the 1990s, the high purity of heroin had made snorting and smoking possible (as opposed to injecting)* The result was that many new users had entered the ranks of the heroin-using population, pushing its numbers well over the half million mark.[49] In 2007, the Department of Justice estimated the population of hard-core heroin users to be greater than 800,000 with hundreds of thousands more using the drug recreationally.[50]

HEROIN CHIC AND THE GEN-X JUNKIE

"Heroin chic" was a fashion trend of the mid-1990s that characterized (and sometimes glorified) the looks of a terminal stage junkie. It typically portrayed gaunt, superanorexic, glassy-eyed, and pale-looking models whose appearance reflected that of heroin addicts—a dirty, drugged out, droopy, and unkempt look. Fashion ads frequently depicted dead-eyed, strung out, and emaciated-looking youths in dirty bathrooms, dingy motels, and other sleazy surroundings.[51] At fashion shows, models sleepwalked down the runways in what appeared to be semidrugged states, clad in clothes by such high-end fashion designers as Gucci, Donna Karan, Gianni Versace, and Calvin Klein.

In the eyes of designers, photographers, and others in the fashion industry, heroin chic was the latest cutting-edge style. But to antidrug groups, parents, and

---

*One of the less common forms of sniffing heroin is a process known as chasing the dragon. Chasing involves placing an oil-rich form of heroin into a piece of tin foil. A flame is then applied directly beneath the drug, with the result that the heroin soon liquefies. Ghostlike plumes of smoke begin to emerge that are then chased and inhaled through a tube. See Marc A. Schuckit, "Chasing the Dragon," *Drug Abuse and Alcoholism Newsletter,* 22 (June 1993).

much of society at large, it was a fashion statement that appeared to advocate drug use. For "Generation-X" (young adult) consumers,* the mid- and late 1990s marketing phenomenon of heroin chic was intended to reflect the times and portray real people.[52] Coinciding with the look were indications that heroin was an "in" drug in trendy segments of the community. Not only was heroin use visible among numerous celebrities, in both Hollywood and the music industry, but in large cities and small towns across the nation annual surveys were finding increases in heroin use among high school students and young adults.[53]

Receiving much of the heat for the glamorization of heroin addiction was Calvin Klein. Controversy had often followed Klein. In 1980, 15-year-old Brooke Shields announced to the world that "Nothing comes between me and my Calvins"; in 1995, Klein's jeans ads featured young models, some only fifteen years old, in provocative poses; and in 1999, his ads were again at the center of controversial attention when a photo depicting children jumping up and down on a sofa in their underwear was viewed by segments of puritanical America as pornographic (it was an advertisement to launch his new line of underwear for children).[54] The peak of the heroin chic dispute surrounding Klein occurred when heroin addict look-alike models adorned a twelve-page spread in the September 1996 issue of *Harper's Bazaar* in an ad for cK Be, a new Calvin Klein fragrance. Advertisers creating this particular spread had actually gone into the streets to seek out heroin users for the sake of developing an authentic addict look that could be adapted to fashion models.

Heroin chic was an outgrowth, in part, of the motion picture industry's growing fascination with the drug. Heroin use has been the subject of several motion pictures, including *Drugstore Cowboy* (1988), *My Own Private Idaho* (1993), *Killing Zoe* (1994), *Pulp Fiction* (1994), *The Basketball Diaries* (1995), *Trainspotting* (1995), and *Permanent Vacation* (1999). In addition, it has also been portrayed in several television productions, including the HBO series "The Corner" (2000).

In 1997, the fashion industry was directly affected by the heroin problem when 20-year-old heroin chic photographer Davide Sorrenti died of a heroin overdose. Reports about Sorrenti's death prompted President Clinton to comment on the dangerous trend: "The glorification of heroin is not creative, it is destructive. It is not beautiful, it is ugly. And it is not about art, it's about life and death."[55] Magazine editors who had featured work by Sorrenti admitted that the glamorized heroin look reflected use among the industry's youth and declared that they would move on with a more upbeat image.

POSTSCRIPT

In retrospect, was heroin chic a reflection of the changing perceptions about heroin among members of Generation X, or did heroin use escalate as a result of the increasing

---

*"Generation-X" has become a negative term to describe the cohort of Americans born between the mid-1960s and late 1970s. Gen-X'ers have been described as members of the MTV generation who are aimless, unfocused, disorganized, unmotivated, uncontrolled, and unpredictable. But as is the case with all stereotypes, some fit the description, but most do not. See Paula M. Poindexter and Dominic L. Lasorsa, "Generation-X: Is the Meaning Misunderstood?" *Newspaper Research Journal,* 20 (Fall 1999), pp. 28–36.

popularity of the look? Or was the increased attention to heroin the result of other factors? No doubt heroin chic played a role, although a very minor one, for other more potent factors had already come to pass. The stigma attached to heroin had faded somewhat as the United States moved from the 1970s through the 1980s and towards the end of the twentieth century. Although the glamour and hip appearance that had been attached to heroin increased, the drug had also metamorphasized. It had become purer and more powerful, enabling users to snort or smoke it, thus taking away the stigma of injection drug use. This attracted younger users, as well as those unwilling to take drugs by needle.

Going further, it was during the late 1960s and early 1970s that the last heroin epidemics had occurred, outbreaks that Generation-X was too young to remember. In the 1980s, powder cocaine was the glamorous drug of choice, which may have paved the way for the attraction to the new forms of heroin. Once thought to be a problem limited to the inner-city communities of the urban United States, by the height of the heroin-chic era of the 1990s, the drug had become popular in all socioeconomic classes. In addition, many revered Hollywood and rock music icons were using heroin.

But perhaps the members of Generation-X who viewed heroin as a glamor drug should have also considered its many casualties over the years, including those in the entertainment industry:

- Janis Joplin, the 27-year-old vocalist who died of a heroin overdose in 1970, at the peak of her career
- Jimi Hendrix, another 27-year-old vocalist who was a heavy heroin user and died of a drug overdose within weeks of Joplin
- Jim Morrison of The Doors, whose death in 1971 at age 27 is a topic of much rock folklore; yet he was heavily involved with heroin prior to his death, which was likely the cumulative effect of his drug-related lifestyle
- Keith Richards, the heroin-using guitarist of The Rolling Stones who was arrested continuously throughout the 1970s for drug offenses
- Sid Vicious of The Sex Pistols, who died of a heroin overdose in 1979 at age 21
- Nikki Sixx of Motley Crue, who overdosed on heroin in 1987
- Will Shatter, the bass player and singer with Flipper, who died of a heroin overdose in 1987 at age 31
- Hillel Slovak, the lead guitarist with Red Hot Chili Peppers, who died of a heroin overdose in 1987 at age 25
- Andrew Wood, the grunge rock vocalist with Mother Love Bone, who died of a heroin overdose in 1990 at age 24
- Johnny Thunders of the New York Dolls rock band, who died of a heroin overdose in 1991
- Stefanie Sargent of the grunge rock band 7 Year Bitch, who died of a heroin overdose in 1993
- River Phoenix, the 23-year-old movie star who died of a heroin overdose in 1993, not too long after portraying a heroin-using street hustler in *My Own Private Idaho*

- Kurt Cobain of Nirvana, one of the founders of grunge rock who died of a self-inflicted gunshot wound in 1994, just days after a near-fatal heroin overdose
- Kristen Pfaff of Hole, who died of a heroin overdose in 1994 at age 27
- Jerry Garcia of The Grateful Dead, who died in 1995 from health complications during withdrawal from heroin
- Shannon Hoon, the 23-year-old lead singer for the alternative rock band Blind Melon, who, a heavy heroin user, died of a drug overdose in 1995 while preparing for a concert in New Orleans
- Jonathan Melvoin of Smashing Pumpkins, who died in 1996 of a heroin overdose at age 34
- Courtney Love, the wife of Kurt Cobain and costar of *The People vs. Larry Flynt,* who struggled with heroin dependence during much of the 1990s
- Dave Gahan, a vocalist with Depeche Mode, who experienced (and survived) a heroin overdose in 1996
- Brad Nowell of the punk rock band Sublime, who died of a heroin overdose in 1996 at age 28

Other celebrities who managed to survive their bouts with heroin include David Bowie, Miles Davis, Boy George, Elvis Presley, Matthew Perry, Christian Slater, Gregg Allman, Chet Baker, Ray Charles, Eric Clapton, Natalie Cole, and Axl Rose to name but a few.

NOTES

1. Ruth R. Levine, *Pharmacology: Drug Actions and Reactions* (Boston: Little, Brown, 1973), p. 336.

2. *New York Times,* 17 August 1972, p. 16.

3. See Alfred W. McCoy, *The Politics of Heroin in Southeast Asia* (New York: Harper & Row, 1972); Editors of Newsday, *The Heroin Trail* (New York: New American Library, 1974); Jon A. Wiant, "Narcotics in the Golden Triangle," *Washington Quarterly,* 8 (Fall 1985), pp. 125–140.

4. For an examination of the hill tribes that populate the Golden Triangle and how opium cultivation impacts on their culture, see Paul Lewis and Elaine Lewis, *Peoples of the Golden Triangle: Six Tribes in Thailand* (London: Thames and Hudson, 1984); Claudia Simms and Thomas Tarleton, "The Lisu of the Golden Triangle," *The World & I,* October 1987, pp. 461–473.

5. Bureau of International Narcotics Matters, *International Narcotics Control Strategy Report* (Washington, DC: Department of State, March 1990), p. 18.

6. Bureau of International Narcotics Matters, *International Narcotics Control Strategy Report* (Washington, DC: Department of State, March 2000).

7. United Nations Office of Drugs and Crime, *2006 World Drug Report* (Geneva: UNODC, 2006).

8. For perspectives on the history of opium, the opium culture, and the processing of opium into heroin, see Dean Latimer and Jeff Goldberg, *Flowers in the Blood: The Story of Opium* (New York: Franklin Watts, 1981); Joseph Westermeyer, *Poppies, Pipes, and People: Opium and Its Use in Laos* (Berkeley: University of California Press, 1982); Peter W. White, "The Poppy," *National Geographic,* February 1985, pp. 142–189.

9. See *U.S. News & World Report,* 6 March 2000, pp. 26–28.

10. Drug Enforcement Administration Press Release, 20 December 2006.

11. Ibid.

12. Dan J. Lettieri, Mollie Sayers, and Helen Wallenstein, eds., *Theories on Drug Abuse: Selected Contemporary Perspectives* (Rockville, MD: National Institute on Drug Abuse, 1980).

13. David P. Ausubel, "Causes and Types of Drug Addiction: A Psychosocial View," *Psychiatric Quarterly,* 35 (1961), pp. 523–531; Jonathan D. Cowan, David C. Kay, Gary L. Neidert, Frances E. Ross, and Susan Belmore, "Drug Abusers: Defeated and Joyless," in *Problems of Drug Dependence,* ed. Louis S. Harris (Rockville, MD: National Institute on Drug Abuse, 1979), pp. 170–176.

14. Calvin J. Frederick, "Drug Abuse: A Self-Destructive Enigma," *Maryland State Medical Journal,* 22 (1973), pp. 19–21.

15. Alfred R. Lindesmith, *Opiate Addiction* (Bloomington, IN: Principia Press, 1947); reprinted edition, *Addiction and Opiates* (New York: Aldine, 1968).

16. Lettieri, Sayers, and Wallenstein.

17. Sandra B. Coleman, "The Family Trajectory: A Circular Journey to Drug Abuse," in *Family Factors in Substance Abuse,* ed. B. Ellis (Rockville, MD: National Institute on Drug Abuse, 1978).

18. Kenneth Chapman, "A Typical Drug Addict," *New York State Health News,* 28 August 1951.

19. Orin Ross Yost, *The Bane of Drug Addiction* (New York: Macmillan, 1964), pp. 68–69, 82.

20. See Harvey B. Milkman and Howard J. Shaffer, eds., *The Addictions: Multidisciplinary Perspectives and Treatments* (Lexington, MA: Lexington Books, 1985).

21. Richard P. Rettig, Manual J. Torres, and Gerald R. Garrett, *Manny: A Criminal Addict's Story* (Boston: Houghton Mifflin, 1977), pp. 33–34.

22. Rettig, Torres, and Garrett, p. 35.

23. Lindesmith, pp. 28–31.

24. David P. Ausubel, *Drug Addiction* (New York: Random House, 1958), p. 26; see also Isidor Chein, Donald L. Gerard, Robert S. Lee, and Eva Rosenfeld, *The Road to H: Narcotics, Delinquency, and Social Policy* (New York: Basic Books, 1964), pp. 113, 248.

25. A. S. Tuchler, "The Narcotic Habit: Further Observations on the Ambulatory Method of Treatment," *California Eclectic Medical Journal,* 38 (1917), pp. 261–264.

26. See Alex W. Young, "Skin Complications of Heroin Addiction: Bullous Impetigo," *New York State Journal of Medicine,* 15 June 1973, pp. 1681–1684; B. W. Pace, W. Doscher, and I. B. Margolis, "The Femoral Triangle: A Potential Death Trap for the Drug Abuser," *New York State Journal of Medicine,* December 1984, pp. 596–598; Wayne Tuckson and Bernard B. Anderson, "Mycotic Aneurysms in Intravenous Drug Abuse: Diagnosis and Management," *Journal of the National Medical Association,* 77 (1985), pp. 99–102; Glenn W. Geelhoed, "The Addict's Angioaccess: Complications of Exotic Vascular Injection Sites," *New York State Journal of Medicine,* December 1984, pp. 585–586. For a comprehensive overview of medical complications associated with heroin dependence, see Jerome J. Platt, *Heroin Addiction: Theory, Research, and Treatment* (Malabar, FL: Robert E. Krieger, 1986), pp. 80–102.

27. For a discussion of the causes of heroin overdose, see Peter G. Bourne, ed., *Acute Drug Emergencies: A Treatment Manual* (New York: Academic Press, 1976); David M. Petersen and Earl L. Mahfuz, "Heroin Overdose Deaths: A Critical Examination of Deaths Attributed to Acute Reaction to Dosage," *Sandoz Psychiatric Spectator,* 10 (1977), pp. 5–8; Platt.

28. Paul J. Goldstein, Douglas S. Lipton, Edward Preble, Ira Sobel, Tom Miller, William Abbott, William Paige, and Franklin Soto, "The Marketing of Street Heroin in New York City," *Journal of Drug Issues,* 14 (Summer 1984), pp. 553–566.

29. Goldstein et al., p. 559.

30. K. W. Bentley and D. G. Hardy, "New Potential Analgesics in the Morphine Series," *Chemical Society Proceedings,* 1963, p. 220. See also B. T. Alford, R. L. Burkhart, and W. P. Johnson, "Etorphine and Diprenorphine as Immobilizing and Reversing Agents in Captive and Free-Ranging Mammals," *Journal of the American Veterinary Medical Association,* 164 (1974), pp. 702–705; Jerry McAdams, "Elephant Juice," *Quarter Horse Track,* August 1981, pp. 6–9.

31. *Newsweek,* 5 January 1981, p. 21.

32. *USA Today,* 15 February 1985, p. 1A; *New York Times,* 24 March 1985, p. 22; *Time,* 8 April 1985, p. 61; *Business Week,* 24 June 1985, pp. 101–102; *U.S. News & World Report,* 5 August 1985, p. 14; *NIDA Notes,* Spring/Summer 1989, pp. 40–41; *Drug Enforcement Report,* 25 October 1988, p. 7; *Street Pharmacologist,* 11 (March 1987), p. 3; *Substance Abuse Report,* 1 March 1991, p. 8.

33. *New York Times,* 4 February 1991, pp. 1, 30, B1, B2.

34. *Drug Enforcement Report,* January 23, 2006; *Substance Abuse Letter,* June 12, 2006; *New York Times,* June 15, 2006, p. A13.

35. Drug Enforcement Administration News Release, March 2000.

36. *Drug Enforcement Report,* 23 October 1991, p. 5.

37. Paul Anderson, "'Homicide' Heroin Problems Spreads through Northeast?" *EmergencyNet News Service,* 11 May 1996.

38. Office of Applied Studies, *1999 Preliminary Emergency Department Data from the Drug Abuse Warning Network* (Rockville, MD: SAMHSA, 2000); Office of Applied Studies, *Drug Abuse Warning Network, 2005: National Estimates of Drug-Related Emergency Department Visits* (Rockville, MD: SAMSHA 2007).

39. *New York Times,* 14 June 2000, p. A3.

40. John C. Ball and Carl D. Chambers, *The Epidemiology of Opiate Addiction in the United States* (Springfield, IL: Chs. C. Thomas, 1970), p. 147.

41. Leon Gibson Hunt, *Recent Spread of Heroin Use in the United States: Unanswered Questions* (Washington, DC: Drug Abuse Council, 1974). See also Joan D. Rittenhouse, ed., *The Epidemiology of Heroin and Other Narcotics* (Rockville, MD: National Institute on Drug Abuse, 1977).

42. *Active Narcotic Addicts as of December 31, 1967, Annual Report* (Washington, DC: Bureau of Narcotics, 1968).

43. Zili Amsel, Carl L. Erhardt, Donald C. Krug, and Donald P. Conwell, "The Narcotics Register: Development of a Case Register," *Thirty-First Annual Meeting of the Committee on Problems of Drug Dependence,* Palo Alto, California, 25 February 1969.

44. Ball and Chambers, pp. 71–73.

45. For the first of these surveys, see Carl D. Chambers, *An Assessment of Drug Use in the General Population* (Albany: New York State Narcotic Addiction Control Commission, 1970). Whereas this first survey focused exclusively on New York, subsequent efforts conducted by the National Institute on Drug Abuse have examined the nation as a whole.

46. Carl D. Chambers, James A. Inciardi, and Harvey A. Siegal, *Chemical Coping: A Report on Legal Drug Use in the United States* (New York: Spectrum Publications, 1975), p. 2.

47. Heroin Indicators Task Force, *Heroin Indicators Trend Report, 1976–1978—An Update* (Rockville, MD: National Institute on Drug Abuse, 1979), p. 16.

48. The White House, Drug Abuse Policy Office, Office of Policy Development, *National Strategy for Prevention of Drug Abuse and Drug Trafficking* (Washington, DC: U.S. Government Printing Office, 1984); National Drug Enforcement Policy Board, *National and International Drug Law Enforcement Strategy* (Washington, DC: Government Printing Office, 1987); Edgar H. Adams, Ann J. Blanken, Joseph C. Gfroerer, and Lorraine D. Ferguson, *Overview of Selected Drug Trends* (Rockville, MD: National Institute on Drug Abuse, Division of Epidemiology and Statistical Analysis, 1988); Bureau of Justice Assistance, Office of Justice Programs, *FY 1988 Report on Drug Control* (Washington, DC: U.S. Department of Justice, 1989).

49. Office of National Drug Control Policy, *National Drug Control Strategy: 2000 Annual Report* (Washington, DC: The White House, 2000), p. 16.

50. U.S. Department of Justice, *National Drug Threat Assessment* (Washington, DC: National Drug Intelligence Center, 2007).

51. Christine L. Harold, "Tracking Heroin Chic: The Abject Body Reconfigures the Rational Argument," *Argumentation and Advocacy,* 36 (Fall 1999), pp. 65–76.

52.   Roy H. Campbell, "Out of It: 'Heroin Chic' Draws Fire from Anti-Drug Groups," *St. Louis Post-Dispatch,* 28 November 1996, p. 13; Pamela Reynolds, "A Fashion World Hooked on 'Heroin Chic'," *Boston Globe,* 26 July 1996, p. C7.

53.   See Christopher S. Wren, "Face of Heroin Is Younger and Suburban," *New York Times,* 25 April 2000, p. A22; Todd G. Pierce, "Gen-X Junkie: Ethnographic Research with Young White Heroin Users in Washington, D.C." *Substance Use & Misuse,* 34 (1999), pp. 2095–2114.

54.   Warren Richey, "Boycott Groups: Klein Ads Carry Scent of 'Heroin Chic'," *Christian Science Monitor,* 26 October 1996, p. 3; Associated Press, "Calvin Klein Pulls Kids' Underwear Ad Amid Controversy," *Dallas Morning News,* 18 February 1999, p. 2D.

55.   Jonathan Peterson, "Clinton Dresses Down Fashion Industry for 'Heroin Chic'," *Los Angeles Times,* 22 May 1997, p. A24.

CHAPTER 6

COCAINE, CRACK, AND OTHER ANALOGS OF "MAMA COCA"

The earliest accounts of coca are contained in the writings of historians who chronicled both the Spanish conquests in South America in the sixteenth century and the Spanish travelers and Jesuit missionaries who followed in their wake. Perhaps the first in this regard was the soldier and historian Pedro de Cieza de Leon (1518–1560), who commented in 1552:

> I have observed in all parts of the *West Indies,* where I have been, that the natives delight in holding herbs, roots, or twigs of trees in their mouths. Thus, in the territory of *Antiocha,* they use a small Herb called *Coca.* . . .
>
> Throughout all *Peru,* from the time they rise in the morning till they go to bed at night, they are never without this *Coca* in their mouths. The reason some *Indians,* to whom I put the question, gave me for so doing, was, that it made them insensible to hunger, and added to them strength and vigor.
>
> This *Coca* is planted in the Mountains *Andes,* where it grows up to little trees, which they cherish and nurse up carefully. So highly was this *Coca* valued in Peru in the years 1548, '49, '50, and '51, that I believe that no plant in the world, except Spice could equal it.[1]

Cieza de Leon attributed the popularity of coca among the natives of Peru to be the result of an ill habit, as he put it, "and fit for such people as they are." He also noted coca's economic value, reporting that many plantations yielded coca crops valued at "80,000 pieces-of-eight a year," and that "several Spaniards got estates by buying and selling Coca, or bartering for it in the Indian markets." What Cieza de Leon likely never imagined was the impact that coca and coca products would eventually have on the state of world affairs and the eventual course of history during the closing decades of the twentieth century.

COCAINE: "THE MOST DANGEROUS SUBSTANCE ON EARTH"

Cocaine has been known by many names—shit, coke, bernice, big C, corrine, girl, lady snow, toot, nose candy, and in some circles, Super Fly (from the 1972 Warner Brothers movie of the same name). Like heroin, LSD, Ecstasy, and methamphetamine, numerous observers have referred to cocaine as the most dangerous substance on earth.

Regardless of the slang names and epithets, the aura surrounding today's coke is quite different from that of Angelo Mariani's Vin Coca, John Pemberton's French Wine Coca, or even Sigmund Freud's cocaine. Cocaine use in the United States today is considered a major health problem, with estimates of the number of regular users in recent years ranging as high as five to ten million.

Adventures along the Cocaine Highway

At the end of the 1880s, when Sigmund Freud and his colleagues discovered that cocaine was not the all-purpose wonder drug that they had hoped for, they quickly withdrew their support for its applications in medical therapy. Despite the drug's use by the patent medicine industry until the passage of the Pure Food and Drug Act in 1906, cocaine moved underground and remained there for the better part of a century. Its major devotees included sex workers, jazz musicians, fortune-tellers, criminals, and a few pockets of African Americans. Its relegation to the netherworlds of vice, crime, and the bizarre should not suggest, however, that people in this country were unconcerned with the use of cocaine by what they referred to as alien subcultures. Quite the contrary.

During the early decades of the twentieth century, commentaries about cocaine took on racial overtones, precipitated by white fears of black sexual and criminal impulses. In 1910, for example, testimony before a committee of the House of Representatives referenced these fears and also included almost every stereotype of African Americans:

> The colored people seem to have a weakness for it [cocaine]. It is a very seductive drug, and it produces extreme exhilaration. Persons under the influences of it believe they are millionaires. They have an exaggerated ego. They imagine they can lift this building, if they want to, or can do anything they want to. They have no regard for right or wrong. It produces a kind of temporary insanity.[2]

In later decades cocaine use was associated with such exotic groups as the beatniks of New York's Greenwich Village, San Francisco's North Beach, Miami's Coconut Grove, and the movie colony of Hollywood, and associated to such an extent with the urban smart set that coke became known as the rich man's drug.

During the late 1960s and early 1970s, cocaine use in the United States began to move from the underground to the mainstream, mostly the result of a series of decisions made unwittingly at the time in Washington, DC. First, the U.S. Senate and the federal drug enforcement bureaucracy sponsored legislation that served to reduce the legal production of amphetamine-type drugs in the United States and to place strict controls on Quaaludes and other abused sedatives. Second, and most importantly, the World Bank allocated funds for the construction of the Pan American Highway through the Huallaga River Valley in the high jungles of Peru. These two factors combined to usher in the cocaine era.

Growing coca leaves had always been popular on the slopes of the Peruvian Andes, but cultivation for the most part was limited to local consumption of the leaves in tea or for chewing. Only relatively small amounts of the leaves were available for processing into cocaine. Travel throughout the rugged Andes terrain was difficult, and the coca leaves had to be carried out by mule pack. The World Bank's construction of a paved thoroughfare through the Huallaga Valley opened up transportation routes for shipping coca, and the reduced availability of amphetamines and sedatives in the United States helped to provide a ready market for the new intoxicant. With the North Americans' increasing usage of cocaine, South American growers and entrepreneurs responded by opening vast new areas for the cultivation of coca.

The cocaine highway begins in the Andes Mountains of South America where the coca leaves are grown.[3] The Chapare, Beni, and Yungas regions of northern and central Bolivia are characterized by spectacular mountain peaks with lofty snow-capped passes and thundering waterfalls that roller coaster down into subtropical valleys and moist tumbling lowlands. In Peru remote high jungles surround the Upper Huallaga River, a tributary of the mighty Amazon. In Ecuador highlands overlook both sides of the equator and areas adjacent to Guayaquil, that nation's largest city. Southeastern Colombia contains the vast and virtually uninhabited Amazonas territory; and East Asia, Bali, and the Caribbean are covered in plantations. In these regions, on some 160,000 hectares (almost 400,000 acres) of mountain slopes and scattered fields, peasant farm families cultivate coca. Virtually all of the coca and cocaine that ultimately reaches Europe and the Americas is grown in Colombia, Bolivia, and Peru, with more than half of the cultivation and 70 percent of the production occurring in Colombia (see Exhibits 6.1 and 6.2).[4]

The production of cocaine begins with the coca leaf. In the natural greenhouses of the Chapare, the Upper Huallaga, and similar forsaken tropical slopes and lowlands in Colombia, rows of *Erythroxylum coca* are neatly planted. At harvest time, the leaves are carefully picked, dried, and bundled for pack carriers who transport them to the clandestine processing laboratories. In Peru's Upper Huallaga, the labs are usually nearby, but in the Bolivian Chapare, the carriers must often bear their loads across hundreds of miles of footpaths to the Beni, a jungle and savanna province the size of Kansas with no paved highways and few roads of any kind.

At the jungle refineries the leaves are sold for just one to two dollars a kilo (2.2 lbs). The leaves are then pulverized, soaked in alcohol mixed with benzol (a petroleum derivative used in the manufacture of motor fuels, detergents, and insecticides),

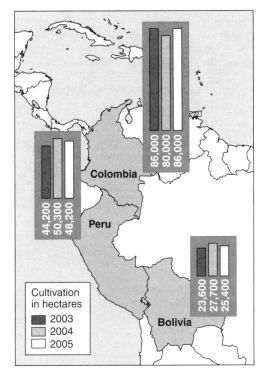

EXHIBIT 6.1   Coca Bush Cultivation, 2003–2005

Source: The United Nations Office on Drugs and Crime, UNODC.

and shaken. The alcohol-benzol mixture is then drained, sulfuric acid is added, and the solution is shaken again. Next, a precipitate is formed when sodium carbonate is added to the solution. When this is washed with kerosene and chilled, crystals of crude cocaine are left behind. These crystals are known as coca paste. The cocaine content of leaves is relatively low—0.5 to 1 percent by weight—as opposed to the paste, which has a cocaine concentration ranging up to 90 percent.*

From the coca fields and refineries, the cocaine highway leads to Amazonia—a land of superlatives and the largest single geographical feature of the South American

---

*Three varieties of coca, a perennial shrub, are cultivated for cocaine production: *Erythroxylum coca* var. *coca*, *Erythroxylum coca* var. *ipadu*, and *Erythroxylum novogranatense* var. *novogranatense*.

> *E. coca* var. *coca*, also called Bolivian or Huanuco coca, is a variety grown in the uplands of Peru and Bolivia, and in sections of Colombia. It has the highest leaf yield and accounts for most of the world's cocaine.
>
> *E. coca* var. *ipadu*, or Amazonian coca, is the variety that has been traditionally grown in Colombia. It has a low leaf yield and a low cocaine alkaloid content.
>
> *E. novogranatense* var. *novogranatense*, or Colombian coca, is also grown in Colombia, where it makes up a small percentage of the coca crop. It is more difficult to process into cocaine.

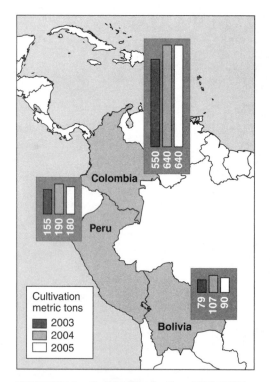

EXHIBIT 6.2   Cocaine Production, 2003–2005

Source: The United Nations Office on Drugs and Crime, UNODC.

continent (see Exhibit 6.3). Amazonia, known to the world as the Amazon, is a river, a valley, and a tropical rain forest. The river begins high in the Peruvian Andes and runs more than 4,000 miles along the equator to the Atlantic Ocean. Drawing its initial strength from hundreds of small mountain streams, it tumbles through steep gorges and eventually opens out into a milewide flow in northern Peru. The Amazon is also fed by two hundred major tributaries, seventeen of which are more than 1,000 miles long. At points along its course in Brazil, the river is several hundred feet deep and often more than 7 miles across. When it finally reaches the Atlantic Ocean, the river discharges 3.4 million gallons of water each minute, staining the sea brown with silt for 150 miles. The river valley and tropical rain forest cover 2.5 million square miles of Brazil, Peru, Colombia, Ecuador, Bolivia, Venezuela, Suriname, and Guyana. If it were a country, Amazonia would be the ninth largest in the world, more than half the size of the United States.[5] Impossible to patrol, yet near cities closely linked to the outside world, Amazonia offers almost limitless potential as a drug base.

At the edge of Amazonia in eastern Bolivia is Santa Cruz (Santa Cruz de la Sierra). Three decades ago the city looked much like a small town on the Texas

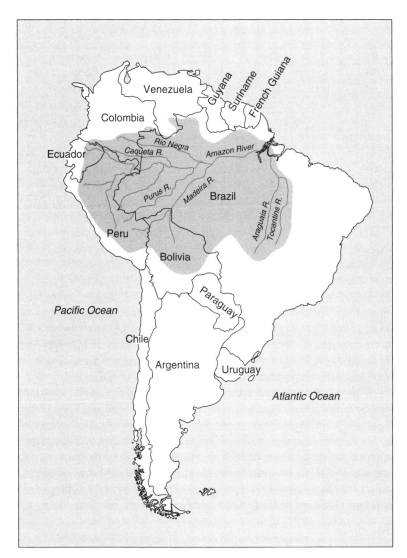

EXHIBIT 6.3   Amazonia

panhandle. Horses roamed its dusty streets, few people could be seen, and about the only sound that could be heard was the howling wind. Then came the discovery of oil and natural gas, and finally the trafficking in cocaine. The once-pathetic outpost suddenly became a boom town. Still hot and dusty, Santa Cruz is now Bolivia's largest city, with a population of more than 1.5 million people. It has a university, an international airport, golf and tennis clubs, and several hotels and restaurants. As a key point along the cocaine highway, the city is a gathering place for Colombian and U.S. buyers of coca leaves, coca paste, and cocaine.*

In the paradise of lush subtropical vegetation of western Amazonia is Tingo Maria, Peru. It is a jungle town of some 20,000 people, situated in the cloud-forest region of the Andes and surrounded by heavy tropical vegetation and often misty hillsides. It is also one of the few places in the world where jet aircraft land on a grass runway. Tingo Maria itself is an architectural nightmare. Most of the buildings appear hastily built of cinder blocks, with little paint or other finishing work. In a few places the streets are paved, but only haphazardly. Just outside Tingo Maria there is a hotel, built during World War II for U.S. military officers and mining engineers. Described as already run-down in the 1950s,[6] it is now the State Tourist Hotel—still run-down but in a state of arrested decay. The primary business enterprise of Tingo Maria is coca leaves and coca paste, which are sometimes openly bartered on its dusty streets.[7] While traders deal in their coca products, a small garrison of the Peruvian military is sometimes present, its efforts directed exclusively against members of the Sendero Luminoso (Shining Path) antigovernment insurgent group.†

Some four hundred miles north of Tingo Maria is Iquitos, deep in Peruvian Amazonia. It is a relatively modern city of 367,000 and is located directly on the west bank of the great river. As a port 2,300 miles upriver from the Atlantic that can be reached by oceangoing freighters, it is a pivotal point in the cocaine commerce. To understand this, one need only visit a few of the many waterfront and backstreet bars in Iquitos. Populated by picturesque adventurers and other characters seemingly from grade B movies, deals in coca paste and cocaine can be readily overheard.

A few hundred miles downriver on the Amazon is Leticia, Colombia, a town of perhaps 23,000. Overpowered outboards as well as Magnums, Cigarettes, Excaliburs, Scarab Sports, and other high-performance, go-fast boats of a vintage that were once seen on TV's "Miami Vice" fill the small marinas that dot the riverbank. Fairly common, too, are rows of small seaplanes docked incongruously among the muddy decay that is characteristic of almost every jungle river town. Parts of Leticia are quite fascinating, particularly the local bustling street markets—typified by stalls selling giant fillets of pirarucú and tucunaré fish the size of garbage can lids, buzzards sitting on

---

*Despite its growth, the influence of drug trafficking has made Santa Cruz a rather unpleasant place. There seems to be no escape, for example, from plainclothes police fining foreigners (particularly North Americans) for one misdemeanor or another, such as having an invalid visa or failing to pay the airport tax on departure, or perhaps even carrying too many U.S. dollars. Failure to pay the appropriate fines can result in a trip to the police station or even to jail. For the U.S. Department of State's analysis of the situation in Santa Cruz, see http://travel.state.gov/travel/cis_pa_tw/cis/cis_1069.html.

†Perhaps most fascinating in the Tingo Maria area is the Cueva de las Lechuzas (Owl's Cave), just six kilometers from town. Reminiscent of the cave on Skull Mountain in the original 1933 RKO production of *King Kong* (and its various remakes), on its towering walls and ceilings are perched any manner of bats, owls, nocturnal parrots, and parakeets. With the help of a torch, one can also see the cave's many other inhabitants, including roachlike bugs the size of mice. A common attraction for hikers, Cueva de las Lechuzas can be dangerous. During late 1990, for example, two British ornithologists were shot to death in the cave, apparently mistaken by Sendero Luminoso insurgents as agents of the U.S. Drug Enforcement Administration (Madrid *EFE,* 1838 GMT, 28 October 1990).

■ ■ ■ ■ ■ ▬▬▬▬▬▬▬▬▬▬▬▬▬▬▬▬▬▬▬▬▬▬▬▬▬▬▬▬

EXHIBIT 6.4

THE JIVARO TSANTA

The Jivaro live in the Amazonian rain forest of Ecuador and Peru in an area known as the *ceja de la selva* (eyebrow of the jungle), located on the eastern slopes of the Andes. A widely known characteristic of Jivaroan society is their persistent intratribal warfare, and tales of the Jivaro have both fascinated and terrified travelers to this part of South America for several centuries. The Jivaro are best known for their now-abandoned customs of head-hunting and shrinking and preserving human heads to make *tsantas,* or trophy heads.

A tsanta consisted of the entire skin removed from an enemy's head and gradually shrunk until it was about one-third its original size. Although the Jivaro practiced this craft for hundreds of years, during the early decades of the twentieth century it was worked by numerous entrepreneurs using the heads of unclaimed dead in Panama, which they then passed off to tourists as authentic Jivaro tsantas.

Although headhunting has been outlawed by the Peruvian and Ecuadorian governments for more than four decades, the process of shrinking heads is not a lost craft. Tsantas appear on the market now and then, but most are made from the heads of monkeys and tree sloths. In Leticia, however, it is claimed that authentic Jivaro tsantas can still be had—for a price. For a discussion of the Jivaro, and the history and significance of tsantas, see Michael J. Harner, *The Jivaro: People of the Sacred Waterfalls* (New York: Doubleday/Natural History Press, 1972); Elman R. Service, *Profiles in Ethnography* (New York: Harper & Row, 1978); Judith Davidson, *Jivaro: Expressions of Cultural Survival* (San Diego: San Diego Museum of Man, 1985). See also www.riversideca.gov/museum/exhibit/jivaro1.htm.

▬▬▬▬▬▬▬▬▬▬▬▬▬▬▬▬▬▬▬▬▬▬▬▬▬▬▬▬▬▬▬▬▬▬

lamp posts after a hard rain spreading their broad wings to dry, and of course, the many coca, coca paste, and cocaine merchants.

In fact, it would appear that Leticia exists for few reasons other than smuggling. The thousands of surrounding small tributaries and inlets make it impossible to control boat and seaplane traffic. Moreover, located just west of Brazil and east of the Peruvian frontier, Leticia is an ideal haven for anyone attempting to move goods from one country to another. The traffic, by the way, is not only in coca products but in stolen art and jewelry, guns, counterfeit money from many nations, rare animals (alive and skinned), and even the notorious Jivaro *tsantas,* the shrunken and preserved skins of human heads (see Exhibit 6.4).

A few steps southeast of Leticia is the port of Tabatinga, Brazil, a place that writers of South America guidebooks seem to leave out. The name used by the aborigines, meaning red mud, aptly portrays this garrison town of some 28,000 inhabitants at the edge of the Solimões River.* Crisscrossed by dirt roads, Tabatinga is constantly under a

---

*At this point in Brazil, the Amazon River does not actually go by the name Amazon. Brazilians refer to it as o Rio Solimões. It is not until the Solimões is joined by the Rio Negro, just west of Manaus, Brazil, that South Americans refer to it as Amazonas.

cloud of dust from the many taxis, trucks, and vans that handle its precarious collective transportation. The enigma of Tabatinga is that although there is no industry and agriculture is one of bare subsistence, the economy is nevertheless bustling. Not surprising, however, is that much of this activity is associated with the drug trafficking that originates in Leticia. A great number of Tabatinga's riverboats, both passenger and fishing, transport coca paste and cocaine to other parts of Brazil.

From Santa Cruz, Tingo Maria, Iquitos, Leticia, Tabatinga, and other remote outposts, the coca paste works its way through Peru, Ecuador, and Brazil to Colombia. In addition, even more of the world's supply of coca leaf and paste originates in the regions within Colombia: Putumayo, Caquetá, and the Vaupes—frontier regions of southeastern Colombia; and San Lucas and Norte de Santander—frontier sections of central Colombia.

The principal destinations in Colombia where coca leaves and coca paste are refined into cocaine include the areas surrounding the cities of Bogotá, Medellín, Cali, Barranquilla, and Cartagena. There the paste is treated with kerosene, washed in alcohol, filtered and dried, dissolved in sulfuric acid, and then processed with potassium permanganate, then with ammonium hydroxide, and filtered and dried once more. What is left is a relatively pure cocaine alkaloid known as cocaine base. Although the base can be smoked, it cannot be inhaled through the mucous membranes in the nose. Thus, to create a cocaine appropriate for snorting, the base is then treated with ether, acetone, and hydrochloric acid, resulting in a cocaine that is typically 85 to 97 percent pure, with no toxic adulterants. From beginning to end: 100 kilos of coca leaves yield 1 kilo of paste; 2.5 kilos of paste yield 1 kilo of base; and 1 kilo of base yields just under 1 kilo of powder cocaine.

The final segment of the cocaine highway extends by air through a series of refueling and transshipping stops in Trinidad, the Bahamas, the Virgin Islands, and other points in the Caribbean, Central America, Cuba, and Mexico to Miami, Tampa, New Orleans, Dallas, New York, Atlanta, Boston, or one of many small Atlantic or Gulf Coast ports (see Exhibit 6.5). The penetration of U.S. borders occurs at major airports, deserted airstrips, and through a variety of obscure air–sea routes chosen because of their impossibility to control. In this regard, a small-time Miami trafficker explained:

> With the combination of good coordination, good connections, good navigation equipment, good navigation skills, plus a few payoffs here and there, coke can be safely brought in at any time. . . . In one operation we had, we had a guy fly out of Cartagena with refueling stops in Jamaica and Nassau. After a little money changed hands there with the right officials, then he headed towards Miami and dropped the 10-kilo watertight package out the window into the water, to a prearranged spot just a few miles offshore just the other side of the reefs. Then he landed at Miami International and went through customs like everyone else and came out perfectly clean. That was on a Saturday night. The next afternoon, when

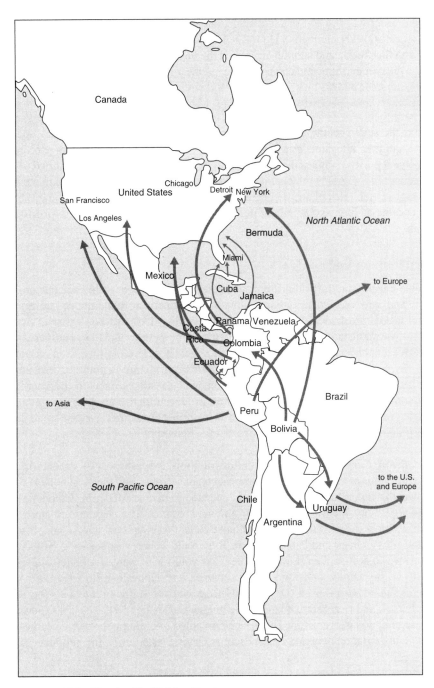

EXHIBIT 6.5   Cocaine Trafficking Routes

the water was full of Sunday boaters, another guy went out with a good set of LORAN numbers.* He located the exact spot, went over the side with fins, mask, and snorkel and found the thing in 40 feet of water. Then he did some fishing and came back late in the afternoon with all the other boaters. He had his girlfriend and her kid with him, so everything looked ordinary and nobody looked suspicious. It's a clean arrangement.

By the time cocaine has been cut several times—with lactose, baking soda, caffeine, quinine, lidocaine, powdered laxatives, or even borax—to an average of 20 to 40 percent purity, it ranges in street price from $40 to $50 a gram. What started out as five hundred kilograms of coca leaves worth about $750 to the grower, ultimately yields eight to ten kilos of street cocaine valued at more than $50,000. In some U.S. cities, cocaine as high as 85 percent purity is sometimes available, selling for $100 per gram.

The Colombian Cocaine Cartels

Colombia-based drug traffickers are responsible for most of the world's cocaine production and wholesale distribution—more than 80 percent. Colombia's strategic location makes it a logical hub for cocaine trafficking. It shares borders with five other Latin American countries—Panama, Brazil, Venezuela, Ecuador, and Peru—and it is reasonably close to the United States. In fact, Bogotá, Colombia's capital and largest city, is only two-and-one-half hours by air from Miami. In addition, because Colombia is the only South American nation with coastlines on both the Pacific Ocean and the Caribbean Sea, a wide variety of air and maritime drug smuggling routes are readily available. And every form of transportation is used to smuggle cocaine out of Colombia: airplanes, ships, trucks, and trains.

The Medellín Cartel.   Historically, the distribution and transport of cocaine has been in the hands of the infamous Colombian cocaine cartels, and the most notable of these was the notorious Medellín Cartel.[8] Headquartered in Medellín, Colombia's second largest city, the cartel was led by a number of men who were ranked among the world's most successful, richest, and most violent criminals—Jorge Ochoa, Jose Gacha, Carlos Lehder, and Pablo Escobar. Jorge Luis Ochoa Vasquez (*el gordo,* the fat man) was a soft-spoken, lower-middle-class youth who wanted a better life for himself and his family, and found it in cocaine. Jose Gonzalo Rodriguez Gacha, known as the Mexican, used the proceeds from cocaine trafficking to buy soccer teams, horses, and vast tracts of land in the jungle. Carlos Lehder Rivas, also known simply as Joe, was a lover of the Beatles and dreamed of building the world's largest cocaine transportation network. Pablo Escobar Gaviria (*el padrino,* the godfather), a

---

LORAN (from *LO*ng *RA*nge *N*avigation) is a navigational device that provides boaters with lines of positions derived from signals emitted from coastal transmitting stations. Any given location offshore, described in terms of its LORAN coordinates (numbers), can be found with reasonable accuracy. In recent years, the use of LORAN has dramatically declined, having been replaced by GPS.

rather flat and boring individual, exchanged a modestly successful career as a kidnapper and car thief for a chance to become a millionaire cocaine trafficker.

Carlos Lehder Rivas was certainly the most colorful of the group. He was drawn to drug trafficking for two reasons: profits and politics. Lehder was an admirer of such political figures as Ernesto "Che" Guevara and Adolf Hitler. He was also intensely anti-American. While in a U.S. prison in the mid-1970s, he conceived of the idea of smuggling cocaine into the United States the same way that it was accomplished with marijuana. Rather than hiding small amounts of cocaine in luggage or on airline passengers, Lehder planned to transport it in large quantities on small, private aircraft. The huge profits he expected to realize from this plan would finance his political ambitions in his native Colombia.

Out of prison in 1976, Lehder eventually bought a sizable portion of Norman's Cay, a small Bahamian island about 225 miles southeast of Miami. There, he built an extended airstrip as a refueling stop for the light planes that transported his cocaine to secret airstrips in Florida and Georgia. His inclination to use violence eventually led to his fall, when he was suspected of involvement in the 1984 assassination of Colombia's Justice Minister, Rodrigo Lara Bonilla. Outraged by the terrorist tactics employed by Lehder and the Medellín organization, the Colombian government turned Lehder over to the Drug Enforcement Administration (DEA) in 1987, which extradited him to the United States. Lehder was convicted and sentenced to 135 years in federal prison. He subsequently cooperated in the U.S. investigation of Panama dictator Manuel Noriega and received a reduced sentence in return for his testimony.

Pablo Escobar, by contrast, may well have been the most violent criminal in history. He was the mastermind behind the 1989 bombing of an Avianca commercial airliner that took the lives of 110 people, reportedly arranging the bombing to kill two people he suspected of being informants. Escobar also placed bounties ranging from one thousand to three thousand dollars on the lives of police officers in Colombia. In June 1991, Escobar surrendered to authorities in exchange for leniency, but escaped from prison a year later. For the next 17 months, Escobar was the target of the largest hunt in Colombian history (see Exhibit 6.6).

The Cali Cartel.   With the gradual elimination of most of the major figures in the Medellín group, ascendancy among traffickers in Colombia passed to groups based in Cali, Colombia, about two hundred miles south of Medellín. Unlike their predecessors in the Medellín Cartel, the members of the Cali Cartel avoided blatant acts of violence and instead tried to pass themselves off as legitimate businesspeople. During the late 1980s and early 1990s, the members of the Cali group generated billions of dollars in drug revenues every year. They operated a sophisticated drug trafficking enterprise that used the best strategies of major international businesses while maintaining the secrecy and compartmentalization of terrorist organizations.

Operating a system of insulated cells in cities throughout the United States, the Cali Cartel employed an army of surrogates who were responsible for every detail of the cocaine trafficking business, from car rentals, to pager and cell phone purchases, to the storage of cocaine in safe houses, to the keeping of inventory and accounts.

■ ■ ■ ■ ■ ▬▬▬▬▬

EXHIBIT 6.6

A REPORT FROM THE FIELD—MEETING PABLO

During a lecture trip to Colombia in 1982, I traveled to Medellín, escorted by an interpreter and a heavily armed bodyguard from the U.S. Embassy. Travel guides at the time said little about Medellín, only that it was a city of 1.5 million located 345 miles northwest of Bogotá; that it was Colombia's industrial hub, manufacturing everything from cigarettes and soft drinks to cement, textiles, and foodstuffs; and that it was not much of a tourist city. What was not spelled out was that Medellín was a city where street crime, brutal violence, terrorism, and cocaine trafficking were prevalent and where bodyguards and armed soldiers were always present, but hardly noticed. Somehow I managed to notice them all.

During lunch on the second day of my visit, my interpreter asked me if I wished to meet a local congressman, who also happened to be an up-and-coming cocaine trafficker. His name was Pablo Emilio Escobar Gaviria. We exchanged greetings, talked about my visit through the interpreter, and then went our separate ways. At the time, I had not heard of Pablo Escobar. Little did I know that he would become one of the most ruthless and powerful drug traffickers Colombia ever had; that he would become head of *El Cartel de Medellín* (the Medellín Cartel), which played a pivotal role in the network of international cocaine trafficking; that he would be suspected of ordering more than 100 murders; and that he would be the prime suspect in the killing of three Colombian presidential candidates and scores of newspaper reporters who would write against him. Interesting fellow.

Pablo Escobar ultimately became one of the most feared people in the Americas, and at the height of his success he was listed in *Forbes Magazine* as one of the wealthiest men in the world. In the final analysis, however, he was little more than a street thug who had become successful by trafficking in cocaine. In 1993, at the age of 44, he was killed during a shoot-out with the Colombian police.

▬▬▬▬▬▬▬▬▬▬

Cali Cartel leaders coerced cooperation from employees by demanding information about their close relatives that could be used later if the employee betrayed the organization or made errors that cost the cartel its profits.

Despite the substantial evidence gathered by federal law enforcement agencies against the heads of the Cali Cartel, it was impossible to extradite them to the United States for trial because extradition had been outlawed by Colombia's constitution in 1991. Therefore, DEA worked with the Colombian National Police to provide information that eventually led to the arrest or surrender of the Cali leaders in Colombia. By 1995, the Cali Cartel had begun to collapse, and by late 1996, all of the Cali kingpins sought by the Colombian National Police had been captured.*

---

*In spite of the abolition of extradition from Colombia in 1991, the United States continued to work with the Colombian government on reinstating extradition. On December 17, 1997, Colombia passed a constitutional amendment that would allow for the extradition of Colombian nationals, with the first occurring in November 1999. See *Houston Chronicle,* 29 November 1997, p. 42A; Bureau of International Narcotics and Law Enforcement Affairs, *International Narcotics Control Strategy Report* (Washington, DC: Department of State, 2000).

The Mexican Drug Cartels

Once known merely as "mules" (carriers) for Colombia's powerful cocaine cartels, since the late 1990s Mexico's major drug traffickers have become the kingpins of the Western Hemisphere's drug trade. The result has been a shifting of the "war on drugs" from South America to just south of the border.

In August 2005, the U.S. Department of State reported that Mexican cartels had leveraged the profits from their delivery routes to wrest control from the Colombian producers. As a result, Mexican drug organizations are in control of what the United Nations estimates is a $142-billion-a-year business in cocaine, heroin, marijuana, methamphetamine, and other illicit drugs.[9]

The new dominance of Mexican cartels has caused a spike in violence along the 2,000-mile U.S.–Mexico border where rival cartels are warring against Mexican and U.S. authorities. Drugs are flown from Colombia to Mexico in small planes. Then they are shipped into the United States by boat, private vehicles, or in commercial trucks crossing the border.

Hotel California?

The Eagles' "Hotel California" is one of the more memorable songs of the 1970s. It is memorable in that almost everyone can sing its opening line, even though they may not know any of the other words. And it is memorable because of arguments as to its actual meaning. Here are some of the theories:

- The Hotel California is a real hotel located in (pick one) Baja California on the coastal highway between Cabo San Lucas and La Paz or else near Santa Barbara. In other words, the song is a hard look at the modern hospitality industry, which is plagued by guests who check out but then never leave.
- The Hotel California is a mental hospital.
- It's about satanism (but then, isn't everything).
- Hotel California is about the pitfalls of living in southern California in the 1970s.

But in all likelihood, "Hotel California" is a metaphor for cocaine dependence, because you can check out, but you can never seem to get away from it.[10]

Fire in the Brain

Lured by the Lorelei of orgasmic pleasure, millions of people in the United States use cocaine each year—a snort in each nostril and the user is up and away for twenty minutes or so. Alert, witty, and with it, users do not suffer from hangovers, lung cancer, holes in the arms, or burned-out cells in the brain. The cocaine high is an immediate, intensely vivid, and sensation-enhancing experience. Moreover, it has the reputation for being a spectacular aphrodisiac: it is believed to create sexual desire, to heighten it, to increase sexual endurance, and to cure frigidity and impotence.

Given all these positives, no wonder cocaine has been the all-American drug for the past three decades. Its use continues to permeate all levels of society into the twenty-first century, from Park Avenue to the inner city: lawyers and executives use cocaine; baby boomers, yuppies, and Gen-X'ers use cocaine; police officers, prosecutors, and prisoners use cocaine; politicians use cocaine; housewives and pensioners use cocaine; Democrats, Republicans, and Socialists use cocaine; students, stockbrokers, children, and athletes use cocaine; even some priests and members of Congress use cocaine.

Yet the pleasure and feelings of power that cocaine engenders make its use a problematic recreational pursuit. In very small and occasional doses it is no more harmful than equally moderate doses of alcohol or marijuana, and infinitely less so than heroin, but there is a side to cocaine that can be very destructive. That euphoric lift, with its feelings of confidence and being on top of things, that comes from but a few brief snorts is short-lived and invariably followed by a letdown.

Because the body does not develop any significant tolerance to cocaine, the drug was once said to be nonaddicting. Yet many question this position, pointing to the many chronic users who compulsively indulge in cocaine. Sidney Cohen of the Neuropsychiatric Institute at the Los Angeles School of Medicine, for example, suggests that the notion that cocaine does not produce dependence comes from the early professional literature, written at a time when quantities of the drug were far smaller than those taken by contemporary users.[11] He adds that the high doses of cocaine currently used, combined with the frequency with which they are taken, produce a withdrawal syndrome characterized primarily by depression.

Dr. Cohen's comments aside, compulsive users seek the extreme mood elevation, elation, and grandiose feelings of heightened mental and physical prowess induced by the drug. When these begin to wane, a corresponding deep depression is felt that is in such marked contrast to the users' previous states that they are strongly motivated to repeat the dose and restore their euphoria and feelings of power. Thus, when chronic users try to stop using cocaine, they are often plunged into a severe depression from which only the drug can arouse them. As such, cocaine dependence is very real.

In addition to the dependence potential, chronic cocaine use typically causes hyperstimulation, digestive disorders, nausea, loss of appetite, weight loss, tooth erosion, brain abscess, stroke, cardiac irregularities, occasional convulsions, and sometimes paranoid psychoses and delusions of persecution.[12] Moreover, repeated inhalation can result in erosions of the mucous membranes, including perforations of the nasal septum. A chronic runny nose is often a mark of the regular cocaine user. The reasons for these effects on the nose are well understood. Cocaine totally numbs the nasal membranes, which then shrink as their blood supply diminishes. When the drug wears off, the mucous membranes demand the blood supply that was withheld, and the nose becomes congested, with the symptoms of a head cold likely to follow. Moreover, any cocaine that remains undissolved in the nose can cause burns and sores, which can eventually lead to degeneration of the nasal mucous membranes or eat through the cartilage itself.[13]

These are the effects of snorting powder cocaine, the most common method of ingestion, but other ways of taking the drug can bring on an added spectrum of complications. One of these methods is freebasing, a phenomenon that has been known in the drug community for more than three decades but moved into mainstream cocaine use only during the 1980s. Cocaine hydrochloride has a high melting point and, thus, cannot be efficiently smoked. As a result, some users change the cocaine salt form to a base form. More specifically, freebase cocaine is actually a different chemical product from cocaine itself.

In the process of preparing freebase, street cocaine, which is usually in the form of a hydrochloride salt, is treated with a liquid base (such as buffered ammonia) to remove the hydrochloric acid. The free cocaine (cocaine in the base state, free of the hydrochloride acid, and hence the name freebase) is then dissolved in a solvent such as ether, from which the purified cocaine is crystallized. These crystals, having a lower melting point, are then crushed and used in a special, heated glass pipe. Smoking freebase cocaine provides a quicker and more potent rush, and a far more powerful high than regular cocaine. Therefore, its use is that much more seductive. However, the freebasing process involves the use of ether, a highly volatile petroleum product that has exploded in the face of many a user.

Cocaine has also been used as a sex aid, a practice that has brought both pleasurable and disastrous results. A sprinkle of cocaine on the clitoris or just below the head of the penis will anesthetize the tissues and retard a sexual climax. But with persistent stimulation, the drug will ultimately promote an explosive orgasm. However, the urethra (the tube inside the penis or the vulva through which urine is eliminated) is very sensitive to cocaine. At a minimum, the drug will dry out the urethral membranes, which must remain moist to function properly. At a maximum, because the absorption rate of cocaine through the walls of the urethra is quite rapid, overdoses have been known to happen.*

As an aphrodisiac, cocaine is highly questionable. Research has found considerable differences in sexual responses to the same dosage level of cocaine, depending primarily on the setting of the usage and the background experiences of the user. Interestingly, the male sexual response to cocaine is different from that of women. For men, cocaine not only helps to prevent premature ejaculation, but at the same time permits

---

*Perhaps the most extravagant complications associated with the intraurethral administration of cocaine were reported from New York Hospital/Cornell Medical Center in 1988. The patient was a 34-year-old male, and his use of cocaine in this manner touched off a series of chain reactions in his body that caused blood abnormalities, skin and muscle deterioration, and gangrene. The eventual consequences included the amputation of his penis, both of his legs above the knees, and nine fingers. See John C. Mahler, Samuel Perry, and Bruce Sutton, "Intraurethral Cocaine Administration," *Journal of the American Medical Association,* 259 (3 June 1988), p. 3126.

prolonged intercourse before orgasm. Among women, achieving a climax under the influence of cocaine is often quite difficult. Finally, research also demonstrates that chronic, heavy users of cocaine typically experience sexual dysfunction.[14]

Among chronic users of cocaine, the injection use of the drug has become more noticeable in recent years. This route of administration produces an extremely rapid onset of the drug's effects, usually within fifteen to twenty seconds, along with a rather powerful high. It also produces the more debilitating effects of psychoses and paranoid delusions, similar to those of the amphetamine speed freak. These occur more rapidly than when cocaine is chronically snorted.*

A related phenomenon is the injection of cocaine in combination with another drug. Known as speedballing, the practice is not at all new. The classic speedball is a mixture of heroin and cocaine. It was referred to as such by the heroin-using community as early as the 1930s, and as whizbang as far back as 1918.[15] Whether the user's primary drug of choice is cocaine or heroin, the speedball intensifies the euphoric effect. It can also be quite dangerous, in that speedball overdoses are not uncommon.†

Whether the pattern of use involves snorting, freebasing, shooting, speedballing, or smoking (discussed later in this chapter), the hazards of cocaine use can go well beyond those already noted. Some individuals, likely few in number, are hypersensitive to cocaine, and as little as twenty milligrams can be fatal. Because cocaine is a potent stimulant that rapidly increases the blood pressure, sudden death can also occur from only small amounts among users suffering from coronary artery disease or weak cerebral blood vessels. Cocaine is also a convulsant that can induce major seizures and cause fatalities if emergency treatment is not immediately at hand. Postcocaine depression, if intense, can lead to suicide. If the dose is large enough, cocaine can be toxic and result in an overdose. For the majority of users, this can occur with as little as one gram, taken intravenously. When injecting cocaine, furthermore, the user is also at high risk of exposure to all those complications that result from the use of unsterile needles—hepatitis, bacterial infections, and even HIV/AIDS (see Chapter 9).‡

---

*When cocaine was first introduced during the latter part of the nineteenth century, intramuscular injections were frequently employed. This mechanism, however, is not reported among contemporary users.

†Heroin is often referred to as *boy* in the street community and cocaine is typically called *girl*. Moreover, like other drugs, speedball is often packaged and sold under brand names, sometimes honoring (or vilifying) well-known men and women. In various times and places, for example, speedball has been sold under such brand names as Samson and Delilah (of Biblical fame), Bill and Hillary (of White House fame), Bill and Monica (of Oval Office fame), and Bond and Beauty (of 007 fame). Speedball has been sold for years in Miami as Rambo and Madonna (who have had homes there).

‡In addition to bacterial and viral infections, numerous cocaine-related deaths have resulted from body packing, a smuggling rather than an ingestion method. Small amounts of cocaine are packed into condoms, which are then swallowed or secreted in the rectum or vagina. Unless the carrier is a suspected cocaine courier or mule, the drug's detection by customs agents is difficult. On many occasions one or more of these condoms have ruptured, releasing lethal amounts of pure cocaine into the carrier's body. See Stephen J. Traub, Robert S. Hoffman, and Lewis S. Nelson, "Body Packing: The Internal Concealment of Illicit Drugs," *New England Journal of Medicine,* 349 (December 25, 2003), pp. 2519–2526.

COCA PASTE AND HURRICANE CRACK: THE SMOKING OF MAMA COCA

Although cocaine can be produced in a number of forms and ingested in a variety of ways, none has received as much media and political attention as smoking crack cocaine. In fact, during the second half of the 1980s, crack was often referred to as the most dangerous substance on earth.

The Discovery of Crack

The first mention of crack cocaine in the major media occurred on November 17, 1985.* Buried within the pages of that Monday edition of the prestigious *New York Times,* journalist Donna Boundy, in writing about a local drug abuse treatment program, unceremoniously commented: "Three teenagers have sought this treatment already this year . . . for cocaine dependence resulting from the use of a new form of the drug called crack or rock-like pieces of prepared freebase (concentrated) cocaine."[16] Although Ms. Boundy, like so many after her, had erred in describing crack as freebase or concentrated cocaine, her mere mention of what was ostensibly an old drug initiated a major media event.

Crack suddenly took on a life of its own, and in less than eleven months the *New York Times, Washington Post, Los Angeles Times,* the wire services, *Time, Newsweek,* and *U.S. News & World Report* had among them served the nation with more than one thousand stories in which crack had figured prominently. As social critic Malcolm Gladwell recalled the episode: ". . . coverage feeding coverage, stories of addiction and squalor multiplying across the land."[17] Then CBS capped their reporting with "48 Hours on Crack Street," a prime-time presentation that reached fifteen million viewers and became one of the highest rated documentaries in the history of television. Not to be outdone, NBC offered "Cocaine Country," culminating a six-month stretch in which the network had broadcast more than four hundred reports on drug abuse.

As the crack hysteria mounted during the summer of 1986, a number of researchers in the drug community were somewhat perplexed. Whereas *Newsweek* claimed that crack was the biggest story since Vietnam and the fall of the Nixon presidency,[18] and other media giants compared the spread of crack with the plagues of medieval Europe, researchers were finding crack to be, not a national epidemic, but a phenomenon isolated to a few inner-city neighborhoods in less than a dozen urban areas. By late August, crack hysteria had reached such proportions that the Drug Enforcement Administration felt compelled to respond. Based on reports from its field agents and informants in cities throughout the country, a DEA report concluded: "With multi-kilogram quantities of cocaine hydrochloride available and with snorting

---

*The media story of crack can actually be traced to the latter part of 1984 when the Los Angeles dailies began reporting on local rock houses where small pellets of cocaine could be had for as little as twenty-five dollars (for example, *Los Angeles Times,* 25 November 1984, pp. CC1, CC8). *Newsweek* (11 February 1985, p. 33) later gave a half page to the Los Angeles item, but the term *crack* was never used, and little attention was given to the matter.

continuing to be the primary route of cocaine administration, crack presently appears to be a secondary rather than primary problem in most areas."[19]

Curiously, most of the major newspapers, networks, and weekly magazines ignored the DEA report, and the frenzy continued. *Newsweek* went on to describe the crack scene as "an inferno of craving and despair,"[20] whereas *Time* stated it somewhat differently: "In minutes the flash high is followed by a crashing low that can leave a user craving another hit."[21] Then the story of Katrina Linton was reported in *USA Today:* "Katrina Linton was 17 when she first walked into a crack house in the Bronx. By then she was selling her body to crack dealers just to support her $900-a-day habit."[22] In these and other stories the implication was clear: crack led the user almost immediately into the nightmare worlds of Stephen King and "The X-Files," from which there was little chance of return.

But to researchers and clinicians in the drug field who remembered the media's portrayal of the PCP epidemic a decade earlier, reports of the pervasiveness of crack were viewed with skepticism. Interestingly, both the media and drug professionals were right about what they were saying. But at the same time, both were very wrong as well. During the summer and fall of 1986, contrary to media claims, crack indeed had not been an epidemic drug problem in the United States. Crack was there all right, but it was not until the beginning of 1987 that it really began to assert itself, eventually becoming perhaps the most degrading drug of the century.

Unraveling Crack Cocaine

The history of crack dates back to at least the early 1970s, to a time when cocaine was still known as charlie, corrine, bernice, schoolboy, and the rich man's drug. But to fully understand the evolution of crack, a short diversion into a few other products of the coca leaf is warranted. More specifically, freebase and coca paste, both briefly addressed previously in this chapter, are prominent players in the story of crack.

From Powder Cocaine to Freebase Cocaine.   During the late 1960s, when cocaine had begun its initial trek from the underground to mainstream society, most users viewed it as a relatively safe drug. They inhaled it in relatively small quantities, and use typically occurred within a social–recreational context.[23] But as the availability of cocaine increased in subsequent years, so too did the number of users and the mechanisms for ingesting it. Some began sprinkling street cocaine on tobacco or marijuana and smoking it as a cigarette or in a pipe, but this method did not produce effects distinctly different from inhalation or snorting.[24] But a new alternative soon became available, freebasing, that is, smoking freebase cocaine.

Freebase cocaine is actually a different chemical product than cocaine itself. As mentioned previously, the process of freebasing transforms cocaine hydrochloride to the base state in a crystalline form. The crystals are then crushed and used in a special glass pipe. By 1977 it was estimated that there were some four million users of cocaine in the United States,[25] with as many as 10 percent of these freebasing the drug exclusively.[26] Yet few outside of the drug-using, drug research, and drug treatment communities were even aware of the existence of the freebase culture. An even lesser number had an understanding of the new complications that freebasing had introduced to the cocaine scene.

The complications are several. First, although ingesting cocaine in any of its forms is highly seductive, the euphoria produced with freebasing is more intense than when the drug is inhaled. Moreover, this profound euphoria subsides into irritable craving after only a few minutes, thus influencing many users to continue freebasing for days at a time—until either they, or their drug supplies, are fully exhausted. Second, the practice of freebasing is expensive. When snorting cocaine, a single gram can last the social user an entire weekend or longer. With street cocaine ranging in price anywhere from forty to two hundred dollars a gram depending on availability and purity, even this method of ingestion can be an expensive recreational pursuit. Yet the cost of freebasing can result in a geometric increase. Habitual users have been known to freebase continuously for three or four days without sleep, using up to 150 grams of cocaine in a seventy-two-hour period.[27] Third, one special danger of freebasing is the proximity of highly flammable ether (or rum when it is used instead of water as a coolant in the pipe) to an open flame. This problem is aggravated by the user suffering from a loss of coordination produced by the cocaine or a combination of cocaine and alcohol. As a result, the volatile concoction has exploded in the faces of many users.

By 1980, reports of the problems associated with cocaine freebasing had begun to reach a national audience, crystallized by the near-death explosion suffered by the late comedian–actor Richard Pryor, presumably the result of freebasing.

From Cocaine and Freebase to Pasta Basica de Cocaína.   Common in the drug-using communities of Colombia, Bolivia, Venezuela, Ecuador, Peru, and Brazil is the use of coca paste, known to most South Americans as basuco, susuko, pasta basica de Cocaína, or just simply pasta.[28] Perhaps best known as basuco, and as mentioned previously in this chapter, coca paste is one of the intermediate products in the processing of the coca leaf into cocaine. It is typically smoked straight or in cigarettes mixed with either tobacco or marijuana.

Smoking coca paste became popular in South America beginning in the early 1970s. It was readily available, inexpensive, had a high cocaine content, and was absorbed quickly. As the phenomenon was studied, however, it was quickly realized that smoking paste was far more serious than any other form of cocaine use. In addition to cocaine, paste contains traces of all the chemicals used to initially process the coca leaves—kerosene, sulfuric acid, methanol, benzoic acid, and the oxidized products of these solvents, plus any number of other alkaloids that are present in the coca leaf.[29] One analysis undertaken in Colombia in 1986 found, in addition to all these chemicals, traces of brick dust, leaded gasoline, ether, and various talcs.[30]

When smoking paste was first noted in South America, it seemed to be restricted to the coca-processing regions of Bolivia, Colombia, Ecuador, and Peru, appealing primarily to low-income groups because of its cheap price compared to refined cocaine.[31] By the early 1980s, however, it had spread to other South American nations, to numerous segments of the social strata, and throughout the decade paste smoking further expanded to become a major drug problem for much of South America.[32]

At the same time, coca paste made its way to the United States, first in Miami, its initial smuggling port of entry, and then elsewhere.[33] Interestingly, the paste quickly became known to young North American users as bubble gum, likely due to the phonetic association of the South American basuco with Bazooka bubble gum.

The Coca Paste/Crack Cocaine Connection.   Contrary to popular belief, crack is not a new substance, having been first reported in the literature during the early 1970s. Among the innovations of the psychedelic era of the late 1960s were the underground guides to illegal drug use. One of the first was Mary Jane Superweed's *Marijuana Consumer's and Dealer's Guide* in 1968.[34] Sold for two dollars at local head shops, this sixteen-page pamphlet provided instructions on how to extract hallucinogenic amides from morning glory seeds to produce two thousand dollars worth of hashish from eighty-five dollars worth of marijuana, thus converting inferior-grade pot into connoisseur "Super-Grass." Other pamphlets offered tips on *cannabis* (marijuana) cultivation, preparing DMT (*di*methyl*t*ryptamine, an LSD-like hallucinogen) at home, and grafting marijuana to other plants.*

One of the early 1970s contributions to the genre was *The Gourmet Cokebook,* a lengthy clothbound publication that seemed to touch on every aspect of cocaine— its history and legends, consumption and sale, refinement and analysis, and effects and legal ramifications.[35] Curiously, the *Cokebook* made passing mention of a rock-like variety of cocaine. Not to be confused with rock cocaine or Bolivian rock— cocaine hydrochloride products for intranasal snorting—what the *Cokebook* was refering to was cocaine reconstituted into the base state in a rock form. That was 1972, and few took notice of it.

In David Lee's *Cocaine Handbook,* published in 1981, the discussion of what appeared to be the same commodity was a bit more explicit. In detailing the freebase process, Lee offered the following brief note:

> A less pure base is sometimes made by dissolving the cocaine hydrochloride in water, making the solution alkaline (sodium bicarbonate is the alkali most often used), and heating the mixture until all the water has evaporated. The waxy base which is produced contains the added alkali and the same adulterants and impurities as did the original cocaine.[36]

That was 1981 and, still, few people took notice of the remark. But what both *The Gourmet Cokebook* and *The Cocaine Handbook* had been talking about was what a few years later would be known as crack cocaine. It was dubbed *crack* in the mid-1980s because of the crackling sound that the sodium bicarbonate (baking soda) makes as it burns during the smoking process. Later commentaries offered explanations for why the crack of the early 1970s never caught on. In 1988, a former resident of San Francisco's Haight-Ashbury community, living in Miami, recalled that it had

---

*In addition to the Mary Jane Superweed series of pamphlets, equally popular was Supermother's *Cooking with Grass,* a collection of recipes for marijuana-containing brownies, soups, meatballs, muffins, and other delicacies.

been available for only a short period of time before it was discarded by freebase cocaine aficionados as an inferior product:

> In the Haight of the early seventies they called it "garbage freebase," because of all the impurities it contained. It was also considered in bad taste to offer that kind of crap. You never saw any of the real coke *diggers* doing garbage.*

Contrary to another popular belief, crack is neither freebase cocaine nor purified cocaine. Part of the confusion about what crack actually is comes from the different ways that the word *freebase* is used in the drug community. *Freebase* (the noun) is a drug, a cocaine product converted to the base state from cocaine hydrochloride after adulterants have been chemically removed. Crack is converted to the base state without removing the adulterants. *Freebasing* (the verb) means to inhale vapors of cocaine base, of which crack is but one form. Finally, crack is not purified cocaine, for during its processing, the baking soda remains as a salt, thus reducing its homogeneity somewhat. Informants in the Miami drug subculture indicate that the purity of crack ranges as high as 80 percent, but generally contains much of the filler and impurities found in the original cocaine hydrochloride, along with some of the baking soda (sodium bicarbonate) and cuts (expanders, for increasing bulk) from the processing.†

The rediscovery of crack seemed to occur simultaneously on the East and West Coasts early in the 1980s. As a result of the Colombian government's attempts to reduce the amount of illicit cocaine production within its borders, it apparently, at least for a time, successfully restricted the amount of ether available for transforming coca paste into cocaine hydrochloride. The result was the diversion of coca paste from Colombia, through Central America and the Caribbean, into South Florida for conversion into cocaine. Spillage from shipments through the Caribbean corridor acquainted local island populations with coca paste smoking. They developed the forerunner of crack in 1980.[37]

Known as baking-soda base, base rock, gravel, and roxanne, the prototype was a smokable product composed of coca paste, baking soda, water, and rum. Migrants from Jamaica, Haiti, Trinidad, the Virgin Islands, and locations along the Leeward and Windward Islands chain introduced the crack prototype to Caribbean inner-city populations in Miami's immigrant undergrounds, where it was ultimately produced from

---

*The Diggers were a Haight-Ashbury clan that adopted the name of a group of 17th-century English radicals who appropriated common land and gave their surplus to the poor. In time, in the Haight and elsewhere, the term *digger* became synonymous with *hippie*. See Allen J. Matusow, *The Unraveling of America: A History of Liberalism in the 1960s* (New York: Harper & Row, 1984), pp. 300–304.

†Some comment seems warranted on the practice of referring to crack as smokable cocaine. Technically, crack is not really smoked. Smoking implies combustion, burning, and the inhalation of smoke. Tobacco is smoked. Marijuana is smoked. Crack, on the other hand, is actually inhaled. The small pebbles or rocks, having a relatively low melting point, are placed in a special glass pipe or other smoking device and heated. Rather than burning, crack vaporizes and the fumes are inhaled.

powder cocaine rather than paste. A Miami-based immigrant from Barbados commented in 1986 about the diffusion of what he referred to as "baking-soda paste":

> Basuco and baking-soda paste seemed to come both at the same time. There was always a little cocaine here and there in the islands, but not too much, and it wasn't cheap. Then 'bout five, maybe six, years ago, the paste hit all of the islands. It seemed to happen overnight—Barbados, Saint Lucia, Dominica, and [Saint] Vincent and [Saint] Kitts—all at the same time.* . . . Then I guess someone started to experiment, and we got the rum-soda-paste concoction. We brought it to Miami when we came in '82, and we saw that the Haitians too were into the same combination.

Apparently, at about the same time, a Los Angeles basement chemist rediscovered the rock variety of baking-soda cocaine, initially referred to as cocaine rock.[38] It was an immediate success, as was the East Coast type, for a variety of reasons. First, it could be smoked rather than snorted. When cocaine is smoked, it is more rapidly absorbed and crosses the blood–brain barrier within six seconds, hence, an almost instantaneous high. Second, it was cheap. Whereas a gram of cocaine for snorting may cost $60 or more depending on its purity, the same gram can be transformed into anywhere from five to thirty rocks. For the user, this meant that individual rocks could be purchased for as little as $2, $5 (nickel rocks), $10 (dime rocks), or $20. For the seller, $60 worth of cocaine hydrochloride (purchased wholesale for $30) could generate as much as $100 to $150 when sold as rocks. Third, it was easily hidden and transportable, and when hawked in small glass vials, it could be readily scrutinized by potential buyers. As a South Miami narcotics detective described it during the summer of 1986:

> Crack has been a real boon to both buyer and seller. It's cheap, real cheap. Anybody can come up with $5 or $10 for a trip to the stars. But most important, it's easy to get rid of in a pinch. Drop it on the ground and it's almost impossible to find; step on it and the damn thing is history. All of a sudden your evidence ceases to exist.

By the close of 1985 when crack had finally come to the attention of the national media, it was predicted to be the wave of the future among users of illegal drugs.[39]

Media stories held crack responsible for rising rates of street crime. As a cover story in *USA Today* put it:

> Addicts spend thousands of dollars on binges, smoking the contents of vial after vial in crack or "base" houses—modern-day opium dens—for days at a time without food or

---

*For those unfamiliar with the geography of the Caribbean, the locations mentioned by this informant are part of the Leeward and Windward Islands. The Leeward Islands are the northern segment of the Lesser Antilles and stretch some four hundred miles in a southerly arc from the Virgin Islands to Dominica. The Windward Islands are the southern part of the Lesser Antilles, stretching some two hundred miles from Martinique south to Grenada. Barbados is located just west of the southern half of the Windward chain, but is not geographically part of it.

sleep. They will do anything to repeat the high, including robbing their families and friends, selling their possessions and bodies.[40]

As the media blitzed the American people with lurid stories depicting the hazards of crack, Congress and the White House began drawing plans for a more concerted war on crack and other drugs, and politicians running for office at federal, state, and local levels began vaulting over one another trying to climb on the antidrug bandwagon. At the same time, crack use was reported in Canada, most European nations, Hong Kong, South Africa, Egypt, India, Belize, Mexico, Venezuela, Bermuda, Barbados, Colombia, Brazil, the Philippines, and other parts of the world.[41]

SKETCHES FROM THE CRACK HUSTLE

Although the use of crack became evident in most major cities across the United States during the latter half of the 1980s, cocaine and crack tend to be associated more often with Miami than other urban areas. In part, this is due to Miami's association with the cocaine wars of the late 1970s and early 1980s, and with South Florida's reputation for cocaine importation and distribution.[42] No doubt the image of the city as the Casablanca on the Caribbean presented in TV's "Miami Vice" during the 1980s contributed as well. But whatever the reasons, crack is indeed a significant facet of Miami street life, and the Miami experience is targeted here to illustrate the players, the situations, the adventures, the degradation, and the tragedies associated with crack use.*

The use of crack and the existence of crack houses proliferated in Miami and elsewhere throughout the 1980s. Crack houses are places to use and/or sell crack, to manufacture and package crack, to exchange sex for crack, and may be actual houses or apartments, small shacks at the rear of empty lots, abandoned buildings, or even the rusting hulks of discarded automobiles. Subsequent to the initial media sensationalism, press coverage targeted the involvement of youths in crack distribution, the violence associated with struggles to control the crack marketplace in inner-city neighborhoods, and the child abuse, child neglect, and child abandonment by crack-addicted mothers.[43]

In Miami, the violence associated with crack distribution never reached the proportions apparent in other urban centers.[44] Nevertheless crack use was a major drug problem.[45] By 1989, the Drug Enforcement Administration had estimated that there were no less than seven hundred operating crack houses in the greater Miami area.[46] As in other urban locales, the production, sale, and use of crack,[47] as well as prostitution and sex-for-drugs exchanges,[48] became prominent features of the Miami crack scene.

---

*Much of the information presented here is based on the author's more than 30 years of street research in Miami, supported in part by grants RO1-DAO1827 and RO1-DAO4862, and contract #271888248/1 from the National Institute on Drug Abuse, and cooperative agreement U64-CCU404539 from the Centers for Disease Control.

Cracks, Hard White, and Eight-Ball

Crack is known by many pseudonyms, most commonly, cracks, hard white, white, or flavor. Others are bricks, boulders, and eight-balls (large rocks or slabs of crack), doo-wap (two rocks), as well as crumbs, shake, and kibbles and bits (small rocks or crack shavings). The dope man or bond man (crack dealer) delivers a cookie (a large quantity of crack, sometimes as much as ninety rocks), which he carries in his bomb bag (any bag in which drugs are conveyed for delivery) to any crack house in his neighborhood territory. The dope man may also deal (sell) or juggle (sell for double its worth) his crack on the street.

In many crack houses, the drug might be displayed on boards (tables, mirrors, or bulletin boards) whereas in the street crack is hawked in small glass vials or plastic bags. In a few locales, these bags are sealed and stamped with a brand name. Like heroin labeling, such a practice affords the illusion of quality control and gives the buyer a specific name for which to ask. In New York City, crack labeling has included brands such as White Cloud, Conan, and Handball, and in Miami, the better known labels of the past two decades included Biscayne Babe (an epithet for sex workers who stroll Miami's Biscayne Boulevard), Olympus (perhaps from Greek mythology), Bogey and Bacall (of Key Largo), Noriega's Holiday (after a former Panamanian dictator), Fidel's Demise (in honor of anti-Castro Cuban refugees), as well as Y2K, M-2000, Tokyo Rose, and the Heat.

Many crack users are uncertain as to what crack actually is. Some know it as cocaine that has been cooked into a hard, solid form called a rock. Exactly what is in crack, in addition to street cocaine, is also debated: some say baking soda whereas others say ether. Actually, most users don't know or care. A few will argue that crack is the purest form of cocaine, but others hold that freebase is. Still others believe that crack *is* freebase.

The rocking up (preparation) of crack is done in a variety of ways, all of which require a cut (expander) of some sort to increase the volume and weight of the crack and, hence, the profits. Typical in this effort are substances such as comeback, swell up, blow up, and rush, all of which are cocaine analogs (novocaine, lidocaine, and benzocaine) that bind with cocaine when cooked. A popular recipe for a substantial quantity of crack is called Miami Magic.

INGREDIENTS FOR MIAMI MAGIC
4 oz. cocaine hydrochloride
4 oz. comeback
2 oz. Arm & Hammer baking soda
water
ice cubes

PREPARATION
Mix the cocaine, baking soda, and comeback with enough water to cover it. Bring to a boil, mixing constantly, and watch the blend draw together. Place the resulting gel in ice water. Let cool into a solid mass. Remove

the crack from water. Let it stand until completely dry and hard. Break into pieces. Serves 1,000.

Although conventional cooking is most common, microwaves are also popular:

> In the microwave I have a little water, little tap water, I put my coke, which was half coke, half baking soda, and I pour it into the glass and I put it in the microwave. And let it start cooking, take the jar and let it start forming into a rock.

Crack is smoked in a variety of ways—special glass pipes, makeshift smoking devices fabricated from beer and soda cans, jars, bottles, and other containers known as stems, straight shooters, ouzies, or, more directly, the devil's dick. A beam (from "Beam me up, Scotty" of TV's original "Star Trek") is a hit of crack. Crack is also smoked with marijuana in cigarettes called geek joints, lace joints, and pin joints. Some users get high from a shotgun—secondary smoke exhaled from one crack user into the mouth of another.

Users typically smoke for as long as they have crack or the means to purchase it—money, sex, stolen goods, furniture, or other drugs. It is rare that smokers have but a single hit. More likely they spend fifty to five hundred dollars during a mission— a three- or four-day binge, smoking almost constantly, three to fifty rocks per day. During these cycles, crack users rarely eat or sleep. Once crack is tried, for many users it is not long before it becomes a daily habit. For example, a recovering crack user indicated:

> I smoked it Thursday, Friday, Saturday, Monday, Tuesday, Wednesday, Thursday, Friday, Saturday on that cycle. I was working at that time. I would spend my whole $300 check. Everyday was a crack day for me. My day was not made without a hit. I could smoke it before breakfast, don't even have breakfast or I don't eat for three days.

A current crack user/dealer reported:

> For the past five months I've been wearing the same pants. And sneakers are new but with all the money you make a day at least $500/$600 a day you don't want to spend $100 on clothes. Everything is rocks, rocks, rocks, rocks, rocks. And to tell you the truth I don't even eat well for having all that money. You don't even want to have patience to sit down and have a good dinner. I could tell you rock is . . . I don't know what to say. I just feel sorry for anyone who falls into it.

"Crack Is My Pimp"

The following quotation, provided by a 28-year-old crack user legally employed as a shipping clerk, clearly illustrates characteristic aspects of both the compulsive nature of crack use and the sex-for-crack phenomenon. This woman had been a marijuana user since age 15, a cocaine user since age 18, and a crack user since age 26. In her comments below, she details her first exchange of sex for crack and how it came about.

I had my last paycheck, that was $107. That day I went straight from there [work] with a friend guy and copped some drugs. I bought $25–5 nickel rocks. I walked up to the apartment, me and the same guy. We drunk a beer, we needed the can to smoke on. So we sat there and we smoked those five rocks and you know like they say, one is too much and a thousand is never enough. And that's the truth. Those five rocks went like this [snaps fingers] and I immediately, I had maybe about $80 left. I had intentions of takin' my grandmother some money home for the kids. But I had it in my mind you know I was, I was just sick. I wanted to continue to get high so push come to shove I smoked up that—that whole day me and him we smoke up. It didn't last till maybe about 8:00 PM cause we started maybe about 12:00 that afternoon.

Okay all the money was gone, all the drugs was gone. About 9:00 we went and sat in the park. Usually when we set in the park people will come over and they'll have drugs. Some friends came over and they had drugs. He walked home. I stayed out because I couldn't give an account for what I had did with the money. My grandmother done thought that I was goin' to pick up my check and comin' back. So I walked around and I walked down this street, you know you got people that will pick you up. So this guy stopped and I got in the car, and I never did any prostituting but I wanted more drugs. So this guy he stopped and he picked me up and he asked me: "How much would you charge me for a head?" That's oral sex. And I told him $40. And so he say how much would you charge me for two hours to have to just sex not oral sex? And so I told him $40 so he say: "Okay get in," and he took me to this hotel.

He had about six rocks. I didn't wanna sex. I wanted to get high so we smoked the rocks and durin' the time I sexed with him. So after I sexed him he gave me the money and after the rocks was gone I still wanted to get high. So this man he gave his car and his keys and gave me more money to go get more drugs. We went into another hotel. By that time it was maybe 6:00 in the morning. He ended up leaving me in the hotel. By that time I done spent all my $40. It wasn't nothing I had done wasted the money. So later on that afternoon, my grandmother done let me get sleep and everything. I think later on that day and the next day I went to my godfather's house and I earned $15, I helped him do some work around the house so he gave me $15.

So I went and stayed home with the kids and waited till they got ready to go to bed that night. I went and got three rocks with that $15. I started off smokin' by myself, but when you sittin' in the park people come to know you and they be tryin' to horn in on what you doin'. So ended up smokin' I think about a rock and a half with somebody that was sittin' in the park. Later on I ended up walkin' down the main strip again and this guy came by and he say: "Well how much money do you want for a head?" So I told him $10. I was really desperate this time around, so I told him $10. He say: "Well I don't have but $5." I say okay I'll take that you know I settle for little or nothin'. So we went down the street and parked in this parkin' lot and I gave him a head. And I immediately went to the drug house, and bought a nickel rock.

It would appear that most of the sex in crack houses is oral and frequent. At the same time, the majority of those performing sex-for-crack exchanges indicate that they do so only while on crack and/or for crack. For example, a 31-year-old male prostitute reported:

As a matter of fact, when you are high on crack you'll do almost anything. We [the respondent and his boyfriend] had sex in front of other people, and one male joined us. Usually I gave the other guy head while we had anal intercourse.

Similarly, a male customer of sex-for-crack exchanges commented:

The next time I ran into this prostitute man dressed like a woman and I paid her/him $10 to have sex. I thought it was a woman. So she bend over and I got in from behind and hey it was just like a woman. And if I wasn't on crack I'm for sure I wouldn't have been doing that.

Finally, although the majority of the sexual activities that take place in crack houses are in a separate room, in many crack houses they occur in the common area where everyone else is smoking. In this regard, one informant reported to the author:

It was like a sex show or somethin' like that. Everybody's sittin' and layin' around smokin' and this lady starts takin' her clothes off, says she's burnin' up. And a guy goes over to her, hands her his pipe in one hand and his meat [penis] in the other. And she starts givin' him a blow job right there.

Another informant reported similarly:

There was this one place where just nobody cared what they did and where they did it. And let's see, I was giving heads for everybody to see 'cause since they didn't care so I didn't either. So I givin' heads all around the room for hits. Even another lady.

THE CRACK BABY MYTH

> The year is 1886. A new bride suffering from melancholia seeks treatment from a local pharmacist, who advises sniffing powdered cocaine. A wonderful new drug, he tells her. And it is. The veil of depression lifts. She feels giddy, euphoric, and energetic. Months later, still taking the miraculous powder, she discovers that she is with child. Her visits to the druggist become even more frequent. What cheers the mother, she reasons, must be good for the baby.[49]

Again, the year was 1886 (see Exhibit 6.7), a century before the world discovered crack cocaine. One wonders what effects the powder cocaine might have had on the woman's developing fetus.

A century later, in 1987, Dr. Ira J. Chasnoff of Northwestern University Medical School in Chicago estimated that 375,000 infants are exposed to drugs each year, and that most of these have been exposed to cocaine—particularly crack. Research on the effects of prenatal substance abuse in the mid-1980s characterized crack-exposed children as moody, often inconsolable, less socially interactive, and less able to bond than other children.[50] Many researchers also found drug-exposed children to be less attentive and less able to focus on specific tasks than nonexposed children.[51] Other harmful effects attributed to prenatal cocaine exposure include high rates of placental abruption (detachment of the placenta from the uterine wall), placenta previa (location of the placenta in front of the birth canal), growth retardation in utero (in the uterus), sudden infant death syndrome (SIDS), withdrawal symptoms, cerebral infarctions (death of brain tissue due to loss of blood supply), low birth weight, physical malformations, microcephaly (small head circumference), and genitourinary tract malformations. Disturbances of feeding, sleep, and vision are also reported. Many studies frequently characterize these effects as irreversible and suggest that no amount of special attention or educational programs will ever be able to turn these cocaine-exposed infants into well-functioning or -adjusted children.

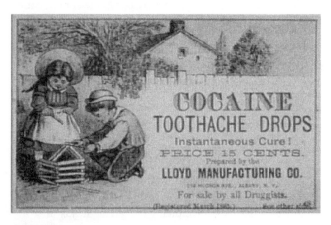

EXHIBIT 6.7

Source: Image taken from www.cocaine.org/cocatooth.htm.

Such dramatic findings sparked a wave of media reports lamenting the fate of a new generation of crack babies. Numerous media stories documented the epidemic numbers of cocaine-addicted infants being born in large urban hospitals across the United States.[52] More often than not, the media publicized case studies of a few children who had been profoundly affected by prenatal exposure to multiple drugs, not exclusively cocaine. However, headlines that read "The Crack Children," "Crack Babies Born to Life of Suffering," "A Desperate Crack Legacy," and "Crack in the Cradle" focused much of the public's attention on the dangers of cocaine and created the image that crack babies were severely damaged human beings. Take, for example, the following excerpts from a story that appeared in the *New York Times* in 1989:

> Babies born to mothers using crack have serious difficulty relating to their world, making friends, playing like normal children, and feeling love for their mother or primary caretakers. Prenatal exposure to illegal drugs, particularly powdered cocaine and crack, seems to be "interfering with the central core of what it is to be human," said Coryl Jones, a research psychologist at the National Institute on Drug Abuse. New research indicates that most babies exposed to illegal drugs appear to be able to develop normal, if low-range intelligence, despite their subnormal emotional development. But the studies suggest that children of addicted mothers may be unable to develop into adults with basic employment skills and unable to form close human relationships.[53]

A similarly disturbing story appeared in *Newsweek* a few months later:

> The problems of crack children are long-term and far more difficult to solve. Educators are frustrated and bewildered by their behavior. "They operate only on an instinctual level, something has been left out," says Geynille Agee of her students. . . . Dr. Judy Howard of the UCLA School of Medicine who has studied hundreds of crack children, says that crack babies are extremely irritable, very lethargic, hyperactive, and may have trouble relating to other people. As part of her research, Dr. Howard compared crack preemies with non-crack preemies. Even at the age of 18 months, the crack kids would hit or throw their toys. "The kids have an impairment that makes them disorganized in everything they do," she says. Dr. Howard says its as if the part of the brain that "makes us human beings, capable of discussion or reflection," has been "wiped out."[54]

Accounts of behavioral disturbances among cocaine-exposed children were particularly commonplace. As frightening reports from weary, disconcerted family members and teachers grew more frequent, public concern over this lost generation increased. Consider the following excerpts that ran in newspapers and magazines across the country. In the *Miami Herald*:

> The tiny angelic looking boy is only 4 but he has long had a reputation around his day care center. For tantrums. He would hurl himself on the floor and bang his head against the concrete. The boy is a cocaine child—his fragile system damaged by the drug while he was still in the womb. . . . "They're like little jekylls and hydes" said a Fort Lauderdale school principal, "all of a sudden, something will set them off. They start throwing tantrums. They start yelling. They can't control their emotions."[55]

In the *Wall Street Journal:*

> One slim six-year-old boy sits on the floor with his classmates happily singing an alphabet song. Two years ago, he used to throw hour-long tantrums. He would build a tower of blocks, then shout that it was on fire and knock it down. Last year, while classmates watched the space shuttle blast off on television, he banged on his desk and cried. Extremes of behavior are common, from apathy to aggression, passivity to hyperactivity, indiscriminate trust to extreme suspicion. Teachers also see more subtle signs of the children's drug exposure and fragmented lives. A girl demands to be left alone, bumps into walls, or stares blankly into space. A boy screams and throws himself on the floor because he wants to be picked up but can't express himself.[56]

Reports that suggested cocaine-damaged children would face insurmountable educational and social obstacles that could doom them to failure in the future and the media's tendency to cite studies with detrimental findings of crack exposure created something of a self-fulfilling prophecy. Children labeled crack babies have been characterized as having little potential for successful outcomes. As such, prospective adoptive parents have been unwilling to care for these kids and school teachers anticipate the worst. Too often the media's stereotypic portrayal of crack babies has obscured the fact that most children who are exposed to cocaine in utero are also exposed to other substances. Crack-using women are much more likely than nonusers to smoke cigarettes and use alcohol during pregnancy.*

More recently, the National Institute on Drug Abuse (NIDA) has indicated that predictions of a lost generation of cocaine-exposed children were overstated.[57] NIDA reported that approximately one-half of all infants born to drug-using mothers have no drug-related health effects and has suggested that previous estimates of epidemic numbers of crack-affected infants resulted from the lack of representative samples and reliable data in early studies. In fact, many early research studies of prenatal cocaine exposure suffered from a variety of methodological flaws that may call their findings into question.[58]

Although thousands of crack-exposed infants are born in the United States each year, crack alone is typically not the issue. Women who use crack during pregnancy are also much more likely than other women to use other illegal drugs, as well as alcohol and cigarettes.[59] A leading cause of mental retardation and birth defects in the United States is fetal alcohol syndrome. Alcohol's effects include dysmorphogenesis (the development of ill-shaped or otherwise malformed body structures), growth abnormalities, and cognitive and language deficits. Several studies have found alcohol use and cigarette smoking during pregnancy to be associated with lower IQ scores and poorer language development and cognitive functioning. Cigarette smoking has also been associated with prenatal complications, low birth weight, and impairment in language and cognitive development. In fact, exposure to alcohol and

---

*Although cocaine seems to be abused equally in all socioeconomic strata, it is reported less frequently among pregnant women of higher socioeconomic status who can afford private obstetric care and who deliver in private hospitals and clinics, making it easier to conceal any evidence of substance abuse.

cigarettes has been determined to have an equal or greater detrimental impact on the infant than exposure to cocaine.[60]

Taking all this one step further, over and above the effects of substance abuse, other variables including nutrition, environment, and delivery date can affect the overall health of a child. Within this context, women drug users have been found to differ from nondrug-using women in a number of important ways. Substance abuse among women is considered a marker for many traits, including lifestyle, demographic characteristics, and socioeconomic status. Drug and alcohol dependence in women have also been linked with low self-esteem, domestic abuse, a history of sexual abuse, and a chaotic lifestyle.

In addition, cocaine-using women tend to suffer from poor nutrition and overall health, a greater exposure to violence, and poor or unsanitary living conditions with greater risk of infections than other women. Importantly, inadequate prenatal care has also been correlated with substance use, particularly with the use of crack. Pregnant women from the nation's inner cities who were not involved in a prenatal care program have also been found to have significantly higher rates of Hepatitis B and syphilis than patients actively participating in a medically supervised prenatal care program. Because of inadequate medical care, many pregnant addicts deliver prematurely and characteristics of premature infants are not unlike those attributed to crack cocaine infants. Perhaps the most significant single predictor of developmental problems for children is the socioeconomic status of the family.[61]

In retrospect, prenatal cocaine exposure has been debated at length, but with little consensus or agreement about whether crack babies per se exist, or whether these babies suffer from a complex of factors at work. Going further, some assert that the crack baby crisis is in fact a myth advanced to fuel a sociopolitical agenda. As explained by one observer:

> The crack-baby myth was so powerful in part because it had something for everyone, whether one's ideological leanings called for enhancing public programs to meet the crisis, or for punishing the drug-addicted mothers seen as responsible for it.[62]

In the final analysis, there is no question that crack and other forms of cocaine can affect the developing fetus, but it has proven difficult to separate the prenatal effects of crack from other potentially negative influences on the development of the fetus and the growing child. In all likelihood, the notion of the crack baby is indeed a myth. So-called cocaine babies and crack babies are more realistically suffering from their mothers' multiple drug use (particularly alcohol) and/or are actually poverty babies afflicted by a lack of medical care and poor nutrition.

POSTSCRIPT

Crack has been called the fast-food variety of cocaine. It is cheap, easy to conceal, it vaporizes with practically no odor, and the gratification is swift: an intense, almost sexual euphoria that lasts less than five minutes. Given these attributes, it would appear that crack cocaine might be a safer alternative to powder cocaine. But such a conclusion is far from accurate. In addition to all the problems associated with cocaine discussed previously in this chapter, there are additional complications with crack use. Smoking cocaine as opposed to snorting it results in more immediate and direct absorption of the drug, producing a quicker and more compelling high, greatly increasing the dependence potential. Moreover, risk of acute toxic reactions, including brain seizure, cardiac irregularities, respiratory paralysis, paranoid psychosis, and pulmonary dysfunction, increases.

The tendency to binge on crack for days at a time, neglecting food, sleep, and basic hygiene, severely compromises physical health. Thus, crack users appear emaciated most of the time. They lose interest in their physical appearance. Many have scabs on their faces, arms, and legs, the results of burns and picking on the skin (to remove bugs and other insects believed to be crawling under the skin). Crack users tend to have burned facial hair from carelessly lighting their smoking paraphernalia; they have burned lips and tongues from the hot stems of their pipes; and they seem to cough constantly. The tendency of both male and female crack users to engage in high-frequency unprotected sex with numerous anonymous partners increases their risk for any variety of sexually transmitted diseases, including HIV/AIDS.

According to national surveys, crack never caught on too well in the general population, and where it did usage rates began to decline at the close of the 1980s.[63] But for reasons difficult to understand, crack's appeal in the majority of the nation's inner cities has endured and will likely remain so for some time.[64] Although the violence associated with crack distribution has subsided in many locales, crack remains a staple in street drug cultures throughout the United States. Perhaps the best explanation of crack's appeal in the inner city comes from anthropologist Philippe Bourgois:

> Substance abuse in general, and crack in particular, offers the equivalent of a born-again metamorphosis. Instantaneously, the user is transformed from an unemployed, depressed high school dropout, despised by the world—and secretly convinced that his failure is due to his own inherent stupidity and disorganization. There is a rush of heart-palpitating pleasure, followed by a jaw-gnashing crash and wide-eyed alertness that provides his life with concrete purpose: Get more crack—fast![65]

NOTES

1. Pedro de Cieza de Leon, *The Seventeen Years' Travels of Pedro de Cieza de Leon through the Mighty Kingdom of Peru* (English translation, London: 1709), p. 211, cited by William Martindale, *Coca and Cocaine* (London: H. K. Lewis, 1894), pp. 2–3.

2. Cited by H. Wayne Morgan, *Drugs in America: A Social History, 1800–1920* (Syracuse, NY: Syracuse University Press, 1981), p. 93.

3. See Nils Noya, "Cocaine Crisis in Bolivia" paper presented at What Works? International Perspectives on Drug Abuse Treatment and Prevention Research, New York, 22–25 October 1989; Rensselaer W. Lee, *The White Labyrinth: Cocaine and Political Power* (New Brunswick, NJ: Transaction Publishers, 1989); Donald J. Mabry, *The Latin American Narcotics Trade and U.S. National Security*

(Westport, CT: Greenwood Press, 1989); Anthony Daniels, *Coups and Cocaine: Two Journeys in South America* (Woodstock, NY: Overlook Press, 1987); Patrick L. Clawson and Rensselear W. Lee, *The Andean Cocaine Industry* (New York: St Martin's Griffin, 1998); Bureau of International Narcotics Matters, *International Narcotics Control Strategy Report* (Washington, DC: Department of State, 1999).

4. United Nations Office of Drugs and Crime, *World Drug Report* (Geneva: United Nations, 2006).

5. For more complete descriptions of Amazonia, see Brian Kelly and Mark London, *Amazon* (San Diego: Harcourt Brace Jovanovich, 1983); Roger D. Stone, *Dreams of Amazonia* (New York: Viking, 1985); Redmond O'Hanlon, *In Trouble Again: A Journey between the Orinoco and the Amazon* (New York: Vintage Books, 1990); Joe Kane, *Running the Amazon* (New York: Alfred A. Knopf, 1989).

6. See Ronald Wright, *Cut Stones and Crossroads: A Journey into the Two Worlds of Peru* (New York: Viking, 1984), p. 42.

7. The coca leaf and paste trades have been so visible over the years in Tingo Maria that they have attracted the attention of the media throughout the Americas. For example, see Lima *Panamericana Television Network,* 0200 GMT, 8 June 1987; Santiago (Chile) *Que Pasa,* 8 February 1990, pp. 41–43; São Paulo *O Estado Se São Paulo,* 29 October 1989, p. 16; Lima *El Nacional,* 3 April 1988, pp. IV–VII; *Miami Herald,* 17 April 1987, p. 8A; *Newsweek,* 31 March 1986, p. 32; Mark Maden, "The Big Push," *Sierra,* 73 (November/December 1988), pp. 66–75; Lima *Television Peruana,* 0100 GMT, 8 February 1990; Lima *La Republica,* 17 October 1993, p. 10; Lima *Caretas,* 1 July 1993, pp. 26–31; Alan Murphy, *Peru Handbook* (Chicago: Passport Books, 1999), p. 458.

8. See United States Attorneys and the Attorney General of the United States, *Drug Trafficking: A Report to the President of the United States, August 3, 1989* (Washington, DC: U.S. Department of Justice, 1989); Guy Gugliotta and Jeff Leen, *Kings of Cocaine* (New York: Simon and Schuster, 1989); Paul Eddy, Hugo Sabogal, and Sara Walden, *The Cocaine Wars* (New York: W. W. Norton, 1988). Of related interest here are Charles Nicholl, *The Fruit Palace: An Odyssey through Colombia's Cocaine Underground* (New York: St. Martin's Press, 1985); Berkeley Rice, *Trafficking: The Boom and Bust of the Air America Cocaine Ring* (New York: Charles Scribner's Sons, 1989); Alvaro Camacho Guizado, *Droga y Sociedad en Colombia* (Cali: Universedad del Valle, 1988).

9. United Nations, 2006.

10. Ed Zotti, *Triumph of the Straight Dope* (New York: Ballentine Books, 1999).

11. Sidney Cohen, "Recent Developments in the Use of Cocaine," *Bulletin on Narcotics,* April–June 1984, p. 9.

12. Roger D. Weiss, Steven M. Mirin, and Roxanne L. Bartel, *Cocaine* (Washington, DC: American Psychiatric Press, 1994); Lawrence Gould, Chitra Gopalaswamy, Chandrakant Patel, and Robert Betzu, "Cocaine-Induced Myocardial Infarction," *New York State Journal of Medicine,* November 1985, pp. 660–661; R. Fishel, G. Hamamoto, A. Barbul, V. Niji, and G. Efron, "Cocaine Colitis: Is This a New Syndrome?" *Colon and Rectum,* 28 (1985), pp. 264–266; Louis Cregler and Herbert Mark, "Relation of Stroke to Cocaine Abuse," *New York State Journal of Medicine,* February 1987, pp. 128–129; A. Naveen Rao, "Brain Abscess: A Complication of Cocaine Inhalation," *New York State Journal of Medicine,* October 1988, pp. 548–550; Frank H. Gawin and Everett H. Ellinwood, "Cocaine and Other Stimulants: Actions, Abuse, and Treatment," *New England Journal of Medicine,* 318 (5 May 1988), pp. 1173–1182; John Grabowski, ed., *Cocaine: Pharmacology, Effects, and Treatment of Abuse* (Rockville, MD: National Institute on Drug Abuse, 1984).

13. See Maria-Elena Rodriguez, "Treatment of Cocaine Abuse: Medical and Psychiatric Consequences," in *Cocaine, Marijuana, Designer Drugs: Chemistry, Pharmacology, and Behavior,* ed. Knife K. Redda, Charles A. Walker, and Gene Barnett (Boca Raton, FL: CRC Press, 1989), pp. 97–111.

14. Patrick T. Macdonald, Dan Waldorf, Craig Reinarman, and Sheigla Murphy, "Heavy Cocaine Use and Sexual Behavior," *Journal of Drug Issues,* 18 (Summer 1988), pp. 437–455.

15. See Eric Partridge, *A Dictionary of the Underworld* (New York: Bonanza Books, 1961), pp. 665, 770; Harold Wentworth and Stuart Berg Flexner, *Dictionary of American Slang* (New York: Thomas Y. Crowell, 1975), p. 507; Richard A. Spears, *Slang and Euphemism* (Middle Village, NY: Jonathan David, 1981), p. 369.

16. *New York Times,* 17 November 1985, p. B12.

17. Malcolm Gladwell, "A New Addiction to an Old Story," *Insight,* 27 October 1986, pp. 8–12. See also Adam Paul Weisman, "I Was a Drug-Hype Junkie," *New Republic,* 6 October 1986, pp. 14–17; Crain Reinarman and Harry G. Levine, "Crack in Context: Politics and Media in the Making of a Drug Scare," *Contemporary Drug Problems,* 16 (Winter 1989), pp. 535–577.

18. *Newsweek,* 16 June 1986, p. 15.

19. Drug Enforcement Administration, *Special Report: The Crack Situation in the United States,* unpublished release from the Strategic Intelligence Section, Drug Enforcement Administration, Washington, DC, 22 August 1986.

20. *Newsweek,* 16 June 1986, p. 18.

21. *Time,* 2 June 1986, p. 16.

22. *USA Today,* 16 June 1986, p. 1A.

23. See Ronald K. Siegel, "Cocaine: Recreational Use and Intoxication," in *Cocaine: 1977,* ed. Robert C. Petersen and Richard Stillman (Rockville, MD: National Institute on Drug Abuse, 1977), pp. 119–136.

24. Lester Grinspoon and James B. Bakalar, *Cocaine: A Drug and Its Social Evolution* (New York: Basic Books, 1985), p. 279.

25. H. Abelson, R. Cohen, R. Schrayer, and M. Rappaport, "Drug Experience, Attitudes and Related Behavior among Adolescents and Adults," in *Annual Report* (Washington, DC: Office of Drug Abuse Policy, 1978).

26. Ronald K. Siegel, "Cocaine Smoking," *Journal of Psychoactive Drugs, 14* (1982), pp. 271–359.

27. Ronald K. Siegel, "Cocaine Smoking Disorders: Diagnosis and Treatment," *Psychiatric Annals, 14* (1984), pp. 728–732.

28. F. Raul Jeri, "Coca-Paste Smoking in Some Latin American Countries: A Severe and Unabated Form of Addiction," *Bulletin on Narcotics,* April–June 1984, pp. 15–31.

29. M. Almeida, "Contrabucion al Estudio de la Historia Natural de la Dependencia a la Pasta Basica de Cocaína," *Revista de Neuro-Psiquiatria,* 41 (1978), pp. 44–45.

30. Bogotá *El Tiempo,* 19 June 1986, p. 2-D.

31. F. R. Jeri, C. Sanchez, and T. Del Pozo, "Consumo de Drogal Peligrosas por Miembros Familiares de la Fuerza Armada y Fuerza Policial Peruana," *Revista de la Sanidad de las Fuerzas Policiales,* 37 (1976), pp. 104–112.

32. See Caracus (Venezuela) *El Universal,* 4 October 1985, pp. 4, 30; Caracus *Zeta,* 12–23 September 1985, pp. 39–46; Manaus (Brazil) *Jornal Do Comercio,* 20 May 1986, p. 16; Bogotá *El Tiempo,* 1 June 1986, p. 3-A; Medellín *El Colombiano,* 22 July 1986, p. 16-A; Bogotá *El Tiempo,* 6 October 1986, p. 7-A; Lima (Peru) *El Nacional,* 14 November 1986, p. 13; La Paz (Bolivia) *Presencia,* 3 March 1988, Sec. 2, p. 1; São Paulo (Brazil) *Folha de São Paulo,* 11 June 1987, p. A29; Buenos Aires (Argentina) *La Prensa,* 20 June 1987, p. 9; São Paulo *O Estado de São Paulo,* 8 March 1988, p. 18; Bogotá *El Espectador,* 2 April 1988, pp. 1A, 10A; La Paz *El Diario,* 21 October 1988, p. 3; Cochabamba (Bolivia) *Los Tiempos,* 13 June 1989, p. B5; São Paulo *O Estado de São Paulo,* 18 June 1989, p. 32; Rio de Janiero (Brazil) *Manchete,* 28 October 1989, pp. 20–29; Philadelphia *Inquirer,* 21 September 1986, p. 25A; Timothy Ross, "Bolivian Paste Fuels Basuco Boom," *World AIDS,* September 1989, p. 9.

33. Curiously, coca paste was reportedly available in Italy during 1987. See Milan *Corriere Della Sera,* 26 October 1987, p. 8.

34. Mary Jane Superweed, *The Marijuana Consumer's and Dealer's Guide* (San Francisco: Chthon Press, 1968).

35. *The Gourmet Cokebook: A Complete Guide to Cocaine* (San Francisco: White Mountain Press, 1972).

36. David Lee, *Cocaine Handbook: An Essential Reference* (San Rafael, CA: What If? 1981), p. 52.

37. James N. Hall, "Hurricane Crack," *Street Pharmacologist,* 10 (September 1986), pp. 1–2.

38. *U.S. News & World Report,* 11 February 1985, p. 33.

39. See *New York Times,* 29 November 1985, p. A1.

40. *USA Today,* 16 June 1986, p. 1A.

41. Windsor (Canada) *Windsor Star,* 26 June 1986, p. A13; Toronto *Globe and Mail,* 2 September 1987, p. A5; Ottawa *Citizen,* 13 February 1988, p. A15; Belfast (Northern Ireland) *News Letter,* 9 July 1986, p. 3; Helsinki (Finland) *Uusi Suomi,* 28 July 1986, p. 8; Rio de Janeiro *O Globo,* 24 May 1986, p. 6; Hong Kong *South China Morning Post,* 2 August 1986, p. 16; Johannesburg (South Africa) *Star,* 23 September 1986, p. 1M; Cape Town (South Africa) *Argus,* 10 March 1987, p. 13; Johannesburg *City Press,* 7 January 1990, p. 5; Milan (Italy) *Panorama,* 3 May 1987, pp. 58–59; Oslo (Norway) *Arbeiderbladet,* 4 June 1987, p. 13; Madrid (Spain) *El Alcazar,* 14 September 1986, p. 11; Nuevo Laredo (Mexico) *El Diario de Nuevo Laredo,* 12 October 1986, Sec. 4, p. 1; Calcutta (India) *Statesman,* 16 October 1986, p. 1; Belize City (Belize) *Beacon,* 25 October 1986, pp. 1, 14; London *Al-Fursan,* 13 September 1986, pp. 51–53; London *Sunday Telegraph,* 12 April 1987, p. 1; Geneva (Switzerland) *Journal de Geneve,* 26 December 1986, p. 1; Brussels (Belgium) *Le Sori,* 10–11 November 1986, p. 3; Munich (Germany) *Sueddeutsche Zeitung,* 18–19 October 1986, p. 12; Lisbon (Portugal) *O Jornal,* 30 January/5 February 1987, p. 40; Hamburg (Germany) *Die Zeit,* 24 April 1987, p. 77; Hamilton (Bermuda) *Royale Gazette,* 3 December 1987, p. 3; Bridgetown (Barbados) *Weekend Nation,* 15–16 January 1988, p. 32; Stockholm (Sweden) *Dagens Nyheter,* 2 January 1988, p. 6; Grand Cayman (Bahamas) *Caymanian Compass,* 20 January 1988, pp. 1–2; Paris (France) *Liberation,* 12 January 1990, p. 33; Bangkok (Thailand) *Siam Rat,* 13 August 1988, p. 12.

42. See T. D. Allman, *Miami: City of the Future* (New York: Atlantic Monthly Press, 1987); David Rieff, *Going to Miami: Exiles, Tourists, and Refugees in the New America* (Boston: Little, Brown, 1987); Patrick Carr, *Sunshine States* (New York: Doubleday, 1990); Edna Buchanan, *The Corpse Had a Familiar Face: Covering Miami, America's Hottest Beat* (New York: Random House, 1987); John Rothchild, *Up for Grabs: A Trip through Time and Space in the Sunshine State* (New York: Viking Press, 1985).

43. See Ron Rosenbaum, "Crack Murder: A Detective Story," *New York Times Magazine,* 15 February 1987, pp. 29–33, 57, 60; *Newsweek,* 22 February 1988, pp. 24–25; *New York Doctor,* 10 April 1989, pp. 1, 22; *U.S. News & World Report,* 10 April 1989, pp. 20–32; *New York Times,* 1 June 1989, pp. A1, B4.

44. James A. Inciardi, "The Crack/Violence Connection within a Population of Hard-Core Adolescent Offenders," in *Drugs and Violence: Causes, Correlates, and Consequences,* ed. Mario De La Rosa, Elizabeth Y. Lambert, and Bernard Gropper (Rockville, MD: National Institute on Drug Abuse, 1990), pp. 92–111.

45. *Miami Herald* ("Neighbors" Supplement), 24 April 1988, pp. 21–25; James A. Inciardi and Anne E. Pottieger, "Kids, Crack, and Crime," *Journal of Drug Issues,* 21 (Spring 1991), pp. 257–270.

46. *Crack/Cocaine: Overview 1989* (Washington, DC: Drug Enforcement Administration, 1989).

47. James N. Hall, "Cocaine Smoking Ignites America," *Street Pharmacologist,* Fall 1988/Winter 1989, pp. 28–30; Steven Belenko and Jeffrey Fagen, *Crack and the Criminal Justice System* (New York: New York City Criminal Justice Agency, 1987); *Newsweek,* 28 November 1988, pp. 64–79; Barbara Wallace, "Psychological and Environmental Determinants of Relapse in Crack Cocaine Smokers," *Journal of Substance Treatment,* 6 (1989), pp. 95–106; Tom Mieczkowski, "Crack Distribution in Detroit," *Contemporary Drug Problems,* 17 (Spring 1990), pp. 9–30; Jeffrey Fagen and Ko-Lo Chin, "Initiation into Crack and Cocaine: A Tale of Two Epidemics," *Contemporary Drug Problems,* 16 (Winter 1989), pp. 579–617; Philippe Bourgois, "In Search of Horatio Alger: Culture and Ideology in the Crack Economy," *Contemporary Drug Problems,* 16 (Winter 1989), pp. 619–649; Paul J. Goldstein, Henry H. Brownstein, Patrick J. Ryan, and Patricia A. Bellucci, "Crack and Homicide in New York City: A Conceptually Based Event Analysis," *Contemporary Drug Problems,* 16 (Winter 1989), pp. 651–687.

48. See James A. Inciardi, Dorothy Lockwood, and Anne E. Pottieger, *Women and Crack-Cocaine* (New York: Macmillan, 1993).

49. Kathy A. Fackelmann, "The Maternal Cocaine Connection," *Science News,* 140 (7 September 1991), p. 152.

50. K. Fackelman, "The Maternal Cocaine Connection: A Tiny Unwitting Victim May Bear the Brunt of Drug Abuse," *Science News* (1991), pp. 140, 152; B. M. Lester, M. J. Corwin, C. Sepkowski,

R. Seifer, M. Peuker, S. McLaughlin, and H. L. Golub, "Neurobehavioral Syndromes in Cocaine-Exposed Newborn Infants," *Child Development,* 62 (1991), pp. 694–705.

51. Ira J. Chasnoff, W. J. Burns, Sidney J. Schnoll, and K. A. Burns, "Cocaine Use in Pregnancy," *New England Journal of Medicine,* 313 (1985), pp. 666–669; Ira J. Chasnoff and D. R. Griffith, "Cocaine-Exposed Infants: Two Year Follow-Up," *Pediatric Research,* 25 (1989), p. 249A.

52. See James A. Inciardi, Hilary L. Surratt, and Christine A. Saum, *Cocaine-Exposed Infants: Social, Legal, and Public Health Issues* (Thousand Oaks, CA: Sage, 1997).

53. S. Blakeslee, "Crack's Toll among Babies: A Joyless View, Even of Toys," *New York Times,* 17 September 1989, p. A1.

54. *Newsweek,* 12 February 1990, pp. 62–63.

55. *Miami Herald,* 16 April 1990, p. A1.

56. *Wall Street Journal,* 27 December 1989, p. A1.

57. *Substance Abuse Letter,* 17 October 1994, p. 3.

58. See Inciardi, Surratt, and Saum.

59. D. C. Van Dyke and A. A. Fox, "Fetal Drug Exposure and Its Possible Implications for Learning in the Preschool and School-Age Population," *Journal of Learning Disabilities,* 23 (1990), pp. 160–163.

60. G. A. Richardson, N. L. Day, and P. McGauhey, "The Impact of Perinatal Marijuana and Cocaine Use on the Infant and Child," *Clinical Obstetrics and Gynecology,* 36 (1993), pp. 302–318; G. A. Richardson and N. L. Day, "Detrimental Effects of Prenatal Cocaine Exposure: Illusion or Reality?" *Journal of the American Academy of Child and Adolescent Psychiatry,* 33 (1994), pp. 28–34.

61. See Inciardi, Surratt, and Saum.

62. K. Greider, "Crackpot Ideas," *Mother Jones,* July/August, 1995, pp. 53–56.

63. Edgar H. Adams, Ann J. Blanken, Lorraine D. Ferguson, and Andrea Kopstein, *Overview of Selected Drug Trends* (Rockville, MD: National Institute on Drug Abuse, Division of Epidemiology and Prevention Research, 1990); Substance Abuse and Mental Health Services Administration, *Results from the 2005 National Survey on Drug Use and Health: National Findings, Cocaine Use in Past Year,* by Age Group, Table 8.37B, NSDUH Series H-30, DHHS Publication No. SMA 06-4194, (Rockville, MD: Office of Applied Studies, 2006).

64. Community Epidemiology Work Group, *City Reports* (Rockville, MD: National Institute on Drug Abuse, 1999); Clair E. Sterk, *Fast Lives: Women Who Use Crack Cocaine* (Philadelphia: Temple University Press, 1999); Mitchell S. Ratner, ed., *Crack Pipe as Pimp: An Ethnographic Investigation of Sex-for-Crack Exchanges* (New York: Lexington Books, 1993); Philippe Bourgois, *In Search of Respect: Selling Crack in the Barrio* (Cambridge: Cambridge University Press, 1995); Sue Mahan, *Crack Cocaine, Crime, and Women: Legal, Social, and Treatment Issues* (Thousand Oaks, CA: Sage, 1996); Bruce A. Jacobs, *Dealing Crack: The Social World of Streetcorner Selling* (Boston: Northeastern University Press, 1999); Dale D. Chitwood, James E. Rivers, and James A. Inciardi, *The American Pipe Dream: Crack Cocaine and the Inner City* (Ft. Worth, TX: Harcourt Brace, 1996); J. A. Inciardi, and H. L. Surratt, "Drug Use, Street Crime and Sex-Trading Among Cocaine-Dependent Women: Implications for Public Health and Criminal Justice Policy," *Journal of Psychoactive Drugs* 33(4) (2001), pp. 379–389; H. L. Surratt and J. A. Inciardi, "HIV Risk, Seropositivity and Predictors of Infection among Homeless and Non-Homeless Women Sex Workers in Miami, Florida, USA," *AIDS Care* 16(5) (2004), pp. 594–604; J. A. Inciardi, *Drug Use, Crime, and Violent Victimization among Indigent, Street Sex Workers in Miami, Florida,* 41st Annual Meeting Academy of Criminal Justice Sciences: Crime Prevention: One Goal, Multiple Approaches, Las Vegas, NV (2004); H. L. Surratt, J. A. Inciardi, et al., "Sex Work and Drug Use in a Subculture of Violence," *Crime & Delinquency* 50(1) (2004), pp. 43–59.

65. Philippe Bourgois, "Just Another Night on Crack Street," *New York Times Magazine,* 12 November 1989, pp. 52–53, 60–65, 94.

■ ■ ■ ■ ■

CHAPTER 7

BARS, FOOTBALLS, OCs, AND WATSON 387

Prescription Drug Abuse and Diversion in the Twenty-First Century

OxyContin, Vicodin, Xanax, Soma? Almost everyone has heard of these prescription drugs, and both the media and government agencies have given widespread attention to the problems associated with their abuse. To some members of Congress, they are the new "most dangerous substances on Earth." But is prescription drug abuse a new phenomenon, or is it just one of those things that keeps coming and going in the American drug scene? A related question is why has the media given so much attention to the abuse of prescription drugs, and particularly OxyContin? And besides OxyContin, as well as Vicodin, Xanax, and Soma, are there other prescription drugs being abused, and how many people are abusing them? Perhaps most interestingly, since you need a prescription to buy any and all of these drugs, how are they getting to the streets?

OPIOIDS, BENZOS, AND PRESCRIPTION STIMULANTS

There are literally thousands of prescription drugs, but the overwhelming majority have little or no abuse potential. Those typically seen on the streets and in the clubs are the *opioids, benzodiazepines,* and a variety of *stimulants.* The opioids are synthetic narcotics used in the treatment of acute and chronic pain. Benzodiazepines, or simply "benzos," a class of drugs with sedative, hypnotic, and muscle relaxant properties, are typically used for the short-term relief of severe, disabling anxiety or insomnia. And finally, stimulants increase alertness and wakefulness. In addition to stimulating the central nervous system, most stimulants also produce a sense of euphoria. The more commonly abused prescription opioids, benzodiazepines, and stimulants are briefly described below.

Opioids

Morphine (MS Contin, Kadian, Avinza, Roxinol), as noted in Chapter 2, is a potent painkiller and is the principal active agent in opium.

Hydrocodone (Vicodin, Lortab, Vicoprofen, Watson 387) is both a cough suppressant and an analgesic agent for the treatment of moderate to severe pain. Studies indicate that hydrocodone is nearly equivalent to morphine for pain relief. Hydrocodone is the most frequently prescribed opioid in the United States, with over 124 million prescriptions dispensed in 2005. There are several hundred brand name and generic hydrocodone products marketed. All are combination formulations, and the most frequently prescribed is hydrocodone with acetaminophen. Although there are scores of brand name and generic varieties of hydrocodone, most people think of them as Vicodin. Moreover, hydrocodone is likely the most abused of all prescription drugs. It has been rumored that Eminem, Courtney Love, and Michael Jackson are on the long A-list of stars who have had problems with it.

Hydromorphone, better known under the name of Dilaudid, is a semisynthetic narcotic analgesic marketed in both tablet and injectable forms. Although shorter acting than morphine, its potency is from two to eight times greater, and hence, it is a highly abusable drug. In some communities, Dilaudid is the substitute drug of choice among narcotics users when heroin supplies are low.

Oxycodone (Percocet, OxyContin, Percodan, and Tylox) is similar to other opioids but more potent and with a higher abuse liability and dependence potential. It is effective orally and is marketed in combination with other drugs for pain relief. Abusers take oxycodone orally, or dissolve the tablets in water, filter out the insoluble material, and inject the active drug.

Oxymorphone, known under the trade names of Opana and Numorphan, is a narcotic analgesic five times more potent than morphine that is used to relieve moderate to severe pain. It is available in tablet and injectable forms.

Fentanyl (Duragesic, Actiq, Sublimaze, and Fentora) is a short-acting analgesic perhaps 100 times more potent than morphine. The clinical use of fentanyl has increased significantly during the past decade. For example, fentanyl prescriptions increased from about 0.5 million in 1994 to 6.95 million in 2005. The drug is currently available in many dosage forms, including oral transmucosal lozenges ("lollipops"), effervescent buccal tablets, transdermal patches, and injectable formulations. Fentanyl is abused for its intense euphoric effects, and it often serves as a direct substitute for heroin in opioid-dependent individuals. Fentanyl patches are abused by removing the liquid contents and then injecting or ingesting the contents. Patches are highly sought after on the street because Fentanyl can not only be eaten or injected but also snorted, smoked, or even freebased. Used patches are attractive to abusers since a large percentage of fentanyl remains in patches even after three days of use.

Methadone, currently available in liquid, tablet, and wafer forms, was first synthesized during World War II by German chemists when supply lines for morphine were interrupted. Although chemically unlike morphine or heroin, it produces many of the same effects. Methadone was introduced in the United States in 1947 and quickly became the drug of choice in the detoxification of those dependent on heroin. Since the 1960s methadone has been in common use for the treatment of heroin dependence. Known as "methadone maintenance," the program takes advantage of methadone's unique properties as a narcotic. Like all narcotics, methadone is cross-dependent with heroin. As such, it is a substitute narcotic that prevents withdrawal. More importantly, however, methadone is orally effective, making intravenous use unnecessary. In addition, it is a longer-acting drug than heroin, with one oral dose lasting up to twenty-four hours. These properties have made methadone useful in the management of chronic narcotic dependence. Methadone is also prescribed by physicians for the treatment of pain.

Meperidine (Demerol) is chemically dissimilar to morphine but resembles it in its analgesic potency. It is used for the treatment of moderate to severe pain, and is administered both orally and by injection. Meperidine is uncommon as a primary drug of abuse. More typically, it is used recreationally by members of the health professions and others who have ready access to it.

Propoxyphine, sold under the trade names of Darvon and PP-Cap, was first marketed in 1957 for the treatment of mild to moderate pain. Less dependence producing than other narcotics, it is also less effective as an analgesic. Once the most widely prescribed analgesic drug in the United States, propoxyphine's questionable effectiveness as a painkiller has led to less widespread use as an analgesic. Nevertheless, it has a significant abuse potential and is occasionally seen on the street.

Pentazocine, sold under the trade name of Talwin, is a potent analgesic that is equivalent in effect to codeine. A recurrent problem with pentazocine has been the periodic appearance of "T's and Blues" (or "T's and B's"). T's and Blues involve a combination of pentazocine (Talwin/T's) and the antihistamine tripelennamine (Blues). Typically, two pentazocine tablets and one tripelennamine are crushed, dissolved in water, and injected intravenously. The injection use of this mixture reportedly produces a "rush" roughly equivalent in intensity to that of heroin, but lasting only five to ten minutes. If several successive injections are made, the euphoric effects are reported to last one to two hours.

Tramadol (Ultram) was introduced in 1995 for the treatment of mild to moderate pain. Postmarketing surveillance studies have documented that rates of abuse tend to be low and that it has not become popular as a street drug. Other forms of tramadol include Ultram ER, Ultracet, and Tramacet.

Benzodiazepines

Alprazolam (Xanax), known on the street as footballs and bars because of the pills' distinctive shapes, is an antianxiety agent used primarily for short-term relief of mild to moderate anxiety and nervous tension. Alprazolam is also effective in the treatment of activity depression or panic attacks. It is also a common "club drug" in the United States and is typically used for its euphoric effects.

Diazepam (Valium) is commonly used in the treatment of anxiety, insomnia, seizures, alcohol withdrawal, and muscle spasms.

Carisoprodol (Soma) is prescribed for the relief of pain, muscle spasm, and the limited mobility associated with painful musculoskeletal conditions. Although technically not a benzodiazepine, the drug shares some similarities with benzos, barbiturates, and alcohol in its pharmacological effects. Hence, it is widely abused as a recreational drug.

Stimulants

Adderall is an amphetamine used to treat attention-deficit hyperactivity disorder (ADHD), narcolepsy, and severe cases of depression.

Methylphenidate (Ritalin, Concerta) also is used in the treatment of attention-deficit hyperactivity disorder. It has a high potential for abuse and produces many of the same effects as cocaine or the amphetamines.

THE EPIDEMIOLOGY OF PRESCRIPTION DRUG ABUSE

The nonmedical use (abuse) of pharmaceuticals and prescription drugs has been a longstanding problem in the United States. It was noted earlier in Chapter 2 that the abuse of drugs in general, and pharmaceuticals in particular, may have started with a form of medicinal opium known as Dover's Powder.

More recently, the abuse of prescription drugs was especially noticeable during the 1960s and 1970s. For example, the first general population survey of drug abuse to be undertaken in the United States was conducted in New York state in 1970—one year before the first National Household Survey on Drug Abuse (NHSDA). The New York survey found the abuse of barbiturates and other sedatives, amphetamines and other stimulants, and other prescription drugs to be commonplace.[1] Subsequent surveys, as well as focused research studies, documented the continuing abuse of prescription drugs in later years,[2] and by the close of the 1990s it had become clear from data gathered through a variety of government agencies that prescription drug abuse was on the upswing, and that this was particularly the case with regard to prescription painkillers.[3] The concerns over the rise in prescription drug abuse is related to the numerous health consequences of such abuse, all of which have been well documented—tolerance, dependence, addiction, overdose, seizures, coma, impairment of functioning, and death, to name but a few.[4]

The precise number of prescription drug abusers is difficult to estimate, given the limitations of general population surveys. Nevertheless, when government attention began to focus on the issue in the early 2000s, some very good indicators were available. Exhibit 7.1 and 7.2, for example, summarize recent national survey data on selected prescription drugs, as compared with a number of illicit drugs, for 12-to-17-year-olds and 18-to-25-year-olds for the period 1999 through 2002.*

---

*Data are limited here to the period 1999 through 2002, the time of the reemergence of prescription drug abuse. More recent data appear in the Postscript of this chapter.

EXHIBIT 7.1   Estimated Numbers (in Thousands) of Lifetime and Past Year Abusers of Prescription and Illicit Drugs Among Persons Aged 12–17, 1999–2002

DRUG	LIFETIME				PAST YEAR			
	1999	*2000*	*2001*	*2002*	*1999*	*2000*	*2001*	*2002*
Any Illicit Drug	6,415	6,288	6,648	7,642	4,584	4,357	4,875	5,494
Benzos	574	595	617	834	362	373	409	568
Cocaine	551	550	525	670	373	389	349	508
Heroin	102	84	73	94	65	49	50	51
Inhalants	2,118	2,079	2,048	2,605	908	826	810	1,078
Marijuana	4,345	4,283	4,638	5,104	3,284	3,136	3,562	3,905
Pain Relievers	1,894	1,964	2,192	2,775	1,266	1,260	1,506	1,870

Source: National Survey on Drug Use and Health Statistics, SAMSHA Office of Applied Studies.

EXHIBIT 7.2   Estimated Numbers (in Thousands) of Lifetime and Past Year Abusers of Prescription and Illicit Drugs Among Persons Aged 18–25, 1999–2002

DRUG	LIFETIME				PAST YEAR			
	1999	*2000*	*2001*	*2002*	*1999*	*2000*	*2001*	*2002*
Any Illicit Drug	14,975	14,846	16,291	18,562	8,287	8,088	9,368	11,000
Benzos	2,239	2,158	2,598	3,473	894	883	1,244	1,144
Cocaine	3,383	3,148	3,803	4,786	1,493	1,274	1,681	2,087
Heroin	498	403	467	487	129	108	147	122
Inhalants	4,014	3,701	3,927	4,867	747	696	719	685
Marijuana	13,326	13,256	14,641	16,680	6,962	6,860	7,870	9,238
Pain Relievers	4,316	4,221	5,329	6,854	2,160	2,108	2,830	3,540

Source: National Survey on Drug Use and Health Statistics, SAMSHA Office of Applied Studies.

YOUTHS (12–17 YEARS)

- Overall, an estimated 568,000 youths ages 12 to 17 reportedly abused benzodiazepines and 1,870,000 abused prescription pain relievers during 2002.
- There was an increase from 1999 to 2002 in lifetime and past year abuse of all drugs except heroin.
- Marijuana/hashish reflected the highest reported use.
- Steady increases in number reporting lifetime abuse of benzodiazepines and pain relievers.
- Lifetime abuse of pain relievers rose from 8.2 percent to 11.2 percent between 1999 and 2002.

YOUNG ADULTS (18–25 YEARS)

- Overall, an estimated 1,144,000 young adults aged 18 to 25 reportedly abused benzodiazepines and 3,540,000 abused prescription pain relievers during 2002.
- Increase overall between 1999 and 2002 in lifetime abuse for all drugs except heroin.
- Marijuana was first in terms of lifetime and past year use; past year use of pain relievers ranked second.
- Among young adults aged 18 to 25, lifetime abuse of pain relievers rose from 15.2 to 22.1 percent.

Other research back in 2002 was documenting not only that the abuse of prescription drugs was widespread, but also that many youths were abusing several different prescription drugs at the same time. The 2002 Delaware Youth Survey, for example, included 84 percent of the state's 8th-graders and 74 percent of 11th-graders and asked questions about the abuse of prescription drugs. The abuse of prescription painkillers in the survey was defined as any use of OxyContin, Percocet, codeine, and/or Tylenol 3 "to get high." For 11th-graders, 15.5 percent reported having ever used painkillers, 10.7 percent reported use in the past year, and 4.2 percent reported use in the past month. Importantly, painkillers were the most abused drugs in the past year by 11th-graders after cigarettes, alcohol, and marijuana. For 8th-graders, 9.2 percent reported having ever used painkillers, 6.3 percent reported use in the past year, and 2.9 percent reported use in the past month. Painkillers were the most abused drugs in the past year by 8th-graders after cigarettes, alcohol, marijuana, and inhalants. Importantly, and as illustrated in Exhibit 7.3, significant proportions of 8th- and 11th-graders used prescription painkillers in the past year, and that those reporting painkiller use were far more involved in the concurrent use of alcohol, tobacco, and other drugs than those who did not use painkillers.[5]

OXYCONTIN: MIRACLE MEDICINE
OR DEVIL DRUG?

Of all the prescription drugs currently on the market, none have captured the attention of so many people as has OxyContin—known on the street as OC, oxy, oxycotton, hillbilly heroin, and the poor man's heroin. When it was first introduced in early 1996, it was hailed as a breakthrough in pain management, and it continues to capture the same positive attention. The medication is unique in that its time-release formula allows patients to enjoy continuous, long-term relief from moderate to severe pain. For many patients who had suffered for years from chronic pain, it gave them relief from suffering. But since the close of the 1990s OxyContin has received a substantial amount of negative attention as well—not for its medicinal effects, but for its addiction liability and abuse potential.[6]

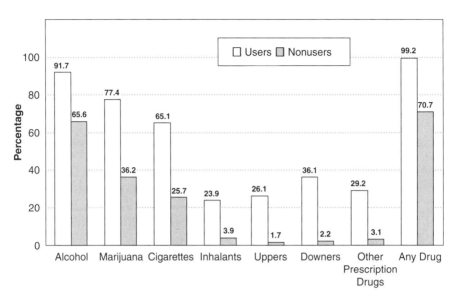

EXHIBIT 7.3   Past Year Use of Selected Drugs by Past Year Users and Nonusers of Painkillers among Delaware 11th-Graders, 2002

Source: J. A. Inciardi, H. L. Surratt, S. S. Martin, and R. E. Gealt, "Prevalence of Narcotic Analgesic Abuse among Students: Individual or Polydrug Abuse?" *Archives of Pediatric and Adolescent Medicine, 158*(5) (2004), pp. 498–499. Copyright © 2004, American Medical Association. All rights reserved.

OxyContin and Oxycodone

The active ingredient in OxyContin is "oxycodone," a drug that has been used for the treatment of pain for almost one hundred years. As noted earlier, oxycodone is a semisynthetic narcotic analgesic most often prescribed for moderate to severe pain, chronic pain syndromes, and terminal cancers. When used correctly under a physician's supervision, oxycodone can be highly effective in the management of pain, and there are scores of oxycodone products on the market—in various strengths and forms. Popular brands include Percocet and Percodan, Roxicet and Roxicodone, and Endocet, OxyIR, and Tylox to name but a few. However, no oxycodone product has generated as much attention as OxyContin.

Produced by the Stamford, Connecticut–based pharmaceutical company, Purdue Pharma L.P., OxyContin is unique because unlike other oxycodone products that typically contain aspirin or acetaminophen to increase or lengthen their potency, OxyContin is a single entity product that can provide up to 12 hours of continuous pain relief. Tablets are available in doses of 10, 20, 40, and 80 milligrams. The company also introduced a 160-milligram dose in July 2000 for its opioid-tolerant patients, only to later withdraw it from the market amidst controversy over its alleged abuse.[7] When the clinical trials for OxyContin were reviewed by the Food and Drug

Administration (FDA), the drug was demonstrated to be an effective analgesic in individuals with chronic, moderate to severe pain. Yet it was also judged by the FDA to carry a substantial risk of abuse because of its properties as a narcotic. As a result, OxyContin was approved by the FDA but placed in Schedule II of the Controlled Substances Act (CSA), which is the tightest level of control that can be placed on an approved drug for medical purposes. The placement of OxyContin in Schedule II warned physicians and patients that the drug carried a high potential for abuse and that it needed to be carefully managed, particularly among those at risk for substance abuse. In addition, in the *Physicians Desk Reference* and on the drug's package insert, OxyContin carries a boxed warning (more commonly known as the infamous "black box"), which boldly indicates:

WARNING:

OxyContin is an opioid agonist and a Schedule II controlled substance with an abuse liability similar to morphine.

Oxycodone can be abused in a manner similar to other opioid agonists, legal or illicit. This should be considered when prescribing or dispensing OxyContin in situations where the physician or pharmacist is concerned about an increased risk of misuse, abuse, or diversion.

OxyContin Tablets are a controlled-release oral formulation of oxycodone hydrochloride indicated for the management of moderate to severe pain when a continuous, around-the-clock analgesic is needed for an extended period of time.

OxyContin 80 mg Tablets ARE FOR USE IN OPIOID-TOLERANT PATIENTS ONLY. These tablet strengths may cause fatal respiratory depression when administered to patients not previously exposed to opioids.

OxyContin TABLETS ARE TO BE SWALLOWED WHOLE AND ARE NOT TO BE BROKEN, CHEWED, OR CRUSHED. TAKING BROKEN, CHEWED, OR CRUSHED OxyContin TABLETS LEADS TO RAPID RELEASE AND ABSORPTION OF A POTENTIALLY FATAL DOSE OF OXYCODONE.

Importantly, this "black box" voluntarily inserted in the packaging information by Purdue Pharma in 2001 alerted potential users with the notice that taking broken, chewed, or crushed tablets leads to rapid release and absorption of a potentially fatal dose of the drug. But even before the insertion of the "black box," drug abusers had figured out how to compromise OxyContin's controlled release formula and set off on a powerful high by injecting or snorting dissolved tablets or by crushing and ingesting them.

Diversion of OxyContin

Prescription drug diversion, discussed in considerable detail later in this chapter, involves the unlawful movement of regulated pharmaceuticals from legal sources to the illegal marketplace, and OxyContin's attractiveness to drug abusers resulted in its diversion in a number of ways. The major mechanisms include the illegal sale of prescriptions by physicians and pharmacists; "doctor shopping" by individuals who visit numerous physicians to obtain multiple prescriptions; the theft, forgery, or alteration of prescriptions by patients; robberies and thefts from pharmacies and pharmaceutical warehouses; and thefts of samples from physicians' offices as well as thefts of institutional drug supplies by health care workers. In all likelihood, OxyContin was, and continues to be, diverted through all of these routes.

Diversion has also occurred by means of fraud, particularly through the abuse of medical insurance programs. Medicaid fraud, in particular, presents an inexpensive mechanism for abusing drugs and oftentimes an easy route to a lucrative enterprise. For example, a Medicaid patient may pay only $3 for a bottle of 100 80-milligram OxyContin tablets. In communities where employment and money are scarce resources, the temptation to sell some of the pills for the going "street price" of $1 per milligram provides an opportunity to earn money. In this example, the $3 bottle from the pharmacy can net the patient up to $8,000 on the illegal market. If the patient needs more pills before a legitimate refill is possible, he or she may simply "doctor shop" a number of physicians for additional prescriptions and pay cash for the new supplies to avoid having the pharmacist check with the Medicaid people.

Going further, just one corrupt physician, pharmacist, health care worker, or other employee in the health care field can have a significant impact on the availability of the product as well. For example, before he was arrested in 2002, a Pennsylvania pharmacist had illegally sold hundreds of thousands of painkillers, including Oxy-Contin, over a three-year period. He made $900,000 on his transactions (only to lose it all in the stock market). Although he operated an independent neighborhood pharmacy, he was reportedly the state's third-largest purchaser of OxyContin.[8] Similarly, a number of physicians in Eastern Kentucky were arrested in 2003 for a variety of diversion schemes. One saw as many as 150 patients each day, writing narcotic prescriptions for them after a visit of less than three minutes. Another physician traded painkillers for sex with female patients whom he had addicted to narcotics. A third opened an office in a shopping mall where he generated prescriptions—one after another—almost as quickly as he could write them.[9]

OxyContin Abuse in the Early 2000s

Although there are several sources of national data on drug abuse that have been operating for decades, the collection of specific data on OxyContin abuse is quite recent. In the Monitoring the Future survey of drug abuse among high school students and young adults that has been conducted annually since 1975, the collection of information on OxyContin began only in 2002, and this was initiated at the request of Purdue

Pharma, the makers of OxyContin. The 2002 survey—conducted near the height of the furor over OxyContin—found that 4 percent of 12th-graders, 3 percent of 10th-graders, and 1.3 percent of 8th-graders had used OxyContin at least once during the past year. Interestingly, the use of Vicodin (hydrocodone) in the past year was at least double that of OxyContin—9.6 percent for 12th-graders, 6.9 percent for 10th-graders, and 2.5 percent for 8th-graders.[10] In the 2001 National Household Survey on Drug Abuse, another survey conducted annually (now called the National Survey on Drug Use and Health, or NSDUH), only "lifetime use" (at least once in a person's lifetime "to get high") data were collected for OxyContin. For persons aged 12 and over, less than one half of one percent reported having ever used OxyContin to get high.[11]

Because the Monitoring the Future and the National Household surveys are conducted with a high degree of scientific rigor, the estimates they generate for society's more "stable" at-home and in-school populations have a high degree of reliability. These should be contrasted with data from the Drug Abuse Warning Network, which tend to be somewhat problematic. More commonly known as DAWN, this large-scale information collection effort was designed to monitor changing patterns of drug abuse in the United States, and to serve as an early warning system for police, prevention, and treatment agencies. Hundreds of hospital emergency rooms and county medical examiners in major metropolitan areas across the United States report regularly to the DAWN system. However, because of the focus on large urban areas, the limitation to drug overdoses and other adverse reactions that result in a trip to the emergency room or county morgue, and the lack of information on specific brands of prescription drugs, DAWN data must be examined with considerable caution. Nevertheless, major pronouncements about drug abuse in the United States are often based solely on DAWN.

With regard to OxyContin, DAWN data indicate that the incidence of emergency room visits related to narcotic analgesic abuse had been on the rise since the mid-1990s, more than doubling between 1994 and 2001. The category with the largest increase during this period was oxycodone, at 352 percent, and most of the increases in narcotic analgesic mentions occurred toward the end of the 1990s, after OxyContin had been released to the market. Oxycodone mentions surged 186 percent from 1999 to 2000 and again by 70 percent from 2000 to 2001.[12] But since DAWN does not publish specific brand names of drugs, it is impossible to ascertain the exact number of episodes specifically related to OxyContin at any given time.

Going further, since many OxyContin overdoses likely occurred outside the DAWN reporting system—in rural areas such as Maine, West Virginia, and Kentucky—DAWN data were of no use for estimating the extent of the problem. To fill this gap, the Drug Enforcement Administration (DEA) started actively collecting and analyzing data from medical examiners in an attempt to establish the extent of the "OxyContin problem." Medical examiner reports from 2000–2001 from 32 states reported that 949 deaths were associated with oxycodone, of which almost half (49%) were "likely" related to OxyContin.[13] However, careful scrutiny of the data paints a more cautious picture; because there are a multitude of oxycodone products on the market, it is impossible to determine the specific brand of drug found in a cadaver. Nevertheless, out of the 949 deaths, DEA reported that 146 were "OxyContin verified," whereas another 318 were "OxyContin likely." To make things even more complicated, the majority of the toxicological analyses reported "poly" or "multiple-drug use," suggesting that the death may have been the result of an overdose induced by a combination of substances, not just oxycodone by itself. When taking all of these factors into consideration, it is very difficult to establish a direct link between OxyContin and cause of death.

A recent study published in the *Journal of Analytical Toxicology* attempted to more scientifically unravel the questions about OxyContin-related deaths. Based on data from over one thousand deaths reported by medical examiners and coroners from twenty-three states from August 27, 1999, through January 17, 2002, the study results were an interesting contrast to those being pushed by DEA. The conclusion was that OxyContin alone was found in only 1.3 percent of the cases examined. Of the 1,014 cases, 90.6 percent of the deaths involved drug abuse; the remainder were due to other causes. Of the drug abuse deaths, 96.7 percent were found to have multiple drugs present.[14] DEA officials countered that polydrug use is often part of patients' overall treatment regimens, such as the coadministration of antidepressants. They emphasized that it should not be surprising to find that many of the deaths were associated with multiple drugs but insist that this should not override the significance of OxyContin's role in the patients' deaths.[15]

The DEA Office of Diversion Control attempted to bolster its case against OxyContin by stressing that property and other crimes related to the abuse of the drug increased by as much as 75 percent in some parts of the United States, with new OxyContin-related arrests increasing from sixty-seven in 2000 to 277 in 2001.[16] Although no one is questioning the validity of these arrest figures, there is a problem with these kinds of data. The nineteenth-century French sociologist Emile Durkheim once commented that a community has as much crime as it has people to count it.[17] In other words, the DEA arrest data, to a very great extent, followed a "Field of Dreams" scenario—"if you look for it, you will find it." If DEA had placed the same focus on the trafficking and illegal distribution of Xanax or Vicodin or Percocet or Ritalin or some other highly abusable prescription drug as it had on OxyContin, increasing numbers of arrests would have occurred as well.

A National OxyContin Epidemic?

OxyContin abuse first surfaced in rural Maine during the late 1990s, soon after spreading down the east coast and Ohio Valley and then into rural Appalachia. Communities in western Virginia, eastern Kentucky, West Virginia, and southern Ohio were especially hard hit, and a number of factors characteristic of these areas seem to correlate with their apparent high rates of abuse. In northern Maine and rural Appalachia, for example, there are aspects of the culture that are markedly different from those in other parts of the country. Many of the communities are quite small and isolated, often situated in the mountains and "hollers" (small crevicelike mountain dens and valleys) a considerable distance from major towns and highways. As a result, many of the usual street drugs are simply not available. Instead, locals make do with resources already on hand, like prescription drugs. In addition, isolation impacts heavily on options for amenities and entertainment—a major contrast to the distractions of metropolitan areas. Many substance abuse treatment patients in these rural areas have told their counselors that they started using drugs because of boredom. Many start abusing drugs quite young, as well. According to one treatment counselor in Maine, the average age of drug experimentation and abuse in that state is nine. Young people begin with marijuana and alcohol, progressing on to other drugs as they move into their teenage years.[18]

Many adults in these rural areas tend to suffer from chronic illnesses and pain syndromes, born out of hard lives of manual labor in perilous professions—coal mining, logging, fishing, and other blue-collar industries—which often result in serious and debilitating injuries. As a result, a disproportionately high segment of the population lives on strong painkillers. The use of pain pills evolves into a kind of coping mechanism, and the practice of self-medication becomes a way of life for many. As such, the use of narcotic analgesics has become normalized and integrated into the local culture. No one understands this cycle better then the people who live in the region and who are most affected by the problem. As the director of Kentucky's Division of Substance Abuse once summarized: "there is a cultural history of solving problems through medication."[19] A Kentucky prosecutor who was focusing on drug crimes concurred: "A lot of places, you got a headache, you'll tough it out," he says. "Down here," he continued, "it's like, 'Well, my grandfather's got some drugs. I'll take that and it'll go away.' And it just escalates."[20]

Based on treatment admissions data from a number of states, it had been suggested in numerous media outlets that the abuse of OxyContin was on the rise, and that its popularity had spread beyond the rural East Coast to other parts of the United States. At the same time, however, there was also concern that the media was playing an integral role in boosting the drug's popularity.

"Hillbilly Heroin" and the Crazed Media Frenzy

Media outlets in Maine began reporting on OxyContin abuse in early 2000. The *Bangor Daily News,* for example, ran several features which included information not only about the properties of the drug, but also about: (1) how to compromise its time-release mechanism, (2) the tactics of diversion that people were using to obtain the drug (including Medicaid fraud), and (3) the concerns of the medical profession about the potential for abusing the drug. In addition, numerous examples of alleged OxyContin-related crimes were described in detail.

A smattering of news articles followed in other parts of the nation, but in May of 2000 the *Boston Globe* became the first major daily to focus on OxyContin. The lead commanded readers' attention by reporting that even a town sheriff in rural Maine was "scared" of the situation—because of an unusually large number of people being arrested for drug-related crimes, the sheriff noted, the inmate population at the local jail had grown well over capacity.[21] The following month, the New Orleans

Times-Picayune quoted a local DEA supervisor who referred to OxyContin as the "new Vicodin" (hydrocodone). In the same article, an anonymous prescription drug abuser added: "You get kind of like a Vicodin feeling, but a little heavier [with Oxy-Contin]."[22]

Media coverage changed dramatically after Kentucky's sensational "Operation OxyFest 2001," when more than one hundred police officers from numerous jurisdictions worked together to arrest 207 OxyContin users and dealers throughout the state. The arrests made for good headlines, and many local officials were more than happy to vie for their personal fifteen minutes of fame. The most colorful of these was Detective Roger Hall of the Harlan County Kentucky Sheriff's Department, who was quoted as saying that abusers "will kick a bag of cocaine aside to get Oxy."[23] Never mind that comparing cocaine, a stimulant, to OxyContin, a depressant, is like comparing Mountain Dew to Chamomile tea, the national media had their hook and a sexy sound bite and they certainly ran with it.

A blitz of national media coverage followed. The Associated Press, *Time, Newsweek,* the *New York Times,* and other media giants, as well as local newspapers across the nation such as the *Orlando Sentinel,* ran alarming stories about the potentially lethal and dangerous new drug. Much of the initial coverage of OxyContin seemed to follow a similar formula: it started off with the personal tale of a chronically ill patient for whom OxyContin had suddenly made life worth living, followed by a contrasting tale of a lowly, depraved junkie who had become a slave to the drug, all the while littering the piece with both information and misinformation about the drug. And slang labels like "OCs," "Oxys," "hillbilly heroin," and the "poor man's heroin" (because it was being used by rural laborers) started to permeate the national vocabulary.

As has always been the case with drugs, coverage of the issue was generally presented in terms of black and white, good versus evil. And much of it was irresponsible—designed more to titillate and expand circulation than to report the truth. "The media presented the drug problem as a war of the holy people against the depraved people, and we haven't gone far past that moralizing tone," noted nationally respected media critic Norman Solomon.[24] Headlines screamed about OxyContin-related crimes, including pharmacy breakins and terrifying accounts of elderly patients' homes being invaded and raided for the drug. Some stories of robberies appeared in local media outlets, only to be followed by a string of copycat attempts. There were numerous stories of physicians who ran "pill mills" to feed the addiction of their clients, as well as contrasting stories of other doctors who had been scared off from prescribing the drug. There were numerous reports of pharmacies that had stopped stocking the drug for fear of inviting crime. All of these things had actually happened, but not to the extent that the media portrayed.

The major television networks, not to be outdone, recognized the potential to capitalize on the OxyContin media frenzy. For example, ABC's "20/20" prime-time news-magazine story was called "What the doctor ordered: Young people hooked on a miracle painkiller." But the story was clearly a setup. In her opening remarks, Barbara Walters gravely warned that every family with children should pay attention to the impending segment. Then correspondent Lynn Sherr talked about her trip to Portsmouth, Ohio, to document one physician's "pill mill" that fed the addiction of locals and others who said they traveled from as far away as Texas to obtain painkiller prescriptions. The camera showed the orthopedic surgeon's dilapidated office, a broken X-ray machine, and even beer cans littering the waiting room. At a dramatic high point in the segment the camera zoomed in on the lengthy list of prescriptions that the aberrant physician had written for his patients. Never mind that most of the scripts had been for Lortab and Soma; the cameras cleverly focused on a few OxyContin prescriptions—highlighting and enlarging them for the audience to see. And then, after detailing a sad story of a young married man's overdose death, blamed on the physician's unscrupulous prescribing practices, and the plea bargain he reached with the local prosecutor, Ms. Sherr closed the story by saying she wasn't sure of the exact statistics, but "several dozen" people in Kentucky had already died from OxyContin overdoses. She called the situation "insidious."[25] Oh well.

Numerous sources likened the "OxyContin epidemic" to that of the "crack epidemic" of the 1980s, and as far as the media coverage of the issues is concerned, there are indeed striking similarities. Media hype tends to have a profound influence on the public's perception of the issues. For example, the journalism watchdog group Fairness and Accuracy In Reporting (FAIR) did an interesting analysis of media coverage and public opinion back in the 1980s, during the height of the crack scare. FAIR reported that in 1985, the *New York Times* published an average of 36 articles per month on drug use and trafficking. In November 1985, crack warranted front-page coverage and the *Times* assigned a full-time reporter to the drug beat. Between July and October 1986, the *Times* increased its coverage to a monthly average of 103 articles, with coverage peaking in September at 169 articles. This coincided with Ronald and Nancy Reagan's infamous "Just Say No" speech, to which Congress responded by approving a new $1.7 billion drug package, apparently appeasing the media and the public alike, as coverage and worries over the drug issue subsided.[26]

A second wave of public drug fear coincided with coverage of George Bush's presidential election in 1988, in which drug abuse was a central campaign issue. In September of that year, in sync with Bush's Oval Office speech on the evils of drugs, the *Times* published 238 articles on drugs, which breaks down to almost seven per day. By the close of September, 64 percent of the American public agreed that drugs were more grave a threat than nuclear war, environmental destruction, AIDS, and poverty.[27]

In a similar manner, the media introduced the OxyContin "epidemic" to the general public. A study published in the *Journal of Toxicology* tracked articles from two large regional newspapers that associated adverse human health effects with drugs, toxins, or other poisonous chemical substances. Within this criterion, articles on chemical and biological warfare (which dramatically spiked after September 11) were the most prevalent topic, followed by therapeutic drugs. Of the individual nonwarfare articles, the two topics with the greatest coverage were medical marijuana (29 stories) and OxyContin abuse (20 stories).[28]

In 2001, the international media began following their American counterparts, as outlets in Europe and more recently Australia began to publish sensational articles about OxyContin. For example, *The Mirror* (UK) featured a story that proclaimed, "A dangerous new drug is on the verge of flooding Ireland's inner city," and that "OxyContin is fast replacing other hard drugs as a way for pushers to trap new customers."[29] An *Observer* (UK) headline reported in April 2002 that an 18-year-old girl became the UK's first OxyContin overdose victim, a drug that "already killed over 300 in America."[30] Interestingly, the story accompanying the headline was actually a feature that had previously appeared in the *New York Times Magazine* in July of 2001. At about the same time, a story called "Epidemic fear as 'hillbilly heroin' hits the streets" described the overdose death of the 18-year-old woman, who reportedly drank, smoked, and ingested "up to seven oxycodone" in a night of partying with her friends. The piece also reported that OxyContin was becoming popular in Manchester and Ireland and reiterated that the drug was responsible for "hundreds of deaths in America . . . prompting fears among police, customs officers and drug workers that it could give rise to a whole new generation of addicts."[31]

Other stories followed, patterning themselves after the media reports seen in the United States. But some readers quickly realized that much of it was media hype. The "Hillbilly Heroin" story in the *Observer* prompted a biting Letter to the Editor from a New Yorker who offered his own perspective on the matter:

> The OxyContin scare in the US is as much a product of the media as it is a genuine "epidemic"; few of the people who become addicted here were taking it for legitimate reasons in the first place. Is it really a surprise that people who already abuse drugs will seek the latest "stronger than heroin" substance?[32]

As the frantic pace of OxyContin stories began to ease in early 2003, pain management specialist Dr. Steven D. Passik wrote in a Letter to the Editor to the *Journal of Pain and Symptom Management* in March 2003:

> . . . I have lost even more respect for the media . . . the media's loss of interest in the story shows that they were less concerned about the suffering in places like Eastern Kentucky and Maine, and more concerned about making headlines and capturing the fickle American attention span and demonizing the pharmaceutical industry. The OxyContin story has gone the way of Monica, Mark McGuire's supplements, and countless other pseudo-scandals.[33]

In retrospect, it would appear that although the abuse of OxyContin was indeed (and continues to be) real, it is just one of many drugs that are abused by individuals whose drug-taking and drug-seeking behaviors focus on prescription painkillers, and others who are looking to get high on the latest fad drug. It also appears that the media stories may have contributed to shifting OxyContin abuse from a regional problem to a national problem. And clearly, OxyContin abuse is anything but an "epidemic." Nevertheless, all of the attention given to OxyContin prompted U.S. government involvement. In response to the heightened awareness of OxyContin abuse, DEA launched its own comprehensive plan to prevent the illegal distribution of the product. Their broad goals include enforcement and intelligence; regulatory and administrative authority; industry cooperation; and awareness, education, and outreach initiatives.

THE DIVERSION OF PRESCRIPTION MEDICATIONS

The Drug Enforcement Administration has estimated that prescription drug diversion, defined earlier in this chapter as the unlawful channeling of regulated pharmaceuticals from legal sources to the illicit marketplace,[34] is a $25 billion-a-year industry,[35] and that diversion can occur along all points in the drug delivery process, from the original manufacturing site to the wholesale distributor, the physician's office, the retail pharmacy, or the patient.[36]

Diversion can occur in many ways, including the illegal sale of prescriptions by physicians and what are referred to on the street as "loose" pharmacists; "doctor shopping" by individuals who visit numerous physicians to obtain multiple prescriptions; theft, forgery, or alteration of prescriptions by health care workers and patients; robberies and thefts from manufacturers, distributors, and pharmacies; and thefts of institutional drug supplies.[37] Furthermore, there is growing evidence that the diversion of significant amounts of prescription opioids and benzodiazepines occurs through residential burglaries as well as cross-border smuggling at both retail and wholesale levels.[38] In addition, recent research has documented diversion through such other channels as "shorting" (undercounting) and pilferage by pharmacists and pharmacy employees, recycling of medications by pharmacists and pharmacy employees, medicine cabinet thefts by cleaning and repair personnel in residential settings, theft of guests' medications by hotel repair and housekeeping staff, and Medicare, Medicaid, and other insurance fraud by patients, pharmacists, and street dealers.[39] Moreover, it would appear that pill-abusing middle and high school students are obtaining their drugs through medicine cabinet thefts, medication trading at school, and thefts and robberies of medications from other students. Finally, a number of observers consider the Internet to be a significant source for illegal purchases of prescription drugs.[40]

Although national surveys and monitoring systems have been documenting widespread abuse of prescription drugs, and numerous scientific papers over the years have discussed the problems associated with diversion,[41] discussions of the scope and magnitude of diversion, as well as patterns of diversion associated with specific drugs of abuse, different user populations, and/or other demographic, sociocultural, and psychosocial factors, are few in number.

Diversion can be described as a disorganized for-profit industry. It is referred to here as "disorganized" because there are so many different players involved in the phenomenon, including physicians, pharmacists, and other health care professionals; drug abusers, patients, students, street dealers, pill brokers, and white collar criminals; and tourists, saloonkeepers, and all types of service personnel to name but a few. The range of diversion is so broad, furthermore, that answers as to what the major sources of diversion are really depend on whom you ask. A few federal agencies maintain that diverted drugs enter the illegal market primarily through "doctor shoppers," inappropriate prescribing practices by physicians, and improper dispensing by pharmacists. Internet sales have also been identified as a major source of diversion by other federal authorities.[42] By contrast, as an adjunct to an ongoing postmarketing surveillance program to monitor the diversion and abuse of oxycodone and a variety of other prescription opioids,[43] in 2005 diversion investigators in 300 police and regulatory agencies participating in this nationwide surveillance program were surveyed. Responses by survey participants reflected a wider assortment of diversion mechanisms.[44] For example, as illustrated in Exhibit 7.4, although almost three-fourths of the survey participants considered drug abusers posing as patients as the major source of diversion (through doctor shopping and prescription theft/forgery), a variety of other mechanisms were also recognized.

Studying Prescription Drug Diversion

In an attempt to develop a better understanding of how specific drug-using populations are diverting prescription opioids and other medications, or obtaining controlled drugs that have already been diverted, during 2004 and 2005 the author of this book participated in a series of studies in Miami, Florida. Focus groups were conducted with individuals from three drug-using street- and club-based populations:

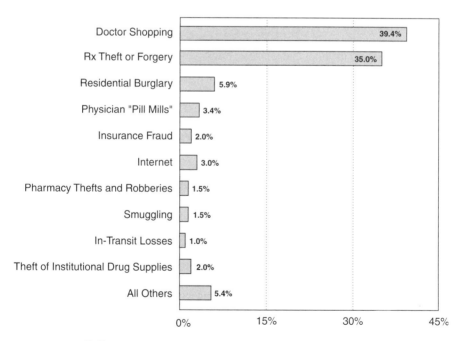

EXHIBIT 7.4   Police and Regulatory Agency Perceptions of the Primary Sources of Prescription Drug Diversion

Source: J. A. Inciardi, H. L. Surratt et al. "Mechanisms of Prescription Drug Diversion Among Drug-Involved Club- and Street-Based Populations," *Pain Medicine 8* (2) (2007), p. 173. Reprinted by permission of Blackwell Publishing.

(1) eight groups with 30 young adult Ecstasy users; (2) four groups with seventeen crack-cocaine and heroin users; and (3) one group of eight methadone maintenance clients. An individual in-depth interview was also conducted with a local prescription drug dealer.* The findings of these inquiries were quite illuminating.

The Club Culture.   Previous work in Miami revealed that in a sample of 186 Ecstasy users recruited from the local club scene, more than 80 percent reported the abuse of opioids, sedatives, and/or stimulants.[45] The average age of onset for the abuse of opioids was 18 years, and in the past twelve months, 23 percent had abused OxyContin, 33 percent other oxycodone products, 40 percent hydrocodone, and 8 percent morphine. None of this prescription drug use was for legitimate medical purposes or under the supervision of a physician. Moreover, polydrug use was common in that 29 percent of the sample reported using one or more prescription medications together with Ecstasy.

To further investigate the unexpected findings of widespread prescription drug abuse in this population, a total of thirty male and female club-drug users aged 18 to 45 from a wide variety of ethnic backgrounds were recruited for participation in eight focus groups. Although a minority of participants described experimenting with prescription drugs in junior and senior high school, most said that their abuse of prescription opioids and tranquilizers quickly followed their introduction to street stimulants, primarily methamphetamine and Ecstasy, for the purpose of easing their coming down from the high that the latter drugs produced. Participants indicated that Ecstasy and methamphetamine were often "packaged" by local drug dealers together with prescription opioids or depressants because of the popular demand for a smooth "landing." Antidepressants were also commonly used by Ecstasy and methamphetamine users to ease withdrawal-related depression.

Three additional patterns of continuing club/prescription polydrug abuse were noted among focus group participants: prescription drugs in combination with, as substitutes for, or as alternatives to, club drugs. The use of prescription drugs in combination with club drugs was for the purpose of achieving "a better high." Focus group participants cited numerous examples of preferred drug combinations, including: marijuana, methylphenidate, and alcohol; depressants and/or opioids with methamphetamine; codeine with Ecstasy; and hydrocodone with cocaine. One individual recalled having had an "excellent" night out after ingesting "4 Seroquels, 3 Lillys (olanzapine), 2 'bars' (2 mg Xanax), alcohol, marijuana, and cocaine," after which he claimed to have successfully driven a carload of friends home. As substitutes, participants described the interchangeability of certain club and prescription drugs for the same intended purpose, as in substituting phentermine for methamphetamine to get high, GHB for painkillers plus alcohol to feel drunk, or Xanax or marijuana to ease withdrawal from stimulants. The third pattern involved the use of

---

*For a detailed discussion of the methods used in this study, see J. A. Inciardi, H. L. Surratt, et al., "Mechanisms of Prescription Drug Diversion among Drug Involved Club- and Street-Based Populations," *Pain Medicine* 8(2) (2007), pp. 171–183.

prescription drugs as alternatives for getting high when club drugs were either unavailable or of poor quality.*

Sources of abused prescription drugs cited by focus group participants were extremely diverse, including their physicians, club drug dealers, parents and other relatives, doctor shopping, leftover supplies following an illness or injury, prescriptions intended for the treatment of mental illness, direct sales on the street and in nightclubs, pharmacy and hospital theft, friends or acquaintances, under-the-door apartment flyers advertising telephone numbers to call, "stealing from grandma's medicine cabinet," and personal visits to Mexico, South America, and the Caribbean.

Several participants noted that a major mechanism for obtaining prescription drugs was through Miami Beach "pill brokers" who routinely worked with elderly patients. One individual commented, for example:

> The main source of how people (pill brokers) get these pills is Medicare and Medicaid fraud. They'll send an old man into a pharmacy or they'll send him to a doctor who's a little bit crooked. He's got a broken arm or a bad hip. He complains of pain. Doctor knows what's going on— he gets kickbacks from patients coming in and stuff through Medicaid. He gets paid for every patient that he sees. We did it with a gentleman who went in to see a doctor and was prescribed OxyContin. So we went right in to Walgreen's to get them. Then someone (the pill broker) comes over and hands us $680 for the OxyContins, I think it was what, 80 pills maybe? He got the pills, and I can only imagine the kind of money he made off of them.

This individual also indicated:

> They (the pill brokers) were in our neighborhood one night asking for people with the red, white, and blue card, which is the Medicare/Medicaid card. And if you had one, they'd sign you up right there. I think they paid them $50 for signing up right there on the spot. They also paid them the $80 for the doctor's visit, and $200 for the pills.

All participants reported having no difficulty in getting prescription medications, although they were often happy to take what was available without seeking out a specific drug or brand name. Those who had relocated to Miami from other cities indicated that the Miami illicit prescription drug market was significantly easier to navigate than other places they had lived, including New York and Boston. Street prices were reportedly much lower in Miami than those offered by domestic and

---

*A number of the participants also described the practice of "colon rolling," also known as "booty bumping"—dissolving prescription and other drugs and then taking the solution rectally with an eye dropper or turkey baster. This anal route of administration was preferred by some because of the slower and more even onset of the effect of the drug. Of particular note in this regard is the "Royal Flush"—a rectally delivered combination of Ecstasy, methamphetamine, and Viagra.

international online pharmacies. For example, whereas OxyContin typically sells for $1 per milligram in most parts of the United States, the street price in Miami is only 50 cents per milligram. Although focus group participants generally described the "high" from prescription drugs as less exciting and less euphoric than that of illicit drugs, prescription drugs were uniformly perceived to be purer, safer, more respectable, more legal, and having fewer withdrawal symptoms.

Street-Based Crack, Cocaine, and Heroin Users. Four focus groups with 17 street drug users were also conducted. Although all had prior or current involvement in prescription drug abuse, their careers in substance abuse typically began with alcohol, marijuana, and cocaine—not prescription drugs. The primary prescription drugs of abuse mentioned were Vicodin, OxyContin, Percocet, Xanax, and Valium. Participants also noted that there was significant abuse among street populations of psychotropic medications used for the treatment of schizophrenia, depression, and anxiety disorders—"psych meds" as they are referred to on the street—such as Zoloft, Paxil, and Seroquel. Although a small number of participants initially acquired prescription drugs to treat legitimate medical conditions, the majority began their involvement in order to moderate the effects of street drugs, or as substitutes for cocaine, crack, and heroin. Specifically, sedative drugs were commonly used to "come down" from crack runs or binges or to "mellow out" without having to purchase and consume alcohol, and prescription analgesics were used as "get-high drugs" when street drugs were unavailable.

A primary focus of the groups was to elucidate the sources of abused prescription drugs reaching the streets. In this population of street drug users, diverse methods of acquisition were mentioned, although they diverged somewhat from those available to higher socioeconomic status individuals. None of the street-based participants, for example, cited the Internet or personal travel as means to access prescription drugs. Among these individuals, the primary sources for acquiring prescription drugs were street dealers, script doctors, illegal sales in small pharmacies, acquaintances who sell their personal prescriptions, doctor shopping, friends and family members, sex workers' clients, disability patients, Medicaid recipients, and personal prescriptions intended for the treatment of drug dependence or mental illness. There was consensus among the participants that script doctors were a reliable source of access to prescription medications, as the supplies available through street dealers and other sources were inconsistent, and tended to wane by the end of each month. Knowledge of particular script doctors was common, as was awareness of the elaborate systems in place to transport individuals with Medicaid coverage to doctors' offices and pharmacies to obtain and fill illegitimate prescriptions for later resale. Commonly described scenarios for prescription drug access included:

> They have people that come pick you up and take you to the clinic, to the pharmacy, put the prescription in, get the pills, and come back. I was introduced to a couple of people in a doctor's office. This was people on Medicaid getting their script drugs and would take it to another source and sell the whole bottle. We're talking like 30 to 60 people and it was like a ring and everybody knew who was getting what and if they wanted

it, they'd call that person up. "Hey, have you been to the doctor yet? I've got a buyer for this." They'd go to the doctor right then.

A repeated theme was the involvement of certain pharmacies in Medicaid fraud. One focus group participant elaborated on the illegal pharmacy sales:

> There is this pharmacy that will sell you the pills through Medicaid and buy them back. One time this girl asked me "Did you get your pills today?" I said, "Yeah, why?" She said . . . she said, "Well next time you can go over there to that pharmacy. He'll give them to you and buy them right back from you. You get them off Medicaid and he'll pay you money for them and put them right back on his shelf and sell them again higher." So, say I pay him $15 for the pills under Medicaid, and they're worth $1,000 on the street. So then he might give me $100 or $500 for them. Then they go back on the shelf and he sells them again, and he sells for $1000 and then he's making that $1000 over and over and over.

A number of focus group participants detailed the process of buying and selling their own medications on the street. For example:

> A lot of people out there are selling their pills. Most of it comes from people you know, but then you get a lot of people coming through that have scripts and they want to sell their pills. You could sell or trade. They want to get rock (crack) or they want cocaine and you switch one for the other. Cocaine for OxyContins. Crack for bars (Xanax). I mean that's how a lot of it comes out here. I mean you don't even have to look for it. It will come to you. Some of them you know from around but some of them you don't even know. They'll drive up to you. They just drive up looking. They will drive up to me and ask me, "You know anybody that wants to buy these?" Or they may ask what you have to sell.

Another focus group member added:

> I'm currently on psychotropic medications and I can get any kind of psych meds I want. All I have to do is go ask my psychiatrist. "Hey I need this." Boom, here it is and I'll get it and most of the time I won't take it because they do knock you down and you can't function. So I sell them on the street.

Methadone Maintenance Treatment Clients.   Eight clients enrolled in a large methadone treatment clinic also participated in a focus group discussion on prescription drug abuse and diversion. All had extensive histories of prescription drug use, both legitimate and illegitimate, primarily with opioids, benzodiazepines, amphetamines, and antipsychotic and antianxiety medications. Several were enrolled in more than one methadone program, and they supplemented their methadone supplies with street purchases of liquid methadone or tablets from pain clinics. For the most part, they echoed the street participants' accounts of prescription drug acquisition, but placed special emphasis on methadone clinics as ideal locations offering virtually unfettered access to any variety of medications. As one participant stated:

> Most people wouldn't think of this but at a methadone clinic, everybody that is either looking to get rid of something, or looking to purchase something, will come around a methadone clinic and will come up to you and say, "I've got Xanax." As a matter of fact, last week I had three people come up to me and tell me they had methadone biscuits and Dilaudid and Xanax.

Another agreed:

> When I was traveling and I was looking for drugs, whether it be prescription or not prescription and I didn't know where to go in the city, the first thing I did was look up the closest methadone clinic. You can always find something at the methadone clinic, no matter where it is. No matter what state it's in.

Other Sources of Diversion

Doctor shoppers, physicians, and the Internet receive much of the attention regarding diversion, yet there is evidence suggesting that residential burglaries, pharmacy robberies and thefts, and "sneak thefts"—the distracting of merchants by one individual while another "sneaks" behind a counter or into a storage room to steal—contribute more to the diversion problem than previously recognized.

Residential Burglary.   According to the Federal Bureau of Investigation, there were an estimated 3.5 million residential burglaries in the United States during 2006, and there is evidence to suggest that prescription drugs are a major target in a significant portion of these crimes. In scores of focus groups and in-depth interviews conducted by the author with hundreds of drug-involved offenders, active street drug users, and recovering addicts in several states over the past decade, there was a consensus that the four items typically sought in residential burglaries are cash, jewelry, guns, and prescription drugs. This contention, furthermore, is substantiated in the many thousands of newspaper articles each year describing the items stolen in burglaries and home invasions[46] and from studies conducted by the Department of Justice[47] and other independent researchers.[48]

Contacts with drug-involved offenders also identified specific types of residential burglaries that target prescription drugs. One of these is known as "obituary shopping." Typically, the perpetrator scans the obituaries in local newspapers looking for the funeral dates and times for individuals who likely passed away as the result of chronic diseases requiring strong pain medications. The home of the deceased is then burglarized during the memorial service or funeral. Another approach involves the stalking of patients attending pain clinics, following them to learn where they reside, and then burglarizing their homes at some later date. A related issue is the filing of false reports to the police and insurance companies regarding burglaries in which prescription opioids were allegedly stolen, with the purpose of getting replacement prescriptions from one or more physicians and/or pharmacists.[49]

Pharmacy Losses.   With respect to robberies, burglaries, and other losses through shoplifting, employee pilferage, and "sneak thefts" by professional thieves from pharmacies, distributors, hospitals/clinics, treatment programs, or any other business or organization where controlled substances are stored, the DEA requires that its Form 106 (Report of Theft or Loss of Controlled Substances) describing such losses be immediately filed. Although Form 106 data are not routinely tabulated and published, what has been released suggests the potential magnitude of losses. During 2001 through 2003, for example, some 563,677 "standard dosage units" of methadone (one methadone dosage unit in DEA terminology = 10 mg) were reported as lost or stolen. Some 37.3 percent of these occurred through night break-ins, 23.1 percent through employee pilferage, 14.3 percent through in-transit losses, 6.4 percent through armed robberies, and 18.6 percent through "all other" mechanisms.[50] For OxyContin, DEA reported that during the period January 2000 through June 2003, almost 1.4 million tablets were lost or stolen in 2,494 separate incidents.[51] Almost half the losses (47.3%) occurred through night break-ins, followed by robberies (29.0%), employee pilferage (16.5%), in-transit losses (6.3%), and customer theft (0.8%). More recently, a request by the University of Wisconsin under the Freedom of Information Act yielded additional data on this topic.[52] During 2000 through 2003 in 22 eastern states, there were a total of 12,894 theft/loss incidents reported to DEA, involving some twenty-eight million dosage units of controlled substances. Almost 90 percent of the reports came from pharmacies. The total number of dosage units lost or stolen for selected opioids were as follows:

Oxycodone	4,434,731
Morphine	1,026,184
Methadone	454,503
Hydromorphone	325,921
Meperidine	132,950
Fentanyl	81,371

In addition, loss estimates for hydrocodone—the most widely prescribed and most frequently diverted of all controlled substances—amounted to some four million dosage units lost or stolen in 2003 alone. As such, these data suggest that massive quantities of prescription opioids, regardless of schedule, are being stolen prior to being prescribed.

The Internet.   Without question, prescription drugs are illegally purchased over the Internet,[53] but its role as a source for drugs may be overstated. A national probability sample of adults polled by the Pew Internet and American Live Project in 2004 found that only 4 percent of Americans had ever used the Internet to purchase drugs and that most sites required a physician's prescription.[54] The major reason for not purchasing from Internet sources was the belief that the drugs were not safe. And interestingly in this regard, during numerous structured interviews and focus groups with scores of prescription drug abusers in the Miami club culture, it was repeatedly emphasized that they deliberately avoided the Internet as a source for drugs, because of "ripoffs," because prescription drugs are generally cheaper on the street than on the Internet, and because "big brother" is always watching.

POSTSCRIPT

By the close of 2006, it appeared that the abuse of prescription medications had become a major public health issue, and that the abuse of prescription medications among youth had become widespread. As illustrated in Exhibit 7.5, marijuana continued to be the

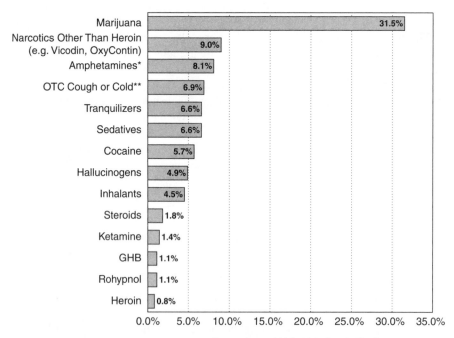

Percentage of U.S. 12th-Grade Students

*Amphetamines include Ritalin (4.4%) and methamphetamine (2.5%).
**Used for the explicit purpose of getting high.

EXHIBIT 7.5   Percentage of U.S. 12th-Grade Students Reporting Past Year Use of Drugs (Other Than Alcohol and Tobacco), 2006

Source: Monitoring the Future study, Institute for Social Research, University of Michigan.

most prevalent illicit drug used among U.S. high school seniors, but after that, the non-medical use of narcotic drugs ranked second. More specifically, nearly one in ten 12th-grade students reported using prescription opioids, such as Vicodin (9.7%) and OxyContin (4.3%), in the past year without a doctor's order. Other drugs used by more than 5 percent of 12th-graders included amphetamines (8.1%), over-the-counter cough or cold medicines (6.9%), tranquilizers (6.6%), sedatives (6.6%), and cocaine (5.7%). The nonmedical use of prescription pain relievers was also the second most prevalent illicitly used drug among the U.S. household population aged 12 and older.

NOTES

1. C. D. Chambers and J. A. Inciardi, *An Assessment of Drug Use in the General Population; Special Report No. 2: Drug Use in New York State, Drug Use in New York City, Drug Use in Selected Geographical Regions of New York State* (Albany, NY: New York Narcotic Addiction Control Commission, 1971).

2. C. D. Chambers, J. A. Inciardi, D. M. Petersen, H. A. Siegal, and O. Z. White, eds., *Chemical Dependencies: Patterns, Costs, and Consequences* (Athens, OH: Ohio University Press, 1987); C. D. Chambers, J. A. Inciardi, and H. A. Siegal, *Chemical Coping: A Report on Legal Drug Use in the United States* (New York: Spectrum Publications, 1975); L. Grinspoon and P. Hedblom, *The Speed Culture: Amphetamine Use and Abuse in America* (Cambridge, MA: Harvard University Press, 1975); R. Hughes and R. Brewin, *The Tranquilizing of America: Pill Popping and the American Way of Life* (New York: Harcourt Brace Jovanovich, 1979); J. A. Inciardi, D. M. Petersen, and C. D. Chambers, "Methaqualone Abuse Patterns, Diversion Paths and Adverse Reactions," *Journal of the Florida Medical Association,* 61 (1974), pp. 279–283; H. Klee, ed., *Amphetamine Misuse: International Perspectives on Current Trends* (Amsterdam: Harwood Academic Publishers, 1997); J. Mondanaro, *Chemically Dependent Women: Assessment and Treatment* (Lexington, MA: Lexington Books, 1989); A. Weil and W. Rosen, *Chocolate to Morphine: Understanding Mind-Active Drugs* (Boston: Houghton Mifflin Company, 1983).

3. J. Zacny, G. Bigelow, P. Compton, K. Foley, M. Iguchi, and C. Sannerud, "College on Problems of Drug Dependence Taskforce on Prescription Opioid Non-Medical Use and Abuse: Position Statement," *Drug and Alcohol Dependence,* 69(3) (2003): pp. 215–232.

4. J. R. Cooper, D. J. Czechowicz, S. P. Molinari, and R. C. Petersen, eds., *Impact of Prescription Drug Diversion Control Systems on Medical Practice and Patient Care,* NIDA Research Monograph vol. 131 (Rockville, MD: National Institute on Drug Abuse, 1993); A.M. Nicholi, Jr., "The Nontherapeutic Use of Psychoactive Drugs: A Modern Epidemic," *The New England Journal of Medicine, 308*(16) (1983), pp. 925–933; D. E. Joranson, K. M. Ryan, A. M. Gilson, and J. L. Dahl, "Trends in Medical Use and Abuse of Opioid Analgesics," *Journal of the American Medical Association, 283*(13) (2000), pp. 1710–1714; M. Meadows, "Prescription Drug Use and Abuse," *FDA Consumer, 35*(5) (2001), pp. 18–24; M. Frischer and A. Blenkinsopp, "Medicine Misuse or Drug Abuse? A Critical Appraisal of Current Issues and Research in the UK," *Critical Public Health, 9*(3) (1999), pp. 181–195; J. Zacny, G. Bigelow, P. Compton, K. Foley, M. Iguchi, and C. Sannerud, "College on Problems of Drug Dependence Taskforce on Prescription Opioid Non-Medical Use and Abuse: Position Statement," *Drug and Alcohol Dependence, 69*(3) (2003), pp. 215–232; B. B. Wilford, J. Finch, D. J. Czechowicz, and D. Warren, "An Overview of Prescription Drug Misuse and Abuse: Defining the Problem and Seeking Solutions," *The Journal of Law, Medicine and Ethics, 22*(3) (1999), pp. 197–203; L. Simoni-Wastila, "The Use of Abusable Prescription Drugs: The Role of Gender," *Journal of Women's Health and Gender-Based Medicine, 9*(3) (2000), pp. 289–297.

5. J. A. Inciardi, H. L. Surratt, S. S. Martin, and R. E. Gealt, "Prevalence of Narcotic Analgesic Abuse among Students: Individual or Polydrug Abuse?" *Archives of Pediatric and Adolescent Medicine, 158*(5) (2004), pp. 498–499.

6. J. A. Inciardi and J. L. Goode, "OxyContin and Prescription Drug Abuse," *Consumers' Research, 86*(7) (2003), pp. 17–21.

7. U.S. Drug Enforcement Administration, Office of Diversion Control, *OxyContin® Diversion and Abuse* (2003, October). Accessed on February 22, 2007, from www.deadiversion.usdoj.gov/drugs_concern/oxycodone/oxy_oct2003.pdf.

8. J. A. Slobodzian, "Delco Pharmacist Pleads Guilty in Illegal Drug Sales," *Philadelphia Inquirer,* December 3, 2002. Accessed on February 20, 2007, from www.philly.com/mld/philly/archives.

9. R. Alford, "Doctors Lured to Help in Appalachia Now Sit in Prison," *Miami Herald,* May 11, 2003, p. 13A.

10. L. D. Johnston, P. M. O'Malley, and J. G. Bachman, *Monitoring the Future National Survey Results on Drug Use, 1975–2002. Volume II: College Students and Adults Ages 19–40* (NIH Publication No. 03-5376) (Bethesda, MD: National Institute on Drug Abuse, 2003).

11. Substance Abuse and Mental Health Services Administration, Office of Applied Studies, *Results from the 2001 National Survey on Drug Use and Health: Volume III* (2002). Accessed on February 21, 2007, from http://oas.samhsa.gov/nhsda/2k1nhsda/vol3/FrontMatter_W.pdf.

12. Substance Abuse and Mental Health Services Administration, Office of Applied Studies, *Narcotic Analgesics: The DAWN Report* (2003). Accessed on February 20, 2007, from https://dawninfo.samhsa.gov/old_dawn/pubs_94_02/shortreports/files/DAWN percent20Report percent 20NA_10.pdf.

13. U.S. Drug Enforcement Administration, Office of Diversion Control, *Summary of Medical Examiner Reports of Oxycodone-Related Deaths* (2007). Accessed on February 20, 2007, from http://www.deadiversion.usdoj.gov/drugs_concern/oxycodone/oxycontin7.htm.

14. B. Goldberger, "Oxycodone Rarely the Sole Cause of Drug Abuse Deaths, New Study Finds: Landmark Analysis Sets Standard for Interpretation of Deaths Involving Drug Abuse," *Journal of Analytical Toxicology* (2003, February 26). Accessed on February 20, 2007, from www.eurekalert.org/pub_releases/2003-02/pn-ort022603.php.

15. DEA, 2007.

16. DEA, 2003.

17. E. Durkheim, *The Division of Labor in Society* (New York: Macmillan Publishing Company, 1933).

18. M. A. Clancy, "Down East High: Washington County Pill Addicts Have Health Officials Worried," *Bangor Daily News,* May 13, 2000, p. 1.

19. V. Gowda, "Not What the Doctor Ordered," *Congressional Quarterly DBA Governing Magazine,* 34 (2003, January).

20. A. G. Breed, In *Appalachia and Beyond, OxyContin Abuse Called 'a Plague'* (2001, June 16). Accessed on January 25, 2005, from LexisNexis Academic database. Gilbert, WV: The Associated Press State & Local wire.

21. D. Gold, "A Prescription for Crime: Abuse of 2 Painkillers Blamed for Rise in Violence in Maine's Poorest County," *The Boston Globe,* May 21, 2000. Retrieved January 2003 from LexisNexis Academic Database.

22. S. Cannizaro, "Potent New Painkiller on the Street, Cops Say; Task Force Investigating Street Sales of 'New Vicodin'," the *New Orleans Times-Picayune,* June 27, 2000. Retrieved January 2003 from LexisNexis Academic Database.

23. S. Kaushik, *Oxycon Game: Anatomy of a Media-Made Drug Scare* (2001, June 4). Accessed on February 19, 2007, from Alternet.org: Drug Reporter, http://opioids.com/oxycodone/oxycon.html.

24. Kaushik, 2001.

25. L. Sherr, "What the Doctor Ordered; Young People Hooked on a Miracle Painkiller," *ABC News 20/20* broadcast, February 9, 2001. Transcript available: www.transcripts.tv/2020.cfm.

26. M. Fink, *Don't Forget the Hype: Media, Drugs, and Public Opinion* (1992, September). Accessed on January 2003 from Fairness and Accuracy In Reporting, www.fair.org/extra/best-of-extra/drugs-hype.html.

27. Fink, 1992.

28. J. Suchard, "Newspaper Coverage of Clinical Toxicology [Abstract]," *Journal of Toxicology: Clinical Toxicology, 40*(5) (2002), p. 629.

29. R. Hafford, "Hillbilly Heroin; New Drug Catches Gardai on the Hop," *The Mirror* (2001, October 27). Accessed on February 2003 from LexisNexis Academic database.

30. P. Tough, "Hillbilly Hell," *The Observer* (2002, April 7). Accessed on February 22, 2007, from http://observer.guardian.co.uk/life/story/0,,679985,00.html#article_continue.

31. T. Thompson, "Epidemic Fear as 'Hillbilly Heroin' Hits the Streets," *The Observer* (2002, March 24). Accessed on February 20, 2007, from www.observer.co.uk/uk_news/story/0,6903, 672984,00.html.

32. M. Szalavitz, "Drug Abuse" [Letter to the Editor], *The Observer* (2002, March 31). Accessed on February 20, 2007, from www.observer.co.uk/letters/story/0,6903,676787,00.html.

33. S. D. Passik, "Same as It Ever Was? Life after the OxyContin Media Frenzy" [Letter to the Editor], *Journal of Pain and Symptom Management, 25*(3) (2003), pp. 199–201.

34. J. A. Inciardi, H. L. Surratt, S. P. Kurtz, and J. J. Burke, "The Diversion of Prescription Drugs by Health Care Workers in Cincinnati, Ohio," *Substance Use and Misuse, 41*(2) (2006), pp. 255–264.

35. M. F. Conlin, "States Starting to Target Rx Drugs Sold on the Streets," *Drug Topics,* 44 (1990, August 6); U.S. General Accounting Office, *OxyContin Abuse and Diversion and Efforts to Address the Problem* [Report to Congressional Requesters, #GAO-04-110], Washington, DC: U.S. Government Printing Office (2003, December).

36. R. A. Weathermon, "Controlled Substances Diversion: Who Attempts It and How," *U.S. Pharmacist, 24*(12) (1999), pp. 32–47.

37. A. M. Gilson, K. M. Ryan, D. E. Joranson, and J. L. Dahl, "A Reassessment of Trends in the Medical Use and Abuse of Opioid Analgesics and Implications for Diversion Control: 1997–2002," *Journal of Pain and Symptom Management, 28*(2) (2004), pp. 176–188; D. A. Forgione, P. Neuenschwander, and T. E. Vermeer, "Diversion of Prescription Drugs to the Black Market: What the States Are Doing to Curb the Tide," *Journal of Health Care Finance, 27*(4) (2001), pp. 65–78; A. Chandra and A. Ozturk, "Health Professionals Beware of Prescription Pain Medication Abuse and Diversion," *Hospital Topics, 82*(4) (2004), pp. 34–37.

38. Inciardi et al., 2006; J. A. Inciardi, *Prescription Drug Diversion,* Paper presented at the Opioid Risk Management Conference, Boston, March 29, 2005; J. A. Inciardi and H. L. Surratt, *Research Issues and Experiences in Studying Prescription Drug Diversion,* Paper presented at the College on Problems of Drug Dependence: Impact of Drug Formulation on Abuse Liability, Safety and Regulatory Decisions Conference, North Bethesda, MD, April 19–20, 2005; A. Valdez and S.J. Sifaneck, "Drug Tourists and Drug Policy on the U.S.-Mexican Border: An Ethnographic Investigation of the Acquisition of Prescription Drugs," *Journal of Drug Issues, 27*(4) (1997), pp. 879–897.

39. Inciardi et al., 2006; Inciardi and Surratt, 2005; J. D. Haddox, *The Standards for Risk Management Plans for High Abuse Potential Medications,* Paper presented at the College on Problems of Drug Dependence: Impact of Drug Formulation on Abuse Liability, Safety and Regulatory Decisions Conference, North Bethesda, MD, April 19–20, 2005; D. B. Leiderman, "Prescription Drugs and the Risks of Abuse, Addiction, and Overdose: Regulatory Challenges," College on Problems of Drug Dependence: Impact of Drug Formulation on Abuse Liability, Safety and Regulatory Decisions Conference, North Bethesda, MD, 2005.

40. CASA (The National Center on Addiction and Substance Abuse at Columbia University), *"You've Got Drugs!": Prescription Drug Pushers on the Internet* [a CASA White Paper] (New York: Author, 2004, February); N. D. Volkow, *Priorities in Prescription Drug Abuse Research,* Paper presented at the College on Problems of Drug Dependence: Impact of Drug Formulation on Abuse Liability, Safety and Regulatory Decisions Conference, North Bethesda, MD, April 19–20, 2005.

41. Inciardi et al., 2006; J. Zacny, G. Bigelow, P. Compton, K. Foley, M. Iguchi, and C. Sannerud, "College on Problems of Drug Dependence Taskforce on Prescription Opioid Non-Medical Use and Abuse: Position Statement," *Drug and Alcohol Dependence, 69*(3) (2003), pp. 215–232; U. Bergman and M.-L. Dahl-Puustine, "Use of Prescription Forgeries in a Drug Abuse Surveillance Network," *European Journal of Clinical Pharmacology, 36*(6) (1989), pp. 621–623; K. Blumenschein, "Prescription Drug

Diversion: Fraudulent Tactics Utilized in the Community Pharmacy," *American Journal of Pharmaceutical Education, 61*(2) (1997), pp. 184–188; S. Borsack, "Hospital Drug Diversion: The Verdict Is In," *Health Matrix, 4*(4) (1986–1987), pp. 27–31; J. R. Cooper, D. J. Czechowicz, R. C. Petersen, and S. P. Molinari, "Prescription Drug Diversion Control and Medical Practice," *Journal of the American Medical Association, 268*(10) (1992), pp. 1306–1310; S. E. McCabe, C. J. Teter, and C. J. Boyd, "The Use, Misuse and Diversion of Prescription Stimulants among Middle and High School Students," *Substance Use and Misuse, 39*(7) (2004), pp. 1095–1116; L. Simoni-Wastila and C. Tompkins, "Balancing Diversion Control and Medical Necessity: The Case of Prescription Drugs with Abuse Potential," *Substance Use and Misuse, 36*(9&10) (2001), pp. 1275–1296; B. B. Wilford, J. Finch, D. J. Czechowicz, and D. Warren, "An Overview of Prescription Drug Misuse and Abuse: Defining the Problem and Seeking Solutions," *The Journal of Law, Medicine and Ethics, 22*(3) (1994), pp. 197–203.

   42. CASA, 2004; U.S. Drug Enforcement Administration, *DEA Unveils International Toll-Free Hotline to Report Illegal Prescription Drug Sales and Rogue Pharmacies Operating on the Internet* (2004, December 15). Accessed on January 25, 2005, from www.usdoj.gov/dea/pubs/pressrel/pr121504.html.

   43. T. J. Cicero, J. A. Inciardi, and A. Muñoz, "Trends in Abuse of OxyContin® and Other Opioid Analgesics in the United States: 2002–2004," *Pain, 6*(10) (2005), pp. 662–672.

   44. J. A. Inciardi and H. L. Surratt, *Trends in the Diversion of Prescription Drugs,* Paper presented at the CPDD 68th Annual Scientific Meeting, Scottsdale, AZ, June 17–22, 2006.

   45. S. P. Kurtz, J. A. Inciardi, H. L. Surratt, and L. Cottler, "Prescription Drug Abuse among Ecstasy Users in Miami," *Journal of Addictive Diseases, 24*(4) (2005), pp. 1–16; S. P. Kurtz, "Prescription Drug Abuse among Ecstasy Users in Miami: Qualitative Research Findings," in *Epidemiologic Trends in Drug Abuse, Advance Report: Prescription Drug Abuse Community Epidemiology Work Group, June 2004,* NIH Publication No. 04-5363A (Rockville, MD, The Institute, November 2004), pp. 43–47.

   46. Associated Press, "Miami Man Gets Prison Time for Illegally Selling Pharmaceuticals (2004, April 2). Accessed on May 31, 2005, from LexisNexis Academic database; P. Breister, "Area Authorities on Alert after Home Invasions," Fon DuLac WI: *The Reporter* (2005), p. 04A; B. Gedan, "Despite 2 Arrests, Break-Ins Still Soar," *Boston Globe,* September 26, 2004, p. 12; D. Harlow, "Drugs Drive Crime in Central Maine," December 29, 2004. Accessed on January 25, 2005, from www.mapinc.org/safe/v04/n1855/a05.html; M. McDonald, "Suspect Held in Rash of Burglaries," *Boston Globe,* December 5, 2004, p. 4; H. Yakin, *Prescription-Drug Crimes on the Rise* (2005, January 3). Accessed on January 28, 2005, from http://archive.recordonline.com/archive/2005/01/03/hyrx.htm.

   47. D. L. Weisel, *Burglary of Single-Family Houses,* Problem-Oriented Guides for Police Series, No. 18 (U.S. Department of Justice, Office of Community Oriented Policing Services, 2004).

   48. M. Wellsmith and A. Burrell, "The Influence of Purchase Price and Ownership Levels on Theft Targets: The Example of Domestic Burglary," *British Journal of Criminology, 45*(5) (2005), pp. 741–764; M. Sutton, "Supply by Theft: Does the Market for Second-Hand Goods Play a Role in Keeping Crime Figures High?" *British Journal of Criminology, 35* (Summer, 2005), pp. 400–416.

   49. J. A. Inciardi, H. L. Surratt, et al., "Mechanisms of Prescription Drug Diversion among Drug Involved Club- and Street-Based Populations." *Pain Medicine, 8*(2) (2007), pp. 171–183.

   50. U.S. Drug Enforcement Administration, *Drug Theft and Loss* (2005). Accessed on January 25, 2005, from www.aatod.org/pdfs/methadone-theft.pdf.

   51. U.S. Drug Enforcement Administration, *OxyContin® Theft and Loss Incidents: January 2000 through June 2003* (2005). Accessed on January 25, 2005, from www.deadiversion.usdoj.gov/drugs_concern/oxycodone/oxylosses_oct2003_1.pdf.

   52. D. E. Joranson and A. M. Gilson, "Drug Crime Is a Source of Abused Pain Medications in the United States," *Journal of Pain and Symptom Management, 30*(4) (2005), pp. 299–301.

   53. R. F. Forman, G. E. Woody, T. McClellan, and K. G. Lynch, "The Availabilty of Web Sites Offering to Sell Opioid Medications without Prescriptions," *American Journal of Psychiatry, 163*(7) (2006), pp. 1233–1238; R. F. Forman, "Availability of Opioids on the Internet," *JAMA 290*(7) (2003), p. 889; R. F. Forman and L. G. Block, "The Marketing of Opioid Medications without Prescription over the Internet," *Journal of Public Policy and Marketing, 25*(2) (2006), pp. 1–2; S. M. Gordon, R. F. Forman, and C. Siatkowski, "Knowledge and Use of the Internet as a Source of Controlled Substances," *Journal of Substance Abuse Treatment, 30*(3) (2006), pp. 271–274.

   54. A. Jesdanun, *Study: Few Americans Buy Drugs Online* (2004, October 10). The Associated Press. Accessed on October 10, 2004, from LexisNexis Academic database.

CHAPTER 8

LEGENDS OF THE LIVING DEAD

Unraveling the Drugs–Crime Connection

Myth is a body of lore regarded as roughly true. It implies collective fantasy, drawing its fabulous plots from notions based more on traditions and convenience than on fact. Myth guides conduct by orienting, sustaining, or suppressing aspects of social behavior.

The chronicle of our nation, from its earliest pages, reflects a noticeable dependence on myth in its perception and understanding of the use of drugs for the enhancement of pleasure or performance. Remarkably, this phenomenon seems to persist despite any contradictions by science and logic. For indeed, many people typically seem to ignore the treasuries of evidence descriptive of drugs, drug users, and drug taking that the fields of pharmacology, medicine, and the social and psychological sciences have provided, in favor of many prevailing mythical systems.

It is generally believed, for example, that all drug users are degenerate and dependent people; that heroin, cocaine, and some prescription drugs are the most dangerous substances on earth; that PCP is a Jekyll and Hyde drug that immediately changes mild-mannered users into raving maniacs; that crack is at the base of all inner-city problems; that the use of marijuana invariably leads to heroin addiction; that more effective policing can eliminate drug use and drug-related crime; that severe punishment of drug users will prevent others from using drugs; that life sentences for drug dealers will curtail drug selling; that heroin addicts are enslaved to their drugs and are forced to commit crimes to support their habits; and that legalizing drugs will solve the drug problem and eliminate the crime associated with illegal drug distribution and use.

This brief listing reflects but a sampling of the mythical images that characterize popular drug awareness. Yet even these few have managed to galvanize the perceptions and responses of legislatures, the media, systems of law enforcement, armchair policy makers, civil libertarians, the public at large, and to some extent even the scientific community. The curiosity, however, is the way in which many drug myths came into being, managing to persist for years hence.

RELIGIOUS ALCHEMY, THE SAGA
OF D. B. COOPER, AND THE GENESIS
OF THE DRUG MYTHS

Myth descends from a process—a series of actions and responses. It passes directly from both literary and folk traditions into belief. The art form of myth is drama, with plot, characters, and dialogue. The performance displays a collection of themes and events, and their interpretation invariably becomes understood as real. Many myths are the result of simple misunderstanding, reinterpretations of fact or deliberate misdirection to suit one's own needs or beliefs, and erroneous or quasiscientific methods of inquiry. This spirit of mythmaking is apparent, for example, in the journalistic sensationalism of the nineteenth-century U.S. "dime novelists," the approximations of fact by armchair historians, and the religious alchemy of generations of Christian writers and contemporary television evangelists.

Among the more curious myths that endured for centuries in much of the world was that of the unicorn, a product of the Bible. The books of the Old Testament were first written in Hebrew and Aramaic, but circa 250 B.C. a group of Hellenistic Jews translated the Scriptures into Greek, producing a version of the Bible known as the *Septuagint.* In the original Scriptures, the Hebrew writers had mentioned with some awe an animal they called *Re'em.* In Job 39:9–12 and Num. 23:22, the Re'em was noted as having great strength. It was characterized as fleet, fierce, indomitable, and especially distinguished by the armor of its brow, but it was never actually described. Later studies discovered that Re'em was *Bos primigenius,* or the urus, a wild ox that is believed to be the feral ancestor of European domestic cattle. But the urus, now extinct, had never been seen by the translators because it no longer existed where they lived. Yet the traits of the Re'em awakened dim recollections of another beast that was believed to be as fierce, mysterious, strange, and remote. They used the Greek word $\mu o\nu\acute{o}\chi\epsilon\rho\omega\zeta$ or *monokeros.*

The monokeros of the ancient Greeks came from the writings of Ctesias, the historian and one-time physician of the Persian King Artaxerxes II. In 398 B.C. he had produced a volume on India, based primarily on the tales and hearsay of travelers. In it he described a wild ass of India that had all the characteristics of the mythical unicorn. Zoologists have determined that Ctesias' monokeros, or wild ass of India, was actually the Indian rhinoceros, with admixtures of features of some other animal. But in English, *monokeros* means unicorn. Re'em was translated as monokeros with one main result: for many centuries to come, the existence of the unicorn would be reiterated, and it could not be doubted, for it was repeatedly mentioned in the Bible.[1]

More entertaining is the myth of D. B. Cooper, the skyjacker who jumped from a Northwest Orient Airlines jetliner on Thanksgiving eve in 1971 with a $200,000 ransom that he had demanded from airline officials. After he parachuted from the plane over Ariel, Washington, the FBI launched a massive manhunt. Cooper was never found, and almost immediately he became a modern-day folk hero—a twentieth-century Robin Hood. Popular mythology holds that he got away, that he beat the system.

Every year on the Saturday after Thanksgiving in Ariel the festivities of D. B. Cooper Day are held. Hundreds of people, some from as far away as England, clog the town's only street to pay tribute to the perpetrator of the only unsolved skyjacking in the United States. It is an article of faith among them that somehow, somewhere, Cooper is managing to live a discreetly decadent life on his marked money.[2] What the cultists do not understand is that when Cooper jumped from the ten-thousand-foot altitude into two-hundred-mile-per-hour freezing rain and air, dressed only in a light business suit and raincoat, it is likely that his body was thrown into immediate shock and that he did not stay conscious long enough even to open his parachute.

In contrast to the tales of the unicorn and D. B. Cooper, the genesis of drug myths is considerably more complex, having come from numerous medical, political, legislative, scientific, and moral arenas of U.S. society. They emerged, in part, from

- The rural creeds of nineteenth-century Methodism, Baptism, Presbyterianism, and Congregationalism, which emphasized individual human toil and self-sufficiency while designating the use of intoxicants as an unwholesome surrender to the evils of an urban morality
- The medical literature of the late 1800s that arbitrarily designated the use of opium, morphine, and cocaine as a vice, a habit, an appetite, and a disease
- The early association of opium smoking with the Chinese—a cultural and immigrant group that had been legally defined as alien, a designation that endured until the early 1940s
- The effects of U.S. narcotics legislation that, in effect, defined heroin users as criminal offenders
- Nineteenth- and twentieth-century police literature that stressed the involvement of professional and other habitual criminals with the use of drugs
- The initiatives of moral crusaders who described drug use as evil and, in so doing, influenced national opinion makers and legislators
- The publicized findings of misguided research efforts, those contaminated by the use of biased samples, impressionistic data, and methodological errors
- Cultural and intellectual lag—that vast and ecumenical gap that stretches between the publication of new discoveries and the ultimate dismissal of earlier proclamations
- The theoretical interpretations of the drug problem offered by armchair observers, academics, and politicians who have had little or no exposure *to,* or experience *with,* the dynamics and complexities of drug-taking and drug-seeking phenomena.

Drug myths are also a product of the mass media, which provide uninformed audiences with misshapen portraits of the worlds of drug use. Consider, for instance, the sentimentalized melodramas and/or irresponsible reporting characteristic of "Miami Vice," *People Weekly, Atlantic Monthly,* "60 Minutes," *Reader's Digest, The New Republic, Rolling Stone, High Times,* "Dateline NBC," "The Closer," "The Shield," and "Law & Order," to name but a few.

THE TALE OF A TERRIBLE VICE

Although opium and its derivatives had been available as general remedies in patent medicines well before the Revolutionary War, it was not until the mid-nineteenth century that concern over their evil effects began to surface. Among the earliest to focus on opiate use as a growing social problem was physician George B. Wood in 1856.[3] Although Wood noted the range of physical impairments that could be attributed to chronic opium intoxication, his treatise focused on evil. Opiate use led to a loss of self-respect, Wood argued; it was a yielding to seductive pleasure, a form of moral depravity, and a vice that led to the lowest depths of evil. Many of Wood's colleagues quickly agreed, and much of the medical literature that examined the opium problem during the next three decades more often stressed moral rather than medical issues.[4] As one commentator put it, "the morbid craving of morphia ranks amongst the category of other human passions, such as smoking, gambling, greediness for profit, and sexual excesses."[5]

To this collection of testimonials ascribing varying levels of stigma to the opiate user, a number of other medical commentators borrowed ideas suggested by the recently introduced theories of biological determinism and criminal anthropology. At the time, the writings of Charles Darwin had become prominent, and Italian physician Cesare Lombroso had just presented his thesis of criminal man.[6] Lombroso argued that there is a born criminal type, that the criminal is an *atavism*—a throwback to an earlier stage in human evolution, a more apelike evolutionary ancestor. There was also Richard L. Dugdale's publication of *The Jukes,* a study that held that crime is caused by bad heredity, and that criminality, degeneracy, and feeblemindedness are biologically transmitted through poor germ plasm.[7] Applying such notions to the drug-using population, it was claimed that addiction was the result of inherited predispositions; therefore, people who take morphine will likely also indulge excessively in alcohol, absinthe drinking, and cocaine use.[8]

Public concern was also mounting over opium smoking in U.S. cities. When gold was discovered in California in 1848, migrants from the Atlantic states as well as from Europe, Australia, and Asia contributed to the gold-seeking population. Among them were some 27,000 Chinese. With the lure of work in the mines and in the construction of railroads across the trans–Mississippi West, by the 1870s the Chinese population had expanded to more than 70,000. The new Asian immigrants had imported their cultural tradition of opium smoking, and they quickly established smoking parlors that were frequented by Celestials, as the Chinese were often called, and Americans alike.[9]

With a Chinatown beginning in 1872 in New York, a city at the very center of the nation's publishing capitals, knowledge of the Chinese way of life and the practice of opium smoking became readily disseminated. Common in mass-market publishing during that time were antiurban exposés, lurid guidebooks describing the many evils of the great metropolis.[10] Chinatown was a popular subject, and the customs of "Orientals" as well as the evil nature of the opium joints were often highlighted. In one volume, published in 1892 under the title *Darkness and Daylight; or,*

Lights and Shadows of New York Life, the descriptions of the opium dens offered clear reflections of the Victorian moral climate of the era. For example:

> Near the farther end of the room was a bunk occupied by four white women, three of them apparently being adept in the vice, and the fourth a novice. Four persons crowd a bunk very closely; two recline their heads upon pillows or headrests, and the other two make use of their companions for the same purpose. A party may consist of either men or women, or it may be made up of both sexes; opium smokers do not stand on ceremony with each other, and strangers will recline on the same bunk and draw intoxication from the same pipe without the least hesitation. The old adage says "Misery loves company"; this is certainly the case with debauchery, and especially of debauchery with opium.[11]

Although the use of opium was not a crime during those years, it was illegal in New York City to operate an opium smoking parlor. Police efforts to close the establishments were vividly presented in the urban guidebooks. Moreover, descriptions of the opium habit and its consequences were dramatized as evil in the police literature of the day, directly associating drug-taking behavior with criminality. In 1884, for example, in a lengthy volume written and published by A. E. Costello, New York's chief of police, the dynamics of opium smoking were related with numerous vivid illustrations. In the commentary, Costello stated:

> A comparatively new criminal agency has been at work in certain sections of the city, spreading the fruitful seeds of contamination, and throwing additional responsibilities on the already overburdened shoulders of the police. The agency in question is what is known as "the opium habit." In a remarkably short space of time this terrible vice has taken deep root, and it is very much to be feared that it will not go down, but that it has come to stay. Unfortunately, this pernicious habit is not confined to the children of the flowery kingdom; a legion of opium smokers to the manner born, and many of them people of respectability and refinement, are slaves of the habit. . . . The most debased and wretched practice of the habit is smoking, which is now engaged in scores of "joints" in New York.[12]

By 1896, the term "dope fiend" had made its way into popular slang usage, implying that taking drugs was, or at least resulted in, an evil obsession.[13]

FABLES AND PARABLES OF THE "LIVING DEAD"

To suggest that during the late nineteenth century a fully committed effort was under way to criminalize the drug user would be somewhat of an overstatement. Indeed, many negative commentaries appeared in the medical and police literature. Also, occasional writers linked drug use with sexual license. Some authorities reported that old smokers of opium used the drug to seduce innocent girls;[14] that "female smokers, if not already lost in the point of virtue, soon become so;"[15] and that "rapes, seductions, and other criminal acts occur, sometimes boldly, or with secretiveness and cunning."[16] These sordid links of drug taking with vice and crime did have their impact on the shaping of public attitudes. In the main, however, people had many ambivalent views about drug abuse.

Experts knew that opium and morphine did not create sexual psychotics, and they were quite vocal about it.[17] Medical, pharmaceutical, and other organizations understood what they considered to be the threats that drug dependence posed for women and youth. Yet while loathing and fearing addiction, at the same time they had sympathy for addicts. They condemned the use of drugs for escape or sensual pleasure, but they also felt that morphinism was a form of physiological slavery that ought to be treated with pragmatic therapy rather than moralism. A growing body of confessional literature also revealed that drug users led lives of despair, that they sought freedom from the superhuman forces of addiction, and they repeatedly underwent rigorous cures.[18]

None of this should suggest, however, that there was no such thing as a criminal addict at this time, for indeed there was. Many contemporary commentators have argued that drug abuse and addiction are social problems created by such unenforceable laws as the Harrison Act of 1914.[19] Evidence for the existence of the pre-Harrison criminal addict appears in the writings of Dr. Perry Lichtenstein, a physician in charge of narcotic addiction treatment in City Prison, Manhattan.[20] Just weeks before the Harrison Act was signed into law, Lichtenstein noted that some 5 percent of the 16,000 prisoners that year were narcotic habitues, and that the numbers had been increasing dramatically since the beginning of the decade. He added that the vast majority of his patients had become addicted not through prescription medications, but had obtained their drugs through access to underworld black-market sources. Moreover, they engaged in prostitution and petty crimes to maintain their drug supplies.

After the passage of the Harrison Act, however, the criminalization process began in earnest. By that time, concerned people viewed heroin use with increasing alarm. Heroin was considered the most threatening drug in history, appealing to a new youthful generation that seemed indifferent to the standards of conduct of the wider society. In addition, as more and more users were arrested for the illegal possession of the drug, the association of heroin with crime became more firmly entrenched.

Chronologically first among the post–Harrison Act crusaders was Mrs. William K. Vanderbilt of New York society's elite "Four Hundred." Jousting for prominence in the society pages of the New York press, the ladies of Gotham's best families pursued causes in the name of social reform. To keep up with her rivals who had become famous as suffragettes during these pre-World War I years, Mrs. Vanderbilt set out on a campaign against heroin. She wanted to prevent the drug from adding to its already engorged prison of lost souls, as she so melodramatically put it. She organized anti-narcotics committees, led marches down Fifth Avenue, and warned New Yorkers of the armies of dangerous fiends roaming Harlem and the Bronx. Her endeavors resulted in a series of newspaper accounts that described an epidemic of heavy addiction within the youth culture and more than 1.5 million violent and dangerous addicts at large in the streets.

The propaganda also included rumors of fiendish enemy agents prowling through urban school yards, passing out candy laced with heroin to seduce innocent children and teenagers into lives of addiction, vice, crime, and despair.[21] The reports quickly spread from the New York dailies to popular national magazines, and *The Literary Digest* offered commentaries on "American enslavement to drugs;"[22] *The Outlook* described how drugs were being trafficked by gamblers, cabdrivers, domestics, vagrants, lunchroom helpers, poolroom employees, porters, and laundry-men;[23] and the *American Review of Reviews* stated that there were five million addicts nationwide, that the trafficker was a criminal of the worst type, and that the drug menace had to be stamped out.[24] All of that was only the beginning. In the 1920s, Captain Richmond Pearson Hobson entered the crusade.

Described by one of his biographers as a man of "virtually unlimited moral indignation,"[25] Hobson was one of the most celebrated heroes of the Spanish-American War. He was also an adept temperance lecturer, but when national Prohibition went into effect he became a reformer without a cause. Hobson soon realized the potential of the addiction issue and began an unprecedented campaign of sensationalism. Through newspaper columns, magazine articles, and national radio broadcasts, he popularized the notion that addicts are beasts and monsters who spread their disease like medieval vampires.

Hobson launched his effort by forming the International Narcotic Education Association, and almost immediately his views were seen in popular magazines and press reports all across the nation. In the May 24, 1924, issue of *The Literary Digest,* he was quoted as saying:

> Every heroin addict, because of the drug's action on his brain, has a mania to spread his addiction to others, the drug is four times as powerful as morphine and comes in a con-venient deceptive form of a white powder called "snow," which is generally "whiffed" into the nostrils.
>
> One "snow party" a day for a week makes a youth an addict. Organized efforts are directed at the young. Besides the professional peddlers we have a million young recruiting agents in our midst insanely trapping our youth into addiction. A sure symp-tom of the activities of this organization is seen in the rising tide of crime.[26]

Hobson pushed heavily the idea that a problem of one million heroin addicts existed, incorporating it into a pamphlet he entitled *The Peril of Narcotics—A Warn-ing to the People of America.* He urged Congress to publish five million copies of the little booklet so that every home in the nation would have one on hand. Even govern-ment antidrug forces, well aware of Hobson's sensationalism and exaggeration, opposed the request. The Federal Narcotics Control Board found the warnings in *The Peril of Narcotics* fantastic: that one ounce of heroin will cause two thousand addicts; that in using any brand of face powder regularly, it is a wise precaution to have a sam-ple analyzed for heroin.[27]

Undaunted, Hobson continued his drive. He managed to have *The Peril of Nar-cotics* read into the *Congressional Record,* and he sent copies under a congressional frank to five thousand superintendents of education, and hundreds of college and uni-versity presidents, officials of parent–teacher associations, and distinguished citizens listed in *Who's Who in America.*[28]

Captain Hobson ultimately achieved his greatest visibility on March 1, 1928, when NBC donated time for the radio broadcast of an emotionally charged address in which addicts were depicted as an army of the living dead. In part:

> To get his heroin supply the addict will not only advocate public policies against the public welfare, but will lie, steal, rob, and if necessary, commit murder. Heroin addiction can be likened to a contagion. Suppose it were announced that there were more than a million lepers among our people. Think what a shock the announcement would produce! Yet drug addiction is far more incurable than leprosy, far more tragic to its victims, and is spreading like a moral and physical scourge.
>
> There are symptoms breaking out all over the country and now breaking out in many parts of Europe which show that individual nations and the whole world is menaced . . . by this appalling foe . . . marching . . . to the capture and destruction of the whole world.
>
> Most of the daylight robberies, daring holdups, cruel murders, and similar crimes of violence are now known to be committed chiefly by drug addicts, who constitute the primary cause of our alarming crime wave.
>
> Drug addiction is more communicable and less curable than leprosy. Drug addicts are the principal carriers of vice diseases, and with their lowered resistance are incubators and carriers of the streptococcus, pneumococcus, the germ of flu, of tuberculosis, and other diseases.
>
> *Upon the issue hangs the perpetuation of civilization, the destiny of the whole world and the future of the human race!*[29]

Hobson's descriptions of addicts suggested to his readers and listeners images of wicked-looking denizens of the urban slime—ugly, scarred, and having all the stereotypic characteristics of the mugger, rapist, and pedophile. Yet the typical heroin user was hardly that. Most were young white males from the slums of eastern cities. They were citizens by birth, although their parents were typically immigrants. Moreover, they were poorly educated, and if they were employed they worked at unskilled or semiskilled jobs. Most addicts spent much of their time on the city streets, running with juvenile gangs.[30] In short, the heroin users of Hobson's time were indistinguishable from most of the urban, second-generation immigrant children—almost all were poor, uneducated, unemployed, and running in the streets. The only differentiating characteristic—if at all observable—was their narcotics use, which usually began with opium smoking in the context of their gang activities. They were indeed vagabonds and petty thieves, but so too were their nondrug-using peers in the Irish, Italian, Jewish, German, and Polish ghettos of the cities. Some heroin users were indeed gamblers and professional criminals, but these generally represented a small minority.

By the middle of the 1930s, Captain Hobson had shifted his energies. He moved to the forefront with Harry J. Anslinger's fight against the evil weed of the fields. As for heroin, Hobson's hysterical rants were no longer needed. Others carried on the crusade. He died in 1937, but by then the image of the addict had been well established. Dope fiends, as they were called, were sex-crazed maniacs, degenerate street criminals, and members of the living dead. Narcotics included marijuana and cocaine and reportedly ravaged the human body; they destroyed morality; addicts were sexually violent and criminally aggressive; they were weak and ineffective members of society; addiction was contagious because users had a mania for perpetuating the social anathema of taking drugs; and finally, once addicted, the user entered into a lifetime of slavery to drugs. Then came the war years and more pressing concerns. The problems of addiction were set aside, at least temporarily, not to be resurrected for almost a decade.

DRUGS, SEX, AND ROCK 'N' ROLL

The United States entered the mid-twentieth century as the most powerful nation on earth. World War II had ended the Great Depression and unleashed a prosperous postwar era; unemployment had stabilized at a uniquely low level, and most people in the United States reveled in a new economic privilege. The period has been called the Fabulous Fifties, for retrospective glances have characterized it as a golden age of simplicity and innocence—the thrilling days of bobby socks and soda fountains, of hot rods and Elvis Presley. There were no real wars, no riots, and no protests. But all was not well.

Along with the postwar prosperity, heroin addiction once more became visible. Having seemingly diminished when the draft sent the young white users off to war, it moved underground into inner-city minority populations, where it began to spread. The 1950s were also a time of youthful rebellion, and many adults in mainstream America feared that heroin use would become epidemic among the children of white society.

Of the many forms of youth rebellion, however, juvenile delinquency, not heroin addiction, became the most visible. Education reporter Benjamin Fine of the *New York Times* predicted in the early 1950s that by the middle of the decade the number of youths being processed by the police would exceed one million. His estimates were quickly realized, and property crimes and car theft were the major juvenile offenses. The young were also committing acts of inexplicable and pointless violence—beatings, rape, and murder. Although statistically few of America's teenage groups were involved in violent crime, those that were had seemingly terrorized entire cities.[31] These were the fighting gangs of the late 1940s and 1950s—the Roman Lords, Young Stars, Pigtown, Scorpions, Tigers, and other urban street gangs as portrayed in Irving Shulman's *The Amboy Dukes* and Hal Ellson's *Jailbait Street.*[32] But such novels were designed more to titillate than to give an objective glimpse at gang life, as evidenced by the promo for *Jailbait Street:*

> Running wild from darkness till dawn—snatching at love in deserted alleys or lonely rooftops—today's tough juvenile punks have turned our city streets into asphalt jungles of terror and lawlessness. This is the savagely realistic story of a teen-age gang, the Sultans, and their mixed-up leader, Silkie Meegan, whose desperate search for manhood drove him into frenzied excesses of violence and vice . . . from the vengeance beating with bicycle chains of a rival gang, to the degraded sharing of sweet, virginal Carol with the rest of the gang. And finally to the fateful family

■ ■ ■ ■ ■

EXHIBIT 8.1

THE FORDHAM BALDIES

Although the Sultans of *Jailbait Street* was a fictional gang, throughout New York City during the 1950s, rumor had it that up in the far reaches of the East Bronx was the most fearsome gang of all, the Fordham Baldies. So terrible were they, with shaved heads as a mark of their membership, that the mere mention of their presence in a local neighborhood would clear the streets of youths—both gang and nongang members alike. But no one ever seemed actually to encounter the Baldies face to face—ever. In the years hence, many concluded that they were a myth, and in all of the literature descriptive of the New York gang-lands of the 1950s, the Baldies are never mentioned. Even in the thousands of issues of the rigorously indexed *New York Times* their name never appears. Yet in an autobiography of a heroin addict, written during the 1970s, its author makes one brief mention of the Baldies, and his remarks suggest how the myth may have started:

> The gangs we used to rumble with mostly were the Hoods, of course, and then the Seven Crowns, the Scorpions, occasionally the Mau Maus, and then the Fordham Baldies. The Baldies were a group of guys made up of the sons of racketeers from the Fordham Road area. The Godfather up Fordham way used to be known as Baldie. So naturally the kids took that name. They were a pretty tough group so we mostly left them alone.

Sources: Richard P. Rettig, Manual J. Torres, and Gerald R. Garrett, *Manny: A Criminal-Addict's Story* (Boston: Houghton Mifflin, 1977), p. 27. See also Eric C. Schneider, *Vampires, Dragons and Egyptian Kings: Youth Gangs in Postwar New York* (Princeton, NJ: Princeton University Press, 1999).

feud with his own father over Charlotte, his father's prostitute mistress, who first taught Silkie her own kind of Jailbait Street love, then hired him to dig up new "business" for her (see Exhibit 8.1).

Curiously, however, although street crime was heavily tied to delinquency, at least as far as the media were concerned, juvenile drug use seemed to be absent from the gang culture. Isidor Chein's *The Road to H,* a pioneering, although theoretically problematic, study of narcotics use among juveniles, reflected what most other informed efforts had found. Adolescent drug use was concentrated in the inner city, most widespread where income and education were lowest. Drug use was not, however, intrinsically tied to gang activities. Some drug users were in organized juvenile gangs, yet these were less often involved in gang fighting.[33]

Extensive gang involvement or not, drug use, and particularly heroin use in the inner city, was indeed spreading at an unprecedented rate (see Exhibit 8.2). Although the media may have oversensationalized their reporting,[34] researchers, clinicians, and law enforcement groups working in the drug field were well aware of the growing

---

EXHIBIT 8.2

ORGANIC SOLVENTS AND INHALANTS

It should be noted here that common gateway drugs (drugs of initiation) for youths then and now are the organic solvents and inhalants. These include a series of highly volatile compounds that act in a central nervous system depressant capacity. Chemically, they exist either in a gaseous state at room temperature, or they rapidly evaporate from a liquid state when exposed to air. The more common organic solvents sought by drug abusers are generally of three varieties:

1. *Coal tar derivatives.* Lacquers, paint thinners and removers; quick-drying glue and cements; gasoline, kerosene, and other petroleum products; lighter and cleaning fluids; nail polish remover; and various aerosols containing active ingredients such as toluene, acetone, benzene, carbon tetrachloride, chloroform, ethyl ether, and various alcohols and acetates
2. *Freon.* A fluorocarbon gas used as a refrigerant and commonly used as a propellant for aerosols prior to 1978 when fluorocarbons were banned from use in household consumer products
3. *Nitrous oxide and related nitrites.* Derivatives of nitric acid, including amyl nitrate

With the exceptions of ether, nitrous oxide (laughing gas), and chloroform, which are used for anesthesia, and amyl nitrate, which has been employed in the treatment of heart pain and asthma, the vast majority of organic solvents and inhalants have no general medical use. Furthermore, most of these compounds are not drugs and, therefore, are not subject to control.

As central nervous system depressants, the effects of the organic solvents and inhalants tend to be similar in many respects to those of alcohol and the sedatives. Reported effects at low-dosage levels include mood elevation and mild euphoria, feelings of sociability, and a lessening of inhibitions. Higher dose levels produce laughing, dizziness, feelings of floating, perceptual distortions, illusions, confusion, blurred vision and slurred speech, and motor incoordination. With even further increases in dosage levels, the general effects of sedation and anesthesia may predominate, with respiratory depression, stupor, and unconsciousness in some cases. Acute intoxication may result in a lack of behavioral control, impaired judgment, or fear. Acute psychoses have been reported, as have abnormalities in kidney and liver functioning.

---

problem. There were, after all, many indicators of the new trend. At New York's Bellevue Hospital during the years 1940–1948, no adolescents had been admitted for treatment with a diagnosis of drug dependence. In 1949 there was one, followed by six in 1950, and eighty-four during the first two months of 1951.[35] In port cities around the nation, the number of heroin seizures had dramatically increased.[36] At the federal drug treatment centers in Lexington, Kentucky, and Fort Worth, Texas, the proportion of youths being admitted was expanding at a geometric rate.[37] In New York and other major cities, the number of youths coming to the attention of the police, the courts, and social work and other human service agencies on drug-related matters was also advancing. Finally, although it could be effectively argued that public pressure to do something about the heroin problem had encouraged selective enforcement of the narcotics laws, drug-related arrests were up in most large U.S. cities.

In terms of the reasons for the new heroin epidemic, *Life* magazine felt it had the answer:

> What had come over today's 15-year-olds? One answer was the brazen pusher, who, needing customers, was now cynically making them among naive youngsters, usually, but not always, from poor homes. Another answer was marijuana, widely available and publicized as nonaddictive—which is scientifically true but tragically misleading since it is usually the first step toward ultimate enslavement by heroin.[38]

Harry J. Anslinger of the Bureau of Narcotics had a different answer. He blamed parents. In the October 1951 issue of *Reader's Digest,* he argued that most juvenile addicts come from families in which there is no proper parental control or training in decent personal habits. "Rarely," he added, "does a boy or girl from a normally balanced family in any income bracket become an addict."[39] In other words, Anslinger was suggesting that decent people just don't use drugs! Finally, the Crime Investigating Committee of the U.S. Senate had the solution to the problem: stiffer penalties for narcotics violators, "for no penalty is too severe for a criminal of such character"; increase the number of agents assigned to narcotics work; cancel the sailing papers of any seaman convicted of a narcotics violation; and initiate a worldwide ban against growing the opium poppy.[40]

Although it seemed clear from both media and scientific reports that heroin use was almost exclusively a problem of the urban inner city, there was considerable concern within segments of the white middle class as to contaminating factors that might induce drug use and other undesirable behaviors among the more socially privileged youth. A prime target of the parental establishment was the new rock 'n' roll music.

When Alan Freed, a disk jockey for Cleveland radio station WJW, introduced the term in 1954, little did he imagine what the impact of rock 'n' roll would be on life in the United States and world social patterns.* The new music had elements of the country and western sounds of the rural white working class, but it was primarily made up of the rhythm and blues of an urbanizing black America. As a product principally of the African American community, it clearly had a racial stigma attached to it.[41] Racism condemned African American tastes in general and race records in particular. When Freed presented rock 'n' roll—a black, inner-city euphemism for both

---

*Various accounts have Alan Freed introducing the term "rock 'n' roll" in 1951, 1952, and 1954. The latter date is likely correct, as 1954 saw the release of what many agree to be the first rock 'n' roll record, *Sh-Boom* by The Chords (a black group) on Cat Records. A white cover (same song, white group) of *Sh-Boom* was recorded by The Crew Cuts the same year and released on Mercury, with an almost identical rendering (with the exception that the "sha-na-na-na-na-na" bridge was a Crew Cut creation).

dancing and sex—to white youth, it was an immediate success.* Some whites had already been listening to the all-black rhythm and blues radio shows, but it was not a taste that the majority cultivated. Freed, a white DJ, put the music in a more familiar and acceptable format, reassuring the majority of repressed and nervous white kids. His framework encouraged them to make the effort to overcome their bland, stereotyped musical background.[42]

The acceptance of rock 'n' roll was part of the new youth rebellion. At the same time it served to threaten every phobia of white America respectability—particularly when children were heard chanting "rock 'n' roll is here to stay!" Parents, members of Congress, and social commentators of the period claimed that it had infected white teenagers all across the country. It introduced them to their sexuality, to interracial contacts, to bizarre dance rituals, and, most seriously and terribly, to drugs! As authors Jack Lait and Lee Mortimer articulated in their 1952 best-seller *U.S.A. Confidential:*

> Like a heathen religion, it is all tied up with tom-toms and hot jive and ritualistic orgies of erotic dancing, weed smoking and mass mania, with African jungle background. Many music shops purvey dope. White girls are recruited for colored lovers. Another cog in the giant delinquency machine is the radio disc jockey. We know that many platter spinners are hopheads. Many others are Reds, left-wingers, or hecklers of social convention. Through disc jocks, kids get to know colored and other hit musicians; they frequent places the radio oracles plug, which is done with design . . . to hook jives and guarantee a new generation subservient to the Mafia.[43]

Lait and Mortimer went on to describe how marijuana use led to addiction and generated orgies of interracial sex.[†]

Yet regardless of the white phobias of the 1950s, rock 'n' roll endured, and its relationship to drugs was never established (see Exhibit 8.3). In spite of media contentions about a connection between drug use and middle-class delinquency, throughout the decade heroin use appeared to remain at a relatively low level in white neighborhoods. Yet narcotics use continued to grow at an alarming rate in the inner city, particularly among African American youths and other minority populations.

---

*The phrase "rock 'n' roll" originally referred to the motions a car makes when two lovers were going at it in the back seat. Hence, rock 'n' roll music became what poured out of the car radio while Johnny B. Goode was trying to mess up Peggy Sue's ponytail or Long Tall Sally's chantilly lace.

†For more widely read observers, what appeared in *U.S.A. Confidential* was no surprise because authors Lait and Mortimer had already established their general ignorance, prejudice, and racism. *New York Confidential* (New York: Viking, 1948), a piece of popular reportorial carrion they had written a few years earlier, stated:

> . . . from the days of earliest slavery in the United States and West Indies, Negroes have swept away their heavy inhibitions, forgotten the burn of the lash and the clank of the shackles with an age-old drug, hashish.
>
> Hashish was used among the ancients to stimulate armies for killing. . . .
>
> There are about 500 apartments in Harlem, known as "tea pads," set up exclusively for marijuana addicts.

■ ■ ■ ■ ■

EXHIBIT 8.3

THE EARLY DAYS OF ROCK 'N' ROLL

Although rock 'n' roll survived and evolved, Alan Freed did not. As depicted in *American Hot Wax,* a 1978 Paramount Pictures release, he was destroyed by the violence of the 1950s mainstream. At a show promoted by Freed in Boston, police interrupted the performance. Later, members of the audience spread through the city, fighting. One person was killed, several were beaten, and Freed was charged with anarchy and inciting to riot. It took him many years and a considerable sum of money before the charges were finally dismissed. Then he was charged in investigations of *payola*—a then-standard practice in the record industry by which bribes were given to disk jockeys to secure air time for certain records. Only the rock 'n' roll industry was targeted, and Freed received only a three hundred dollar fine, but his career was ruined. He moved from station to station, drinking heavily and continually pursued by harassing indictments. He died in 1965 at the age of forty-three.

Contemporary rock has also experienced some repression. Perhaps best known in this behalf was the federal court decision in 1990 that ruled that rap group 2 Live Crew's album *As Nasty As They Wanna Be* was obscene. The decision was an unfortunate one, for not only did it compromise the integrity of the First Amendment, but it awarded fame and fortune to a less-than-average rap group. Rap, for the uninitiated, is rhythmic chant, rhyme set to drums or the thundering cacophony of heavy metal, a musical culture filled with self-assertion, with cartoonish stories marked by exaggeration and often sex, anger, violence, and hate. What was declared obscene in *As Nasty As They Wanna Be* were lyrics about tearing and damaging vaginas, forcing anal sex on a young woman, and then forcing her to lick excrement.

For an examination of the rap and 2 Live Crew controversy, see David Mills, "Rap Music That Guns for Violence," *Insight,* 25 September 1989, pp. 54–56; *Newsweek,* 19 March 1990, pp. 56–63; *U.S. News & World Report,* 19 March 1990, p. 17; *Miami Herald,* 7 June 1990, pp. 1A, 10A; *New York Times,* 8 June 1990, p. A10; 11 June 1990, p. A14; 17 June 1990, pp. E1, E5.

For many of them, drug use had become a way of life, and street crime was typically a part of their drug-taking and drug-seeking activities.[44]

THE RIDDLE OF THE SPHINX

The Sphinx was a monster of Greek mythology that had the face of a woman, the body of a lion, and the wings of a bird. For years she perched on Mount Phicium, near the ancient city of Thebes, posing a riddle to all passersby. "What goes on four feet," she would ask, "on two feet, and three, but the more feet it goes on the weaker it be?" Those who could not answer her riddle were promptly devoured—which were all, save one. Oedipus answered her directly. "It is *man,*" he stated, "for he crawls as an infant, walks upright as an adult, and totters with a staff in old age." Upon hearing this, the Sphinx slew herself. Oedipus was made king of Thebes, and went on to other adventures.

In the drug field, for as long as commentators were sensationalizing crimes allegedly the maniacal handiwork of heroin, cocaine, and marijuana users, researchers argued a corresponding riddle. Is criminal behavior antecedent to addiction, or does criminality emerge subsequent to addiction? More specifically, is crime the result of or a response to a special set of life circumstances brought about by the addiction to narcotic drugs? Or conversely, is addiction per se a deviant tendency characteristic of individuals already prone to offense behavior? Moreover, and assuming that criminality may indeed be a preaddiction phenomenon, does the onset of chronic narcotics use bring about a change in the nature, intensity, and frequency of deviant and criminal acts? Does criminal involvement tend to increase or decrease subsequent to addiction? There were also related questions. What kinds of criminal offenses do addicts engage in? Do they tend toward violent acts of aggression? Or are their crimes strictly profit oriented and geared toward the violation of the sanctity of private property? Or is it both?

As early as the 1920s, researchers had been conducting studies—many studies—seeking answers to these very questions. Particularly, Edouard Sandoz at the Municipal Court of Boston and Lawrence Kolb at the U.S. Public Health Service examined the backgrounds of hundreds of heroin users, focusing on the drugs–crime relationship.[45] Their conclusions were relatively informed ones, however ignored. Basically, what they found within criminal justice and treatment populations were several different types of cases. Some drug users were habitual criminals, and likely always had been; others were simply violators of the Harrison Act, having been arrested for no more than the illegal possession of narcotics. Moreover, with both types a record of violent crimes was absent.

The analyses provided by Sandoz, Kolb, and others established the parameters of several points of view:

- Addicts ought to be the object of vigorous law-enforcement activity, since the majority are members of a criminal element and drug addiction is simply one of the later phases of their deviant careers.
- Addicts prey upon legitimate society, and the effects of their drugs do indeed predispose them to serious criminal transgressions.
- Addicts are essentially law-abiding citizens who are forced to steal to adequately support their drug habits.
- Addicts are not necessarily criminals but are forced to associate with an underworld element that tends to maintain control over the distribution of illicit drugs.[46]

The notion that drug abusers ought to be the objects of vigorous police activity, a posture that might be called the criminal model of drug abuse, was actively and relentlessly pursued by the Federal Bureau of Narcotics and other law enforcement groups. Their argument was fixed on the notion of criminality, for on the basis of their own observations, the vast majority of heroin users encountered were members of criminal groups. To support this view, the Bureau of Narcotics pointed to several studies that demonstrated that most drug users were already criminals before they began using heroin.[47] Addicts, the Bureau emphasized, represent a destructive force confronting the people of America. Whatever the sources of addiction might be, they are members of a highly subversive and antisocial group.

For the bureau, this position did indeed have some basis in reality. Having been charged with the enforcement of a law that prohibited the possession, sale, and distribution of narcotics, what bureau agents were confronted with were criminal addicts, often under the most dangerous of circumstances. It was not uncommon for agents to be wounded or even killed in arrest situations, and analyses of the careers of many addicts demonstrated that their criminal records were lengthy. Moreover, the matter of professional underworld involvement with narcotics was a point that Commissioner Anslinger himself commented on in 1951:

> It is well established that a larger proportion of the pickpocket artists, the shoplifters, the professional gamblers and card sharks, the confidence men operating fake horse race or fake stock sale schemes, the "short con" men such as the "shortchange artists" or the coin matchers, are addicted to the use of narcotic drugs.[48]

Anslinger was referring to the world of professional thieves, and studies have demonstrated that predators of this kind were involved not only in the use of narcotics but in trafficking as well.[49] Anslinger was wrong, however, in his belief that all heroin users are from the same mold. Studies of drug-using populations of his time have referenced the existence of numerous and alternative patterns of narcotic addiction. The professional thieves about which Anslinger spoke were a group of highly skilled yet essentially nonviolent criminals who made a regular business of stealing. Crime was their occupation and means of livelihood, and as such, they devoted their entire time and energy to stealing. They operated with proficiency; they had a body of skills and knowledge that was used in planning and executing their work; and they were graduates of an informal developmental process that included the acquisition of specialized skills, knowledge, attitudes, and experience.

Finally, in identifying themselves with the world of crime, professional thieves were members of an exclusive fraternity that extended friendship, understanding, sympathy, security, safety, recognition, and respect.[50] Their pattern of addiction revolved around using heroin or morphine by needle or smoking opium. Spree use of drugs was also common, generally to reduce the boredom associated with incarceration or as part of pleasure-seeking activities.

By contrast, during the years between 1900 and 1960, a different pattern of addiction was characteristic of a core of middle-aged white southerners. Identified through patient records at federal drug treatment facilities, they were usually addicted to morphine or paregoric, and their drugs had been obtained from physicians through legal or quasilegal means. As patients under treatment for some illness, these addicts were not members of any deviant subcultures and did not have contacts with other addicts.[51]

There were also groups of hidden addicts who, because of sufficient income and/or access to a legitimate source of drugs, had no need to make contacts with visibly criminal cultures to obtain drugs. Among these were musicians, physicians, and members of other segments of the health professions.[52]

Finally, there was the stereotyped heroin street addict—the narcotics user of the inner cities of whom the mass media spoke. Heroin street addicts were typically from the socially and economically deprived segments of the urban population. They began their careers with drug experimentation as adolescents for the sake of excitement or thrills, to conform with peer-group activities and expectations, and/or to strike back at the authority structures that they opposed. The use of alcohol, marijuana, inhalants, codeine, or pills generally initiated them into substance abuse, and later drug intake focused primarily on heroin. Their status of addiction was often said to have emerged as a result of an addiction-prone personality, and they supported their habits through illegal means. Also among this group were polydrug users—those who concurrently abused a variety of drugs.*

Most law enforcement agencies focused their attention and their commentary on those who manifested the pattern of heroin street addiction. In what may be one of the most scientifically prejudiced and ignorant studies targeting this group, FBI agent James P. Morgan, a former detective in the narcotics bureau of the New York City Police Department, compiled data in 1965 to prove conclusively that addiction was indeed a criminal problem.[53] His population included 135 narcotics users he had personally arrested during preceding years. Playing the roles of both police officer and scientific researcher, Morgan extensively questioned his quarries regarding their careers in crime and addiction. In terms of the validity and reliability of the responses received, Morgan was quite confident that his information was accurate. In fact, he said so himself: "I do not believe that any false answers were given to the questions." Morgan's analysis indicated that "only fifteen of the addicts studied were able to prove that they were lacking a criminal background." So logically, and with apparent confidence, he concluded: "The statistical results of this study revealed that those addicts studied become what they are, not by accident, but as a result of criminal tendencies which they had already exhibited."

Reading on in Morgan's essay, and in more serious works that address the issue of criminal tendencies, one could not avoid recalling Cesare Lombroso's thoughts on born criminals and atavisms and inherited predispositions to crime of a century earlier. Aside from Morgan's problems with sample bias and misguided interpretation, perhaps if given more time he might have resurrected Lombroso's ideas. After all, if his addicts did indeed have criminal tendencies, maybe their head shapes and sizes could have been significant in understanding their behaviors, as Lombroso had so foolishly argued.

What Agent Morgan and company were responding to in their commentaries were the clinicians and social scientists of the 1950s and early 1960s who had put forth the notion of what might be called a medical model of drug abuse, as opposed to the criminal view of law enforcement. The medical model, which physicians first proposed in the late nineteenth century, held that addiction was a chronic and relapsing disease. The addict, it was argued, should be dealt with as any patient suffering from

---

*This list of patterns of addiction is by no means exhaustive; there were, and still are, many more types.

some physiological or medical disorder. At the same time, numerous proponents of the view sought to mitigate addict criminality by putting forth the enslavement theory of addiction. The idea here was that the monopolistic controls over the heroin black market forced sick and otherwise law-abiding drug users into lives of crime to support their habits.

AMERICA'S FIRST WAR ON DRUGS

For the better part of the twentieth century, hundreds of studies of the relationship between crime and addiction were conducted.[54] Invariably, when one analysis would appear to support the medical model of addiction, the next would affirm the criminal model. Given these repeated contradictions, something had to be wrong—and indeed was. The theories, hypotheses, conclusions, and other findings generated by almost the entire spectrum of research were actually of little value, for there were awesome biases and deficiencies in the very nature of their designs.

Data-gathering enterprises on criminal activity had usually restricted themselves to drug users' arrest histories, and there can be little argument about the inadequacy of official criminal statistics as measures of the incidence and prevalence of offense behavior.[55] Those studies that did manage to go beyond arrest figures to probe self-reported criminal activity were invariably limited to either incarcerated heroin users or those in treatment settings. The few efforts that did manage to locate active heroin users in the street community typically examined the subjects' drug-taking behaviors to the exclusion of their drug-seeking behaviors. Given the many methodological difficulties, it was impossible to draw many reliable conclusions about the nature of drug-related crime—about its magnitude, shape, scope, or direction.

Moreover, and perhaps most importantly, the conclusions being drawn from the generations of studies were not taking into account a number of important features of the drug scene: that there were many different kinds of drugs and drug users; that the nature and patterns of drug use were constantly shifting and changing; that the purity, potency, and availability of drugs were dynamic rather than static; and that both drug-related crime and drug-using criminals were undergoing continuous metamorphosis.

Meanwhile, in 1956, while the U.S. mainstream was persecuting Alan Freed and the Fordham Baldies were terrorizing the imaginations of New York youth, Senator Price Daniels of Texas was repeating an oft-quoted message: "Addiction is bad enough in itself. But with it goes crime, committed to pay for the habit. This combination of addiction and crime is a very communicable disease."[56] If one had not known otherwise, one might have thought the words had come from the ghost of Captain Richmond Hobson, echoing lines from his enthusiastic living dead sermon of almost three decades earlier. Senator Daniels, however, did Hobson one better. He claimed that he had established a startling fact: that narcotic addiction was directly responsible for one-fourth of all the crimes committed in the United States. His declaration was an interesting one, for not only was the nature and extent of drug-related crime virtually unknown but, further, absolutely no one had even the vaguest idea of how much crime of any kind existed in the nation.

Then came the 1960s, a decade that occupies an individual summit in Americans' jagged images of the crime and violence in their midst. It began with the assassination of John Fitzgerald Kennedy, the fourth president of the United States to die by such violent means. But Kennedy's death was only the beginning. His alleged assassin, Lee Harvey Oswald, was shot to death within thirty-six hours of the president. In 1965, Black Muslim leader Malcolm X died violently in New York City. In 1967 American Nazi Party leader George Lincoln Rockwell was murdered by one of his followers. The next year the lives of civil rights leader Dr. Martin Luther King, Jr., and Senator Robert Kennedy were taken by assassination. Of less political renown, the 1960s also saw the cold-blooded murders of three young civil rights workers by members of the Ku Klux Klan in Mississippi, with the connivance of local law enforcement officers; the fire bombing of the freedom riders in Alabama; the bloody battles at Kent State, "Ole Miss," and other campuses across the nation, spurred by U.S. involvement in the Vietnam War; the ghetto riots in Los Angeles, Newark, Detroit, and numerous other densely populated urban areas; and the police riot at the 1968 Democratic Convention when Chicago's Mayor Richard J. Daley unleashed a force of 18,000 police officers, members of the Illinois National Guard, and regular Army troops armed with rifles, flamethrowers, and bazookas against peace marchers demonstrating their opposition to the Vietnam War. There was also street crime.

During the first half of the decade alone, reported crimes of violence had increased by one-half, property crimes by two-thirds, and the overall crime rate by almost one-half. In response, newly elected President Lyndon Johnson announced a war on crime during an address to the Eighty-Ninth Congress on March 8, 1965. A centerpiece in his war was the President's Commission on Law Enforcement and Administration of Justice, established by Johnson to study the problems of crime and justice in the United States.[57] A major task of the commission, at a time when politicians, parents, and the press were claiming that addiction was responsible for up to half the crime in the nation, was to examine the drug problem and its relation to crime.

When the commission's work was complete, the task force assigned to study narcotics and drug abuse made the following embarrassing, however honest, announcement:

> The simple truth is that the extent of the addict's or drug abuser's responsibility for all nondrug offenses is unknown. Obviously it is great, particularly in New York City, with its heavy concentration of users; but there is no reliable data to assess properly the common assertion that drug users or addicts are responsible for 50 percent of all crime.[58]

Professionals in the drug field applauded the announcement, hoping that, finally, resources would be made available to measure the phenomenon in question. To their chagrin, however, no federal funds were earmarked for focused studies of the drugs–crime connection, and on into the next decade the issue remained unresolved.

By that time, common assertions had pushed the amount of crime presumed to have been committed by drug users up to 90 percent.

Then, when Richard M. Nixon assumed the presidency of the United States, he spoke of a war on drugs and a war on heroin. He established a Special Action Office for Drug Abuse Prevention, but according to investigative reporter Edward Jay Epstein, the real purpose of the war was to increase the power of the White House bureaucracy. Epstein maintained that under the aegis of a war on heroin, Nixon had established two new agencies—the Office of Drug Abuse Law Enforcement and the Office of National Narcotics Intelligence—created for the purpose of investigating the president's political enemies.[59] Whether this was really so, Nixon's war seemed to accomplish little.

Yet Nixon's *screwworm* project[60] was an effort by the White House, the Department of Agriculture, and NASA to create a wonderfully wicked weevil that, when released in Turkey and the Golden Triangle, would eat the plants that produced the pod that contained the opium that supplied the drug that obsessed poor Richard Nixon. A screwworm as such was actually created, but its developers feared that, if released, it might start eating rice, wheat, and other plants once it had devoured the world's poppy crop. That, combined with the possibility of its crossing international boundaries to attack Soviet poppies, ultimately led to the little bug's demise.

In 1972, the fear of crime climbed to new heights. According to a Gallup Poll in that year, almost half of those surveyed were afraid to walk in their neighborhoods at night, and drug addiction was cited among the major reasons for the high crime rate.[61] By January 1973, crime was ranked highest among the nation's urban problems, with drug abuse ranking third.[62] President Nixon, by that time in his second term and all too busy denying his complicity in the Watergate coverup, nevertheless responded with a statement reemphasizing his war on drugs:

> No single law-enforcement problem has occupied more time, effort, and money in the past four years than that of drug abuse and drug addiction. We have regarded drugs as "public enemy number one," destroying the most precious resource we have—our young people—and breeding lawlessness, violence and death.[63]

Although often accused of exaggeration, this time many of the President's claims were quite accurate. Estimated federal expenditures for drug abuse prevention and law enforcement were indeed staggering for the era—increasing from $150.2 million in 1971 to $654.8 million just two years later.[64] But Nixon's descriptions of the drug problem and its relation to crime often went beyond the parameters of reasonable estimate. He referred to heroin use as a plague that threatened every man, woman, and child in the nation with the hell of addiction, and maintained that addict crime—largely in the form of crime in the streets—cost the nation roughly $18 billion a year. Yet the billions of dollars of losses from thefts and robberies that Nixon claimed addicts were committing to buy their heroin supplies was actually more than 25 times greater than the value of all property stolen and unrecovered throughout the United States in 1971.[65]

HEROIN, COCAINE, AND CRIME IN THE STREETS

In the aftermath of Watergate and Nixon's resignation, the Pittsburgh Steelers' victory over the Minnesota Vikings in Super Bowl IX, Evel Knievel's unsuccessful attempt to leap across Idaho's 1,600-foot-wide Snake River Canyon on a motorcycle, and five decades of banter about the nature and extent of drug-related crime, the National Institute on Drug Abuse (NIDA) convened a one-day workshop in 1975 for the purpose of establishing a federal drugs–crime research agenda. Subsequently, a panel of experts was assembled to examine any available data and prior research on the topic, to determine what questions could be readily addressed, and to recommend research approaches for studying questions that remained unanswered.

The ultimate conclusion of the panel was politically disturbing, to at least a few government drug officials at any rate. Many studies had heretofore demonstrated a statistical correlation between drug use and crime. From such data, policy makers had drawn an inference of causality—that is, that drug use causes crime. Yet the panel, on the basis of existing data and prior research, called the inference of causality into question, suggesting that the drug-use-causes-crime conclusion could not be drawn from what was known.

Moreover, in holding that any such linkage could not be demonstrated, the panel was questioning a fundamental assumption of U.S. drug control policy—that by reducing the demand for drugs through prevention and treatment initiatives, the criminality of the addict could be eliminated.[66] Nevertheless, NIDA established a federal drugs–crime research agenda. In the years hence, both NIDA and the National Institute of Justice funded a series of studies in many parts of the nation that began the building of a more meaningful database on the elusive drugs–crime connection.

On the basis of extensive follow-up studies of addict careers in Baltimore, for example, John C. Ball of Temple University and David N. Nurco of the University of Maryland School of Medicine found high rates of criminality among heroin users during the periods when they were addicted and markedly lower rates during times of nonaddiction.[67] This finding was based on the concept of the *crime-days per year at risk*. The crime-day was defined as a twenty-four-hour period during which an individual committed one or more crimes. Thus, crime-days per year at risk was a rate of crime commission that could vary anywhere from 0 to 365. For the addiction careers of the Baltimore addicts studied, the average crime-days per year at risk was 230, suggesting that their rates of criminality were not only persistent on a day-to-day basis, but also tended to continue over an extended number of years and periods of addiction.[68]

In a series of New York studies, the investigators operated from a storefront. During their many projects, they conducted interviews with hundreds of criminally active drug users recruited from the streets of east and central Harlem. The findings on drug-related criminality tended to confirm what was being learned elsewhere and provided insights as to how heroin and cocaine users functioned on the streets—how they purchased, sold, and used drugs; the roles that drugs played in their lives; and how the street-level drug business was structured.[69]

A series of studies conducted in Miami demonstrated that the amount of crime drug users committed was far greater than anyone had heretofore imagined, that drug-related crime could at times be exceedingly violent, and that the criminality of heroin and cocaine users was far beyond the control of law enforcement.[70] Other research investigations were arriving at similar conclusions.[71] What most seemed to be saying was that although the use of heroin and other drugs did not necessarily initiate criminal careers, it tended to intensify and perpetuate them. In that sense, it might be said that drug use freezes offenders into patterns of criminality that are more acute, dynamic, unremitting, and enduring than those of other law violators.

THE DRUGS–VIOLENCE CONNECTION

It has been a recurring theme over the years that drugs instigate users to acts of wanton violence. Richmond Pearson Hobson and many others before and after him said it about heroin; Harry J. Anslinger and members of other antimarijuana contingents made a similar proclamation about the evil weed of the fields; and at various times the same has been said about cocaine, the amphetamines, and PCP. More recently, the same arguments are made about cocaine and crack. Moreover, there is a lengthy literature on the issue, with inconsistencies and contradictions on both sides of the argument.

During the 1920s, after Captain Hobson had launched his ravings against the quagmire of heroin use, Dr. Lawrence Kolb of the U.S. Public Health Service responded with what turned out to be one of the most often-quoted statements in the literature on drugs and violence:

> There is probably no more absurd fallacy prevalent than the notion that murders are committed and daylight robberies and holdups are carried out by men stimulated by cocaine or heroin which has temporarily distorted them into self-imagined heroes incapable of fear. . . . Violent crime would be much less prevalent if all habitual criminals were addicts who could obtain sufficient morphine or heroin to keep themselves fully charged with one of these drugs at all times.[72]

Kolb's argument was based on his belief that all preparations of opium capable of producing dependence tend to inhibit aggressive impulses and, furthermore, that the soothing narcotic properties of the opiates have the effect of making psychopaths less likely to commit crimes of violence. From a strictly pharmacological point of view Kolb was correct, for the opiates do indeed depress the central nervous system. In the decades hence, others reiterated his position. In 1957, for example, the Council on Mental Health of the American Medical Association clearly stated that the belief that opiates per se directly incite otherwise normal people to violent assaultive criminal acts, including sexual crimes, is not tenable.[73] During the 1960s the President's Commission on Law Enforcement and Administration of Justice reached the same conclusion.[74]

What the American Medical Association and the President's Commission were reacting to was the growing body of studies that were empirically documenting that drug users were not coming to the attention of the criminal justice system for the commission of violent crimes. In 1957, for example, sociologist Harold Finestone's study of a jail population found that heroin users engaged primarily in nonviolent property crimes.[75] The perspective that developed from the work of Finestone and others was that narcotics users tended toward burglary and prostitution—low-risk activities that generated the income necessary to purchase drugs. Thus, noneconomically productive crimes, such as assault, were avoided.

Other studies have argued that individuals who are involved in violent crime become less so after initiation into drug use.[76] Perhaps all that was so in the 1920s through the 1960s. Perhaps the addict was indeed nonviolent. Or perhaps the findings were the result of the long-standing tradition in drug abuse research to study only treatment populations and to assess criminality on the basis of arrest records alone.

In 1972, in an obscure paper published in what may be the most remote corner of the social science/criminology literature, a New York University graduate student challenged the position that heroin users were nonviolent.[77] Based on the growing number of studies of polydrug abusers, an emergent cohort of multiple drug users that had evolved from the drug revolution of the 1960s, it was argued that a new and different breed of heroin user was living on the streets of American cities. They used not only heroin, but other drugs as well. Most importantly, their criminality was situational in nature. Rather than repeatedly committing burglaries, they lacked any type of criminal expertise and specialization. They engaged in a wide variety of crimes—including assaults, muggings, and armed robberies—selected according to the nuances of situational opportunity. Shortly thereafter, other research studies began reporting the same phenomenon.[78] All this was sometime before the research literature began examining the criminality of cocaine users, and well before the rediscovery of crack cocaine.

In the mid-1980s, Dr. Paul J. Goldstein, at the time a researcher with New York City's Narcotic and Drug Research, Inc., conceptualized the whole phenomenon of drugs and violence into a useful theoretical framework.[79] The *psychopharmacological model of violence* suggests that some individuals, as the result of short-term or long-term ingestion of specific substances, may become excitable, irrational, and exhibit violent behavior. The *economically compulsive model of violence* holds that some drug users engage in economically oriented violent crime to support costly drug use. The *systemic model of violence* maintains that violent crime is intrinsic to the very involvement with any illicit substance. As such, systemic violence refers to the traditionally aggressive patterns of interaction within the systems of illegal drug trafficking and distribution.

The early statements attributing violent behavior to drug use generally focused on the psychopharmacological argument. More recently this model has been applied to cocaine, barbiturates, and PCP, and with a major focus on the amphetamines, crank, and crack. In study after study, it was reported that the chronic use of amphetamines produced paranoid thought patterns and delusions that led to homicide and other acts of violence.[80] The same was said about cocaine. The conclusion is a correct one, although it did not apply to *every* amphetamine and cocaine user. Violence was most typical among the hard-core, chronic users.

Contrary to everything that has been said over the years about the quieting effects of narcotic drugs, recent research has demonstrated that there may be as much, and perhaps more, psychopharmacological violence associated with heroin use than that of any other illegal drug. Goldstein's studies of heroin-using sex workers in New York City during the 1970s, for example, found a link between the effects of the withdrawal syndrome and violent crime.[81] The impatience and irritability caused by withdrawal motivated a number of prostitutes to rob their clients rather than provide them with sexual services. This phenomenon was found to be common in Miami, and not only among sex workers but among other types of criminals as well. For example, one sex worker declared:

> . . . there are lots of shortcuts to get the john's money without having to go down on him. Sometimes you can con him out of it. Sometimes you just rob them outright. . . . Most of the time when me and the other girls are feeling sick and we just want to get back out in the street to fix . . . somethin' just seems to come over us. More than one time we felt so bad that I just cut a guy just to get out'a there and get straight. One time I was so crazy I just cut this guy and didn't even take his money.

A methadone patient stated: "Many times when you're sick you might do things you don't normally [do] . . . you can get so desperate and uptight that you don't see straight. . . . I cut a connection more than once just so I didn't have to argue over the price of shit." A low-level street dealer added: "I'm just talkin' to this guy and all of a sudden, bam! He hits me. I know he wasn't feelin' too good, but the cocksucker just hits me and walks away." To these can be added the many incidents of violence precipitated by the irritability and paranoia associated with crack use.[82]

The economically compulsive model of violence best fits the aggressive behavior of contemporary heroin, cocaine, and crack users. Among 573 narcotics users interviewed in Miami, for example, more than one-third engaged in a total of 5,300 robberies over a one-year period as one source of income.[83] Some of these were strong-arm robberies or muggings with the victim attacked from the rear and overpowered whereas the majority occurred at gunpoint. In fact, more than one-fourth of the respondents in this study used a firearm in the commission of a crime.

A similar phenomenon was found among a cohort of 429 nonnarcotics users in Miami, with weapon use most common among those who were primarily cocaine users.[84] Also, of 611 adolescent drug users (primarily crack) in Miami, 59 percent had participated in over 6,000 robberies during the one-year period prior to interview.[85] A more recent study in Miami included 699 crack and cocaine users, the majority of whom were actively using drugs and committing crimes in the community at the time that they were contacted. All subjects were interviewed at length about the number of their crimes and arrests during the previous ninety days. The study found that the incidence of crime was strikingly high whereas the rate of arrest was almost insignificant. There were a total of 1,766,630 offenses, but less than 1 percent resulted in arrest. Although most of these offenses were the so-called victimless crimes of procuring, drug sales, prostitution, and gambling, the number of violent crimes was significant—almost 5,000 robberies and assaults.[86]

In the systemic model, acts of drug-related violence can occur for a variety of reasons: territorial disputes between rival drug dealers; assaults and homicides committed within dealing and trafficking hierarchies as means of enforcing normative codes; robberies of drug dealers, often followed by unusually violent retaliations; elimination of informers; punishment for selling adulterated, phony, or otherwise bad drugs; retribution for failing to pay one's debts; and general disputes over drugs or drug paraphernalia.

Most street drug users report having been either the perpetrator or victim of drug-related violence.[87] In this regard, a Miami heroin dealer made the following comment about one of his street-level sellers:

> Just the other day we caught this dumb junky nigger stiff with his hand in the till messin' with the money. We took care of him outright so as the word would get around quick. . . . We cut three of the stupid motherfucker's fingers off and fed them to his dog.

Many women drug users reported over the years that they were the victims of rape at the hands of drug dealers. One 24-year-old cocaine and marijuana user stated:

> In the last few years I've been beaten and raped at least 10 times when I was trying to make a buy. One time this Cuban pimp drug dealer smacked me across the mouth, tied me to a bed, and then had all his friends try to fuck me to death—all the time sayin', "pretty white girl, ya just love it don't ya." If I ever find the bastard I'll blow his fucking brains out.

Violence associated with disputes over drugs has been common to the drug scene probably since its inception. Two friends come to blows because one refuses to give the other a taste. A husband beats his wife because she raided his stash. A woman stabs her boyfriend because he didn't cop enough drugs for her too. A kingrat (the owner of a crack house) beats and rapes his house girl (a woman who exchanges sex for crack in a crack house) because she asks for too much crack. A cocaine injector kills another for stealing his only set of works (injection equipment). In short, systemic violence seems to be endemic to the parallel worlds of drug dealing, drug taking, and drug seeking. This has been the case especially in the crack markets.[88]

DRUG USE, SEX WORK, AND THE SUBCULTURE
OF VIOLENCE

If systemic violence is endemic to drug dealing, drug taking, and drug seeking, it would appear that systemic violence reaches epidemic levels in the netherworlds of drug use and sex work in the inner city. In fact, drug-involved women sex workers are so often the victims of violence that the street sex industry has been referred to as a "subculture of violence."[89]

The concept of a "culture of violence," with origins in the fields of both sociology and anthropology, has been used to explain high rates of homicide and other violent behaviors in certain cultures and segments of society. The concept expresses the notion that cultural values and social conditions, rather than simply individual biological or psychological factors, are significant causes of violent behavior. For example, the culture of violence thesis has been used to explain the higher rates of violent crime in urban inner-city areas,[90] as well as the propensity among males in the American south to use violence to settle disputes.[91] In anthropological writings, the culture of violence concept has been considered when comparing the values, attitudes, and behaviors characteristic of generally peaceful cultures, such as the Limbu of Nepal, with those of violent societies like the Yanomano of Brazil or the Bena Bena of New Guinea.[92]

In the criminology and delinquency literature, a "subculture of violence" thesis was introduced several decades ago for the purpose of explaining social-structural causes of violence in urban areas. The general model of such a subculture is one characterized by dense concentrations of socioeconomically disadvantaged persons with few legitimate avenues of social mobility, lucrative illegal markets for forbidden goods and devices, a value system that rewards only survival and material success, and private enforcement of the rules of the game. In this context, the subculture of violence thesis emphasizes Emile Durkheim's idea of *anomie* rather than normative socialization.[93] According to sociologist Robert K. Merton, furthermore, inner-city minority nihilism is sourced in the disparity between the cultural ideal of equal opportunity and real structural inequalities.[94] Richard Cloward and Lloyd Ohlin once emphasized that the form which deviant or criminal behavior takes in response to these anomic conditions—criminal, violent, or retreatist (drug addiction)—depends on the opportunity structures for illegitimate activity.[95] Too, socialization remains an aspect of concern here because the exposure of generations of children to violent life experiences refashions inner-city norms to favor violence over nonviolence.[96] This rendering of the subculture of violence concept has been used to analyze juvenile gang violence,[97] adolescent delinquency,[98] violence committed by black women against black men,[99] as well as generalized violence in urban inner-city neighborhoods.[100]

Perhaps the best known elucidation of the subculture of violence thesis appeared back in the 1960s in the work of Marvin Wolfgang and Franco Ferracuti, which concluded that young, lower socioeconomic class African Americans possessed a value system in which violence was an acceptable and "normal" part of everyday life in the inner city.[101] In recent years, however, Wolfgang and Ferracuti's point of view has been widely criticized because of its stereotyping of young African American males and its failure to address the social-structural sources of the values in question, including the differential treatment of blacks and whites by criminal justice agencies and the media.[102] Despite these limitations, the subculture of violence thesis can be a useful approach for understanding the extent to which certain types of violence are socially situated, rather than focusing exclusively on individual factors.

Within this context, it has been well documented that women sex workers who walk the boulevards and back streets of urban centers are typically at high risk for assault, rape, and other forms of physical violence—including murder—from a variety of individuals, including muggers, serial predators, drug dealers, pimps, police, "dates" ("johns" or customers), and even passersby.[103] Furthermore, street sex workers are embedded in the same violent social spaces where street violence and other subcultures of violence exist. As such, it would appear that to a considerable extent, street sex workers ply their trade in a subculture of violence.

The violence experienced by sex workers has been attributed to a number of enduring social problems, including gender inequality and discrimination against women, as well as the attempts by many men to exercise sexual control over women.[104] Class and racial discrimination is also an issue, because a great majority of street sex workers are indigent minority women, many of whom lack the social and work skills that offer alternative options. In addition, many street-based sex workers are also embedded in a complex of social situations that are independently associated with violent victimization, including homelessness and drug abuse.[105] As such, the sex worker milieu can be an extremely violent one. Furthermore, numerous studies have documented that although sex workers are victimized by a variety of different types of perpetrators, most of the violence they experience comes from their own customers, or dates, many of whom are drug users.[106] This situation was most recently demonstrated in studies of street sex workers in Miami, Florida.[107]

It would appear that among drug-involved sex workers in Miami, virtually all drift back and forth between commercial solicitation on the streets and sex-for-drugs exchanges in automobiles, empty lots and backyards, crack houses, shooting galleries, "stroll" motels, and behind fences, along the sidewalks of darkened streets, and in the many back alleys that are a characteristic part of the downtown Miami geography. And although most sex workers prefer commercial solicitation along the "stroll," they also resort to sex-for-drugs exchanges when they have an immediate need for drugs and when money is scarce, and paying dates are few in number.

The study under consideration here was conducted with sex workers recruited from Miami's well-known Biscayne Boulevard, a more than 15-mile long major thoroughfare extending from the Broward County line into downtown Miami. An 80-block stretch at the lower end of "the Boulevard" is a major sex worker "stroll." To the east are several gated, barricaded, and somewhat gentrified neighborhoods fronting Miami's Biscayne Bay, whereas to the west are mainly African American and Haitian residential areas long steeped in poverty. Numerous services for the homeless are found along the southern end of the Boulevard strip as it enters downtown Miami. Despite more than a decade of gradual revitalization, the Boulevard stroll continues its long-held reputation for prostitution, sex trading, drug dealing, fencing operations, and the widespread availability of cheap motels which cater not only to locals, but also to those who participate in Miami's sexual tourism industry.

More than three hundred sex workers were recruited into the study, and the substantial level of drug use and sex work engaged in by these women was often associated with violent encounters in their daily lives. In fact, the "subculture of violence" thesis might suggest that interpersonal conflict and violence has permeated the lives and experiences of these women from an early age. Interesting in this regard are the historical self-reports of trauma experienced by the women when they were children and adolescents. For example, nearly half reported a history of childhood physical abuse, and just over half reported childhood sexual abuse. And going further, almost half of the women had some violent encounter while engaging in sex work in the past year, including being "ripped off" (forcibly taking back money paid for sex) by a customer or date, being beaten by a date, being threatened with a weapon by a date, and being raped by a date. And importantly for the subculture of violence thesis, current violent victimization was consistently correlated with childhood victimization.

Overall, the survey data collected on this cohort of drug-involved female sex workers documented that their historical and current life experiences were replete with episodes of victimization and violence. The prevalence of both physical and sexual victimization, in childhood and adulthood, was extremely elevated by comparison with national estimates. In fact, a recent National Violence Against Women survey sponsored by the National Institute of Justice and the Centers for Disease Control and Prevention placed the percentage of women experiencing rape or physical assault in the past 12 months at 0.3 percent and 1.9 percent, respectively.[108] In this analysis of drug-involved sex workers, the rates of date violence alone were some 43 and 13 times higher, supporting the contention that female sex workers are enmeshed in a social milieu wherein violence is commonplace and victimization is expected. In fact, one of the sex workers commented:

> Prostitution, drugs, and violence go hand in hand; it's all in one palm, ok? And because the prostitute is out there to get drugs and because she has an addiction and—whether it be violence from the date or violence from the dope boy, either way we're looking at it, there's still violence involved.

Another reported:

> I think people who have been abused, like from childhood, sexual, or physical . . . I think they become co-dependent [on it]. Like my first boyfriend . . . I was like co-dependent on him, even though he was violent, a drug dealer, a drug addict, and you know, I was used to that kind of lifestyle anyway 'cause that's what I had in my parents home. Violence and drugs.

And still another reported:

> It's like there are two worlds, there's a good world and then there's a violent world and it's like alls we know is violence, alls we know is violent men.

POSTSCRIPT

Researchers in the drug field have long maintained that narcotics addicts are responsible for tens of millions of crimes each year in the United States.[109] In addition, an unknown and perhaps greater level of crime is committed by cocaine, crack, and other drug users. A result has been the extraordinarily high crime rates in the United States since the early 1960s. But in recent years, crime rates have been falling. Why has this been so, particularly since it would appear that rates of drug use continue to escalate? Moreover, although crime rates have declined in many parts of the country, why have they gone up in others? Does this have anything to do with the drugs–crime connection?

Although no single answer can explain all of the changes occurring throughout the United States, a few interpretations address the downward trend in crime rates. First, there is the economy. Because of greater prosperity and reduced unemployment, youths in particular have more hope of finding legal jobs and view crime as a less desirable option. Second, there is prevention. The 1990s witnessed an increased number of early intervention programs for high-risk youths and after-school programs during the 3 P.M. to 8 P.M. peak hours for juvenile violent crime. Third, rates of incarceration are higher. Between 1979 and 1991, the number of offenders sent to prison for violent crimes doubled. From 1991 through the beginning of 2006, there was yet another doubling of violent offenders being sent to prison,[110] and as the noted political scientist James Q. Wilson put it: "Putting people in prison is the single most important thing we've done."[111] Fourth, policing is better in a number of jurisdictions. Not only are more police on the streets, but the use of community policing techniques has increased. Fifth, and perhaps most importantly, the number of street-corner crack markets has dramatically reduced. The withering of these markets lessened the violence associated with (1) rivalries in the crack distribution system, (2) the large number of drug transactions among highly agitated buyers and sellers, and (3) the number of handguns that users and dealers carry to protect themselves from robberies. Yet by contrast, the increased rates of violent crime in many midsized cities was likely the result of crack markets arriving there late. As criminologist Alfred Blumstein of Carnegie Mellon University recently put it:

> Smaller cities are going through what bigger cities went through five years ago. There is a lag effect in the smaller cities, caused not necessarily by the saturation of drugs in the big cities but the propagation of markets. There may be entrepreneurs from the big cities looking to expand or new entrepreneurs in small cities looking to get involved.[112]

As a final point here, and returning to questions posed previously in this chapter, are drug users—and particularly cocaine, crack, heroin, and other narcotics users—driven to crime, driven by their enslavement to expensive drugs that can be afforded only through continual predatory activities? Or is it that drugs drive crime, that careers in drugs intensify already existing criminal careers? Contemporary data tend to support the latter position more than any other explanation.

NOTES

1. For a more complete analysis of the unicorn myth, see James A. Inciardi, Alan A. Block, and Lyle A. Hallowell, *Historical Approaches to Crime: Research Strategies and Issues* (Beverly Hills, CA: Sage, 1977), pp. 11–13.

2. Robert J. Trotter, "Psyching the Skyjacker," *Science News,* 101 (12 February 1972), pp. 108–110; *New York Times,* 25 November 1979, p. 45; *People,* 3 March 1980, pp. 45–46; *Newsweek,* 26 December 1983, p. 12; *USA Today,* 28 November 1988, p. 3A; *Los Angeles Times,* 6 December 1996, p. 1; *Buffalo News,* 24 November 1999, p. B4.

3. George B. Wood, *A Treatise on Therapeutics and Pharmacology of Materia Medica* (Philadelphia: J. B. Lippincott, 1856).

4. See, for example, F. E. Oliver, "The Use and Abuse of Opium," in *Third Annual Report,* Massachusetts State Board of Health (Boston: Wright and Potter, 1872), pp. 162–177; J. M. Hull, "The Opium Habit," in *Third Biennial Report,* Iowa State Board of Health (Des Moines, IA: George E. Roberts, 1885), pp. 535–545.

5. E. Levinstein, "The Morbid Craving of Morphia," cited in Charles E. Terry and Mildred Pellens, *The Opium Problem* (New York: Bureau of Social Hygiene, 1928), p. 139.

6. Cesare Lombroso, *Crime, Its Causes and Remedies* (Boston: Little, Brown, 1911).

7. Richard L. Dugdale, *The Jukes* (New York: Putnam, 1911).

8. W. G. Thompson, *Textbook of Practical Medicine* (Philadelphia: Lea Brothers, 1902).

9. See Frank Soule, John H. Gilran, and James Nisbet, *The Annals of San Francisco* (San Francisco: A. L. Bancroft, 1878); Herbert Asbury, *The Barbery Coast* (Garden City, NY: Garden City, 1933).

10. J. W. Buel, *Sunlight and Shadow of America's Great Cities* (Philadelphia: West Philadelphia Publishing Co., 1891); Edward Crapsey, *The Nether Side of New York* (New York: Sheldon, 1872); Gustav Lening, *The Dark Side of New York Life and Its Criminal Classes* (New York: Frederick Gerhard, 1873); Edward Winslow Martin, *Sins of the Great City* (Philadelphia: National, 1868).

11. Helen Campbell, Thomas Knox, and Thomas Byrnes, *Darkness and Daylight; or, Lights and Shadows of New York Life* (Hartford, CT: A. D. Worthington, 1892), p. 570.

12. A. E. Costello, *Our Police Protectors* (New York: Author's Edition, 1884), pp. 516–524. See also Thomas Byrnes, *Professional Criminals of America* (New York: G. W. Dillingham, 1895), pp. 39–40.

13. Harold Wentworth and Stuart Berg Flexner, *Dictionary of American Slang* (New York: Thomas Y. Crowell, 1960), p. 161.

14. Alonzo Calkins, *Opium and the Opium Appetite* (Philadelphia: J. B. Lippincott, 1871), pp. 324–330.

15. H. H. Kane, *Opium Smoking in America and China* (New York: G. P. Putnam's, 1881), p. 81.

16. Thomas D. Crothers, *Morphinism and Narcomaniacs from Other Drugs* (Philadelphia: W. B. Saunders, 1902), pp. 88, 112–113.

17. For example, see J. B. Mattison, "The Impending Danger," *Medical Record,* 22 January 1876, pp. 69–71.

18. H. Wayne Morgan, *Yesterday's Addicts: American Society and Drug Abuse: 1865–1920* (Norman: University of Oklahoma Press, 1974), p. 28.

19. For example, see the forward by Walter C. Bailey in James W. Brown, Roger Mazze, and Daniel Glaser, *Narcotics Knowledge and Nonsense* (Cambridge, MA: Ballinger, 1974), p. xiii.

20. Perry Lichtenstein, "Narcotic Addiction," *New York Medical Journal,* 100 (14 November 1914), pp. 962–966.

21. See Rufus King, *The Drug Hang-Up: America's Fifty-Year Folly* (New York: W. W. Norton, 1972), pp. 23–27.

22. *Literary Digest,* 26 April 1919, p. 32.

23. *The Outlook,* 25 June 1919, p. 315.

24. *American Review of Reviews,* July 1919, pp. 331–332.

25. Cited in David T. Courtwright, *Dark Paradise: Opiate Addiction in America before 1940* (Cambridge, MA: Harvard University Press, 1982), p. 33.

26. *Literary Digest,* 24 May 1924, p. 32.

27. Committee on Education of the House of Representatives, Conference on Narcotic Education, *Hearings on HJR 65,* 69th Cong., 1st sess. 16 December 1925, pp. 2–3.

28. David F. Musto, *The American Disease: Origins of Narcotic Control* (New Haven, CT: Yale University Press, 1973), p. 322.

29. National Broadcasting Company, "The Struggle of Mankind against Its Deadliest Foe," 1 March 1928.

30. Courtwright, p. 91.

31. Douglas T. Miller and Marion Nowak, *The Fifties: The Way We Really Were* (Garden City, NY: Doubleday, 1977), pp. 279–287.

32. Irving Shulman, *The Amboy Dukes* (Garden City, NY: Doubleday, 1947); Hal Ellson, *Jailbait Street* (Derby, CT: Monarch Books, 1959).

33. Isidor Chein, Donald L. Gerard, Robert S. Lee, and Eva Rosenfeld, *The Road to H: Narcotics, Delinquency, and Social Policy* (New York: Basic Books, 1964). See also Harold Alksne, *A Follow-Up Study of Treated Adolescent Narcotics Users* (New York: Columbia University School of Public Health and Administrative Medicine, 1959); Isidor Chein and Eva Rosenfeld, "Juvenile Narcotic Use," *Law and Contemporary Problems,* Winter 1957, pp. 52–68; A. S. Meyer, *Social and Psychological Factors in Opiate Addiction* (New York: Columbia University Bureau of Applied Social Research, 1952).

34. *Newsweek,* 25 June 1951, pp. 19–20; 11 June 1951, pp. 26–27; 17 September 1951, p. 60; *Life,* 25 June 1951, pp. 21–24; *The Survey,* July 1951, p. 328; *Time,* 26 February 1951, p. 24; 7 May 1951, pp. 82, 85; 3 October 1955, pp. 63–64; *Reader's Digest,* December 1957, pp. 55–58; *The Nation,* 31 August 1957, pp. 92–93; *Ladies' Home Journal,* March 1958, pp. 173–175.

35. *Newsweek,* 13 August 1951, p. 50.

36. *Newsweek,* 11 June 1951, p. 26.

37. *Newsweek,* 20 November 1950, pp. 57–58.

38. *Life,* 11 June 1951, p. 116.

39. *Reader's Digest,* October 1951, pp. 137–140.

40. *Time,* 10 September 1951, p. 27.

41. Ian Whitcomb, *After the Ball: Pop Music from Rag to Rock* (New York: Viking, 1974), pp. 219–241.

42. Miller and Nowak, p. 295.

43. Jack Lait and Lee Mortimer, *U.S.A. Confidential* (New York: Crown, 1952), pp. 37–38.

44. David M. Wilner, Eva Rosenfeld, Donald L. Gerard, and Isidor Chein, "Heroin Use and Street Gangs," *Journal of Criminal Law, Criminology and Police Science,* November–December 1957, pp. 399–409.

45. Edouard C. Sandoz, "Report on Morphinism to the Municipal Court of Boston," *Journal of Criminal Law and Criminology,* 13 (1922), pp. 10–55; Lawrence Kolb, "Drug Addiction and Its Relation to Crime," *Mental Hygiene,* 9 (1925), pp. 74–89.

46. James A. Inciardi, "The Vilification of Euphoria: Some Perspectives on an Elusive Issue," *Addictive Diseases: An International Journal,* 1 (1974), p. 245.

47. U.S. Treasury Department, Bureau of Narcotics, *Traffic in Opium and Dangerous Drugs for the Year Ended December 31, 1939* (Washington, DC: U.S. Government Printing Office, 1940).

48. Harry J. Anslinger, "Relationship between Addiction to Narcotic Drugs and Crime," *Bulletin on Narcotics,* 3 (1951), pp. 1–3.

49. James A. Inciardi and Brian R. Russe, "Professional Thieves and Drugs," *International Journal of the Addictions,* 12 (1977), pp. 1087–1095.

50. For detailed descriptions and analyses of the history, social organization, occupational structure, and criminal activities of professional thieves, see Edwin H. Sutherland, *The Professional Thief* (Chicago: University of Chicago Press, 1937); James A. Inciardi, *Careers in Crime* (Chicago: Rand McNally, 1975).

51. John C. Ball, "Two Patterns of Narcotic Addiction in the United States," *Journal of Criminal Law, Criminology and Police Science,* 52 (1965), pp. 203–211; John A. O'Donnell, "The Rise and Decline of a Subculture," *Social Problems,* Summer 1967, pp. 73–84.

52. Charles Winick, "Physician Narcotic Addicts," *Social Problems,* Fall 1961, pp. 174–186; Charles Winick, "The Use of Drugs by Jazz Musicians," *Social Problems,* Winter 1961, pp. 240–253.

53. James P. Morgan, "Drug Addiction: Criminal or Medical Problem," *Police,* July–August 1966, pp. 6–9.

54. For bibliographies and analyses of the literature on drug use and crime, see Harold Finestone, "Narcotics and Criminality," *Law and Contemporary Problems,* Winter 1957, pp. 72–85; Florence Kavaler, Donald C. Krug, Zili Amsel, and Rosemary Robbins, "A Commentary and Annotated Bibliography on the Relationship between Narcotics Addiction and Criminality," *Municipal Reference Library Notes,* 42 (1968), pp. 45–63; Jared R. Tinklenberg, "Drugs and Crime," in *Drug Use in America: Problem in Perspective,* Appendix, vol. I, National Commission on Marihuana and Drug Abuse (Washington, DC: U.S. Government Printing Office, 1973), pp. 242–267; Gregory A. Austin and Dan J. Lettieri, *Drugs and Crime: The Relationship of Drug Use and Concomitant Criminal Behavior* (Rockville, MD: National Institute on Drug Abuse, 1976); Research Triangle Institute, *Drug Use and Crime: Report of the Panel on Drug Use and Criminal Behavior* (Springfield, VA: National Technical Information Service, 1976); Stephanie W. Greenberg and Freda Adler, "Crime and Addiction: An Empirical Analysis of the Literature, 1920–1973," *Contemporary Drug Problems,* 3 (1974), pp. 221–270; Robert P. Gandossy, Jay R. Williams, Jo Cohen, and Henrick J. Harwood, *Drugs and Crime: A Survey and Analysis of the Literature* (Washington, DC: United States Department of Justice, National Institute of Justice, 1980); David N. Nurco, John C. Ball, John W. Shaffer, and Thomas Hanlon, "The Criminality of Narcotic Addicts," *Journal of Nervous and Mental Disease,* 173 (1985), pp. 94–102.

55. For a review essay on the unreliability of official criminal statistics, see James A. Inciardi, "The Uniform Crime Reports: Some Considerations on Their Shortcomings and Utility," *Public Data Use,* 6 (November 1978), pp. 3–16.

56. *Reader's Digest,* June 1956, p. 21.

57. President's Commission on Law Enforcement and Administration of Justice, *The Challenge of Crime in a Free Society* (Washington, DC: U.S. Government Printing Office, 1967).

58. Task Force on Narcotics and Drug Abuse, President's Commission on Law Enforcement and Administration of Justice, *Task Force Report: Narcotics and Drug Abuse* (Washington, DC: U.S. Government Printing Office, 1967), p. 11.

59. Edward J. Epstein, *Agency of Fear* (New York: G. P. Putnam's, 1977), p. 8.

60. Epstein, pp. 148–151.

61. *New York Times,* 23 April 1972, p. 23.

62. *Washington Post,* 16 January 1973, p. A3.

63. Cited by Carl D. Chambers and James A. Inciardi, "Forecasts for the Future: Where We Are and Where We Are Going," in *Drugs and the Criminal Justice System,* ed. James A. Inciardi and Carl D. Chambers (Beverly Hills, CA: Sage, 1974), p. 221.

64. Chambers and Inciardi, p. 222.

65. Epstein, pp. 179–181.

66. For a complete discussion of the operations of the drugs–crime "panel" and the structuring of the federal drugs–crime research agenda, see Richard R. Clayton, "Federal Drugs–Crime Research: Setting the Agenda," in *The Drugs–Crime Connection,* ed. James A. Inciardi (Beverly Hills, CA: Sage, 1981), pp. 17–38.

67. John C. Ball, Lawrence Rosen, John A. Flueck, and David N. Nurco, "The Criminality of Heroin Addicts: When Addicted and When Off Opiates," in *The Drugs–Crime Connection,* ed. James A. Inciardi (Beverly Hills, CA: Sage, 1981), pp. 39–65; John C. Ball, John W. Shaffer, and David N. Nurco, "The Day-to-Day Criminality of Heroin Addicts in Baltimore—A Study in the Continuity of Offense Rates," *Drug and Alcohol Dependence,* 12 (1983), pp. 119–142.

68. David N. Nurco, John C. Ball, John W. Shaffer, and Thomas E. Hanlon, "The Criminality of Narcotic Addicts," *Journal of Nervous and Mental Disease,* 173 (1985), p. 98.

69. See Bruce D. Johnson, Paul J. Goldstein, Edward Preble, James Schmeidler, Douglas S. Lipton, Barry Spunt, and Thomas Miller, *Taking Care of Business: The Economics of Crime by Heroin Abusers* (Lexington, MA: Lexington, 1985). See also Paul J. Goldstein, "Getting Over: Economic Alternatives to Predatory Crime among Street Heroin Users," in *The Drugs–Crime Connection,* Inciardi, ed. (Beverly Hills, CA: Sage, 1981) pp. 67–84.

70. See James A. Inciardi, "Heroin Use and Street Crime," *Crime and Delinquency,* July 1979, pp. 335–346; Susan K. Datesman and James A. Inciardi, "Female Heroin Use, Criminality, and Prostitution," *Contemporary Drug Problems,* 8 (1979), pp. 455–473; James A. Inciardi, "Women, Heroin, and Property Crime," in *Women, Crime, and Justice,* ed. Susan K. Datesman and Frank R. Scarpitti (New York: Oxford University Press, 1980), pp. 214–222; James A. Inciardi, "The Impact of Drug Use on Street Crime," *Thirty-Third Annual Meeting of the American Society of Criminology,* Washington, DC, November 1981 pp. 11–14; Anne E. Pottieger and James A. Inciardi, "Aging on the Street: Drug Use and Crime among Older Men," *Journal of Psychoactive Drugs,* April–June 1981, pp. 199–211; Charles E. Faupel, "Drugs and Crime: An Elaboration of an Old Controversy," *Thirty-Third Annual Meeting of the American Society of Criminology,* Washington, DC, November 1981 pp. 11–14; Susan K. Datesman, "Women, Crime, and Drugs," in *The Drug–Crime Connection,* ed. James A. Inciardi, (Beverly Hills, CA: Sage, 1981), pp. 85–105; Carl D. Chambers, Sara W. Dean, and Michael Pletcher, in "Criminal Involvements of Minority Group Addicts," ed. James A. Inciardi, pp. 125–154; Anne E. Pottieger, "Sample Bias in Drugs/Crime Research: An Empirical Study," in *The Drugs–Crime Connection,* ed. James A. Inciardi, (Beverly Hills, CA: Sage, 1981), pp. 207–238; James A. Inciardi, Anne E. Pottieger, and Charles E. Faupel, "Black Women, Heroin and Crime: Some Empirical Notes," *Journal of Drug Issues,* Summer 1982, pp. 241–250; James A. Inciardi, "The Production and Detection of Fraud in Street Studies of Crime and Drugs," *Journal of Drug Issues,* Summer 1982, pp. 285–291; James A. Inciardi and Anne E. Pottieger, "Drug Use and Crime among Two Cohorts of Women Narcotics Users: An Empirical Assessment," *Journal of Drug Issues,* 16 (Winter 1986), pp. 91–106; Leon Pettiway, "Partnership in Crime Partnerships by Female Drug Users: The Effects of Domestic Arrangements, Drug Use, and Criminal Involvement," *Criminology,* 25 (August 1987), pp. 741–766.

71. Charles E. Faupel and Carl B. Klockars, "Drugs–Crime Connections: Elaborations from the Life Histories of Hard-Core Heroin Addicts," *Social Problems,* 34 (February 1987), pp. 54–68; Marcia R. Chaiken and Bruce D. Johnson, *Characteristics of Different Types of Drug-Involved Offenders* (Washington, DC: National Institute of Justice, 1988); Jose E. Sanchez and Bruce D. Johnson, "Women and the Drugs–Crime Connection: Crime Rates among Drug Abusing Women at Rikers Island," *Journal of Psychoactive Drugs,* 19 (April–June 1987), pp. 205–216; Eric D. Wish, Kandace A. Klumpp, Amy H. Moorer, Elazabeth Brady, and Kristen M. Williams, *An Analysis of Drugs and Crime among Arrestees in the District of Columbia* (Washington, DC: National Institute of Justice, 1981); George Speckart and M. Douglas Anglin, "Narcotics Use and Crime: An Overview of Recent Research Advances," *Contemporary Drug Problems,* Winter 1986, pp. 741–769; M. Douglas Anglin and Yih-Ing Hser, "Addicted Women and Crime," *Criminology,* 25 (May 1987), pp. 359–397.

72. Lawrence Kolb, "Drug Addiction and Its Relation to Crime," *Mental Hygiene,* 9 (1925), p. 78.

73. American Medical Association, Council on Mental Health, "Report on Narcotic Addiction," *Journal of the American Medical Association,* 7 December 1957, p. 1834.

74. Task Force on Narcotics and Drug Abuse, pp. 10–11.

75. Harold Finestone, "Use of Drugs among Persons Admitted to a County Jail," *Public Health Reports,* 90 (1957), pp. 553–568.

76. For a review of the issues and early research on drugs and violence, see Duane C. McBride, "Drugs and Violence," in *The Drugs–Crime Connection,* ed. James A. Inciardi, pp. 105–123.

77.   James A. Inciardi, "The Poly-Drug Abuser: A New Situational Offender," in *Politics, Crime and the International Scene: An Inter-American Focus,* ed. Freda Adler and G. O. W. Mueller (San Juan, PR: North-South Center for Technical and Cultural Exchange, 1972), pp. 60–68.

78.   Richard C. Stephens and Rosalind D. Ellis, "Narcotics Addicts and Crime: Analysis of Recent Trends," *Criminology,* 12 (1975), pp. 474–488; Margaret A. Zahn and Mark Bencivengo, "Violent Death: A Comparison between Drug Users and Non-Drug Users," *Addictive Diseases: An International Journal,* 1 (1974), pp. 283–296.

79.   Paul J. Goldstein, "The Drugs/Violence Nexus: A Tripartite Conceptual Framework," *Journal of Drug Issues,* 15 (Fall 1985), pp. 493–506.

80.   See Everett H. Ellinwood, "Assault and Homicide Associated with Amphetamine Abuse," *American Journal of Psychiatry,* 127 (1971), pp. 1170–1175; Roger C. Smith, "Speed and Violence: Compulsive Methamphetamine Abuse and Criminality in the Haight-Ashbury District," in *Proceedings of the International Conference on Drug Abuse,* ed. Chris Zarafonetis (Philadelphia: Lea & Febiger, 1972), pp. 435–448; S. Asnis and Roger C. Smith, "Amphetamine Abuse and Violence," *Journal of Psychedelic Drugs,* 10 (1978), pp. 317–378.

81.   Paul J. Goldstein, *Prostitution and Drugs* (Lexington, MA: Lexington, 1979), p. 126.

82.   See Duane C. McBride and James A. Swartz, "Drugs and Violence in the Age of Crack Cocaine," in *Drugs, Crime and the Criminal Justice System,* ed. Ralph Weisheit (Cincinnati: Anderson Publishing Co., 1990), pp. 141–169; Arthur J. Lurigio and James A. Swartz, "The Nexus Between Drugs and Crime: Theory, Research, and Practice," *Federal Probation,* 63 (June 1999), pp. 67–72; Karen McElrath, Dale D. Chitwood, and Mary Comerford, "Crime, Victimization, and Injection Drug Users," *Journal of Drug Issues,* 27 (1997), pp. 771–783.

83.   James A. Inciardi, *The War on Drugs: Heroin, Cocaine, Crime, and Public Policy* (Palo Alto, CA: Mayfield, 1986), pp. 122–132.

84.   Ibid.

85.   James A. Inciardi, "The Crack/Violence Connection within a Population of Hard-Core Adolescent Offenders," in *Drugs and Violence: Causes, Correlates, and Consequences,* ed. Mario DeLaRosa, Elizabeth Y. Lambert, and Bernard Gropper (Rockville, MD: National Institute on Drug Abuse, 1990), pp. 92–111.

86.   James A. Inciardi and Anne E. Pottieger, "Drug Use and Street Crime in Miami: An (Almost) Twenty-Year Retrospective," *Substance Use & Misuse,* 33 (1998): pp. 1839–1870.

87.   Harvey A. Siegal, Russell S. Falck, Jichuan Wang, and Robert G. Carlson, "Crack-Cocaine Users as Victims of Physical Attack," *Journal of the National Medical Association,* 92 (2000), pp. 76–82.

88.   See Ansley Hamid, "The Political Economy of Crack-Related Violence," *Contemporary Drug Problems,* 17 (1990), pp. 31–78; James A. Inciardi and Anne E. Pottieger, "Crack-Cocaine Use and Street Crime," *Journal of Drug Issues,* 24 (Winter/Spring 1994), pp. 273–292; James A. Inciardi and Anne E. Pottieger, "Kids, Crack, and Crime," *Journal of Drug Issues,* 21 (1991), pp. 257–270.

89.   Hilary L. Surratt, James A. Inciardi, Steven P. Kurtz, and Marion C. Kiley, "Sex Work and Drug Use in a Subculture of Violence," *Crime & Delinquency,* 50 (January 2004), pp. 43–59.

90.   R. Gottesman and R. M. Brown, *Violence in America: An Encyclopedia,* vol. 2 (New York: Charles Scribner's Sons, 1999).

91.   H. P. Lundsgaarde, *Murder in Space City* (New York: Oxford University Press, 1977); W. L. Montell, *Killings: Folk Justice in the Upper South* (Lexington, KY: University Press of Kentucky, 1986); R. E. Nisbett and D. Cohen, *Culture of Honor: The Psychology of Violence in the South* (Boulder, CO: Westview Press, 1996).

92.   L. L. Langness. "Ritual, Power and Male Dominance," *Ethos,* 2(3) (1974), pp. 189–212; G. Northrup, "The Residential Treatment of Violent Youth Viewed as a Process of Acculturation," *Milieu Therapy,* 4(1) (1985), pp. 51–59.

93.   Emile Durkheim, *The Division of Labour in Society* (Paris: P.U.F., 1893).

94.   Robert K. Merton, *Social Theory and Social Structure* (New York: Free Press, 1968).

95. Richard Cloward and Lloyd Ohlin, *Delinquency and Opportunity: A Theory of Delinquent Gangs* (Glencoe, IL: Free Press, 1960).

96. C. M. Clark, "Deviant Adolescent Subcultures: Assessment Strategies and Clinical Interventions," *Adolescence, 27*(106) (1992), pp. 283–293; C. Shaw and H. D. McKay, *Social Factors in Juvenile Delinquency* (Washington, DC: Government Printing Office, 1931).

97. Clark, 1992; L. W. Kennedy and S. W. Baron, "Routine Activities and a Subculture of Violence: A Study of Violence on the Street," *Journal of Research in Crime & Delinquency, 30(1)* (1993), pp. 88–112; R. J. Thompson and J. Lozes, "Female Gang Delinquency," *Corrective & Social Psychiatry & Journal of Behavior Technology, Methods & Therapy, 22*(3) (1976), pp. 1–5; M. L. Walker, L. M. Schmidt, and L. Lunghofer, "Youth Gangs," in *Handbook for Screening Adolescents at Psychological Risk,* ed. M. I. Singer, L. T. Singer, et al. (New York: Lexington Books/Macmillan, Inc., 1993), pp. 400–422.

98. J. G. Bernburg and T. Thorlindsson, "Adolescent Violence, Social Control, and the Subculture of Delinquency: Factors Related to Violent Behavior and Nonviolent Delinquency," *Youth and Society, 30*(4) (1999), pp. 445–460.

99. M. C. Ray and E. Smith, "Black Women and Homicide: An Analysis of the Subculture of Violence Thesis," *The Western Journal of Black Studies, 15*(3) (1991), pp. 144–153.

100. J. W. Clarke, *The Lineaments of Wrath: Race, Violent Crime, and American Culture* (Tucson, AZ: University of Arizona Press, 1998); S. W. Baron and T. F. Hartnagel, "Street Youth and Criminal Violence," *Journal of Research in Crime and Delinquency, 35*(2) (1998), pp. 166–192.

101. M. E. Wolfgang and F. Ferracuti, *The Subculture of Violence: Towards an Integrated Theory in Criminology* (London: Tavistock Publications, 1967).

102. E. Madriz, "Overview II," in *Violence in America: An Encyclopedia,* vol. 1, ed. R. Gottesman and R. M. Brown (New York: Charles Scribner's Sons, 1999), pp. 298–302.

103. A. Carmen and H. Moody, *Working Women: The Subterranean World of Street Prostitution* (New York: Harper & Row, 1985); E. M. Miller, *Street Woman* (Philadelphia: Temple University Press, 1986); J. A. Inciardi, "Kingrats, Chicken Heads, Slow Necks, Freaks, and Blood Suckers: A Glimpse at the Miami Sex-for-Crack Market," in *Crack Pipe as Pimp: An Ethnographic Investigation of Sex-for-Crack Exchanges,* ed. M. Ratner (New York: Lexington Books, 1993), pp. 37–68; L. Maher, *Sexed Work: Gender, Race and Resistance in a Brooklyn Drug Market* (Oxford, UK: Clarendon Press, 1997); J. A. Inciardi and H. L. Surratt, "Drug Use, Street Crime, and Sex-Trading among Cocaine-Dependent Women: Implications for Public Health and Criminal Justice Policy," *Journal of Psychoactive Drugs, 33*(4) (2001), pp. 379–389; J. M. Teets, "The Incidence and Experience of Rape among Chemically Dependent Women," *Journal of Psychoactive Drugs, 29*(4) (1997), pp. 331–336.

104. R. Weitzer, ed., *Sex for Sale: Prostitution, Pornography, and the Sex Industry* (New York: Routledge, 2000).

105. N. J. Davis, "From Victims to Survivors: Working with Recovering Street Prostitutes," in *Sex for Sale: Prostitution, Pornography, and the Sex Industry,* ed. R. Weitzer (New York: Routledge, 2000), pp. 139–158; S. L. Wenzel, B. D. Leake, and L. Gelberg, "Risk Factors for Major Violence among Homeless Women," *Journal of Interpersonal Violence, 16*(8) (2001), pp. 739–752; J. Baseman, M. Ross, and M. Williams, "Sale of Sex for Drugs and Drugs for Sex: An Economic Context of Sexual Risk Behaviors for STDs," *Sexually Transmitted Diseases, 26*(8) (1999), pp. 444–449; R. S. Falck, J. Wang, R. G. Carlson, and H. S. Siegal, "The Epidemiology of Physical Attack and Rape among Crack-Using Women," *Violence and Victims, 16*(1) (2001), pp. 79–89; L. Gilbert, N. El-Bassel, V. Rajah, A. Foleno, and V. Frye, "Linking Drug-Related Activities with Experiences of Partner Violence: A Focus Group Study of Women in Methadone Treatment," *Violence and Victims, 16*(5) (2001), pp. 517–536.

106. Maher, 1997; C. T. M. Coston and L. E. Ross, "Criminal Victimization of Prostitutes: Empirical Support for the Lifestyle/Exposure Model," *Journal of Crime and Justice, 21*(1) (1998), pp. 53–70; S. Church, M. Henderson, M. Barnard, and G. Hart, "Violence by Clients towards Female Prostitutes in Different Work Settings: Questionnaire Survey," *British Medical Journal, 322* (2001), pp. 524–525;

M. Farley and H. Barkan, "Prostitution, Violence and Posttraumatic Stress Disorder," *Women and Health, 27*(3) (1998), pp. 37–49; C. Hoigard and L. Finstad, *Backstreets: Prostitution, Money and Love* (University Park: Pennsylvania State University Press, 1986); J. A. Inciardi, D. Lockwood, and A. E. Pottieger, *Women and Crack Cocaine* (New York: Macmillan, 1993).

107. Steven P. Kurtz, Hilary L. Surratt, James A. Inciardi, and Marion C. Kiley. "Sex Work and 'Date' Violence," *Violence against Women,* 10 (April 2004), pp. 357–385.

108. P. Tjaden and N. Thoennes, "Prevalence, Incidence, and Consequences of Violence against Women: Findings from the National Violence Against Women Survey," in *National Institute of Justice/Centers for Disease Control and Prevention: Research in Brief* (Washington, DC: U.S. Department of Justice, Office of Justice Programs, National Institute of Justice, 1998).

109. John C. Ball, Lawrence Rosen, John A. Flueck, and David N. Nurco, "The Lifetime Criminality of Heroin Addicts in the United States," *Journal of Drug Issues,* 12 (1982), pp. 225–239.

110. Bureau of Justice Statistics. *Prisoners in 2005.* (2006, November). Accessed on June 21, 2007, from www.ojp.usdoj.gov/bjs/pub/pdf/p05.pdf.

111. Cited in Gordon Witkin, "The Crime Bust," *U.S. News & World Report,* 25 May 1998, pp. 28–37.

112. *New York Times,* 15 January 1998, p. A16.

■ ■ ■ ■ ■

CHAPTER 9

MAINLINING IN THE SHADOW OF DEATH

Probing the HIV/AIDS– Drugs Connection

George Gordon Byron, the nineteenth-century English poet better known as Lord Byron, is credited with coining the phrase "truth being stranger than fiction." So often that seems to be the case. Consider, for instance, the best-selling science fiction novel by Michael Crichton, *The Andromeda Strain.* This gripping story involved a space-borne organism that wiped out an entire U.S. town before mutating into a harmless germ. Little would the readers of Crichton's book, written in the late 1960s, have suspected what was about to begin in their country, and across the globe.

AIDS: A STRANGE DISEASE OF UNCERTAIN ORIGINS

Acquired immunodeficiency syndrome (AIDS) has been called many things. In 1986 the United States Surgeon General referred to the disease as the most serious health issue since the bubonic plague of the fourteenth century.[1] Similarly, in 1988 the U.S. Secretary of Health and Human Services called AIDS the number one public health problem in the United States.[2] In 1998, almost two decades after AIDS was first noticed, the Assistant Secretary General of the United Nations emphasized that the disease was as fierce as the greatest epidemics in history.[3] And in 2000, top officials in President Bill Clinton's administration declared that AIDS was a disease that could destroy nations and was a major threat to U.S. national security.[4] By contrast, however, both God and nature have also been brought into discussions about the epidemic. To some, AIDS is nature's revenge for the crime of homosexuality, or God's retribution for the perversions committed by junkies, perverts, queers, and whores.[5] To many more AIDS has become like syphilis, leprosy, and the plague—the contemporary metaphor for corruption, decay, and consummate evil.

The linking of AIDS with the sexual practices of gay men, and with drug use, makes it easily susceptible to these and perhaps many other metaphorical interpretations, as are other diseases transmitted through taboo behaviors or those with unknown causes. But these should not distract from the seriousness of the disease. AIDS confronts everyone with a variety of concerns, including risk factors and disease vectors, as well as susceptibility, contagion, and the spread of a disorder that eventually kills the majority of those who contract it.

The Emergence of AIDS

Acquired immune deficiency syndrome was first described as a new and distinct clinical entity during the late spring and early summer of 1981.[6] First, clinical investigators in Los Angeles reported five cases of *Pneumocystis carinii* pneumonia (PCP) among gay men to the Centers for Disease Control (CDC). None of these patients had an underlying disease that could have been associated with PCP, or a history of treatment for a compromised immune system. All, however, had other clinical manifestations and laboratory evidence of immunosuppression. Second, and within a month, twenty-six cases of Kaposi's sarcoma (KS) were reported among gay men in New York and California.

What was so unusual was that prior to these reports, the appearance of both PCP and KS in populations of previously healthy young men was unprecedented. PCP is an infection caused by the parasite *P. carinii,* previously seen almost exclusively in cancer and transplant patients receiving immunosuppressive drugs (see Exhibit 9.1). KS, a cancer or tumor of the blood vessel walls typically appearing as blue-violet to brownish skin blotches, had been quite rare in the United States—occurring primarily in elderly men, usually of Mediterranean origin. Like PCP, KS had also been reported among organ transplant recipients and others receiving immunosuppressive therapy. This quickly led to the hypothesis that the increased occurrences of the two disorders in gay men were due to some underlying immune system dysfunction. This hypothesis was further supported by the incidence among gay men of *opportunistic infections*—infections caused by microorganisms that rarely generate disease in persons with normal immune defense mechanisms. For this reason, the occurrence of KS, PCP, and/or other opportunistic infections in a person with unexplained immune dysfunction became known as the acquired immune deficiency syndrome, or more simply, AIDS.*

With the recognition that the vast majority of the early cases of this new clinical syndrome involved gay men, it seemed logical that the causes might be related to the lifestyle unique to that population. The sexual revolution of the 1960s and 1970s was accompanied not only by greater sexual permissiveness among both heterosexuals and gays, but also by a more positive social acceptance of homosexuality. The emergence of commercial bathhouses and other outlets for sexual contacts among gays

---

*By early 1982 the disease was known by a variety of names and acronyms. The most popular of these was GRID, for gay-related immune deficiency. But staff members at the Centers for Disease Control despised the GRID acronym and refused to use it, particularly because they were well aware that the disease was not restricted to gay men. When someone finally suggested the sexually neutral yet snappy acronym AIDS during the middle of 1982, it immediately replaced all others. See Randy Shilts, *And the Band Played On: Politics, People, and the AIDS Epidemic* (New York: St. Martin's Press, 1987), p. 171.

■ ■ ■ ■ ■

EXHIBIT 9.1

P. CARINII **AND KS**

Prior to the age of AIDS, *Pneumocystis carinii* pneumonia was one of the perhaps thousands of malevolent microorganisms that lurked on the fringes of human existence. PCP was first observed in guinea pigs and identified in 1910 by a Brazilian scientist known in the literature only as Dr. Carini. Three years later, physicians at the Pasteur Institute in France found that the same microbe lived quite comfortably in the lungs of Parisian sewer rats. Dr. Carini's discovery of the organism combined with its cystlike makeup resulted in its designation *Pneumocystis carinii.* As one of tens of thousands of creatures that exist in almost every corner of the world's inhabited terrain, but easily held in check by a normally functioning immune system, *P. carinii* was identified in human lungs during World War II in Europe. In 1956, it was diagnosed in the United States for the first time among immuno-suppressed patients. See Randy Shilts, *And the Band Played On: Politics, People, and the AIDS Epidemic* (New York: St. Martin's Press, 1987), p. 34; Jeffrey A. Golden,"Pulmonary Complications of AIDS," in *AIDS: Pathogenesis and Treatment,* ed. Jay A. Levy (New York: Marcel Dekker, 1989), pp. 403–447; W. T. Hughesg,"Pneumocystis Carinii," in *Principles and Practices of Infectious Diseases,* ed. G. L. Mandell, R. G. Douglous, and J. E. Bennett (New York: John Wiley, 1979), pp. 2137–2142.

Sarcoma* is a medical term describing a tumor that is often malignant, and Kaposi's sarcoma has been observed in a number of non-AIDS populations. First described in 1872 by the Viennese dermatologist Moritz Kaposi as a "multiple pigmented sarcoma of the skin," it was an extremely rare malignancy for more than a century in both the United States and Europe. Elderly men, particularly of Mediterranean or Jewish origin would occasionally develop this variety of cancer. Clinically, it appeared most frequently as a tumor of the feet and lower extremities. It was not accompanied by immune depression, other than the expected immunological attrition associated with aging.

During the early 1960s, studies in Uganda revealed that KS was a common cancer—accounting for up to 9 percent of all cancers in the region. But again, no associated immunodeficiency was determined, although a few reports of particularly aggressive cases, often in the young, were recorded.

The only non-AIDS population to develop KS with parallels to current AIDS-related cases were patients receiving immunosuppressive therapy following kidney transplants. As with many AIDS patients, the cancer was often aggressive. However, KS in transplant patients often regressed completely after the withdrawal of the immunosuppressive drugs. See P. A. Volberding, M. A. Conant, R. B. Strickler, and B. J. Lewis, "Chemotherapy in Advanced Kaposi's Sarcoma: Implications for Current Cases in Homosexual Men," *American Journal of Medicine,* 74 (1983), pp. 652–656; Bureau of Hygiene and Tropical Diseases,"Kaposi's Sarcoma: More Questions Than Answers," *WorldAIDS,* November 1990, p. 11

further increased promiscuity, with self-selected segments of the male gay population viewing promiscuity as a facet of gay liberation.

In fact, among early patients diagnosed with AIDS, sexual recreation typically occurred within the anonymity of bathhouses with similarly promiscuous men. Some had as many as twenty-thousand sexual contacts and more than eleven-hundred sex partners.* To complicate matters, active gay men with multiple sex partners were manifesting high rates of sexually transmitted diseases—gonorrhea, syphilis, genital herpes, anal warts, and hepatitis B.[7] To this could be added the matter of enteric diseases. As the late Randy Shilts (who died of AIDS in 1994) described it:

> Another problem was enteric diseases, like amebiasis and giardiasis, caused by organisms that lodged themselves in the intestinal tracts of gay men with alarming frequency. At the New York Gay Men's Health Project . . . 30 percent of the patients suffered from gastro intestinal parasites. In San Francisco, incidence of the "Gay Bowel Syndrome," as it was called in medical journals, had increased by 8,000 percent since 1973. Infection with these parasites was a likely effect of anal intercourse, which was apt to put a man in contact with his partner's fecal matter, and was virtually a certainty through the then-popular practice of rimming, which the medical journals politely called oral-anal intercourse.[8]

Because of this, it is not surprising that factors such as frequent exposure to semen, rectal exposure to semen, exposure to amyl nitrate and butyl nitrate (better known as poppers used to enhance sexual pleasure and performance), and/or a high frequency of sexually transmitted diseases were themselves considered potential causes of AIDS.

Although it was apparent that AIDS was a new disease, most of the gay lifestyle factors were not particularly new, having changed only in a relative sense. As such, it was difficult to single out immediately specific behaviors that might be related to the emerging epidemic. Nevertheless, in the minds of many Americans, AIDS was an immunity disease linked to homosexual practices and the homosexual condition. AIDS came along just when the old religious, moral, and cultural arguments against homosexuality seemed to be moderating. As the spread of AIDS became linked in the public imagination to men who have sex with men, the gay visibility and affirmation of the past decade allowed for some nasty scapegoating. Some were even asking whether Anita Bryant had been right after all.

The Rise and Fall of Anita Bryant

For those too young to remember, Anita Bryant had been a beauty queen (Miss Oklahoma in 1958), a Miss America contender (second runner-up in 1959), and a pop singer (such cloyingly maudlin inspirational ballads as "It's a Sin to Flirt," "Paper Roses," and "My Little Corner of the World"). In the 1970s, she divided much of her time between being the national spokesperson for the Florida Citrus Commission and doing concert tours in the state fair and convention circuits. She was also a devout born-again Christian and assertedly antigay. On January 18, 1977, despite highly publicized opposition by Bryant, Miami, Florida, became the first southern city in the United States to pass a gay rights ordinance, prohibiting housing and employment discrimination

---

*For an examination of the gay bathhouses of the 1970s and early 1980s, as well as the author's ethnographic studies of the gay baths of the early 1990s, see Clyde B. McCoy and James A. Inciardi, *Sex, Drugs, and the Continuing Spread of AIDS* (Los Angeles: Roxbury Publishing Co., 1995).

against gay men and lesbians.[9] Bryant quickly countered the ordinance by organizing the Save Our Children movement to overthrow the new legislation and by announcing:

> The ordinance condones immorality and discriminates against my children's rights to grow up in a healthy, decent community. Before I yield to this insidious attack on God and His laws, I will lead such a crusade to stop it as this country has never seen before. If homosexuality were the normal way, *God would have made Adam and Bruce!*[10]

Bryant was very clever. Rather than focusing her campaign on homosexuality per se, the real issue was saving children from recruitment by homosexuals. In her view, if teachers could not be fired for being gay, then Miami's children would not be safe from indoctrination into becoming gay. On March 20th, Bryant took out a full-page ad in the *Miami Herald* in which she proclaimed:

> Homosexuality is nothing new. Cultures throughout history have dealt with homosexuals almost universally with disdain, abhorrence, disgust—even death. The recruitment of our children is absolutely necessary for the survival and growth of homosexuality. Since homosexuals cannot reproduce, they *must* recruit, *must* freshen their ranks. And who better qualifies as a likely recruit than a teenage boy or girl who is surging with sexual awareness.[11]

The reactions to Anita Bryant's diatribe were mixed. On one side of the issue, the Arkansas State House of Representatives unanimously passed a special resolution applauding Bryant for her antigay crusade. In fact, the lawmaker who introduced the resolution remarked, "When you go against God's law, you have no human rights." Shortly thereafter, in a countywide referendum, voters in Miami repealed the controversial gay rights ordinance by a margin of two to one. In response, a firestorm of controversy emerged; Florida orange juice was boycotted throughout the gay community nationwide; Bryant was hit in the face with a pie at one of her Save Our Children press conferences; and syndicated columnist Mike Royko named Anita Bryant on his list of "The Ten Most Obnoxious Americans" and questioned: "If God hates gays so much, how come he picked Michelangelo, a known homosexual, to paint the Sistine Chapel while assigning Anita to go on TV and push orange juice?"[12]

Although Anita Bryant was successful in her campaign, she paid a high price for her victory. Her crusade galvanized the gay pride movement; she lost her job with the Florida Citrus Commission; and her celebrity status slowly faded.*

Shifting back to the early 1980s, the notion that AIDS was some form of gay plague was quickly extinguished. The disease was suddenly being reported in other populations, such as intravenous and other injection drug users, blood transfusion patients, and hemophiliacs.[13] These reports suggested to the scientific community that an infectious etiology for AIDS had to be considered.

---

*Fast forward to 1998: A gay advocacy group called SAVE-DADE was formed to pursue equal rights for gays and lesbians. A new measure was passed on December 1, and once again it is illegal to discriminate against gay men and women in Miami. As for Anita Bryant, with debts of more than ten million dollars, she and her husband declared bankruptcy in 1997. Poor Anita. Let's all have a glass of orange juice.

Exploring the Viral Frontier

Almost immediately after the first cases of AIDS were reported in 1981, researchers at the Centers for Disease Control began tracking the disease backward in time to discover its origins. They ultimately determined that the first cases of AIDS in the United States probably occurred in 1977. By early 1982, AIDS had been reported in fifteen states, the District of Columbia, and two foreign countries, but the total remained extremely low—158 men and one woman. Although more than 90 percent of the men were either gay or bisexual, interviews with all the patients failed to provide any definite clues about the origin of the disease.

Although it was suspected that AIDS might be transmitted through sexual relations among sexually active gay men, the first strong evidence for the idea did not emerge until the completion of a case control study in June 1982 by epidemiologists at the Centers for Disease Control.[14] In that investigation, data were obtained on the sex partners of thirteen of the first nineteen cases of AIDS among gay men in the Los Angeles area. Within five years before the onset of their symptoms, nine had had sexual contact with people who later developed Kaposi's sarcoma or *P. carinii* pneumonia. The nine were also linked to another interconnected series of forty AIDS cases in ten different cities by one individual who had developed a number of the manifestations of AIDS and was later diagnosed with Kaposi's sarcoma. Overall, the investigation of these forty cases indicated that 20 percent of the initial AIDS cases in the United States were linked through sexual contact—a statistical clustering that was extremely unlikely to have occurred by chance.

Yet even in the face of this evidence, some doubted that AIDS was caused by a transmissible agent. However, when AIDS cases began to emerge in other populations—among individuals who had been injected with blood or blood products but had no other expected risk factors—the transmission vectors for the disease became somewhat clearer. Such cases were confirmed first among people with hemophilia, followed by blood transfusion recipients and injection drug users who shared hypodermic needles. Then, when cases of AIDS among heterosexual partners of male injection drug users were documented, it became increasingly evident that AIDS was a sexually transmitted disease and that sexual preference was not necessarily the only risk factor.[15]

In 1983 and 1984, scientists at the Institute Pasteur in Paris and the National Institutes of Health in the United States identified and isolated the cause of AIDS—human T-cell lymphotropic virus, Type III (HTLV-III), or lymphadenophy-associated virus (LAV). Later, this virus would be renamed human immunodeficiency virus, more commonly known as HIV. More specifically, HIV is a *retrovirus*, a type of infectious agent that had previously been identified as causing many animal diseases. The designation *retrovirus* derives from the backward (or *retro*) flow of genetic information from RNA to DNA, which reverses the normal flow of genetic messages.*

---

*DNA is the carrier of genetic information for all organisms except the RNA viruses. See Institute of Medicine, National Academy of Sciences, *Mobilizing against AIDS: The Unfinished Story of a Virus* (Cambridge, MA: Harvard University Press, 1986), pp. 62–63.

Subsequent studies demonstrated that HIV is transmitted when virus particles or infected cells gain direct access to the bloodstream. This can occur through all forms of sexual intercourse, through sharing contaminated needles and other injection equipment, through mingling blood and blood products, and through infected mothers passing the virus to their unborn or newborn children. Within this context, HIV is a continuum of conditions associated with immune dysfunction, and AIDS is best described as a severe manifestation of infection with HIV (see Exhibit 9.2).

Subsequent to the discovery of HIV, an early priority was to fully verify its association with the diseases in question. Using a variety of different laboratory tests, researchers in virology and molecular biology searched for antibodies against HIV in

■　■　■　■　■

EXHIBIT 9.2

HUMAN IMMUNODEFICIENCY VIRUS

HIV has been isolated from blood, semen, vaginal secretions, urine, cerebrospinal fluid, saliva, tears, and breast milk of infected individuals. Transmission could theoretically occur from contact with any of these fluids, but the concentration of HIV found in saliva and tears is extremely low. Moreover, no cases of HIV infection have been traced to saliva or tears. The virus is found in greater concentration in semen than in vaginal secretions, which supports the hypothesis that transmission occurs more readily from male to female than from female to male.

More than one strain of human immunodeficiency virus (HIV) exists. HIV-1 is the most common form. A second variety, discovered in late 1985 and subsequently termed human immunodeficiency virus type 2 (HIV-2), was isolated from two West African patients with AIDS. In evolutionary terms, HIV-2 is clearly related to HIV-1. The two viruses are similar in their overall structure and both can cause AIDS. Although differences in the relative infectiousness of HIV-1 and HIV-2 have not yet been determined, it would appear that HIV-2 is a less virulent pathogen.

Importantly, HIV-1 has ten genetically distinct subtypes. Subtype B, which is most commonly transmitted through anal intercourse and injection drug use, is primarily found in the Americas, Europe, Australia, Japan, and the Caribbean. Subtype C, most often found in South Africa and India, seems to be more infectious with a higher potential for heterosexual transmission. For the sake of simplicity, all references to HIV-1 throughout this chapter are designated *HIV.*

HIV manifests itself in a variety of conditions, complicating efforts to define AIDS. The Centers for Disease Control formulated an initial definition of AIDS in 1982 that relied on the presence of certain opportunistic infections and malignancies. *Opportunistic infections* in this original case definition included pneumonia, meningitis, and encephalitis caused by nine different viruses, bacteria, fungi, and protozoa; esophagitis (inflammation of the esophagus) caused by candidiasis, cytomegalovirus, or herpes simplex; progressive brain disease with multiple lesions; chronic inflammation of the intestine caused by certain protozoan parasites (lasting more than four weeks); and unusually persistent herpes simplex infections of the mouth or rectum (lasting more than five weeks).

the blood of AIDS patients. Ultimately, they found that almost 100 percent of AIDS patients had HIV antibodies.[16] The presence of specific antibodies in the blood indicates that a previous infection registered on the body's immune system. The antibody molecules that remain in the bloodstream act as scouts, so to speak: if the virus appears again, the scouts recognize it immediately and attempt to prevent it from getting a foothold.

In 1985 this research led to the widespread availability of a commercial test for antibodies to HIV. The basic test is an enzyme-linked immunosorbent assay, more commonly known as ELISA or EIA. It is not a test for AIDS, nor does it detect the presence of the virus itself. What the test does indicate is whether HIV has been noticed by an individual's immune system.

The Origins of HIV/AIDS

As to where AIDS and HIV actually originated, speculation has been piled on both supposition and conjecture. However, there has always been considerable agreement that the source may have been Central Africa. The AIDS problem in Africa first became evident in 1982 when physicians in Belgium began seeing patients from Zaire (now called the Democratic Republic of the Congo) and Burundi.[17] Prior to gaining their independence in the early 1960s, Zaire and Burundi were part of the Belgian Congo. For many years their citizens with financial means traveled to Belgium for their major medical care. Many showed signs and symptoms virtually identical to what was being called AIDS in the United States. Further investigation led to a number of different theories. The first was that HIV existed for decades, nestled in remote regions of Africa and limited to small, relatively isolated populations.[18] The social mores of those populations may not have been conducive to the rapid spread of the disease, and the few cases that did develop could likely have escaped detection against the backdrop of multiple life-threatening infections common to the region.

A number of factors eventually changed this pattern. African cities grew dramatically after World War II, principally the result of many African countries gaining their independence. As in other parts of the world, the urbanization of Africa was accompanied by social changes and family disruptions, combined with the anonymity of urban life—all of which increased the likelihood of behaviors that contributed to the spread of sexually transmitted diseases (multiple sex partners and prostitution). In time, the prevalence of HIV increased sufficiently to make AIDS visible as a new clinical entity in Africa, and elsewhere.

An alternative theory suggested that the natural home of the AIDS virus is in an animal. The African green monkey was singled out as an initial suspect, with the hypothesis that somehow, the virus mutated and jumped species, entering the human population when monkeys bit hunters who were attempting to capture them for food.[19] Several investigations have also suggested that AIDS and HIV may have made their way to North America from Africa, via Haiti. More specifically, from the early 1960s through the mid-1970s, there was considerable migration from Zaire to

Haiti, and many of these immigrants are believed to have settled in the United States.[20] In addition, several commentators have argued that African green monkeys were imported to Haiti from Zaire and kept as pets in male houses of prostitution.[21] Finally, there is the point of view that Haiti was a popular vacation spot for gay people who brought the disease to the United States with them and infected the mainland population.[22]

There have been a number of conspiratorial theories, as well, about the origins of AIDS. Perhaps the most widely circulated was an opinion introduced by the press of the then Soviet Union. During the summer months of 1987, a number of Soviet-sponsored articles stated that the AIDS virus had been created by Pentagon experiments; that the experiments had been carried out at Fort Detrick, Maryland; and that they were initiated to develop a subtle biological weapon. The articles appeared not only in Soviet outlets, but in newspapers in Kenya, Peru, Sudan, Nigeria, Mexico, and Senegal as well. On November 4, 1987, however, members of the Soviet Academy of Sciences distanced themselves from the rumor, and their disavowals were published in *Izvestia,* the Soviet government newspaper.[23]

Then, in a letter dated February 25, 1987, written and widely circulated by Frances Cress Welsing, a Washington, DC, psychiatrist, an alternative theory that AIDS was a manmade virus was forcefully presented. Reminding readers of the Tuskegee syphilis experiments (see Exhibit 9.3), Dr. Welsing implied that AIDS was an instrument of genocide, likely introduced into African American and other undesirable populations for the purpose of a systematic depopulation agenda.[24] As proof

---

EXHIBIT 9.3

THE TUSKEGEE STUDY

The Tuskegee Study, as it has come to be known, involved a sample of some four hundred syphilitic African American men in Macon County, Alabama, who were deliberately denied treatment. The purpose of the study was to determine the course and complications of untreated latent syphilis in African American males and to ascertain whether it differed from the course of the disease in whites. Syphilitic men chosen for the Tuskegee sample were told that they were ill and promised free care. Unaware that they were participants in an experiment, all subjects believed that they were being treated for *bad blood*—a rural southern colloquialism for syphilis.

The project endured from 1932 through 1972, undertaken with the complicity of the United States Public Health Service. For the full story of the Tuskegee Study, see Molly Selvin, "Changing Medical and Social Attitudes toward Sexually Transmitted Diseases: A Historical Overview," in *Sexually Transmitted Diseases,* ed. King K. Holmes, Per-Anders Mardh, P. Frederick Sparling, and Paul J. Wiesner, (New York: McGraw-Hill, 1984), pp. 13–14; J. H. Jones, *Bad Blood: The Scandalous Story of the Tuskegee Experiment* (New York: Free Press, 1981).

of her contention, Dr. Welsing went on to quote the following paragraph from *A Survey of Chemical and Biological Warfare:*

> The question of whether new diseases could be used [for biological warfare] is of considerable interest. Vervet monkey disease may well be an example of a whole new class of disease-causing organisms. Handling of blood and tissues without precautions causes infection. It is unaffected by any antibiotic substance so far tried and is unrelated to any other organism. It causes fatality in some cases and can be venereally transmitted in man.[25]

To substantiate her thesis, Dr. Welsing pointed out that the vervet monkey was none other than the African green monkey.

Dr. Welsing's theory is easily refuted, for the disease of which she spoke is of a category known as viral hemorrhagic fever.* In 1967, an outbreak of a particular strain of hemorrhagic fever occurred in Germany and Yugoslavia (now known as the State Union of Serbia and Montenegro) among laboratory workers engaged in processing kidneys from African green monkeys for cell culture production. Additional cases involved medical personnel attending these patients. A total of thirty-one cases, including six secondary cases, and seven deaths occurred. A virus was isolated from the blood and tissues of the patients. The virus, named Marburg virus after the town in Germany where the first cases were described, was found to be unique and unrelated to any other known human pathogen.[26]

In subsequent years there were a few small and short-lived outbreaks of the disease, and clinical studies found that the secondary spread occurred through close contact with infected persons, or contact with infected blood or body secretions or excretions.[27] Sexual transmission of the disease has occurred, and the virus has been isolated from seminal fluid up to two months after illness.[28] Although this would suggest some similarities with HIV infection, the incubation period for Marburg virus ranges from only three to nine days—a marked difference with the months to years between initial HIV infection and the appearance of AIDS.†

Although speculative and conspiratorial theories of AIDS attract little attention and tend to fade as quickly as they appear, there was one exception. A relatively new hypothesis was published in the March 19, 1992, issue of *Rolling Stone,*[29] and it quickly drew the attention of scientists throughout the nation. The author of the article, Houston freelance writer Tom Curtis, speculated that some as-yet-undiscovered simian (monkey) form of HIV may have contaminated a polio vaccine formulated

---

*The term *viral hemorrhagic fever* refers to the illness associated with a number of geographically restricted viruses. It is characterized by fever and, in the most severe cases, shock and hemorrhage. See S. P. Fisher-Hoch and D. I. H. Simpson, "Dangerous Pathogens," *British Medical Journal,* 41 (1985), pp. 391–395.

†For the longest time, AIDS researchers believed that people exposed to HIV developed antibodies within six months of infection. In June, 1989, however, researchers from the UCLA Medical Center reported that one-fourth of a group of 133 gay men who engaged in high-risk sexual behavior were infected but for long periods did not produce HIV antibodies, thus causing some uncertainties about the test. See D. T. Imagawa, H. L. Moon, S. M. Wolinsky, K. Sano, F. Morales, S. Kwok, J. J. Sninsky, P. G. Nishanian, J. Giorgi, J. L. Fahey, J. Dudley, B. R. Visscher, and R. Detels, "Human Immunodeficiency Virus Type 1 in Homosexual Men Who Remain Seronegative for Prolonged Periods," *New England Journal of Medicine,* 320 (1989), pp. 1458–1462.

decades ago by researchers at the prestigious Wistar Institute in Philadelphia. Curtis suggested that the antecedent virus might have come from monkey kidney cells in which the polio vaccine had been cultured. The vaccine was tested during the late 1950s in what is now Zaire, Rwanda, and Burundi, where it was spray-injected into the mouths of several hundred thousand people. Piling speculation upon speculation, Curtis intimated that HIV infection might have occurred through mucosal cells, lesions in the mouth, or via aerosolized virus trickling into the lungs.

At least to those unfamiliar with the nature of viruses and the production of vaccines, the *Rolling Stone* thesis seemed plausible. In the first place, the Wistar Institute had indeed used monkeys in the preparation of the polio vaccine. Second, it was widely distributed in the Belgian Congo in the late 1950s. Perhaps most importantly, numerous HIV-related viruses are found in monkeys.[30] Soon after the recognition of AIDS in people, several clinical reports described outbreaks of severe infections, wasting disease (see Exhibit 9.4), and death in several colonies of Asian macaque monkeys housed at primate centers in the United States.[31] This was subsequently referred to as simian AIDS (or SAIDS), and SIV (simian immunodeficiency virus) was found to be the causative agent. The SIVs constitute a family of naturally occurring viruses indigenous to certain simian species in Africa. In their natural hosts—African green monkeys, sooty mangabeys, and mandrills—they apparently cause no disease. But accidental infection of macaques with certain strains of SIV causes persistent infection, with eventual death from simian AIDS.[32] By contrast, no real evidence supports the Curtis thesis that appeared in *Rolling Stone.* When his work was severely criticized by AIDS researchers for its lack of documentation, Curtis admitted that, unlike science, journalism allows for theories without hard proof.[33]

■ ■ ■ ■ ■ ▬▬

EXHIBIT 9.4

AIDS WASTING DISEASE

Wasting disease is characterized by involuntary weight loss combined with chronic diarrhea, fever, fatigue, and weakness. In parts of Central Africa, this illness in humans is often referred to as slim disease.

During late 1982, a new epidemic disease was reported in a small village on the shores of Lake Victoria near the Uganda–Tanzania border. Seventeen people were complaining of intestinal troubles and weight loss. Because all the patients were smugglers, it became known as robbers disease. But when the illness began attacking others whose honesty was not in doubt, it was called slim. The name came from the English word connoting an extremely lean condition, because, in later stages of the disease, patients resembled living skeletons before they eventually died in a state of total debilitation.

In 1987, slim was included in the Centers for Disease Control's definition of AIDS. See D. Serwadda, R. D. Mugerwa, and N. K. Sewankambo, "Slim Disease: A New Disease in Uganda and Its Association with HTLV-III/LAV Infection," *Lancet,* 2 (1985), pp. 849–852; Centers for Disease Control, "Revision of the CDC Surveillance Case Definition for Acquired Immunodeficiency Syndrome," *Morbidity and Mortality Weekly Report,* 36 Supplement (1987), pp. 3–15.

By the close of the 1990s, and despite the many conspiracy theories, scientists exploring all sectors of the viral frontier were almost certain as to the origins of HIV. The clear suspect was a subspecies of chimpanzee called *Pan troglodytes troglodytes.*[34] The chimp lives in West Central Africa, the very region where HIV was first thought to have originated. The plausible mode of transmission from chimp to human is believed to have been from the blood of animal carcasses, used for food, entering hunters' bodies through superficial wounds. It would appear that the virus jumped species on at least three occasions and evolved into the HIV strains recognized today.

MAINLINING DEATH

The ready transmission of HIV/AIDS among intravenous and other injection drug users is the result of sharing injection equipment, combined with the presence of cofactors. Cofactors include any behavioral practices or microbiological agents that facilitate the transmission of HIV. The risk factors that relate to injection drug users are summarized in Exhibit 9.5.

Shooting Galleries and Injection Drug Use

In most urban locales where rates of injection drug use are high, common sites for injecting drugs (and sometimes purchasing drugs) are the neighborhood shooting galleries, also referred to in some communities as safe houses or get-off houses. After purchasing heroin, cocaine, amphetamines, or some other injectable substance in a local copping (drug-selling) area, users are faced with three logistical problems: how

EXHIBIT 9.5   Possible Routes of HIV-1 Acquisition and Transmission among Injection Drug Users

BLOOD
Contaminated needles, syringes, spoons, cookers, and cottons
Needle/syringe sharing, booting, jacking, frontloading, and backloading
Use of contaminated drug paraphernalia in shooting galleries

SEX
Sex partner of injection drug user
Sex worker using injection drug
Gay or bisexual male injection drug user

PERINATAL
Prepartum transplacental
Peripartum HIV-infected genital secretions or blood
Postpartum HIV-infected breast milk

to get off the street quickly to avoid arrest for possession of drugs, where to obtain a fit or set of works (drug paraphernalia) with which to administer the drugs, and where to find a safe place to get off (inject the drugs). As such, shooting galleries occupy a functional niche in the world of injection drug use, where for a fee of two or three dollars users can rent an injection kit and relax while getting off. After using a syringe and needle, the user generally returns them to a central storage place in the gallery where they are held until someone else rents them. On many occasions, however, these works are simply passed to another user in the gallery.

In general, shooting galleries have not been systematically studied. However, based on the author's observations combined with reports from a variety of ethnographic and other research studies in drug communities in several parts of the United States, their more obvious roles and characteristics can be described.[35] Most shooting galleries are situated in basements and backrooms, apartments and hotel rooms, and even house trailers in the rundown sections of cities where drug-use rates are high. Typically, they are only sparsely furnished, not clean, and reports suggest many similarities from city to city. In West Oakland, California, for example:

> It was in a ratty, condemned house up over an old-time nightclub. They used two rooms and a hallway. It had lights, but no running water, and they just shit out the windows. And the lights were hooked up from outside, you know, somebody else's shit.[36]

And in Miami, an outreach worker described a popular get-off house as follows:

> The place is really gross. It's just a small house with an upstairs, in the middle of the block set further back than the other houses and has a garage in the back. The owner lives upstairs and uses part of the downstairs. There are two back rooms which he uses as the get-off and they're cut off from his front rooms by wood paneling nailed over the doorway. It's filthy, probably not ever been cleaned.
>
> There's an old couch, two tables, couple of chairs, some buckets. One room is real small, and has a sink that works—probably was a kitchen at one time. No bathroom, so they piss in the sink, or right on the floor or out the windows. Smells like it too. One of the windows has no glass, so sometimes there's all kinds of creepies to watch out for. There's all kinds of junk on the floors, like needle wrappers, old needles and syringes that don't work any more, bloody cotton and bandaids. Stuff like that. In the corner of the room there's a table with three of four containers of syringes. They look like the Chinese food take-out buckets. There's matches on the table, and a file to sharpen needles, some caps and baby food jars for water, and a bag of cotton balls.

Other galleries are in abandoned buildings, darkened hallways, alleys, and under railroad bridges and highway ramps. Characterized by the stench of urine and littered with trash, human feces, garbage, and discarded injection paraphernalia, the conditions are extremely unsanitary and rarely is there heat, running water, or functional plumbing. For example, an informant in Miami reported:

> Before the county came along and cleaned out the junkies and the homeless, there was this section under Rt. 395 near Biscayne Blvd. known as the "shit hole." There were some dumpsters up at one end near the walls of the overpass. When you were behind them you could see out but no one could see you, so there would be folks shooting up back there on and off every day and night.

Most galleries are run by drug users or drug dealers. Neighborhood heroin and cocaine sellers may operate galleries as a service to customers—providing them with a nearby location to inject for a slight charge, perhaps two or three dollars. More often, however, gallery operators are drug users themselves who provide a service for a small fee or a taste (sample) of someone else's drugs.

For the majority of injection drug users, shooting galleries are considered to be the least desirable places to patronize. Most prefer to use their own homes or apartments or those of drug-using friends. These are considered safer than galleries, and few users relish having to pay a fee to use someone else's drug paraphernalia. For a minority of hard-core injectors, there is also the matter of personal hygiene. As one heroin user summed it up:

> Galleries ain't where it's at. We wasn't brought up like that. They be definitely hard-core junkies and they don't give a damn no more about how their appearance is or nothing like that. Ain't nobody want to give another two dollars. Their works . . . all dirty, man. An' people be shootin' blood all over you.[37]

For many drug injectors, however, the use of shooting galleries is routine and commonplace. Moreover, in the lives of all injection drug users, including the most hygienically fastidious types, galleries become necessary on occasion. If they have no works of their own, or if friends or other running partners have no works, then a neighborhood gallery is the only recourse. Similarly, users who purchase drugs far from home also gravitate toward the galleries. This tendency is based on the heightened risk of arrest when carrying drugs and drug paraphernalia over long stretches. In addition, for the heroin or cocaine user undergoing withdrawal, getting somewhere close by to inject after copping is imperative. Moreover, the gallery operator often serves as a middleman between drug user and drug dealer, thus making the get-off house the locus of exchange. For example, as one Miami heroin user explained the situation:

> OK, let's say I'm white, but the only place I can cop some smack (heroin) is in the black neighborhoods, but I'm afraid that I'll be ripped off (robbed) there. But, then there's this gallery an' I know the man there, he's *right* (trusted) by the buyers and sellers. So I go there an' he cops for me for a few dollars and maybe a taste. For another $3 I can use his works and house to lay up in for a little while.

Finally, some drug injectors actually prefer local galleries because of the opportunities they provide to socialize with other drug users. For example, a Miami cocaine user explained:

> When you live on the street you need a place to go, to see people, to relax, to hear things, to be in the know. You need to connect with your friends, with your running partners; you need to know where the drugs are, where the police are working, who the snitches are, where the fences are, who's in jail and who's out, who's HIV positive and who's bought it with an OD [overdose], and who's full of shit and who isn't.

Interestingly, this clearinghouse role is not something unique to shooting galleries and the drug scene. Criminal hangouts have served the identical role for a variety of segments of the underworld down through the ages. For example, a Brooklyn-born sneak thief and burglar with a criminal history spanning the Prohibition Era through the late 1960s once reflected on some of New York City's hangouts for professional thieves:

> The bars along 48th and 49th streets from 6th to 8th Avenues are to me what the golf and country clubs are to the execs. That's where we do our business, where we meet key people, and where we relax. Whenever you get in town you know where you need to go and each of us has our favorites.[38]

There are other reasons for using a shooting gallery. For homeless persons, there is nowhere else to go. For those with no money or drugs, hanging out in a gallery is a way to get some free drugs—a taste at any rate. Too, the gallery is a place where the user can find a street doc or house doc. More specifically, some users are squeamish about sticking needles into their veins and injecting themselves. Some are just not particularly adept at it. Others, because of deep or collapsed veins, can't orchestrate a proper hit or register (drops of blood in the syringe as evidence of connecting with the vein).[39] Under these circumstances the street or house doc will inject the drugs into the user for a small fee (money or a taste of drugs). For example, a heroin- and cocaine-using house doc in Miami reported:

> I was a med-tech in Nam, so I've had a lot of experience. I can shoot into any vein in the body—arms, legs, neck, between the fingers and toes, wherever. Most of the time I just sit here and wait 'till someone comes in and wants me to fix them. Sometimes I got to make house calls, to an apartment, a house, an alley, a car. Someone comes and tells me, and I go make the call. That's why they call me the "doc." And some docs simply sell their skills and rely on house works, but I carry my own outfit. I keep it clean, and people know that, so they always call me.

In short, despite its unsavory character, the shooting gallery does indeed occupy a functional role in the street worlds of injection drug taking and drug seeking.

Shooting Galleries and Viral Contamination

As mentioned earlier in this chapter, the sharing of hypodermic needles, syringes, and other parts of the injection kit is the most likely route of HIV acquisition and transmission among injection drug users. The mechanism is the exchange of the blood of the previous user that is lodged in the needle, the syringe, or elsewhere. Because most injection drug use is intravenous (into the vein), the very nature of mainlining virtually guarantees contact between the paraphernalia and the user's blood. Further, the problem is exacerbated through the practice of booting, also known as kicking. Booting involves the use of a syringe to draw blood from the user's arm, mixing the drawn blood with the drug already taken into the syringe, and injecting the blood/drug mixture into the vein.

There are three reasons for booting. First, most injectors draw blood into the syringe for the sake of vein registration, that is, to ensure that the needle is properly placed in the vein. Second, many injectors draw large amounts of blood into the syringe, pumping it in and out several times to mix the blood with the drug solution, believing that this practice potentiates a drug's effects. Third, many users wish to test the strength or effect of the drug before injecting the entire amount.[40] In any case, booting leaves traces of blood in the needle and syringe, thus placing subsequent users of the injection equipment at risk.

In addition to booting, there is also jacking, a practice more common to cocaine injectors than users of other injection drugs. Jacking is *staged shooting:*

> . . . that is, some injectors prefer to shoot the drug in stages rather than the full amount all at once. For example, if an IDU (injection drug user) has 50cc of dissolved cocaine, he or she might shoot 15cc and then pull 15cc of blood back into the syringe, wait for the rush to subside, inject 25cc and pull back 25cc of blood, wait again for the rush to pass, and then inject the remaining mix, perhaps jacking one more time to make sure no cocaine is left in the syringe.[41]

The booting/jacking process further increases the likelihood that traces of potentially infected blood remain in the needle/syringe, thus placing the next user at risk. Moreover, because of the way that injection equipment is cleaned and distributed in galleries, the potential for coming in contact with an infected needle/syringe is high. The user pays his or her fee to use the gallery, and a needle/syringe is taken from those available on a table or in a container. In some galleries, the user is given a syringe by the gallery operator and has no choice in the matter. In either case, the equipment is not usually scrutinized for traces of blood, but rather for dull or clogged needles. Should such an impairment be evident, only then will the user return it for a substitute.

Moreover, needles are generally not cleaned prior to use. Shooting up as quickly as possible is the matter of prime importance. After injecting and before returning the needle/syringe to the common container, the user is expected to rinse it—not necessarily for the sake of decontamination, but to prevent any drug/blood residue from hardening and causing an obstruction. Sometimes this rinsing is indeed done, but with water, which does not deactivate HIV. Sometimes the rinsing is done with infected water taken from a container to rinse other needles.

Although systematic research and clinical observation suggest that the use of shooting galleries, the sharing of needles and other drug paraphernalia, and the practices of booting and jacking combine to explain the increasing proportion of injection drug users infected with HIV, little is known about the prevalence of HIV antibodies in needle/syringe combinations used by drug injectors. In this behalf, samples of needle/syringe combinations from major shooting galleries in Dade County (Miami), Florida, were collected for the sake of analyzing their contents for the presence of HIV antibodies.[42]

A total of 212 needle/syringe combinations were collected and then labeled, visually graded as to condition—clean (if they contained no visible dirt, stains, or blood), dirty (if they contained dirt or stains but no visible blood), and visible blood (if they appeared to contain any liquid or dried blood). Of a total collected, 62 could not be analyzed for the presence of HIV antibodies because of clogging, broken plungers, or other physical damage, leaving 150 available for laboratory analysis. Of the 150 needles tested, 15 were found to be seropositive (positive for HIV antibodies), 133 were seronegative, and in two cases serostatus was indeterminate. As such, the overall seropositivity rate was 10 percent, and, interestingly, a strong relationship was found to exist between the graded condition of needle/syringe combinations and the presence of HIV antibodies. Of the 55 needle/syringe combinations graded clean through visual inspection, only 5.5 percent were found to be seropositive, with a similar rate (4.7 percent) for dirty needles and syringes. By contrast, 20 percent of the needle/syringe combinations containing visible blood were found to be HIV positive—a clearly significant relationship between the appearance of a needle/syringe and the presence of HIV antibodies.

Viral contamination can also occur through indirect sharing practices. For example, water contaminated through the rinsing of a syringe is often used for rinsing other syringes and for mixing the drug. Similarly, spoons, cookers, and cottons are parts of the injecting kit that also represent potential reservoirs of disease. Spoons and cookers are the bottle caps, spoons, baby food jars, and other small containers used for mixing the drug, whereas cottons refer to any materials placed in the spoon to filter out undissolved drug particles. Filtering is considered necessary because undissolved particles tend to clog injection equipment. The risks of HIV infection from spoons and cottons are due to their frequent sharing, even by drug users who carry their own syringes.

Transmission of the virus might also result from *frontloading* and *backloading,* techniques for distributing a drug solution among a drug-injecting group.[43] When frontloading, the drug is transferred from the syringe used for measuring by removing the needle from the receiving syringe and squirting the solution directly into its hub. Common in shooting galleries is the intercontamination of drug doses through the mixing and frontloading of speedball (heroin and cocaine). Because heroin is cooked (heated in an aqueous solution), whereas cocaine is not during its preparation for injecting, separate containers are used for the mixing process. Those who share speedball draw the heroin into one syringe and the cocaine into another; remove the needle from the cocaine syringe and discharge the heroin into it through its hub; and return half the speedball mixture back into the syringe that originally contained the heroin. If either syringe contains virus at the start of such an operation, both are likely to contain it afterward.[44]

The backloading of speedball has also been observed in many shooting galleries. Backloading involves essentially the same process, but the plunger, rather than the needle, is removed from the receiving syringe. Frontloading seems to be the preferred mixing/sharing method, with backloading as a substitute when syringes with detachable needles are unavailable.

Both frontloading and backloading have been reported by inmate informants in Delaware, Florida, New York, Maryland, and Ohio penitentiaries. Illicit drugs are generally available in most U.S. prisons, but typically in limited quantities and at considerable cost, often resulting in the sharing of injectable heroin, cocaine, and speedball by groups of three to four prisoners. Backloading is the preferred mixing/measuring technique. Because hypodermic syringes are closely controlled in prisons, makeshift injection equipment is manufactured from securable materials. The most common works in the penitentiary is an eye dropper, with the glass or plastic end sharpened to an angular point. Backloading is accomplished by removing the squeeze bulb. Regarding the practice, an inmate in Miami's Dade County Stockade indicated:

> There's times when a "mixed" (backloaded) dose is all you can get, with drugs bein' so scarce and all inside. They'll be someone with some dope and a few droppers with sharpened ends. You get your share by havin' yours pointed down with your finger covering the tip while someone loads it in.

An alternative method of drug sharing is referred to by some injecting drug users as shooting back and drawing up. This practice has been observed in instances when every member of the drug-sharing group has a syringe. After the heroin, cocaine, or speedball is thoroughly mixed, it is discharged from the mixing syringe into a common spoon, cap, or container. Each member of the sharing group then draws a specific amount.

Rip Offs and Running Partners

Booting, frontloading, and backloading are not the only aspects of injecting drugs that place users at risk for HIV infection. The street subculture of illegal drug use is characterized by exploitation and danger. Moreover, it is a perpetually embattled subculture, conditioned by scarcity—scarce money, scarce drugs, scarce needles, scarce places in which to be safe. Within this relentless context, users must temper trust with streetwise wariness and vigilance. Deals gone sour, bad drugs, bad deals, bogus sterilized needles, rip offs, and outright violent assaults combine with the omnipresent threat of arrest, worry about drug availability, and the generalized anxiety associated with poverty and the inner city to create an environment that is bleak and harrowing, threatening and exciting.

But within this subculture can be found fragile threads of social support and bonding—structures necessary to sustain users in the face of external hostility and internal danger. Ironically, these very patterns of social support increase the pathways for HIV contamination. The issue is this: All forms of needle/syringe and indirect sharing tend to occur among running partners (or running buddies), that is, injection drug users who are lovers, good friends, crime partners, or live together. They serve as lookouts for one another—one watches for police and other intruders while the other cops (purchases), prepares, or injects the drugs. Running partners also provide other elements of safety, such as monitoring each other's responses to the drugs they use to prevent overdoses or other acute reactions. In this regard, as a 32-year-old, former heroin-using sex worker in Miami related, having a running partner can mean the difference between life and death for some injection drug users:

> Without my partner I'd be dead. He was big, and more than once he saved my ass from being beat on. . . . We weren't lovers or anything like that, although we did sleep together a few times when I was really down. He was no pimp either. We were just really good friends. We could depend on each other.
>
> One time I was cut up pretty bad and he got me patched up. One of my "dates" (customers) had really worked me over—one of them sado-blood freaks, tied me to a bed and worked over my "change purse" (vagina) with a coat hanger. Another time when I was bein' ripped off by a bunch of street kids who wanted all of my "shit" (money and drugs), he came to the rescue, like the Lone-fucking-Ranger.

For many decades, needle sharing has been a prominent aspect of the subculture of the street drug scene, and all its associated practices are generally learned during initiation to drug use.[45] A user's first episode of sharing is typically unplanned. Because novice injectors rarely have their own injection kit, they often borrow a more experienced user's equipment. After becoming a regular user, association with a running partner may begin and sharing both drugs and needles serves as a convenience and a symbol of friendship and trust. Because a running partner is often a lover, a surrogate family member, or a replacement family, refusing to share a needle would be viewed as an indication of mistrust. For running partners who are also sex partners, injecting drugs as a pair can serve as an even deeper symbol of emotional bonding. In addition, the mixing of blood while injecting and the booting of each other's blood is not uncommon, symbolizing a brotherhood or bond between running partners. The risks of such ritual blood exchanges, of course, are obvious, and are likely responsible for scores of HIV and other infections.* Consequently, shooting galleries represent a significant health problem as far as the spread of HIV and other blood-borne infections is concerned.

---

*In addition to the risk of contracting HIV during blood exchanges, mixing even small amounts of blood of a type different than your own can result in a *bone crusher.* Described by one user as "a brain freeze of the bones," a bone crusher is the street term used to describe the pressure felt on a person's bones when such blood mixing occurs.

VIRAL HEPATITIS AND INJECTION DRUG USE

Viral hepatitis, a cluster of diseases causing inflammation of the liver, has killed millions of people throughout history. As many as one-half of the inhabitants of Western nations are likely infected with at least one of the hepatitis viruses, but because of asymptomatic cases (infections in which symptoms are not evident), inaccurate diagnoses, and underreporting, only 10 percent of new cases are reported to the Centers for Disease Control each year. Hepatitis viruses A through E (abbreviated HAV, HBV, HCV, HDV, and HEV) account for 95 percent of all reported cases (see Exhibit 9.6). Among injection drug users, HBV and HCV are the types most commonly observed.

Hepatitis B (HBV) is a DNA virus that is transmitted primarily through sexual contact and the sharing of contaminated injection equipment.[46] Although HBV is a preventable and treatable disease, high rates of the infection nevertheless have been documented among both drug users and sex workers.[47] Furthermore, although high rates of HBV are apparent in numerous parts of the United States, education and prevention programs are few in number. Data from the National Institute on Drug Abuse indicate that 6.6 percent of women drug users and 7.4 percent of women sex traders reported having been diagnosed with HBV at some time.[48]

Hepatitis C virus is the most common chronic blood-borne infection in the United States.[49] During the 1980s an average of 230,000 new infections occurred each year, but the incidence of new cases declined by 80 percent in the 1990s, and approximately 30,000 to 40,000 currently occur each year. An estimated four million people in the United States are currently infected with HCV, although many may be unaware of their infection because they remain asymptomatic.[50] HCV infected persons are at risk for chronic liver disease, cirrhosis, and liver cancer. Studies indicate that 40 percent of all chronic liver disease is HCV-related, and results in eight thousand to ten thousand deaths each year. Chronic liver disease associated with HCV is the most frequent indication for liver transplantation among adults.

HCV is transmitted primarily through percutaneous (under the skin) exposure to blood. Although blood transfusion accounted for a substantial proportion of HCV infections in the 1980s, more recent blood screening procedures have virtually eliminated new transfusion-related cases.[51] The major exposure category to HCV is now injection drug use, which currently accounts for approximately 60 percent of infections. HCV is acquired more rapidly after initiation of injecting than other viral infections, including hepatitis B and HIV, and rates of infection among young injection drug users are four times higher than rates of HIV. Studies estimate that within six to twelve months of injecting, as many as 80 percent of all users are infected with HCV.

Other modes of HCV transmission are less clearly defined. The evidence for HCV transmission through sexual activity is mixed. A low prevalence of HCV infection has been reported in studies of long-term sex partners of patients with chronic HCV infection and hemophiliacs who had no other risk factors for infection.[52] Other studies have provided substantial evidence of elevated HCV infection rates acquired through sexual contact. Among patients at STD (sexually transmitted disease) clinics, women with HCV-positive male partners were significantly more likely to be

EXHIBIT 9.6   Characteristics and Effects of Viral Hepatitis

FACTORS	HEPATITIS A	HEPATITIS B	HEPATITIS C	HEPATITIS D	HEPATITIS E	HEPATITIS G
INCUBATION PERIOD	15–50 days	45–180 days	14–160 days	21–45 days	15–60 days	14–35 days
VIRAL-INFECTED SUBSTANCES	Blood Feces Saliva	Blood and serum-derived fluids (e.g., bloody saliva or respiratory secretions; menstrual fluids) Liver tissue Semen Vaginal secretions	Blood Liver tissue	Blood Liver tissue	Feces	Blood
DISEASE ONSET	Sudden	Insidious* or sudden	Insidious	Sudden	Sudden	Unknown
JAUNDICE	Children: <5% Adults: ~30%	≤20%	≤10%	Unknown	Unknown	Percentage unknown
ASYMPTOMATIC	>90% in infants; percentage decreases with increased age at infection	Most children Adults: 50%	~70 to 75%	Few	Few	Percentage unknown
CHRONIC DISEASE	None	>90% infants; percentage decreases with increased age at infection	~85%	~10 to 15%	None	Percentage unknown; young children are the most susceptible

*When referring to a disease, *insidious* means developing so gradually as to be well established before becoming apparent.

HCV-positive than women with HCV-negative partners.[53] Male patients' infection rates did not differ according to the seropositivity of their female partners, suggesting that, similar to other blood-borne viruses, sexual transmission of HCV from males to females may be more efficient than from females to males. What all of this suggests is that injection drug users and their sex partners, as well as noninjection drug users who engage in unprotected sex, are at risk for the acquisition and transmission of not only HIV, but hepatitis as well.

THE DILEMMAS OF DRUGS, SEX, HCV AND HIV/AIDS

In addition to themselves, injection drug users also represent a group primarily at risk for transmitting HIV and hepatitis infections to noninjecting gay and bisexual men, heterosexuals, and pediatric cases. At the close of 2005, almost one million confirmed cases of AIDS had occurred in the United States since the beginning of the epidemic, and of these, almost a third had occurred among injection drug users (see Exhibit 9.7). In addition, much of the high-risk heterosexual contact cases involved sex with an injection drug user. And importantly, although there have been comparatively few pediatric cases of AIDS in recent years, half of all reported pediatric AIDS cases since the beginning of the epidemic have some association with injecting drug use—mothers at risk of HIV infection through injection drug use and/or sex with an injection drug user.

Many of the issues surrounding the spread of HIV infection to sex partners are rooted in subcultural issues of trust, because the lives of most injection users are beset with insecurity, apprehension, fragile relationships, and minimal kinship. As a result, the kinds of behavioral changes appropriate for HIV risk reduction have the potential for introducing elements of suspicion into a relationship. It has been argued, for example, that to ask a sex partner to use a condom is in direct contradiction to the gender roles existing in the injection drug street culture.[54] More specifically, a woman's request of her man to use a condom not only compromises her prescribed role in the relationship, but also suggests that she believes her partner to be contaminated in some way. The reverse can also be the case when a male injection user begins using condoms with his partner. Quite clearly, a substantial asymmetry of power and risk exists in sexual relationships between male drug users and female partners who do not inject drugs.

The existence of shooting galleries across the urban landscape combined with the drug-taking and sexual behaviors of injection drug users pose a dilemma. Most, if not all, injection drug users are aware of AIDS and the risk of infection through sharing needles and having unprotected sex. However, because heroin and cocaine are highly seductive drugs, in many instances the prevention messages are either not heard or not heeded. For those dependent on them, heroin and cocaine become life consuming. They become mother, father, spouse, lover, counselor, confessor, and confidant. Because they are short-acting drugs, they must be taken regularly and repeatedly. Most heroin users, and a growing number of cocaine users, inject their drugs to

EXHIBIT 9.7   AIDS Cases by Age Group, Exposure Category, and Gender, 2005 and Cumulative,[a] United States

ADULT/ADOLESCENT EXPOSURE CATEGORY	MALES				FEMALES				TOTAL			
	2005		Cumulative Total		2005		Cumulative Total		2005		Cumulative Total	
	NUMBER	(%)	NUMBER	(%)	NUMBER	(%)	NUMBER	(%)	NUMBER	(%)	NUMBER	(%)
Men who have sex with men	18,939	(43)	454,106	(48)					18,939	(43)	454,106	(48)
Injecting drug use	5,806	(13)	168,695	(18)	3,179	(7)	73,311	(8)	8,985	(20)	242,006	(26)
Men who have sex with men and inject drugs	2,190	(5)	66,081	(7)					2,190	(5)	66,081	(7)
High-risk heterosexual contact[b]	5,208	(12)	61,914	(7)	8,278	(19)	102,936	(11)	13,486	(31)	164,850	(17)
Other[c]	287	(.7)	13,967	(1)	253	(.6)	6,575	(.7)	540	(1)	20,542	(2)
Adult/Adolescent Total	32,430	(73)	764,763	(81)	11,710	(27)	182,822	(19)	44,140	(100)	947,585	(100)

PEDIATRIC (<13 YEARS OLD) EXPOSURE CATEGORY	NUMBER	(%)	NUMBER	(%)
Hemophilia/coagulation disorder	0	(0)	226	(2)
Mother with/at risk or HIV infection:	57	(98)	8,438	(93)
Injecting drug use	4		3,196	
Sex with injecting drug user	1		1,388	
Sex with bisexual male	1		202	
Sex with person with hemophilia	0		36	
Sex with transfusion recipient with HIV infection	0		22	
Sex with HIV-infected person, risk not specified	25		1,501	
Receipt of blood transfusion, blood components, or tissue	0		143	
Has HIV infection, risk not specified	25		1,949	
Receipt of blood transfusion, blood components, or tissue +	0	(0)	372	(4)
Risk not reported or identified	0	(0)	42	(0)
PEDIATRIC TOTAL[d]	58	(100)	9,078	(100)

Note: These numbers do not represent reported case counts. Rather, these numbers are point estimates, which result from adjustments of reported case counts. The reported case counts have been adjusted for reporting delays and for redistribution of cases in persons initially reported without an identified risk factor, but not for incomplete reporting.

[a] From the beginning of the epidemic through 2005

[b] Heterosexual contact with a person known to have, or to be at high risk for, HIV infection

[c] Includes hemophilia, blood transfusion, perinatal exposure, and risk factor not reported or not identified.

[d] Cumulative total includes 33 children of unknown race or multiple races. Because column totals were calculated independently of the values for the subpopulations, the values in each column may not sum to the column total.

Source: Centers for Disease Control and Prevention, *HIV/AIDS Surveillance Report, 2005,* vol. 17.

experience the more rapid onset and more powerful euphoric high produced when taken intravenously.

Collectively, these effects result in a majority of chronic users more concerned with drug taking and drug seeking than with careers, relationships, or health. Consequently, altering the risk behaviors of drug users might prove difficult. As one cocaine-injecting sex worker summed it up:

> Every day I risk my health, and my life for that matter, when I shoot up. Every time I go out to cop (buy drugs) I risk getting cut (stabbed) or even killed. Every time I'm strolling (walking the streets soliciting clients) at night, there are all kinds of crazies, geeks, thugs, and death freaks out there just waiting to carve up my ass. Now they say that if I use some dirty needle I can get sick, even die in a few years. So I care? I'm probably already dead. Why should I care?

In other words, preventing behavior that may cause sickness and death in two or five years or more is difficult when the injection drug user is confronted with violence, sickness, and death almost every day; motivating behaviors aimed at preventing death in the future is difficult when the population is already at high risk of imminent death and struggling to survive in the present from moment to moment.

HIV Risk Reduction among Injection and Other Drug Users

By the mid-1980s, risk-reduction efforts geared toward injection drug users were focusing on issues of needle contamination and sexual behavior. During the latter half of the decade, however, some programs included not only education, but also proactive intervention techniques such as distributing needle cleaning supplies, latex condoms, and establishing needle exchange centers. According to most reports, outreach workers and intervention and treatment programs succeeded in educating drug users about the risks of infection and prevention methods.[55] A number of these evaluations also noted some positive changes in needle-sterilizing practices.

Trojans, Rubbers, Frogskins, and Bishops: A Brief Discourse on Condoms, Both Male and Female

No doubt everyone has heard of condoms, also known as bags, baggies, scum bags, rubbers, and skins.* The condom is a thin latex or membranous sheath worn over the penis during intercourse as a contraceptive device and/or for the prevention of sexually

---

*Over the years condoms have also been referred to as balloons, bishops, buckskins, cheaters, condos, condominiums, diving suits, dreadnoughts, eel skins, envelopes, fish skins, French letters, French safes, Frenchies, frogs, frog skins, Italian letters, jo-bags, johnnies, joy bags, letters, lubies, one-piece overcoats, phallic thimbles, Port Said Garters, prophos, raincoats, safes, safeties, safety sheaths, shower caps, and spitfires. See Richard A. Spears, *Slang and Euphemism* (Middle Village, NY: Jonathan David Publishers, 1981), p. 121.

transmitted diseases. In history and folklore the term *condom* has been attributed to a certain Dr. Condom, reputedly a physician in the court of King Charles II of England (1630–1685) who developed it to control the number of illegitimate offspring being sired by His Majesty.[56] Alternatively, John S. Farmer and William E. Henley's *Slang and Its Analogues,* published in seven volumes between 1890 and 1904, refers to the *cundum* as an obsolete appliance so-called from the name of its inventor, a colonel in the Guards of Charles II.[57] Interestingly, no mention of either the condom or the cundum appears in the respected *Oxford Dictionary of English Etymology,*[58] but the term most likely comes from the Latin *condus,* a receptacle.

The Male Condom. The condom is not a new invention. It has been reported that the early Egyptians used animal membranes to cover the penis, and in 1504 the Italian anatomist Gabriel Fallopius designed a medicated linen sheath that was pulled on over the penis. The first dictionary to discuss the condom was Captain Francis Grose's *A Classical Dictionary of the Vulgar Tongue,* published in London in 1785. Captain Grose included the following entry:

> *Cundum.* The dried gut of a sheep, worn by men in the act of coition, to prevent venereal infection; said to have been invented by one Colonel Cundum. These machines were long prepared and sold by a matron of the name of Phillips at the Green Canister, in Half-Moon St., in the Strand.[59]

The earliest rubber condom carried a seam along its entire length, and was likely uncomfortable for all parties involved. Hand-dipping with glass formers began during the latter part of the nineteenth century, and the continuous production process, in which formers are dipped in latex and then cured, dates from the 1930s. Electronic testing of condoms (for leakage and breakage) was introduced in 1951; silicon lubricants were offered in the 1960s; and spermicidally lubricated condoms became available in 1975.[60]

The popularity of condoms in past years would be difficult to reckon. What is clear, however, is that prior to the age of AIDS, they were continually maligned. In 1667, three aristocratic British courtiers, wits, and poets—Rochester, Roscommon, and Dorset—issued their *A Panegyroc Upon Cundum,* satirically eulogizing the penile device.[61] In his *Memoirs,* the eighteenth-century Italian adventurer and rogue Giovanni Casanova likened the condom to an English overcoat. Furthermore, only as recently as 1977 the United States Supreme Court abolished state laws that restricted the advertisement and display of condoms.

Since the emergence of AIDS, condoms have come out from behind the counter and are now sold openly—even having entire retail shops devoted exclusively to their promotion and sale. For the wearer, condoms provide a mechanical barrier that greatly reduces the risk of infections acquired through penile exposure to infectious cervical, vaginal, vulvar, or rectal secretions or lesions. For the wearer's partner, the proper use of condoms prevents semen deposition, contact with urethral discharge, and exposure to lesions on the head or shaft of the penis. In study after study, condoms have been found to be effective in the prevention and transmission of HIV.[62]

The Female Condom.   Although HIV and AIDS in the United States are still concentrated among gay and bisexual men and injection drug users, the new prevalence data suggest that the direction of the epidemic is toward heterosexual women. Indications show that many of the traditional HIV prevention/intervention programs have not had a major impact in reducing high-risk sexual behaviors among women. Increased knowledge about HIV transmission, AIDS, and associated risk behaviors does not appear to bring about major reductions in sexual risk behaviors among those women who are at the greatest risk for HIV acquisition and transmission. This finding is apparent among numerous groups of women at high risk for HIV infection, including sex workers contacted on the street,[63] heroin-addicted sex workers,[64] incarcerated women,[65] arrestees,[66] and indigent women of color.[67]

One of the difficulties is that risk-reduction methods are often not feasible for women at greatest risk for HIV infection. Historically, the most common and effective risk-reduction method is condom use. However, many women report not using condoms on a regular basis, particularly with regular sex partners.[68] The lack, or irregular use, of condoms is typically related to social and lifestyle circumstances. For example, condom use is more likely to occur with women who are confident in their negotiating power during sexual encounters.[69] However, many women at risk are unable to negotiate or insist on condom use with their partners.[70] This results partially from some women's dependence on sex for drugs or money, and customers and sex partners frequently refuse to use a condom.[71] Moreover, insistence on condom use may result in violence.

The risk factors associated with HIV acquisition and transmission specific to women are multiple and interrelated. Sex without condoms represents a major risk for acquiring HIV.[72] However, the higher levels of unsafe sex associated with drug use increases the potential for infection by sex-for-crack exchanges,[73] by injection drug users,[74] and by numerous anonymous partners.[75] In fact, studies indicate that drug use may overshadow sexual activity as a risk factor for HIV.[76]

In addition, women's health status is strongly associated with risk. Women with a sexually transmitted infection (STI) who have sex without a condom are more susceptible to HIV infection than women who do not have an STI.[77] Other research substantiates the STI/drug-use connection. Women who use crack are more likely to have STIs than those who do not.[78] Crack-using women also have a greater likelihood of high-risk sexual behaviors, such as not using condoms and having numerous sex partners.

Socioeconomic circumstances have also been associated with increased risk of HIV infection. Poor women are at greater risk than middle- or upper-class women.[79] Women who are dependent on trading sex to support themselves increase their risk of HIV acquisition.[80] For many women of color, particularly those of low socioeconomic status, AIDS is only one of many life problems facing them and often is rated by them as being less serious than unemployment, lack of access to child care, and crime victimization.[81] Therefore, prevention and intervention as well as methods of risk reduction must take into account the entire life circumstances of women if they are to be successful.

To date, few prevention/education programs specifically tailored for women address the entire life spectrum, and developing such programs is one of the greater challenges facing prevention experts who must address the many issues spanning that spectrum. For instance, women need to be educated on how to use condoms with regular sex partners. This often means changing long-standing practices, which, as noted previously in this chapter, may involve introducing mistrust into a relationship. Similarly, women need to be taught how to negotiate safe sex, particularly in situations where insistence on condom use may result in physical abuse or even serious violence.[82]

Education programs need to address sexually transmitted diseases, their diagnosis and treatment, and their relationship to HIV acquisition and transmission. Many women, particularly African Americans and Latinas, as well as HIV-positive women, are less likely to access health care services. Therefore, education programs need to teach women how to access these services, including how to use limited resources to obtain appropriate care. Prevention/intervention programs must be culturally sensitive, and they must be administered by culturally competent health educators, taking into consideration the traditional gender roles as well as culturally specific gender roles of African American and Latina women.

Perhaps most important, few women-controlled methods of sexual risk reduction are available to women at risk of HIV infection, and what is available is not effective in preventing HIV infection. For example, both the effectiveness and the side effects of spermicides have raised questions about their feasibility as an HIV risk-reduction technique.[83] Therefore, developing and promoting an effective woman-controlled risk-reduction method is essential if HIV acquisition and transmission are to be reduced among women at high risk.

During the 1990s, such a method became available—the Reality Vaginal Pouch, or, simply, the female condom. The first female condom, made of rubber with a steel coil rim, was introduced in the 1920s.[84] However, it was not until the late 1980s that a more acceptable device was developed—the Femidom female condom, which has been commercially available in the United Kingdom since 1992 and received FDA approval in the United States in 1993. The female condom is a polyurethane sheath with a flexible inner ring that secures the condom against the cervix and an outer ring that holds the condom in place, preventing it from slipping (and spilling) into the vaginal canal. The design combines features of the male condom and the diaphragm (see Exhibit 9.8).

The female condom has several advantages over the male condom, both as a contraceptive and as an STI prevention method. First, it is controlled by the woman. With the female condom, women are not as dependent on the cooperation of sex partners to protect themselves from HIV and other sexually transmitted diseases. Second, the female condom is inserted before intercourse, providing additional protection against infections from preejaculated fluids. Third, the female condom protects a greater proportion of the vagina, providing additional protection against STIs. Fourth, it has less risk of rupture than the male condom.[85] Other advantages are that because of its loose fit, it causes less loss of sensitivity, it permits penetration before

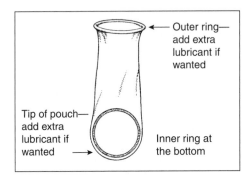
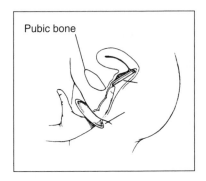

EXHIBIT 9.8   The Female Condom

Source: Reprinted courtesy of The Female Health Company.

complete erection of the penis, and it permits continued intimacy in the resolution phase of intercourse since it need not be removed immediately.

When the female condom first became available in the United States, the media response was less than enthusiastic. In fact, it was a public relations disaster. Many articles focused on the reactions of middle-class women who were not at particularly high risk for HIV. They compared it to a plastic sock, a vacuum cleaner bag, a parched jelly fish, a Trojan on steroids, a Hefty bag, a windsock, and an elephant's trunk.[86] No doubt, if they had tried it, they would have felt differently. Numerous studies have examined the acceptability of the female condom, with extremely positive results.[87]

Needle/Syringe Exchange

Needle/syringe exchange programs provide sterile needles for contaminated or otherwise used needles, thereby increasing access to sterile needles and removing contaminated ones from circulation. Equally important, needle/syringe programs establish contact with hard-to-reach populations to deliver health services, such as HIV testing and counseling, as well as referrals to drug abuse treatment.[88] The need for needle exchange programs is a result of the drug paraphernalia laws that limit their availability in most jurisdictions.

In Europe, many needle exchange programs were organized early in the AIDS epidemic. Several of these programs were evaluated during their early years and found to be effective in increasing the supplies of sterile needles in the street community.[89] The first needle exchange program began in the Netherlands during 1984. According to its founders, the rate of infection among injection drug users did not rise significantly after its inception.[90] Positive evaluations were also reported for a British program initiated two years after the Dutch piloted their experiment,[91] and other early needle exchange programs reported similar successes.[92]

In the United States, government-approved needle exchange programs did not begin until 1988, the delay due mainly to the illegal status of needles and syringes in most parts of the country. In the overwhelming majority of state jurisdictions, injection equipment may not be legally purchased without a physician's prescription. However, privately funded activist groups began distributing sterile equipment as early as 1986. Among the first was that operated by John Parker, a graduate student at Yale University. In 1986, Parker founded the Boston AIDS Brigade and began distributing needles in those neighborhoods with high rates of injecting drug use.[93] He legally secured his needles in Vermont and transported them to Boston for distribution.

Since then, more than a hundred legally sanctioned needle exchange schemes have been implemented in the United States, beginning with a pilot program in New York City.[94] Other cities commenced similar operations, all of which were designed to provide injection drug users with sterile needles in exchange for their used ones.

From their outset, the needle exchange programs were mired in controversy.[95] Some observers feared a repeat performance of the black-market diversion incidents that plagued methadone maintenance programs.[96] In April 1989, New York Congressman Charles Rangel, a fierce opponent of syringe exchange, introduced a bill banning federal funds or assistance to exchange programs and others that dispensed sterilizing materials.[97] Rangel argued that "addicts think that their habit is safe when the government provides the needles . . . this lends an air of approval to a practice that prolongs drug addiction." Also, claims were made that distribution of sterile needles enabled addicts to keep their habits, which—given their higher rates of injection drug use—amounts to genocide of African Americans and Hispanics.[98] In response to these accusations, exchange advocates pointed to statistics from the apparently successful projects elsewhere in the world that suggested that since the exchanges began, treatment entries had increased and the rate of AIDS infection had stabilized.[99]

One can understand some of the initial opposition to needle exchange back in the late 1980s. After all, it was something new, something untested, and something that, for a few observers, smacked of legitimizing street drug use. But in the face of the body of literature empirically documenting the effectiveness of syringe exchange, it is difficult to comprehend opponents' continued paranoia and hysteria. Scores of scientific reports from all over Europe, Australia, Brazil, and the United States have systematically demonstrated that syringe exchange programs are effective in removing contaminated injection paraphernalia from the streets, expanding HIV testing and counseling services, referring drug users into substance abuse treatment, and, most importantly, reducing the numbers of new HIV infections—all without creating populations of new injectors.[100] Perhaps most dramatic in this regard is the success of the syringe exchange program in Hawaii. Authorized in 1990, Hawaii became the first jurisdiction to fund statewide needle exchange as an AIDS prevention measure, and since 1996 no new cases of HIV infection have been found among needle exchange participants.[101]

POSTSCRIPT

During the late spring and early summer of 1981, when researchers in Los Angeles and New York City were first reporting a new and distinct clinical entity associated with immune dysfunction among young gay men, HIV infection and AIDS were already on an upward climb. Although the number of cases was small, evidence suggests that hundreds of thousands of infections had already occurred in North America, many urban areas of sub-Saharan Africa, and some parts of the Caribbean. HIV had also been introduced into the large cities in Western Europe and Oceania. But HIV and AIDS were not understood, and even if an HIV test had been available at the time, the testing of sexually active adults on a comprehensive scale would not have been possible. Moreover, restricting the travel and sexual practices of those identified as infected would have been equally infeasible. The national and global spread of HIV and AIDS could not have been prevented. However, it could have been dramatically slowed!

Many mistakes were made that resulted in the failure to respond effectively: lethargy and indecision, official disinterest in many governmental quarters, and many unfortunate political decisions—based more on ideology and fear than on humanitarian concerns and the best interests of public health. Given the past, where do we go from here? Several actions seem warranted:

1. The federal government, and the great majority of state jurisdictions, effectively encourage drug injectors to share needles, syringes, and other parts of the injection kit by treating the paraphernalia as contraband. Laws should be altered, and needle exchange programs should be implemented wherever they are needed.

2. For injection drug users and crack users who exchange sex for drugs, drug abuse treatment is likely the most effective mechanism of AIDS prevention. Thus, funding for drug abuse treatment and treatment research need to be greatly increased.

3. For students, prisoners, sex workers, and persons who cannot afford to purchase them, condoms should be made readily available on a widespread basis.

Despite the hard work of so many people in the HIV/AIDS prevention field, politics continues to raise its unsightly head and bare its appalling fangs. For example, during the closing months of 2003 the United States National Institutes of Health (NIH) was asked by a congressional committee to justify the funding of almost 200 research grants focusing on a variety of topics that some "right wing" groups found offensive.[102] The list of grants had been compiled earlier in the year by the Traditional Values Coalition, a conservative advocacy group in Washington, DC, which claimed to represent 43,000 churches across the United States. The list included projects headed by researchers studying female condoms, HIV-related stigma, cancer in men living with HIV, the epidemiology of AIDS among opiate users, HIV transmission in rural communities, and HIV prevention programs for street-based sex workers.[103] In fact, one of the projects specifically targeted by the Traditional Values Coalition was headed by the author of this book. Called "Women Protecting Women," the project was designed to reduce the HIV risk behaviors of street sex workers in Miami, Florida.[104] Such grants, argued Andrea Lafferty, executive director of the Traditional Values Coalition, were a waste of taxpayer dollars. "We know for a fact that millions and millions of dollars have been flushed down the toilet over the years on this HIV/AIDS scam and sham," Lafferty said.[105]

The comments by Lafferty and the congressional review were referred to as "scientific McCarthyism" by Representative Henry Waxman (D-CA) and were strongly criticized by the American Association for the Advancement of Science, the American Foundation for AIDS Research, and the Global AIDS Council, as well as by infectious disease researchers throughout the world. Criticisms of the congressional review were even discussed in the March 3, 2003, episode of NBC's award-winning TV series "The West Wing."

In response to critics of research focused on the study of HIV among vulnerable populations, the data found in the Women Protecting Women project document the importance of prevention research among sex workers as well as the significance of science-based interventions for women in the sex industry. One of the findings of the study was that as a result of the project, HIV-positive women sex workers were 2.4 times more likely than the HIV-negative women to enter residential treatment for drug abuse, 2.2 times more likely to decrease the number of their sex partners, 1.9 times more likely to decrease the frequency of unprotected sex, 1.9 times more likely to reduce their levels of alcohol use, and 2.3 times more likely to decrease their crack use.[106]

These findings are critically important from a public health perspective given that it is well documented that sex work facilitates the spread of HIV and other infectious diseases into the general population.[107] The findings also support a growing and significant body of research demonstrating that HIV interventions targeting drug-using women reduce HIV risk behaviors,[108] and that drug abuse treatment is effective in reducing HIV risks.[109]

Collectively these findings suggest that rather than placing studies of HIV prevention programs for sex workers on a "hit list," support for these and similar initiatives should be expanded dramatically. In addition, future research should address a number of concomitant life problems faced by street sex workers, including high levels of homelessness, poverty, drug abuse, and violent victimizations that serve as barriers to drug abuse treatment and other needed health and social services.

In the final analysis, one can only hope that AIDS will go the way of smallpox, which was squeezed relentlessly into a smaller and smaller area in Somalia. In 1977, the last potential carrier was vaccinated, and smallpox had nowhere to go. But hopefully, AIDS will not endure for as long as smallpox before it is finally conquered. The pockmarked mummified face of Ramses V is mute testimony to the presence of smallpox as long ago as ancient Egypt.

NOTES

1. C. Everett Koop, *Surgeon General's Report on Acquired Immune Deficiency Syndrome* (Washington, DC: Department of Health and Human Services, 1986).

2. O. R. Bowen, "In Pursuit of the Number One Public Health Problem," *Public Health Reports,* 103 (May–June 1988), pp. 211–212.

3. Lawrence K. Altman, "In Africa, a Deadly Silence about AIDS Is Lifting," *New York Times,* 13 July 1999, p. F7.

4. Barton Gellman, "A Disease That Could Destroy Nations," *Washington Post National Weekly Edition,* 8 May 2000, p. 15.

5. David Black, *The Plague Years: A Chronicle of AIDS, The Epidemic of Our Times* (New York: Simon and Schuster, 1986).

6. Centers for Disease Control, "Pneumocystis Pneumonia—Los Angeles," *Morbidity and Mortality Weekly Report,* 30 (5 June 1981), pp. 250–252; Centers for Disease Control, "Kaposi's Sarcoma and Pneumocystis Pneumonia among Homosexual Men—New York City and California," *Morbidity and Mortality Weekly Report,* 30 (3 July 1981), pp. 305–308; M. S. Gottlieb, R. Schroff, H. Schanker, J. D. Weismal, P. T. Fan, R. A. Wolf, and A. Saxon, "Pneumocystis Carinii Pneumonia and Mucosal Candidiasis in Previously Healthy Homosexual Men: Evidence of a New Acquired Cellular Immunodeficiency," *New England Journal of Medicine,* 305 (10 December 1981), pp. 1425–1431; H. Masur, M. A. Michelis, J. B. Greene, I. Onorato, R. A. Vande Stouwe, R. T. Holzman, G. Wormser, L. Brettmen, M. Lange, H. W. Murray, and S.Cunningham-Rundles, "An Outbreak of Community-Acquired Pneumocystis Carinii Pneumonia: Initial Manifestation of Cellular Immune Dysfunction," *New England Journal of Medicine,* 305 (10 December 1981), pp. 1431–1438.

7. Anne Rompalo and H. Hunter Handsfield, "Overview of Sexually Transmitted Diseases in Homosexual Men," in *AIDS and Infections of Homosexual Men,* ed. Pearl Ma and Donald Armstrong (Boston: Butterworths, 1989), pp. 3–11.

8. Randy Shilts, *And the Band Played On: Politics, People, and the AIDS Epidemic* (New York: St. Martin's Press, 1987), pp. 18–19.

9. Clyde B. McCoy and James A. Inciardi, *Sex, Drugs, and the Continuing Spread of AIDS* (Los Angeles: Roxbury Publishing Co., 1995), p. 7; Peter N. Carroll, *It Seemed Like Nothing Happened: The Tragedy and Promise of America in the 1970s* (New York: Holt, Rinehart and Winston, 1982), p. 290.

10. Carroll, pp. 290–291.

11. *Miami Herald,* 20 March 1977.

12. Leigh W. Rutledge, *The Gay Decades* (New York: Plume Books, 1992), pp. 100–112.

13. Centers for Disease Control, "Epidemiologic Aspects of the Current Outbreak of Kaposi's Sarcoma and Opportunistic Infections," *New England Journal of Medicine,* 306 (28 January 1982), pp. 248–252.

14. D. M. Auerbach, W. W. Darrow, H. W. Jaffe, and J. W. Curran, "Cluster of Cases of Acquired Immune Deficiency Syndrome: Patients Linked by Sexual Contact," *American Journal of Medicine,* 76 (March 1984), pp. 487–492.

15. For a discussion of the early history of AIDS, see Ann Giudici Fettner, "The Discovery of AIDS: Perspectives from a Medical Journalist," in *AIDS and Other Manifestations of HIV Infection,* ed. Gary P. Wormser, Rosalyn E. Stahl, and Edward J. Bottone (Park Ridge, NJ: Noyes Publications, 1987), pp. 2–17.

16. Institute of Medicine, National Academy of Sciences, *Mobilizing against AIDS: The Unfinished Story of a Virus* (Cambridge, MA: Harvard University Press, 1986), p. 20.

17. N. J. Clumeck, H. Sonnet, and H. Taelman, "Acquired Immunodeficiency Syndrome in African Patients," *New England Journal of Medicine,* 210 (1984), pp. 492–497.

18. Institute of Medicine, National Academy of Sciences, *Mobilizing against AIDS* (Cambridge, MA: Harvard University Press, 1989), p. 107.

19. See Max Essex and Phyllis J. Kanki, "The Origins of the AIDS Virus," in *The Science of AIDS,* ed. Jonathan Piel (New York: W. H. Freeman, 1989), pp. 27–37; *New York Times,* 21 November 1985, p.A1.

20. Vincent T. DeVita, Samuel Hellman, and Steven A. Rosenberg, *AIDS: Etiology, Diagnosis, Treatment, and Prevention* (Philadelphia: J. B. Lippincott, 1985), p. 304.

21. Dennis Altman, *AIDS in the Mind of America: The Social, Political, and Psychological Impact of the New Epidemic* (Garden City, NY: Doubleday, 1987), p. 72; *Newsweek,* 7 May 1984, pp. 101–102.

22. Altman, p. 72.

23. See *New York Times,* 5 November 1987, p. A31.

24. Frances Cress Welsing, unpublished letter, Washington, DC, 25 February 1987.

25. J. Cookson and J. Nottingham, *A Survey of Chemical and Biological Warfare* (New York: Monthly Review Press, 1969), pp. 322–323.

26.   Frederick A. Murphy, "Marburg and Ebola Viruses," in *Virology,* ed. Bernard N. Fields (New York: Reven Press, 1985), pp. 1111–1118; G. A. Martini and R. Siegert, *Marburg Virus Disease* (Berlin, Germany: Springer-Verlag, 1971).

27.   J. P. Luby and C. V. Sanders, "Green Monkey Disease ('Marburg Virus' Disease): A New Zoonosis," *Annals of Internal Medicine,* 17 (1969), pp. 657–660; F. W. Van der Walls, K. L. Pomeroy, J. Goudsmit, D. M. Asher, and D. C. Gajdusek, "Hemorrhagic Fever Virus Infections in an Isolated Rainforest Area of Central Liberia: Limitations of the Indirect Immunofluorescence Slide Test for Antibody Screening in Africa," *Tropical and Geographical Medicine,* 38 (1986), pp. 209–214; J. S. S. Gear, G. A. Cassel, A. J. Gear, B. Trappler, L. Clausen, A. M. Meyers, M. C. Kew, T. H. Bothwell, R. Sher, G. B. Miller, J. Schneider, H. J. Koornhof, E. D. Gomperts, M.Isaacson, and J. H. S. Gear, "Outbreak of Marburg Virus Disease in Johannesburg," *British Medical Journal,* 29 (1975), pp. 489–493.

28.   D. H. Smith, B. K. Johnson, and M. Isaacson, "Marburg Virus Disease in Kenya," *Lancet,* 1 (1982), pp. 816–820.

29.   Tom Curtis, "The Origin of AIDS," *Rolling Stone,* 19 March 1992, pp. 54–61, 106.

30.   See Thierry Huet, Remi Cheynier, Andreas Meyerhans, Georges Roelants, and Simon Wain-Hobson, "Genetic Organization of a Chimpanzee Lentivirus Related to HIV-1," *Nature,* 345 (1990), pp. 356–359; P. J. Kanki, J. Alroy, and M. Essex, "Isolation of T-Lymphotropic Retrovirus Related to HTLV-III/LAV from Wild-Caught African Green Monkeys," *Science* (1985), pp. 951–954; Lisa Chakrabarti, Mireille Guyader, Marc Alizon, Muthiah D. Daniel, Ronald C. Desrosiers, Pierre Tiollais, and Pierre Sonigo, "Sequence of Simian Immunodeficiency Virus from Macaque and Its Relationship to Other Human and Simian Viruses," *Nature,* 328 (1987), pp. 543–547.

31.   Myron Essex, "Origins of AIDS," in *AIDS: Etiology, Siagnosis, Treatment, and Prevention,* ed. Vincent T. DeVita, Samuel Hellman and Steven A. Rosenberg (Philadelphia: J. B. Lippincott, 1988), pp. 3–10.

32.   R. C. Desrosiers and N. L. Letvin, "Animal Models for Acquired Immunodeficiency Syndrome," *Reviews of Infectious Diseases,* 9 (1987), pp. 438–446; M. B. Gardner and P. A. Luciw, "Simian Immunodeficiency Viruses and Their Relationship to Human Immunodeficiency Viruses," *AIDS,* 2 Supplement 1 (1988), pp. S3–S10.

33.   Jon Cohen, "Debate on AIDS Origin: *Rolling Stone* Weighs In," *Science,* 255 (1992), p. 1505; Nancy Touchette, "Wistar Panel Disputes Polio Vaccine-HIV Link," *Journal of NIH Research,* 4 (1992), p. 42.

34.   Feng Gao, Elizabeth Bailes, David L. Robertson, Yalu Chen, Cynthia M. Rodenburg, Scott F. Michael, Larry B. Cummins, Larry O. Arthur, Martine Peeters, George M. Shaw, Paul M. Sharp, and Beatrice H. Hahn, "Origin of HIV-1 in the Chimpanzee Pan Troglodytes Troglodytes," *Nature,* 397 (4 February 1999), pp. 436–441.

35.   Michael Agar, *Ripping and Running: A Formal Ethnography of Urban Heroin Addicts* (New York: Seminar Press, 1973); Seymour Fiddle, *Portraits from a Shooting Gallery* (New York: Harper & Row, 1967); Leroy Gould, Andrew L. Walker, Lansing E. Crane, and Charles W. Lidz, *Connections: Notes from the Heroin World* (New Haven, CT: Yale University Press, 1974); Bill Hanson, George Beschner, James M. Walters, and Elliott Bovelle, *Life with Heroin: Voices from the Inner City* (Lexington, MA: D. C. Heath, 1985); Bruce D. Johnson, Paul J. Goldstein, Edward Preble, James Schmeidler, Douglas S. Lipton, Barry Spunt, and Thomas Miller, *Taking Care of Business: The Economics of Crime by Heroin Users* (Lexington, MA: D. C. Heath, 1985); Richard P.Rettig, Manual J. Torres, and Gerald R. Garrett, *Manny: A Criminal Addict's Story* (Boston: Houghton Mifflin, 1977); Sheigla Murphy and Dan Waldorf, "Kickin' Down to the Street Doc: Shooting Galleries in the San Francisco Bay Area," *Contemporary Drug Problems,* 18 (1991), pp. 9–29; J. Bryan Page, "Shooting Scenarios and Risk of HIV-1 Infection," *American Behavioral Scientist,* 33 (1990), pp. 478–490; J. Bryan Page, Dale D. Chitwood, Prince C. Smith, Normie Kane, and Duane C. McBride, "Intravenous Drug Abuse and HIV Infection in Miami," *Medical Anthropology Quarterly,* 4 (1989), pp. 57–72; J. Bryan Page, Prince C. Smith, and Normie Kane, "Shooting Galleries, Their Proprietors, and Implications for Prevention of AIDS," *Drugs and Society,* 3 (1990), pp. 69–85.

36.   Murphy and Waldorf, p. 12.

37.   Hanson et al., p. 43.

38. James A. Inciardi, *Careers in Crime* (Chicago: Rand McNally, 1975), p. 53.

39. Murphy and Waldorf, p. 15.

40. Lawrence Greenfield, George E. Bigelow, and Robert K. Brooner, "HIV Risk Behavior in Drug Users: Increased Blood Booting during Cocaine Injection," *AIDS Education and Prevention*, 4 (1992), pp. 95–107.

41. Lawrence J. Ouellet, Antonio D. Jimenez, Wendell A. Johnson, and W. Wayne Wiebel, "Shooting Galleries and HIV Disease: Variations in Places for Injecting Illicit Drugs," *Crime and Delinquency*, 37 (1991), pp. 64–85.

42. Dale D. Chitwood, Clyde B. McCoy, James A. Inciardi, Duane C. McBride, Mary Comerford, Edward Trapido, H. Virginia McCoy, J. Bryan Page, James Griffin, Mary Ann Fletcher, and Margarita A. Ashman, "HIV Seropositivity of Needles from Shooting Galleries in South Florida," *American Journal of Public Health*, 80 (1990), pp. 1–3.

43. Jean-Paul Grund, Charles Kaplan, and Nico F. P. Adriaans, "Needle Exchange and Drug Sharing: A View from Rotterdam," *Newsletter of the International Working Group on AIDS and IV Drug Use*, 4 (1989), pp. 4–5; Jean-Paul C. Grund, Charles D. Kaplan, Nico F. P. Adriaans, Peter Blanken, and Jan Huismanm, "The Limitations of the Concept of Needle Sharing: The Practice of Frontloading," *AIDS*, 4 (August 1990), pp. 819–821.

44. James A. Inciardi and J. Bryan Page, "Drug Sharing among Intravenous Drug Users," *AIDS*, 5 (1991), pp. 772–774.

45. Don C. Des Jarlais and Dana Hunt, *AIDS and Intravenous Drug Use*, National Institute of Justice AIDS Bulletin (February 1988); Richard C. Stephens and Duane C. McBride, "Becoming a Street Addict," *Human Organization*, 15 (1976), pp. 87–93.

46. A. G. Barthwell and C. L. Gilbert, *Screening for Infectious Diseases among Substance Abusers* (Rockville, MD: Center for Substance Abuse Treatment, 1993).

47. K. W. Elifson, J. Boles, W. W. Darrow, and C. E. Sterk, "HIV Seroprevalence and Risk Factors among Clients of Female and Male Prostitutes," *Journal of Acquired Immune Deficiency Syndrome Human Retrovirology*, 20 (1999), pp. 195–200; L. Rosenblum, W. Darrow, J. Witte, J. Cohen, J. French, P. S. Gill, J. Potterat, K. Sikes, R. Reich, and S. Hadler, "Sexual Practices in the Transmission of Hepatitis B Virus and Prevalence of Hepatitis Delta Virus Infection in Female Prostitutes in the United States," *Journal of the American Medical Association*, 267 (1992), pp. 2477–2481; S. R. Tabat, D. L. Palmer, W. H. Wiese, R. E. Voorhees, D. R. Pathak, "Seroprevalence of HIV-1 and Hepatitis B and C in Prostitutes in Albuquerque, New Mexico," *Public Health Briefs*, 82 (1992), pp. 1151–1154.

48. CSR Incorporated, *Cooperative Agreement for AIDS Community-Based Outreach/Intervention Research Program, National User's Guide* (Bethesda, MD: CSR, 1998).

49. Centers for Disease Control and Prevention, "Recommendations for Prevention and Control of Hepatitis C Virus (HCV) Infection and HCV-Related Chronic Disease," *Morbidity and Mortality Weekly Report*, 47 (RR19), 16 October 1998, pp. 1–39.

50. A. M. Di Bisceglie, "Hepatitis C," *Lancet*, 351 (1998), pp. 351–355.

51. Di Bisceglie, 1998.

52. N. F. Hallam, M. L. Fletcher, S. J. Read, A. M. Majid, J. B. Kurtz, and C. R. Rizza, "Low Risk of Sexual Transmission of Hepatitis C Virus," *Journal of Medical Virology*, 40 (1993), pp. 251–253; R. Wyld, J. R. Robertson, R. P. Brettle, J. Mellor, L. Prescott, and P.Simmonds, "Absence of Hepatitis C Virus Transmission but Frequent Transmission of HIV-1 from Sexual Contact with Doubly-Infected Individuals," *Journal of Infection*, 35 (1997), pp. 163–166.

53. D. L. Thomas, J. M. Zenilman, H. J. Alter, J. W. Shih, N. Galai, A. V. Carella, and T. C. Quinn, "Sexual Transmission of Hepatitis C Virus among Patients Attending Sexually Transmitted Diseases Clinics in Baltimore—An Analysis of 309 Sex Partnerships," *Journal of Infectious Diseases*, 171 (1995), pp. 768–775.

54. R. Conviser and J. H. Rutledge, "The Need for Innovation to Halt AIDS among Intravenous Drug Users and Their Sexual Partners," *IV International Conference on AIDS*, Stockholm, 12–16 June 1988.

55. J. Sorensen, J. Guydish, and M. Constantini, "Changes in Needle Sharing and Syringe Cleaning among San Francisco Drug Abusers," *New England Journal of Medicine*, 320 (1989),

p. 807; Jeffrey A. Kelly and Janet S. St. Lawrence, *The AIDS Health Crisis: Psychological and Social Interventions* (New York: Plenum Press, 1988); *AIDS Education: Reaching Populations at Higher Risk* (Washington, DC: U. S. General Accounting Office, 1988); John C. Ball, W. Robert Lange, C. Patrick Myers, and Samuel R. Friedman, "Reducing the Risk of AIDS through Methadone Maintenance Treatment, *Journal of Health and Social Behavior,* 29 (September 1988), pp. 214–226; Robert L. Hubbard, Mary Ellen Marsden, Elizabeth Cavanaugh, J. Valley Rachel, and Harold M. Ginzburg, "Role of Drug-Abuse Treatment in Limiting the Spread of AIDS," *Reviews of Infectious Diseases,* 10 (March–April 1988), pp. 377–384; Sandra Baxter, "AIDS Education in the Jail Setting," *Crime and Delinquency,* 37 (January 1991), pp. 48–63; Barry S. Brown and George M. Beschner, eds., *Handbook on Risk of AIDS: Injection Drug Users and Sexual Partners* (Westport, CT: Greenwood Press, 1993).

56. Hugh R. K. Barber, "Condoms (Not Diamonds) Are a Girl's Best Friend," *Female Patient,* 15 (1990), pp. 14–16.

57. John S. Farmer and W. E. Henley, *Slang and Its Analogues, Past and Present: A Dictionary, Historical and Comparative, of the Heterodox Speech of All Classes of Society for More Than Three Hundred Years,* Vol. II (New York: Arno Press, 1970, reprint of the 1891 edition), p. 229.

58. C. T. Onions, ed., *The Oxford Dictionary of English Etymology* (New York: Oxford University Press, 1966).

59. Francis Grose, *A Classical Dictionary of the Vulgar Tongue* (London: C. Chappel, 1785).

60. Malcolm Potts and Roger V. Short, "Condoms for the Prevention of HIV Transmission: Cultural Dimensions," *AIDS,* 3 (1989, Supplement1), pp. S259–S263.

61. See Eric Partridge, *The Macmillan Dictionary of Historical Slang* (New York: Macmillan, 1973), p. 231.

62. For example, see Roger Detels, Patricia English, Barbara R. Visscher, Lisa Jacobson, Lawrence A. Kingsley, Joan S. Chmiel, Janice P.Dudley, Lois J. Eldred, and Harold M. Ginzburg, "Seroconversion, Sexual Activity, and Condom Use among 2,915 HIV Seronegative Men Followed for up to Two Years," *Journal of Acquired Immune Deficiency Syndromes,* 2 (1989), pp. 77–83; Joseph A. Catania, Thomas J. Coates, Susan Kegeles, Mindy Thompson Fullilove, John Peterson, Barbara Marin, David Siegel, and Stephen Hulley, "Condom Use in Multi-Ethnic Neighborhoods of San Francisco: The Population-Based AMEN (AIDS in Multi-Ethnic Neighborhoods) Study," *American Journal of Public Health,* 82 (1992), pp. 284–286; John L. Peterson, Thomas J. Coates, Joseph A. Catania, Lee Middleton, Bobby Hilliard, and Norman Hearst, "High-Risk Sexual Behavior and Condom Use among Gay and Bisexual African-American Men," *American Journal of Public Health,* 82 (1992), pp. 1490–1494; J. B. F. de Witt, T. G. M. Sandford, E. M. M. de Vroome, G. J. P. Van Griensven, and G. J. Kok, "The Effectiveness of Condom Use among Homosexual Men," *AIDS,* 7 (1993), pp. 751–752.

63. Nzilambi Nzila, Marie Laa, Manoka Abib Thiam, Kivuvu Mayimona, B. Edidi, Eddy Van Dyck, Frieda Behets, Susan Hassig, Ann Nelson, K. Mokwa, Rhoda L. Ashley, Peter Piot, and Robert W. Ryder, "HIV and Other Sexually Transmitted Diseases among Female Prostitutes in Kinshasa," *AIDS,* 5 (1991), pp. 715–721.

64. David J. Bellis, "Fear of AIDS and Risk Reduction among Heroin-Addicted Female Street Prostitutes: Personal Interviews with Seventy-two Southern California Subjects," *Journal of Alcohol and Drug Education,* 35 (1990), pp. 26–37.

65. Jennifer Davis-Berman and Debra Brown, "AIDS Knowledge and Risky Behavior by Incarcerated Females: IV and Non-IV Drug Users," *Social Science Review,* 75 (1990), pp. 8–11.

66. Joseph B. Kuhns and Kathleen M. Heide, "AIDS-Related Issues among Female Prostitutes and Female Arrestees," *International Journal of Offender Therapy and Comparative Criminology,* 36 (1992), pp. 231–245.

67. Adeline Nyamathi, Crystal Bennett, Barbara Leake, Charles Lewis, and Jacquelyn Flaskerud, "AIDS-Related Knowledge, Perceptions, and Behaviors among Impoverished Minority Women," *American Journal of Public Health,* 83 (1993), pp. 65–71.

68. Nancy S. Padian, "Prostitute Women and AIDS: Epidemiology," *AIDS,* 2 (1988), pp. 413–419; Robert F. Schilling, Nabila El-Bassel, Louisa Gilbert, and Steven P.Schinke, "Correlates of Drug Use,

Sexual Behavior, and Attitudes toward Safer Sex among African-American and Hispanic Women in Methadone Maintenance," *Journal of Drug Issues,* 21 (1991), pp. 685–698; Ronald O. Valdiserri, Vincent C. Arena, Donna Proctor, and Frank A. Bonati, "The Relationship between Women's Attitudes about Condoms and Their Use: Implications for Condom Promotion Programs," *American Journal of Public Health,* 79 (1989), pp. 499–501.

69.   William P.Sacco, Brian Levine, David L. Reed, and Karla Thompson, "Attitudes about Condom Use as an AIDS-Relevant Behavior: Their Factor Structure and Relation to Condom Use," *Psychological Assessment: A Journal of Consulting and Clinical Psychology,* 3 (1991), pp. 265–272.

70.   Dooley Worth, "Sexual Decision-Making and AIDS: Why Condom Promotion among Vulnerable Women Is Likely to Fail," *Studies in Family Planning,* 20 (1989), pp. 297–307; Michael J. Rosenberg, Arthur J. Davidson, Jian-Hua Chen, Franklyn N. Judson, and John M. Douglas, "Barrier Con- tracep- tives and Sexually Transmitted Diseases in Women: A Comparison of Female-Dependent Methods and Condoms," *American Journal of Public Health,* 82 (1992), pp. 669–674; Stephanie Kane, "AIDS, Addiction and Condom Use: Sources of Sexual Risk for Heterosexual Women," *Journal of Sex Research,* 27 (1990), pp. 427–444.

71.   James A. Inciardi, Dorothy Lockwood, and Anne E. Pottieger, *Women and Crack-Cocaine* (New York: Macmillan, 1993).

72.   Michael J. Rosenberg and Jodie M. Weiner, "Prostitutes and AIDS: A Health Department Prior- ity?" *American Journal of Public Health,* 78 (1988), pp. 418–423.

73.   Carole A. Campbell, "Prostitution, AIDS, and Preventive Health Behavior," *Social Science Medicine,* 32 (1991), pp. 1367–1378; Marsha F. Goldsmith, "Sex Tied to Drugs = STD Spread," *JAMA,* 260 (1988), p. 2009.

74.   Nancy J. Padian, J. Carlson, R. Browning, L. Nelson, J. Grimes, and L. Marquiss, "Human Immunodeficiency Virus (HIV) among Prostitutes in Nevada," *Third International Conference on AIDS,* Washington, DC, June 1987.

75.   Harvey A. Siegal, Robert G. Carlson, Russel Falick, Mary Ann Forney, Jichuan Wang, and Ling Li, "High-Risk Behaviors for Transmission of Syphilis and Human Immunodeficiency Virus among Crack Cocaine–Using Women," *Sexually Transmitted Diseases,* 19 (1992), pp. 266–271; Moira L. Plant, Martin A. Plant, David F. Peck, and Jo Setters, "The Sex Industry, Alcohol and Illicit Drugs: Implications for the Spread of HIV Infection," *British Journal of Addiction,* 84 (1989), pp. 53–59; Inciardi, Lockwood, and Pottieger, 1993.

76.   Robert E. Fullilove, Mindy Thompson Fullilove, Benjamin P. Bowser, and Shirley A. Gross, "Risk of Sexually Transmitted Disease among Black Adolescent Crack Users in Oakland and San Fran- cisco," *Journal of the American Medical Association,* 263 (1990), pp. 851–855; Robert T. Rolfs, Martin Goldberg, and Robert G. Sharrar, "Risk Factors for Syphilis: Cocaine Use and Prostitution," *American Journal of Public Health,* 80 (1990), pp. 853–857.

77.   Padian, 1988.

78.   Sevgi O. Aral and King K. Holmes, "Sexually Transmitted Diseases in the AIDS Era," *Scientific American,* 264 (1991), pp. 62–69.

79.   Vivian T. Shayne and Barbara J. Kaplan, "Double Victims: Poor Women and AIDS," *Women and Health,* 17 (1991), pp. 21–37.

80.   Worth, 1989; Campbell, 1991.

81.   Seth C. Kalichman, Tricia L. Hunter, and Jeffrey A. Kelly, "Perceptions of AIDS Susceptibility among Minority and Nonminority Women at Risk for HIV Infection," *Journal of Consulting and Clin- ical Psychology,* 60 (1992), pp. 725–732.

82.   Zena A. Stein, "HIV Prevention: The Need for Methods Women Can Use," *American Journal of Public Health,* 80 (1990), pp. 460–462.

83.   Zena A. Stein, "Editorial: The Double Bind in Science Policy and the Protection of Women from HIV Infection," *American Journal of Public Health,* 82 (1992), pp. 1471–1472.

84.   Editorial, "The Female Condom," *British Journal of Family Planning,* 18 (1992), pp. 71–72.

85.   Mary Ann Leeper and M. Conrardy, "Preliminary Evaluation of Reality: A Condom for Women to Wear," *Advances in Contraception,* 5 (1989), pp. 229–235; Walli Bounds, John Guillebaud, Laura Stewart, and Stuart Steele, "A Female Condom (Femshield): A Study of Its User Acceptability," *British Journal of Family Planning,* 14 (1988), pp. 83–87; Erica L. Gollub and Zena A. Stein, "Commentary:

The New Female Condom—Item I on a Woman's AIDS Prevention Agenda," *American Journal of Public Health,* 83 (1993), pp. 498–500.

86. For example, see L. Blumenfeld, "The New Sexual 'Reality'," *Washington Post,* 9 March 1992; L. Jackson, "The Female Condom Gets Mixed Reviews," *Philadelphia Daily News,* 18 October 1994, p. 4.

87. See, for example, Hilary L. Surratt, Wendee M. Wechsberg, Linda B. Cottler, Carl G. Leukefeld, Hugh Klein, and David P. Desmonf, "Acceptability of the Female Condom among Women at Risk for HIV Infection," *American Behavioral Scientist,* 41 (May 1998), pp. 1157–1170; Hilary L. Surratt and James A. Inciardi, "Introducing the Female Condom to Drug Users in Brazil," *Population Research and Policy Review,* 18 (1999), pp. 169–181.

88. David Vlahov and Benjamin Junge, "The Role of Needle Exchange Programs in HIV Prevention," *Public Health Reports,* 113, Supplement1 (June 1998), pp. 75–80.

89. C. A. Raymond, "U. S. Cities Struggle to Implement Needle Exchanges Despite Apparent Successes in European Cities," *Journal of the American Medical Association,* 260 (1988), pp. 2620–2621.

90. E. Buning, T. Reid, H. Hagan, and L. Pappas, "Needle Exchange V: Update on the Netherlands and the United States," *Newsletter of the International Working Group on AIDS and IV Drug Use,* 4 (June 1989), pp. 9–10; C. Hartgers, E. C. Buning, G. W. Van Santen, A. D. Verster, and R. A. Coutinho, "The Impact of the Needle and Syringe-Exchange Programme in Amsterdam on Injecting Risk Behavior," *AIDS,* 3 (1989), pp. 571–576.

91. *New York Times,* 29 February 1988, p. A4; *Alcoholism and Drug Abuse Week,* 26 April 1989, p. 5.

92. G. V. Stimson, "Editorial Review: Syringe-Exchange Programmes for Injecting Drug Users," *AIDS,* 3 (1989), pp. 253–260; M. C. Donoghoe, G. V. Stimson, K. Dolan, and L. Alldritt, "Changes in HIV Risk Behavior in Clients of Syringe-Exchange Schemes in England and Scotland," *AIDS,* 3 (1989), pp. 267–272; G. J. Hart, A. L. M. Carvell, N. Woodward, A. M. Johnson, P.Williams, and J. V. Parry, "Evaluation of Needle Exchange in Central London: Behaviour Change and Anti-HIV Status over One Year," *AIDS,* 3 (1989), pp. 261–265; *World Press Review,* June 1988, pp. 31–32.

93. *International Journal on Drug Policy,* September–October 1989, p. 5.

94. C. A. Raymond, "First Needle Exchange Program Approved: Other Cities Await Results," *Journal of the American Medical Association,* 259 (1988), pp. 1289–1290.

95. See "Needle Exchange Goes on Trial," *International Journal on Drug Policy,* 1 (1989), p. 5.

96. B. T. Farid, "AIDS and Drug Addiction Needle Exchange Schemes: A Step in the Dark," *Journal of the Royal Society of Medicine,* 81 (1988), pp. 375–376.

97. *Alcoholism and Drug Abuse Week,* 26 April 1989, p. 5.

98. *Drug Abuse Report,* 22 November 1988, p. 1.

99. Hartgers et al., 1989.

100. For example, see Robert Heimer, "Syringe Exchange Programs: Lowering the Transmission of Syringe-Borne Diseases and Beyond," *Public Health Reports,* 113 Supplement 1 (June 1998), pp. 67–74; Judith A. Hahn, Karen M. Vranizan, and Andrew R. Moss, "Who Uses Needle Exchange? A Study of Injection Drug Users in Treatment in San Francisco, 1989–1990," *Journal of Acquired Immune Deficiency Syndromes and Human Retrovirology,* 15 (1997), pp. 157–164; Edward H. Kaplan and Robert Heimer, "HIV Incidence among New Haven Needle Exchange Participants: Updated Estimates from Syringe Tracking and Testing Data," *Journal of Acquired Immune Deficiency Syndromes and Human Retrovirology,* 10 (1995), pp. 175–176; Robert Heimer, Kaveh Khoshnood, Dan Bigg, Joseph Guydish, and Benjamin Junge, "Syringe Use and Reuse: Effects of Syringe Exchange Programs in Four Cities," *Journal of Acquired Immune Deficiency Syndromes and Human Retrovirology,* 18 Supplement 1 (1998), pp. S37–S44; N. Braine, D. C. Des Jarlais, S. Ahmad, D. Purchase, and C. Turner, "Long-Term Effects of Syringe Exchange on Risk Behavior and HIV Prevention," *AIDS Education and Prevention,* 16(3) (2004), pp. 264–275.

101. Don C. Des Jarlais, "Prevention of HIV and Hepatitis in Drug Using Populations," *Drug Use, HIV, and Hepatitis, Bringing It All Together,* May 7–10, 2000, Baltimore, MD; Don C. Des Jarlais, Darlene Rodriguez and Suzette Smetka, *Hawaii Statewide Syringe Exchange Program: 1999 Evaluation Report* (Honolulu, HI: Community Health Outreach Work Project, 2000).

102. A. I. Leshner, "Don't Let Ideology Trump Science," *Science,* 302 (November 28, 2003), p. 1479.

103. B. Herbert, "The Big Chill at the Lab," *New York Times,* 3 November 2003, p. A19; J. Kaiser, "NIH Roiled by Inquiries over Grants Hit List," *Science,* 302 (October 31, 2003), p. 758; M. Navarro,

"Experts in Sex Field Say Conservatives Interfere with Health and Research," *New York Times,* 11 July 2004, pp. 1, 16.

104. H. L. Surratt, S. P. Kurtz, J. C. Weaver, and J. A. Inciardi, "The Connections of Mental Health Problems, Violent Life Experiences, and the Social Milieu of the 'Stroll' with the HIV Risk Behaviors of Female Street Sex Workers," *Journal of Psychology and Human Sexuality,* 17 (1/2) (2005), pp. 23–44; H. L. Surratt, "Mental Health Problems and Criminal Justice Involvement among Female Street-Based Sex Workers," *Law Enforcement Executive Forum,* 6 (3) (2006), pp. 121–134; J. A. Inciardi, H. L. Surratt, and S. P. Kurtz, "HIV, HBV, and HCV Infections among Drug-Involved, Inner-City, Street Sex Workers in Miami, Florida," *AIDS and Behavior,* 10 (2) (2006), pp. 137–147; S. P. Kurtz, H. L. Surratt, M. C. Kiley, and J. A. Inciardi, "Barriers to Health and Social Services for Street-Based Sex Workers," *Journal of Health Care for the Poor and Underserved,* 16 (2) (2005), pp. 345–361.

105. S. Russell, "AIDS, Sex Scientist on Federal List Fear Their Research Is in Jeopardy," *San Francisco Chronicle,* 28 October 2003, p. A3.

106. J. A. Inciardi, H. L. Surratt, S. P. Kurtz, and J. C. Weaver, "The Effect of Serostatus on HIV Risk Behavior Change among Women Sex Workers in Miami, Florida," *AIDS Care,* 17 (Supplement 1) (2005), pp. S88–S101.

107. P. D. Ghys, C. Jenkins, and E. Pisani, "HIV Surveillance among Female Sex Workers," *AIDS,* 15 (2001), pp. S33–S40; L. T. Giang, N. T. Son, L. T. L. Thao, L. Vu, E. S. Hudes, and C. Lindan, "Evaluation of STD/HIV Prevention Needs of Low- and Middle-Income Female Sex Workers in Ho Chi Minh City, Vietnam," *AIDS and Behavior,* 4 (2000), pp. 83–91; C. M. Lowndes, M. Alary, C. A. B. Gnintougbe, E. Bedard, L. Mukenge, N. Geraldo, P. Jossou, E. Lafia, F. Bernier, E. Baganizi, J. Joly, E. Frost, and S. Anagonou, "Management of Sexually Transmitted Diseases and HIV Prevention in Men at High Risk: Targeting Clients and Non-Paying Sexual Partners of Female Sex Workers in Benin," *AIDS,* 14 (2000), pp. 2523–2534; L. Morison, H. A. Weiss, A. Buve, M. Carael, S.-C. Abega, F. Kaona, L. Kanhonou, J. Chege, and R. J. Hayes, "Commercial Sex and the Spread of HIV in Four Cities in Sub-Saharan Africa," *AIDS,* 15 (2001), pp. S61–S69.

108. J. B. Cohen, L. E. Poole, L. E. Dorman, C. A. Lyons, T. J. Kelly, and C. B. Wofsy, "Changes in Risk Behavior for HIV Infection and Transmission in a Prospective Study of 240 Sexually Active Women in San Francisco," Fourth International Conference on AIDS, Stockholm, Sweden, June 13–14, 1988; N. Corby, P. Barchi, R. J. Wolitsky, P. Smith, and D. Martin, "Effects of Condom-Skills Training and HIV-Testing on AIDS Prevention Behaviors among Sex Workers," Sixth International Conference on AIDS, San Francisco, CA, June 23, 1990; C. E. Sterk, K. W. Elifson, and K. P. Theall, "Effectiveness of an HIV Risk-Reduction Intervention among African American Women Who Use Crack Cocaine," in *Strategies to Improve the Replicability, Sustainability, and Durability of HIV Prevention Interventions for Drug Users,* NIDA/CAMCODA Working Meeting, Washington, DC, May 6–7, 2002 (Bethesda, MD: National Institute on Drug Abuse, 2003); G. M. Wingood, "Designing HIV Relapse Prevention Program for African American Women," in *Strategies to Improve the Replicability, Sustainability, and Durability of HIV Prevention Interventions for Drug Users,* NIDA/CAMCODA Working Meeting, Washington, DC, May 6–7, 2002 (Bethesda, MD: National Institute on Drug Abuse, 2003).

109. D. Burrows, "Drug Abuse, Infectious Diseases, and HIV/AIDS," in *Proceedings of the Global Research Network on HIV Prevention in Drug-Using Populations: HIV and Drug Use—the Global Situation,* Satellite Session, XIV International AIDS Conference, Barcelona, Spain, July 2002, (Bethesda, MD: National Institute on Drug Abuse), pp. 27–30; M. Farell, L. Gowing, R. Ali, and W. Ling, "A Presentation of Work in a Progress on a Review of the Evidence for the Impact of Drug Treatment on HIV Prevention," in *Proceedings of the Global Research Network on HIV Prevention in Drug-Using Populations: HIV and Drug Use—the Global Situation,* Satellite Session, XIV International AIDS Conference, Barcelona, Spain, July 2002 (Bethesda, MD: National Institute on Drug Abuse), pp. 31–34; National Institute on Drug Abuse, *Principles of HIV Prevention in Drug-Using Populations,* NIH Publication No. 02-04733 (Bethesda, MD: National Institute on Drug Abuse, 2002).

CHAPTER 10

THE GREAT DRUG WAR

Policies and Programs
to Reduce Drug
Supply and Demand

Historically, the federal approach to drug abuse and drug control has included a variety of avenues for reducing both the supply of and the demand for illicit drugs. Early in the twentieth century, during the period when the Harrison Act was contrived, the supply-and-demand reduction strategies were grounded in the classic deterrence model: through legislation and criminal penalties, individuals would be discouraged from using drugs; by setting an example of traffickers, the government would force potential dealers to seek other economic pursuits. For most people who had a significant investment in the social system, the model worked—at least for a time.

As the United States moved toward midcentury, other components were added: treatment for the user; education and prevention for the would-be user; and research to determine how best to develop and implement plans for treatment, education, and prevention. By the early 1970s, when it appeared that existing drug control strategies had won few, if any, battles, new avenues for supply reduction were added. Federal interdiction initiatives included Coast Guard, Customs, and Drug Enforcement Administration operatives charged with intercepting drug shipments coming to the United States from foreign ports; and attempts in the international sector to eradicate drug-yielding crops at their source. On the surface, none of these strategies seemed to have substantial effects. Drugs managed to slip through the borders to the streets of urban America, and illicit drug use continued to spread.

Legislation and enforcement alone were not enough to solve the problem, and early education programs using scare tactics quickly lost their credibility among youth. For social scientists, clinicians, and most other people who had humanitarian ideals—which probably included the majority of the people in the United States—treating drug abuse as a medical problem seemed to be the logical solution. But the difficulty with that approach was threefold. First, the medical model of treatment was structured around a belief in the stereotypical addiction-prone personality—that deep-rooted personality disorder used to characterize just about everyone with a drug problem. However, all drug abusers were *not* the same. The result was high program failure rates, regardless of the method of treatment.[1] Second, from what is now known about the course of drug abuse treatment, most treatment regimens in the 1950s and 1960s were not long enough to have significant and lasting impacts. And third, not enough treatment beds were available to meet the demand.

During the late 1970s, given the perceived inadequacy of the traditional approaches to drug abuse control, federal authorities began drawing plans for a more concerted assault on drugs, both legislative and technological, and both on the supply and the demand sides.

SUPPLY-REDUCTION STRATEGIES

Richard Nixon may have launched a war on heroin in the early 1970s, but the first real war on drugs did not actually begin until a decade later. The time was ripe during the early 1980s to witness a significant political shift to the conservative right, as clearly evidenced by the election of Ronald Reagan to his first term as president of the United States. Voters left no doubt as to what they wanted. The 1980 election represented the strongest shift in three decades, hinting at a conservative domination that would reign in Congress for the remainder of the twentieth century. Quite telling, in this regard, was the shift back to some traditional values by the nation's youth, especially on college campuses.

Each year, the University of California and the American Council on Education develop a national profile of the characteristics and attitudes of first-year college students. As illustrated in Exhibit 10.1, which highlights selected areas of student

EXHIBIT 10.1   Selected Attitudes of the Classes of 1977, 1984, and 1987

	PERCENT		
ATTITUDE	*CLASS OF 1977*	*CLASS OF 1984*	*CLASS OF 1987*
Poltical Views			
Far left	2.2	2.1	1.9
Liberal	32.6	19.6	19.2
Middle-of-the-road	50.7	60.0	60.3
Conservative	13.9	17.1	17.5
Far right	0.6	1.2	1.2
Proportions Who Agree That			
Courts are too concerned with the rights of criminals	50.1	65.9	68.8
The death penalty should be abolished	43.3	34.5	28.9
Marijuana should be legalized	48.2	39.3	25.7

Source: The Chronicle of Higher Education, February 11, 1974, p. 8; February 9, 1981, p. 8; February 1, 1984, p. 14.

response from this profile, it is clear that liberalism as a political ideology had lost some of its radiance. Comparing the graduating classes of 1977, 1984, and 1987, the number of students calling themselves liberals declined whereas conservatives and middle-of-the-roaders increased. Perhaps most significant was the trend toward more conservative views with respect to the rights of the accused, the death penalty, and the legalization of marijuana. These data, combined with the growing conservatism among older people, suggested that an enhanced war on drugs would be well received. As both drug use and crime escalated during the 1980s, the federal government, as well as legislators and criminal justice systems at all jurisdictional levels, responded.

Fat Albert, Blue Thunder, and Posse Comitatus: Weapons for the New War on Drugs

Federal policy makers instituted dramatic increases in funding for a new war on drugs, with much of the additional monies earmarked for law enforcement and interdiction activities. It began with RICO (Racketeer-Influenced and Corrupt Organizations) and CCE (Continuing Criminal Enterprise) statutes. What RICO and CCE accomplish is the forfeiture of the fruits of criminal activities. Their intent is to eliminate the rights of traffickers to their personal assets, whether these be cash, bank accounts, real estate, automobiles, jewelry and art, equity in businesses, directorships in companies, or any kind of goods or entitlements that are obtained in or used for a criminal enterprise.[2]

Added to the perceived strength offered by RICO and CCE was a new extradition treaty between the United States and the Republic of Colombia, signed on September 14, 1979, and entered into force on March 4, 1982.[3] The treaty was notable in that it added to the list of extraditable crimes a variety of offenses related to drug trafficking, aircraft hijacking, obstruction of justice, and bribery. In addition, Article 8 of the treaty was a considerable innovation in international affairs in that it imposed an obligation on the government of Colombia to extradite all persons, including its nationals, when the offense was a punishable act in both countries and was intended to be consummated in the United States (i.e., the export of cocaine and/or marijuana into the United States from Colombia by Colombian citizens).*

The new and evolving federal strategy considered it crucial to include the U.S. military in its war on drugs, but to do so something had to be done about the Posse Comitatus Act, originally passed by the Forty-Fifth Congress more than a century earlier, on June 18, 1878. The act had been a response to post–Civil War reconstruction policies that permitted U.S. marshals in occupied southern states to call on federal troops to enforce local laws. It had been the goal of southern members of Congress to prevent such a practice, and the Posse Comitatus Act accomplished exactly that. It prohibited the army (and eventually other branches of the military) from enforcing federal, state, and local civilian law, and from supplementing the efforts of civilian law enforcement agencies.[4]

---

*As noted earlier in Chapter 6, this extradition treaty was outlawed by Colombia's constitution in 1991, but on December 17, 1997, Colombia passed a constitutional amendment that once again permitted the extradition of its nationals to the United States.

But the Posse Comitatus Act was never a constitutionally mandated statute. In fact, its wording permitted the assistance of the military if specifically authorized by an act of Congress.* As a result, when Congress passed, and President Reagan signed into law, the Department of Defense Authorization Act of 1982, it included several amendments to the century-old Posse Comitatus Act. Although military personnel were still prohibited from physically intercepting suspected drug vessels and aircraft, conducting searches and seizures, and making arrests, the entire war chest of U.S. military power did become available to law enforcement—for training, intelligence gathering, and detection. Moreover, members of the U.S. Army, Navy, Air Force, and Marines could operate military equipment for civilian agencies charged with the enforcement of drug laws.†

Beginning in 1982, the war on drugs had a new look. Put into force was the Bell 209 assault helicopter, more popularly known as the "Cobra." None in the military arsenal were faster, and in its gunship mode it could destroy a tank. In addition, the awesome Sikorsky Black Hawk assault helicopter was assigned for operation by U.S. Customs Service pilots. Customs also had the Cessna Citation, a jet aircraft equipped with radar originally designed for F-16 fighters. In addition was the Navy's EC-2, an aircraft equipped with a radar disk capable of detecting other aircraft from as far as three hundred miles away. The U.S. Coast Guard also strengthened its equipment, and U.S. Customs put Blue Thunder into service, a vessel specifically designed to outrun the high-performance ("go-fast") speedboats that traffickers use in Florida and Caribbean waters. A thirty-nine-foot catamaran with 900 horsepower, Blue Thunder cut through six-foot seas at speeds better than sixty miles per hour (see Exhibit 10.2).

NASA satellites could spy on drug operations as far apart as California and Colombia; airborne infrared sensing and imaging equipment could detect human body heat in the thickest underbrush of Florida's Everglades; in addition a host of other high-technology devices could be put into operation. Fat Albert and his pals were aerostat surveillance balloons 175 feet in length equipped with sophisticated radar and listening devices. Based in the Florida Keys, Fat Albert could not only pick up communications from Cuba and Soviet satellites, but also detect traffic in Smugglers' Alley, a wide band of Caribbean sky that is virtually invisible to land-based radar systems. In all, drug enforcement appeared well equipped for battle.[5]

The Conch Republic Rebellion

Although the intent of the new war on drugs was quite serious, one of its first battles provided considerable comic relief to many observers throughout the nation. On April 23, 1982, the U.S. Border Patrol set up a blockade in front of Skeeter's Last

---

*Over the years, Congress has authorized the use of the military to control civil disorder. It was for this reason that Chicago's Mayor Daley was able to call in the Illinois National Guard, as well as regular army troops, to control the perceived threat of disorder by antiwar protestors at the Democratic National Convention in 1968.

†It should be noted here that the Posse Comitatus Act never prevented the U.S. Coast Guard from intercepting and seizing vessels at sea that were transporting contraband to U.S. ports.

EXHIBIT   10.2
BLUE THUNDER AND THE FLORIDA STRAITS

Blue Thunder was designed by the late Don Aronow, the creator of such internationally rec-ognized "go-fast boats" as Formula, Donzi, Magnum, and the most famous powerboat ever—the Cigarette. Nicknamed the "Ferrari of the open seas, " the Cigarette became the boat desired by both the famous and infamous throughout the world, from former presi-dents Richard M. Nixon and Lyndon B. Johnson to the Shah of Iran, fugitive financier Robert Vesco, and likely every bandit and drug-runner that carried contraband across the Florida Straits. What distinguished Blue Thunder from the Cigarette was not its speed, but its ability to sustain high speeds in extremely heavy seas without breaking up.

Also known as "ocean racers, " go-fast boats are still popular with both smugglers and law enforcement. Some of these high-performance watercraft are as long as sixty feet, pow-ered by twin and triple 1,000-hp engines, and can reach speeds exceeding 100 mph. For an examination of the making of Blue Thunder and the gangland-style murder of Don Aronow in 1987, see Thomas Burdick and Charlene Mitchell, *Blue Thunder* (New York: Simon and Schuster, 1990).

Chance Saloon in Florida City, Florida. Skeeter's is located on U.S. Highway 1, at the entrance to the Florida Keys (or the exit, depending on which direction you are facing—see Exhibit 10.3). All northbound traffic was stopped and searched for illegal drugs and illegal aliens, and the roadblock portrayed the Keys residents as non–U.S. citizens who had to prove their citizenship to drive onto the Florida mainland.

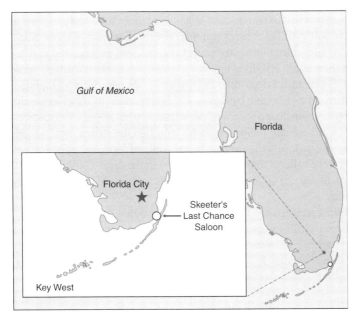

EXHIBIT 10.3   The Florida Keys and Skeeter's Last Chance Saloon

Because ensuing traffic jams effectively stymied the Florida Keys tourism industry, Key West Mayor Dennis Wardlow hatched a scheme to save the Keys economy. Wardlow and a number of other local citizens went to the federal district court in Miami to seek an injunction against the federal blockade. But their efforts were to no avail. As Mayor Wardlow descended the courthouse steps, he announced to the world, by way of assembled TV reporters: "Tomorrow at noon, the Florida Keys will secede from the United States of America!"

At noon on the day of secession, at Mallory Square in Key West, Wardlow read the proclamation of secession and declared that the new Conch Republic (pronounced "konk," and named after the queen conch—that cherished mollusk that children hold to their ears to hear the ocean) was an independent nation, separate from the United States. Wardlow then symbolically began the Conch Republic's civil rebellion by breaking a loaf of stale Cuban bread over the head of a man dressed in a U.S. Navy uniform. After just one minute of rebellion, Wardlow, now the Prime Minister of the Conch Republic, turned to the admiral in charge of the navy base at Key West and surrendered to the U.S. forces, demanding one billion dollars in foreign aid and war relief to rebuild the nation. Almost immediately, the roadblock was discontinued and the Keys economy was saved. But the Conch Republic lives on, and in April every year, from Key Largo to Key West, there is a ten-day birthday bash to celebrate the independent spirit of the Florida Keys.[6]

Zero Tolerance

As the drug war escalated, the 1980s also witnessed the rediscovery of crack cocaine, and, as discussed earlier in Chapter 6, the U.S. crack experience was vividly reported in the media during the second half of that decade. Highs and binges followed crashes that induced crack users to sell their belongings and their bodies in pursuit of more crack. The high abuse liability of the drug instigated users to commit any manner and number of crimes to support their habit. Rivalries in crack distribution networks turned some inner-city communities into urban dead zones where homicide rates were so high that police had written them off as anarchic badlands. The involvement of many inner-city youths in the crack business included scores of peewees and wannabees—those street-gang acolytes in grade school and junior high who patrolled the streets with walkie-talkies in the vicinity of crack houses, serving in networks of lookouts, spotters, and steerers, and aspiring to be rollers (short for high rollers) in the drug distribution business. Perhaps worst of all was the child abuse, child neglect, and child abandonment by crack-addicted mothers.

The hysteria over crack created enthusiasm for additional drug war weaponry. What appeared to be politically important to the Republican administration in this regard was zero tolerance, a 1988 White House antidrug policy that was never clearly articulated in the national media. It would appear that zero tolerance was (and is) based on a number of premises:

1. If there were no drug abusers there would be no drug problem.
2. The market for drugs is created not only by availability, but also by demand.

3. Drug abuse starts with a willful act.

4. The perception that drug users are powerless to act against the influences of drug availability and peer pressure is mistaken.

5. Most illegal drug users can choose to stop their drug-taking behaviors and must be held accountable if they do not.

6. Individual freedom does not include the right to self- and societal destruction.

7. Public tolerance for drug abuse must be reduced to *zero*.[7]

As such, the zero-tolerance policy expanded the war on drugs from suppliers and dealers, to users as well—especially casual users—and meant that planes, vessels, and vehicles could be confiscated for carrying even the smallest amount of a controlled substance.

Not surprisingly, the policy quickly became unpopular, particularly with non-drug-using owners of confiscated boats. As a case in point, during May 1988 the Coast Guard seized the *Ark Royal,* a $2.5 million, 133-foot yacht that was in international waters between Mexico and Cuba. The drug stash on board was one-tenth of an ounce of marijuana, and because only the captain and crew were on board at the time of the raid, it was not even apparent that the drug had been that of the vessel's owner.[8] Similar incidents led to an easing of the zero-tolerance policy, and an innocent-owner's defense was established to protect against vessel and vehicle confiscation when someone else's drugs for personal use were found.[9]

Presidents, Czars, Chiefs, and Generals: Leadership for the War on Drugs

Winning any war requires strong and decisive guidance on all fronts. It demands unified and attentive strategies, and the cooperation of the joint chiefs of staff. But in terms of leadership and cooperative strategy, the war on drugs has, at times, looked more like the rag-tag antics of a banana republic dictator than an effort orchestrated by the most powerful nation on earth. For example, in the 1980s there were no less than eleven cabinet departments, thirty-two federal agencies (from the FBI and the National Parks Service to the Department of Education), and at least five independent agencies with some responsibility for drug control. Not unexpectedly, such a situation could undermine drug control endeavors through duplications of effort and agency turf battles, and it did.

To remedy this situation, on more than one occasion during the 1980s, Senator Joseph R. Biden (a Democrat from Delaware) sponsored a bill known as the National Narcotics Leadership Act that called for a new cabinet-level position to head the federal war on drugs, a post that the media dubbed "drug czar." Biden argued: "Without some central, coordinated mechanism in place, with the statutory and political authority to do the job, each agency will continue to pursue its own narrow agenda, with little or no concern for the effectiveness of the overall program."[10] Biden's idea for a drug czar seemed to be logical, if for no other reason than it would be more cost effective. As a bonus, it had the potential for adding some professionalism to the U.S.

supply reduction efforts, and maybe even some humanity. But President Reagan rejected the drug czar idea, and the war on drugs went on—stumbling, fumbling, and bungling onward.

The Bush Strategy.   With the coming of George Bush (the first one) to the White House in 1989, it was apparent that the drug czar concept and a new drug initiative appealed to him. Not surprisingly, Democrats in the House and Senate began going through the motions that politicians usually do when they suspect that someone in the other party is about to do something special. So the Democrats began hastily drafting their own approaches to drug control. A host of antidrug strategies were at first modest but gathered some rather expensive moss as they were rolled from committee to committee. Knowing that a new drug war was close at hand and that it was politically acceptable, politicians across the nation—Democrats and Republicans alike—began vaulting over one another, hoping to reach the frontlines of the antidrug parade, attempting to demonstrate how thoroughly and unconditionally they disapproved of crack, cocaine, heroin, marijuana, and other illegal drugs. It was politics at its best and politics at its worst, and it became clear to many people that their representatives all too often appeared more interested in narrow political advantage than the welfare of the country. However, what did result was the passage of Title I of the Anti-Drug Abuse Act of 1988 (21 U.S.C. 1504), which was the National Narcotics Leadership Act. Finally, the United States would have its first drug czar. Was it a good idea? Only time would tell.

During the early months of 1989, William J. Bennett, Ph.D., J.D., was selected, appointed, anointed, and confirmed as the head of the Office of National Drug Control Policy (ONDCP)—the drug czar.* A former U.S. Secretary of Education, former college football player, and a lifelong rock 'n' roll fan, Bennett was an iconoclastic, irreverent neoconservative with an acerbic tongue, a taste for the bully pulpit, and a mission that most people felt was impossible. At best, Bennett knew that his job would be difficult, for he was a czar without an empire and a general without troops. The difficulty was that when President Bush appointed Bennett, his position was not of cabinet rank, and ONDCP was given only a modest operating budget. Accordingly, the new drug warrior had neither the power nor the funds to wage an organized war. But this was not Bennett's only problem.

Bennett's second problem was the Democrats. Although Bennett had no army of his own, it was clear from the outset that a multibillion-dollar antidrug package would be available, and that his thoughts would influence how these funds would be allocated. In fact, Bennett's initial mandate was to prepare a national drug control strategy by September 1, 1989, that would function as the President's blueprint for the nation's new war on drugs. As it began to take shape, partisan politics kicked in, or as Senator Biden put it:

---

*Bennett hated the label "drug czar," but the more he objected to it, the more the media used it.

Quite frankly, the President's plan is not tough enough, bold enough, or imaginative enough to meet the crisis at hand. The President says he wants to wage a war on drugs, but if that's true, what we need is another "D Day," not another Vietnam, not another limited war fought on the cheap and destined for stalemate and human tragedy.[11]

Bennett's third problem was Washington, DC, Mayor Marion S. Barry, Jr. Months before the National Drug Control Strategy was unveiled on September 1, 1989,[12] Bennett characterized the nation's capitol as a high-intensity drug-trafficking area and designated the city a "shock treatment" test case in the war on drugs. Bennett was not exaggerating the District's problems. During the first three months of 1989, Washington, DC, had had 120 murders—most of them drug related, and almost double the number during the same period in 1988.[13] Moreover, police seemed virtually powerless to stop the warfare in the streets between rival drug dealers.

The Bennett plan ultimately called for additional DEA and FBI agents for drug enforcement duties in the Washington area, the increased use of mandatory prison sentences for certain drug-related crimes, a special narcotics prosecution unit in the court system, three hundred slots to be added to the existing drug treatment system, and an expansion of drug education in the city school system.[14] But the complication in Mr. Bennett's Washington strategy was DC's Mayor Barry. While struggling to gain control over the city's drug epidemic, Barry was also battling allegations that he himself used drugs. Later in the year Barry was arrested.

During his six-week trial, government witnesses testified that Barry had indeed used drugs—cocaine, opium, and marijuana—more than two hundred times in homes and hotels, on ships, and even at the 1988 Democratic National Convention. An FBI videotape showed Barry twice inhaling from a crack pipe in a downtown Washington hotel room to which he had been invited by a former girlfriend. The jury found Barry guilty of one misdemeanor count of possessing cocaine, acquitted him on a second drug possession charge, but deadlocked on twelve other counts, including three felony charges of lying to a grand jury.[15] Unquestionably, Barry's use of cocaine not only disgraced his office and city, but undermined the fight against drugs. As William Bennett put it: "It's kind of hard to fight a war against drugs when your chief executive officer is a user."[16]

The Barry verdict did not play in Bogotá, Medellín, and other cities in Colombia where judges, prosecutors, and journalists had been casualties of their country's war against the cocaine cartels.[17] The Barry trial was seen as a symbolic test of the U.S. commitment to reduce drug consumption, and with his conviction on only one of fourteen counts, the United States was accused of having a double standard.* *Semana,* Colombia's leading news weekly wrote in a cover story on the Barry verdict: "In the war against drugs, the United States is ready to fight to the last Colombian."[18]

---

*In October of 1990, Barry was sentenced to a term of six months. But he was a survivor. In 1992 he was elected to the DC city council, and two years later he was reelected to serve his fourth term as mayor of the nation's capital. He did not seek a fifth term.

Bennett's fourth problem was what can only be described as a rather lopsided approach to addressing the drug problem. It had been Bennett's view from the outset that to reduce drug use and sales, and the related crime and violence, the nation had to take back the streets from the dealers and violent predators. No one could argue with him that the violence in the streets had to be addressed, but without going into all the details of what was unveiled in the National Drug Control Strategy, the new scheme called for the government to do essentially more of what it had been doing for years with only marginal success: make tougher laws, hire and train more police officers, expand street-level enforcement, make more arrests, build more prisons, intensify efforts to break up drug-trafficking organizations, escalate drug testing in the workplace, elevate the certainty of punishment for drug crimes, increase the penalties for casual users, and cut back foreign aid to drug-producing nations not cooperating with coca- and poppy-eradicating efforts.

In retrospect, one could argue that taking back the streets from the drug dealers and violent predators is important, for, after all, an essential benefit of living in a free society should be freedom from fear. At the time that Bennett released his first National Drug Control Strategy in 1989, the streets in many cities were indeed unsafe. For example, total violent crime in the United States increased by 22.4 percent during the 1980s, and the rate of violent crime increased by 11.1 percent. Moreover, keeping heroin and cocaine off the streets and out of the country are integral aspects of a coordinated supply-reduction strategy. But to the disappointment of those who actually understood the drug problem in the United States, supply reduction represented roughly 70 percent of the Bennett/Bush strategy—a ratio that had remained essentially the same since Richard M. Nixon's war on heroin two decades earlier. It was the same old agenda—more police, more enforcement, and more interdiction, with little attention to reducing the demand for drugs through prevention, education, treatment, and research (see Exhibit 10.4).

Bennett announced his resignation from government on November 8, 1990, to pursue his interests in writing and fostering conservative ideas. He was replaced by former Florida governor Bob Martinez—dubbed by the press as the "bad-news drug czar."[19] Martinez was laidback and amiable, traits quite the opposite of those exhibited by his predecessor but unworkable for the leader of a war on drugs. As a result, his tenure as drug czar was plagued by tumult, staff turnover, disorganization, and a lack of support from President Bush. In 1993, he retired to political obscurity in his hometown, Tampa, Florida.

The Clinton Strategy. Ever since the law-and-order days of Barry Goldwater and the presidential election of 1964, crime control in U.S. politics had been safe Republican territory. Republicans were viewed as tougher on crime than Democrats, with a greater willingness to expand government powers to fight crime, even at the cost of individual rights. By contrast, President Bill Clinton, a Democrat, embraced greater voter backing on the crime issue. He supported the death penalty and presided over four executions in Arkansas during his twelve years as governor. On gun control, he espoused modest regulation, a position held by the majority of people in the United States. During the first

"WE HAVE THE ENEMY IN OUR SIGHTS, CHIEF"

EXHIBIT 10.4   **"We have the enemy in our sights, Chief"**

two years of his presidency, Clinton signed the Brady Handgun Violence Prevention Act as well as a major crime bill that, among other things, increased law enforcement initiatives, expanded the scope of the federal death penalty, and called for mandatory life sentences for three-time felony offenders.

As for the drug problem, Clinton was relatively silent during the presidential campaign, focusing on more pressing economic issues. With the onset of his presidency, however, his position departed from that of the Reagan/Bush years. It appeared that the Republican war on drugs and its emphasis on supply reduction would be taking a back seat. Clinton seemed to favor a demand-reduction strategy, stressing education, prevention, and treatment while maintaining basic law enforcement initiatives. However, the implementation of his drug strategy was slow, and much of the policy of previous administrations tended to endure.

In 1993, Dr. Lee P. Brown, who had previously headed the Atlanta, Houston, and New York City police departments, was appointed the director of the Office of National Drug Control Policy. Brown became Clinton's first drug czar but announced his resignation after only two years, expressing frustration at the political climate in Washington: "At a time when we see a rise in the use of illegal drugs by our adolescents, the proposed budget cuts in drug-fighting are wrong-headed and must be reversed."[20] During Brown's tenure, however, Clinton raised the status of the drug czar to cabinet level, but the department's budget and staff had been dramatically cut. The mission of Brown's office had been criticized by members of Congress, who called for a stiffer antidrug message from the White House. Brown, himself, was frequently criticized for putting too much emphasis on prevention and treatment. Once again, partisan politics took center stage. But Brown should be credited for advocating treatment for chronic drug abusers as the most humane and effective way to reduce overall demand for cocaine and heroin. However, he was no more successful than others in moving the White House and Congress toward a more progressive position on drug control.*

During President Clinton's State of the Union address on January 23, 1995, he nominated General Barry McCaffrey to fill the vacancy left by Lee Brown's resignation. Caving in to political pressure, Clinton selected General McCaffrey because he was a decorated veteran of both the Vietnam War and the Gulf War. As commander-in-chief of the U.S. Southern Command, McCaffrey had been heavily involved in U.S. drug war efforts in Latin America. Clinton's choice was an obvious political attempt to compete for votes in the coming election year by appearing to be as tough on drugs as the Republicans. With McCaffrey, the President had a real general, and hoped to remove all doubt that he was committed to the drug war. But despairingly to most observers in the drug field, McCaffrey's experience was with interdiction—perhaps the least-efficient drug control strategy. For those who supported prevention and treatment, it was feared that McCaffrey's military background might lead to further militarization of the drug war—both domestically and internationally. Early on, however, some thought McCaffrey might be a blessing in disguise, for during his tenure as czar he did emphasize the importance of treatment. Little did they know what was yet to come—the 2000 National Drug Control Strategy.[21]

Reactions to the 2000 strategy were mixed. Indeed, in reviewing all the goals and objectives, there was something for everyone: education, prevention, partnerships with the media, drug abuse treatment, research, enforcement, foreign assistance initiatives, interdiction, protection of U.S. borders, medications development, provision of health services for drug abusers, and much more. But not everyone was satisfied. In a press release from the Criminal Justice Policy Foundation, a Washington, DC–based organization focusing on drug policy reform, the strategy received a blistering indictment:

> The latest National Drug Control Strategy attempts to sweep monumental failure under a rug. Gen. McCaffrey sounds like a broken record. He insists that "we are winning" our fight against drug abuse, but his scoreboard must be broken—deaths are up, high school kids can get drugs more easily than ever, drug use by junior high kids has tripled, drug

---

*After leaving his post as drug czar, Dr. Brown joined the faculty at Rice University, where he taught sociology during the 1996–1997 academic year. In 1997, he was elected mayor of Houston and overwhelmingly reelected to a second term in 1999.

prices are at historic lows, drug purity is as high as ever, and we are still not treating most of the millions of addicts desperate for help. It is time for us to have the courage to do something different.

The indices that Gen. McCaffrey is most proud of are the least important—the declines in casual use of cocaine and marijuana. Casual drug users are not the cancer at the core of America's drug crisis.[22]

Some reasons for these harsh reactions were justified because drug abuse was *not* under control by any means, and it appeared that billions more taxpayer dollars were being allocated for approaches that were not working. One major objection to the drug strategy was an initiative called Plan Colombia, a $1.3 billion aid package to assist the Colombian government in its efforts to reduce heroin and cocaine production within its borders. Colombia's efforts to attack the drug trade have been hampered over the years by the activities of insurgent guerillas and paramilitary groups that control the country's drug-producing regions. Moreover, organized drug cartels run the international aspects of Colombia's drug trade. For years a vicious circle has existed—the money produced by the drug trade enriches the outlaw groups, which generate violence and corruption in government, which threaten the country's democratic institutions.

The backbone of Plan Colombia was supplying thirty Blackhawk and thirty-three Huey helicopters for the Colombian Army and police forces, as well as almost $600 million to train and equip three Colombian Army battalions for antidrug operations. This plan had numerous critics in addition to the Criminal Justice Policy Foundation—even in the U.S. Congress. Many observers warned that the United States would be drawn deeply into a convoluted civil conflict, a Vietnam-like quagmire, in a country where two leftist guerilla armies were fighting the government, where right-wing paramilitary forces were fighting the guerillas, and where civilians were trapped in the middle. As Representative Jose E. Serrano, a New York Democrat, stated: "We're getting involved in a civil war for which we're going to pay a high price."[23] Nancy Pelosi, a California Democrat, and the current Speaker of the House explained: "This really doesn't get to the heart of the matter: the drug problem in our country. Some 5.5 million Americans need substance abuse treatment, and only 2 million are getting it."[24]

U.S. drug policy is easy to criticize. In fact, doing so has been quite fashionable for decades, particularly by academics, intellectuals, and other armchair observers who know little about drug abuse, drug trafficking, or how the U.S. government works. But in this case, the critics had two valid points: (1) the supply-reduction initiatives were not working well at all; and (2) not only were some aspects of the poorly funded demand-reduction ventures quite effective, but others were showing great promise. Interestingly, when the U.S. Senate voted on the Plan Colombia appropriation on June 21, 2000, Senator Paul Wellstone of Minnesota proposed an amendment shifting $225 million from military funding to domestic drug abuse treatment.[25] Not surprisingly, the Wellstone amendment was overwhelmingly defeated by a vote of eighty-nine to eleven, and, once again, the U.S. Congress demonstrated its lack of understanding of how to deal with the phenomenon of drug abuse in the United States.

The Bush/Walters Strategy

With the inauguration of George W. Bush as forty-third president of the United States in 2001, General McCaffery stepped down from his position as drug czar, and was replaced later in the year by John P. Walters. Having been deputy director for supply reduction during William Bennett's tenure as head of the Office of National Drug Control Policy, the issues of supply reduction and demand reduction were not altogether unknown to the new drug czar. And not surprisingly, he essentially followed in the footsteps of Bennett—deemphasizing demand reduction and throwing major support to supply reduction. By 2007, the budget request for drug control was $12.9 billion, with only one-third earmarked for demand reduction. And Plan Colombia not only endured, but grew substantially.

DEMAND-REDUCTION STRATEGIES

Demand reduction, as its very designation suggests, includes policies and programs designed to reduce the demand for drugs. The logic behind demand reduction is essentially the same as the basic premise of zero tolerance—if there are no drug users, there will be no drug problem. However, approaches to demand reduction versus zero tolerance are dramatically different. Rather than attempting to legislate drug use out of existence through mandatory sentences, asset forfeiture, and drug-testing policies, demand reduction focuses on two specific areas—substance abuse prevention and substance abuse treatment.

Substance Abuse Prevention

The history of drug education and prevention reflects a collection of highly problematic approaches. For the better part of the twentieth century, programs attempted to scare people away from using illegal drugs. But the tactic did not work. One need only look back to the reefer madness era of the 1930s, 1940s, and 1950s for evidence of this. Marijuana was portrayed in the media as the devil drug and assassin of youth, but such messages failed to discourage use. The problem was simple—the propaganda was a series of untruths, and most of those in the target audiences knew it. Moreover, the way that marijuana was portrayed actually enticed many into trying it.

By the 1960s, drug prevention approaches continued to be naive and unsophisticated, but in a very different way. Educators assumed that the more information young people had about drugs and their effects, the more negative their attitudes would become, and the lower the likelihood that they would try or use illegal drugs.[26] This illusion was shattered in the 1970s, however, when studies demonstrated that students who knew the most about drugs had the most positive attitudes toward their use.[27] Moreover, of four programs studied, all were equally effective in increasing knowledge about drugs, but equally ineffective in changing drug-related attitudes or behavior.[28] A number of observers began wondering whether drug education actually encouraged drug use. In 1973, the Special Action Office for Drug Abuse Prevention—what the White House drug policy office was named at that time—called a halt to the production of all federally funded drug prevention materials, and issued a set of guidelines regulating the content of all subsequent materials, including an end to all scare tactics, stereotyping of drug users, and exaggerated and dogmatic statements.[29]

Since the 1980s, a variety of different drug abuse prevention programs have been tried. Curiously, those that have been the most visible also appear to be the least effective, for example, "Just Say No," DARE, and numerous well-funded media campaigns.

"Just Say No."   Not too long after Ronald Reagan moved into the White House in 1981, Nancy Reagan, his wife, began making speeches with an antidrug theme. It was from her office as First Lady that the "Just Say No" slogan emerged. However, the slogan and its accompanying drug education programs came under fire almost immediately after they were announced. Some called the "Just Say No" premise unrealistic and unworkable; others suggested that drug educators should just say no to "Just Say No," claiming the program was ineffective and was taking time away from more practical forms of drug education. In addition, although years of "Just Say No" education may have taught some youths about the dangers of heroin, cocaine, marijuana, and other illegal drugs, it is speculated that this education neglected to address legal substances (alcohol and prescription drugs) and everyday household items (solvents and inhalants) that have a high potential for abuse. One need only visit a rave or dance club to confirm this suspicion.

A major criticism of "Just Say No" has been its no-use message, considered simplistic by many because of the noninteractive method by which drug prevention messages are delivered. A three-year study of California's drug education programs, for example, that were grounded in the "Just Say No" concept, clearly demonstrated this point.[30] Based on interviews with more than five thousand students, respondents indicated that the drug education had no effect, particularly as they got older. The everyday experiences of youths, such as seeing their parents use alcohol in moderation, seemed to undo what was being taught in the program—the message that no drugs should be used in any amount or under any circumstances.*

Drug Abuse Resistance Education (D.A.R.E.).   The most widespread and popular approach embodying the "Just Say No" principle has been the well-known Drug Abuse Resistance Education (D.A.R.E., or DARE) program. Implemented both nationally and internationally, DARE was founded in Los Angeles in 1983 and was designed to give youths the skills they need to avoid involvement in drugs, gangs, and violence. Roughly three-fourths of all school districts in the United States have adopted DARE. Most versions run for one hour a week for seventeen weeks, beginning in kindergarten and running through senior high school. Uniformed police officers teach the program, which includes informational messages, group interaction, role-playing, and homework.

DARE programs have been extremely popular because of the image they project—police officers working with kids to reduce the problem of drug abuse. In

---

*As a footnote to the "Just Say No" era, even its critics admitted that the slogan was catchy. To capitalize on its popularity, when Senator Bob Dole ran against Bill Clinton for the presidency in 1996, Dole came up with an antidrug slogan of his own—"Just Don't Do It." It was about as effective as Dole's run for the White House.

fact, parents and politicians consider DARE so sacred that approximately $220 million each year (almost all of which is from taxpayer funding) is devoted to it. But numerous studies, including five- and ten-year follow-ups of students, have demonstrated that DARE is a failure, that it has no sustained effects on adolescent drug use.[31] Although it has shown some short-term positive effects with regard to attitude changes, it has never been shown to have any lasting effects on the likelihood of children using drugs in later life.[32]

Despite criticism and doubt about the effectiveness of the program, DARE endures around the country (with massive federal and corporate subsidies) and also around the world. And it continues because it is highly visible, making police and politicians look good. But as recent as January 2003, even the United States General Accounting Office concluded that DARE was not effective in preventing the use of drugs among youth.[33]

Drug Prevention Media Campaigns.   Like DARE, antidrug media campaigns are politically popular because they give the appearance that something is being done and because they are delivering the messages that their promoters want national audiences to hear. Foremost in this regard has been Partnership for a Drug-Free America. Started in 1986, the Partnership is a small private, nonprofit, and nonpartisan coalition of professionals from the communications industry. Its stated mission is to reduce the demand for illicit drugs in the United States through the use of media communication and to change attitudes about drugs by denormalizing drug use. Over the years, the Partnership has received almost $3 billion in media exposure donations.*

Beginning in early 1998, Partnership for a Drug-Free America, in conjunction with (and through the support of) the Office of National Drug Control Policy and The Advertising Council, launched the National Youth Anti-Drug Media Campaign. The initiative draws on a variety of media and messages that are designed to reach young people and that are influential in their lives. The messages address a wide variety of drug problems and target several different ethnic and geographic audiences.

At the core of these youth-targeted messages are the concepts that most teens do not use drugs or approve of drug use, that using specific drugs has many negative consequences, that remaining drug free has many benefits, that young people can learn skills to enable them to stay drug free, and that young people can use their time in positive ways after school and on weekends. Parents and adults are informed that their children are at risk for using drugs, that parents are a strong influence on whether their child uses drugs, and that adults can take simple actions to help children avoid getting involved with drugs.

---

*It is the Partnership for a Drug-Free America that came up with the well-known "this is your brain on drugs" message, which was but one of its numerous thirty-second fear-oriented TV spots. The Partnership has been heavily criticized for its narrow focus, dissemination of false information, and potential conflicts of interest arising from its sources of funding. For a lengthy examination of these issues, see David R. Buchanan and Lawrence Wallack, "This Is the Partnership for a Drug-Free America: Any Questions?" *Journal of Drug Issues,* 28 (1998), pp. 329–356.

With all of this effort, do the media campaigns really work? Many observers in the drug field suspected from the outset that they would have little impact on youths. In 2002, the Westat Corporation and the Annenberg School of Communication at the University of Pennsylvania completed a preliminary evaluation of the campaign.[34] The findings were quite damaging. In general, there was little evidence of direct favorable effects on youth. Moreover, for some youth cohorts, those with the highest exposure to the media ads appeared more likely to initiate marijuana use. But does all of this suggest that drug education and prevention programming should be eliminated? The answer here is that there are many research-based prevention programs that appear to do some good. In fact, research over the past twenty-five years has identified many factors that put young people at risk for drug abuse. Moreover, research has also identified protective factors that decrease the likelihood that young people will use or abuse drugs.[35]

Although drug abuse has many risk factors, the most crucial ones are those that influence a child's early development within the family. These risk factors include parents who abuse drugs or suffer from mental illness; lack of strong parent–child attachments in a nurturing environment; poor parental monitoring; and ineffective parenting, particularly with children who suffer from conduct disorders or have difficult temperaments. Other risk factors involve a child's interaction in environments outside the family—in school, among peers, or in the community at large. These risk factors include inappropriate classroom behavior or failing school performance, poor social skills or affiliation with deviant peers, and a perception that drug use is acceptable within peer, school, or community environments.[36]

Like risks, the most important protective factors come from within the family but include factors that influence a child in other environments. Among protective factors identified by research are strong bonds and clear rules of conduct within a family, involvement of parents in a child's life, successful school performance, strong bonds with positive institutions such as school and religious organizations, and a child's agreement with the social norm that drug use is not acceptable.[37]

Clearly, risk factors and protective factors are quite broad, and it is likely that every child in the United States is exposed to some of each. However, a number of prevention programs based on these ideas have been shown to be noteworthy.[38] Project Star, for example, is an initiative that reaches the entire community population with a comprehensive school program, a mass media effort, and a parent program, combined with initiatives for community organization and health policy change. Similarly, the Life Skills Training Program is a classroom effort designed to address a wide range of risk and protective factors for drug abuse by teaching general personal and social skills in combination with drug resistance skills and normative education. Numerous other programs have shown great promise as well. Overall, drug abuse prevention is important, but it should not be expected to prevent all drug use.*

Importantly, by the close of the 1990s, there appeared to be dramatic and perhaps unnecessary increases in the number of school-aged children taking such

---

*Extensive materials on effective drug abuse prevention programming can be found on the website of the National Institute on Drug Abuse (www.drugabuse.gov).

EXHIBIT 10.5   Kids! Just Say NO to Drugs
Source: © Tribune Media Services. All rights reserved. Reprinted with permission.

prescription psychoactive drugs as Ritalin, Adderall, Prozac, and Zoloft for the treatment of hyperactivity, depression, anxiety, or some other disorder (see Exhibit 10.5).[39] At the same time, this ready availability of medications in school led to increases in early experimentation with drugs. Some youths began taking the Ritalin prescribed to their friends, as well as other drugs they found in their medicine cabinets at home.[40]

In 2007, The National Youth Anti-Drug Media Campaign released a report showing that teens were turning away from street drugs, such as marijuana and cocaine, and were now abusing prescription drugs to an even greater extent. For example:

- There were more new users of prescription drugs than any illegal drug, including marijuana.
- Pain relievers, such as OxyContin and Vicodin, were the most commonly abused prescription drugs by teens.
- One-third of all new abusers of prescription drugs in 2005 were 12- to 17-year-olds.
- Prescription drugs were the drug of choice among 12- to 13-year-olds.
- Girls were more likely than boys to intentionally abuse prescription drugs to get high.
- The majority of teens (57%) who abused these products said they obtained them for free from a relative or friend (47%) or took them from a relative or friend (10%) without asking. An additional 10 percent purchased pain relievers from a friend or relative.

■ Adolescents were more likely than young adults to have become dependent on prescription medications.[41]

Apparently, the cleaner, safer appearance of prescription drugs—drugs that youths observed their parents and peers using—challenged the efforts of antidrug programs.

Substance Abuse Treatment

Treatment programming for substance abuse has a long and well-documented history. Programs of seemingly every variety have been tried, everything from diet and exercise to inpatient and outpatient therapy, electric shock, water cures, chemical detoxification, hot-air and light boxes that mimicked equatorial climate conditions, psychoanalysis, injections of fluid from fever blisters (now called herpes simplex), colon irrigation therapy, and penitence through prayer;[42] but the majority of approaches never received any form of independent evaluation. By contrast, a considerable body of literature has described and documented the effectiveness of the six major modalities of substance abuse/dependence treatment: chemical detoxification, methadone maintenance, buprenorphine treatment, drug-free outpatient treatment, self-help groups, and residential therapeutic communities. Each has its own particular view of substance abuse/addiction, each affects the client in different ways, and each has demonstrated an ability to reduce the drug-taking and drug-seeking behaviors of many (but certainly not all) substance abusers. Moreover, all exist in one form or another in almost every jurisdiction in the United States.[43]

Chemical Detoxification.   Designed primarily for persons dependent on narcotic drugs, chemical detoxification programs are typically situated in inpatient settings and endure for seven to twenty-one days. The rationale for detoxification as a treatment approach is grounded in two basic principles. The first is a conception of addiction as craving drugs, accompanied by physical dependence that motivates continued usage, resulting in a tolerance to the drug's effects and a syndrome of identifiable physical and psychological symptoms when the drug is abruptly withdrawn. The second is that negative aspects of the abstinence syndrome discourage many addicts from attempting withdrawal, and hence influences them to continue using drugs. Given this, the aim of chemical detoxification is the elimination of physiological dependence through a medically supervised procedure.

Methadone, a synthetic narcotic, is the drug of choice for the detoxification of narcotics users. Generally, a starting dose of the drug is gradually reduced in small increments until the body adjusts to the drug-free state. Whereas many detoxification programs address only the patient's physical dependence, some provide individual or group counseling in an attempt to address the problems associated with drug abuse, and a few refer clients to other longer-term treatments.[44]

Almost all narcotics users have been in a chemical detoxification program at least once. Studies document, however, that in the absence of supportive psychotherapeutic services and community follow-up care, virtually all relapse. In all detoxification programs, success depends on following established protocols for drug administration and withdrawal. In a recent assessment of research literature on the effectiveness of detoxification, rates of program completion appear to be increasing.[45] Yet many clinicians feel that mere detoxification from a substance is not drug abuse treatment and does not relate to staying off drugs. From this perspective, for detoxification to be successful, it must be the initial step in a comprehensive treatment process. Thus, detoxification is a temporary regimen that provides heroin users with the opportunity for reducing their drug intake; for many, this means that the criminal activity associated with taking and seeking drugs is interrupted. Finally, given the association between injection drug use and HIV/AIDS, detoxification also provides counseling to reduce AIDS-related risk behaviors.

Methadone Maintenance. As noted previously in this book, methadone was synthesized during World War II by German chemists when supply lines for morphine were interrupted. Although chemically unlike morphine or heroin, it produces many of the same effects. Methadone was introduced in the United States in 1947, and since the mid-1960s the drug has been in common use for the treatment of heroin dependence. Known as methadone maintenance, the program takes advantage of methadone's unique properties as a narcotic. Like all narcotics, methadone is cross-dependent with heroin. As such, it is a substitute drug that prevents withdrawal. More importantly, however, methadone is orally effective, making injection use unnecessary. In addition, it is longer acting than heroin, with one oral dose lasting up to twenty-four hours.

These properties have made methadone useful in the management of chronic heroin dependence.[46] During the first phase of methadone treatment, the patient is detoxified from heroin on dosages of methadone sufficient to prevent withdrawal without either euphoria or sedation. During the maintenance phase, the patient is stabilized on a dose of methadone high enough to eliminate the craving for heroin. Although this process seems to substitute one narcotic for another, the rationale behind methadone maintenance is to stabilize the patient on a less debilitating drug and to make counseling and other treatment services available.

Studies have demonstrated that although few methadone maintenance patients have remained drug free after treatment, those who remain on methadone have favorable outcomes in a number of areas. More specifically, a number of investigations have found that patients continued to use high levels of nonopiate drugs such as cocaine and marijuana.[47] On the other hand, much of the research has concluded that those on methadone maintenance have been more likely to reduce their criminal activity, become employed, and generally improve in psychosocial functioning.[48] Well-designed programs, furthermore, tend to be integrated with other forms of treatment and social services.

For these reasons, methadone maintenance is effective for blocking heroin dependency. However, methadone is also a primary drug of abuse among some narcotics users, resulting in a street market for the drug. There was a time when most illegal methadone was being diverted from legitimate maintenance programs by methadone patients. Hence, illegal supplies of the drug were typically available only where such programs existed. However, times have changed.

In January 2004, the White House Office of National Drug Control Policy (ONDCP) reported that the diversion and abuse of methadone was emerging as a major problem in a number of metropolitan areas across the United States.[49] This warning came on the heels of a GAO report that methadone-related overdose deaths and abuse were also becoming problems in several states.[50] It was asserted that much of the methadone abuse was the result of its inappropriate use as a safer alternative to OxyContin for pain relief. More recently, there has been extensive coverage in the print and television media, such as in Maine, Kentucky and Florida,[51] indicating large increases in abuse and overdose deaths and that in some areas methadone had surpassed OxyContin as the most widely abused drug. All of this is a result of the fact that methadone is being increasingly prescribed for pain management and, as a result, abuse, diversion and overdose deaths have risen markedly.[52]

On a lighter note, there is an interesting piece of folklore about methadone. In describing how the drug was first synthesized in Germany as a substitute for morphine during the early 1940s, a number of sources, including a few textbooks, repeat the myth that the drug was given the trade name of Dolophine after Adolf Hitler.[53] The early literature on methadone, however, makes no such suggestion but repeatedly indicates that the Germans referred to it as compound 10820, or Amidon.[54] The word *Dolophine,* however, comes from the Latin *dolor,* meaning pain. In fact, based on this Latin root, at least one textbook on the market misspells the drug as *Dolorphine* in all of its editions.[55] To set the record straight, Dolophine is a trade name for methadone, adopted by Eli Lilly and Co. after the end of World War II when patents for the drug were made available to U.S. pharmaceutical manufacturers. Lilly's purpose in using that particular designation was to convey the notion of pain relief.[56] Exactly how the association between Dolophine and Hitler found such an enduring place in the drug literature is not fully clear. Perhaps it all began with Alexander King, the surrealist comedian and nonconformist editor of *Life* magazine, who made the following comment about his drug treatment at Lexington, Kentucky in a 1958 autobiography: "We got shots four times a day and an additional barbiturate sedative at night. They gave us a synthetic horror called Dolofine [sic] which was invented in Germany under the Nazis and named after the great Adolph!"[57]

Buprenorphine. Within the past few years a new drug called buprenorphine has been made available for use in heroin addiction therapy. Buprenorphine has two formulations. The first is Subutex, which is pure buprenorphine, and it is designed to be used in the initial stages of addiction treatment. Suboxone, on the other hand, contains a component designed to be used in the maintenance stage of treatment. Like methadone, both formulations of buprenorphine block the effects of heroin while reducing cravings and easing withdrawal symptoms. Buprenorphine is the only heroin addiction therapy drug that can be prescribed in a physician's office; others must be dispensed in a clinic. This method of distribution is advantageous to many heroin addiction therapy patients because it is more convenient and less stigmatizing than clinic-based therapy, which typically involves methadone. Like methadone, however, buprenorphine is susceptible to abuse. Despite safety measures in place to guard against diversion of the drug, illegal distribution and abuse of buprenorphine have been reported in the United States.[58]

Drug-Free Outpatient Treatment. Drug-free outpatient treatment encompasses a variety of nonresidential programs that do not employ methadone or other pharmacotherapeutic agents. Most are based on a mental health perspective, and the primary services include individual and group therapy, while some offer family therapy and relapse prevention support. An increasing number of drug-free outpatient programs are including case management services as adjuncts to counseling. The basic case management approach is to assist clients in obtaining needed services in a timely and coordinated manner.[59] The key components of the approach are assessing, planning, linking, monitoring, and advocating for clients within the existing nexus of treatment and social services.

Evaluating the effectiveness of drug-free outpatient treatment is difficult because programs vary widely—from drop-in rap centers to highly structured arrangements that offer counseling or psychotherapy as the treatment mainstay. A number of studies have found that outpatient treatment has been moderately successful in reducing daily drug use and criminal activity.[60] However, the approach seems to be inappropriate for the most troubled and for antisocial users.

Self-Help Groups. Self-help groups, also known as twelve-step programs, are composed of individuals who meet regularly to stabilize and facilitate their recovery from substance abuse. The best known is Alcoholics Anonymous (AA), in which sobriety is based on fellowship and adhering to the Twelve Steps of recovery. The twelve steps stress faith, confession of wrong-doing, and passivity in the hands of a higher power, and move group members from a statement of powerlessness over drugs and alcohol to a resolution that they will carry the message of help to others and will practice the principles learned in all affairs.[61] In addition to AA, other popular self-help groups are Narcotics Anonymous (NA), Cocaine Anonymous (CA), and Drugs Anonymous (DA); all follow the twelve-step model. All these organizations operate as stand-alone fellowship programs but are also used as adjuncts to other modalities. Although few evaluation studies of self-help groups have been carried out, the weight of clinical and observational data suggests that they are crucial to facilitating recovery.

Residential Therapeutic Communities. The therapeutic community, or TC as many people call it, is a total treatment environment in which the primary clinical staff are typically former substance abusers—recovering addicts—who themselves were rehabilitated in therapeutic communities. The treatment perspective of the TC is that drug abuse is a disorder of the whole person—that the problem is the person and not the drug, that addiction is a symptom and not the essence of the disorder. In the TC's view of recovery, the primary goal is to change the negative patterns of behavior, thinking, and feeling that predispose drug use. Therefore, the overall goal is a responsible drug-free lifestyle. Recovery through the TC process depends on positive and negative pressures to change, and this is brought about through a self-help process in which relationships of mutual responsibility to every resident in the program are built.

In addition to individual and group counseling, the TC process has a system of explicit rewards that reinforce the value of earned achievement. Privileges are earned. In addition, TCs have their own specific rules and regulations that guide the behavior of residents and the management of their facilities. Their purposes are to maintain the safety and health of the community and to train and teach residents through the use of discipline. TC rules and regulations are numerous, the most conspicuous of which are total prohibitions against violence, theft, and drug use. Violation of these cardinal rules typically results in immediate expulsion from a TC. Therapeutic communities have been in existence for decades, and their successes have been well documented.[62]

POSTSCRIPT

Before examining alternatives to the current war on drugs, a few other points need to be noted. First, the budget for drug control activities in 1981 was just over one billion dollars, with two-thirds of the funding allocated for domestic enforcement, interdiction, and international initiatives. As illustrated in Exhibit 10.6, twenty-six years later the budget for drug control was approaching thirteen billion dollars, with two-thirds allocated for domestic enforcement, interdiction, and international initiatives. Funding had increased dramatically, but the proportions for supply reduction

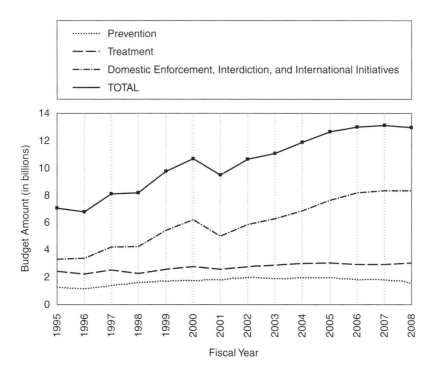

EXHIBIT 10.6   National Drug Control Budget, 1995–2008 (in billions)

Source: Office of National Drug Control Policy, *National Drug Control Strategy: FY 2008 Budget Summary* (Washington, DC: Executive Office of the President, February 2007). *National Drug Control Strategy. FY 2004 Summary,* February 2003.

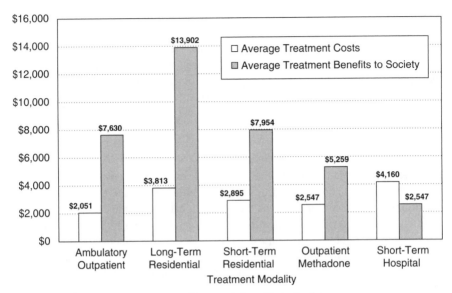

EXHIBIT 10.7 **Average Treatment Costs and Benefits to Society by Treatment Modality**

Source: Center for Substance Abuse Treatment.

versus demand reduction remained virtually unchanged. Is there anything wrong with this picture? More importantly, has the war on drugs generated many benefits?

One set of gains is certainly evident. As illustrated in Exhibit 10.7, the average benefits of substance abuse treatment—in terms of increased employment and reduced hospitalizations, crime, and expenses of criminal justice processing—exceed the costs by three to one, although the benefits vary significantly by treatment modality. Ambulatory outpatient and long-term residential treatment have the highest benefit to cost ratios (3.7 and 3.6 to 1, respectively). Only short-term hospital stays have costs that exceed the related benefits. What does this suggest regarding the relative importance of supply reduction versus demand reduction?

One final point requires mentioning. Earlier in this chapter, Exhibit 10.1 examined some of the attitudes of the college graduating classes of 1977, 1984, and 1987, highlighting the fact that over time fewer considered themselves liberals and that their views were becoming more conservative. How are students oriented now? As illustrated in Exhibit 10.8, it would appear that we might be witnessing a shifting away from the conservative agenda. From 1987 through 2007, although there have been only slight increases in the proportions considering themselves to be either liberal or conservative, there seems to be a definite movement away from the more conservative ideology. Increasing proportions favor the abolition of the death penalty and the legalization of marijuana, whereas fewer feel that the courts are overly concerned with the rights of criminals.

EXHIBIT 10.8   Selected Attitudes of the Classes of 1987, 1997, and 2007

	PERCENT		
ATTITUDE	*CLASS OF 1987*	*CLASS OF 1997*	*CLASS OF 2007*
Poltical Views			
Far left	1.9	2.5	2.8
Liberal	19.2	24.7	24.2
Middle-of-the-road	60.3	49.9	50.3
Conservative	17.5	21.4	21.1
Far right	1.2	1.5	1.6
Proportions Who Agree That			
Courts are too concerned with the rights of criminals	68.8	67.6	61.1
The death penalty should be abolished	28.9	22.1	32.6
Marijuana should be legalized	25.7	28.2	38.8

Source: CIRP Freshman Survey, Higher Education Research Institute, UCLA.

NOTES

1. See Raymond Glasscote, James N. Sussex, Jerome H. Jaffe, John Ball, and Leon Brill, *The Treatment of Drug Abuse: Programs, Problems, Prospects* (Washington, DC: American Psychiatric Association, 1972); Marvin R. Burt, Sharon Pines, and Thomas J. Glynn, *Drug Abuse: Its Natural History and the Effectiveness of Current Treatments* (Cambridge, MA: Schenkman, 1979); Barry S. Brown, ed., *Addicts and Aftercare: Community Integration of the Former Drug User* (Beverly Hills, CA: Sage, 1979).

2. See John Dombrink and James W. Meeker, "Beyond 'Buy and Bust': Nontraditional Sanctions in Federal Drug Law Enforcement," *Contemporary Drug Problems,* 13 (Winter 1986), pp. 711–740; John Dombrink and James W. Meeker, "Racketeering Prosecution: The Use and Abuse of RICO," *Rutgers Law Journal,* 16 (Spring/Summer 1985), pp. 632–654; James Meeker and John Dombrink, "Criminal RICO and Organized Crime: An Analysis of Appellate Litigation," *Criminal Law Bulletin,* 20 (July–August 1984), pp. 309–320; *U.S. News & World Report,* 5 December 1988, pp. 20–22; U.S. General Accounting Office, *Profitability of Customs Forfeiture Program Can Be Enhanced* (Washington, DC: U.S. General Accounting Office, 1989); *New York Times,* 7 January 1990, p. 13; *Drug Enforcement Report,* 23 April 1990, p. 8.

3. Committee on Foreign Relations, *Extradition Treaty with the Republic of Colombia,* Senate Report to Accompany Treaty Doc. No. 97-8, 20 November 1981; Mary Ann Forney, "Extradition and Drug Trafficking," in *Handbook of Drug Control in the United States,* ed. James A. Inciardi (Westport, CT: Greenwood Press, 1990), pp. 327–338.

4. See *Drug Law Enforcement: Military Assistance for Anti-Drug Agencies* (Washington, DC: U.S. General Accounting Office, 1987); David C. Morrison, "The Pentagon's Drug Wars," *National Journal,* 6 September 1986, pp. 13–19; Steven Zimmerman, "Posse Comitatus," *Drug Enforcement,* Summer 1982, pp. 17–22; *Drug Enforcement,* Summer 1984, p. 33; *United States Statutes at Large,* 45th Cong., 1877–1879, Vol. 20, p. 152.

5. For descriptions of the military involvement and high technology approaches to drug enforcement, see *Wall Street Journal,* 5 August 1982, pp. 1, 8; *Newsweek,* 9 August 1982, pp. 14–15; *Motor*

Boating & Sailing, September 1982, pp. 46–49, 107–109; *National Law Journal,* 1 November 1982, pp. 3, 17; *Miami Herald,* 23 January 1983, p. 11A; *Miami Herald,* 17 July 1983, p. 1A; *National Law Journal,* 13 February 1984, pp. 1, 27–28; *Time,* 22 January 1990, pp. 22–23; U.S. General Accounting Office, *DOD Counter-Drug Activities: GAO Review of DOD's Compliance with FY 1989 DOD Authorization Act* (Washington, DC: U.S. General Accounting Office, 1989); Richard Mackenzie, "Borderline Victories on Drug War's Front Line," *Insight,* 14 January 1991, pp. 8–17.

6. *Miami Herald,* 21 April 2000, p. B1.

7. For a discussion of the philosophy of zero tolerance, see *Drug Abuse Report,* 19 April 1988, p. 6; *Drug Abuse Report,* 3 May 1988, pp. 1–3; U.S. Department of Transportation, Office of Public Affairs, *Transportation Facts,* "Zero Tolerance Policy on Illegal Drugs," 6 June 1988; Department of the Treasury, U.S. Customs Service, "Zero Tolerance Made Plain," *Southern Boating,* October 1988, pp. 86–88; *New York Times,* 12 April 1988, pp. A1, A10; *Drug Enforcement Report,* 8 July 1988, pp. 1–2; *U.S. News & World Report,* 6 June 1988, p. 11.

8. *Time,* 23 May 1988, p. 55; *Boat/U.S. Reports,* XXIV (May 1989), pp. 1, 7.

9. *National Law Journal,* 7 November 1988, pp. 3, 9; *In Command,* Fall 1989, p. 5; *Miami Herald,* 20 May 1988, pp. 1A, 24A; *Drug Enforcement Report,* 8 June 1988, p. 3; *Drug Enforcement Report,* 23 September 1988, p. 6; *Drug Enforcement Report,* 8 March 1989, p. 4; *Drug Enforcement Report,* 24 April 1989, p. 4; *Drug Enforcement Report,* 8 November 1989, p. 4; *Boat/U.S. Reports,* XXIII (November–December 1988), pp. 1–2.

10. Quoted in James A. Inciardi, "Revitalizing the War on Drugs," *The World & I,* February 1988, pp. 132–139.

11. *Alcoholism and Drug Abuse Week,* 6 September 1989, p. 3.

12. The White House, *National Drug Control Strategy* (Washington, DC: Executive Office of the President, Office of National Drug Control Policy, September 1989).

13. *Time,* 3 April 1989, p. 24.

14. *New York Times,* 18 March 1989, p. 7; *Drug Enforcement Report,* 24 April 1989, p. 3.

15. *Time,* 20 August 1990, p. 48; *Washington Post,* 12 August 1990, pp. A1, A14–A17.

16. *USA Today,* 13 November 1990, p. 2A.

17. Bogotá *Radio Cadena Nacional,* 1200 GMT, 27 October 1990; Madrid *EFE,* 2246 GMT, 17 August 1990; Bogotá *El Tiempo,* 14 August 1990, p. 5A.

18. *New York Times,* 27 August 1990, p. A6.

19. *U.S. News & World Report,* 10 February 1992, p. 33.

20. Pierre Thomas and Jim McGee, "Brown Ends Two-Year Tenure as Drug Policy Chief," *Washington Post,* 13 December 1995, p. A27.

21. Office of National Drug Control Policy, *National Drug Control Strategy, 2000 Annual Report* (Washington, DC: Executive Office of the President, 2000).

22. Criminal Justice Policy Foundation, "Release of Newest Anti-Drug Strategy Conceals Monumental Failure," press release, 22 March 2000.

23. Eric Schmitt, "House Passes Bill to Help Colombia Fight Drug Trade, *New York Times on the Web,* 31 March 2000.

24. Schmitt, 2000.

25. *New York Times,* 22 June 2000, pp. A1, A12.

26. Erich Goode, *Drugs in American Society,* 5th ed. (Boston: McGraw-Hill, 1999), p. 365.

27. John D. Swisher, J. Crawford, R. Goldstein, and M. Yura, "Drug Education: Pushing or Preventing?" *Peabody Journal of Education,* 49 (October 1971), pp. 68–75.

28. John D. Swisher, R. W. Warner, C. C. Spence, and M. L. Upcraft, "Four Approaches to Drug Abuse Prevention at the College Level," *Journal of College Student Personnel,* 14 (May 1973), pp. 231–235.

29. Goode, 1999.

30. Joel H. Brown, Marianne D'Emidio-Caston, and John A. Pollard, "Students and Substances: Social Power in Drug Education," *Educational Drug Education and Policy Analysis,* 19 (Spring 1997), pp. 65–82.

31. Richard R. Clayton, Anne M. Catarello, and Bryan M. Johnstone, "The Effectiveness of Drug Abuse Resistance Education (Project DARE): 5-Year Follow-Up Results," *Preventive Medicine,* 25

(1996), pp. 307–318. See also Donald R. Lynam, Richard Milich, T. K. Logan, Catherine Martin, Carl G. Leukefeld, and Richard Clayton, "Project DARE: No Effects at 10-Year Follow-Up," *Journal of Consulting and Clinical Psychology,* 67 (August 1999), pp. 590–593.

32.   Ryan H. Sager, "Teach Them Well," *National Review,* 52 (1 May 2000), pp. 30–32.

33.   U.S. General Accounting Office, *Youth Illicit Drug Use Prevention: DARE Long Term Evaluations and Federal Efforts to Identify Effective Programs*, #GAO-03-172r (Washington, DC: U.S. Government Printing Office, January 15, 2003).

34.   R. Hornik, D. Maklan, D. Cadell, A. Prado, and C. Barmada, *Evaluation of the National Youth Anti-Drug Media Campaign: Fourth Semi-Annual Report of Findings* (Rockville, MD: Westat Inc., May 2002).

35.   Robert Mathias, "Putting Science-Based Drug Abuse Prevention Programs to Work in Communities," *NIDA Notes,* Vol. 14, No. 6 (1999), pp. 10–11; "Developing Successful Drug Abuse Prevention Programs," *NIDA Notes,* Vol. 14, No. 6 (1999), pp. 14–15.

36.   Judith S. Brook, Martin Whiteman, and David W. Brook, "Transmission of Risk Factors across Three Generations," *Psychological Reports,* 85 (1999), pp. 227–241; J. S. Brook, M. Whiteman, E. B. Balka, and B. A. Hamburg, "African-American and Puerto Rican Drug Use: Personality, Familial and Environmental Factors," *Genetic, Social, and General Psychology Monographs,* 118 (November 1992), pp. 417–438; J. S. Brook, M. Whiteman, E. B. Balka, and P. Cohen, "Drug Use and Delinquency: Shared and Unshared Risk Factors in African American and Puerto Rican Adolescents," *Journal of Genetic Psychology,* 158 (March 1997), pp. 25–39; J. S. Brook, D. W. Brook, M. De La Rosa, L. F. Duque, E. Rodriquez, I. D. Montoya, and M. Whiteman, "Pathways to Marijuana Use among Adolescents: Cultural/Ecological, Family, Peer, and Personality Influences," *Journal of the American Academy of Child and Adolescent Psychiatry,* 37 (July 1998), pp. 759–766; J. S. Brook, E. B. Balka, and M. Whiteman, "The Risks for Late Adolescence of Early Adolescent Marijuana Use," *American Journal of Public Health,* 89 (October 1999), pp. 1549–1554; J. S. Brook, R. C. Kessler, and P. Cohen, "The Onset of Marijuana Use from Preadolescence and Early Adolescence to Young Adulthood," *Developmental Psychopathology,* 11 (Fall 1999), pp. 901–914; J. S. Brook, M. Whiteman, and D. W. Brook, "Transmission of Risk Factors across Three Generations," *Psychological Reports,* 85 (August 1999), pp. 227–241.

37.   For example, see G. J. Botvin, E. Baker, L. Dusenbury, E. M. Botvin, and T. Diaz, "Long-Term Follow-Up Results of a Randomized Drug Abuse Prevention Trial in a White Middle-Class Population," *Journal of the American Medical Association,* 273 (1995), pp. 1106–1112; G. J. Botvin, S. P. Schinke, J. A. Epstein, and T. Diaz, "Effectiveness of Culturally Focused and Generic Skills Training Approaches to Alcohol and Drug Abuse Prevention among Minority Adolescents: Two-Year Follow-Up Results," *Psychology of Addictive Behaviors,* 9 (1995), pp. 183–194; G. J. Botvin, E. Baker, A. D. Filazzola, and E. M. Botvin, "A Cognitive-Behavioral Approach to Substance Abuse Prevention: One-Year Follow-Up, *Addictive Behaviors,* 15 (1990), pp. 47–63; J. S. Brook, M. Whiteman, and D. W. Brook, "Sibling Influences on Adolescent Drug Use: Older Brothers on Younger Brothers," *Journal of the American Academy of Child and Adolescent Psychology,* 30 (November 1991), pp. 958–966; J. S. Brook, M. Whiteman, S. J. Finch, and P. Cohen, "Young Adult Drug Use and Delinquency: Childhood Antecedents and Adolescent Mediators," *Journal of the American Academy of Child and Adolescent Psychiatry,* 35 (December 1996), pp. 1584–1592; J. S. Brook, E. B. Balka, M. D. Gursen, D. W. Brook, J. Shapiro, and P. Cohen, "Young Adults' Drug Use: A 17-Year Longitudinal Inquiry of Antecedents," *Psychological Reports,* 80 (3 Pt. 2), pp. 1235–1251; J. S. Brook, P. Cohen, and L. Jaeger, "Developmental Variations in Factors Related to Initial and Increased Levels of Adolescent Drug Involvement," *Journal of Genetic Psychology,* 159 (June 1998), pp. 179–194; J. S. Brook, M. Whiteman, E. B. Balka, P. T. Win, and M. D. Gursen, "Similar and Different Precursors to Drug Use and Delinquency among African Americans and Puerto Ricans," *Journal of Genetic Psychology,* 159 (March 1998), pp. 13–29; J. S. Brook, M. Whiteman, S. Finch, and P. Cohen, "Mutual Attachment, Personality, and Drug Use: Pathways from Childhood to Young Adulthood," *Genetic, Social, and General Psychology Monographs,* 124 (November 1998), pp. 492–510; J. S. Brook, E. B. Balka, D. W. Brook, P. T. Win, and M. D. Gursen, "Drug Use among African Americans: Ethnic Identity as a Protective Factor," 83 (3 Pt. 2), pp. 1427–1446.

38.   For example, see Institute of Medicine, *Annual Report of the Institute of Medicine Committee on Comprehensive School Health Programs* (Washington, DC: National Academy Press, 1995); M. A. Pentz, J. H. Dwyer, D. P. MacKinnon, B. R. Flay, W. B. Hansen, E. Y. Wang, and C. A. Johnson, "A

Multi-Community Trial for Primary Prevention of Adolescent Drug Abuse: Effects on Drug Use Prevalence," *Journal of the American Medical Association, 261* (1989), pp. 3259–3266.

39. Peter R. Breggin, "Kids Are Suffering Legal Drug Use," *Boston Globe,* 26 September 1999, p. E7.

40. Kate Zernike, "Added Drug Risk for the Young Turning to Abuse of Legal Substances," *Boston Globe,* 3 May 1997, pp. A1, A4.

41. Office of National Drug Control Policy, Executive Office of the President, *Teens and Prescription Drugs: An Analysis of Recent Trends on the Emerging Drug Threat* (2007, February). Accessed on February 26, 2007, from www.mediacampaign.org/teens/brochure.pdf.

42. See William L. White, *Slaying the Dragon: The History of Addiction Treatment in America* (Bloomington, IL: Chestnut Health Systems, 1998).

43. Robert L. Hubbard, Mary Ellen Marsden, J. Valley Rachel, Henrick J. Harwood, Elizabeth R. Cavanaugh, and Harold Ginzberg, *Drug Abuse Treatment: A National Study of Effectiveness* (Chapel Hill: University of North Carolina Press, 1989); Jerome J. Platt, Charles D. Kaplan, and Patricia J. McKim, *The Effectiveness of Drug Abuse Treatment* (Malabar, FL: Robert E. Krieger, 1990); Joel A. Egertson, Daniel M. Fox, and Alan I. Leshner, *Treating Drug Abusers Effectively* (Malden, MA: Blackwell, 1997).

44. D. R. Gerstein and H. J. Harwood, eds., *Treating Drug Problems* (Washington, DC: National Academy Press, 1990).

45. R. P. Mattick and W. Hall, "Are Detoxification Programmes Effective," *Lancet,* 347 (1990), pp. 97–100.

46. Vincent P. Dole and Marie Nyswander, "A Medical Treatment for Diacetylmorphine (Heroin) Addiction: A Clinical Trial with Methadone Hydrochloride," *Journal of the American Medical Association,* 193 (1965), pp. 80–84.

47. Carl D. Chambers, W. J. Taylor, and Arthur D. Mofett, "The Incidence of Cocaine Abuse among Methadone Maintenance Patients," *International Journal of the Addictions,* 7 (1972), pp. 427–441.

48. John C. Ball and A. Ross, *The Effectiveness of Methadone Maintenance* (New York: Springer-Verlag, 1991).

49. Office of National Drug Control Policy and Executive Office of the President, *Pulse Check: Drug Markets and Chronic Users in 25 of America's Largest Cities* (2004, January). Accessed on February 26, 2007, from www.whitehousedrugpolicy.gov/publications/drugfact/pulsechk/january04/january2004.pdf.

50. National Drug Intelligence Center, U.S. Department of Justice, *Methadone Abuse Increasing* [Information Bulletin] (Product No. 2003-L0424-004) (2003, September). Accessed on February 26, 2007, from http://0225.0145.01.040/ndic/pubs6/6292/6292p.pdf.

51. *Maine Drug-Related Mortality Patterns: 1997–2012,* Office of Substance Abuse, Bangor, Maine; "Methadone Abuse Hits State Hard," *Louisville Courier Journal,* 9 May 2004.

52. Theodore J. Cicero and James A. Inciardi, "Diversion and Abuse of Methadone Prescribed for Pain Management," *Journal of the American Medical Association,* 293 (3) (January 19, 2005), pp. 297–298.

53. For example, see Patricia Jones-Witters and Weldon Witters, *Drugs & Society: A Biological Perspective* (Monterey, CA: Wadsworth Health Sciences, 1983), p. 242. In addition, see the web pages of Oxford Brookes University in Oxford, England, as well as that of the Imperial College of Science, Technology and Medicine in London.

54. Charles C. Scott and K. K. Chen, "The Action of 1,1-diphenyl-1-(dimethylaminoisopropyl), butanone-2, a Potent Analgesic Agent," *Journal of Pharmacology and Experimental Therapeutics,* 87 (1946), pp. 63–71; Nathan B. Eddy, "A New Morphine-Like Analgesic," *Journal of the American Pharmaceutical Association,* November 1947, pp. 536–540; H. B. Haag, J. K. Finnegan, and P. S. Larson, "Pharmacologic Observations on 1,1-diphenyl-1-(dimethylaminoisopropyl), butanone-2," *Federation Proceedings,* 6 (1947), 334.

55. Charles F. Levinthal, *Drugs, Behavior, and Modern Society* (Boston: Allyn & Bacon, 1996), p. 161; Charles F. Levinthal, *Drugs, Behavior, and Modern Society,* 2nd ed. (Boston: Allyn & Bacon, 1999), p. 104.

56. Personal communication with Dr. Ivan Bennett of Eli Lilly and Co., 14 January 1976.

57. Alexander King, *Mine Enemy Grows Older* (New York: Simon & Schuster, 1958), p. 39.

58. Theodore J. Cicero and James A. Inciardi, "Potential for Abuse of Buprenorphine in Office-Based Treatment of Opioid Dependence," *New England Journal of Medicine,* 353 (17) (2005), pp. 1863–1865.

59. Harvey A. Siegal and Richard C. Rapp, *Case Management and Substance Abuse Treatment* (New York: Springer, 1996).

60. Barbara C. Wallace, *The Chemically Dependent: Phases of Treatment and Recovery* (New York: Brunner/Mazel, 1992); William R. Miller and Nick Heather, *Treating Addictive Behaviors* (New York: Plenum, 1986).

61. *Alcoholics Anonymous Comes of Age* (New York: Alcoholics Anonymous World Services, 1985).

62. George DeLeon, *Community as Method: Therapeutic Communities for Special Populations and Special Settings* (Westport, CT: Praeger, 1997); Marc Galanter and Herbert D. Kleber, *The American Psychiatric Press Textbook of Substance Abuse Treatment* (Washington, DC: American Psychiatric Press, 1994); Frank M. Tims, James A. Inciardi, Bennett W. Fletcher, and Arthur MacNeill Horton, *The Effectiveness of Innovative Approaches in the Treatment of Drug Abuse* (Westport, CT: Greenwood Press, 1997).

CHAPTER 11

THE GREAT DRUG DEBATE

The War on American Drug Policy

At a meeting of the U.S. Conference of Mayors in 1988, Baltimore Mayor Kurt L. Schmoke called for a national debate on U.S. drug control strategies and on potential benefits of legalizing marijuana, heroin, cocaine, crack, and other illicit substances. Schmoke's argument was that for generations the United States had been pursuing policies of prosecution and repression that resulted in little more than overcrowded courts and prisons, increased profits for drug traffickers, and higher rates of addiction.[1]

Schmoke's comments certainly did not pass unnoticed. From a broad assortment of metaphorical garrets and cloisters and cellars and towers responses came—from a highly vocal minority of academicians and attorneys, editors and economists, and liberals and libertarians, capped by a fragmentary sampling of Marxist criminologists, blue-chip conservatives, and marijuana smokers and enthusiasts. There they were, all sharing the same podium. It was a curious mixture, like an odd and mismatched arrangement of roses, dandelions, ornamental grasses, and shaggy weeds crowded into a small rooftop flower garden. They captured the attention of the television networks, *Time* and *Newsweek,* the major dailies, House and Senate committees, the TV talk-show circuit, and even Oprah and Geraldo.

The drug legalization debate received considerable attention in 1988 and 1989, but in the years hence interest in the topic (or at least media coverage of it) has dwindled. At the same time, many former supporters of legalization moved on to embrace philosophies of decriminalization and harm reduction, approaches to the drug problem that have different meanings to different people, and terms that are often considered euphemisms for *legalization.* What do these terms mean, and are these approaches good ideas?

LEGALIZATION OF DRUGS: THE PROFESSED BENEFITS

Arguments posed by the supporters of drug legalization seem all too logical. First, they argue, drug laws have created evils far worse than the drugs themselves, namely, corruption, violence, street crime, and disrespect for the law. Second, legislation passed to control drugs has failed to reduce demand. Third, it is impracticable to make illegal that which a significant segment of the population in any society is committed to doing. You simply cannot arrest, prosecute, and punish such large numbers of people, particularly in a free society, a democracy. In a liberal democracy the government must not interfere with personal behavior if liberty is to be maintained. Fourth, legalizing marijuana, cocaine, crack, heroin, methamphetamine, Ecstasy, and other drugs would result in a number of positive outcomes:

1. Drug prices would fall.
2. Users could obtain their drugs at low government-regulated prices and would no longer be forced to engage in prostitution, burglaries, robberies, muggings, and other street crimes to support their habits.
3. Levels of drug-related crime would significantly decline, resulting in less crowded courts, jails, and prisons, and freeing law enforcement personnel to focus their energies on the real criminals in society.
4. Drug production, distribution, and sale would be removed from the criminal arena; no longer would it be within the province of organized crime, and criminal syndicates such as the Colombian cartels and the Jamaican posses would be decapitalized, eliminating the violence associated with drug distribution rivalries.
5. Government corruption and intimidation by traffickers as well as drug-based foreign policies would be effectively reduced, if not eliminated entirely.
6. The often draconian measures undertaken by police to enforce the drug laws would be curtailed, thus restoring to the public many of its hard-won civil liberties.[2]

To these contentions can be added the argument that legalization in any form or structure would have only a minimal impact on current drug-use levels. Apparently, those favoring drug legalization assume that, given the existing levels of access to most illegal drugs, current levels of use closely match demand. Thus, no additional health, safety, behavioral, and/or other problems would accompany legalization. Finally, a few proponents of legalization make one concluding point. Through government regulation of drugs, the billions of dollars spent annually on drug enforcement could be better used. Moreover, by taxing government-regulated drugs, revenues would be collected that could be used for preventing drug abuse and treating those harmed by drugs.

In the long and the short, the argument for legalization seems to boil down to the basic belief that U.S. prohibitions against marijuana, cocaine, heroin, and other drugs impose far too great a cost in terms of tax dollars, crime, and infringements on civil rights and individual liberties. Although the overall argument may be well intended and seem quite logical, it is highly questionable in its historical, sociocultural, and empirical underpinnings, and demonstrably naive in its understanding of the negative consequences of a legalized drug market.[3]

UNRESOLVED ISSUES IN THE QUEST FOR A LEGALIZED DRUG MARKET

At the outset, it can be argued that current proposals to legalize drugs are not proposals at all. Although legalizing drugs has been debated ever since the passage of the Harrison Act in 1914, never has an advocate of the position structured a concrete proposal.* Any attempt to legalize drugs would be extremely complex, but proponents tend to proceed from somewhat simplistic shoot-from-the-hip positions without first developing any sophisticated proposals. Even amid the clamor for legalization in the late 1980s and 1990s, specific proposals that addressed all the complex control issues could not be found. In this regard, many questions need to be addressed:

1. Which drugs should be legalized? Marijuana? Heroin? Cocaine? If cocaine is designated for legalization, should proposals include coca products such as crack and freebase cocaine? Should the list include basuco (coca paste), that potent and highly toxic processing derivative of the coca leaf discussed previously in Chapter 6? Other drugs must be considered as well. Which hallucinogenic drugs should be legalized? LSD? Peyote? Mescaline? Should Quaaludes be returned to the legal market? Should Ecstasy and the other popular club drugs be included? In short, which drugs should be legalized, according to what criteria, and who should determine the criteria?

2. Assuming that some rationally determined slate of drugs could be designated for legalization, what potency levels should be permitted? For example, 80-, 100-, and 151-proof rum; marijuana with 5, 10, and 14 percent THC content? Should legalized heroin be restricted to Burmese No. 3 grade, or should Mexican black tar and the mythical China White be added to the ledger?

3. As with alcohol, should age limits determine who can and cannot use drugs? Should those old enough to drive be permitted to buy and use drugs? Which drugs? Should 16-year-olds be permitted to buy pot, but have to wait until age 18 to buy cocaine and crack, and age 21 for heroin?

4. Should certain drugs be limited to those only who are already dependent on them? In other words, should heroin sales be restricted to heroin addicts and cocaine sales to cocaine addicts? If this approach were deemed viable, what would we say to the heroin users who want to buy cocaine? In other words, do we legalize heroin and cocaine sales but forbid speedballing? What about drug experimenters? Should they

---

*There was one exception to this statement, in 1991, from Richard B. Karel, a Washington, DC area journalist. Karel advocated the idea of cocaine chewing gum—available in packages of twenty, each piece containing ten to twenty milligrams of pharmaceutical cocaine, dispensed through vending machines activated by ATM bank cards, with purchases limited to one package every forty-eight to seventy-two hours. Karel offered similar proposals for other drugs, but they were so ludicrous that they could not be taken seriously. See Richard B. Karel, "A Model Legalization Proposal," in *The Drug Legalization Debate,* ed. James A. Inciardi (Newbury Park, CA: Sage, 1991), pp. 80–102.

be permitted access to the legal drug market? Assuming that these issues could be decided, in what amounts could users—regardless of their drugs of choice—purchase heroin, cocaine, marijuana, Quaaludes, and other chemical substances?

5. Where should drugs be sold? Over the counter in drug and grocery stores as is the case with many pharmaceuticals? Through mail-order houses and the Internet? In special vending machines strategically located in public restrooms, hotel lobbies, and train and bus stations where cigarettes and condoms are dispensed? In tax-supported drug shacks as Representative Charles Rangel (Democrat—New York) satirically asked some years ago?[4] Should some, or all, of the newly legalized drugs be available only on a prescription basis? If this were the case, would a visit to a physician be necessary to obtain a prescription? For how many tabs, lines, lids, bags, rocks, or whatever should prescriptions be written? How often should these prescriptions be refillable?

6. Where should the raw material for the drugs originate? Would cultivation be restricted to U.S. lands, or would foreign sources be permitted? Coca from Bolivia and Peru, or from all of South America and Java, as well? Marijuana from Colombia and Jamaica? Opium from Colombia, Mexico, Laos, Thailand, or from the Golden Crescent countries of Iran, Afghanistan, and Pakistan? Should trade restrictions of any type be imposed—by drug, amount, potency, purity, or by country? Should legalization policies permit the introduction of currently little-known drugs of abuse into the United States from foreign ports, such as qat from Yemen or bekaro from Pakistan?*

7. If drugs are to be legalized, should the drug market be a totally free one, with private industry establishing the prices as well as levels of purity and potency? What kinds of advertising should be permitted? Should advertisements for some drugs but not others be allowed? Should people like Whitney Houston, Darryl Strawberry, Charlie Sheen, and Robert Downey, Jr., be permitted to endorse certain drugs or brands of drugs as part of advertising programs?

8. If drugs are to be legalized, what types of restrictions should be placed on their use? Should transportation workers, nuclear plant employees, or other categories of workers be forbidden to use them at all times, or just while they are on duty?

9. As is the case with alcohol, will certain establishments be permitted to serve drugs (and which drugs) to their customers? And similarly, as is the case with cigarettes, should there be separate drug-using and nondrug-using sections in restaurants, on planes and trains, and in the workplace? As with coffee and cigarette breaks, should users be permitted pot and coke breaks as part of their union contracts or management/labor policies?

---

*Qat (also known as khat) is the evergreen shrub *Catha edulis,* whose leaves and buds are chewed or brewed as a beverage. Qat produces stimulant effects similar to, but milder than, those induced by the amphetamines, and dependence has been known to develop. Bekaro, the seeds of the Tula tree (*Pterygota alata*), is well known in parts of India and Pakistan as an effective substitute for opiates. See Shelagh Weir, *Qat in Yemen: Consumption and Social Change* (London: British Museum Publications, 1985); William Emboden, *Narcotic Plants* (New York: Macmillan, 1979).

10. For any restrictions placed on sales, potency levels, distribution, prices, quantity, and advertising in a legalized drug market, which government bureaucracy should be charged with the enforcement of the legalization statutes? The Federal Bureau of Investigation (FBI)? The Drug Enforcement Administration (DEA)? The Food and Drug Administration (FDA)? The Bureau of Alcohol, Tobacco, and Firearms (ATF)? State and local law enforcement agencies? Or should some new federal bureaucracy be created for the purpose? Going further, what kinds of penalties ought to be established for violation of the legalization restrictions?

This list is by no means exhaustive and many more questions are likely, questions both sarcastic and sardonic. But they are intended to make a point—that the whole idea of even articulating a legalization policy is very complex. Not only have proponents failed to answer the questions, but they have yet to even pose most of them. Moreover, those attempting to structure a serious proposal highlighting the beneficial expectations of a legalization policy will find little support for their arguments in either published research data or clinical experience. By contrast, numerous legitimate arguments against the legalization of drugs have considerable empirical, historical, pharmacological, and/or clinical support.

THE PUBLIC HEALTH AND BEHAVIORAL CONSEQUENCES ARGUMENT

Considerable evidence suggests that the legalization of drugs would create behavioral and public health problems to a degree that would far outweigh the current consequences of the drug prohibition. There are some excellent reasons why marijuana, cocaine, crack, heroin, and other drugs are now controlled, and why they ought to remain so.

Marijuana. Considerable misinformation exists concerning marijuana. To the millions of adolescents and young adults who were introduced to the drug during the social revolution of the 1960s and early 1970s, marijuana was a harmless herb of ecstasy. As the new social drug and a natural organic product, it was deemed to be far less harmful than either alcohol or tobacco.[5] More recent research suggests, however, that marijuana smoking is a practice that combines the hazardous features of both tobacco and alcohol with a number of pitfalls of its own. Moreover, many questions about marijuana's effect on the vital systems of the body, on the brain and mind, on immunity and resistance, and on sex and reproduction are disturbing.[6]

One of the more serious difficulties with marijuana use relates to respiratory damage. Recent findings in this area should put to rest the rather tiresome argument by marijuana devotees that smoking just a few joints daily is less harmful than regularly smoking several times as many cigarettes. Researchers at the University of California (Los Angeles) reported in 1988 that the respiratory burden in smoke particulates and absorption of carbon monoxide from smoking just one marijuana joint is some four times greater than from smoking a single tobacco cigarette.[7] Specifically, it was found that one toke of marijuana delivers three times more tar to the mouth and lungs than one puff of a filter-tipped cigarette; that marijuana deposits four times more tar in the throat and lungs and increases carbon monoxide levels in the blood four- to fivefold. Furthermore, in 1999, a National Academy of Sciences panel concluded that cellular, genetic, and human studies all suggest that marijuana smoke is an important risk factor for the development of respiratory cancer.[8]

Marijuana apologists tend to downplay, if not totally ignore, three distinct sets of facts about its chemical structure, its persistence-of-residue effect, and its changing potency.

First, the *cannabis sativa* plant from which marijuana comes is a complex chemical factory. Marijuana contains 426 known chemicals that are transformed into 2,000 chemicals when burned during the smoking process. Seventy of these chemicals are cannabinoids, substances that are found nowhere else in nature. Because they are fat soluble, they are immediately deposited in those body tissues that have a high fat content—the brain, lungs, liver, and reproductive organs.

Second, the fact that THC (delta-9-tetrahydrocannabinol), the active ingredient and most potent psychoactive chemical in marijuana, is soluble in fat but not in water has a significant implication. The human body has a water-based waste disposal system—blood, urine, sweat, and feces. A chemical such as THC that does not dissolve in water becomes trapped, principally in the brain, lungs, liver, and reproductive organs. This is the persistence-of-residue effect. One puff of smoke from a marijuana cigarette delivers a significant amount of THC, half of which remains in the body for several weeks. As such, if a person is smoking marijuana more than once a month, the residue levels of THC are not only retained, but also building up—in the brain, lungs, liver, and reproductive organs. It is not yet clear what the long-term effects of this build-up might be.[9]

Third, the potency of marijuana has risen dramatically over the years. During the 1960s the THC content of marijuana was only two-tenths of 1 percent. By the 1980s the potency of imported marijuana was up to 5 percent, representing a twenty-five-fold increase. California *sinsemilla,* on the other hand, a seedless, domestic variety of marijuana, has a THC potency of 14 percent.* In fact, so potent is sinsemilla that it has become a pot of choice both inside and outside the United States. Moreover, at times sinsemilla has been traded on the streets of Bogotá, Colombia, for cocaine on an equal weight basis.[10] Because smoked marijuana causes diminished psychomotor performance, which impairs a user's ability to operate machinery and motor vehicles,[11] high-potency marijuana can exacerbate this effect.

Finally, aside from the health consequences of marijuana use, research on the behavioral aspects of the drug suggests that it severely affects the social perceptions of heavy users. Findings from the Center for Psychological Studies in New York City,

---

*Marijuana seized in the United States has an average potency of 5 percent. The most potent marijuana, having a THC content of 16 percent, is grown in the Netherlands by HortaPharm for the manufacture of certain pharmaceuticals.

for example, found that adults who smoked marijuana daily believed the drug helped them to function better—improving their self-awareness and relationships with others.[12] In reality, however, marijuana serves as a buffer, so to speak, enabling users to tolerate problems rather than face them and make changes that might increase the quality of their social functioning and satisfaction with life. The study found that the research subjects used marijuana to avoid dealing with their difficulties, and the avoidance inevitably made their problems worse—on the job, at home, and in family and sexual relationships.

What this research documented was what clinicians had been saying for years. Personal growth evolves from learning to cope with stress, anxiety, frustration, and the many other difficulties that life presents, both small and large. Marijuana use (and the use of other drugs as well, including alcohol), particularly among adolescents and young adults, interferes with this process, and the result is a drug-induced arrested development.[13]*

Cocaine and Crack.   As already detailed in Chapter 6, the pleasure and feelings of power that cocaine engenders make its use a rather unwise recreational pursuit. Its euphoric lift, with its feelings of pleasure, confidence, and being on top of things, that comes from but a few brief snorts is short-lived and invariably followed by a letdown. When the elation and grandiose feelings begin to wane, a corresponding deep depression is often felt that is in such marked contrast to users' previous states that they are strongly motivated to repeat the dose and restore the euphoria. This leads to chronic, compulsive use. When chronic users try to stop using cocaine, they are typically plunged into a severe depression from which only more cocaine can arouse them. Also problematic are the physiological consequences of cocaine use—convulsions, hyperstimulation, and overdose—also discussed in Chapter 6.

To these can be added what is known as the cocaine psychosis.[14] As dose and duration of cocaine use increase, the development of cocaine-related psychopathology is not uncommon. Cocaine psychosis is generally preceded by a transitional period characterized by increased suspiciousness, compulsive behavior, fault finding, and eventually paranoia. When the psychotic state is reached, individuals may experience visual and/or auditory hallucinations, with persecutory voices commonly heard. Many believe that they are being followed by police or that family, friends, and others are plotting against them. Moreover, everyday events tend to be misinterpreted in a way that support delusional beliefs. When coupled with the irritability and hyperactivity that the stimulant nature of cocaine tends to generate in almost all its users, the cocaine-induced paranoia may lead to violent behavior as a means of self-defense against imagined persecutors.

Finally, what has been said about cocaine also applies to crack (also examined at length in Chapter 6), and perhaps more so. Crack's low price (as little as two dollars per rock in some locales) has made it an attractive drug of abuse for those with

---

*The medical marijuana issue is discussed in the Postscript of this chapter.

limited funds, particularly adolescents and the indigent. Its rapid absorption brings on a faster onset of dependence than is typical with cocaine, resulting in higher rates of addiction, binge use, and psychoses. The consequences include higher levels of cocaine-related violence and all the same manifestations of personal, familial, and occupational neglect that are associated with other forms of drug dependence.

Heroin.   As discussed in detail in earlier chapters, the abuse liability and dependence potential of heroin is extremely high, and, historically, the drug has been associated with addiction and street crime. Although heroin overdose is not uncommon (unlike alcohol, cocaine, tobacco, and many prescription drugs), the direct physiological damage caused by heroin use tends to be minimal. For this reason the proponents of drug legalization include heroin in their arguments. By making heroin readily available to users, they argue, many problems could be sharply reduced if not totally eliminated, including the crime associated with supporting a heroin habit; the overdoses resulting from problematic levels of heroin purity and potency; the HIV and hepatitis infections brought about by the sharing of drug paraphernalia; and the personal, social, and occupational dislocations resulting from the drug-induced criminal lifestyle.[15]

The belief that legalizing heroin would eliminate crime, overdose, infections, and life dislocations is for the most part a mirage, for it is likely that the heroin-use lifestyle would change little for most users, regardless of the legal status of the drug. Ample evidence supports this argument—in biographies and autobiographies of narcotics users, in clinical assessments of heroin dependence, and in treatment literature.[16] To this evidence can be added the many thousands of conversations conducted with heroin users over the past three decades.

The point is, heroin is a highly abusable drug. To reiterate what has been stated elsewhere in this book, heroin becomes life consuming for those dependent on it. Because heroin is a short-acting drug, with its effects lasting at best four to six hours, it must be taken regularly and repeatedly. Because a more rapid onset occurs when taken intravenously, most heroin users inject the drug. Because heroin has depressant effects, a portion of the user's day is spent in a semistupefied state. Collectively, these effects result in a user more concerned with taking drugs than with health, family, work, or anything else.

As a final note to this section, and perhaps most important, research by professors Michael D. Newcomb and Peter M. Bentler of the University of California at Los Angeles has documented the long-term behavioral effects of drug use on teenagers.[17] Beginning in 1976 a total of 654 Los Angeles County youths were tracked for a period of eight years. Most of these youths were only occasional users of drugs and alcohol, using them moderately at social gatherings, whereas upwards of 10 percent were frequent, committed users. The impact of drugs on these frequent users was considerable. For teenagers, drug use tended to intensify the typical adolescent problems with family and school. In addition, drugs contributed to such psychological difficulties as loneliness, bizarre and disorganized thinking, and suicidal thoughts. Moreover, frequent drug users left school earlier, started jobs earlier, and formed families earlier, thus moving into adult roles with the maturity levels of adolescents.

The consequences of this pattern included rapid family breakups, job instability, serious crime, and ineffective personal relationships. In short, frequent drug use prevented the acquisition of coping mechanisms that are part of maturing; it blocked teenagers' learning of interpersonal skills and general emotional development.

THE CRIME AND ENSLAVEMENT ARGUMENT

In 1974, at a time when heroin and Quaaludes were the major drugs of abuse and cocaine had only begun its trek from the high jungles of the Andes Mountains to the streets of the United States, the noted psychiatrist Thomas Szasz commented in his book *Ceremonial Chemistry:*

> The plain historical facts are that before 1914 there was no "drug problem" in the United States; nor did we have a name for it. Today there is an immense drug problem in the United States, and we have lots of names for it. Which came first: "the problem of drug abuse" or its name? It is the same as asking which came first: the chicken or the egg? All we can be sure of now is that the more chickens, the more eggs, and vice versa; and similarly, the more problems, the more names for them, and vice versa. My point is simply that our drug abuse experts, legislators, psychiatrists, and other professional guardians of our medical morals have been operating chicken hatcheries: they continue—partly by means of certain characteristic tactical abuses of our language—to manufacture and maintain the "drug problem" they ostensibly try to solve.[18]

Szasz certainly does have a way with words. He was suggesting something that nominalists have been saying for centuries: that a thing does not exist until it is imagined and given a name. For Szasz, a hopeless believer in this position, the drug problem in the United States did not exist before the passage of the Harrison Act in 1914, but only became a reality when the behavior under consideration was labeled a problem. If one were to read Szasz's entire volume, despite the numerous errors of fact and poor scholarship, his point would be clear: the drug problem in the United States was created in great part by the very policies designed to control it. On the other hand, one could save a good bit of time by just glancing at the subtitle of his book—*The Ritual Persecution of Drugs, Addicts, and Pushers*—which seems to convey the same message.

The position taken by Szasz has been fashionable for quite some time. Others have attacked U.S. drug control policies with equal vigor and zeal. Washington attorney Rufus King described the issue as a fifty-year folly, a misguided and ineffective endeavor.[19] David F. Musto's classic *The American Disease* offered a similar perspective, although accomplished with considerable scholarship.[20] In addition, a number of early social scientists were among the first to speak out against the federal approach to drug control. Alfred R. Lindesmith, for example, who probably spent a good part of his professional career condemning federal policies, summed up his position in a 1956 issue of *The Nation:*

For 40 years the United States has tried in vain to control the problem of drug addiction by prohibition and police suppression. The disastrous consequences of turning over to the police what is an essentially medical problem are steadily becoming more apparent as narcotic arrests rise each year to new records and the habit continues to spread, especially among young persons. Control by prohibition has failed; but the proposed remedies for this failure consist mainly of more of the same measures which have already proved futile.[21]

Lindesmith's words have a familiar ring to them, in that he was suggesting that drug users receive treatment instead of incarceration. But for Dr. Szasz, the solution to the drug problem was simple. Ignore it, and it will no longer be a problem. After all, he maintained, there was precedent for it:

What does this larger view show us? How can it help us? It shows us that our present attitudes toward the whole subject of drug use, drug abuse, and drug control are nothing but the reflections, in the mirror of "social reality," of our own expectations toward drugs and toward those who use them; and that our ideas about and interventions in drug-taking behavior have only the most tenuous connection with the actual pharmacological properties of "dangerous drugs." The "danger" of masturbation disappeared when we ceased to believe in it: when we ceased to attribute danger to the practice and to its practitioners; and ceased to call it "self-abuse."[22]

What Szasz seems to be suggesting is that heroin, cocaine, and other dangerous drugs be legalized; hence, the difficulties associated with their use would go away. Even the problems of crime would go away, because he was a firm believer in what might be called the enslavement theory of addiction. The whole notion of enslavement theory is intricately tied to the complex relationship between drug abuse and criminal behavior, for it suggests that essentially law-abiding individuals become criminals as the result of drug use. That is, the drug black market imposes such high prices that users are forced to commit crimes to support their habits. Thus, criminality is the result of enslavement to drugs and the drug black market.

Although the origins of the theory date back to the nineteenth century with the early clinical writings about morphine dependence, its most complete statement appears in the work of David W. Maurer and Victor H. Vogel. In the third edition of their *Narcotics and Narcotic Addiction,* Maurer and Vogel stated:

First, the potential addict begins to take very small doses of some addicting drug, let us say morphine, or heroin. He either does not realize what the drug will do to him, or he knows that others have become addicted but believes that it will never happen to him. . . .

Second, the addict notices that the amount of the drug he has been taking does not "hold" him, and, if he is addiction-prone, he no longer experiences the intense pleasure which he felt in the very early stages of the use of the drug. If he has been "pleasure-shooting" (taking small doses at intervals of several days or several weeks) he notices that he must increase these in size to continue to get any pleasure from the drug; eventually, of course, he will also increase the frequency until he is taking a shot four to six times daily. . . .

Third, as the habit increases in size over a period of weeks or months, the addict who must buy his drugs from bootleg sources finds that more and more of his wages go for drugs and that he has less and less for the other necessities; in fact, other things come to mean less and less to him, and he becomes heavily preoccupied with simply supporting his habit. . . .

Fourth, it becomes obvious to him that he must have increasing amounts of money on a regular basis, and that legitimate employment is not likely to supply that kind of money. *Therefore, some form of crime is the only alternative.*[23]

The theory, of course, is not without some logic. As already pointed out in Chapter 2, during the latter part of the nineteenth century and the early years of the twentieth, the use of narcotics was fairly widespread, and both morphine and heroin were readily available through legal channels. When the Harrison Act was passed, users had to embrace the black market to obtain their drugs. Since that time, the possession of heroin has remained a crime, and most users seem to have criminal records.

The theory also has a basis in empirical research. As noted in Chapter 8, from the 1920s through the 1970s, the findings of many research studies suggested that narcotics use preceded criminal activity. Hence, as the enslavement theorists suggested, the inference of causality seemed clear—drug use caused crime, because users had to embrace the black market and commit crimes to support their habits. Perhaps it was so, at least for some drug users, but more likely such findings were an outgrowth of research biased by the reliance on arrest records as the sole indicators of criminality. For it is clear, particularly within highly criminal populations, that only an insignificant proportion of the offenses committed by drug offenders actually result in arrest.[24] There were other biases as well, for, as pointed out in Chapter 8, subsequent research demonstrated that whereas drug use tends to intensify and perpetuate criminal careers, it does not necessarily initiate them.

Given the premises of the enslavement theory of addiction, supporters of drug legalization argue that if the criminal penalties attached to heroin and cocaine possession and sale were removed, three outcomes would occur: the black market would disappear, the prices of heroin and cocaine would decline significantly, and users would no longer have to engage in street crime to support their desired levels of drug intake. But no solid empirical evidence has ever supported the contentions of enslavement theory.

Yet as also pointed out in Chapter 8, research since the middle of the 1970s with active drug users from the streets of New York, Miami, Baltimore, and elsewhere has demonstrated that enslavement theory has little basis in reality, and that the contentions of the legalization proponents in this behalf are mistaken.[25] All these studies of the criminal careers of heroin and other drug users have convincingly documented that whereas drug use tends to intensify and perpetuate criminal behavior, it usually does not initiate criminal careers. In fact, the evidence suggests that among the majority of street drug users who are involved in crime, their criminal careers were well established prior to the onset of narcotics, cocaine, or crack use.

THE DRUGS/VIOLENCE ARGUMENT

In terms of the drug legalization/violence connection, recall the three models of drug-related violence addressed in Chapter 8.[26] The psychopharmacological model of violence suggests that some individuals, as the result of short-term or long-term ingestion of specific substances, may become excitable, irrational, and exhibit violent behavior. The paranoia and aggression associated with the cocaine psychosis fit into the psychopharmacological model, as does most alcohol-related violence. The economically compulsive model of violence holds that some drug users engage in economically oriented violent crime to support drug use. This model is illustrated in the many studies of drug use and criminal behavior that have demonstrated that although drug sales, property crimes, and prostitution are the primary economic offenses committed by users, armed robberies and muggings do indeed occur. The systemic model of violence maintains that violent crime is intrinsic to the very involvement with illicit substances. As such, systemic violence refers to the traditionally aggressive patterns of interaction within systems of illegal drug trafficking and distribution.

An overview of recent studies of drug-related violence documents that alcohol and other drugs have psychopharmacological effects that result in violence.[27] Cocaine in all its forms is linked to aggressive behavior as a result of the irritability and paranoia it engenders. Also, alcohol and cocaine have been found to be present in both the perpetrators and victims of violence. Alcohol is legal and cocaine is not, suggesting that the legal status of a drug is unrelated to the issue of psychopharmacological violence. Hence, it is unlikely that such violence would decline if drugs were legalized.

Studies of economically compulsive violence also suggest that in a legalized market, crime would not necessarily decline. Users who engage in predatory behaviors do so for a variety of reasons—not only to obtain drugs, but also to support themselves. Typically, as many studies suggest, drug-involved offenders were involved in crime before the onset of their careers in drugs. Too, even when a drug is inexpensive, it still may not be affordable when dependence and compulsive use exist. This is amply illustrated by the experience with crack.

As for systemic violence, much of it is unrelated to the use of drugs. When it is drug linked, the overwhelming majority seems to be associated with the use of alcohol or crack, and this brings up another interesting consideration. The illegal drug most associated with systemic violence is crack cocaine, and of all illicit drugs, crack is the one that seems to have been responsible for the most homicides. In a study conducted in New York City, for example, crack was found to be connected to 32 percent of all homicides and 60 percent of all drug-related homicides.[28]

Taking this point further, violence stems from many of the dysfunctional aspects of society other than drug use. In a different study of the violence associated with crack distribution in Manhattan neighborhoods, researchers concluded that crack had been integrated into behaviors that were evident before drug sellers' involvement with crack or its appearance on New York City streets.[29] In other words, the crack users and dealers were often immersed in violent and crime-involved lifestyles that existed independent of their involvement with crack. Furthermore, although evidence shows that crack sellers were more violent than other drug sellers, this violence was not confined to the drug-selling context—violence potential seemed to precede involvement in selling.[30]

Although crack has been blamed for increasing violence in the drug marketplace, perhaps this violence actually stemmed from the psychopharmacological consequences of crack use. Crack dealers are generally crack users, and because crack has a high dependence potential, yet is comparatively inexpensive, the demand for it is continual. This leads to the competition that generates violence. As a result, legalizing crack would likely reduce the competition but increase the demand. Furthermore, researcher Ansley Hamid reasoned that increases in crack-related violence were due to the deterioration of informal and formal social controls throughout communities that had been destabilized by economic processes and political decisions.[31] Can all these complex social problems that contribute to crack-related violence be improved on through the simple act of legalizing drugs?

Finally, one more interesting point can be added here. The great majority of studies of crack-related violence occurred during the late 1980s, a time when crack use was occurring at seemingly epidemic levels in some locales and when violence in drug markets was also at epidemic levels. During the 1990s, crime rates in general, and homicide rates in particular, began to recede dramatically. In fact, during the early months of 2000, the Federal Bureau of Investigation announced that serious crime in the United States had declined in 1999—the eighth consecutive annual reduction. The FBI also reported that the rate of violent crime was the lowest since 1987 and the nation's murder rate had dropped to a thirty-year low. Some of the greatest decreases in crime during the 1990s occurred in the country's largest cities, such as New York and Los Angeles, but to the surprise of many observers, violent crime increased dramatically in many midsize cities. In Louisville and Nashville, for example, the number of murders increased by more than 50 percent during the decade, and in Cincinnati murders went up almost 75 percent in just one year.

Although no single answer can explain all the changes that occurred throughout the United States, a few interpretations address the downward trend in crime rates. First is the economy. Because of greater prosperity and reduced unemployment, youths in particular had more hope of finding legal jobs and viewed crime as a less desirable option. Second is prevention. The 1990s witnessed an increased number of early intervention programs for high-risk youths, including after-school programs during the 3 P.M. to 8 P.M. peak hours for juvenile violent crime. Third is the higher rates of incarceration. Between 1979 and 1991, the number of offenders sent to prison for violent crimes doubled, and as the noted political scientist James Q. Wilson put it: "Putting people in prison is the single most important thing we've done."[32] Fourth is better policing in a number of jurisdictions. Not only are more police on the streets, but use of community-policing techniques has increased.* Fifth, and most

---

*Community policing is a collaborative effort between the police and the community to identify the problems of crime and disorder and to develop solutions within the community. See James A. Inciardi, *Elements of Criminal Justice,* 2nd ed. (Ft. Worth, TX: Harcourt Brace, 2000), pp. 130–134.

important to this discussion, is the dramatic reduction in the number of street-corner crack markets. The withering of these markets lessened the violence associated with rivalries in the crack distribution system, the large number of drug transactions among highly agitated buyers and sellers, and the number of handguns that users and dealers carried to protect themselves from robberies. It was not legalizing crack that had this impact but, in great part, dramatically reducing the use of crack. Finally, the increased rates of violent crime in many midsized cities was the result of crack markets arriving there late.[33] As criminologist Alfred Blumstein of Carnegie Mellon University put it:

> Smaller cities are going through what bigger cities went through five years ago. There is a lag effect in the smaller cities, caused not necessarily by the saturation of drugs in the big cities but the propagation of markets. There may be entrepreneurs from the big cities looking to expand or new entrepreneurs in small cities looking to get involved.[34]

THE EXPANDED MARKET ARGUMENT

An often-neglected argument revolves around the assumption that legalization would have minimal impact on use; that most or all those who would use drugs are already using them. Such an assumption appears to ignore one of the most powerful aspects of U.S. tradition: the ability of an entrepreneurial market system to create, expand, and maintain high levels of demand.

As noted previously, explicit legalization proposals are few, and there has yet to be a serious discussion of how the issues of advertising and marketing might be handled. However, if the treatment of other legal drugs, such as alcohol and tobacco, are used as models of regulatory control, then it is reasonable to assume an application of free speech rights to legalized drugs. This indeed would be logical, for, after all, the drugs would be legal products. Similarly, it would not seem unreasonable to assume that the U.S. market economy would become strongly involved in expanding and maintaining demand for the legalized substances. The successes of tobacco and alcohol advertising programs are eminently conspicuous. The linking of smoking with women's rights has been masterful. The linking of alcohol with the pursuit of happiness after work, in recreational activities, and in romantic liaisons has been so effective that people in the United States spend tens of billions of dollars each year on beer, wine, and distilled spirits.

In a United States where drugs are legal, how far would advertisers go? Would they show students, executives, and truck drivers—overworked and faced with tight schedules and deadlines—reaching for a line of cocaine instead of a cup of coffee? Would cocaine be touted as the mark of success in an achievement-oriented society? Would heroin be portrayed as the real way to relax after a harried day? Would the new Marlboro Man be smoking marijuana or crack instead of tobacco? These are not fanciful speculations, for many controlled substances are regularly advertised, even if only in medical journals. Regardless, the focus of advertising is to market a product by creating and maintaining demand.

The issue, then, of whether the market is saturated fails to recognize the ability of a free enterprise system to expand demand. Epidemiological data confirm that there is considerable room for increasing the demand for drugs. Estimates projected from the 2005 National Survey on Drug Use and Health suggest that only 6 percent of the general population of the United States aged twelve years and older were current users (use during the past month) of marijuana, and less than 1 percent were current users of cocaine.[35] These are very small proportions. The survey also demonstrated, however, that one-fourth of U.S. adolescents and the majority of young adults are current users of the major available legal drug—alcohol—and that, in all, there were no less than 60 million current users of cigarettes and more than 126 million current users of alcohol. Such numbers represent very significant proportions. To assume that the legalization of drugs would maintain the current, relatively low levels of drug use when rates of both alcohol and tobacco use are high seems rather naive. Moreover, it considerably underestimates the deterrent effect of the law, as well as the advertising industry's ability to create a context of use that appears integral to a meaningful, successful, liberated life.

SOPHISM, LEGALIZATION, AND ILLICIT DRUG USE

For some reason that is difficult to understand, numerous members of the prolegalization lobby argue that if drugs were to be legalized, usage would likely not increase very much, if at all.[36] The grounds, they state, are that drugs are everywhere, and that everyone who wants to use them already does. But the data beg to differ. For example, as indicated in Exhibit 11.1, drawn from the Monitoring the Future surveys, slightly over half of U.S. high school seniors in 2005 had never used an illicit drug in their lifetimes.[37] Monitoring the Future data also indicate that only 30 percent had ever used an illicit drug other than marijuana in their lifetimes (Exhibit 11.2). Even smaller proportions had used illicit drugs in the past year or past thirty days. True, these surveys did not include dropout populations in which usage rates are higher, but nevertheless, the absolute numbers in these age cohorts who have never even tried any illicit drugs are in the tens of millions. Most significant to the argument that drugs are everywhere, with the exception of marijuana, almost half of all high school seniors in 2005 did not feel that they were easy to obtain.

Furthermore, as indicated in Exhibit 11.3, most people in the general population do not use drugs. Granted, these data are limited to the general population, which excludes such hard-to-reach populations as members of deviant and exotic subcultures, the homeless, and others living on the streets, and particularly those for which drug use rates are highest. However, the data do document that the overwhelming majority of people in the United States do not use illicit drugs. This suggests two explanations: (1) that the drug prohibitions may be working quite well and (2) that a large population might use drugs if they were legal and readily available.

This relates to the concept of sophism. The Sophists were Greek philosophers of the fifth century B.C., masters of the arts of rhetoric and persuasion. They were the

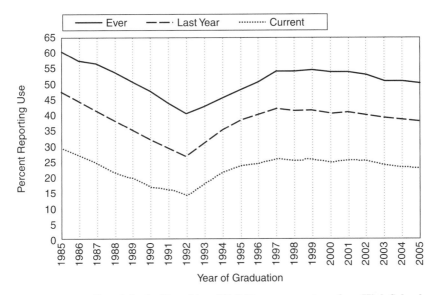

EXHIBIT 11.1   Trends in the Use of Any Illicit Drug among American High School Seniors, 1985–2005
Source: Monitoring the Future study, Institute for Social Research, University of Michigan.

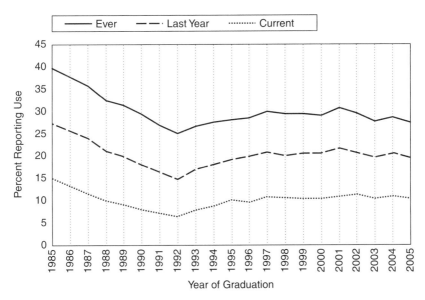

EXHIBIT 11.2   Trends in the Use of Illicit Drugs Other Than Marijuana among High School Seniors, 1985–2005
Source: Monitoring the Future study, Institute for Social Research, University of Michigan.

EXHIBIT 11.3 Percentage and Estimated Number of Users (in Thousands) of Illicit Drugs, Alcohol, and Tobacco in the U.S. Civilian, Noninstitutionalized Population Aged 12 or Older in Their Lifetime, the Past Year, and Past Month, 2005

| Drug | ONCE EVER IN LIFETIME | | PAST YEAR | | PAST MONTH | |
	(%)	*NUMBER (IN THOUSANDS)*	*(%)*	*NUMBER (IN THOUSANDS)*	*(%)*	*NUMBER (IN THOUSANDS)*
Illicit Drugs[a]	46.1	112,085	14.4	35,041	8.1	19,720
Marijuana/hashish	40.1	97,545	10.4	25,375	6.0	14,626
Cocaine	13.8	33,673	2.3	5,523	1.0	2,397
Crack	3.3	7,928	0.6	1,381	0.3	682
Heroin	1.5	3,534	0.2	379	0.1	136
Hallucinogens	13.9	33,728	1.6	3,809	0.4	1,088
LSD	9.2	22,433	0.2	563	0.0	104
PCP	2.7	6,603	0.1	164	0.0	48
MDMA (Ecstasy)	4.7	11,495	0.8	1,960	0.2	502
Inhalants	9.4	22,745	0.9	2,187	0.3	611
Nonmedical Use of Psychotherapeutics[b]	20.0	48,709	6.2	15,172	2.6	6,405
Pain Relievers	13.4	32,692	4.9	11,815	1.9	4,658
OxyContin®	1.4	3,481	0.5	1,226	0.1	334
Tranquilizers	8.7	21,041	2.2	5,249	0.7	1,817
Stimulants	7.8	19,080	1.1	2,771	0.4	1,067
Methamphetamine	4.3	10,357	0.5	1,297	0.2	512
Sedatives	3.7	8,982	0.3	750	0.1	272
Illicit Drugs Other Than Marijuana[a]	29.5	71,822	8.3	20,109	3.7	8,963
Alcohol	82.4*	198,220*	65.1*	156,686*	51.8	126,028
Cigarettes	66.6	161,863	29.1	70,832	24.9	60,532
Smokeless tobacco	18.4	44,793	4.3	10,442	3.2	7,682

*Data for 2004

[a]Illicit drugs include marijuana/hashish, cocaine (including crack), heroin, hallucinogens, inhalants, or prescription-type psychotherapeutics used nonmedically. Illicit drugs other than marijuana include cocaine (including crack), heroin, hallucinogens, inhalants, or prescription-type psychotherapeutics used nonmedically.

[b]Nonmedical use of prescription-type psychotherapeutics includes the nonmedical use of pain relievers, tranquilizers, stimulants, or sedatives and does not include over-the-counter drugs.

Source: SAMHSA, Office of Applied Studies, *National Survey on Drug Use and Health,* 2004 and 2005.

first professional teachers of Greece, and the first to give practical help in politics. Because rhetorical training was the key to political power, these teachers emphasized the art of persuasion.

Originally, *sophist* was the Greek term for any highly skilled craftsman or artist. However, it was later applied to scholars who devoted themselves to wisdom.

Because the Sophists were in the service of the rich, a class then inimical to democracy and held in contempt by Plato and Aristotle, the word *sophist* was given a pejorative sense by these two philosophers. They felt that the object of the Sophists was not genuine knowledge, and the word *sophist* in a general sense came to mean anyone who made the worse reason appear the better or who used fallacious arguments to prove a point.

An interesting variety of sophist reasoning pervades segments of the prolegalization thesis. It is argued repeatedly that drugs should be legalized because they do not really do much harm. Those making this contention point to data from the Drug Abuse Warning Network, more commonly known as DAWN. Noted earlier, DAWN is a large-scale data-collection effort designed to monitor changing patterns of drug abuse in the United States. Hundreds of hospital emergency rooms, as well as county medical examiners in major metropolitan areas, regularly report to the DAWN system. The result is extensive data on deaths and emergency room episodes associated with illicit drug use. The supporters of legalization use these data to demonstrate that not too many people actually have adverse encounters with heroin, cocaine, and other illicit drugs, as compared with the hundreds of thousands of deaths each year linked to alcohol and tobacco use. But interestingly, it is never stated that proportionately few people actually use illicit drugs, and that the segment of the population at risk for overdose or other physical complications from illegal drug use is but an insignificant fraction of that at risk for disease and death from alcohol and tobacco use.

PROHIBITION VERSUS REGULATION

An important point to be discussed here involves the circular thinking on the part of many proponents of the legalization of drugs, typically evident in their portrayals of the drug control establishment as an ineffective, inefficient, power hungry, and sometimes corrupt bureaucracy attempting to enforce impossible laws. Yet this cynical disdain for drug enforcement is replaced with a naive faith in the effectiveness of government regulation. Don't criminalize drugs, they argue, legalize and regulate them. Although the specifics of regulation have yet to emerge, all the legalization proposals actually involve increased regulation. Yet with alcohol and tobacco, it is clear that regulation does not work very well. Using the alcohol analogy, the proponents of legalizing drugs seem to be suggesting that the best defense against the use of cocaine and crack by youths is to distribute the drugs to those 21 years and older, but only after carefully explaining to them that they must not share their government-sanctioned and -supplied drugs with adolescents. The point is that it is naive to believe that drug laws are unenforceable but drug regulations are easily enforced. A good case in point here are the number of people abusing prescription drugs. These are quite heavily regulated, and of course, they are legal.

Shifting to an alternative segment of the debate, many drug legalization proponents seem to believe that the willingness of political conservatives and free-market economists to support their arguments somehow provides them with at least the appearance of broad-based social and even moral support. Yet the fact that a few free-market economists support legalization should be seen for the purely material, or at least intellectual, self-interest that it is. Nineteenth-century capitalists were willing to fight a war in China to keep opiates legal. From a free-market economic perspective, producing, distributing, and expanding the market for a product that is immediately consumed and readily addictive would appear to be a fantasy come true.

Research has documented that illegal drug use is concentrated in many inner-city communities of the United States. Under the free-market arrangement, would the so-called market segmentation practices be applied that the alcohol and tobacco industries use for targeting their products toward African Americans and other minorities in these inner cities? Even if this were prohibited, under the free-market system, drug use, in all likelihood, would expand dramatically in socioeconomically marginal neighborhoods. Urban inner-city areas are not particularly pleasant places in which to live. There is vice, crime, and littered streets. There is the desolation of people separated culturally, socially, materially, and politically from the mainstream. There are the disadvantages of a tangle of economic, family, and other problems—delinquency, teenage pregnancy, unemployment, child neglect, poor housing, sub-standard schools, inadequate health care, and limited opportunities. There are many modes of adaptation to inner-city life. One of them is drug use, perhaps the main cause of higher drug-use rates in inner cities. It is for this reason that a free market for heroin, cocaine, crack, and other drugs would be a nightmare.

The social fabric of the inner city is already tattered, and drugs are further shredding what is left of fragile inner-city families. A great number of them are headed by women, and, for reasons that are not at all clear, women seem to be more disposed to become dependent on crack cocaine than men—further increasing the problems of child neglect. Within this context, the legalization of drugs would, in large part, function as a program of social management and control that would legitimate the chemical destruction of an urban generation and culture. As such, legalization would be an elitist and racist policy supporting the old neocolonialist views of underclass population control.

As a final point here, in untangling the logic of the legalization thesis, a more focused look should be directed toward those who make up the prolegalization lobby. In all likelihood their arguments are born of frustration—frustration with the lack of immediate major successes in the prevention and control of drug use. Part of the problem is reflected in the old saying about a little bit of knowledge being dangerous. As academics, economists, and civil libertarians from outside the drug field, their experiences have rarely, if at all, exposed them to the full dynamics of drug dependence, drug craving, and drug-taking and drug-seeking behaviors. Stated differently, it would appear that arguing about why drugs should be legalized is little more than a parlor game played by intellectuals who have only a limited understanding of the drug problem. It should be noted as well that those who have spent their lives and careers in the trenches researching the drug problem, treating the drug problem, or otherwise coping with the drug problem feel that legalization would initiate a public health problem of unrestrained proportions.

POSTSCRIPT

Contemporary discussions of U.S. drug policy have been framed by a variety of terms—
prohibition, legalization, decriminalization, medicalization, and *harm reduction:*

> *Prohibition* reflects current policy, with its supporters focusing on the neces-
> sity for prohibiting illegal drugs through severe penalties for their use, distribu-
> tion, and sale.

> *Legalization* rests at the other end of the continuum from prohibition, and calls
> for the elimination of drug prohibitions and for the institution of some form of
> government regulation.

> *Decriminalization* refers to the removal of the criminal penalties associated
> with the possession of illegal drugs.

> *Medicalization* advocates giving physicians the responsibility for treating drug
> abusers, including the decision to maintain some users on the drug on which
> they have become dependent.

> *Harm reduction* is an approach that emphasizes a public health model for
> reducing the risks and consequences of drug abuse.[38]

Before going further, two points must be emphasized. The first is that none of
these approaches are mutually exclusive, for each contains elements of the others. Prohibition, for example, includes elements of harm reduction in the forms of substance
abuse prevention and treatment. Furthermore, methadone maintenance programs fall
under the prohibition, medicalization, and harm reduction approaches. At the same
time, legalization proposals often include aspects of both decriminalization and medicalization. The second point is that each of these five drug policy approaches mean
different things to different people, with the most confusion associated with harm
reduction.

What *Is* Harm Reduction?

CHARLOTTE, N.C., May 20, 2000. In a speech before more than two thousand cheering members of the National Rifle Association, NRA president Charlton Heston—a.k.a.
Moses, Judah Ben-Hur, and Taylor (in *Planet of the Apes*) in previous incarnations—
dramatically lifted a replica of a Revolutionary War–era musket and shouted:

> "I'll give up my gun when you take it from my cold, dead hands. As we
> set out this year to defeat the divisive forces that would take freedom
> away, I want to say those words again for everyone within the sound of
> my voice to hear and to heed . . . from my cold dead hands!"[39]

Mr. Heston, representing the NRA membership, was expressing his concern
for what has become known as the slippery-slope hypothesis. As it relates to gun
control, the slippery slope refers to the belief that if even the slightest controls are

placed on gun ownership, eventually, through additional legislation, the possession of *all* guns will become illegal—except for the military, law enforcement, licenced security guards, licenced gun collectors, and licenced sporting clubs. Similarly, opponents of physician-assisted suicide argue that legalizing assisted suicide for the terminally ill would put the medical community on a slippery slope toward allowing assisted suicide in other circumstances—such as for the disabled, the chronically ill, the clinically depressed, the mentally ill, or the elderly.

In just the same way, the U.S. government's official opposition to harm reduction is based on a belief in both a slippery slope and a hidden agenda. As stated by General McCaffrey in 1998: "[Harm reduction is] a hijacked concept that has become a euphemism for drug legalization. It's become a cover story for people who would lower the barriers to drug use."[40] These sentiments, offered by President Clinton's drug czar, explain why there is so much difficulty in unraveling what harm reduction is really all about.

Harm reduction is a concept that is difficult to define with any degree of precision. Its essential feature, however, is the attempt to ameliorate the adverse health, social, legal, and/or economic consequences associated with the use of mood-altering drugs. As such, harm reduction is neither a policy nor a program but, rather, a principle that holds that managing drug abuse is more appropriate than attempting to stop it altogether. Within this context, harm reduction, or *harm minimization* as it is also termed in a number of countries, can be interpreted differently by different people, groups, cultures, and nations. Most broadly, it can refer to any variety or combination of policies and policy goals, including

1. *Advocacy for changes in drug policies.* Legalization, decriminalization, ending the drug prohibition, reduction of criminal sanctions for drug-related crimes, and changes in drug paraphernalia laws
2. *HIV/AIDS-related interventions.* Needle/syringe exchange programs, HIV prevention/intervention programs, bleach and condom distribution programs, referrals for HIV and other sexually transmitted disease (STD) testing, referrals for HIV and other STD medical care and management, and referrals for HIV/AIDS-related psychological care and case management
3. *Broader drug treatment options.* Methadone maintenance by primary care physicians, changes in methadone regulations, heroin substitution programs, new experimental treatments, and treatment on demand
4. *Drug abuse management for those who wish to continue using drugs.* Counseling and clinical case management programs that promote safer and more responsible drug use
5. *Ancillary interventions.* Housing and other entitlements, healing centers, and support and advocacy groups[41]

So yes, as General McCaffery indicated, for some people, harm reduction includes legalization. But for most supporters of harm reduction, legalization is not part of the agenda. Advocating harm reduction does not necessarily mean promoting the legalization of heroin, cocaine, or other currently illegal drugs. Rather, it can focus on many different alternatives, including drug abuse education, prevention, and treatment; it can include modifying, but not necessarily eliminating, some of the penalties for the possession of illegal drugs; and it can mean expanded rehabilitative services for drug-involved offenders who come to the attention of the criminal justice system.

One of the more controversial issues falling under the harm reduction label is the medicalization of marijuana—the use of marijuana for medical purposes. Supporters of medical marijuana point to its usefulness in five specific areas:

1. *Cancer chemotherapy.* Marijuana's active ingredient THC reduces vomiting and nausea caused by chemotherapy; alleviates pretreatment anxiety.
2. *AIDS-related wasting.* Marijuana improves appetite and forestalls the loss of lean muscle mass.
3. *Multiple sclerosis.* Marijuana reduces the muscle pain and spasticity caused by the disease; may also help some patients with bladder control and may relieve tremor.
4. *Epilepsy.* Marijuana may prevent epileptic seizures in some patients.
5. *Glaucoma.* The leading cause of blindness in the United States is caused by increased pressure inside the eyeball. Marijuana, when smoked, reduces pressure within the eye, but it may also reduce blood flow to the optic nerve, exacerbating the loss of vision.

Although a number of state jurisdictions support the concept of medical marijuana, the federal government sees it as another slippery slope. For example, during hearings before the U.S. Congress in 1999, a Drug Enforcement Administration official emphatically stated: "I suspect that medical marijuana is merely the first tactical maneuver in an overall strategy that will lead to the eventual legalization of all drugs."[42] Wow!

Because public opinion on medical marijuana has been so divided, in 1997 the Office of National Drug Control Policy asked the highly respected and prestigious Institute of Medicine of the National Academy of Sciences to conduct a review of the scientific evidence to assess the potential health benefits and risks of marijuana. In 1999, the Institute of Medicine reported on its findings. One of its many conclusions that received considerable attention is as follows:

> Marijuana is not a completely benign substance. It is a powerful drug with a variety of effects. However, the harmful effects to individuals from the perspective of possible medical use of marijuana are not necessarily the same as the harmful physical effects of drug abuse.
>
> Although marijuana smoke delivers THC and other cannabinoids to the body, it also delivers harmful substances, including most of those found in tobacco smoke. In addition, plants contain a variable mixture of biologically-active compounds and cannot be expected to provide a precisely defined drug effect. For those reasons, this report concludes that the future of cannabinoid drugs lies not in smoked marijuana, but in

chemically-defined drugs that act on the cannabinoid systems that are a natural component of human physiology. Until such drugs can be developed and made available for medical use, this report recommends interim solutions.[43]

Based on the evidence, the conclusion is logical, and the interim solutions included calls for further research, including clinical trials of cannabinoid drugs with the goal of developing rapid-onset, reliable, and safe delivery systems. Not surprisingly, the federal drug establishment took this conclusion by the Institute of Medicine as its passport for continued, total prohibition of medical marijuana. But another, especially significant conclusion was ignored: "Until a nonsmoked, rapid-onset cannabinoid drug delivery system becomes available, we acknowledge that there is no clear alternative for people suffering from *chronic* conditions that might be relieved by smoking marijuana, such as pain or AIDS wasting."[44]

As a final point here, one of the first and oldest harm reduction initiatives in the world—methadone maintenance—originated in the United States more than three decades ago. Furthermore, such federal agencies as the Centers for Disease Control and Prevention, the National Institutes of Health, and the Department of Justice, to name but a few, have been in the harm reduction business for decades. They just use different terminology. But as William Shakespeare once said: "What's in a name? That which we call a rose, By any other name would smell as sweet."

NOTES

1. Kurt L. Schmoke, "Forward," *American Behavioral Scientist,* 32 (January–February 1989), pp. 231–232.

2. For some of the major discussions in support of drug legalization, see Milton Friedman and Rose Friedman, *Tyranny of the Status Quo* (San Diego: Harcourt Brace Jovanovich, 1984), pp. 132–141; Milton Friedman, "An Open Letter to Bill Bennett," *Wall Street Journal,* 7 September 1989, p. A14; Ethan A. Nadelmann, "U.S. Drug Policy: A Bad Export," *Foreign Policy,* 70 (Spring 1988), pp. 83–108; Ethan A. Nadelmann, "The Real International Drug Problem," paper presented at the *Defense Academic Research Support Conference,* National Defense College, Defense Intelligence Analysis Center, Washington, DC, 2–3 June 1987; Ethan A. Nadelmann, "The Case for Legalization," *The Public Interest,* 92 (Summer 1988), pp. 3–31; Ethan A. Nadelmann, "Drug Prohibition in the United States: Costs, Consequences, and Alternatives," *Science,* 245 (1 September 1989), pp. 939–947; Arnold S. Trebach, "Effects of the Drug War on Constitutional Guaranties," *Drug Law Report,* 2 (January–February 1989), pp. 248–258; Arnold S. Trebach, "A Bundle of Peaceful Compromises," *Journal of Drug Issues,* 20 (Fall 1990), pp. 515–531; David Boaz, *The Crisis in Prohibition* (Washington, DC: Cato Institute, 1990); William J. Chambliss, "Testimony," *Legalization of Illicit Drugs: Impact and Feasibility, Hearing before the Select Committee on Narcotics Abuse and Control,* House of Representatives, One Hundredth Congress, Second Session, September 29, 1988, Washington, DC; Drug Policy Foundation, *National Drug Reform Strategy* (Washington, DC: Drug Policy Foundation, 1992); Richard Lawrence Miller, *The Case for Legalizing Drugs* (Westport, CT: Praeger, 1991); Chester Nelson Mitchell, *The Drug Solution* (Ottawa: Carelton University Press, 1990); Thomas S. Szasz, *Our Right to Drugs: The Case for a Free Market* (Westport, CT: Praeger, 1992); Steven Wisotsky, *Breaking the Impasse in the War on Drugs* (Westport, CT: Greenwood Press, 1986); Steven Wisotsky, "Crackdown: The Emerging 'Drug Exception' to the Bill of Rights," *Hastings Law Journal,* 38 (July 1987), pp. 889–926; Steven Wisotsky, "Testimony," *Legalization of Illicit Drugs: Impact and Feasibility,*

Hearing before the Select Committee on Narcotics Abuse and Control, House of Representatives, One Hundredth Congress, Second Session, September 29, 1988, Washington, DC.

3. The arguments *against* legalization presented here are drawn from Duane C. McBride, Yvonne M. Terry, and James A. Inciardi, "Alternative Perspectives on the Drug Policy Debate," in *The Drug Legalization Debate,* 2nd ed., ed. James A. Inciardi (Thousand Oaks, CA: Sage, 1999), pp. 9–54; James A. Inciardi and Duane C. McBride, "Legalization: A High-Risk Alternative in the War on Drugs," *American Behavioral Scientist,* 32 (January–February 1989), pp. 259–289; James A. Inciardi and Duane C. McBride, "Debating the Legalization of Drugs," in *Handbook of Drug Control in the United States,* ed. James A. Inciardi (Westport, CT: Greenwood Press, 1990), pp. 283–299.

4. See *Drug Abuse Report,* 17 May 1988, p. 7.

5. See Lester Grinspoon, *Marihuana Reconsidered* (Cambridge: Harvard University Press, 1971); David E. Smith, ed., *The New Social Drug: Cultural, Medical, and Legal Perspectives on Marijuana* (Englewood Cliffs, NJ: Prentice-Hall, 1970); Larry Sloman, *Reefer Madness: The History of Marijuana in America* (Indianapolis: Bobbs-Merrill, 1979).

6. For a thorough discussion and analysis of these points, see Institute of Medicine, *Marijuana as Medicine: Assessing the Science Base* (Washington, DC: National Academy Press, 1999); Helen C. Jones and Paul W. Lovinger, *The Marijuana Question* (New York: Dodd, Mead, 1985).

7. Donald Ian Macdonald, "Marijuana Smoking Worse for Lungs," *Journal of the American Medical Association,* 259 (17 June 1988), p. 3384; C. Nora Chiang and Richard L. Hawks, eds., *Research Findings on Smoking of Abused Substances* (Rockville, MD: National Institute on Drug Abuse, 1990).

8. Institute of Medicine, p. 119.

9. Institute of Medicine, pp. 125–127.

10. *Street Pharmacologist,* May–June 1988, p. 5.

11. Institute of Medicine, p. 5.

12. Herbert Hendin, Ann Pollinger Haas, Paul Singer, Melvin Ellner, and Richard Ulman, *Living High: Daily Marijuana Use among Adults* (New York: Human Sciences Press, 1987).

13. See Robert L. DuPont, *Getting Tough on Gateway Drugs* (Washington, DC: American Psychiatric Press, 1984), pp. 80–83; John W. Spencer and John J. Boren, eds., *Residual Effects of Abused Drug on Behavior* (Rockville, MD: National Institute on Drug Abuse, 1990).

14. Roger D. Weiss and Steven M. Mirin, *Cocaine* (Washington, DC: American Psychiatric Press, 1987), pp. 50–53.

15. This point of view is most thoroughly articulated in Arnold S. Trebach, *The Heroin Solution* (New Haven: Yale University Press, 1982).

16. See Anonymous, *Twenty Years in Hell, or the Life, Experience, Trials, and Tribulations of a Morphine Fiend* (Kansas City, MO: Author's Edition, 1903); William Burroughs, *Junkie* (New York: Ace, 1953); Seymour Fiddle, *Portraits from a Shooting Gallery* (New York: Harper & Row, 1967); Florrie Fisher, *The Lonely Trip Back* (New York: Bantam, 1972); Phil Hirsch, *Hooked* (New York: Pyramid, 1968); Leroy Street, *I Was a Drug Addict* (New York: Random House, 1953); Leroy Gould, Andrew L. Walker, Lansing E. Crane, and Charles W. Litz, *Connections: Notes from the Heroin World* (New Haven: Yale University Press, 1974); Richard P. Rettig, Manual J. Torres, and Gerald R. Garrett, *Manny: A Criminal-Addict's Story* (Boston: Houghton Mifflin, 1977); Marsha Rosenbaum, *Women on Heroin* (New Brunswick, NJ: Rutgers University Press, 1981); David E. Smith and George R. Gay, eds., *"It's So Good, Don't Even Try It Once"* (Englewood Cliffs, NJ: Prentice-Hall, 1971); Marie Nyswander, *The Drug Addict as a Patient* (New York: Grune & Stratton, 1956); Jerome J. Platt, *Heroin Addiction* (Malabar, FL: Robert E. Krieger, 1986); Stanton Peele, *The Meaning of Addiction* (Lexington, MA: Lexington Books, 1985); David Courtwright, Herman Joseph, and Don Des Jarlais, *Addicts Who Survived: An Oral History of Narcotic Use in America, 1923–1965* (Knoxville: University of Tennessee Press, 1989).

17. Michael D. Newcomb and Peter M. Bentler, *Consequences of Adolescent Drug Use: Impact on the Lives of Young Adults* (Newbury Park, CA: Sage, 1988).

18. Thomas Szasz, *Ceremonial Chemistry: The Ritual Persecution of Drugs, Addicts, and Pushers* (Garden City, NY: Anchor Press, 1974), pp. 11–12.

19. Rufus King, *The Drug Hang-Up: America's Fifty-Year Folly* (New York: W. W. Norton, 1972).

20. David F. Musto, *The American Disease: Origins of Narcotic Control* (New Haven, CT: Yale University Press, 1973).

21. *The Nation,* 21 April 1956, p. 337. See also Alfred R. Lindesmith, *Addiction and Opiates* (Chicago: Aldine, 1968).

22. Szasz, p. 180.

23. David W. Maurer and Victor H. Vogel, *Narcotics and Narcotic Addiction,* 3rd ed. (Springfield, IL: Chas. C. Thomas, 1978), pp. 286–287 (italics added).

24. See James A. Inciardi, "Heroin Use and Street Crime," *Crime and Delinquency,* July 1979, pp. 335–346.

25. See James A. Inciardi, *The War on Drugs: Heroin, Cocaine, Crime, and Public Policy* (Palo Alto, CA: Mayfield, 1986), pp. 115–143; Bruce D. Johnson, Paul J. Goldstein, Edward Preble, James Schmeidler, Douglas S. Lipton, Barry Spunt, and Thomas Miller, *Taking Care of Business: The Economics of Crime by Heroin Users* (Lexington, MA: Lexington Books, 1985); David N. Nurco, John C. Ball, John W. Shaffer, and Thomas F. Hanlon, "The Criminality of Narcotic Addicts," *Journal of Nervous and Mental Disease,* 173 (1985), pp. 94–102; Richard C. Stephens and Duane C. McBride, "Becoming a Street Addict," *Human Organization,* 35 (1976), pp. 87–93; Duane C. McBride and Clyde B. McCoy, "Crime and Drugs: The Issues and the Literature," *Journal of Drug Issues,* Spring 1982, pp. 137–152; James A. Inciardi and Anne E. Pottieger, "Kids, Crack, and Crime," *Journal of Drug Issues,* 21 (Spring 1991), pp. 257–270; Jose E. Sanchez and Bruce D. Johnson, "Women and the Drugs–Crime Connection: Crime Rates among Drug Abusing Women at Rikers Island," *Journal of Psychoactive Drugs,* 19 (April–June 1987), pp. 205–216; Eric D. Wish, Kandace A. Klumpp, Amy H. Moorer, Elizabeth Brady, and Kristen M. Williams, *An Analysis of Drugs and Crime among Arrestees in the District of Columbia* (Washington, DC: National Institute of Justice, 1981); George Speckart and M. Douglas Anglin, "Narcotics Use and Crime: An Overview of Recent Research Advances," *Contemporary Drug Problems,* Winter 1986, pp. 741–769; M. Douglas Anglin and Yih-Ing Hser, "Addicted Women and Crime," *Criminology,* 25 (May 1987), pp. 359–397.

26. Paul J. Goldstein, "Homicide Related to Drug Traffic," *Bulletin of the New York Academy of Medicine,* 62 (June 1986), pp. 509–516.

27. For an analysis of these studies, see James A. Inciardi, "Legalizing Drugs: Would It Really Reduce Violent Crime?" in *The Drug Legalization Debate,* 2nd. ed., ed. James A. Inciardi (Thousand Oaks, CA: Sage, 1999), pp. 55–74.

28. Paul J. Goldstein, Henry H. Brownstein, P. J. Ryan, and P. A. Bellucci, "Crack and Homicide in New York City, 1988: A Conceptually Based Event Analysis," *Contemporary Drug Problems,* 16 (1989), pp. 651–687.

29. Jeffrey Fagan and Ko-lin Chin, "Violence as Regulation and Social Control in the Distribution of Crack," in *Drugs and Violence: Causes, Correlates, and Consequences,* ed. Mario De La Rosa, Elizabeth Y. Lambert, and Bernard Gropper (Rockville, MD: National Institute on Drug Abuse Research, 1990).

30. Fagan and Chin, 1990.

31. Ansley Hamid, "The Political Economy of Crack Related Violence," *Contemporary Drug Problems,* Spring 1990, pp. 31–78.

32. Cited in Gordon Witkin, "The Crime Bust," *U.S. News & World Report,* 25 May 1998, pp. 28–37.

33. *Louisville Courier-Journal,* 28 December 1998, p. A1; *New York Times,* 28 December 1998, p. A16.

34. Cited in *New York Times,* 15 January 1998, p. A16.

35. Substance Abuse and Mental Health Services Administration, Office of Applied Studies, *Results from the 2005 National Survey on Drug Use and Health: National Findings,* NSDUH Series H-30, DHHS Publication No. SMA 06-4194 (Rockville, MD: Office of Applied Studies, 2006). Accessed on February 26, 2007, from http://oas.samhsa.gov/nsduh/2k5nsduh/2k5results.pdf.

36. For example, see Chambliss, 1988; Boaz, 1990; Miller, 1991.

37. University of Michigan News and Information Services, *Monitoring the Future,* December 19, 1999.

38. Erich Goode, *Between Politics and Reason: The Drug Legalization Debate* (New York: St. Martin's Press, 1997); Duane C. McBride, Yvonne Terry, and James A. Inciardi, "Alternative Perspectives on the Drug Policy Debate," in *The Drug Legalization Debate,* 2nd ed., ed. James A. Inciardi (Thousand Oaks, CA: Sage, 1999), pp. 9–54.

39. *New York Times,* 21 May 2000, p. 28.

40. *New York Times,* 18 June 1998, p. A29.

41. James A. Inciardi and Lana D. Harrison, "The Concept of Harm Reduction," in *Harm Reduction: National and International Perspectives,* ed. James A. Inciardi and Lana D. Harrison (Thousand Oaks, CA: Sage, 2000), p. viii.

42. Statement by Donnie Marshall, Deputy Administrator of the Drug Enforcement Administration, before the Subcommitttee on Criminal Justice, Drug Policy and Human Resources, June 16, 1999.

43. Institute of Medicine, *Marijuana as Medicine: Assessing the Science Base* (Washington, DC: National Academy Press, 1999), p. vii.

44. Institute of Medicine, p. 8.

CHAPTER 12

WAR IS NOT THE ANSWER

Most Americans experienced the media feeding frenzy during the closing weeks of 2002 that detailed Senator Trent Lott's veiled, but nevertheless resounding, endorsement of the politics of segregation.* His remarks demonstrated exactly how myopic, insensitive, obtuse, dull-witted, and self-serving some (and likely most) of our political leaders can be at times. And it seems to make little difference whether the issue happens to be civil rights, crime control, national defense, the environment, budgetary issues, or other domestic and international affairs. Anachronistic thinking combined with a partisan political style contrived more for getting votes rather than for establishing sound public policy seems to be far too commonplace. This situation appears to be especially the case with regard to American drug policy and how it impacts law and justice, as well as the prevention and treatment of drug abuse and the management of drug-involved offenders. Given this, the closing commentary addresses some of these issues, as well as a few of the bright spots in drug policy alternatives.

THE GOLDEN FLEECE AWARD

Does anyone remember Wisconsin Senator William Proxmire?[†] He had many accomplishments during his long career, but what history will most remember him for is his

---

*For readers who may stumble upon this book a decade or more from now, a brief recap of the Trent Lott bungle appears warranted. Lott, the Republican senator from Mississippi, provoked widespread criticism on December 5, 2002, for commenting that the United States would have been better off if then-segregationist candidate Strom Thurmond had won the presidency in 1948. Speaking at a 100th birthday party and retirement celebration for Senator Thurmond, Lott said, "I want to say this about my state: When Strom Thurmond ran for president, we voted for him. We're proud of it. And if the rest of the country had followed our lead, we wouldn't have had all these problems over all these years, either." Thurmond, then governor of South Carolina, was the presidential nominee of the breakaway Dixiecrat Party in 1948. He declared during his campaign against Democrat Harry S. Truman and Republican Thomas Dewey: "All the laws of Washington and all the bayonets of the Army cannot force the Negro into our homes, our schools, our churches" (See Thomas B. Edsell, "Lott Decried for Part of Salute to Thurmond," *Washington Post*, 7 December 2002, p. A6).

[†]The late Edward William Proxmire (1915–2005) was a member of the Democratic Party, serving in the United States Senate from Wisconsin from 1957 to 1989.

"Golden Fleece Award." Proxmire issued one of these every month between March 1975 and December 1988. In his own words, the award singled out a "wasteful, ridiculous or ironic use of the taxpayers' money." Through the Golden Fleece Award, Senator Proxmire fought for American taxpayers by focusing public attention on budgetary waste in every department of government. A number of the programs or projects he targeted were curtailed, modified, or canceled, helping to save American taxpayers millions of dollars.

The dubious distinction of a Golden Fleece was not awarded to just any example of government waste, but to federal programs that most Americans would agree were outrageous and wasteful. For example, although Senator Proxmire believed that the military's MX Missile was a waste of money, he never gave a Fleece to that program. More importantly, projects receiving the Golden Fleece Awards did not necessarily have high costs, but rather violated a principle of responsible government spending. Some examples included a $27,000 study to determine why inmates want to escape from prison, and his favorite was a study to find out whether sunfish that drink tequila are more aggressive than sunfish that drink gin.

Over the years, almost every federal agency received a Golden Fleece Award. Among the more memorable Golden Fleece recipients are the following:

- The National Endowment for the Humanities for a $25,000 grant in 1977 to study why people cheat, lie, and act rudely on local Virginia tennis courts
- The Office of Education for spending $219,592 in 1978 to develop a curriculum to teach college students how to watch television
- The Department of the Army for spending $6,000 in 1981 to prepare a seventeen-page document that told the federal government how to buy a bottle of Worcestershire sauce
- The Environmental Protection Agency for spending an extra $1 million to $1.2 million in 1980 to preserve a Trenton, New Jersey, sewer as an historical monument

If Senator Proxmire were alive today and still a member of the United States Congress, one wonders what he would be saying about American drug control policies and the budgetary allotments for supply-reduction strategies versus demand-reduction strategies. What would Proxmire have thought about the billions of dollars for Plan Colombia, for counternarcotics in a country where mass murders have been commonplace for decades and where guerrillas control almost half of the national territory? By contrast, what would he have thought about the fact that for every dollar invested in drug abuse treatment, the benefits to society are threefold?[1] And although Plan Colombia may represent one of the more expensive debacles in drug policy making, fear not—there have been numerous others in the history of American drug policy.*

INCARCERATING DRUG-INVOLVED OFFENDERS

Researchers, clinicians, and observers in the fields of substance abuse and public policy have repeatedly expressed concerns over the mass imprisonment of drug-involved offenders. Many different sets of figures have been bandied about—some based on government statistics, others drawn from individual studies, and a few from speculation, educated and otherwise. It has been noted, for example, that drug arrests have tripled since 1980, with more than four-fifths being for simple posses-sion violations; that in any given year, twice as many people are convicted for a drug felony than are convicted for a violent felony; that drug offenses account for more than a third of felonies in federal courts and almost half in state courts; that the over-whelming majority of mandatory drug sentences are imposed on first offenders; and that most of the women and men in federal prisons for drug offenses are first-time, nonviolent offenders, who were arrested for having small amounts of drugs for per-sonal use.[2] The general consensus of advocates for drug policy reform has been that the "war on drugs" is ineffective, having accomplished little more than incarcerating hundreds of thousands of individuals whose only crime was the possession of drugs, and in so doing, disenfranchising them in the areas of voting, employment opportu-nities, and housing, to name but a few.[3] The big question concerns the extent of such incarcerations.

In 2000, the Bureau of Justice Statistics published the findings of its 1997 *Survey of Inmates in Federal and State Correctional Facilities,*[4] and two years later the Washington, DC–based prisoner advocacy organization, *The Sentencing Pro-ject,* released its analysis of the government's survey of inmates.[5] The Sentencing Project's report received considerable national attention, highlighting that 58 per-cent of drug prisoners had no history of violence or high-level drug activity; that three-fourths of the drug offenders in state prisons had only been convicted for drug and/or nonviolent offenses; and that one-third of the total had only been con-victed of drug crimes. The report concluded that the mass incarceration of drug

---

*One of the more entertaining items in this regard was the MODUS project. With funding from the National Institutes of Health, the purpose of MODUS (Model of Drug Use Spread) was to determine, from existing data and policies, what factors contributed to the drug abuse problem in particular Latin American countries. From these data, science-based solutions for reducing drug abuse would be developed. In the-ory, it was a good idea, but after more than a year's effort, the solutions offered were a bit simplistic. For example, some of the suggested remedies for solving the drug problem included: 1) arrest drug traffickers, 2) keep drugs away from youth, 3) make treatment available to drug abusers, 4) strengthen antidrug legis-lation, and 5) offer economic alternatives to poppy and coca cultivation. See *The MODUS Project: Model of Drug Use Spread* (Miami, FL: Health Services Research Center, University of Miami School of Medi-cine, September 1996).

offenders was misguided and inappropriate, and that national drug policy needed constructive redirection.

Unfortunately, the Sentencing Project's analysis of the data suffered from a major gap. In 2004, a more thorough analysis of the same 1997 *Survey of Inmates in Federal and State Correctional Facilities* was published.[6] Entitled "Kingpins or Mules: An Analysis of Drug Offenders Incarcerated in Federal and State Prisons," it confirmed the Sentencing Project finding that most incarcerated drug offenders showed no evidence of being either violent or having a major organizational role. In other words, few were "kingpins." Beyond that, however, the interpretations offered by the "Kingpins or Mules" analysis differed markedly from those of The Sentencing Project, demonstrating that less than 2 percent of federal inmates and less than 6 percent of state inmates were unambiguously low-level offenders. This finding, among others detailed in the paper, dampened any hopes of dramatically reducing prison populations by releasing or diverting the lowest level offenders.

CALIFORNIA'S PROPOSITION 36

Moving on, in November 2000, California voters approved the Substance Abuse and Crime Prevention Act, otherwise known as "Proposition 36," which gave adults convicted of nonviolent drug possession offenses the option of participating in drug treatment in lieu of incarceration. Proposition 36 was a relatively recent entry to the long tradition of criminal justice diversion—the removal of offenders from the application of the criminal law at any stage of the police and court processes.* Diversion implies the formal halting or suspension of traditional criminal proceedings against individuals who have violated criminal statutes, in favor of processing them through some noncriminal disposition or nonincarcerating alternative.

Criminal justice diversion has probably existed in an informal fashion for thousands of years, ever since the inception of organized social control. In both ancient and modern societies, informal diversion has occurred in many ways: a police officer removes a public drunk from the street to a Salvation Army shelter; a prosecutor decides to *nolle pros.* a petty theft; a magistrate releases with a lecture an individual who assaulted a neighbor during the course of an argument. These are generally discretionary decisions, made at random and off the record, and they tend to be personalized and inconsistent. They are often problematic in that they may reflect individual, class, or social prejudices or preferences. Moreover, they serve only to remove offenders from the application of criminal penalties; there is no attempt to provide appropriate alternatives.

---

*"Criminal justice diversion," which involves the removal of offenders from the application of the criminal law, must be differentiated from "prescription drug diversion," described in Chapter 7 as the channeling of prescription medications to the illegal marketplace.

Although these haphazard and unsystematic practices will always be with us, more formal diversion programs place offenders in social–therapeutic programs in lieu of conviction and/or punishment. These initiatives began to emerge within the juvenile justice system almost a century ago. Among the first was the Chicago Boys' Court, founded in 1914 as an extralegal form of probation.[7] As criminal justice diversion continued to evolve, the arguments in its favor increased. It was felt that it would reduce court backlog, provide early intervention before the development of full-fledged criminal careers, ensure some consistency in selective law enforcement, reduce the costs of criminal processing, and enhance an offender's chances for community reintegration. More importantly, however, many social scientists and penal reformers had long since concluded that the criminal justice process, which was designed to protect the public from criminals, often contributed to the very behavior it was trying to eliminate.

Primarily as a result of massive federal funding for the prevention and reduction of crime, criminal justice diversion programs of many types emerged during the 1970s and expanded throughout the nation during the ensuing decades. Most were designed for youths, for individuals who committed minor crimes (such as nonaggravated assaults, simple thefts, and property damage resulting from neighborhood disputes), or for special offenders whose crimes were related to problem drinking or drug abuse.

The first of the nationwide diversion programs targeting drug-involved offenders was Treatment Alternatives to Street Crime, or simply TASC, which began during the early 1970s in Delaware.[8] Known today under the less value-laden and perhaps more politically correct (but nevertheless meaningless) name of Treatment Accountability for Safer Communities, the TASC initiative is designed to be a liaison between the criminal justice system and community treatment programs. As a diversion effort combining treatment and case management for substance-abusing arrestees, probationers, and parolees, its more than 200 sites in 30 states makes it one of the most widely supported forms of court diversion in the United States.

Even more widespread are drug courts—almost 1,600 in all across America (operating or in development). The label "drug court" is actually a generic term for several different kinds of approaches designed to cope with the growing number of drug cases entering the justice arena. They include special courts or judges, distinctive case management systems, and/or pretrial diversion programs. Many of these entities function as traditional courts by hearing evidence and adjudicating guilt, whereas others serve as special "plea bargaining" forums. Many handle only first offenders, with others having no such limitations. The majority, however, have the responsibility of handling drug-abusing offenders through comprehensive supervision, drug testing, treatment services, and intermediate sanctions and incentives.

It is difficult to assess the overall value and impact of the national diversion effort. The great majority of programs have never been evaluated, and estimations of their effectiveness have been based on little more than clinical intuition and hunch. Among those that have undergone rigorous assessment, the findings have ranged from promising to bleak. But as jail and prison populations have continued to grow well beyond capacity, diversion programs remain popular because they permit judges to impose intermediate sanctions yet still avoid incarcerating offenders.

It was within this context, at least partially anyway, that the Proposition 36 agenda was launched. Although it followed the generic diversion, TASC, and drug court model and philosophy of moving drug-involved offenders into treatment rather than prison, there were a few things that were quite unique about it. First, it resulted from a California ballot initiative that was supported by 61 percent of the electorate. Second, and most importantly, the impetus for, and campaign support behind, the promotion of Proposition 36 came primarily from George Soros (President of Soros Fund Management), Peter Lewis (philanthropist and CEO of Progressive Insurance), and John Sperling (CEO of The Apollo Group, Inc.) — billionaire financiers who view American drug policy as an all-embracing failure and wish to change its focus, including a liberalization (and perhaps elimination) of some or all of the nation's drug laws. However, given a recent study documenting high rates of arrest among Proposition 36 clients,[9] one wonders if California was really ready for Proposition 36. California voters were probably ready for it, but was the state's treatment system prepared for the sudden influx of so many new clients?

It can be argued that diversion programs, TASC, drug courts, and now Proposition 36, can be only as good as the treatment programs to which the drug-involved offenders are sent. Given the scores of scientific studies conducted over the years, we know that drug abuse treatment works.[10] However, because the overwhelming majority of existing programs have never been evaluated, little is known as to which ones have demonstrated long-term effectiveness, which ones are only marginally helpful, and which ones should be immediately shut down. Going further, there are simply not enough programs to meet the need—nationwide *and* in California.

Research has documented that a significant majority of the drug-involved offenders coming to the attention of the criminal justice system are in need of long-term residential treatment.[11] As a result, beginning in the mid-1980s there was a movement to increase the number of treatment programs and beds in correctional institutions. This culminated in the passage of the Residential Substance Abuse Treatment for State Prisoners (RSAT) legislation in 1994, which provided tens of millions of dollars each year for residential treatment programs in state and local correctional facilities. However, in the community-based settings to which Proposition 36 and other diversion clients were channeled, residential treatment beds tended to be quite scarce. As such, the great majority of clients ended up being "under-treated" in outpatient programs.

It wasn't always this way. In 1990, for example, there were more than 16,000 substance abuse treatment facilities in the United States: about 55 percent were residential or inpatient-hospital, some 30 percent were outpatient, and the balance were methadone maintenance programs.[12] By 2001, there were 2,000 fewer programs, and the overwhelming majority were abstinence-oriented outpatient programs.[13] One could argue that there was a redirection of resources from community-based residential programs to the RSAT initiative. This might have been so in a few instances, but RSAT funds were new federal monies made available for correctional agencies. In the main, the elimination of residential slots evolved from transformations in the management of health care and the preference for lower-cost, short-term outpatient care.[14]

Perhaps the greatest problem affecting Proposition 36 and other treatment initiatives was (and still is) that the infrastructure of the nation's community-based drug abuse treatment system is crumbling. This was most vividly demonstrated in a study of the treatment system recently published in the *Journal of Substance Abuse Treatment*.[15] Based on systematic inquiries made with a representative sample of the nation's 13,484 treatment programs, the findings were quite disturbing. Results indicated that during the sixteen-month period prior to contact, 15 percent of the facilities had closed or had stopped addiction treatment, and an additional 29 percent had been reorganized under a different agency. Moreover, there had been a 53 percent turnover among program directors and a similar rate among counselors within just the previous year. Only about half of the programs had even a part-time physician on staff, and outside of methadone maintenance programs, less than 15 percent of programs had a nurse, and very few programs had a social worker. The predominant form of treatment was abstinence-oriented group counseling. Overall, the study called into question the ability of the national treatment system to meet the complex needs and demands of both the patients that enter the system and the agencies that refer clients to it.

What does this suggest for the California treatment system's ability to meet the demands of Proposition 36? The answer is that it is not meeting the demand. One could speculate that Soros, Lewis, Sperling, and the others who pushed for the passage of Proposition 36 had not done their homework and failed to realize that the system was underfunded, understaffed, underequipped, and had too few residential beds. However, one could also speculate that they had indeed done their homework and had done it very well. Perhaps the intention was to force tens of thousands of new clients into a system that they knew could not handle them properly. In demonstrating that neither incarceration nor treatment was effective in dealing with drug abuse, the ground would then be fertile for a drug policy liberalization initiative.[16]

TREATING DRUG-INVOLVED OFFENDERS IN CORRECTIONAL SETTINGS

An important question that should be raised here is whether the war on drugs should even continue? In all likelihood, it probably should not. Or perhaps, war is not the answer; peaceful solutions should be sought. However, because drug laws and drug control will persist, and because drug-involved offenders will continue to be arrested and prosecuted, one peaceful strategy is to use harm reduction approaches for making a more humane use of the criminal justice system.

In this regard, amidst the billions funneled into drug control, there have been a few bright spots. One of these was RSAT, briefly described above. Given the hundreds of thousands of drug-involved offenders coming to the attention of the nation's prison systems, the RSAT initiative provided states with funding for substance abuse treatment in correctional settings. The rationale for RSAT was that although there is a need to punish offenders, it is important that they do not return to prison. Hence, the RSAT initiative is an attempt to break the cycle of drug use and crime, and at the same time, make the inmate's prison time more productive. The RSAT program is, to a great extent, an outgrowth of the success experienced by a treatment system that had been evolving in the Delaware correctional system since the late 1980s. Although drug treatment in prison settings was not new, what had emerged in Delaware was somewhat unique at the time.

The Delaware program was based on the notion that for drug-involved individuals who come in contact with the criminal justice system, "drug abuse" and "criminality" are but symptoms of a complex behavioral disorder that cannot be properly addressed through short-term outpatient treatment, vocational rehabilitation, or imprisonment. The aspects of this disorder might be referred to as crime-related "impedimenta" to social functioning.[17] The major "impedimenta" include inadequacy, immaturity, dependency, limited social skills, inadequate education, vocational maladjustment, cognitive deficiency, compulsive pathology, organic pathology, antisocial attitudes, catalytic impulsivity, habitual impulsivity, and substance dependency, including alcoholism or drug addiction or both (see Exhibits 12.1).

EXHIBIT 12.1
IMPEDIMENTA TO SOCIAL FUNCTIONING

"Inadequacy" is characterized by a pervasive feeling of inability to cope with needs; a generalized feeling of helplessness; the inability to plan ahead; frequent feelings of despair, negativism, and cynicism; diffuse anxiety, not seen as related to a specific cause; the perception of tasks as likely to lead to failure rather than success; and a disproportionate fear (and anticipation) of rejection.

"Immaturity" is characterized by the inability to postpone gratification; a general attitude of irresponsibility; a preoccupation with concrete and immediate objects, wishes, and needs; an orientation of the individual as "receiver" and a tendency to view others as "givers"; manipulativeness; selfishness; and petulance.

"Dependency" is characterized by difficulty in coping with unstructured or complex environments; anxiety in situations requiring independent action; feelings of guilt with respect to the above elements of dependency; and feelings of resentment toward what is believed to be the source of dependency.

"Limited social skills" is characterized by a lack of ability to articulate feelings and ideas, and a resulting inability to communicate meaningfully with others except at superficial levels; lack of ability to function in subordinate–superordinate roles (e.g., inability to take orders from a superior in a work situation); inability to "take the role of the other" (i.e., empathize with others); and, inadvertent, socially disapproved behavior (e.g., use of language inappropriate to various social situations, dress inappropriate for job interviews, failure to conform to norms of personal hygiene).

"Inadequate education" is characterized by functional illiteracy or a conspicuous disproportion between the individual's level of education and his or her potential level or both.

"Vocational maladjustment" is characterized by a lack of appropriate technical skills for employment that would be meaningful to the individual, or a conspicuous disproportion between the aptitudes of the individual and realistic opportunities or both.

"Cognitive deficiency" is characterized by a state of mental retardation, restricted mental potentiality, or incomplete development existing from birth or early infancy, as a result of which the individual is confused and bewildered by any complexity of life, overly suggestible and easily exploited, and able to achieve a mental age within a range of only 8 to 12 years.

"Compulsive pathology" is characterized by a sense that criminal behavior is forced upon the individual against his or her will; inability to obtain any lasting satisfaction from the act committed (e.g., no apparent gain to the individual from act nor any reason for injury to another); and repetition of such acts.

"Organic pathology" involves such things as glandular and neurological anomalies (e.g., brain damage, organic brain disease). Conduct stemming from organic pathology is not usually typified by any single behavioral pattern.

"Antisocial attitudes" consist of a configuration of values and viewpoints which are defined by society as delinquent, criminal, and antisocial. An individual who possesses antisocial attitudes demonstrates positive affective toward trouble, toughness, smartness, excitement, fate, autonomy, and short-run hedonism.

"Catalytic impulsivity" is a characteristic that requires the presence of a catalyst for it to appear (i.e., criminal acts only occur while the normally overcontrolled person is affected by the catalyst). The catalyst may take the form of alcohol or an overwhelming need stemming from psychic or physical dependence (e.g., narcotics) or a specific emotional stimulus (e.g., cursing one's mother). The central concept of catalytic impulsivity is the impulsive, spontaneous, unplanned nature of the criminal act while the offender is under the influence of, or is affected by, the catalyst. Under normal circumstances the catalytic impulsive individual is not antisocial and possesses adequate and even excessive self-control. Under the influence of the catalyst, however, there is first a recognition of the imminence of the criminal act, and then the criminal act almost invariably precipitates and there is total disregard for the consequences of such acts.

"Habitual impulsivity" differs from catalytic impulsivity by the absence of the need for a catalyst as a trigger. A habitually impulsive individual may use alcohol or drugs, but the crucial aspect is that these substances are neither necessary nor sufficient for the criminal act to occur. The act itself is always spontaneous and unplanned, and the individual who possesses this characteristic is temperamental, exhibits a low frustration tolerance and high reactivity. His or her volatile temperament typically demonstrates rapid mood swings. The triggering source for impulsive criminal acts cannot be definitively indicated. Such a characteristic may be seen in individuals who react variously to situations of temptation, slight provocation, and frustration. Rages may be a typical reaction for one offender, whereas another may react by random shoplifting or driving dangerously.

Offenders with "substance dependency" typically (1) have several years experience as a street drug addict or alcoholic, (2) have many failed treatment experiences, (3) are driven to use their chosen substance regardless of consequences while on the street, (4) are preoccupied with thoughts about their substance of choice while institutionalized, and (5) intend using the preferred substance on discharge.

These characteristics may appear singly, or in combinations of two, three, four or more in any individual at any given time. And the drug abuse treatment and psychiatric literatures have documented the presence of "impedimenta" among substance abusers through literally hundreds of studies.[18]

To reiterate, drug addiction is typically one symptom of a complex of problems that cannot be addressed by any easy solution. Moreover, there is a whole literature which suggests that drug abuse is "over-determined" behavior. That is, physical dependence is secondary to the wide range of influences that instigate and regulate drug-taking and drug-seeking behaviors. Drug abuse is a disorder of the whole person, affecting some or all areas of functioning. In the vast majority of drug offenders, there are cognitive problems, psychological dysfunction is common, thinking may be unrealistic or disorganized, values are misshapen, and frequently there are deficits in educational and employment skills. The research and clinical literature also documents that the great majority of drug abusers were victims of physical abuse, sexual abuse, and/or neglect as children.[19] As such, drug abuse is a response to a series of social and psychological disturbances. Thus, the goal of treatment should be "habilitation" rather than "rehabilitation." Whereas *rehabilitation* emphasizes the return to a way of life previously known and perhaps forgotten or rejected, *habilitation* involves the client's initial socialization into a productive and responsible way of life. What the large drug offender population needs is habilitation in long-term residential treatment.

Within this context, numerous drug abuse clinicians and researchers have expressed the opinion that the "therapeutic community" (described earlier in Chapter 10), commonly referred to as the "TC," is perhaps the most viable form of treatment for drug-involved offenders, particularly for those whose criminality has resulted in incarceration.[20] Drug-involved offenders who come to the attention of state and federal prison systems are typically those with long arrest histories and patterns of chronic substance abuse, and the intensive nature of the TC regimen tends to be best suited for their long-term treatment needs.[21] Moreover, the therapeutic community is especially efficacious in a correctional institution because the TC is a total treatment environment isolated from the rest of the prison population—separated from the drugs, the violence, and other aspects of prison life that tend to militate against rehabilitation.

Based on a wide body of literature in the fields of both treatment and corrections, combined with clinical and research experiences with correctional systems and populations, it would appear that the most effective strategy would involve three stages of therapeutic community treatment intervention. Each stage in this continuum is an adaptation to the client's changing correctional status: incarceration, work release, and parole (or other form of community supervision).[22]

The primary stage of treatment should consist of a prison-based therapeutic community. Segregated from the negativity of the prison culture, recovery from drug abuse and the development of prosocial values in the prison TC involve essentially the same mechanisms seen in community-based TCs. Therapy in this stage is an ongoing and evolving process over twelve months, with the potential for the resident to remain slightly longer, if needed. Moreover, it is important that TC treatment for inmates begin *while they are still in the institution.* In a prison situation, time is one of the few resources that most inmates have in abundance. The competing demands of family, work, and the neighborhood peer groups are absent. Thus, there is the time and opportunity for focused and comprehensive treatment, perhaps for the first time in a drug offender's career. In addition, there are other new opportunities presented: to interact with "recovering addict" role models, to acquire prosocial values and a positive work ethic, and to initiate a process of understanding the addiction cycle.

The secondary stage of treatment should be a "transitional" therapeutic community in a work release setting. Since the 1970s, work release has become a widespread correctional practice for felony offenders. It is a form of partial incarceration whereby inmates who are approaching their release dates are permitted to work for pay in the free community, but must spend their nonworking hours either in the institution or, more commonly, in a community-based work release facility. Although graduated release of this sort carries the potential for easing an inmate's process of community reintegration, there is a negative side as well, especially for those whose drug involvement served as the gateway to prison in the first place. Inmates are exposed to groups and behaviors that can easily lead them back to substance abuse, criminal activities, and reincarceration. Since work release populations mirror the institutional populations from which they come, there are still the negative values of the prison culture, but in addition, street drugs and street norms abound. As such, the transitional work release TC should be similar to that of the traditional therapeutic community. There should be the "family setting" removed from as many of the external negative influences of the street and inmate cultures as is possible. However, the clinical regimen in the work release TC must be modified to address the correctional mandate of "work release." That is, in addition to intensive therapeutic community treatment, clients must prepare for and obtain employment in the free community.

In the tertiary stage (aftercare), clients will have completed work release and will be living in the community under the supervision of parole or some other supervisory program. For those individuals who entered work release after serving mandatory fixed sentences, there is no parole requirement, and hence, no community supervision. Treatment intervention in this stage involves outpatient counseling and group therapy. Clients are encouraged to return to the work release TC for refresher/reinforcement sessions, to attend weekly groups, to call on their counselors on a regular basis, and to spend one day each month at the facility.

This multistage model has been operating in the Delaware correctional system since the mid-1990s, and a comprehensive research program has been established to examine the effectiveness of various components of, and combinations of, the model. The findings of the research have vividly demonstrated that drug-involved offenders receiving prison-based treatment, followed by transitional treatment in a work release therapeutic community, followed by aftercare, will have significantly lower rates of relapse and recidivism, in both the short and long term, than those receiving little or no treatment.[23]

POSTSCRIPT

The findings from the Delaware experiment clearly demonstrate not only that the treatment of drug-involved offenders works, but that it can work quite well. Studies of similar programs in other parts of the United States reflect similar levels of effectiveness.[24] Overall, for drug-involved offenders who receive a full complement of treatment and aftercare in a correctional setting, when compared with those who receive no treatment at all, the chances are three times greater for remaining drug free and arrest free. And consider the implications—reduced crime, safer communities, and reduced costs for police activity, court processing, and incarceration. In addition, drug-free prison releasees who are working in legitimate jobs are contributing to the national economy as taxpayers, and their dependents are no longer in need of public assistance. Unfortunately, many political observers feel that if treatment fails to have positive outcomes 100 percent of the time, it is ineffective. But anyone who has ever been on a diet, or has tried to stop drinking or smoking, understands that relapse is commonplace for many, and that recovery is typically a long and often difficult process.

The federal government has embraced the idea of corrections-based treatment, as well as the processing of many offenders through drug courts and other justice-related treatment programs.[25] But the calamity of it all is that treatment is only as good as the programs to which clients are sent. Because of the cuts in treatment budgets over the years, the misplaced emphasis on enforcement and interdiction initiatives, and the support of Plan Colombia and similarly imprudent, unsound, and torpid uses of drug control funds, the infrastructure of the nation's residential treatment system is in a state of disarray. There appear to be fewer programs each year, and rates of staff burnout and turnover are high. No doubt this is affecting the quality of treatment.

In the final analysis, what legislators and other politicians need to better understand is that we cannot legislate our way out of the drug problem by passing mandatory sentencing and asset forfeiture laws, we cannot police our way out of the drug problem by further expanding narcotic enforcement activities both domestically and internationally, and we cannot build our way out of the drug problem by constructing more penitentiaries and prison cells. The alternative is science-based treatment and prevention activities to reduce the demand for drugs. For after all, if there were no drug users, there would be no drug problem.

NOTES

1. Center for Substance Abuse Treatment, *The Costs and Benefits of Substance Abuse Treatment* (Bethesda, MD: CSAT, 1999).

2. Samuel, Walker, *Sense and Nonsense about Crime and Drugs: A Policy Guide* (Belmont, CA: Wadsworth, 1994); Barry Stimmel, *Drug Abuse and Social Policy in America: The War That Must Be Won* (New York: Haworth Press, 1996); Marc Mauer, Cathy Potler, and Richard Wolf, *Gender and Justice: Women, Drugs, and Sentencing Policy* (Washington, DC: The Sentencing Project, 1998); James

P. Gray, *Why Our Drug Laws Have Failed and What We Can Do About It: A Judicial Indictment of the War on Drugs* (Philadelphia: Temple University Press, 2001); Meda Chesney-Lind, "Imprisoning Women: The Unintended Victims of Mass Imprisonment," in *Invisible Punishment: The Collateral Consequences of Mass Imprisonment,* ed. M. Mauer and M. Chesney-Lind (New York: New Press, 2002).

3. John Irwin and James Austin, *It's About Time: America's Imprisonment Binge* (Belmont, CA: Wadsworth, 1997); Michael Tonry, *Penal Reform in Overcrowded Times* (New York: Oxford University Press, 2001).

4. U.S. Department of Justice, Bureau of Justice Statistics, U.S. Department of Justice and Federal Bureau of Prisons, *1997 Survey of Inmates in State and Federal Correctional Facilities* [Computer file], compiled by U.S. Department of Commerce, Bureau of Census, ICPSR ed. (Ann Arbor, MI: Inter-University Consortium for Political and Social Research [producer and distributor], 2000).

5. Ryan S. King and Marc Mauer, *Distorted Priorities: Drug Offenders in State Prisons* (Washington, DC: The Sentencing Project, 2001).

6. Eric L. Sevigny and Jonathan P. Caulkins, "Kingpins or Mules: An Analysis of Drug Offenders Incarcerated in Federal and State Prisons," *Criminology and Public Policy,* 3 (July 2004), pp. 401–434.

7. J. M. Braude, "Boys' Court: Individualized Justice for the Youthful Offender," *Federal Probation,* 12 (1988), pp. 9–14.

8. M. D. Anglin, D. Longshore, and S. Turner, "Treatment Alternatives to Street Crime: An Evaluation of Five Programs," *Criminal Justice and Behavior,* 26 (1999), pp. 168–195; James A. Inciardi and Duane C. McBride, *Treatment Alternatives to Street Crime (TASC): History, Experiences, Issues,* DHHS Pub. No. (ADM)91-1749 (Rockville, MD: National Institute on Drug Abuse, 1991).

9. David Farabee, Yih-ing Hser, M. Douglas Anglin, and David Huang, "Recidivism among an Early Cohort of California's Proposition 36 Offenders," *Criminology and Public Policy,* 3 (November 2004), pp. 563–584.

10. Institute of Medicine, *Treating Drug Problems: A Study of the Evolution, Effectiveness, and Financing of Public and Private Drug Treatment Systems,* vol. 1 (Washington, DC: National Academy Press, 1990); C. G. Leukefeld, F. Tims, and D. Farabee, eds., *Treatment of Drug Offenders: Policies and Issues* (New York: Springer Publishing Company, 2002).

11. J. A. Inciardi, ed., *Drug Treatment and Criminal Justic* (Newbury Park, CA: Sage Publications, 1993).

12. *Uniform Facility Data Set* (Rockville, MD: Substance Abuse and Mental Health Services Administration, October 1990).

13. *National Survey of Substance Abuse Treatment Services* (Rockville, MD: Substance Abuse and Mental Health Services Administration, October 2001).

14. Institute of Medicine, *Managing Managed Care: Quality Improvement in Behavioral Health* (Washington, DC: National Academy Press, 1997).

15. A. T. McLellan, D. Carise, and H. D. Kleber, "Can the National Addiction Treatment Infrastructure Support the Public's Demand for Quality Care?" *Journal of Substance Abuse Treatment,* 25 (2003), pp. 117–121.

16. James A. Inciardi, "Proposition 36: What Did You Really Expect?" *Criminology and Public Policy,* 3 (November 2004), pp. 593–598.

17. Douglas S. Lipton, *The Theory of Rehabilitation as Applied to Addict Offenders* (New York: Narcotic and Drug Research, Inc., 1989).

18. For example, see Dean R. Gerstein and Henrick J. Harwood, eds., *Treating Drug Problems* (Washington, DC: National Academy Press, 1990); George De Leon, "Psychopathology and Substance Abuse: What is Being Learned in Therapeutic Communities," *Journal of Psychoactive Drugs,* 21 (April–June 1989), pp. 177–188; H. Westley Clark and Joan Ellen Zwerben, "Legal Vulnerabilities in the Treatment of Chemically Dependent Dual Diagnosis Patients," *Journal of Psychoactive Drugs,* 21 (April–June 1989), pp. 251–258; J. Calvin Chatlos, "Adolescent Dual Diagnosis: A 12-Step Transformational Model," *Journal of Psychoactive Drugs,* 21 (April–June 1989), pp. 189–202; Sheila B. Blume, "Dual Diagnosis: Psychoactive Substance Abuse and Personality Disorders," *Journal of*

Psychoactive Drugs, 21 (April–June 1989), pp. 135–138; John C. Ball and Alan Ross, *The Effectiveness of Methadone Maintenance Treatment* (New York: Springer-Verlag, 1991).

19. See P. A. Harrison, J. A., Fulkerson, and T. J. Beebe, "Multiple Substance Use Among Adolescent Physical and Sexual Abuse Victims," *Child Abuse & Neglect,* 21 (1997), pp. 529–539; T. Ireland and C. S. Widom, "Childhood Victimization and Risk for Alcohol and Drug Arrests," *The International Journal of the Addictions,* 29 (1994), pp. 235–274; L. W. Johnsen and L. L. Harlow, "Childhood Sexual Abuse Linked with Adult Substance Use, Victimization, and AIDS-Risk," *AIDS Education and Prevention,* 8 (1996), pp. 44–57; M. A. Medrano, D. P. Desmond, W. A. Zule, and J. P. Hatch, "Histories of Childhood Trauma and the Effects on Risky HIV Behaviors in a Sample of Women Drug Users," *American Journal of Drug and Alcohol Abuse,* 25 (1999), pp. 593–606; M. A. Medrano, W. A. Zule, J. Hatch, and D. P. Desmond, "Prevalence of Childhood Trauma in a Community Sample of Substance-Abusing Women," *American Journal of Drug and Alcohol Abuse,* 25 (1999), pp. 449–463.

20. Carl G. Leukefeld and Frank M Tims, eds., *Compulsory Treatment of Drug Abuse: Research and Clinical Practice,* Research Monograph No. 86 (Rockville, MD: National Institute on Drug Abuse, 1988); Frank M. Tims, George De Leon, and Nancy Jainchill, eds., *Therapeutic Community: Advances in Research and Application,* Research Monograph No. 144 (Rockville, MD: National Institute on Drug Abuse, 1994); Carl G. Leukefeld and Frank M. Tims, eds., *Drug Abuse Treatment in Prison and Jails,* Research Monograph No. 118 (Rockville, MD: National Institute on Drug Abuse, 1994).

21. George De Leon, *The Therapeutic Community: Theory, Model, and Method* (New York: Springer, 2000).

22. Steven S. Martin, Clifford A. Butzin, and James A. Inciardi, "Assessment of a Multistage Therapeutic Community for Drug Involved Offenders, *Journal of Psychoactive Drugs,* 27 (1995), pp. 109–116; James A. Inciardi, Dorothy Lockwood, and Steven S. Martin, "Therapeutic Communities in Prison and Work Release: Some Clinical and Policy Implications," in *Therapeutic Community: Advances in Research and Application,* Research Monograph No. 144, ed. Frank M. Tims, George De Leon, and Nancy Jainchill, (Rockville, MD: National Institute on Drug Abuse, 1994), pp. 259–267.

23. James A. Inciardi, Steven S. Martin, Clifford A. Butzin, Robert M. Hooper, and Lana D. Harrison, "An Effective Model of Prison-Based Treatment for Drug-Involved Offenders," *Journal of Drug Issues,* 27 (1997), pp. 261–278; Steven S. Martin, Clifford A. Butzin, Christine A. Saum, and James A. Inciardi, "Three-Year Outcomes of Therapeutic Community Treatment for Drug-Involved Offenders in Delaware: from Prison to Work Release to Aftercare," *Prison Journal,* 79 (1999), pp. 294–320.

24. See Gary Field, "Oregon Prison Drug Treatment Programs, in *Drug Abuse Treatment in Prisons and Jails,* Research Monograph No. 118, ed. Carl G. Leukefeld and Frank M. Tims, (Rockville, MD: National Institute on Drug Abuse, 1992), pp. 142–155; M. W. Forcier, "Substance Abuse, Crime and Prison-Based Treatment: Problems and Prospects," *Social Practice Review,* 2 (1991), pp. 123–131; C. J. Mumola, *Substance Abuse and Treatment, State and Federal Prisoners* (Washington, DC: National Institute of Justice, 1999); M. Prendergast, D. Farabee, and J. Cartier, "Corrections-Based Substance Abuse Programs: Good for Inmates, Good for Prisons," *Offender Substance Abuse Report,* 2 (2002), pp. 81–96; H. K. Wexler, G. Melnick, L. Lowe, and J. Peters, "Three Year Reincarceration Outcomes for Amity In-Prison therapeutic Community and Aftercare in California," *Prison Journal,* 70 (September 1999), pp. 321–336; Kevin Knight, D. Dwayne Simpson, and Matthew L. Hiller, "Three Year Reincarceration Outcomes for In-Prison Therapeutic Community Treatment in Texas," *Prison Journal,* 79 (September 1999), pp. 337–351.

25. See D. P. Mears, L. Winterfield, J. Hunsaker, G. E. Moore, and R. M. White, *Drug Treatment in the Criminal Justice System: The Current State of Knowledge* (Urban Institute: Washington, DC, 2002); D. P. Mears, G. E. Moore, J. Travis, J. and Winterfield, L., *Improving the Link Between Research and Drug Treatment in Correctional Settings—Summary Report* (Urban Institute: Washington, DC, 2003); G. E. Moore and D. P. Mears, *Voices from the Field: Practitioners Identify Key Issues in Corrections-Based Drug Treatment* (Urban Institute: Washington, DC, 2002); G. E. Moore and D. P. Mears, *A Meeting of the Minds: Researchers and Practitioners Discuss Key Issues in Corrections-Based Drug Treatment* (Urban Institute: Washington, DC, 2002).

GENERAL DRUG TERMS AND CONCEPTS

A common difficulty in many published discussions of drug abuse is the limited attention given to the basic concepts used to describe and analyze the problem. Appendix A provides widely accepted definitions of drug abuse phenomena.

A. BASIC DRUG GROUPS

Drugs. Any natural or artificial substances (aside from food), that by their chemical nature alter the functioning of the body.

Psychoactive Drugs. Drugs that alter perception and consciousness, including analgesics, depressants, stimulants, and hallucinogens.

Analgesics. Drugs used for the relief of varying degrees of pain without rendering the user unconscious. There are both *narcotic* and *nonnarcotic* varieties of analgesics.

Depressants. Drugs that act on and lessen the activity of the central nervous system (CNS), diminishing or stopping vital functions.

Sedatives. CNS depressant drugs that produce calm and relaxation. Alcohol, barbiturates and related compounds, and minor tranquilizers are sedative drugs.

Hypnotics. CNS depressant drugs that produce sleep; barbiturates, methaqualone, and chloral hydrate and hypnotic drugs. A number of drugs are both sedatives *and* hypnotics.

Stimulants. Drugs that stimulate the central nervous system and increase the activity of the brain and spinal cord. Amphetamines and cocaine are CNS stimulant drugs.

Hallucinogens. Drugs that act on the central nervous system producing mood and perceptual changes varying from sensory illusions to hallucinations. Sometimes referred to as psychedelics, hallucinogenic drugs include marijuana, hashish, LSD, PCP, and psilocybin.

B. USE, ABUSE, AND DEPENDENCY TERMS

Drug Misuse.   The inappropriate use of a prescription or nonprescription drug, that is, using it in greater amounts than, or for purposes other than, it was intended.

Drug Abuse.   Any use of an illegal drug, or the use of a legal drug in a manner that can cause problems for the user.

Addiction.   Drug craving accompanied by physical dependence, which motivates continuing usage, resulting in a tolerance to a drug's effects and a syndrome of identifiable symptoms when the drug is abruptly withdrawn. Narcotics, barbiturates, and cocaine are addicting drugs.

Dependence.   A concept that indicates the central role that a substance has come to play in an individual's life, with evidence of problems relating to control of intake and the development of physical and psychological difficulties, despite which the individual continues to use the substance.

Neuroadaptation.   The chemical and biological changes that occur within the brain in response to the use of psychoactive drugs.

Tolerance.   A state of acquired resistance to some or all effects of a drug. Tolerance develops after the repeated use of certain drugs, resulting in a need to increase the dosage to obtain the original effects.

Cross Tolerance.   Among certain pharmacologically related drugs, tolerance to the effects of one will carry over to most or all others. For example, a person who has become tolerant to the euphoric effects of secobarbital is likely to be tolerant to the euphoric effects of all other short-acting barbiturates.

Cross Addiction.   Also referred to as cross dependence, a situation in which dependence on drugs of the same pharmacological group is mutual and interchangeable. For example, persons addicted to heroin can use methadone or some other narcotic in place of the heroin without experiencing withdrawal.

Withdrawal.   The cluster of reactions and behavior that ensue on the abrupt cessation of a drug on which the user's body is dependent.

Detoxification.   The removal of physical dependency.

C. DRUG REACTIONS

Potentiation.   The ability of one drug to increase the activity of another drug when the two are taken simultaneously. This can be expressed mathematically as $a + b = A$. For example, aspirin, a, plus caffeine, b, increases the potency of the aspirin, A.

Synergism.   Similar to potentiation, a situation in which two or more drugs are taken together and the combined action dramatically increases the normal effects of each drug. A synergistic effect can be expressed mathematically as $1 + 1 = 5$, and typically occurs with mixtures of alcohol and barbiturates.

Antagonism.   A situation in which two drugs taken together have opposite effects on the body. An antagonistic reaction can be expressed mathematically as $1 + 1 = 0$, and typically occurs with certain mixtures of depressants and stimulants.

Idiosyncracy.   An abnormal or peculiar response to a drug, such as excitation from a depressant or sedation from a stimulant.

Side Effect.   Any effect other than what the drug was intended for, such as stomach upset from aspirin.

D. ROUTES OF DRUG ADMINISTRATION

Intravenous (IV).   Injected into the vein.

Intramuscular (IM).   Injected into the muscle.

Cutaneous.   Absorbed through the skin.

Subcutaneous.   Inserted under the skin.

Insufflation (inhalation).   Drawn into the lungs through the nose or mouth.

Oral.   Swallowed and absorbed through the stomach.

Vaginal.   Absorbed through vaginal tissues.

Anal.   Absorbed through rectal tissues.

Sublingual.   Absorbed through the tissues under the tongue.

E. PHARMACEUTICAL TERMS

Tablets.   Tablets are solid dosage forms of medication prepared by molding or compressing into dies. More specifically, they are made by compressing powdered, crystalline, or granular materials in a tablet machine. This may be either a single punch or a rotary punch machine. The former is more likely to be used in clandestine manufacture because it is cheaper, smaller, and easier to use. The best method of making tablets is to use what is known as the wet-granulation method, which requires the use of a bowl or blender in which to mix the components of the tablet, water and/or alcohol, a mesh screen, shallow trays and a drying cupboard. Tablets may be of many shapes, sizes, and colors.

Capsules.   Capsules are doses of solids contained in a soluble shell of hard or soft gelatine. They are usually artificially colored. Hard capsules are normally made in two halves, the end of one slipping over the end of the other. Soft capsules are permanently flexible and may be round, oblong, or elliptical.

Pills.   Pills are small, round dosage forms made by rolling the pharmaceutical material into a cylinder and cutting the cylinder to provide individual doses. Although once a common variety of pharmaceutical preparation, pills have been largely replaced by tablets and capsules.

Tinctures.   Tinctures are alcoholic solutions of extracts of plant material containing a drug.

Extracts.   Extracts are concentrated forms of plant drugs typically prepared through distillation or percolation.

Syrups.   Syrups are solutions of medicine in a concentrated form of sugar dissolved in water.

F. NOMENCLATURE OF MEDICINES

Proprietary Names.   Designations given by manufacturers to particular drugs or combinations of drugs. More commonly known as trade or brand names, they generally are not related to the chemical composition of the drug. Moreover, with so many companies manufacturing pharmaceutical products, virtually the same drug or medicine may appear in pharmacies under many different names.

Chemical Names.   Chemical compositions of drugs. Health authorities in many nations, including the United States, have passed legislation requiring the use of chemical names in drug labeling to allow physicians, pharmacists, and patients to identify the contents of medications. However, chemical names tend to be long, complicated, and virtually impossible to remember.

International Nonproprietary Names (INN).   Also known as generic names, INNs were developed by the World Health Organization as substitutes for chemical names. They may be used by any manufacturer without legal restrictions, thus providing a system for the easy identification of pharmaceuticals, for example:

1. **INN: methadone**
   Chemical name: 6-dimethylamino-4,4-diphenyl-3-heptanone
   Proprietary names: Dolophine, Intensol, Physeptone
2. **INN: phenobarbital**
   Chemical name: 5-ethyl-5-phenylbarbituric acid
   Proprietary names: Donnatal, Belladenal, Kinesed, Quadrinal
3. **INN: diazepam**
   Chemical name: 7-chloro-1,3-dihydroi-1-methyl-5-phenyl-2H-1-4-
      benzodiazepin-2-one
   Proprietary names: Valium, T-Quil

SCHEDULING PROVISIONS OF THE FEDERAL CONTROLLED SUBSTANCES ACT

The regulatory scheme of the federal Controlled Substances Act classifies drugs into five categories, or schedules, based on the drug's accepted medical value, and its potential for abuse and dependence.

The categories are based on characteristics of drugs such as potential for abuse, accepted medical use, and propensity to create a psychological or physiological dependency for users. Classifications of drugs and periodic updating and republication of lists of drugs included in each category are the responsibility of the U.S. Drug Enforcement Administration (DEA).

Schedule I.   Schedule I drugs, the most strictly controlled, are considered to have a high potential for abuse, no currently accepted medical use in the United States, and no acceptable safe level of use under medical supervision. Many narcotics, such as heroin and other opium derivatives, as well as marijuana, mescaline, peyote, psilocybin, LSD, and Ecstasy are listed in Schedule I.

Schedule II.   Schedule II drugs have a high potential for abuse, and their use may lead to severe dependence; however, they have some recognized medicinal value. Drugs in this category include cocaine, morphine, methamphetamine, and PCP, to name but a few.

Schedule III.   Schedule III drugs have less potential for abuse and dependence than Schedule I or II drugs, but have some accepted medical use. Substances listed in Schedule III include limited quantities of some narcotic drugs; amphetamines; and derivatives of barbituric acid.

Schedule IV.   Schedule IV drugs have a low potential for abuse compared to those in Schedule III, and although they may lead to limited dependence, they have a currently accepted medical use. Substances in Schedule IV include phenobarbital, chlordiazepoxide hydrochloride (Librium), diazepam (Valium), and propoxyphene hydrochloride (Darvon).

Schedule V.   Schedule V drugs have a low potential for abuse compared to substances in Schedule IV and a currently accepted medical use; use may lead to limited dependence relative to Schedule IV substances. Substances in Schedule V include narcotic compounds containing a limited quantity of narcotic drugs together with one or more nonnarcotic medicinal ingredients.

NAME INDEX

SUBJECT INDEX

Abstinence syndrome, 7
Academic problems, 70
Acetaminophen, 154
Acquired immune deficiency syndrome (AIDS),
 61, 77–78, 104. *See also* HIV (human
 immunodeficiency virus)
 definition of, 223
 emergence of, 218–220, 226, 245–246
 epidemiology of, 224–228, 239, 246
 fundraising for, 77
 gay community and, 222
 tracking, 222–224
 transmission of, 228–235
Adderall, 156
Addiction, 102
 criminal model of, 195, 197
 defined, 5–8
 enslavement theory of, 293, 294
 medical model of, 197–198
 ontological, 44
 pseudo-, 7
 symptom of other problems, 319
 withdrawal distress and, 99
Addiction-prone personality, 40, 100, 195
Addiction Research Center in Baltimore, 74
Addictive behavior, 99
Addicts, 5, 187, 188
Adulteration
 of club drugs, 82–85
 of heroin, 105
 of party drugs, 82–85
Afghanistan, 96
African Americans, 38, 41, 117, 207
Aggressive behavior, 56
AIDS. *See* Acquired immune deficiency syndrome
 (AIDS)
Alcohol, 65–70
 brain and, 67–68
 effects of, 50, 68
 history of, 2, 65–66
 ingestion of, 66–67
 overdose of, 68
 types of, 66
 violence and, 295
 widespread use of, 298
Alcohol abuse, 70
Alcohol dependence, 70
Alcoholic content, 66
Alcoholics Anonymous (AA), 276
Alprazolam (Xanax), 155
Altered states, 8, 27, 56

AMA Drug Evaluations, 49
Amazonia, 119–121
Ambrosia, 66–68
America as a Civilization (Lerner), 38
American Disease, The (Musto), 292
American drug policy. *See* Drug policy issues
American Foundation for AIDS Research, 247
American Medical Association (AMA), 26, 203
American Medical Oil Company, 25
Amidon, 275
Amphetamines, 48, 57, 73, 101, 156, 203
Analgesics, 154
Andes Mountains, 118
Angel dust, 56. *See also* PCP (phencyclidine)
Anti-Drug Abuse Act of 1988, Title I, 262
Antidrug legislation, 27–28
Aphrodisiacs, 131–132
Aqua Vitae, 66–68
Ark Royal, 261
Atavism, 184
Atropa belladonna, 84–85
Atropine, 85
Attention Deficit-Hyperactivity Disorder
 (ADHD), 75, 156
AZT (zidovudine), 77

Backloading, 233–234
Baking-soda cocaine, 137, 138
Barbiturate drugs, 49
Basuco, 135, 138
Bayer Laboratories, 23–25
Beer, 66, 67
Belladonna alkaloids, adulteration of, 84–85
Belladonna psychosis, 85
Bell 209 assault helicopter (Cobra), 258
Bennies, 48
Benzedrine, 47
Benzodiazepines, 76, 153, 155–156, 168
Bhang, 32
Bindis, 72
Binge drinking, 68–70
Birney's Catarrah Cure, 25
Black beauties, 48
Black-market drugs, 29
Blood alcohol content (B.A.C.), 68
Blue Thunder, 259
Bogotá, Colombia, 289
Booting, 232, 234
Brady Handgun Violence Prevention Act, 265
Brain, 7–8, 67–68, 74
 cocaine and, 129–132